Teresa: A Woman

A BIOGRAPHY OF TERESA of AVILA

Victoria Lincoln

87367

EDITED WITH INTRODUCTIONS

by

Elias Rivers and Antonio T. de Nicolás

State University of New York Press

ALBANY

Published by
State University of New York Press, Albany

© 1984 State University of New York

Printed in the United States of America

For information, address State University of New York
Press, State University Plaza, Albany, N.Y., 12246

Library of Congress Cataloging in Publication Data

Lincoln, Victoria, 1904-1981
   Teresa, a woman.

   (SUNY series in cultural perspectives)
   Bibliography: p.xxiv
   1. Teresa, of Avila, Saint, 1515-1582. 2. Christian
saints — Spain — Avila — Biography. 3. Avila (Spain) —
Biography. I. Rivers, Elias L. II. De Nicolas,
Antonio T. III. Title. IV. Series.
BX4700.T4L475 1984 282'.092'4 [B]   84-8561
ISBN 0-87395-936-1
ISBN 0-87395-937-X (pbk.)

Contents

The Chapters

Introduction

Through Love the intercourse of the divine and wo/man transpires.[1]

Plato

Introduction

It has been the custom among writers on saints and mystics to clean up their lives so much that hardly anything human was left. No matter how inspiring this attitude might have been, the moment anyone was written off as a saint he or she was automatically written off as a human being. The antiseptic environment pious writers inflicted on the saints had little to do with their actual lives. It was difficult for the rest of us to even imagine in what capacity their lives had anything to contribute to ours. Teresa de Avila, perhaps, has been the greatest victim of biographers, pious writers, and scholars. Regardless of what else these writers tried to accomplish they certainly failed in trying to answer the problems raised by Teresa's own writings and in particular her letters.[2]

This kind of one-dimensional writing has its roots in the fact that these writers approached the saint with only one text[3] IN HAND and that this text made or unmade their lives and images.

Suddenly, in the last ten years, a new wave of writers has emerged insisting on the human qualities of the saints. In the case of Teresa de Avila, this volume I am honored to introduce by Victoria Lincoln, *Teresa: A Woman*, is the first of the new wave in English. These writers, in particular those writing on Teresa, have changed the game of saint-watching into something more immediate and vital for all of us. They do this mostly by incorporating new and sensational discoveries about their humanity, through new and undisclosed documents which the earlier texts did not consider, ignored, or covered up. Victoria Lincoln, in particular, accomplishes this task by weaving through the letters of Teresa a seamless text, previously hinted at but never fully finished.

This new attitude may be summarized as follows:

Saints cannot be judged by a selective criterion of external behavior only, for this may be embellished by any antiseptic text. The saints, like the rest of us, were sinners with dark secrets, and unless this basic humanity can be brought forward, there is no room in them for divine transformation. The measure of the divine transformation is in direct proportion to the depth of the humanity that needs to be transformed: social, individual, human. A fancy of God over some man or woman will not do. The effort of the saint to reach that middle ground where the divine and the human meet is an effort repeatable by any of us. The saint embodies the form of the desire of the world made public through their own ability to read the texts of their own transformation and to will them to us. This biography of Victoria Lincoln answers these points in an exemplary manner.

Teresa's Bumpy Road

In view of this new attitude, Teresa's life is covered best by the image of a woman riding a long, bumpy, Castilian road. The image of the vertical flight of an angel does not fit anymore. In this new reading Teresa's image is wholly human and her feet are deeply rooted in the values, perspectives, crusades, prejudices, and images of Old Castile where she lived and died.

Teresa's life (1515-1582) was spent in Castile, with the exception of the Seville foundation where, in disobedience or half deceived by her adored Father Gracián, she mingled with Andalusians, "a strange and deceitful people," [4] "not my kind of people."[5]

Castile was at the time "the intellectual and spiritual capital of Spain,"[6] and Teresa's task of reform would be difficult to imagine had she been born in any other province of Spain. Teresa's life unfolded at a unique time and coincided with far-reaching changes and dreams in the political, economic, and religious orientation of Castilians. With the arrival of Carlos I (Charles V of Hapsburg) and his multi-territorial legacy, Castile changed in a short time from being a province to becoming the capital of Europe.[7] She also witnessed the passage of an open Castile into a hardened isolation ("tibetization") forced on her by Philip II.[8] Castile thus became closed to Europe but opened to heaven, slave to its own customs under the watchful eyes of the Inquisition in search of heresies. Teresa's reformation cannot be understood without understanding the Castilian external "crusade." Teresa's *Life* and the *Foundations* are more than a convincing argument for a woman engaged in a crusade equal to the Castilian crusade for the "Peace of the Counter Reformation." Teresa linked her foundations to the wealthy urban centers of Castile for the security of her nuns and appeared totally immersed in the life of her times.[9] We learn through her writings of the popularity of the Inquisition,[10] her dissatisfaction with the process of Portugal's annexation,[11] her concern for the rebellion of the *moriscos*,[12] the failure of Philip II's military project and policy against the Protestants, the difficulties arising from the imminent religious wars in France, and the spiraling inflation which forced her to increase enormously the economic provisions for the survival and security of her monasteries.[13]

Teresa was also a part of the inner struggles of a Castile seemingly unified in religious matters but hopelessly divided in practices. Teresa's writings reveal at times unconcern, at others apprehension at "the difficult times." The hostility in Castile between well-defined groups and others not so well defined was in part due to the new trends in inner prayer brought on by "Illuminism," Erasmus' writings, the new translations of the Bible into the vernacular, and Protestantism. The reigning climate of suspicion identified Lutheranism, Illuminism, recollection, internal prayer, and mystical practice as being in the same unorthodox camp. Anyone engaged in inner prayer was always on the verge of being branded a heretic. The theologians of the Inquisition, more keen on theoretical unity than on a direct encounter with the orginial God—more daring an encounter even than Protestantism's—were completely unresponsive to these practices. The Inquisition was ready at the least suspicion of heresy to bring the whole machinery of their theology crashing down on the suspected heretics.[14] No one was spared, not even Teresa. Without taking this into account it is impossible to have a clear idea of the struggles of her reform, conceived precisely in the meeting of women dedicated to inner prayer; nor is it possible to understand her struggle for the recognition of a woman's right to the inner prayer of recollection. It is no wonder Teresa herself was astounded, in her death bed, and summarized these struggles with her sigh of relief: "In the end I die a daughter of the Church."[15]

But then, too, few people knew how to handle men better than Teresa. She used *letrados*, confessors, and theologians the way she needed them. She easily convinced them that her writings were not from the devil. They were willing friends and she knew how to praise them, write about their value and contributions, praise the Inquisition, charm them, and form intimate friendships with them, some more intimate than a nun should have allowed. "For more than eighteen years of the twenty-eight years since I began prayer, I suffered this battle and conflict between friendship with God and friendship with the world" (*Life*, 8, 3). It was a long time before Teresa heard the inner command: "No longer do I want you to converse with men but with angels" (*Life* 24, 5-6), but in Teresa's human terms this became translated as: "I have never again been able to tie myself to any friendship or to find consolation in or bear particular love for any other person than those *I understand love Him and strive to serve Him*" (*Life* 24, 5-6). But as one reads her letters, especially as they uncover and tie her life as in the present biography written by Victoria Lincoln, the story is more complex. Teresa was bound with the greatest of fidelities to her inner "voice," the signs from her meditations. Her external obedience to confessors and theologians is more sophistic. She was tied to several theologians, confessors and superiors at the same time; to some because of their position, to others as confessors, to one, Gracián, with a vow of obedience. This situation allowed Teresa to follow her "voice," for there would always be one of them to command as the "voice" wished. In Chapter 75 of the present biography, Victoria Lincoln shows the tragic consequences of this attitude for the friendship between Juan de la Cruz (John of the Cross) and Teresa when they met for the last time, parting in unfriendly terms never to see one another again. We even see some of these men turning around and becoming pupils instead of teachers. They confess their sins to her; follow her manner of inner prayer; some even fall in love with her; they even disagree with one another in the correction of her writings for the Inquisition.

In her own manner Teresa managed to disobey the Inquisition by letting her *Life* fall into the hands of the Princess of Eboli. The Princess took advantage of this indiscretion and used the *Life* to laugh at it, passed it to the servants so that they would do the same, and then accused her to the Inquisitor General. Teresa had friends in high places. Philip II came to her side and the book of the *Life* eventually ended up in his library.

For a woman of such warm love for friends, she also showed some dislikes for "strangers." We have already seen her reaction to Andalusians, and she also expressed her deep dislike of rural areas: for there lived the "vilest and lowest peasants and Jewish converts in the whole world." Even if, as Egido suggests, this report of Teresa's words has most probably been embellished by Gracián,[16] we still have a list of direct quotations from Teresa's writing about her absolute dislike of the nobility.

But, perhaps, in order to understand more fully the human Teresa we have to delve deeper into her woman's secrets.

Teresa's Dark Secrets

The center of the human Teresa had escaped scholars until about twelve years ago. Suddenly these external inconsistencies of the Foundress seemed to tie together at a deeper recess of her own humanity. Castile, and therefore Teresa, lived by a silent and binding code of sensibilities, more demanding and vital than wealth, health, or even religion. This secret and vital code of human values bound Castilian society with chains stronger than those that bound slaves to the galleys. This code allowed freedom of social mobility or caused with impunity the social death of individuals and families. This secret code was the Castilian code of "honor." It involved not only personal character, but through social consent to the code, public reputation. The social consent predominated over the personal honor. Every Castilian was slave to the opinion of others. Every Castilian had to be watchful for easy attack on an unprotected reputation.[17]

Honor took two particular manifestations for immediate, and consequently, easy social action. The first one was personal honor which affected women exclusively (sexual decorum, publicly acknowledged virginity in the unmarried, fidelity in the married); the second one was hereditary honor, an untainted lineage (absence of ancestors of Jewish and Moorish blood), with a direct impact on men. A loss of honor in the first sense might be forgiven but there was no possibility of repairing a breach of honor in the second sense (at least in theory, for in practice one could with money cover the traces of the past by buying titles of *Hidalgo*, moving to another town, or going to the Indies where it was easier to acquire titles and erase the past).[18]

Teresa's honor was tainted on both counts of Castilian honor. She was not a virgin. Teresa confesses in her *Life* how she entered the convent for the first time by the hand of her father, "through the total loss of my honor and the suspicion of my father" (*Life* 2, 6). Teresa was also first-generation Christian. Her grandfather and father had publicly done penance and worn the *sanbenito* habit in Toledo for having returned to the old religion of Israel, then became converts to Christianity and spent the rest of their days buying titles of *Hidalgos* and behaving as if they were "old Christians."[19]

It is this second breach in the code of Castilian honor that holds the key to most of the writings and to the transformation of Teresa's life. Honor comes at the most unexpected places through all her writings. Even when Teresa liked everything about religious life she was not inclined to "suffer anything that would look as loss of self esteem" (*Life* 5, 1); even her reasons for fostering suspicious friendships, or the conversations in the convent parlor with a male benefactor were justified by Teresa because: "I was not losing my honor, but rather was gaining it" (*Life* 7, 7). This broken honor could also explain her concern for the spiritual life and death of her father and the tears she shows in letters to her brothers and relatives concerning the kind of jobs they were taking that could give away the secret.

Astonishing as it might seem, Teresa's Jewish background was not discovered until a few years ago. Teresa's family, who testified at her beatification and canonization, managed to cover up this fact. Biographers invented an aristocratic old-Christian image of the Saint and polished that image to reach us as an inhuman and sterile image. And yet, though Teresa never told a soul of her true "social" dishonor, all her writings explode with allusions and hints and strategies of honor for the truly religious convert: "tampering these points of honor underfoot," she writes, is a prerequisite to entering the path of perfection, because "the soul's profit and what the world calls honor can never go together" (*Way of Perfection*, 36, 3).[20] Teresa's *Way of Perfection* is a programmatic path of "losing a thousand honors for You." (*Way* 3, 7). On this path the pride in untainted ancestors is replaced with the divine lineage of the soul. Teresa removes from her convents all titles and prerogatives, even those of seniority and religious names of reverence. "She who is of more noble birth should speak less of her parentage; all must be equal" (*Life* 37, 7, to end); for as Christ teaches her, "I have always esteemed virtue more than lineage" (*Foundations* 15, 15).

It is undeniable that Teresa's progress as a mystic begins only when her human honor begins to mutate for the divine. She understood this clearly when, in referring to another nun, she exclaims: "what the love of God was able to do when she was no longer concerned with her honor" (*Foundations* 26, 12-13). No story of the sainthood of Teresa is possible if the three vulnerable points of her human honor are not held in perspective: she lost her woman's honor, she was always on the verge of being exposed and losing her social honor, and she was in danger of losing her spiritual honor if the Inquisition convicted her for her prayer of recollection. It is only from these depths that the flight of the phoenix gathers height. It is because of these human foundations that Victoria Lincoln's biography is invaluable.

A Woman's Transformation

Victoria Lincoln's biography of Teresa holds firm to these human roots and by doing so also opens human possibilities on a grand scale. Teresa did not change from human to angel, but rather explored and transformed the human to the point of divine contact. One witnesses, between successes and failures, always a woman stretching the human to its outermost limits, to the middle ground where the divine and human meet. But Teresa never stops being a woman, and in her all the human desires of the rest of us are present.

Teresa discovered a new style of life and to this new style she dedicated with passion her fidelity (*honradez*). This new style was based on a new kind of prayer practiced on herself and recorded for the public domain: "This is," she writes, "another new book from here on" (*Life* 23:1). Teresa's honor is bound now to this new-found book even if in the beginnings it is slow reading and boring.

Until 1554, Teresa confesses in her *Life* 9:1, 8, her way of directing the will and regathering it in prayer was through readings:

> And very often, for some years, I was more anxious for the hour I had determined to spend in prayer be over than I was to remain there . . . and so unbearable was the misery I felt on entering the oratory, that I had to master all my courage. (*Life* 8:7)

She was so dependent on books that when the Inquisitor Valdés published the *Index of Forbidden Books* (1559) her spiritual life seemed to come to a standstill (*Life* 26:5). And, again, it is in reading that her humanity finds its limits:

> If a mystery [of Christ's life] came to me I would represent it interiorly; but I would spend most times reading good books; they were all my entertainment; God did not give me talent to reason with my understanding, nor of taking advantage of the imagination, which in me is so inept that even to think and represent the humanity of Our Lord in me I could never succeed. (*Life*, 4)

But in the end books only prepared the way, for she writes: "I was able to learn little from books, because there was nothing I understood until his Majesty gave me understanding through experience" (*Life* 22:3). The exercise eventually pays off and so Teresa writes:

> God arrives at times very late, but [then] He pays generously and with such high interest, all at once, as He has been granting others for many years. I spent fourteen years unable to do meditation unless it were accompanied by reading. (*Way of Perfection*, 26)

But all this changed, suddenly, while looking at a picture of the wounded Christ and again while reading the *Confessions* of St. Augustine (*Life* 9:7-8). Signs of a different kind started to appear: enormous feelings, representations, consolations, which Teresa turned to a reading text and returned to the public domain (*Life*, 6:4).

Reading, Writing, and the Public Opinion

The act of reading, for Teresa, immersed as she was in an oral culture, was a different kind of act than it is for us. It did help her in meditation to the degree that the technology of reading was primarily directed to *hold memory together* and then visualize the image or images, rather than to gain information and content. Reading, for most of the people of the sixteenth century, was an act closer to listening than reading proper. It was more an exercise in memory than intellection.

But, as soon as the signs of meditation appeared in Teresa's life she turned to reading, searching for the public domain of that interior life. She learned to describe it in terms others had used in books before. When her confessor asked her to write down what she understood by "prayer" Teresa handed over to him the book *Subida del Monte Sión* (1535), by Francisco de Salcedo, with underlinings under the descriptions that fitted her own experience of prayer (*Life*, 23). Similarly, she marked Osuna's *Third Spiritual Alphabet* so that through the readings she could speak to others about prayer. In short, the readings helped her as a preparation for prayer exercising memory and will. For another they helped her find the public domain to express herself and thus understand. She did not learn meditation through books. She exercised the will, memory, images till the door of meditation burst open, for as she said: "Meditation proper begins with the will" (*Interior Castle* 4, 1). But for Teresa finding the public domain was of the greatest importance: "For a long time, even though God favored me, I did not know what words to use to explain His favors; and this was no small trial" (*Life* 12, 6). And she adds completing Osuna: "For it is one grace to receive the Lord's favor, another to understand which favor and grace it is; *a third, to know how to describe it*" (*Life* 17, 5). Once the door of inner signs opens, however, Teresa does not hesitate to affirm her knowledge: "I know from experience that what I say is true" (*Life* 27, 11). This certitude proper of the mystics is a challenge to theology and to them to comply with obedience: "The mystery of the Blessed Trinity and other sublime things are so explained that there is no theologian with whom [the mystic's soul] would not dispute in favor of the truth of these sublime things" (*Life* 27, 9). The reason is simple: these experiences and knowledge "do not come from my head, but my heavenly Master tells them to me" (*Life* 39, 8). This telling is the experience itself of meditation: "for it the Lord didn't show me, I was able to learn little from books, because there was nothing I understood until His Majesty gave me understanding through experience" (*Life*, 2:3).

Transformation as the World's Desire

Teresa's need and search for the public domain is the revelation of the human in its totality of desire. Teresa reconfirms, through her inner life, that what she wills for has been the will of the world and is in the public domain of the world. The mystics have a larger role than personal gain, they embody the world's desire by turning their inner life into a code of signs for the world and the divinity. If there is a code, there is a world. Teresa is more careful than most in distinguishing, separating, accounting, for those human characteristics that encompass the human spectrum of possibilities and desires.

The faculties, Teresa writes, are like "wild horses"; they run in all directions. Meditation proper begins through the technologies that gather them within. There the faculties are not lost, nor do they sleep; only the will is occupied: "without knowing how, it becomes captive; it merely consents to God allowing Him to imprison it as one who well knows how to be captive of its lover" (*Life*, 14:2). The signs, now, change; prayer does not tire one; the intellect obtains more water than it pulled out of the well; joy accompanies tears; there is no effort (*Life*, 14:4). "This little spark is the sign or the pledge God gives to his soul that He now chooses it for great things *if it will prepare itself to receive them*" (*Life*, 15:5).

xvii

What this preparation consists in, for Teresa, is always a human effort, accessible to all. In the third degree of prayer Teresa finds no better way to describe the preparation than to call it the sleep of all the faculties. They do not fail to function, nor to understand how they function: "the water of grace rises up to the throat of this soul"; memory and imagination gather unto themselves and become quiet (Life, 16:1). Here Teresa boldly opposed that other chauvinist text of Christianity started by St. Augustine in his *De Trinitate* Book 14, Chapter 4, where he writes: "The image of God is sought in the immortality of the rational soul. How a Trinity is demonstrated in the mind." This Teresa calls a "nuisance" for, as she says, the natural faculties "fleeting from one thing to another, like little moths at night, bothersome and annoying, though they do not do any harm they are a nuisance and the only distance to total union" (*Ibid.*).

Total transformation, for Teresa, takes place in the fourth degree of prayer and the signs of union and rapture affect the whole human complex: soul/body/world. No one can help this happening. Joy is of great intensity. The soul and the body are drained of power (Life, 18, 1). The spirit rises higher and links with heavenly love; the detachment from creatures is deeper and more subtle; but the instances last but a moment (Life, 18, 12). The whole soul/body complex ceases to live by itself and is as if sensitized by someone else (Life, 18, 14); at last soul and body, imagination, memory, and intellect are unified by "an understanding [that lives] by not understanding."

As Teresa describes for us these last passages of the soul/body transformation there is little we dare to add: "The soul undergoes a change; it is always absorbed. . . the intellectual vision is represented to the imagination so that in conformity to our weakness this presence may last in the memory and keep the thought well occupied. These two kinds of visions almost always come together" (Life 28, 9). Teresa established very clearly that God is not the product of the imagination: but it is through the imagination that God becomes present (Life, 28, 10). And she reminds us, with her Castilian irony: "The toad does not fly" (Life 23, 13).

It is in this transformation stage that the great raptures of Teresa took place. The spiritual raptures overcame the body too: "The natural body heat fails the body, the body gradually grows cold, and there is no remedy to avoid this" (Life 20, 3). These raptures took many physical manifestations: in movement (levitation), smells, colors, temperature, and so forth (Life 20, 4).

> For in the pain that is experienced in those impulses, the body feels it along with the soul, and both seem to have a share in it. [The soul raises to a distant place.] God places it in a desert so distant from all things. . . it doesn't find a creature on earth that might accompany it. . . it desires only to die in that solitude. . . . (*Ibid.*, 9)

The soul has found the middle regions where the divine and wo/man have intercourse: "It seems to me that the soul is crucified since no consolations come to it from heaven, nor visit heaven; neither does it desire any from earth, nor is it on earth. . . . it is as though crucified between heaven and earth . . . the intense pain takes away sensory consciousness. . . and this experience resembles the death agony with the difference that the suffering bears along with it great happiness. . . .It is arduous, delightful martyrdom" (*Ibid.*, 20, 11).

Conclusion

I would like to conclude this brief presentation by returning the reader to Teresa herself as we read her at the beginning of her journey of meditation and at the end of that journey, her own testimony.

> At one time I took advantage for my soul in seeing field, water, flowers; in those things I used to find memory of the Creator; that is, they would wake me up and recollect myself, they were as a book. (*Life* 9)

This was the beginning. This was her end in the form of the world's desire:

> I saw close to me an angel in bodily form. . . not very large, but small; very beautiful, his face aflame, he must have been one of the highest angels. . . . In his hand I saw a golden dart, long, the tip of the dart red with some fire. This dart would enter my heart many times and reach my insides; in drawing out the dart it seemed he was taking them with it; he left me all inflamed in great love for God. The pain was so deep that it made me moan; and it was so excessive the sweetness this unbearable pain plunged me into, that there was no way for me to wish it to stop, nor was the soul satisfied with any less than God Himself.   (*Life*, 29, 13)

The total transformation of Teresa's body was discovered by accident. Two years after her death, in trying to return her body to her first convent, it was found that her body had not decomposed. This transformation started the process of reading the texts of her life and her canonization.

But the ultimate testimony and text of her life lies forever in the body of her own writings. We owe a great debt to a writer like Victoria Lincoln for bringing us closer than anyone before to the human depths of Teresa, the woman. Let's hear, now, the authentic voice.

Antonio T. de Nicolás
Professor of Philosophy
State University of New York
Stony Brook

NOTES AND BIBLIOGRAPHY

1. In order to avoid the awkward "men and women," or the fashionable "men," though correct, to apply to both men and women, I have chosen the expression wo/men as their substitute.

2. Teófanes Egido (1980) "The Historical Setting of St. Teresa's Life," in *Carmelite Studies*. Washington, D.C.: ICS Publications, p. 123.

3. Reading technologies involve two kinds of texts: first a primary text that allows us to read. This is primary because it is the condition of possibility of the others. This is, in this notation called 'text₁.' There is a secondary text that

includes signs or such like material and equals some form of information. The primary text, 'text$_1$' is not only interpretative but it is also causal in the sense that it not only creates the conditions of possibility for reading but it also shapes the signs and objects that appear causally. The causal character of this 'text$_1$' is derived from a radical embodiment of the humans using it and the technologies involved. This human embodiment of "text$_1$' is completely transparent to those using it or adept in using it. But this causality is not on a par with physical causality where the effect is proportionate to the cause. It is rather a causality more similar to biological causality where an effect may be disproportionate to its cause, as when the prick of the spur on the flank of the horse produces an exuberant jump totally disproportionate to the cause. And vice versa, no matter how much a horse is pricked by the spur sometimes it does not move.

These two texts, a primary one, 'text$_1$', and a secondary one, 'text$_2$,' are the texts we will be referring to throughout this paper. The primary text, 'text$_1$,' has to do with the embodiment of certain acts needed to create; the secondary text, 'text$_2$,' refers to the signs originated by the primary text in the acts of its exercise and repetitions, like consolations, tears, visions, etc., as we point out later in the paper. It is also obvious how texts derived from imaginative embodiments differ radically from texts derived from cognitive embodiments and why through history they have been antagonistic or subservient to one another. It is also obvious why plurality of texts is a radical necessity and why theoretical uniformity is a crime against humanity.

4. Letter to Padre Rubeo, June 18, 1575, 6; Letter to María de San José, September 9, 1576.

5. Letter to María Bautista, April 29, 1576, 12. The translations from the Spanish, unless otherwise staged, are my own. I will, however, give the reader the quotations as coming from the following English edition so that they may follow better the plot: St. Teresa of Avila (1976) *The Collected Works*, trans. Kieran Kavanaugh and Otilio Rodriguez. 2 vol. ICS Publications: Washington, D.C.

The Letters are not in this English edition but may be found in several Spanish editions, including the *Obras Completas*, Editorial Plenitud, Madrid, 1964.

6. Pierre Chaunu (1973) *L'Espagne de Charles Quint*, Vol. 1. Paris. p. 307.

7. Egido, *Loc. cit.*, p.127.

8. *Ibid.*, p. 128.

9. *Ibid.*, p. 126.

10. *Life*, 33, 5.

11. Letter to Gracián, August 19, 1578, 2; Letter to Don Teutonio de Braganza, July 22, 1579.

12. Letter to María de San José, July 4, 1580, 14.

13. Egido, *Loc. cit.*, p. 124.

14. The fundamental work on the spirituality of the sixteenth century is: Marcel Bataillon (1966) *Erasmo y España*. Fondo de Cultura Economica: Mexico.

Other works:

Antonio Marquez (1972) *Los Alumbrados*, Madrid. M. Andres (1973) *Nueva vision de los alumbrados de 1525*, Madrid (1976); *El misterio de los alumbrados de Toledo desvelado por sus contemporáneos*, Burgos.

15. Quoted by Egido, *Loc. cit.*, p. 130.

16. *Ibid.*, p. 158.

17. *Ibid.*, pp. 150-154.

18. Américo Castro, *The Structure of Spanish History*, pp. 466-551.

19. Egido, *Loc. cit.* The reader is advised to go to this source for a more balanced evaluation of these facts than is customary. On page 140 the document found in Toledo attesting to the facts here discussed appears.

On page 134 the reader will find how the secret was never revealed, not even to Teresa's beloved Gracián despite his diggings in that direction and Teresa's misapprehensions.

In practice new Christians were excluded from religious orders; from the military; from higher education; from holding offices and benefices. . . but always exposed to denunciations and taxes.

20. *Ibid.*, p. 157. Teresa's own recognition was that the success of her reform was due to the hand of God, since "it cannot have been because I was of illustrious descent that He did me this honor" (*Foundations* 27, 12).

As a footnote to this section I would like to add the following reflection. Castile, which did not undergo Teresa's transformation, is not very different today as in her time when it comes to the code of honor. I remember, as I grew up in that part of the world, the mixture of castes and practices associated with honor. In the same tiny village unleavened bread, crosses, "marranos," "new Christians," "old Christians," lived under the same fears and insults as four hundred years ago. People still cheated on account of honor and hid ancestral roots or left the village for the same reason.

Editor's Foreword

When the American novelist Victoria Lincoln died in Baltimore on June 13, 1981, she left an uncorrected final draft of a new biography of the Spanish saint Teresa of Avila (1515-1582). In her Preface—reconstructed from notes after her death by her widower Victor Lowe, Professor emeritus of Philosophy at the Johns Hopkins University—she explains her purpose: to avoid hagiography while narrating the life of a woman of flesh and blood who became dedicated to a rediscovered Christian faith, a conversion that led her to reform the Carmelite Order to which she belonged. Victoria Linclon spent the last dozen years of her life recreating Teresa's experiences from all the documentation, old and new, available.

The result is not just another academic or religious biography of Teresa of Avila. Miss Lincoln discovered in Teresa a kindred spirit, a semi-liberated woman who seemed never to have been properly understood from a human point of view. To decipher her life, frequently expurgated by the pious and overlaid by legends of all sorts, was not a simple task. Victoria Lincoln realized that Teresa's own autobiographical writings, especially her *Life* and her *Foundations*, no matter how fascinating, could not always be taken at face value, for they were written by order, and under the direction, of her confessors, and were shaped for the religious edification of her sister-nuns; there were, to say the least, some omissions. The major source of supplementary information and insights was Teresa's correspondence, over four hundred surviving letters written to members of her family, to fellow Carmelites, to Jesuit confessors, and to other prelates and members of Spanish society. In these letters, despite their occasional censorship, Miss Lincoln discovered the inner workings of a vibrant personality, an active "Jewish mother," intensely involved with brothers, sisters, and cousins, with politicians of Church and State, and with wealthy patrons.

This revisionist view of Teresa was also indebted to a new understanding of Spanish history developed after 1940, principally under the influence of the historian Américo Castro. He emphasized the importance of the symbiosis of Semitic religions—Christian, Muslim, and Jewish—in medieval Iberia, and was able to explain many cultural phenomena of sixteenth-century Spain as the results of the conversion of Jewish families, the conflict between Old Christians and New Christians, and the eventual assimilation of *converso* families into orthodox Spanish society. Castro realized that Teresa must have known of her Jewish ancestry and of her grandfather's persecution by the Inquisition in Toledo before she was born. The function of the Spanish Inquisition as an agent of religious and social assimiliation has also become clearer in recent years. The relevance of this to Teresa of Avila was made emphatically evident by the publication of E. Llamas Martinez's *Santa Teresa de Jesús y la Inquisición espanola* (Madrid, 1972). This book documents fully how, during her lifetime, Teresa was frequently denounced to the Inquisition and accused of heresy and immorality. It was a classical case of guilt by association: her Jewish ancestors, her illuminism ("heretical" mysticism and/or sexual hysteria), her embarrassing demand for mental prayer and the reform of conventual life, her being a woman (*"mulieres in ecclesia taceant"*). . . . It was apparently her political shrewdness and personal charm, more than her religious sincerity, that saved her from imprisonment and formal trial.

Victoria Lincoln's biography of Teresa is based on many historical documents such as those mentioned above, and on others such as Teresa's accounts of conscience (*cuentas de conciencia)* and the testimony given by many individuals for her beatification and canonization (1622). But it is less a work of scholarship than a novel-like story of one woman's discovery of the truth about another woman. The reader is plunged into the social and psychological life of sixteenth-century Spain, the life of convents and churches, of intrigue, hypocrisy, and mental derangement. But, despite her bad health, Teresa's eminently sane humanity is seen as her true sanctity, within a mad and confusing world of patriarchal domination. And Miss Lincoln's text is that of a novelist: in it the narrator's voice merges with that of the protagonist. Teresa's words are sometimes quoted in direct discourse, but in a free, colloquial translation, close to the style of twentieth-century America; there are Teresa's own breathless sentences, and repetitions, and non-sequiturs, the freest written style of sixteenth-century Spanish literature. There is also indirect discourse: Victoria Lincoln's paraphrases of Teresa's letters, her empathetic imitation of Teresa's style, the merging of two women's thought.

As editor of the text, I have changed as little as possible. With the help of other readers — Professors Audrey Lumsden-Kouvel, Ciriaco Morón Arroyo, Antonio de Nicolás — I have corrected many Spanish names. But I have not done the radical revising and documenting demanded by scholars; Victoria Lincoln's text is an almost seamless garment, with many movements back and forth in time and space. To help the non-specialized reader, I have added an essential bibliography, a map, a list of proper names, and a chronology.

Despite residual obscurities and even inaccuracies, this novel-like biography is an important first attempt at radically revising the too sanctimonious view of a very human Spanish woman. Scholars will later sift and refine upon Victoria Lincoln's discoveries and intuitions concerning Teresa of Avila; meanwhile we can all immerse ourselves in an authentic encounter between twentieth-century America and sixteenth-century Spain.

Elias L. Rivers
SUNY at Stony Brook
March, 1984

Essential Bibliography

Santa Teresa de Jesús, *Obras completas,* eds. Efrén de la Madre de Dios and Otger Steggink. Madrid, 1962. This handy single volume contains the complete works of Teresa: *Libro de la vida (The Book of her Life), Camino de perfección (Way of Perfection), Meditaciones sobre los Cantares (Meditations on the Song of Solomon), Moradas del castillo interior (Mansions of the Inner Castle), Cuentas de conciencia (Accounts of conscience), Exclamaciones (Exclamations), Poesisas (Poetry), Libro de las fundaciones (The Book of Foundations), Constituciones (Constitutions), Visita de Descalzas (The Visitation of Discalced Nuns), Avisos (Warnings), Ordenanza de una cofradia (Rules for a Brotherhood), Epistolario (Correspondence), Apuntaciones (Notes), Desafio espiritual (Spiritual Challenge),* and *Vejamen (Rebuke),* with indexes.

Jerónimo de Gracián, *La peregrinación de Anastasio,* Brussels, 1605.

Diego de Yepes, *Vida, virtudes y milagros de la bienaventurada virgen Teresa de Jesús. . . ,* Zaragoza, 1606.

Silverio de Santa Teresa, *Vida de Teresa de Jesús,* Burgos, 1935-37.

_____ *Procesos de beatificación y canonización de Santa Teresa de Jesús,* Burgos, 1934-35.

Henry Kamen, *The Spanish Inquisition,* London, 1965.

Efrén de la Madre de Dios and Otger Steggink, *Tiempo y vida de Santa Teresa,* Madrid, 1968.

Américo Castro, *The Spaniards: An Introduction to Their History,* Berkeley, 1971.

E. Llamas Martínez, *Santa Teresa de Jesús y la Inquisición española,* Madrid, 1972.

Stephen Clissold, *St. Teresa of Avila,* London, 1979. (This excellent brief biography was published too late to be of use to Victoria Lincoln.)

Chronology

1515	On March 28 Teresa de Ahumada is born on her mother's farm in Gotarrendura (near Avila), the daughter of Alonso Sánchez de Cepeda (from Toledo) and Beatriz de Ahumada (from Olmedo, near Valladolid).
1519	Her brother Lorenzo de Cepeda is born.
1520	Her uncle Francisco Alvarez de Cepeda married María de Ahumada. Her brother Antonio de Ahumada is born.
1521	Her brother Pedro de Ahumada is born.
1522	She tries to run away from home, with her brother Rodrigo, "to the land of the Moors." Her brother Jerónimo de Cepeda is born.
1525	Her maternal grandmother, Teresa de las Cuevas, dies in Olmedo.
1527	Her brother Agustín de Ahumada is born.
1528	Her sister Juana de Ahumada is born. Her mother writes her will and dies at Gotarrendura.
1531	Her older half-sister María de Cepeda marries Martín de Guzmán y Barrientos; in the spring she enters the Augustinian convent of Santa María de Gracia (Our Lady of Grace).
1532	In the fall she leaves the convent because of illness.
1533	She is at the home of her uncle Pedro Sánchez de Cepeda (in Hortigosa) and at that of her half-sister María (in Castellanos de la Cañada). She tells her father of her religious vocation.
1534	Her brother Hernando de Ahumada leaves for Peru.
1535	Her brother Rodrigo de Cepeda leaves for Río de la Plata. On November 2 she runs away to the Carmelite convent of the Encarnación de Avila.
1536	On October 31 her religious dowry is signed. On November 2 she dons the Carmelite habit at the Encarnación.
1537	On November 3 she professes as a Carmelite nun.
1538	In the fall she leaves the convent because of illness and heads for Becedas, stopping with her sister in Castellanos de la Cañada, where she reads Osuna's *Third Spiritual Alphabet*.
1539	In April she goes on to Becedas, to be treated by a female healer. In July she returns to Avila very ill. On August 15 she asks for confession, collapses for three days, and is prepared for burial. She returns to the convent of the Encarnación, where she remains an invalid for three years.
1542	In April she feels herself cured by the intercession of St. Joseph (San José), but has trouble praying.
1543	On December 26 she witnesses her father's death.
1544	In the fall Father Vincente Barrón exhorts her not to abandon prayer.
1548	In the summer she makes a pilgrimage to the Jeronimite monastery of Guadalajara.
1551	The Jesuits found a center in Avila.

1554	During Lent she undergoes a conversion in the presence of an image of the suffering Christ. The Jesuit Father Diego de Cetina is sent to Avila and becomes her confessor.
1555	In May the Jesuit Father Juan de Prádanos arrives in Avila.
1556	In May she makes her mystic betrothal. She travels to Alba de Tormes and to Villanueva del Aceral. The Jesuit Father Baltasar Alvarez arrives in Avila.
1557	She is in Aldea del Palo with Doña Guiomar de Ulloa ("Yomar") taking care of Father Prádanos. In the winter the Jesuit Father (later Saint) Francisco de Borja (Borgia) passes through Avila and gives her advice.
1558	Her friends decide that her spiritual graces are sent by the devil.
1559	On June 29 she has her first intellectual vision of Christ.
1560	On January 25 she has a vision of the Risen Christ; she is ordered to ward off her visions. She experiences transverberation at Doña Guiomar's house. In August Pedro de Alcántara visits her in Avila. She has a fearful vision of Hell. In September she holds an evening meeting in her cell and resolves to reform the Carmelite Order. In October she consults Dominican Father Pedro Ibáñez about it, and writes her first "Account of Conscience." At Christmas a confessor refuses her absolution unless she gives up her reform movement.
1561	A new Jesuit rector, Father Gaspar de Salazar, arrives. On August 12 Saint Clare promises her help. At the end of August she resuscitates her nephew Gonzalo de Ovalle. At Christmas she is ordered to leave for the home of widowed Doña Luisa de la Cerda in Toledo.
1562	From January to June, at Doña Luisa's home in Toledo, she confesses with Jesuit Father Pedro Domenech and meets Dominican Father García de Toledo. On February 7 Pope Pius IV grants her a brief for the founding of San José de Avila. In June she finishes her *Life* and leaves Toledo for Avila, finding the papal brief there waiting for her. In August Pedro de Alcántara persuades the Bishop of Avila, Don Alvaro de Mendoza, to permit the founding of San José without an endowment. On August 24 the Reformed convent is opened and four novices don the habit, leading to ecclesiastical and municipal opposition. On August 29 there is a mass meeting and a lawsuit. Finally, in December, she is permitted to transfer four nuns from the Encarnación to San José. She begins to write *The Way of Perfection*.
1563	She becomes prioress of San José as the new year begins. On May 5 María Bautista (Ocampo) joins her. In July she removes her shoes, giving her reform the name of Discalced. In August the Carmelite Provincial confirms permission for a year, under the Bishop of Avila. She writes the *Constitutions* (approved in 1565 by Pius IV).
1564	On August 24 the Nuncio renews permission for San José to continue. More nuns profess.
1565	On July 17 Pius IV confirms the status of San José. More nuns profess.
1566	She writes the first draft of her *Meditations on the Song of Songs*.

1567   On February 18 Father Rubeo, general of the Carmelite Order, visits both the Encarnación and San José. In April he presides over a provincial Chapter held in Avila and approves Teresa's vow of perfection, permitting her to found other female Reformed (Discalced) convents, except in Andalusia. On August 13 she leaves Avila to found a convent in Medina del Campo on August 15. Father Rubeo permits Reformed (Discalced) male monasteries (except in Andalusia).

1568   Between January and March she travels from Medina to Toledo via Alcalá. In April, with Doña Luisa de la Cerda, she travels to Malagón, where she founds a Discalced convent. In May she leaves for Avila via Toledo and Escalona. In June she leaves for Medina del Campo via Duruelo. On August 9 she leaves Medina for Valladolid with Juan de la Cruz, founding a convent on August 15. On November 28 a Reformed monastery for friars is founded in Duruelo by Juan de la Cruz. Teresa plans another foundation in Toledo.

1569   She leaves Valladolid on February 22, visiting Medina and Duruelo, and staying two weeks in Avila. On March 24 she reaches Toledo, founding there on May 14. Leaving Toledo on May 30, and after ten days at the Descalzas Reales in Madrid, she founds a Discalced nuns' convent in Pastrana on June 28 and a friars' monastery there on July 13; Mariano de San Benito and Juan de la Miseria don the habit. On July 21 she returns to Toledo, sending Isabel de Santo Domingo to be prioress at Pastrana and taking Ana de los Angeles from Malagón to be prioress at Toledo. She writes her *Exclamations*.

1570   On July 10 Teresa attends the professions of Mariano de San Benito and Juan de la Miseria at Pastrana. She travels to Alba de Tormes via Medina and returns to Toledo via Medina and Valladolid. In August she goes to Avila. On October 31 she arrives at Salamanca with María del Sacramento, founding there on November 1.

1571   On January 25 Teresa founds in Alba de Tormes with Juan de la Cruz. Early in March she returns to Salamanca with Inés de Jesús and stays with the Count and Countess of Monterrey. From there she goes to Medina. She is elected prioress of San José, and in July the Visitor of Castile invites Teresa to be prioress of the Encarnación; after some hesitation she accepts, leaving Medina for Avila on July 11. On July 13 she renounces the Mitigated (Calced) rule at San José de Avila and returns to Medina for August and September. She returns to the Encarnación de Avila to take over as prioress; she is also put in charge of the Salamanca convent.

1572   On January 19 the Virgin appears to Teresa. On March 25 Jerónimo Gracián dons the Carmelite habit in Pastrana. Teresa summons Juan de la Cruz as confessor to the Encarnación de Avila. In September she writes the *Spiritual Challenge*. On November 16 she receives the grace of spiritual matrimony.

1573   Between February 2 and 12, in Alba, Teresa approves a copy of the *Way of Perfection*. On July 31 she arrives at Salamanca, and on August 25, by order of her Jesuit confessor Jerónimo Ripalda, she begins to write the *Foundations*.

1574   In January Teresa goes from Salamanca to Alba, returning in February. In March she returns to Alba and then sets out for Segovia, with Julián de Avila, Antonio Gaitán, and Juan de la Cruz; she founds in Segovia on March 19. On April 6 and 7 she transfers the Discalced nuns of Pastrana to Segovia. Gracián becomes Carmelite Provincial and Reformer for Andalusia. On September 30 she leaves Segovia, arriving at the Encarnación de Avila early in October, completing her triennium as prioress there and returning to San José on October 6. She writes the second draft of her *Meditations on the Song of Songs*. About December 20 she goes to Valladolid on business.

1575   In January Teresa leaves Valladolid, stops in Medina, and arrives at Beas on February 21, founding there on February 24. In April and May she sees Father Gracián in Beas, leaving for Seville by his order on May 18. Passing through Córdoba, in Ecija she makes a vow of obedience to Father Gracián. Arriving in Seville on May 27, she founds there on May 29. In June and July the Dominican Father Domingo Báñez approves her *Meditations* and her *Life*. On August 12 her successful brother Lorenzo arrives from the Indies with three children and with their brother Pedro. In December a novice denounces the Seville Discalced nuns to the Inquisition; Teresa is ordered to retire to a convent in Castile.

1576   On January 1 Ana de San Alberto, acting for Teresa, founds in Caravaca. Teresa is interrogated in Seville for the Inquisition. On June 4 she leaves Seville with her brothers and family, arriving at Malagón June 11 and at Toledo June 26. In August she writes the *Visitation of Discalced Nuns*, and in November she finishes Chapter 27 of the *Foundations*.

1577   On May 28, in Toledo, Gracián orders Teresa to write the *Dwellings of the Inner Castle*. In July she goes to Avila to transfer San José's obedience from the Bishop of Avila to the Carmelite Order. On November 27 she completes in Avila *The Dwellings*. On December 3 the Calced friars imprison Juan de la Cruz and Germán de San Matías; Teresa writes to King Philip II asking him to intervene. On December 24 she falls down a stairway at San José and breaks her left arm.

1578   In May a healer sets Teresa's arm. On July 23 Gracián is removed by the Nuncio Sega as Apostolic Visitor. On August 9 the Royal Council forbids the Discalced to obey the Nuncio. Gracián visits Teresa in Avila. On August 9 a Discalced Chapter, meeting in Almodóvar, elects Antonio de Jesús Heredia as Father Superior. On October 16 the Nuncio annuls the Chapter's decisions and orders all Carmelites to submit to the Calced authorities; on December 20 he orders Father Gracián imprisoned at the Carmelite college in Alcalá.

1579   On April 1 the Nuncio removes the Calced authorities and appoints Father Angel de Salazar as vicar general of the Discalced. On June 6

Teresa writes her *Four Warnings* for Discalced friars. On June 25 she leaves Avila and, after a few days in Medina, arrives in Valladolid on July 3. On July 30 she leaves Valladolid, and after a few days each in Medina and Alba, arrives in Salamanca on August 14. She returns to Avila toward the end of October. In mid-November she leaves Avila and, passing through Toledo, reaches Malagón on November 25 to direct construction work.

1580	Authorized to found a Discalced convent in Villanueva de la Jara, Teresa leaves Malagón on February 13, spends three days in La Roda, arriving at Villanueva on February 21 and founding on February 25. She hurts her left arm again. On March 20 she leaves Villanueva, arriving in Toledo on March 26, seriously ill. On May 5 Gracián is reinstated as provincial. Teresa leaves Toledo, passes through Madrid, and arrives in Segovia on June 13. On June 22 a papal brief orders a separate province for the Discalced. Yanguas and Gracián revise *The Dwellings* in Segovia with Teresa. On June 26 her brother Lorenzo dies; she goes to Avila for family reasons on July 6. In August she goes to Valladolid via Medina, despite serious illness, and then to Segovia on August 23. She goes via Valladolid to Palencia, where she founds on December 29.
1581	In February Teresa prepares Gracián for the first Discalced Chapter, meeting in Alcalá on March 3; Gracián is elected provincial and the new constitutions are ratified. On May 9 Teresa leaves Palencia for Soria, stopping in Burgo de Osma; she founds in Soria on June 3. On August 16 she meets Diego de Yepes in Osma. She arrives in Segovia on August 23, then goes to San José de Avila, via Villacastín, on September 6. She is elected prioress on September 10. She does not go with Juan de la Cruz to Granada.
1582	On January 2 Teresa leaves Avila with Gracián for Burgos, stopping in Medina, Valladolid, and Palencia. Ana de Jesús founds in Granada on January 20; Teresa arrives in Burgos on January 26 and founds there on April 19. On May 7 Gracián and Teresa part for the last time. On July 26 Teresa leaves Burgos and goes to Palencia, Valladolid, and Medina. From there Father Antonio de Jesús Heredia orders her to Alba on September 19. She faints next day in Peñaranda. She arrives in Alba on September 21; on September 29 she goes to bed mortally ill. Announcing her death on October 1, Teresa receives the last rites on October 3 and dies at 9 P.M. on October 4.

List of People and Places

While place-names are relatively stable, personal names are quite unstable in sixteenth-century Spain: there were multiple surnames, and children chose the surname(s) of either or both parents; members of religious orders normally dropped surnames and adopted popular religious names that were frequently repeated. The relatively simple case of Teresa herself will illustrate this: born in 1515 on her mother's farm at Gotarrendura (near Avila), the daughter of Alonso Sánchez de Cepeda and Beatriz de Ahumada, she chose to call herself Teresa de Ahumada, but some of her siblings chose Cepeda. When she entered religious life, she took the name Teresa de Jesús, but she is widely known as Saint Teresa de Avila.

Agustín de los Reyes (Carrasco y Góngora), 1552-96. Became a Discalced Carmelite in Pastrana (1571). Prior of Almodóvar (1577) and Granada (1580).

Ahumada. Surname of Teresa's mother, Beatriz, 1495(?)-1529. Some of her children took her surname, others that of her husband, Alonso Sánchez de Cepeda (q.v.).

Ahumada, Agustín de, 1527-91. Teresa's brother. Went to the Indies in 1546.

Ahumada, Hernando de, 1510-(?). Teresa's oldest brother. Went to the Indies in 1534 with Pizarro.

Ahumada, Juana de, 1528-87. Teresa's younger sister. Married Juan de Ovalle. Helped with San José de Avila; closely associated with Teresa. See Ovalle.

Ahumada, Pedro de, 1521-89. Teresa's brother. Went to the Indies in 1548; returned to Spain in 1575 with their brother Lorenzo de Cepeda.

Ahumada, Teresa de ("Teresica"), 1566-1610. Teresa's niece, daughter of her brother Lorenzo de Cepeda, born in Quito. Entered Seville convent in 1574, novice in San José de Avila 1576, professed in 1582.

Alba, Duchess of. See *Enríquez de Toledo, Doña María.*

Alba de Tormes. Town seat of the Duke of Alba; Discalced foundation of 1571.

Alberta Bautista (Mencía Ponce de León y Ramírez), 1548-83. Professed in 1569, elected prioress of Medina in 1577.

Alcántara: see *Pedro de Alcántara.*

Almodóvar del Campo. Male Discalced foundation of 1575; chapters celebrated in 1576, under Father Gracián, and in 1578, under Father Antonio de Jesús Heredia.

Altomira (small town): site of male Discalced foundation in 1572.

Alvarez, Baltasar, 1533-80. Confessor of Teresa while Jesuit rector of Avila (1559-64); helped her found in Medina (1567).

Alvarez, García (Garciálvarez). Priest in Seville who helped Discalced founda-tion of 1575 and became confessor; removed by Archbishop after scandals.

Alvarez, Rodrigo, 1523-87. Jesuit confessor of Teresa in Seville; defended her as an Inquisitor in 1575.

Alvarez del Aguila, Hernando, 1510-72. Jesuit of Avila, Francisco de Salcedo's brother-in-law; occasional confessor of Teresa.

Ambrosio de San Pedro. Professed in Pastrana 1571; vicar of Almodóvar 1575. Accompanied Ana de San Alberto at Caravaca foundation (1576).

Ana de Jesús (Lobera), 1545-1621. Professed in Salamanca 1571; went with Teresa to Beas, where she was prioress; founded in Granada in 1582.

Ana de la Encarnación (Tapia), 1536-1601. Went with Teresa from Encarnación de Avila to Medina in 1567; prioress there and in Salamanca.

Ana de los Angeles (Ana Ordóñez). First mother superior of San José de Avila. Prioress in Malagón.

Ana de San Alberto (Salcedo). Daughter of Alonso de Avila and Ana de Salcedo. The second nun to profess in Malagón (1569). Founded in Caravaca (1576) for Teresa and was prioress there until 1591.

Ana de San Bartolomé, 1549-1626. Daughter of Hernando García and María Manzanas. Entered San José de Avila in 1570. Teresa's amanuensis and nurse during her last years.

Ana de San Pedro (Wasteels), 1540-88 ("La Flamenca"). Entered San José de Avila as a widow.

Angela. One of Teresa's nicknames in her correspondence with Gracián, whom she calls "Eliseo" or "Paul."

Antonio de Jesús (Heredia), 1510-1601. Carmelite priest who helped organize San José de Avila. Attended general chapter in Rome 1564. Named prior of Medina in 1567. Joined Juan de la Cruz in Duruelo in 1568. Prior of Toledo, 1573-75; founded in Almodóvar (1575). Visitor with Gracián in Andalusia. With Teresa at her death.

Avila (city). Site of Calced Carmelites of the Encarnación and Discalced Carmel-ites of San José.

Avila, Julián de, 1527-1605. Priest and chaplain of San José from 1563 to 1604.

Avila, Saint Juan de, 1500-69. Spiritual reformer in Andalusia; read Teresa's *Life* with enthusiasm.

Azzaro: see *Mariano de San Benito.*

Baltasar de Jesús (Nieto), 1524-90. Carmelite who, with his brothers Gaspar and Melchor, rebelled against General Rubeo (q.v.). Prior of Pastrana, 1570-75. Founded in Granada (1573). Denounced Gracián to King Philip II in 1577.

Báñez, Domingo, 1528-1604. Dominican defender of San José de Avila in 1562; Teresa's confessor, and friend from then until her death.

Beamonte y Navarra, Doña Beatriz, 1523-1600. Widow with nieces; gave her palace for a convent in Soria (1581).

Beas (town in Andalusia). Teresa founded there in 1575, meeting Father Gracián for the first time.

Beatriz de Jesús (Cepeda y Ocampo). Daughter of Teresa's cousin Francisco de Cepeda. Moved from Encarnación to San José de Avila in 1574, renouncing the mitigated rule in Malagón. With Teresa at Villanueva foundation.

Brianda de San José (Temiño). Professed 1571. With Teresa at Descalzas Reales in Madrid. Prioress at Malagón and at Toledo.

Burgos (major city of Old Castile). Discalced foundation, Teresa's last, in 1582.

Caravaca (in Andalusia). Ana de San Alberto made Discalced foundation in 1576.

Carleval, Dr. Bernadino. Professor at the University of Baeza; enthusiastic disciple of Saint Juan de Avila.

Cepeda. Second surname of Teresa's father, Alonso Sánchez de Cepeda, 1480(?)-1543. Surname of several of her siblings and of numerous other relatives.

Cepeda, Francisco Alvarez de, 1493-(?). Younger brother of Teresa's father, Alonso Sánchez de Cepeda. Married María de Ahumada in 1520 and had many children, surnamed Cepeda, Cimbrón, or Tapia.

Cepeda, Francisco de, 1560-1617. Son of Teresa's brother Lorenzo; married Orofrisia de Mendoza y Castilla in 1580, inheriting his father's estate, 'La Serna.'

Cepeda, Jerónimo, 1522-75. Teresa's brother; went to the Indies in 1540. The father of several illegitimate children.

Cepeda, Lorenzo, 1519-1580. Teresa's brother; went to the Indies in 1540 and became rich. Close to her after his return to Seville in 1575. The father of Francisco de Cepeda (1560), Lorenzo de Cepeda (1562), and Teresica de Ahumada (1566).

Cepeda, Lorenzo, 1562-1627. Born in Quito, the son of Teresa's brother Lorenzo; inherited his father's property in America.

Cerda, Doña Luisa de, 1517 (?)-96. Daughter of the Duke of Medinaceli. Widowed in 1561, befriended by Teresa; offered money for founding at Malagón.

Chaves, Diego de, 1507-92. Philip II's Dominican confessor; helped Teresa.

Corro, María del. Denounced Teresa to the Inquisition in Seville.

Cuevas, Juan de las, 1524-99. Dominican, named Commissary of the Discalced by Pope Gregory XIII and Philip II, presided at Alcalá Chapter of 1581, which declared the separation of Calced and Discalced Carmelites.

Dantisco, Doña Juana, 15(?)-1601. Daughter of the Polish ambassador, married Diego Gracián de Aldrete; close friend of Teresa. Mother of Father Jerónimo Gracián.

Diego de la Trinidad: see *Juan de Jesús.*

Doria, Nicoleo (Nicolás de Jesús María), 1539-94. Genoese businessman in Seville; ordained priest, professed as Discalced Carmelite in 1578 and became vicar of Los Remedios, prior of Pastrana. Opposed Father Gracián and finally had him expelled (1592).

Duruelo (small town near Avila). Site of first male Discalced foundation (1568), moved to Mancera in 1570.

Eboli, Princess of: see *Mendoza, Doña Ana de.*

Elías de San Martín (Heriz), 15(?)-1614. Professed in Pastrana 1573. Famous as preacher. Founded in Toledo (1586).

Enríquez de Toledo, Doña María. Wife of third Duke of Alba, strong supporter of Teresa. With Duke, read Teresa's *Life.*

Fernández Orellana, Pedro, 1527-80. Dominican prior in Segovia and in Madrid. Apostolic Visitor of Castilian Carmelites (1569) and associate of Nuncio in Discalced affairs (1579). Supported Teresa.

Gaitán, Antonio. Under Teresa's spiritual direction, went with her to found at Segovia and at Beas.

Garciálvarez: see *Alvarez, García.*

Germán de San Matías (Ruiz de Alda y Navarrete), (?)-1579. Professed at Pastrana in 1573. Imprisoned with Juan de la Cruz in Toledo by Calced friars.

Gotarrendura (village near Avila). Site of the estate of Teresa's mother, Beatriz de Ahumada, whose children were born there.

Gracián, Jerónimo de la Madre de Dios, 1545-1614. Son of Diego Gracián and Juana Dantisco. Brilliant student at Alcalá; ordained priest 1570, professed as Carmelite in 1573 and became superior of Discalced in Andalusia. Founded in Seville (1574). Met Teresa at Beas in 1575; Teresa took a vow of obedience to him. Involved in political struggles, was elected first Discalced provincial in 1581. Expelled by Doria in 1592, after Teresa's death.

Gregorio Naciano (Martínez y López), 15(?)-1599. Ordained priest in 1563, after studies at Alcalá. Traveled with Teresa from Beas to Seville; professed 1576. Novice master at Los Remedios, prior at La Roda.

Guiomar, "Yomar": see *Ulloa, Doña Guiomar de.*

Gutiérrez, Nicolás. Teresa's friend and helper in Salamanca; six of his daughters became Discalced Carmelites.

Gutiérrez de la Magdalena, Juan ("El Magdaleno"), 1537-79. Calced Carmelite, responsible for the imprisonment of Juan de la Cruz and Germán de San Matías.

Heredia, Antonio de: see *Antonio de Jesús.*

Hernándcz, Pablo. Jesuit confessor of Teresa while she was with Doña Luisa de la Cerda; helped with Malagón foundation.

Inés de Jesús (Tapia). Teresa's cousin, who helped her found San José de Avila (1562) and attended the foundations at Medina (1567), where she became prioress, and at Palencia (1580), where she also became prioress.

Isabel de San Pablo, 1547-82. Daughter of Teresa's cousin Francisco de Cepeda. Entered the Encarnación de Avila with two sisters; followed Teresa to San José in 1563, and to foundations in Toledo, in Pastrana (1569), and in Segovia (1574).

Isabel de Santo Domingo (Ortega), 1537-1623. Entered San José de Avila in 1563, professed in 1565. In 1569 went with Teresa to Toledo as prioress; founding prioress at Pastrana. Left Pastrana with her nuns for Segovia, where she became prioress in 1574.

Jerónima del Santo Espíritu (Villalobos), 15(?)-1599. Professed with her sister at Salamanca in 1576. Teresa sent her as prioress to Malagón in 1579; she helped Teresa revise *El camino de perfección.*

Juan de Jesús (Roca), 1543-1614. Gracián's fellow student, he professed at

Pastrana in 1573 and was prior at Mancera, Pastrana, etc. In 1579 went to Rome with Diego de la Trinidad to get a separate province for the Discalced.

Juan de la Cruz (Yepes), 1542-91. Studied at Salamanca as a Carmelite; joined Teresa to found at Valladolid and at Duruelo (1568). From 1572 to 1577 appointed by Teresa as confessor at the Encarnación de Avila; imprisoned with Germán de San Matías for nine months by his Calced brothers (1577-78). Held high offices with the Discalced; defended Gracián. A major poet, mystic, and saint of the Reformed Carmelites.

Juan de la Miseria (Narduch), 1526(?)-1616. Neapolitan painter, friend, and associate of Mariano Azzaro; professed at Pastrana in 1570.

Laiz, Teresa de. Founding patroness (in association with the Duchess) at Alba.

Lárez, Antonio. Jesuit rector in Avila, Teresa's confessor.

Malagón (town between Toledo and Almodóvar). Discalced foundation in 1568.

Mancera (town in the region of Avila). The Duruelo community was moved to Mancera in 1570.

María Bautista (de Ocampo), 1543-1603. Daughter of Diego de Cepeda, Teresa's cousin. Professed in San José de Avila in 1564; went with Teresa to found at Medina and at Valladolid.

María de Cristo (del Aguila), 1544(?)-90. Professed in San José de Avila in 1568; first elected prioress there in 1577, resigning in favor of Teresa in 1581.

María de San Jerónimo (Dávila), 1541(?)-1602. Daughter of Alonso Alvarez Dávila, Teresa's cousin; professed in San José in 1565, where she often substituted for Teresa as prioress.

María de San José (Salazar), 15(?)-1603. With Doña Luisa de la Cerda in Toledo, met Teresa in 1562. Professed in Malagón in 1571. In 1575 went with Teresa to found in Beas and in Seville, where she stayed on as prioress, corresponding frequently with Teresa.

Mariano de San Benito (Azzaro), 1510-94. Italian theologian and scientist; introduced in 1569 to Teresa, who persuaded him to join the Discalced in Pastrana. Professed in 1570, went to Andalusia with Gracián in 1573, ordained priest in 1574.

Medina del Campo (market town southwest of Valladolid). Site of Discalced foundation in 1567.

Mendoza, Don Alvaro. Became Bishop of Avila in 1560; supported Teresa's first reform plans. Named Bishop of Palencia in 1577. His sister María was an influential friend of Teresa.

Mendoza, Doña Ana de (Princess of Eboli), 1540-92. Married to Ruy Gómez de Silva, Philip II's favorite. Met Teresa at Doña Luisa de la Cerda's home in Toledo and encouraged her to found in Pastrana (1569); entered that convent at husband's death in 1573, causing nuns to flee surreptitiously to Segovia in 1574. Imprisoned 1578.

Mendoza, Doña María Sarmiento de. Sister of Don Alvaro de Mendoza, Bishop of Avila; widow of Francisco de los Cobos, Charles V's secretary. Became Teresa's friend in 1562 and helped her with influence at Court and with money for Valladolid foundation (1568).

Mendoza y Castilla, Orofrisia de, 1564-1617. Married Francisco de Cepeda, Teresa's nephew, in 1580; inherited part of Lorenzo de Cepeda's estate, but had financial problems.

Nieto. Surname of three Andalusian Carmelite brothers, denounced by Father Rubeo. See *Baltasar de Jesús (Nieto).*

Orellana, Juan de. Dominican who denounced Teresa to the Inquisition.

Ormaneto, Nicholas. Bishop of Padua, became Nuncio to Philip II in 1572; active in matters pertaining to Carmelite Reform.

Ovalle Godínez, Juan de, 15(?)-1595. Married Teresa's sister Juana de Ahumada in 1553. Their daughter Beatriz (1560-1639) eventually became a Discalced Carmelite, in 1585.

Pastrana (town in province of Guadalajara). Site of Discalced foundation in 1569.

Pedro de Alcántara, 1499-1562. Franciscan reformer and saintly author of pious works; met Teresa through Guiomar de Ulloa.

Prádanos, Juan de, 1528-97. Jesuit priest who in 1555 replaced the Jesuit Diego de Cetina as Teresa's spiritual director in Avila.

Quiroga, Gaspar de, 1507(?)-94. Named Grand Inquisitor in 1572 and Primate Archbishop of Toledo in 1577. Teresa refers to him as "Angel Mayor" (i.e., Grand Inquisitor) in her correspondence.

Ripalda, Jerónimo, 1535-1618. While rector of Jesuits in Salamanca, confessed Teresa (1573) and ordered her to write *Foundations.*

La Roda (town in eastern Spain). Site of male Discalced foundation in 1572.

Rubeo, Juan Bautista (Giovanni Battista Rossi), 1507-78. Italian Carmelite, elected in 1564 to be General of the Order. Went to Spain in 1566 and met Teresa in Avila in 1567; before leaving Spain he ordered her to found Reformed convents and monasteries (except in Andalusia, where the Nieto brothers had left things in bad shape).

Salamanca (major university city in Old Castile). Site of Discalced foundation in 1570.

Salazar, Angel de. Carmelite provincial of Castile, attending general chapter in Rome, with Heredia, in 1564. Gave Teresa tentative support.

Salazar, Gaspar de, 1529-93. Jesuit confessor of Teresa in 1561. Apparently unstable later on.

Salcedo, Francisco de, (?)-1580. Native of Avila who, when widowered in 1570, became a priest and served the Discalced nuns of Avila. Left his impoverished estate to San José.

Sánchez de Cepeda, Rodrigo. The brother of Teresa's father Alonso (see *Cepeda);* married Isabel del Aguila about 1513, producing two daughters, Mencía and Elvira.

San José: see *María de San José.*

San Matías: see *Germán de San Matías.*

Sega, Felipe, 1537(?)-96. Named Nuncio to Spain in 1577, where he attacked the Discalced Reform; he later yielded to Philip II's demand for Discalced independence.

Seville (major city of Andalusia). Site of male Discalced foundation in 1574, female in 1575.

Toledo, Fernando Alvarez de, 1507-82. The famous third Duke of Alba, married to María Enríquez. Read Teresa's *Life* while imprisoned.

Toledo, García de, (?)-1590. Dominican father superior at Santo Tomás de Avila; as Teresa''s confessor (1562) ordered her to write her *Life*.

Tolosa, Catalina de, 1538-1608. A widow with two sons and six daughters, several of whom became Discalced Carmelites.

Tostado, Jerónimo. Carmelite from Portugal, named Visitor in 1575; persecuted the Discalced.

Ulloa, Doña Guiomar de ("Yomar"), 1527-85(?). A widow at 25, with three children, became identified with Teresa and Carmelite reform.

Valladolid (city in Old Castile). Site of Discalced foundation in 1568.

Velázquez, Dr. Alonso. Theologian and professor at Toledo, where he was Teresa's confessor. Later Bishop of Osma.

Villanueva de la Jara (town in eastern Spain). Site of Discalced convent (1580).

Yanguas, Diego de, 1535(?)-1607. Dominican from Segovia, where he met Teresa and was her confessor and counselor. In 1580, with Gracián, he censored her *Moradas* in her presence; he ordered her to burn her *Meditations*.

Yepes, Diego de, 1529-1613. Jeronimite friar, met Teresa in 1576; wrote a life of Teresa in 1587.

Preface

There have been countless books about Saint Teresa of Avila, and for my sins I have read most of them—most, that is, which were written in English, Spanish or French. I have read only one that tried to do what I have spent eleven years on trying to do here. Gabriela Cunningham-Grahame wrote a biography as opposed to a piece of hagiography: a serious, two-volume life, published in 1894, to which she was inspired by Teresa''s own writings as she found them in their first halfway complete and honest edition, that of De La Fuente (1861). But Teresa's collected writings received their pioneer scholarly edition in the 1920's and had an incomparably better job done on them in 1963, further revised and updated in 1968. It is only since 1972 that all the material for a biography has been available to anyone who can read Spanish and is willing to study the period—for the story cannot be divorced from its background.

As Mrs. Cunningham-Grahame was writing her book in 1894, she was shut off from the necessary facts, yet somehow she caught Teresa's tone, her spirit. And she saw to a remarkable extent how it contrasted with the greater part of what was written about her after the "miraculous" event, a year after Teresa''s death, which changed her reputation.

That event calls for a word here. Teresa's wake was held on the day she died, at Alba de Tormes, in 1582. On the following morning, fifteen hours after her death, her body was sealed away in the wall of a crypt—a prompt, dry cold-storage. A year later one branch of the faction-torn Order that she had founded—in its reality very far from her founding dream—arranged a body-snatching. The thin lid of the pinewood box in which she was thrust away had broken under the mortar and rubble piled over it before the wall was rebuilt, and the body was found to be miraculously preserved—white as wax and celestially fragrant, by all accounts save one.

That one comes from Ribera, her first and best contemporary biographer. He had met her only twice, and at a time when the opinion held of her by his Order, the Jesuits, was one that they have long wished to forget and have forgotten. He believed in Teresa's great purpose. His attempt to research and celebrate her life, alone among such contemporary writings, caught the vital quality celebrated four hundred years later by Mrs. Cunningham-Grahame.

Her name was Teresa de Ahumada; by the Spanish custom which allowed a choice between the mother's surname and the father's, she used her mother's. The name, like many English surnames, can be that of prince or peasant; the de Ahumadas in her background were untitled farm folk and as such (as Sancho Panza boasted of his sole unstained virtue) "ever a mortal enemy to the Jews." Her father came of a distinguished old Jewish family. To anyone familiar with sixteenth-century Spain, there was no dishonesty, disloyalty or snobbery in his ceasing to be Señor Alonso Pina in his thirties and becoming (illegally) Don Alonso de Cepeda, then legally so as the result of a lawsuit in Avila.

This biography had its origin in my reading of a curious book now called *The Life of St. Teresa of Avila by Herself.* I *believed* all that we have been expected to disbelieve piously ever since the miraculous preservation of her corpse. I did not know the extenuating circumstances which surrounded her loss of virginity, but I believed her account of a "reputation very very badly damaged," though nobody could say anything "for sure"; and I was touched by her account of how she made her adored and adoring father believe her protestations of innocence "because he loved me so much and I lied to him so much."

The Spanish Church is justly proud of its twelve saints of the Counter Reformation while still remaining reluctant to admit that Spain ever gave them anything much to reform. Only an Italian, the Carmelite General Rubeo (Giovanni Battista Rossi), tells us of the conditions that he found in Spanish convents and monasteries. His report, "A Visit to Spain," was first given proper attention, after four centuries of moldering in the Vatican Archives, in 1968. I believed what Teresa wrote about her twenty years as a repeatedly fallen Magdalen in one of those sprawling Renaissance convents which made it only too easy for a Magdalen to fall.

We cannot appreciate the courage that Teresa's career demanded — from its small-scale beginnings when she was forty-seven to its nationwide scope which began when she turned fifty-three and ended with her death at sixty-seven — unless we know what it meant to be of Jewish blood in her time and place: Spain, 1515 to 1582. There were truths that she could not tell without endangering the military careers of seven brothers or destroying her sole chance to serve Christ's church by other means than supporting the foredoomed futility of holy wars.

Somehow or other, I believed Teresa's great confession from the start, and was moved when her chance discovery of Saint Augustine, translated for the first time into Spanish, taught her the central truth of Christianity — that God forgives.

Teresa is celebrated for the miracle of the Transverberation — the physical piercing of her heart by one thrust of an angel's flame-tipped lance. This miracle is founded on her own honest account, set down unwillingly at an Inquisitor's orders, of a *recurrent* dream experience in which the angelic lance penetrated her body "repeatedly," causing delight intense as pain until she "felt that her very entrails would be pulled out with it." Bernini's beautiful, and sexually loaded, Baroque masterpiece, "The Ecstasy of St. Teresa," is faithful to her words as he depicts the immediate aftermath of one such experience: the swooning nun whose face I once heard a man call the world's only beautiful depiction of a woman in orgasm, beautiful with the love always so sadly missing from pornography.

I suggest a very different miracle, one which would not suggest itself to a woman born much later than I — in 1904, that is. I grew up in changing times, but I remain instinctively, though no longer intellectually, a child of the double standard. Teresa reminded one unquestioningly, throughout her life: the redemption and forgiveness of Mary Magdalen was a far greater wonder than that of the repentant King David, and both were irrelevant to her own certain damnation "since they, once called, did not fall again." Then, when she was forty, she read Augustine, who had prayed, "God make me chaste—but not yet." And amazingly, she read him not as a man, judged by the double standard, but as a human soul. "I felt as if I were reading the story of my own life." Her conversion and her founding of the reformed or Discalced Carmelite convents sprang from a total identification with the oft-fallen Augustine. She fell in love with the all-forgiving Christ, the Rival with whom no man could compete.

The time I had spent with Teresa de Ahumada was all totally rewarding. Hardly a day of it did not bring some new understanding. If her many lies of omission had sprung from cowardice or ambition, they would soon have bored me. But the more I discovered about her lies, from many dependable sources — lawsuits, papal briefs, convent expense accounts, and over four hundred letters she had written during her last ten years — the more I knew that I myself would have told those that protected her family, and I had to admit humbly that I should have lacked the courage and stamina to tell those which protected her great reforming work. When I read her description of that work in the book that was interrupted by her death, I could only fear that in her place I would have abandoned hope, told the whole truth, and taken the advice of Job's counsellors to curse God and die.

It was still more moving to discover the subject about which, to use her own phrase, she could never "dissemble a little." This made her confession so inconvenient to the Carmelites of her day that it was suppressed during her lifetime and only published to be disbelieved after she died and became "the saint of raptures."

Teresa was pitilessly honest about herself, but from the time she ceased to deserve it — at forty — scandals about her love affairs with confessors pursued her until the time she was sixty, such tales reaching imaginative heights of prurient fancy which betray an amazing will to believe in the Spanish conservatives of her day. Why were these tales believed when her own confession of her twenty years as a Carmelite nun who feared God too much to love Him and loved at least one man too much to deny him was suppressed, both while she lived and when her canonization made it incredible? (For except for the saint of her deepest devotion, the Magdalen, the double standard for saints is inflexible.)

My slow discovery of answers to questions like this went on for decades; from time to time it sent a newly invalidated carton of manuscript up to the attic and left me back at page one, but always with a sense of deepened friendship with Teresa and a quickened excitement over digging for the facts *and* using them once they were exhumed. Summers were devoted to material in the British Museum, including correspondence between the Vatican and the Court of Philip II. Each discovery of having been fooled by years of pious

concealment brought some new illumination of an obscure or cautiously oblique passage in Teresa's letters.

The story of Augustine"s conversion was her release from "the way of fear"
and her healing discovery of "the way of love." It was *not* this which brought on
the "raptures" with which Teresa's name is associated. Raptures were typical
of an epidemic disorder in the life of the Spanish church when she was
converted — a wave of neo-Protestant hysteric illuminism. As experienced in
the organized groups of such *alumbrados*, they commonly went hand in hand
with unbridled sexuality, though on occasion they were allied with a masochis-
tic excess of bodily penance: this the Spanish temperament responded to with
holy awe, though John of the Cross called it "the penances of beasts."

At three times Teresa had to struggle against *arrobamientos*, raptures. Her
final word on them was expressed to the brother with whom she could be
wholly open, as he with her. They had come back, she said; he should pray
that she be delivered from them, at least in public, where they constituted a
real danger. And danger or no, they were worthless: "they do not even help
one to pray better."

Teresa came to agree with the Inquisition on the validity of "raptures," as
did Domingo Báñez, the Dominican scholar to whose rationalism and pragmatism she owed much, and as did that great mystic, John of the Cross, the first
friar of the Order that she founded once Rome allowed her to begin her
astounding public career. The Inquisition contested her threatened canonization for many years after the prompt discovery of her miraculous preservation. Such miracles were too common to notice if they lacked political
significance; Teresa's canonization, forty years after her death, was a political
triumph for the Spanish crown, a compromise on the part of the Vatican, and a
defeat for the Inquisition. It was also a defeat for Teresa, one of which she died
mercifully unaware. Canonization on any grounds could never have seemed
less ludicrously unlikely than it did at her deathbed, least of all canonization
on the grounds which had for so long kept her in danger of the stake.

So far as I know, this book is the first since 1894 that has tried to go to source
materials a historian would respect and to write with complete honesty a
biography covering every episode of Teresa's life. She died in 1582, but I
can count on my fingers the friends who have been more fully alive to me
in my lifetime.

Victoria Lincoln
May, 1981

Acknowledgments

As the inheritor of the manuscript of this book by my late wife, I owe thanks for reading it to her friend, the author Rhoda Truax, and to Professor Richard Kagan of the Johns Hopkins University, and thanks for helpful suggestions to Professor Robert S. Fitzgerald of Johns Hopkins. When the four hundredth anniversary of St. Teresa's death was observed in 1982 at the Catholic University of America in a symposium organized by Father John Sullivan, O.C.D., I was impressed by a paper, "The Vernacular Mind of St. Teresa," given by Professor Elias L. Rivers, and overjoyed to find that he was willing to edit Victoria Lincoln's manuscript. Thanks are also due to Professor Keith Egan of Marquette University for his interest in it and to Professor Antonio T. de Nicolás for writing the Introduction and helping with the editing.

Victor Lowe
March, 1984

Chapter 1 ❁ Juan Sánchez, Teresa's Jewish Grandfather

The massive, red-brown walls that surround Avila date from the eleventh century, yet they look uncannily new. The effect, I think, is due less to the fact that they are still in mint condition than that they are so inexplicably mismatched to the gray stone buildings, the gray cobbled streets, or indeed to any stone in the surrounding landscape. Looking at them, one feels that they are a barrier through which time oozes in the slowest of slow leaks; and indeed, when Teresa's grandfather chose Avila for the place in which to rebuild a life that Torquemada had disrupted, it was blessedly out of date. Its temper of opinion, like its walls, belonged to the days when St. Ferdinand, King of Castile (1217-1252), put down a Moorish uprising, gave himself the proud title of King of the Three Religions, and thus established the only nation in Europe where the Jews of the Middle Ages could prosper unpersecuted.

At the height of his career, Torquemada (1420-1498), the founder of the Spanish Inquisition, had unwisely chosen that ancient, upland city in which to build the splendid Dominican monastery of Santo Tomás, and he retired to it, an unhappy recluse, when the expulsion of the Jews in 1492 plunged Spain into financial chaos and made him equally unpopular everywhere. Or, almost everywhere: when six years later he died in Avila, his monks buried him in an unmarked grave, and Avila drew a deep breath.

Avila had mourned when the brilliant, witty, benevolent Moisés Rubén de Bracamonte, with his noble wife and their titled children—for *hidalguía* could be inherited from either side of the house—fled to Flanders to save his fortune. Avila rejoiced when the news of Torquemada's death brought Moisés Rubén home, and was both gratified and amused when he celebrated his return by giving the city a remarkable church—not cruciform, as usual, but hexagonal, as if it were built around the points of a six-sided star. The Inquisition briefly halted its construction, and then decided that, all things considered, it had better be overlooked.

Avila, not to put too fine a point on it, was an ugly hotbed of religious toleration. Juan Sánchez knew what he was doing when he chose it for the place in which to rebuild a life that Torquemada had disrupted.

He was Teresa's grandfather; and if it had not been for the war against Granada, he would never have left Toledo. He was in the cloth trade, and like his father before him, he "lived magnificently." His first wife, Teresa's grandmother, came from a family which included the international financier Simon de Fonseca Pina and Archbiship Alonso de Fonseca, the editor and chief translator of Cardinal Cisneros' Polyglot Bible, in which the Hebrew, Greek, and Aramaic might be compared with the Latin of St. Jerome.

Families like theirs were a peculiarly Spanish product of the Renaissance, which in Italy produced its merchant princes. In Spain, the Don Quixote of the nations, the *hidalguía* knew that all employment was dishonorable except for the Army or the Church; those who elected neither could sit at home "with much linen on the table but little food," as the saying went. In consequence, the Spanish Jews became Spain's lifeline to the world's changing economic realities, the wealthiest often married into the nobility, the most scholarly entered the Church, and the conversion rate increased. Many of the conversions were genuine; many were merely expedient. Juan Sánchez was not unusual in being, like his father, a nominal Christian and a secret Jew.

The war against Granada changed his world. Wars are expensive, and the money was where Spain had put it, in the hands of the Jews. Luckily, it was a war against the Moors, hence a holy war to save the One True Faith — which, by extension, made it obvious that the Jews were a dangerous fifth-column. So the Spanish Inquisition was born of an anti-Semitism that it never outgrew. It was popular in Seville, on the edge of the war zone down in Andualusia. Aragon was another matter; to get a chapter into Teruel, King Fernando had to call in the troops, and in Zaragoza the presiding Inquisitor was assassinated as the result of a conspiracy headed by Gabriel Sáchez, the King's treasurer. While the treasurer was too valuable to sacrifice, fourteen members of his family were arrested and their fortunes impounded. But this cost more than it was worth; the Aragonese government was largely *converso* — and popular. There were riots which threatened to develop into a civil war. By the time the chapter sent to New Castile had got as far as Ciudad Real, it was realized that Toledo would have to be handled differently.

First, the city was introduced to a medieval entertainment which Castile, thanks to King Ferdinand the Saint, had never enjoyed. The village Jew who had cut out the heart of a Christian child in ritual murder was apprehended, brought into town, and burned at the stake.

Thereafter, the rabbis were invited ouside the city gates and promised immunity if they would inform on the secret Jews in their congregations; they were also instructed to let this request leak. That done, heralds went through the wealthiest *barrios*, proclaiming that all who confessed and repented would be punished lightly; no more would be expected of them than public penance and a suitable thank-offering.

Juan Sánchez was a widower, recently remarried — to a less distinguished wife; Inés López was the daughter of a merchant from Tordesillas. The Inquisition, at that stage of the game, was not interested in women, but Sánchez's three sons by his first marriage were old enough to make their public confessions — though the youngest of them, Teresa's father, Alonso Pina, using his mother's surname, just barely qualified. (Until a child started to learn a little Hebrew, at ten, he was not considered apostate.)

The oldest boy, Hernando Sánchez, rebelled. He had heard horror stories from Seville and Aragon even before the poor Jew was burned in Toledo. It was one thing to be a secret Jew, another to go before those murderers and publicly forswear the God of Israel. Juan Sánchez gave him his blessing and ar-

2

ranged for him to run away to Salamanca and read for the bar; a cousin, Francisco Sánchez, one of Archbishop de Fonseca's collaborators on the Polyglot Bible, taught at the University. But the boy would have to change his name—and he chose one that his niece, Teresa, would have appreciated, as she, too, was blessed with laughter. He became Fernando de Santa Catalina. His family had been Jew, Christian, Jew, and were about to be Christian again; and the symbol of Santa Catalina—St. Catherine—is the wheel.

The Inquisition's docket for June 22, 1485 was crowded; Teresa's grandfather, her father, and his twelve-year-old brother Alvaro are listed only as "Juan Sánchez and his sons," and when Juan Sánchez confessed to "grave crimes of apostacy and heresy against our Holy Catholic Faith" the Inquisitors saved time by a simple pronouncement to the boys: "We have and hold you to have confessed on the word of your father."

Fines varied according to the penitent's means, but all were condemmed to go in penitential procession "on seven successive Fridays to all the Churches in Toledo, wearing the *sambenitillo con sus cruces.*" The *sambenito*, a full-length garment painted with flames and devils, was worn to the stake. The *sambenitillo* was knee-length, yellow, and marked with black crosses, shoulder to hem, front and back. Bystanders knew that to deny it a proper rain of stones and spittle was to show oneself weak in the faith; and Toledo, a big city for its day, was a maze of narrow streets which held a vast number of churches. The boy who became Teresa's father would long remember the faces of those who cursed, spat, and threw stones to the greater glory of Christ's Church.

Not all of Juan Sánchez's fortunes was demanded as a thank-offering for that mercy; but such publicity is bad for business. Sánchez left Alvaro and Alonso with his sister, and took his young wife to Ciudad Real, the city from which the Inquisition had just come, and thus the least likely for it to revisit soon.

He also felt it wise to change his name—though for one that would be legally that of any children he might have by his second marriage. Inés López's brother was named Pedro de Cepeda, so Juan Sánchez became Juan de Cepeda, shopkeeper. By 1492, he had done well enough in the sale of luxury fabrics to have reunited his family comfortably—if that year had not forced him to think ahead. In 1492, Torquemada expelled the Jews, thereby creating financial chaos which the government tried to rectify by a tax-structure so crippling that a man of less financial intelligence than Sánchez would have despaired.

Sánchez did not. He saw that tax-gathering would be, in a matter of years, the only sound business. By a quaint law, based on the belief that a knight is by definition too noble to skim off a bit of the cream, one had to purchase a knighthood in order to become a tax-gatherer. (Those born to knighthood would not stoop to it.) These curious knighthoods were, unlike all others of their day, non-hereditary; Sánchez would be Don Juan, his wife Doña Inés, while the children remained plain *señores* and *señoritas*.

This purchase would take time. The courts moved slowly. But meantime, friends in Avila saw to it that an opening would be ready for Don Juan de Cepeda once the knighthood was his. Meanwhile, to establish the Avilan connection, Juan de Cepeda bought a "rich shop in San Andrés Street," arranged for a Toledan cousin, Antón de Villalba, to go there and run it, and sent Alonso — now nineteen — to live with him and learn the trade. Alvaro, already established in business, preferred to stay in Toledo.

That was in 1494. In Ciudad Real, Inés had given Sánchez four more children: Lorenzo, Ruy, Elvira, and Francisco. As they grew old enough to need good clothes and good company more than a mother's care, they were sent on to Avila, one by one. Only Francisco, a four year old, was still with his parents when the case was won, in 1500, and Don Juan de Cepeda came to Avila with his wife, Doña Inés, and set up housekeeping with their untitled offspring.

Teresa's father, Alonso Pina, was almost twenty-five. Avilans set him apart from his half-siblings with a nickname: El Toledano. By that time, Torquemada was two years dead in his unmarked grave, and Moisés Rubén de Bracamonte, back from Flanders, was drawing up the plans for his famous six-pointed church. Yet Juan Sánchez's far-sighted plans had nearly failed. Within six months of his becoming Don Juan de Cepeda, tax-gatherer for Church and State, a law was passed forbidding the sale of such titles to "recent New Christians."

That law could have meant real trouble for Teresa's father in her childhood if Avila had not still been Avila.

Chapter 2 ❋ Teresa's Father and Mother; Her Birth in Gotarrendura

I

Avila, I repeat, was an ugly hotbed of religious toleration. When Juan Sánchez's offspring by his second marriage grew up, it was no more surprising that Pedro married an Old Christian *hidalga* than that Elvira married a prosperous *converso* merchant.

Alonso's two marriages were another matter; both times he married farmer's daughters, and few farmers could not have echoed Sancho Panza's boast that whatever his other failings, he had at least "been ever a mortal enemy to the Jews." We know that Alonso's marriage to Catalina del Peso came dear. The *carta de dote* or dowery document (drawn up by his brother, the Salamancan lawyer, Fernando de Santa Catalina) literally covers the bride with gold from top to toe: a gold head piece, gold slippers and a stunning array of necklaces, broaches and golden girdle in between — plus hard cash, in a day when husbands were bought for brides, not vice versa. In contrast, Catalina's dowry consisted chiefly of money to be paid to the church yearly for the good of her soul. Furthermore, though a *carta de dote* was normally signed on the eve of the wedding, Alonso's marriage was put off for a whole year. I suspect that the papers were drawn up and signed before Catalina's parents had finally re-

4

solved their disagreement on the basic issue: Old Christian principles versus peasant greed.

At the year's end, Alonso bought a house from a Bracamonte for his bride; his signature, Alonso Pina, is on the bill of sale. Catalina gave birth to María, then Juan, and after less than two years of marriage she died of the plague. So did Juan Sánchez and Fernando de Santa Catalina; Inés Lopez had died before that. (Alonso's papers record a small bequest "from my mother." Death in childbirth and remarriage were so common in those days that words like "stepmother" or "half-sister" rarely occur outside of lawsuits. Teresa's writings never indicate that María, unlike her sister, Juana, was not her mother's child.)

Incidentally, the wills of "Inés López, native of Tordesillas" and "Juan Sánchez y Cepeda, native of Toledo," were published early in this century and disappeared shortly thereafter. Some French Carmelites, researching in Avila, had made the happy discovery that Teresa's background was as bourgeois as that of their St. Thérèse, the little Flower. As they were weak in Spanish history, they did not know that they were letting a Jewish cat out of the bag, and were surely baffled when the only place they could print their findings turned out to be in England, on the lowly press of a Catholic boy's industrial school.

II

Those deaths coincided with the failure of "the rich shop in San Andrés Street." Alonso was a widower at thirty-two, father of two children and the guardian of young Francisco. He was also hard up, and a financial incompetent —as his pack-rat collection of papers still goes to prove. (It also proves that his brother Alvaro, in Toledo, and his well-married sister Elvira were generous, often lending him money that they did not expect to see again.)

Pedro's wife had a little estate in Hortigosa which was run as a farm; he could move there. Lorenzo had just decided to enter the Church; he had not been stoned and spat upon for "seven successive Fridays." Elvira's husband would see to it that Ruy was respectably employed. But what could Alonso do for his children and Francisco?

He had one relative who could advise him.

Juan de Fonseca was the son of his mother's cousin, the Archbishop of Santiago. When Alonso first came to Avila, de Fonseca was still only a canon of the Cathedral in Seville. But in 1492, when two *converso* bankers of his acquaintance put up the money for Columbus's voyage to the Indies, de Fonseca smelled opportunity. It was always said of him that his talents "were more those of a Biscayan than a Bishop." (Biscayans had a name for shrewd trading.) So he offered to buy, outfit and man the ships and have them ready by the time Columbus was free to set sail; and he did. This remarkable show of efficiency in a cleric caught the King's attention and thus became the first step on the upward path.

When Juan Sánchez died, de Fonseca was Bishop of Palencia with the further title of Commissar of the Crusade, i.e., chief fund raiser for Spain's (invariably) holy wars.

Bishop de Fonseca's advice was typically Biscayan. Alonso was well-liked, and his father had been, too. Tax-gatherers can be a nasty lot. If Don Alonso de Cepeda placed his little brother, Don Francisco, as a page in the Bishop's household, rejoined his brother and sister, Doña Elvira and Don Ruy, and announced his decision to act as tax-gatherer in his late father's place — an *hidalgo*, like his siblings, on the maternal side — Avila would relish it, just as Avila relished the six-pointed Church of Moisés Rubén de Bracamonte.

De Fonseca was right; he had a mind for politics and one need not wonder that he ended up an Archbishop. Juan Sánchez's children entered the Old Christian *hidalgua* by common consent. Nobody was decieved, and everybody chose to forget that Alonso had been Alonso Pina, distinguished from his half-siblings by the nickname "El Toledano." After all, politics aside, Alonso was the ideal tax-gatherer — vague about money, and generous to a fault.

So Teresa's mother, Beatriz de Ahumada, that pathetic little Doña Quixote, never knew Don Alonso de Cepeda by any other name.

III

Beatriz's father had died of the plague, leaving her mother with six children. Her cousin, Señora del Peso, took Beatriz in. Alonso saw her when he came to visit his little girl, María. (Baby Juan was farmed out with a wet-nurse.)

Beatriz was extremely beautiful; and shortly before her thirteenth birthday or just after it, Beatriz was pregnant. But Alonso wasted no time on asking Beatriz's parents for her hand. Having learned the hard way that farmers had strong feelings about "pure blood," he simply announced their betrothal.

Up in Olmeda, Beatriz's mother let a priest know that her principles, unlike those of the late Catalina's parents were not for sale. The priest reassured her: canon law forbade marriage with a deceased wife's cousin. The betrothal was declared void, and Beatriz and Alonso were excommunicated before Señora de Ahumada discovered that Beatriz was pregnant.

Fortunately Bishop de Fonseca, as Commissar General of the Crusade, was expected to raise money by selling dispensations; the marriage could eventually take place, though procuring the dispensation from Rome would take time. And Beatriz's mother owned a lean little sheep farm in the village of Gotarrendura on the mountain pass that connects Old and New Castile. If worst came to worst, and the birth came before the dispensation, Beatriz could be hidden there; her lost honor need never be known. (The double standard was never more striking than in the times when a priest could acknowledge his offspring and a pregnant girl had to be hidden away.)

That farm — to which Beatriz returned to bear all her children, as if to underline that the first was born there only at her whim — became in later years the subject of a lawsuit at which a witness stated that he had been sent from Gotarrendura (population 85) to Olmeda, when he was a boy of sixteen, to fetch Beatriz and her mother in an ox-cart. He also remembered that though the only wedding-guests were his fellow villagers, the bride "wore splendid silks and ornaments, all the gifts of the groom." These, it was being claimed, were hand-me-downs from the late Catalina, and hence the sole property of her daughter María.

It seems likely. Alonso was at considerable expense. All such dispensations were an upper-class luxury, bought oftenest to keep a family fortune intact. Even his—which shades down the relationship and permits "Don Alonso de Cepeda to marry his first wife's cousin in the fourth degree for a certain sum of money" (delicately left unspecified)—could not have come cheap. And to top it, on the day the dispensation came, Alonso signed a *carta de dote* for "one thousand florins of pure gold of just weight and value according to the law and stamp of Aragon in honor of the bride's virginity." (This paper, Beatriz's mother, Teresa de Ocampo, signed with a cross—"her mark.") As to the bride's virginity, the relevant pages are torn from the baptismal book in the village church, but Alonso kept a notebook in which he recorded the births of all his children; so we know that within fifteen months from the day of her wedding Beatriz had given birth, successively, to two healthy, normal sons.

It should be pointed out that in all this Alonso showed unusual tenderness for his little Doña Quixote. The most that any gentleman would have been expected to do under the circumstances was to assume financial responsibility for the care of the child—as some of his sons would do for their begettings—and some would not. If Alonso had not wanted to save Beatriz from grief and shame, Teresa de Ocampo could have done nothing about it.

But Beatriz treasured her "honor" as any high-born lady would have done. And she was dead in love with her title; so much so that Alonso, to please her on their return to Avila, had a carved stone shield set up over their door, bearing the combined arms of de Cepeda and de Ahumada. (There were, in fact, titled families of that name; similarly, two de Guzmáns enter Teresa's story—one a plain dirt farmer and one a royal princess. Beatriz's surname was de Ahumada, but her mother's will, still in the legal archives of Valladolid, names six children, with only one *don* or *doña* among them: Doña Beatriz, by virtue of her marriage to Don Alonso.)

Alonso humored Beatriz's dream of *hidalguia*. He even fed it, by teaching her to read, and she became "an *aficionada* of books about knights." And Beatriz's shame at being driven to that place of hiding in an ox-cart until the church allowed Alonso to save her honor brought back memories to him of those "seven successive Fridays" which had been his first encounter with Christian charity. He gave Beatriz's first son the true name of Fernando de Santa Catalina, Hernando: the brother who had refused to forswear the God of his fathers.

A year later, Beatriz went back to Gotarrendura and gave birth to Rodrigo. And shortly thereafter Alonso received his "invitation," as a knight, to join in the conquest of Navarre. His papers record the purchase of "a magnificent war-horse," a mule for his armor-bearer, plate armor, chain mail, lance, sword, and the proper shields to go with them, the round and the long.

He was gone for three years, and it was four years to the day from Rodrigo's birth that Alonso recorded in his notebook the birth of the girl who would always be his favorite child:

"On Wednesday, March 28, 1515, my daughter Teresa was born at five in the morning, give or take half an hour, as that Wednesday was just about to dawn."

Teresa begins her own story, with its many omissions, when she was eight, and Charles V had brought about the events that cost her oldest brother's life and forever shattered poor Doña Quixote's dream.

Chapter 3 ❋ Teresa's Siblings

I

The so-called War of the Comuneros was sincerely seen by many as a war of succession. Queen Juana la Loca, Joanna the Mad, by that wishful thinking was not mad but only a political prisoner in Tordesillas and the Hapsburg, Charles V, was a usurper. Unfortunately for Charles, he not only spoke Spanish with a heavy German accent, he had also inherited a shaky economy, a lunatic tax-structure, and an atmosphere of civil discontent.

The actual fighting did not break out until 1520, and it was crushed within a year. However, by 1519 Toledo was in ferment under the leadership of Juan de Padilla, a priest, but by descent a merchant-class Jew; and the two Castilian cities most furiously on Doña Juana's side were Avila and Segovia—both strongholds of the powerful, and Jewish, de Bracamontes. Consequently, from the start the rebellion could be widely propagandized as a Jewish plot; and trials which would discredit prominent Jews were useful to the Crown.

A little research turned up a highly promising case. A Toledan Jew, passing himself off in Avila as an Old Christian hidalgo, was illegally collecting taxes for Church and Crown and doubtless—you know those Jews—making the taxes seem even more onerous than they were.

A little more research would have shown how the case was flawed. While Avila had never known "the brothers Sánchez (as they were accused) under that name, they knew and liked one Pina and three de Cepedas who had become *hidalgos* as the only way to circumvent an impracticable law passed in 1500. Furthermore, Alonso was not only delightfully inept as a tax collector, he was a true gentleman who had many friends and no enemies. We may be sure that the first Avilan questioned by a Toledan spy would have hurried to give Don Alonso warning.

The whole family fled. They were hunted down and papers served on "the brothers Sánchez" at Don Pedro's wife's estate in Hortigosa, but the Avilan court delayed the trial until 1522, when the revolt had been put down and the case lacked political relevance. As for the trial itself, a less friendly court would have found the evidence less than conclusive.

One witness for the defense let it slip that the brothers had come to Avila as *pecheros*—commoners—and that Don Alonso had been plain "Alonso Pina" when he first married; then, catching himself up, he said that Alonso had married at *eighteen* — hence, was still unborn when Juan Sánchez was "reconciled," and thus a birthright Christian and Doña Ines's son — an *hidalgo* after all. The prosecution produced Ines's brother who identified himself as "Pedro de Cepeda, merchant of Tordesillas" — no *hildago;* but he, in turn, assured the court that all Juan Sánchez's sons, Hernando included, had been "reconciled" — not one Jewish subversive left among them.

This his namesake, Don Pedro, who was religious, sadly denied. Called to the stand, he said that Hernando "had not been reconciled then or at any other time," but they had an out-of-town brother, Lorenzo, who was a priest, and another, Francisco, who had been "in the household of the Bishop of Palencia," and their father had been "a friend" of the Archbishops of Santiago and of Toledo. (He could claim no closer relationship with the de Fonseca churchmen as Alonso was now, of necessity, Doña Ines's child.)

Fortunately, all Avila found the trial distasteful; it did not matter that a Toledan witness had seen Juan Sánchez in the *sambenitillo*, or that he had come to Avila as a recent New Christian with a bought title, or that his wife's brother was a *converso* merchant, or that Alonso, El Toledano, was obviously a son by another marriage. The true question in that court was whether Avila had done well to preserve the tradition of St. Ferdinand, King of the Three Religions. The verdict in favor of "the brothers Sánchez" was one in the eye for Charles V and the ghost of Torquemada. Thereafter, so far as Avila was concerned, Don Alonso de Cepeda had inherited his *hidalguía* from his mother "Doña Inés de Cepeda."

Ruy shrugged off the victory, dropped the *don* and went back to Toledo as Ruy Sánchez. Alonso showed Avila more gratitude.

But so far as Alonso's private life went, the verdict came too late.

II

A court verdict is one thing; town talk is quite another. And boys can be cruel; there was teasing. Hernando, a tough customer who ended up as a Governor in the Indies, could take it in his stride; Juan could not. He had been proud of his noble lineage; to live in Avila as a half-Jewish commoner was unbearable. He had run away and joined the infantry; there was great need of cannon fodder, and it was shockingly easy for a well-grown boy of fourteen to fill that need. He was shipped to North Africa and killed by the Moors in his first engagement. The word of his death came back before Teresa's ninth birthday.

The routine comfort given the families of all such victims of Spain's holy wars was "he died a martyr." At eight, Teresa could believe it. And Alonso, God know, would have said nothing that might deprive her or her mother of that comfort. But he must always have wondered if that tragedy was not caused by Beatriz — his poor, silly Doña Quixote — who thereafter lived as a recluse, wearing the shabby black of an old woman, and chainreading her "books about knights."

The whole story begins to come clear through Beatriz's will.

She died in childbirth, in Gotarrendura, when Teresa was not quite fourteen. Wills were dictated from the deathbed, and on her deathbed Beatriz poured out an astonishing catalogue of the brilliant dresses that she no longer wore: silk, satin, paduasoy, gold-worked brocade, in vivid colours, crimson, orange, violet, azure blue, and all lovingly detailed down to their very contrasting bindings and embroideries, a wardrobe far too large, too fine, to have been the hand-me-downs of a first wife, twenty years dead after a scant two years of marriage. But Beatriz had been beautiful, she had been in love with a dream, and Alonso was generous; his gifts always outran his means.

That loving catalogue alone would be something to think about, but the will does not end there. Beatriz ended it with a request that her body should be brought back to Avila by night and buried in secret. Buried as she had lived through her last nine years, hidden from any who might hide a smile behind clasped hands over the downfall of Doña Beatriz de Ahumada.

She had come, a frightened girl not yet fourteen, from Olmeda, to Gotarrendura in an ox-cart, her only escort a farm-boy of sixteen. She was carted back from Gotarrendura by night for that secret burial.

Another will, Alonso's, tells us more.

Teresa's story mentions nine brothers. We know of seven who went to the Indies with the bought captaincies permitted to the *hidalguía*. It was also long admitted that an eighth, Juan de Cepeda, joined the infantry and died young in North Africa. Only Alonso's will, unpublished for centuries, names Juan de Ahumada.

On his deathbed, with little to bequeath, Alonso listed his still-dependent children in the order of their age — explaining one, as if the lawyer might not have heard of him: "Juan de Ahumada (Juan de Cepeda being dead), Jerónimo, Agustín, and Juana."

Juan de Cepeda would have been older by thirteen years than those provided for: and Alonso was old, but his mind, in those last hours, had gone back to a time of grief for which he unjustly though typically blamed himself: for that will ends with his orders that he, like his poor Beatriz, be buried in secret.

I have seen Juan de Ahumada variously explained away since his existence was first admitted. He became a monk— though never cited as evidence of La Santa's pious background; alternatively, he was an illegitimate child born out of town — though not identified by the customary legal form, "my natural son." I myself find him no mystery.

It was customary to give a child the name of one recently dead. Beatriz, in that time of grief and stress, had a son, Pedro, who lived in his older brother Lorenzo's care, though nobody liked to admit in so many words that he was not quite all there. My mother, also in a time of stress, gave birth to premature twins, one of whom died and the other lived into his thirties with the intelligence of an eight months old baby. In my day, brain-damage at birth was understood. In Teresa's, a child so handicapped was believed to result from a genetic flaw; idiocy and madness "ran in families." In the background of a saint, a severely retarded brother was as much to be hidden as a Jewish grandfather or a dubious title of *hidalguía*.

Indeed, for the sake of her dear father's memory and for the well-being of her whole family, Teresa had much to hide when she sat down and began her great confession with a brief picture of the Eden from which she fell.

Chapter 4 ✸ *Teresa as a Child and as a Very Young Woman in Avila*

That Eden, Teresa had to say, was above all, truly Catholic.

"Having good, godfearing parents should have been enough to make me good if I had not been so vile." She hesitates, fumbles for the evidence. Her father "liked good books and had some in Spanish for his children to read." (Good books meant books on religious subjects; she has not said that Don Alonso's own good books were in Latin, the language of scholars, and those in Spanish only laid in for the little ones; but the reader's imagination is left free.) And her mother taught her, when she was only six or seven, to say her prayers "and be devoted to Our Lady and several saints." Both were paradigms of virtue.

Her tone warms suddenly as she remembers her father, her first love. Remembers him, and remembers the qualities that made his true conversion to the Church so belated — and so moving — when it came, many years later.

"My father was a man who had much charity for the poor and pity for the weak, and even for servants, so much so that he could never bear to keep slaves; and when one — she belonged to his brother — was staying in our house he pampered her as much as his own children. He used to say he couldn't bear the pity of her not being free. He was utterly truthful. I never heard him curse or complain. Very chaste, *en gran manera*." (A phrase which then as now oftenest meant "by and large." Teresa was always a child of the double-standard.)

In that first chapter, at least, she tried to do as much for Beatriz.

"My mother also had many virtues and passed her life as a great invalid. The greatest chastity; though she was extremely beautiful I never saw her give herself a chance to make anything of it, for though she died at thirty-three she made a point of dressing like an old woman. Very quiet and intelligent. The troubles that came in her life were very great. She died most Christianly."

But again she remembers her father's love:

"We were twelve, three sisters and nine brothers. All took after their parents by the grace of God, though I was my father's dearest; and before I began to sin against God, I think he had a point, for it grieves me to think of the good tendencies I had and the bad use I made of them. . . ."

Now she comes to her other childhood love and has to tell one lie. Rodrigo was not seven years old but twelve; but the truth would have raised questions about that dear dreamer who preferred the company of an imaginative little girl to that of boys his age—a Catholic twelve-year old who had not learned that heaven and hell, unlike purgatory, are permanent conditions of the life to come.

"I had one brother almost my age. He was the one I loved most, though I loved them all very much and they loved me. We got together to read the lives of the saints. When I read that women saints got to be martyrs for God' [death in battle, like Juan de Cepeda's, not being a prerequisite] 'it struck me that they bought their joy of God at a big bargain and I wanted to die like that very much—not for any love of God that I might have thought myself to have but just to enjoy so fast all the great riches I read that they have in heaven, and I got together with this brother of mine to talk over how it might be managed."

The book was doubtless the *Flos Sanctorum*, a best seller that was in every house that had any books at all. One of its woodcuts shows St. Inez, about to strike Juan de Cepeda's "big bargain." She is bound to a stake in a bonfire which leaves her miraculously unscorched, but she smiles happily, for a Moor—so indicated by his curious nightcap and curved scimitar—is just about to decapitate her and send her on her way to instant riches.

"We agreed that we should take off for the land of the Moors, begging our way for the love of God, so that they would cut our heads off there—but having parents struck us as the great difficulty."

It was tempting, and it was feasible; Juan de Cepeda had been only two years older than Rodrigo when "he died a martyr"—as so many had told them. But his parents mourned his loss. How much more they would mourn at losing not one but three, and one of them her father's dearest! As Teresa tells it, they renounced their greedy dream because they were too kind. Ribera, Teresa's first biographer, says that they ran away but were found and brought back by her Uncle Fernando. Pope Gregory XIII says that Teresa, so young, was inspired by her flaming love of God to seek martyrdom, but was circumvented by Christ who was "enamored of her virgin breast." I like her story best.

"It shocked us when we read that pain and glory last forever. We often talked about it and liked to say it over and over, *forever, forever....* So long as I remained a child it kept me impressed with the way of truth." (But not thereafter. As she later sums it up, "I could not be led by the way of fear.")

Next they thought of being hermits; one can be a hermit in the patio, causing little grief. But the hermitages they tried to build of stones "always fell in on [them]"—so they had to settle for saying rosaries, like Beatriz, and giving alms from their scanty pocket-money, like Alonso.

For girls, growing up meant a choice between marriage and the convent, with the convent likelier, since the eligible young men were leaving like lemmings for the Indies—as would seven of Alonso's sons. So Teresa finds one more pious childhood memory;

"When I played with other little girls, I like playing convent and pretending to be nuns very much, and I think I even wanted to be one too—though not as much as the other things I've told about."

That was all Teresa tells of her lost Eden, but she ends the chapter with a displaced memory more suited to that time than to anything that she would tell about thereafter.

When her mother's body was brought back to Avila for its secret burial, Teresa was almost fourteen, older than Beatriz when she became pregnant with Hernando. It is revelatory that she reduces her age by two years, and that she presents her story as a delayed reaction, but above all, that it stands alone in all her writings as an expression of any feelings for Our Lady other than a proper reverence.

For one aged fourteen, Teresa knew a good bit about her parents, and she loved her father. She surely felt Beatriz's secret burial as a cruelty to him and hard to forgive. So here is her misplaced story as she told it:

"I remember that when my mother died I was a little under twelve. When I began to realize what I had lost, I ran crying to a statue of Our Lady and begged her to be my mother, with many tears. It seems to me that though it was done as a silly child it was worth something to me, for I have certainly found that Sovereign Virgin insofar as I have commended myself to her, and she has finally turned me back to Herself." (The Carmelites are the Order of Our Lady of Mt. Carmel.) "It weighs on me when I see that and think about how I did not keep on with the good desires I set out with."

But her grief for the sinful years to come is genuine. The dam breaks, the Sovereign Virgin is forgotten, and Teresa's own voice cries out to the God made Man:

"Oh, my own Lord, since You have determined to save me, I beg Your Majesty that it may be so. And since You have shown me so many mercies, wouldn't it be better — not for Your benefit but for the sake of your own esteem — that this inn where You have to dwell should not be so defiled? It troubles me to say this, Lord, since I know that the fault is all mine; for it seems to me that even when I was back at that age You spared no effort to make me wholly Yours."

This is typical Teresa. She sees nothing odd in reminding Christ that it would do His own reputation no good if He let her fall again. Mystics always have trouble with Teresa's highly human conception of the Divine Humanity.

It is also pure Teresa to utter the spontaneous cry from the heart and get right back to the task in hand. Having said, in effect, "No, Christ, I can't blame You," she goes on, "When I try to blame my parents I can do that just a little, for I saw nothing in them but good and care for my soul.

"Then, outgrowing childhood, I began to understand the bodily charms the Lord had given me — they were very great, according to what people say — and when I should have given thanks for them, I began to use them to sin against Him, as I will tell you now."

II

To tell that part of the story Teresa had to resurrect Beatriz, though briefly. And for us to understand her, we must realize that "books about knights" were no *Idylls of the King*. Our great English example of the genre is Malory's *Morte d'Arthur*, in which — as in Beatriz's chosen reading, *Tristan, Floristan, Esplandian,* and the like—knights take their brisk succession of ladies to bed "with great joy and pleasaunce," as Malory put it. (And ladies, in result, are sometimes forced to leave a babe in the care of kindly shepherds.)

Teresa knew that such reading needed no description when she tried to defend her mother's tastes and still explain why her father made it necessary for her to read them on the sly.

"She was fond of books about knights; and she got less harm from them than I did, for she did not lose her purity by reading them . . . perhaps she did it to keep from thinking about her troubles, and to occupy her children so that they would not indulge in other ruinous affairs. This troubled my father so much that she had to take care that he wouldn't see it."

And, father was right—even though she, Teresa, still "feared falling into mortal sin," and yet more that her "honor should be wholly lost." But she began to dress *de gala*, to use scents and lotions, to study new ways to arrange her hair. In consequence, her father forbade all young men the house except for some cousins with whom he let her "go everywhere": a further mistake, as what they had to confide to her was "not all good."

Worse still, she had a chaste older sister from whom she "learned nothing" and the friendship of a young woman from whose "wanton talk" she learned much, nor could this "wanton" friend—for reasons that Teresa leaves unexplained—be forbidden the house.

The "wanton" is sadly easy to place. During the trial for false *hidalguía*, Francisco—to whom Alonso was a second father— got María de Ahumada, Beatriz's young cousin, pregnant. Alonso saw to their marriage and set them up in an adjoining house which shared a common patio. This María and an equally "wanton" friend got themselves such a name for "gallantry" that Francisco eventually had to move away from Avila. Meantime, it amused them to educate poor Alonso's budding beauty; she surely learned, among other things, why she and all her siblings were born in Gotarrendura.

As for the "chaste" sister from whom Teresa "learned nothing," María de Cepeda was no advertisement for the rewards of virtue. She had passed the market-age for marriage—fifteen or so—before the trial was over. She was now twenty-five, worthy, dull, and born to be overlooked. She might have had status in a convent as one of the many brides of Christ for whom no earthly husband had been found; but Alonso was quietly determined to give no child of his to the Church. He remembered the faces, the stones and spittle, in Toledo; he remembered poor little Beatriz hiding away until her dispensation to marry came "for a certain sum of money." Unlike his brother Fernando de Santa Catalina, Alonso was technically "reconciled"; but there was a point at which he drew the line.

Teresa was a great beauty, her love for her father and her brother had set a pattern: she was love-prone. Her safeguard was her fear of "losing her honor in the eyes of the world." We can believe her when she says that "unchaste behavior made her shrink" and that her downfall began with her love for "good conversation." But "good conversation" can be wonderfully seductive. "He finds me congenial, intelligent," becomes, "He loves me"; and love is beautiful.

Teresa was sixteen when for three unhappy months the servants helped her slip in and out of the house secretly, by dark. Unhappy, she says, "for I knew that I was in the hand of danger and I was putting my father and my brothers into it, too."

The danger was real. She was no farm girl but Doña Teresa, her father and brothers were *hidalgos*, not commoners—as a court had proved. If she had "lost all" and the man would not marry her, it would have meant a duel—or worse, a vendetta. Fortunately, the gossip began before worse came to worst.

Her honor, as she says, was "very, very badly damaged," even though "nobody could say anything for certain." But what mattered most to Teresa was that her father should not believe "his dearest" guilty of more than innocent indiscretion.

He believed her, she says, because she "lied to him so much and he loved her so much." At least, he wanted her to believe that he believed her, and he gave prompt and touching proof that she was indeed his dearest.

III

The man was not for sale, nor could Alonso have afforded any husband that Teresa would accept. All he could do was to put her out of the public eye and hidden from her seducer until the scandal went stale and the poor child came to her senses.

The right place was obvious. Just outside the city wall, five minutes walk from their house, a strictly enclosed Augustinian convent took in young lady boarders who were kept in seclusion as rigid as that of the nuns. But, Alonso knew, to put her there with no good excuse would only fuel the scandal; the town would say that Teresa's father had found her out and locked her away.

Teresa gave a remarkably oversimplified account of the solution.

"God freed me in a way that was much against my will . . . for they put me in a convent in the neighborhood where they took care of girls like me, only not so evil in their ways; and it was done with so much dissembling that nobody knew about it but me and a certain man related to me because they waited for an excuse that would not look strange—because with my sister married it wasn't good for me to live without a mother."

Husbands were so scarce that even young, attractive, and moneyed girls were overcrowding the big unenclosed convents. Yet according to legend, poor, drab María, ten years past market age, suddenly happened to marry Don Martín de Guzmán, an *hidalgo* who lived on an estate near Castellanos de Canadá.

But Teresa herself had told the truth—in part.

The "certain man" who knew the facts was Teresa's Uncle Lorenzo. He was the village priest in Villatoro—where Francisco had already moved away with María de Ahumada. Father Lorenzo knew enough about that wanton wife to pity a young girl whom she had led astray. He also preached around the countryside; if some respectable farmer were available for a price, Father Lorenzo would know. And María de Cepeda always did as she was told.

Alonso was too honest to see that the excuse was ludicrously transparent. The dowry which bought Martín de Guzmán—a disagreeable and irreligious

15

farmer — was a joke in Villatoro which improved in the telling; years later, when Alonso's will was contested, one witness inflated that purchase price to a sum which would have bought a nobleman. De Guzmán would have been no bargain at half his cost, but at least poor María had one satisfaction. The arms of de Cepeda and de Guzmán are on a carved stone shield still over the door of her husband's farmhouse in Castellanos de la Cañada.

And so, as Teresa says, "with much dissembling" she was sent to board at Our Lady of Grace because "with my sister married it wasn't good for me to live without a mother."

Chapter 5 ❁ *Her Life in an Augustinian Convent*

I

Our Lady of Grace stands on the edge of a steep drop just outside the city walls. It faces a breathtaking view of the Guadarramas, their jagged peaks rising on the far side of the valley below, but the view is wasted. In the gaunt little building, too tall for its width, the windows are set so high and small as to exclude all but a patch of sky. You ring the bell, hear the unseen porteress ask your business, and are admitted to a little stone-floored room furnished with a single bench set aginst one wall. Across the room from you, two wall-to-wall iron grilles are set one before the other, far enough apart so that if you should dare to spring up and try to touch your daughter's hand at a visit, it could not be done.

Two chairs stand behind those grilles against the further wall. The nun you have come to visit appears and sits down with another besider her, a silent but censoring presence. I went there once with a young couple come to visit the man's sister. They made a small-talk, as casually as if it were over a cup of tea in a neighbor's kitchen, which somehow increased my own mounting claustrophobia.

Teresa was locked away so for nineteen months. Her fear that the other boarders would know why she was there quickly proved groundless; Our Lady of Grace was an innocent world apart. She was also eased by a tolerant confessor and a few friends she quickly made and confided in:

"The affair had been with someone I had believed would bring it to a good end by marrying me, and when my confessor and some others heard about that, they told me that in a good many ways I had not sinned against God."

Attempts to send her presents and messages from outside were foiled. So, she says, she settled down and "as God gave her a gift for making herself liked" she became a general favorite. Sometimes she even felt that she was returning to the "good desires" of childhood. But up to the end, the place was alien to Teresa.

She judged herself by its standards, but while she was impressed by the nuns who wept so much over the sufferings of Christ crucified, she found herself "so hard-hearted" that she "could read through the whole Passion without shedding one tear." She was also instinctively repelled by the nuns who fasted to near-starvation and "did themselves violence" in excesses of bodily penance. Yet she did not doubt that they were earning heaven, and that heaven and hell go on forever . . . forever . . .

To the end of those nineteen months she hated the thought of being a nun; but the thought of marriage "frightened her just as much." And small wonder; she knew what sort of marriage could be bought for a girl in her eighteenth year and with her "honor very, very badly damaged." She asked the nuns to pray that God would lead her to "whatever way would please Him best." The young nuns told her that she would do well in a convent; the older and more percipient disagreed. She herself believed that being a nun would insure her against hell, and tried to persuade herself that being a nun in a big, unenclosed Carmelite convent, like her friend Juana Suárez, would be better at least than marriage to a man one could not love or a spinsterhood which would surely lead her back on the road to eternal torment.

She began to have fainting spells and to run a high fever. She was genuinely ill; for the rest of her life she would have a weak heart and rheumatoid arthritis to ignore and live with.

Alonso took her home. Teresa's book makes no further mention of Our Lady of Grace, though in time it became her example of all that an inclosed convent should avoid if God is to be truly served. She only says, without comment, that once she was well enough, her father took her to her sister's home "in a village."

Of María and de Guzmán, Teresa says only, "My sister loved me very much, as did her husband—or, at least he showed me all affectionate attention even though that was chiefly due to the Lord." (It fits in well with what we know of de Guzmán that Teresa could only attribute such amiability as he displayed to divine intervention.) However, that visit was important only because it had begun with a stop-over in Hortigosa with Uncle Pedro.

II

Uncle Pedro had become increasingly religious—in what Teresa, in time, would call "the way of fear." He brooded on the perils of this wicked world and the endless torture awaiting its victims in the world to come. He read a great deal on the subject, in Spanish for he knew no Latin, and he asked Teresa to read aloud to him.

Teresa disliked his gloomy talk and his books, but she loved to give pleasure. She listened and read so well that, when she left, Uncle Pedro gave her books to read on María's farm, and among them was a translation of the sermons of St. Jerome.

Jerome is a great writer, and the first that Teresa, a born great appreciator, had ever read. But the painters who usually depict him as kneeling in the desert, breast bared while he gashes his hated flesh with a stone, grasp something central. One cannot imagine Jerome telling a lovely penitent that her seduction had not, really, been much of a sin.

Teresa read Jerome, and "the way of fear" took over totally. She was sure that if she had died of the illness that released her from Our Lady of Grace, she would have gone to hell.

She knew that nuns go to heaven, and that her friend Juana Suárez in the big, cheerful, unenclosed convent of the Incarnation had struck the best possible bargain with the awful Judge. She told herself that being a nun "would be no worse than an equal time in Purgatory" and that only the devil was making her feel that she could not bear convent life. It took her three months of such inner war to make up her mind to it that her choice lay only between the convent and hell. Three months, she says: and reading, one remembers that it had also been for three months that she "risked losing all" and put her father and brothers "in the hand of danger."

She made her decision; and immediately suffered a relapse into fever and fainting-fits. Whatever their source, the fever was real. Alonso had to come and take her home again.

Teresa wrote the book now called *The Life* to celebrate her long-delayed discovery of God's forgiveness and "the way of love." She had spelled it out that her childhood dream of martyrdom was a get-rich-quick scheme unmixed with any love of God; and again she laid it on the line that the sole motive for becoming a nun was a "slavish fear." But—she was not confessing for anyone else. Her father, she says, would not consent: "Because he loved me too much."

He did love her, so unselfishly that he renounced her dear company, hiding her first in Our Lady of Grace and then in the guarded seclusion of María's farm. As a nun of the big, lax convent of the Incarnation, she would be free to come and go, dine at home if she liked, and be alone with him for hours on end. He loved her and hated to deny her anything. But he was also essentially religious and a man of conscience; nothing could shake his determination to give no child of his to the Church.

Teresa pleaded with him and persuaded others to plead for her. It was useless. This went on for two years, though she does not say so and ends her chapter abruptly:

"He would only say that when he was dead I might do as I pleased. . . . I had already begun to fear my frailties of the flesh to which I might turn back, and I determined to manage it by another way, as I will tell you now."

III

Once more, Teresa's story needs filling in.

Hernando, the eldest of Alonso's living sons, bought his captaincy and left for the Indies with Pizarro in the year that Teresa came back from María's farm. He was made for Army life, did well, and ended up a governor in Peru.

Rodrigo was a reader and a dreamer. At twelve he had been happiest in the company of an imaginative child of eight; and when he was nineteen and

Teresa fifteen they wrote a novel of chivalry in collaboration. It seems to have shown promise, for Ribera says that it "amazed" the friends who saw it.

Rodrigo left for the Indies in the year Teresa turned twenty. Both he and Hernando left at least one illegitimate child behind, but a gift for celibacy, though admired, was still not expected of the priesthood. A taste for books was what counted when an hidalgo chose the Church instead of the Army.

That choice was not open to Rodrigo. Ribera, researching Teresa's first biography, was told that he drowned in the River Plata and that Teresa "was comforted that he died a martyr." (His name does appear on a list of those bound for the River Plata.) However, María de San José has it that he was killed by the Aztecs, twenty-five years later; and the story from Peru — that he simply deserted and disappeared — purports to come from military records, records now destroyed. This, by itself, is inconclusive; but since Rodrigo is the only one of Teresa's seven brothers whose career in the Indies is undocumented after the record of his embarcation and the only one about whom conflicting stories are told, that desertion and disappearance seems only too likely. Rodrigo was not born for Army life, and Alonso would give no child of his to the Church.

Rodrigo and Teresa had always been close, and they were close now in a common predicament. Teresa was convinced that only by being a nun could she avoid "turning back" to her "frailties of the flesh" and earning hell; but to become a nun one needed a dowry. One could not become a bride of Christ for nothing. And Rodrigo did what he could for her.

Wills were dictated from the deathbed, but before Rodrigo set sail he went to a lawyer and dictated a will. He was leaving a mistress and at least one baby girl behind him; it was also common for these young adventurers to settle down and marry in Peru. Nonetheless, he left what little he owned and all he hoped to acquire to his sister Teresa.

Teresa herself does not mention that will. She does not mention Rodrigo after their childhood, though we know that she ran away to the Carmelites directly after he made his will and set sail. However, many others cite that will as proof of the enduring bond between "the glorious virgin, Teresa de Jesús" and the brother with whom, according to Gregory XIII, "she would, so young, have gained the martyr's crown if the Sovereign Spouse, enamored of her virgin breast, had not saved her in order that its former strengths might be restored to the Order of Carmel without the spilling of her virgin blood."

Let me suggest — for the first time, I believe — that both Rodrigo and Teresa assumed that the Carmelites would admit her to the Convent of the Incarnation on receiving legal assurance that they would eventually receive all that Rodrigo might win in the land of gold.

Nonetheless, I think that Teresa saw Rodrigo leave with forboding, and that this explains something else long in need of filling-in: Teresa's futile effort to save a younger brother from the same fate.

Teresa was almost eight months past twenty. Lorenzo, the next youngest, was seventeen. Though a cheerful womanizer who did not get around to marrying until Teresa was forty-six, he was all warmth and competence: Juan Sánchez reborn. He was, in fact, the brother with whom Teresa, after her girlhood, had most in common. But the next youngest brother, Antonio, would never outgrow the instability which he must have shown at sixteen. Teresa doubtless believed that in a monastery he would live a protected life, so she persuaded him to run away with her.

The Dominicans at Santo Tomás turned him down after a brief novitiate. Later, he ran away again, to the Jeronimites: an odd choice, since their order excluded those of "impure blood." Apparently his background was discovered, for he left them "on grounds of ill-health" — according to their records — and joined the Army. He was killed in the battle of Quito when Teresa was thirty-four. She herself is on the Incarnation's record as having made a pilgrimage to Guadalajara "for the good of her brother Antonio's soul."

About Antonio, Teresa simply avoided explanations. She could not say that her father also "loved him too much," as he could readily spare sons to the Army if not to the Church. Her story of how they ran away is one of her most striking exercises in the task of telling the truth about herself — and herself alone.

IV

"In those days, while I went on with my decisions, I had persuaded a brother of mine to become a friar by talking to him about the vanity of the world, and we made our plans to go one day, very early, to the convent of that friend I was so fond of, though by that time I had got to the point of being willing to go to any convent where I might serve God better or that my father might prefer — for I had already got to caring more about saving my soul and absolutely nothing about taking things easy.

"I can remember completely what it was like, and in sober truth I don't think that the pain will be more when I die than when I walked out of my father's house, for I felt as if my very bones were being pulled apart. Since I had no love of God to free me from my love for my father and my family, the whole thing did me such great violence that if the Lord had not helped me, my own concerns would not have been enough to make me go on with it. Right here, he gave me the spirit to confront myself in such a way that it was done.

"As soon as I took the habit the Lord made me understand how he does favor to those who force themselves to serve him — which nobody saw in me, but on the contrary, the utmost self-indulgence."

Antonio is forgotten along with Alonso. The memory of her life on-for-forty sweeps her into a further attempt to bare her own truth while simultaneously white-washing her world.

She recalls her wonder at finding herself happier while doing the menial tasks assigned to novices than she had ever been in her days of self-indulgence and sinful vanities, a great discovery all too soon forgotten. She pictures a convent from whose "many servants of God" she might have learned by example; it sounds like a second Eden. Then:

"I don't know how to go on from here, when I remember what my profession was like, and the great determination and contentment with which I made it, and the espousal I made with You. It cannot be told without tears, and they should be tears of blood and my heart should be shattered—and that would be little to feel for what I did wrong You afterwards. Now it seems to me that I would have been right not to want such great honor, since I would make such bad use of it." For now, she goes on, it seems that she only vowed to break all her vows through those next twenty years through which God waited for her. And still her grief for those sins is lessened by her joy in thinking of the use to which God put them, as proof of His endless patience, mercy, forgiveness.

"In whom, Lord, could they shine forth as in me, who so clouded with my evil deeds the great mercies You had begun to show me?"

This is true, alas, "for [her] sins had repaid the love He had begun to show her, she could have spent her love on nobody but Him—and that would have been the cure for all that went wrong. But since she neither had nor merited such good fortune, may God now grant [her] mercy!"

It came out in a passionate rush like that surprising end to her Eden chapter, in which she begs Christ—for the sake of His own good name as well as hers—not to let her fall again.

And, as before, she recalls herself to telling what little—as she first sees it—need to be told.

The " 'change' in life-style and diet" so injured her health that despite her inner contentment she once more fell dangerously ill and had to be taken away. From the onset of winter until the spring she stayed at her sister's house, gathering strength to undergo the torments of a famous cure. The friend of whom she has spoken before went with her.

They stopped at her uncle's house in Hortigosa, and he gave her a book, *The Third Alphabet.* It was her introduction to true prayer and led to constant reading of similar books, her only guides for eighteen years, for she could find no *maestro*, no confessor to guide her in such reading or to teach her how to resist the subtle attacks by which the devil led her into occasions of sin from which she did not flee in time. But for those first nine months, while she was careless about venial sins, she took great care to avoid mortal sins— and would to God it had always been so!

(She is remembering an "occasion" which did not lead to mortal sin when she went to the cure in Becedas.)

She ends the chapter with telling of how God, for His own great purposes, has now made many blind to her wicked past, able to see only the virtues which He "almost forced upon her." And she repeats, as in her preface, that if she told her story in detail, it would make the world know how much she owes to God—"since it is all forgotten."

Seven long chapters ahead, Teresa faced it that no life-story can be told *in vacuo.* Reactions without their causes make pointless telling. Furthermore she had a duty to warn parents against sending young girls to convents like the Incarnation. Such places keep up a front; Juana Suárez had confided little to her about the easy terms at which her convent offered eternal bliss.

Not to put too fine a point on it, Teresa lied when she blamed her third severe breakdown on a change of life-style and diet. She throve on the spartan year of her novitiate; the breakdown only came after that year in which she learned how much more easily a Carmelite nun could "lose all," both here and hereafter, than could one, however beautiful, however frail and love-prone, who stayed at home.

Chapter 6 ❀ *Teresa as Nun in the Unenclosed Carmelite Convent of the Incarnation*

I

Teresa took four short chapters to tell this much of her life, and five more to cover her next twenty years: all, she felt, that was necessary to make her readers believe that God can forgive a Magdalene as readily as an Augustine, and that the way to this forgiveness is through prayer: prayer that begins as reaching out and ends as pure reception of God's own grace, life-changing, inexhaustible, the source of all life that is truly worth the living.

That done, she could hope to be believed as she gave her book its true substance in a twelve-chapter treatise on a subject then widely distrusted: "mental prayer" as it was called, prayer thought out, felt out from the inner life, as opposed to "verbal prayer"—the recitation of Aves and Paternosters. This treatise, three chapters longer and far deeper than all that went before, ended her book as she intended it. Where and why it was written, we will see.

Some years later, under pressure from the Inquisition, Teresa was forced to expand the five chapters which had told, she felt, enough of her life as a nun and of her conversion in a way that made her finely conceived little book not twenty-one chapters long, but forty. This was ordered because many of the post-conversion experiences for which she is now celebrated as the saint of raptures had been a dangerous embarrassment to the convent of the Incarnation. Far from being unusual, such visionary and ecstatic experiences were typical of a national epidemic, seen as evidence of hersey: heresy, moreover, of a kind to which those of Jewish blood, and particularly women, were most prone. They were also seen as going hand-in-hand with sexual laxity. Much as Teresa had wanted to rethink and re-evaluate them, she had known the danger of doing so in black and white.

Teresa wrote this nineteen-chapter addendum at top speed. It was never her custom to rewrite or even to reread what she had already written, or to avoid self-interruptions or irrelevancies which came to her by free association; indeed, as she once told her brother Lorenzo in a letter, any other way of writing is a waste of time. But as a result, the book now called the *Life* must be reread incessantly if it is not to mislead us both in ways that Teresa intended and in ways that she struggled to avoid; and the last nineteen chapters fill in the intendedly lean autobiographical first five with unintended, unexpected flashbacks.

These flashbacks, however, can only be understood in a context of history that the Spanish Church still finds distasteful. They don't even like to remember that the Carmelites headed Philip II's list of the three religious orders most flagrantly in need of reform.

But, I repeat, Teresa did not know what she was getting into.

II

Rodrigo's will made no impression. (Eventually, Teresa made it over to her sister Juana, who found it equally useless.) The prioress sent for Alonso, who came and gave in.

The poorest nuns at the Incarnation slept in dormitories, the next well-off had their own cells, the richest, two-room suites. Alonso arranged that Teresa should have two rooms as soon as she took the veil and that a feast be given in her honor on that day. The document which bears his signature calls her "Doña Teresa de Ahumada, daughter of noble parents and family connections and a person of praiseworthy morals."

However, throughout the year-long novitiate one slept in a dormitory, got one full meal a day with meat three times a week, except for the six-weeks' fasts of Advent and Lent, and "took the discipline" on Monday, Wednesdays and Fridays. The novices saw no visitors, immediate family included, and were allowed to talk with no nuns except for the novice mistress.

Teresa does not mention these rules, though she grants the year a flashback in which she confesses to "imperfections." She resented being blamed for things that were not her fault and was hurt because when she wept for her past sins the others thought she wept for discontent. She was also too proud to learn to say her offices properly. (True, to her last day her Latin remained intractably original: *Agnus Dei*, for example, is *anusdei*.) But she was ashamed of such self-centered pettiness, and when she cleaned the infirmary and saw the patience of a woman dying with a cancerous wound in her belly through which she defecated, she prayed for some equal test of her own patience and the strength to endure it.

The year ended, Teresa suddenly found herself the convent beauty, the convent wit, the center of men's attention in the parlors — parlors which were a magnet for the town's bored young married men.

The convent housed one hundred and fifty nuns, few as well dowered as Teresa. It needed alms, and in consequence the nuns were encouraged to take *devotos*, supposedly for purposes of spiritual guidance.

The nuns were attractive. They wore their veils set back to show their curls, brightened their habits with colored sashes and much jewelry, fluttered bright fans, and used perfumes: a conventual favorite was called "angel-water." They also "kept many little lap-dogs."

They were remarkably free to come and go. After the Council of Trent passed stricter rules for the unenclosed convents, a nun told their General, come from Italy on a tour of inspection, how well she kept those rules: "She never went out without telling the Prioress." Others told him of how these rules were sidestepped by meeting one's *devoto* in the dusky chapel or in a confessional, which in those days were small rooms in which priest and penitent were not divided.

The confessors were Carmelite friars. For years they told Teresa that "her mortal sins were only venial, and her venial sins no sin at all," which she blames on their being "half-educated," saying that when she finally found the guidance of *letrados* — scholars — she "was never misguided."

Of such faulty guidance I think it might be said, "A man's reach should exceed his grasp or what's heaven for?" Teresa set her sights higher than on those friars. The story she tells comes in a flashback that can be dated, for we know when she wrote that second part of her book, and "twenty-six years ago" was her first year as a professed nun.

She only calls the man "a certain person." Over-innocent translators, leaning on the fact that *persona* is an invariable feminine, taking the pronoun *she* regardless of the person's sex, can be blamed for V. Sackville-West's bit of wishful thinking: "Her name is linked with that of Sappho." This fits no part of Teresa's story, least of all that passionate outpouring of grief in which, remembering her profession at the end of that novitiate, she mourns for her faithlessness to Him who had made her His bride.

The man was probably García de Toledo, no less noble for being an illegitimate son of the ducal house of Alba. He was a Dominican — a profession which he took as lightly as did most noblemen; he came to the Incarnation often to visit two lady cousins, daughters of the Marquis of Velada. His friendship with Teresa was twice interrupted, once by his going back to the Indies where he had grown up, and once by her conversion. It is only during their second and third times of association that he can be firmly placed, but we can say at least that Teresa would have found no *devoto* more flattering and few men more endearing.

When their "fondness" (*afición*) first began, Teresa says, she did not think it wrong. Such associations were the accepted thing, and she did not stop to think that while such intimacies "might be harmless to those who were naturally good, it was a great danger to me. An older nun, a relative by marriage, warned me that I was endangering my honor."

To this, Teresa retorted that "the attentions of one so distinguished did honor to the whole convent!" But in her heart of hearts she knew that the old nun was right. The man, she adds, would come back into her life again, and "in time there would be others"; but, "He was the one who most disturbed my soul . . . because I felt so much fondness for him."

The "fondness" and guilt intensified together. Once Teresa saw an ugly reptile scutter across the floor; other nuns saw it too, and screamed. It was probably a lizard come up from Andalusia in a shipment of fruit, but Teresa took it for a warning from hell. Then as she was going to her room after a long talk with that man "who most disturbed her soul," she saw Christ, her Spouse, staring at her with accusing eyes. She told herself that it was "only imagination," but it felt like a reality.

Once more she began to run fevers, suffer fainting-spells. The doctors said that she was fatally ill of consumption, and her father took her to Maria's farm, to gain enough strength to survive the famous "cure" in Becedas.

How far had Teresa "endangered her honor?" Not far, I think. She fell in love, but she was still obsessed with the fear of hell. She broke down not because she fell, but because she had fled for safety to a place she learned to call "an inn just off the road to hell." Well on in her book she makes a sudden plea to parents: if they care at all for their daughters' honor, their chastity, they must keep them out of the unenclosed covents. At home, she urges, girls can only misbehave for a short time before they are found out and with luck saved from themselves. In a great, sprawling, ill-supervised convent of one hundred and fifty souls, a love-affair could run on until "God laid it bare." What future is there for a pregnant nun? Forget these convents, Teresa begs; instead, marry the girl off, even if it has to be to one of far lowlier station in life!

For the tragedy, she goes on, is that so many of "the poor little things" come to such convents believing that they have escaped the sinful world's temptations only to find themselves "in seven worlds rolled into one," and given a choice of two ways, of which the road to hell was by far the easier to find.

Teresa made no excuses for the woman she was; but her pity for girls no wiser than she had been at the end of her novitiate was passionate.

However, as a direct result of that breakdown Teresa took her first step into religious maturity through help from a surprising quarter. Uncle Pedro had discovered religious books of a kind that would eventually be taken from Teresa by the Inquisition.

Chapter 7 ✿ Osuna's *Third Spiritual Alphabet;* "Mental Prayer"

I

Though Juana Suárez, Teresa's girlhood friend, went to María's farm with her as her companion, she thereafter disappears from Teresa's story. Juana was due to be outgrown.

In Hortigosa, Teresa found Uncle Pedro changed almost beyond recognition. The new vogue in "good books" was for what was then called "mystical theology"; its essence was "mental" as opposed to "verbal" prayer — prayer, that is, as a reaching for direct religious experience. Uncle Pedro had discovered it, and obsession with sin and hell were forgotten. With his lovely niece, a dying nun so enviably near to eternal joy, he was as eager to share his new revelation as, earlier, he had been to snatch her from the burning. He sent Teresa off to María's farm with the book that had initiated his new understanding.

Its author, Francisco de Osuna, was a Franciscan monk, and his book *The Third Spiritual Alphabet*, is sane, simple, and moving. It became the nucleus of Teresa's own little library which she built up, bit by bit, until she was forty-five and the Inquisition çondemmed all her books as being tainted with humanism, illuminism, Lutheranism, and similar pitfalls. Other books would come to mean more to her, such as Erasmus's *Enchiridion: The Handbook of the Militant Christian* — his great pronouncement on the unholy futility of holy wars which somehow escaped the fate of his other writings until 1559. But in the winter before Teresa turned twenty-three, Osuna brought her life to its first major turning point, one that would not be outreached until she was forty.

He taught her for the first time that prayer can be more than the recitation of holy Latin words — that it can also be a kind of inner conversation, a listening. This, she says, "was the first time [she] ever got any satisfaction from prayer." She discovered the peace, the sense of opening that mystics call "the prayer of quiet."

Osuna warns that the sense of new insight into spiritual truths can be an intoxication, a source of destructive spiritual pride. Bellerophon, he says, knew that from time to time he must bring Pegasus down, and touch the earth. This Teresa did not grasp; she believed that at times she reached even that final perfection of religious experience called "the prayer of union." The absurdity hardly matters; she had at least discovered prayer as something more than a means of barter in discovering it as a means of self-transcendence. Teresa had begun to gain a source of strength that would never wholly fail her.

Eventually she was well enough to go for the cure. In Becedas, while she waited for the cure to begin, Teresa sought out the village priest. She was eager to talk about what she calls "the things of God," for which the farm denied all opportunity.

Ideally, Teresa once wrote, a confessor should combine scholarship with virtue; but this was rare, and while she found that a *letrado* never misled her whatever the quality of his own life, the "half-educated" needed perfect virtue if they were not to be "far worse than nothing." The priest of Becedas was a half-educated sinner. So, Teresa says, "The devil began right then and there to disturb my soul," though in the end, "God drew good out of the situation."

The story goes best in her own words.

"When I began to confess to the one I've just told about, he developed an excessive affection for me. . . . It wasn't that the fondness was bad in itself, but rather that such fondness comes to no good end. He understood that nothing could make me sin against God and assured me that it was the same with him, and so we had much conversation.

"But . . . intoxicated as I was with the things of God, what I most relished was talking about His works. And as I seemed such a girl, it threw him into great confusion to see this. So what with that and the great fondness he had for me, he began to declare his own perdition to me."

He had, in fact, kept a mistres for seven years, and not with decent discretion, but blatantly "giving scandal." "He had lost his honor and his good name, and still nobody dared to speak out against him. This filled me wiht great pity, for I loved him very much; in my wantoness and blindness I saw it as a virtue to be grateful and loyal to those who loved me.

"Damned be such loyalty when it even befouls our loyalty to God!... May it please you, God, to make me utterly ungrateful to the world and not opposed to you in anything! But, for my sins, it has all gone the other way."

She asked about him in the village and learned that he was not wholly at fault. The woman had put a spell on him by persuading him to wear a copper idol hung about his neck. (Copper brings down the influence of Venus; anyone, Teresa assumes, would know *that*.)

"I don't believe that this witchcraft business is definitely true, but I will tell you what I saw, so as to warn men against women who want to hold them by such means.... Evil as I have been, I have never fallen into anything like that — nor have I even wanted to force them to feel such fondness for me... for the Lord kept me from that. But if He had left me, I should have done that along with all the rest, for there is nothing to trust in me."

(Not that she needed witchcraft; when she was sixty and looking a youthful forty, men were still drawn to her "like flies to honey.")

So, having learned about the copper idol, she "began to show him more love."

"My intention was good, the means bad, to do any good, however great, one should not have to do even a little evil. Most of the time I talked to him about God, and this ought to have done him good — though I believe it's more to the point that he loved me so much; for, to please me, he gave me the idol, which I had thrown into a river right away." (Such spells can be washed away by running water.)

The priest awoke "as if from a dream," looked back in horror at his sins and wept for his soul. Our Lady helped him because he always gave the village "a big fiesta on the feast of the Immaculate Conception," and — since Teresa kept in touch with him and his friends — she could give her story a happy ending: Pedro Hernández, the priest of Becedas, without backsliding, died a year later in a state of grace.

The story ends with a coda: "I never saw that the love he had for me was bad, though there might have been more purity in it. Just the same there were occasions — on account of which his sins might have been more serious if he had not been kept in the sight of God." (*Ocasión* is shorthand for *occasion of sin*, i.e., temptation plus opportunity.) "As I have said, at that time I would not have done anything I understood to be a mortal sin... and I think that men can't help being fonder of women they see as wanting to be good — and even for the sake of getting what they aim at in this world women can get more out of men that way, as I'll tell you later."

(A promise never specifically kept.)

"I am sure he is on the way to salvation. He died very well, and free of the earlier occasion. It seems as if the Lord wanted to save him by these means."

It *seems:* she is not sure. Indeed, Teresa would never settle the problem of ends and means, though, unlike most of us, she tried.

The cure when it finally began came close to killing her. The most superficial study of such cures leaves one marvelling that anyone survived them. Some did, and since the cures were seen as a last hope, their survivors made more of an impression than the fatalities. One popular treatment, for example, was to bind a split chicken to an incision in the patient's flesh; since like attracts like, the fowl's decay drew off the putrefactions in the patient's blood.

Teresa barely survived Becedas. The hysteric factor in her most recent breakdown cannot be denied, but I think it played little part in the damage she suffered from the cure. Her supposed complaints, consumption and heart-disease, were treated with daily purges and vomitings induced by a near-deadly brew of local plants from which her digestive system would take years to recover. Her body rapidly wasted away from simple starvation; she was literally skin and bone, all muscle-tone lost and every nerve shrieking in exquisite pain. She was too weak to do anything but let out an occasional scream.

The *curandera* diagnosed this final state as rabies, and sent for Alonso. Shortly before mid-August he brought her home on a litter to die. She was critically ill, and probably from more than the cure; her resistance was nil, and a cure, so long as it left one mobile, also left one exposed to the infections of the other patients.

The crisis came on the Feast of the Assumption. This Teresa mentions without comment, but it raised a question: did Our Lady's summer festival remind her of Her other, Her winter feast when the priest of Becedas always gave his village its "big fiesta"? Teresa had saved him, but only "by showing him more love." That morning, Teresa asked for a priest.

Whatever was on her mind, she would still have wanted to confess. The Carmelites are "the Virgin's Order" and that day was her most holy day of obligation: one of the surprisingly few when Carmelite nuns confessed and received communion. Any Catholic would have know why his Carmelite daughter asked for a priest on that day. Teresa tries to cover Alonso's refusal:

"They [not he] thought it was because I was afraid I was going to die." But she feels the inadequacy and tries to better it with an excess of whitewash: "Oh, too great love of mortal flesh, that such a Catholic and well-informed father should do me such harm! For he was that, and very much so, and it couldn't have been from ignorance!"

Teresa had neither taste for the lie direct nor skill at it. She protests too much, and calls attention to the wrong things by protesting them. It is too bad that Teresa wrote her book when a new wave of dangerous antisemitism made it impossible for her to tell the whole story. Alonso's conversion, when it came, was deep, sincere, and oddly moving.

That night Teresa's fever shot up perilously. She became delirious, suffered a severe epileptoid convulsion, bit her tongue to shreds and passed into deep coma. Alonso, in anguish for his darling, felt his first real onslaught of religious doubt: "Was I wrong?" I am glad to believe that it was for her, not for himself, that he was overcome by the icy logic of Pascal's wager.

He sent for the priest, who could only give her supreme unction. She was unconscious for four days; her coma was so deep that she appeared to be dead. When she came to herself, there was wax on her eyelids: someone had prematurely sealed the eyes of a corpse.

"My father's grief at not having let me confess was great; many cries and prayers to God. Blessed be He who heard them because for a day and a half my grave had been open in the convent waiting for my body, and the office of the dead had been read in a friary in another place when the Lord willed me to come to myself again."

The "other place" was Villatoro. Alonso, desperate, had turned once more to his brother Lorenzo, the priest; and Lorenzo, assuming that his niece, the Carmelite nun, was dead, asked the local Carmelite friars to say the office for the repose of her soul.

Poor Alonso, asking himself questions: What if his child had been right? Surely, God would understand by this that it was his fault, not hers, that she died unconfessed? His fault, of which he repented?

Now Alonso was only too glad to let Teresa confess and receive communion. She wept throughout, but only from physical pain, not in penitence as the priest believed. Looking back, she would believe that if she had died then, her chances of salvation would have been slim: "Because my confessors were so ignorant and I was so vile, and a lot of things." But it was still more terrifying to think that she might have died years later "when my soul was in a thousand times greater danger."

"I don't believe that I exaggerate much when I say a thousand times, though it may start a quarrel with the one who ordered me to play down the account of my sins—and mightly prettified it is all coming out! I beg him for the love of God to cut out nothing about my sins, for it is just there that the glory of God is shown—by what He will put up with in a human soul."

Fortunately for those who profited by her canonization, Father García de Toledo had his own good reasons for leaving her plea unanswered; her story has huge gaps in it. However, she truly believed herself to be converted once and for all when she converted Alonso, "as I will tell you now."

Chapter 8 ✸ Teresa's Recovery from Serious Illness

Teresa recovered slowly. At first she was helpless and in such pain that she could not endure being handled. To move her, it was necessary to lift her by the four corners of the sheet. She wanted only to be left alone; when the room was still, the pain seemed less acute. In time it became only intermittent, not a continuous torment. She was delighted, and even more delighted when by early spring she could crawl about the room on her hands and knees.

She insisted upon being taken back to the convent, where she spent three years in the infirmary. Along with what sounds like rheumatoid arthritis, from which she would thereafter always suffer crippling seizures, she had probably contracted malaria, for she speaks of the wracking chills that followed her recurrent fevers; in river towns like Becedas many got the "quartan ague" in mosquito season.

Convents treasured a holy invalid, so long as her symptoms were not revolting like those of the cancerous nun whom Teresa envied. She had also become the convent's miracle, their little Lazarus raised from the dead. Teresa, as the apt phrase goes, could have enjoyed poor health for the rest of her days.

She rejected the role. From that time until her death at sixty-seven every illness including her last was always "getting better" and she fought to lead a remarkably active life. It shows the dark side of Spanish religion that Teresa always had to apologize for her conviction that life offers us worthier crosses to bear than the cross of pain; but after that illness she felt it strongly even before she had thought it out. Furthermore, she wanted to escape the infirmary. It offered neither solitude or real companionship. She could and did read there, avidly; but to think and pray in that place was impossible. One could say rosaries, but that was not what she wanted.

Nor could she explain her needs, least of all to her Carmelite confessors. But her father began to understand her. He had always been a reader, and now he kept her supplied with the kind of books she wanted and read them himself. "Mystical theology" was a far cry from his introduction to the Faith by the Inquisition, nor did it confuse him with figures like "Our Lady and several saints" — the alien deities to whom Beatriz had prayed. Teresa's books talked comprehensibly about God. Still, they raised questions: questions that only Christian scholars could answer.

Alonso began to pray, and since the Dominicans were known to be scholars, he went to the monastary of Santo Tomás for help; and Fr. Vicente Barrón, a man of distinguished mind and sterling character, became his confessor.

When Teresa wrote her book, the fires of the Inquisition were newly burning in Valladolid. She could say that after reading her books her father became increasingly devout, though she could not admit the vast change in his attitude. Yet she saw and understood that change, and her understanding bred a conviction that most Spaniards of her day found shocking, if not downright heretical.

In her lifetime she found few to whom she could confess that she, like Erasmus, believed that "souls are not won by the sword."

Her three years in that infirmary were chiefly obsessed with a desire to escape it. Sometimes she had fears that with health regained she would revert to her old ways and be "lost forever," but she put them aside. She had her friends pray for her, with the stipulation that their devotions "should only be the most approved, for I never liked that other kind that some people, especially women, find so inspiring. Later I learned that they are superstitious."

For herself, she chiefly appealed to St. Joseph, the father-figure to whom, she was sure, His Majesty Jesus Christ would refuse nothing.

Yet while fathers are wise and indulgent, they also make mistakes, and Teresa both blamed and exonerated St. Joseph for her return to health. Though renewed health was, she says, "her ruin," she always gave the convent a fiesta on St. Joseph's day, and on that day made some special request of him; but St. Joseph, having learned from his mistake in restoring her health, granted her request only if he found it wise, and if not "he gave [her] something else." And, as she always does for Alonso, she goes still further to put St. Joseph in a favorable light. She had been wrong to sidestep Jesus Christ by appealing to the father whom He could not easily refuse, but: "I see now how that father and my Lord saved me from that folly, just as they would save me in time from greater dangers to my reputation, as well as from the loss of my soul."

Teresa never doubted that her slow struggle back to health was a miracle brought about by St. Joseph; and as such it is now famous. But she also considered it a miracle that her sins were not discovered in the year when she lost not only all virtue but all discretion: a miracle worked because both the saint and his foster Son saw that a nun with a bad name could not carry out the work for which God intended to use her.

This second miracle, which she mentions specifically not once but twice, is now reverently forgotten. But Teresa saw it as the greater by far, and in gratitude she named many convents in St. Joseph's honor.

When Teresa got back to the parlors and their "occasions" she had suffered agonies of boredom for three long years. She was twenty-six, but she looked far younger; her striking beauty was wholly restored. But she went back with noble intentions and she expresses a real amazement when she writes, "Who would have thought that I would fall so soon!"

II

Teresa's next three years were the antithesis of the three just passed. She rushed "from pastime to pastime, from vanity to vanity, from occasion to occasion" and finally into "a very great occasion" with the one "who had most power to disturb her soul."

An "occasion" we have translated. A "vanity" can be anything from an unseemly worldliness to behavior like that which had put her father and brothers "in the hand of danger"—of which she wrote, "I had not been three months in these vanities when ..." We should also remember that as one

31

apparently raised from the dead and thereafter restored to health by St. Joseph, Teresa had become a convent legend. She was given even more trust and freedom than "the poor little things" whom she so learned to pity.

"It did me terrible harm not to be in an enclosed convent, for the same liberty that those who are naturally good can use to good purpose would have carried me straight to hell, wicked as I was, if the Lord had not drawn me out of that danger by many means. . . . And so . . . in convents where women are given such liberty it seems to me more like a step on the road to hell than a cure for the frailities of the flesh."

And what of the friars who should guide these nuns?

"Oh, greatest, greatest evil of the monastic life—and I am not talking about women more than men—a religious house where there is no real care for religion . . . where a monk or a nun who has begun to follow a real vocation has more reason to be afraid of the others in his house than of all the devils in hell."

Her anger was directed at a system in which girls were not only unprotected but were taught that it was no sin to play with fire until God, or physiology, "laid it bare." Thus placed, "the poor little things" did not even feel guilt; taught that their mortal sins were only venial and their venial sins no sin at all, they blundered to hell "blinded like the unfortunate heretics."

For herself she made no such excuse. In prayer she had felt herself receiving the love of Christ, and from the start she had known that what she felt for the man "who had most power to disturb her soul" was at best a spiritual adultery. But she could not break away from such "fondness." She had come to think of "mental prayer" as a way into Christ's living company, and towards the end of those three years she relinquished it—because, as she says, "she was only fit to associate with demons."

In time she would come to see that self-condemnation as the most cruel temptation ever sent her by the devil. Now she only dared pray her prayers of daily obligation, by rote, like the child who had said rosaries to buy her way into heaven. Yet she longed to give others what she had lost. When she saw some small leaning towards religion in other nuns, she tried to teach them "how to make a meditation" and lent them the books that had once opened her spirit. This, to her horror, only increased her reputation for holiness. Teresa means it when she says that "hypocrisy" and vainglory were always the two sins which she shrank from in such sheer distaste that the devil gave her up for a lost cause in that respect at least. "Even back then it weighed heavy on me to be so well thought of when I knew my own secret. . . ."

Still, she guarded that secret. She did not want to be thought holy but neither did she want to hurt the convent's reputation, for its alms came from the pious and overtrusting quite as much as from *devotos* with earlier hopes.

She was trusted in part, she says, because she looked so young for her years; and still more because she did none of the things that are easily detected and give a convent a bad name. (But forced to "prettify" General Rubeo's report of assignations in the dark chapel and the confessionals, she only says that nuns had secret talks "through crannies and over walls and by night.")

"It seemed to me that it would be wicked to risk the honor of so many nuns because I was wicked — as if the other things I was doing were good!"

Yet once Teresa denied herself any emotional satisfaction in prayer, things slipped from bad to worse.

III

Meanwhile, Alonso had become a devout Catholic. He barely noticed that his finances were on the rocks; he was laying up treasures in heaven. He loved to visit the convent and talk with Teresa about the friendship they shared with the Christ who so perfectly embodied the virtues by which he had always tried to live: the charity that does not judge, pity for human suffering and forgiveness of human frailties. He talked about prayer as she herself had conceived it: a privileged conversation in which one was lifted up, set right, made better.

Teresa had always been her father's dearest, and she knew that fathers, like all other lovers, love a curious blend of truth and illusion. She had a native gift for "dissembling" as she called it, but from the time that religion came to mean more to her than future-life insurance, it was the one subject on which she could neither deceive herself or others. In years to come, this quirk would save her sanity. Now it tormented her. She had to tell Alonso that she no longer prayed; but she could not bear to tell him why. She said that she was not well enough to pray more than her "verbal" prayers of obligation.

Alonso loved her; he knew that "mental prayer" demands no physical strength, but he could not give her the lie direct. And Teresa tried to believe that he believed her, as she had when she "lied to him so much" about the affair that ended with her being shut up in Our Lady of Grace. At least, she knew, he wanted to believe her. But his visits became less frequent and shorter. He would talk for a little and then get up restlessly saying that he was wasting the time that his soul needed to get ready for death.

She tells about that, as if to admit that he knew the truth, and ends with one cold line of self-condemnation: "As I was wasting my time on other vanities, I hardly noticed."

He was old and in failing health, but she did not notice that, either. Lost in love for "the one who always had most power to disturb [her] soul," she was shut off from all the other ways of love.

That indifference to her beloved father was something that she could not bear to remember; and that his death did not send her at once to the confessor who had also loved his gentle soul is the one shame that she ever deliberately concealed on her own account.

IV

Alonso's death flashes out of her enforced generalities with startling reality.

Only one sentence of it blurs, as she struggles against censorship to tell what state her own life was in when they called her to his deathbed in that December before she turned twenty-nine.

"I went to take care of him more sick in soul than he was in body, involved in many vanities, though not in such a way as to be in mortal sin—so far as I understood—throughout all that time that was more worth of damnation than I am telling, because if I had understood it, it never would have been."

I suppose that this unconstruable sentence means, "At least there was still no actual sexual intercourse." But from here on in, the account of Alonso's death is vivid and in sharp contrast with those four words spent on her mother: "She died most Christianly."

"I suffered the utmost strain throughout his illness; perhaps it paid back some part of all he had gone through with mine. Though I was utterly sick at heart and though in losing him I was losing all good and comfort—for he gave me all that summed up in his one life—I managed to be brave enough to show him no pain; and while I went on acting as if there were nothing to grieve over right up to his death, I felt as if my own soul was being torn out of me, for I loved him much.

"He charged us to commend him to God and pray God to have mercy on him, and that we should serve Him always and remember that everything comes to an end. And he told us with tears what great pain it gave him that he had no served Him—and that he should have wanted to be a monk—I mean in one of the strictest orders that exist. . . .

"His chief suffering was a terribly severe pain in the shoulders that never let up. Sometimes it seized him so intensely that he suffered cruelly. Because he was always so moved to devotion when he thought of the Lord carrying the cross on His back, I told him that he could think His Majesty wanted him to share something of what He had gone through in just such pain. He was so comforted that I never heard him complain again.

"He was unconscious for three days. On the day he died, the Lord brought him to himself so completely that we were amazed and he died halfway through the Creed, saying it himself. He died like an angel. You could say that he always seemed like one to me, both in soul and disposition—they were so good.

"I don't know why I should have told all this if it isn't to blame my wicked life still more after having seen such a death and known such a life. To make myself like my father in any way at all I should have grown better. His confessor, a very scholarly Dominican, had no doubt that he went straight to heaven, for he had confessed him for several years and praised the purity of his conscience."

The writing is awkward, ground out through remembered pain; it rings true. But it is not the whole story of Alonso's death. Teresa could tell of her father's tears for the time when he had not served God; and the account gains meaning when we realize that even one of Torquemada's converts could not claim "invincible ignorance" to exonerate fifty-one years of quiet inner rejection of the Faith. Nor could Teresa tell of her father's last request.

We know of it, as we know of the defective child, Juan de Ahumada, because Alonso's will was contested. (The legal archives of Valladolid are much harder to rob than collections of private papers.)

Alonso, dying, remembered Beatriz, a frightened, pregnant child in Gotarrendura, a Doña Quixote whose dreams he had nourished in mistaken tenderness. And his will directs that he, like Beatriz, be buried in secret.

Teresa had always idolized her father. Though she could only call him chaste *en gran manera*, she knew (as she once wrote to her brother Lorenzo of his own persistent sexual drive) that the de Cepedas were "of the sanguine humor," warm-blooded. She would have seen any infidelity for which Alonso begged God to shorten his stay in Purgatory as the natural outcome of her mother's protracted fear of bearing another child like poor Juan De Ahumada. But Teresa had treasured the belief that she understood the father whose gentle soul "could not be won by the sword"; she had loved him far more than she loved her mother, and believed that he loved her more than anyone else alive or dead.

I find it hard to believe that she could have heard him ask to be buried in secret, like poor Beatriz, without feeling a sense of betrayal; and a born father's daughter, like Teresa, never feels complete without some man's love.

The first impulse of one who feels so betrayed—at whatever level, or however consciously it be denied—is all too often to seek reassurance from another man.

By omission, Teresa lets us believe that she took her father's confessor for her own immediately after his death. Barrón's own records show that she waited for ten months.

He would not have told her that her mortal sins were only venial, and she knew it. I am not surprised that she could not bear to hear him say so until those ten months had passed.

Chapter 9 ❀ *Inner Conflict; Teresa's Second Conversion following Her Reading of St. Augustine's Confessions*

I

Lorenzo took over the care of his mildly retarded brother, Pedro, and left for the Indies, to be gone for thirty years; when he could he sent for Jeronimo, to whom he became a second father, and Agustín, the one bad apple in the family basket. Juan de Ahumada remained hidden away. The dowry left to Juana, then a boarder at the Incarnation, bought her an out-at-elbows *hidalgo* from Alba de Tormes who promptly contested Alonso's will with Martín de Guzmán.

Their suits and countersuits over largely non-existent property (supposedly their wive's respective dowries and due inheritance) continued until, seventeen years later, de Guzmán dropped dead.

While we only know from Father Barrón's records that Teresa put off seeing him for ten months, she does call that time "the most sinful year of my life." Of Barrón she says, "He was very good and fearful of his God." One remembers that she said of her conversion, ten years later, "I could not be led by the way of fear." Yet I doubt that she would have gone back so soon to the "half-educated" Carmelites if Barrón had not been offered a priorate for which he left Avila in a matter of months.

Once Teresa went to him, Barrón told her that she was heading straight for hell. He directed her "to take communion once a fortnight" and told her that she had been wrong to give up her "mental prayer."

"He said that there was no way in which it would not do me good."

Teresa believed him, and her belief led to a long agony of inner conflict. She would remember it (inaccurately) as having been "for twenty years cast up and down upon that stormy sea." But when Barrón left, she did not seek out another *letrado*. Her next confessor was a twenty-two-year-old Carmelite, Pedro de la Purificación. He lived to join the Order that she founded and left an interesting bit of testimony which is still in the Carmelite archives:

"One thing worried me about that glorious Mother which I noted many times, and it troubled me to think about it; and that was that when a visitor had to be with her on business, she would talk with him for three or four hours at a time, quite as often in private as in company."

"Had to be with her on business" is cautious in the matter of Teresa's beatification; Brother Pedro was not yet quite sure how the cookie would crumble when he set down this reminiscence, though frequent four-hour meetings, closeted alone on some unexplained business, is striking, even before he describes, from his own experience, the quality of such meetings: "Her conversation was so sublime, her words so sweet, her mouth so full of laughter that one never grew weary or could make oneself go away from her."

Teresa was thirty when Brother Pedro replaced Father Barrón. She was forty when Father Miguel Carranza met her in the course of a tour of inspection he made with the Provincial of her Order:

"We reached Avila . . . and went . . . to the Convent of the Incarnation. . . . Doña Teresa de Ahumada was a distinguished lady, both for her noble lineage and for her talents. She was young . . . very gay and witty . . . and as people say, she did have her *devotos* in the Order then; but I never heard that the said Doña Teresa was given to evil behavior or that she exceeded the limits set the religious life — though she did behave with a certain liberty, as was customary in that convent and in many convents before the Council [of Trent]."

She was young. . . . At forty, Teresa looked well under thirty; and at sixty like a still-beautiful forty; that would be her misfortune. *Very gay and witty . . . her mouth so full of laughter. . . .* That was her blessing. Almost to the end of her life she could laugh at herself and her world, and without bitterness. She could also keep up a front. Father Carranza, *nota bene*, saw her in a time of inner conflict and suffering.

Tastes had gone more baroque when Teresa was canonized. Ana Maria of the Incarnation testifies that when Teresa had spoken, "even briefly, with a visitor at the screen" (a barrier installed after the Council of Trent), she withdrew at once to her cell and "lashed herself with the utmost cruelty." Another nun, from Segovia, betters it: the glorious Mother habitually lacerated her flesh with the pronged whip "until the walls of her cell dripped with gore." But Brother Pedro and Father Carranza were accurate. Teresa never wore her heart upon her sleeve.

Still, she could describe those ten years, once they were behind her:

"I went through a life of the greatest conflict, for in prayer I could see my failings for what they were. On the one hand, God called me; on the other, I followed the world." She struggled to harmonize "the spiritual life . . . and the life of sensual pleasures and pursuits," but "the spirit was not master but slave." She could not "withdraw into [herself] to pray without shutting a thousand vanities in with [her]."

"Now it amazes me that I could have borne it without giving up one or the other. . . . Oh, God help me, if I were only allowed to tell about the occasions of sin that God freed me from in those years, and how I used to turn back and throw myself into them, again and again! And the dangers of totally losing my reputation that He saved me from! I have deliberately done things to uncover what I was, and the Lord would cover the evil over again . . . so that even when my vanities were perfectly transparent people wouldn't believe it because they saw other things that looked like goodness to them."

That was God's plan, she explains, because He knew that her past would have to seem virtuous if she were to be trusted once she began to act in his service. He also knew that once her need for love was rightly channeled, she would use it for the healing of his schism-torn Church: so she described the Rival Love that she bore for ten years without "giving up the other."

"Oh, Lord of my soul, how could I ever exaggerate the mercies You showed me in those years? Or explain to myself how, even when I was sinning against You most, You would fill me with ecstasy? . . . Truly, my King, You chose the most delicate and painful punishment for me that could ever have been: for, like one who understood what would hurt me most, You chastized my soul with great caressings."

This is the stage that Teresa outgrew. Her conversion brought about a change of direction and the release of a wasted genius, but at this point, however, we are left asking, "What actually happened? How far did these 'great affections' really go?" At my own guess, she only "lost all" shortly before her father's death; the year in which she put off seeing Father Barrón for those ten months of what she calls "the most sinful year of my life." Women of my generation can remember lovemaking that was both passionate and technically chaste; lovemaking ideally suited to leave a Teresa torn between guilt and desire.

Those ten years were nearly over — the years of which she says, of men, "and in time there would be others" — when García de Toledo, long absent, "the one who always had the most power to disturb [her] soul," came back to Avila.

García became in time the most anxious censor of Teresa's book. He appears (admittedly) in the story first when Teresa, at forty-seven, had long since left the Incarnation: she describes him as a friend of former days who was *muy, muy principal*. Accurate, for though illegitimate, he was the openly accepted cousin of the Duke of Alba. Nobles were nobles; Don John of Austria was no less royal for being illegitimate. García was also in holy orders, and it was as both priest and worldling that he brought Teresa to the breaking-point. She could see him as on neither side in her inner conflict, or worse, on both sides at once. The confusion fed the conflict, and the conflict tore her apart.

García had been made subprior at Santo Tomás; no less position would have been suitable for one so *muy principal*. It was natural for him to visit the Incarnation often to see his cousins, the daughters of the Marquis of Velada. He also preached sermons there which are said to have been stirring, and Rubeo's report names him as a "favorite confessor."

At his return, Teresa had broken off a friendship which had become overfond, and formed no other "for nearly a year." But she was trapped in "the way of fear," and García's return caused a suffering about which she was forbidden to be specific:

"Then the torment of hearing sermons was no small thing, and I was so fond of them that if I heard someone preach well and with spirit, a particular love drew him close to me without my trying for it — and I don't know who got me into it. I never got tired of talking about God or hearing about Him . . . so on the one hand I got much comfort from these sermons, and on the other hand it was torture to me — for right then and there I could see that the love, in large part, was not what it should have been.

"I begged God to help me, but what I must have lacked — I see it now — came through my not putting all my confidence in Him and losing every shred of it in myself. I wanted to live, for I saw perfectly well that I was not living but only struggling with a shadow of death — and I had nobody to give me life and I could not take it. . . .

"So then my soul was going on in weariness, and though I longed for rest, the wicked ways I had would not let me find it.

"One day I happened to go into an oratory and see a statue they had put there for safekeeping; they had borrowed it for a certain celebration to be held in the convent. It was of Christ, much wounded, and it was so devout that when I saw it I was completely stirred up to see Him like that, for it showed so well what He went through for us. My grief over the wickedness with which I had deepened those wounds was so great that I threw myself down before Him in a tremendous flood of tears, pleading with Him to give me strength, once and for all, not to sin against Him any more.

"I was much devoted to the glorious Magdalen, and I often thought about her conversion, especially when I took communion, for knowing that the Lord was truly within me right then and there, I would set myself at His feet, believing that my tears were not rejected. (And I didn't know what I was saying!

As if He did a lot for Himself when He let me shed them and when I forgot such feelings so quickly!) And I would commend myself to that glorious saint, in the hope of her winning me forgiveness.

"But that last time, before that image I told you about, it seemed to me that it did me more good, for I felt the deepest distrust of myself and put all my confidence in God. I think I told Him that I would not get up from that place until He did what I was praying for. I know for certain that it did me some good, for I was much bettered from that time on."

She was "much bettered" but no more than that. Perfect fear casteth out love, and Teresa could not believe that her repentance had come in time to save her from the hell that she had earned through all those years when she wept her Magdalen tears at the altar rail and then, so quickly, fell back into sin again. The next months, like those that followed her father's death, were nothing that she could write about. But she elides them less skillfully. We know, at least, that at some time not long thereafter she told a priest about her disturbing friendship with one who was not in any deep sense religious, and he laughed it off as a scruple, certainly no occasion of sin.

No priest would have said anything else if her scruple concerned the subprior of the Dominicans. But I am convinced that she confessed it to García himself. Teresa's handbook for nuns, *The Way of Perfection*, treats of the scruples that nuns feel over unencouraged, unwilling "particular loves." They must not brood over it, she says, if they feel a great personal fondness for a confessor; and, above all, they must not confess it to him. The thing to do is simply to ignore it unless they begin to feel that the fondness is being returned. If that happens, she says, change confessors.

Such wisdom is only gained the hard way.

But she does not expand on the subject here. Instead, she begins to lay the ground for a more urgent kind of special pleading, not for her sins, but for her conversion. She was eventually ordered to tell the whole story—by an Inquisitor. Once we have put it into the context of history, we will understand why the Inquisition tried to block her canonization for a full eleven years after her "miraculous preservation" was discovered, and how only a genuine, justified fear for her safety made her friends drive her to the outer limits of sanity. That she saved herself by unsparing self-analysis joined to an inspired sense of basic Christian values, and did it with no loss of her unquestioning Catholic orthodoxy, can be considered a miracle, though it is the miracle that her Church chooses to forget.

II

Teresa would eventually admit that García de Toledo, like most career churchmen of his day, "was not Christ's friend." However, he was Teresa's friend; and when she took him for her confessor and poured out the story of her temptations, her many falls, and her trap of self-despair, he was too civilized and percipient to be swayed by his own desires and belittle her sins like a "half-educated Carmelite."

And he believed that he knew how to help her. Augustine, who prayed through many years, "God make me chaste—but not yet," had long been forbidden reading to non-latinists, and hence to women. But now, as all courtiers like García knew, he was for the first time available in Spanish.

The Portugese who made the translation was forced to have it printed in the Lowlands; but, intelligently, he dedicated it to Doña Leonora de Mascareñas, the Portuguese noblewoman who had been Philip II's governess and still remained part of his inner circle. He sent her the book, Doña Leonora was flattered, Philip was pleased by this public gesture of respect for her piety, and the censure of a translation dangerous to "women and idiots" was forestalled.

This happened in 1555, the year that Teresa turned forty. Outside of court circles she was one of the first to read the *Confessions* in Spanish. And, *incipit vita nova*. Lord, we know not what we do. García, a spiritual lightweight, would only have wanted to cheer Teresa up by releasing her from "the way of fear."

This is how she tells it; note the impersonal *they* which she always uses to shield someone or to avoid introducing a character into her story at the wrong time:

"At that time, they gave me the *Confessions* of St. Augustine; it seems as if the Lord ordained it, for I did not try to get it for myself and had never seen a copy.

"Oh, God help me, how all that harsh resistance of my soul to all the help God gave me shocks me now! It frightens me to see ... how I kept myself shackled just to keep from making up my mind to give myself wholly to God. When I started reading the *Confessions* it seemed to me that I was seeing my own self right there. When I got as far as his conversion and read how he heard that voice in the garden, it was just as if the Lord gave it to me, too, to judge from the grief that filled my heart. For a long time I was wholly undone by my weeping, and with Augustine's very same love and anguish within my own self, too. . . .

"Oh, God help us, what a soul suffers when it loses the freedom to rule itself that it would have! I wonder that I could have lived so long in such torment! God be praised who gave me life so that I could rise up from such a mortal death!"

Yes, death is generally mortal. Teresa was not writing as a woman of letters. She was pouring out a story intended to give hope to the hopeless; to do for others what Augustine, so often called and often fallen, had done for her.

The voice in the garden, you remember, directed Augustine to pick up his Bible and read and he opened to these words of St. Paul: "Not in rioting and drunkenness, not in whorings and lasciviousness, not in quarrelings and jealousy, but take on the nature of the Lord Jesus Christ and give no more thought to the lusts of the flesh."

Augustine thereafter loathed the flesh in the familiar pattern of the libertine turned puritan. Woman, he said, is a temple built over a sewer. Pious souls rarely mean anything else when they say, "The greatest saints were the greatest sinners."

Teresa's conversion filled her with a love for the all-forgiving Christ that no man could rival; but she did not turn puritan. She would always take it for granted that girls needed to be guarded from temptation and make excuses for those who fell: "They were young ... not properly watched over ... set a bad example." And she would always take it for granted that men will be men, living as they do in "the world's occasions" and tempted as well by that free-floating sexuality which few women ever really understand. This we know, at long last, from her letters.

Teresa's conversion was above all a release from her obsession with the sins of the flesh. Little by little it freed her to take up arms against the sins that more gravely endangered the life of the Church: hypocrisy, greed, ambition — and in time, against the superstition encouraged by her most powerful opponents and the hysteria embraced by all too many as mystic experience. But this came slowly.

Teresa would go on learning until she died; but she had already learned much when, at forty-six, she wrote the intended end to her book, *Concerning God's Mercies*, her treatise on the ascending stages of prayer from which she turns back, at the very end, to sum up the message of hope implicit in her own conversion:

"Oh, Lord of my soul, if only somebody could find the words to make others understand what You give to those who have faith in You, and what they lose who find that very faith and still hang back in their own company! You cannot want this, Lord, for you did still more; You came to an inn as evil as my own. May you be blessed forever without end, amen."

Yes, in those six years since her conversion she had learned much, and none of it cheaply. 1555 was not a safe year in which to undergo a deep and intensely emotional conversion: not in Spain.

"Mental prayer" was suspect, a flirtation with heresy. It was known (and, be it admitted, with considerable corroborative evidence) to endanger women more that men, and *conversos* more than those of "pure blood." Furthermore, the temper of opinion had changed in Avila since it had cheerfully shrugged off that Don Alonso de Cepeda was Alonso Pina, Torquemada's convert.

Even in Avila, where Moisés Rubén de Bracamonte's six-pointed church had been seen as so amusing.

Chapter 10 ❄ Jesuit Confessors; Teresa's Desire to Escape from the Incarnation

Teresa had learned from Augustine that she was not irrevocably damned; that even those who hear the call, repent, and fall again, as she had for twenty years as Christ's unfaithful bride, cannot outwear His forgiveness and His Love. Perhaps we may call it a miracle that she, so utterly a child of the double-standard, could accept his story, a man's, with such an utter sense of identification.

It changed the whole quality of her religious life, though she could never explain it. Since girlhood, she had often tried to imagine Christ in the Garden of Gethsemane praying that the cup might pass. At Our Lady of Grace the nuns had told her that imagining it would bring "many indulgences." As a woman — and seeking no indulgences — she imagined herself beside Him in the Garden, longing to wipe the sweat from His forehead and "not daring, because [her] sins showed themselves as so grave." But those imaginings had been only holy daydreaming from which, she says, she "could either win or lose a great deal" — since her mind had a way of drifting off into earthier phantasies.

Looking at holy pictures had helped; so did reading "good books" or going out of doors "to look at a field, or water, or flowers, and thinking about their Creator." But it was conscious effort and while at times she could feel that she was praying as she had in her days of comparative innocence, the sense of being at one with God was fleeting; it had no effect on her daily life, and it only came through conscious effort.

Now she was certain, God Himself took over. She would fall into a state which rarely lasted "longer than an Ave Maria" (say fifteen seconds) and "never as long as half-an-hour," in which she seemed to think nothing, imagine nothing, and afterwards could remember nothing about it, but the after-effect was a sense of wonder, holy joy, like a foretaste of the joy that the blessed must feel in heaven, a moment of total accord between the soul's desires and God's will. She believed that this state was supernatural because it came by no effort of her own. Indeed, when she tried to convince herself that it was self-induced and attempted to stave it off, it would still seize her.

But this in itself was frightening, for if it did not come from God, it came from the devil to seduce and deceive her soul. He had done just that to Fernanda Hernández and her followers; they slept with monks to prove that they were miraculously freed from sin. Others he lured into the still deadlier sin of heresy, by making them believe that they knew more than any *letrados*. Magdalen of the Cross had probably believed herself inspired when she first gained her name for holiness, though she ended up by receiving the stigmata — with ochre dye — before the Inquisition exposed and punished her.

Such thoughts tormented Teresa: God had forgiven her, but the devil does not quickly relinquish his hopes. How could she know that these strange, overpowering seizures of holy joy were really holy, God-given? And what priest could advise her? The Carmelites were useless, and García would only be kind and uncomprehending.

She finally consulted a man whose wife was related to her Uncle Pedro's late wife. Her book, which names no names, calls him "the saintly gentleman." Francisco de Salcedo was, among other things, a holy innocent who visited the Incarnation to be edified by the sight of so much sanctity. He also prayed much, in "verbal prayer," and took courses in religion at Santo Tomás. His confessor, Master Daza ("Master" because he had taken a university degree), was a worthy parish priest. They were both good—but wholly unsuited to Teresa's needs. Francisco de Salcedo was incurably "led by the way of fear." And Daza had a distaste for mysticism: he was *bien incrédulo de revelaciones*.

One meeting in the confessional convinced Daza that he wanted nothing to do with a woman who was apparently trying to bolster a shaky reputation with talk about a mystical conversion. He told Teresa that he was too busy to confess her again.

Francisco de Salcedo was sorry. He had always admired Teresa, and while her apparent disturbance, so unlike her, baffled him, he wanted to help. She tried to tell him about her conversion and the sinful years that had gone before. He assumed that her nun's pure conscience was making Alps out of anthills, and tried to tell her about his own little failings: nothing, she says, even remotely improper for a man of the world.

Finally, her need to be understood forced her to a degree of honesty that shocked him. He told her that her supposed religious experiences could not have been given by God to one as vile as she claimed to be; he could help her no more. But quite possibly his brother-in-law, a Jesuit, could.

The Jesuits, newly come to Avila, had a name for understanding such things. Their founder, Ignatius of Loyola, was said to have learned all theology through a single revelation; furthermore, he approved of "mental prayer" and taught it to his followers. Francisco would ask if they would give her a confessor.

The Jesuits showed courage in accepting her as their penitent when they did. Father Andrés González, who got himself transferred from Avila after a year, wrote to Ignatius of Loyola about the distrust "the Company" faced there. Sermons, he said, were being preached against them in which it was said that they called themselves apostles when they were only dangerous innovators, that their show of unworldly detachment was "artful hypocrisy," and that their dressing like the secular priesthood was a scandalous refusal to wear the monastic garb "of mortification and humility." Furthermore, though Father González did not mention it, they were suspected of an improper lack of antisemitism—which Avila had just begun to see as a sin.

That last charge was true at the time; indeed, Loyola said that he was sorry to have no Jewish blood, for it would have given him a deeper sense of human kinship with Christ and Our Lady.

This, of course, Teresa never mentions; she had her work and the welfare of her family to think about. Nor does she mention one other unpopular tenet of Loyola's teaching that she had long embraced. Loyola believed, as firmly as

Erasmus, that there are no holy wars and that the true Christian soldier's sole armaments are the Word, the Sacraments, and righteousness.

II

Teresa learned with some anxiety that she would be sent a Jesuit confessor. As she says, "They had the name of being saints." She did not know what to expect and made a futile effort to keep the convent from learning that one of the Company was coming to confess her. Actually, the Company was also anxious, which is why they sent her Diego de Cetina: but I doubt that Teresa ever saw him as he was. Her chief need at the time was to be taken seriously.

"What a thing it is, " she exclaims, "to understand a soul!"

The Company (as Teresa always calls the Jesuits, when she does not misname them the Theatines) had a hard time getting accepted by Avila. Little de Cetina had been tossed to Teresa as the most expendable among them.

He was only twenty-three and not very intelligent. Nine years later, when his superiors were trying to find some suitable niche for him, he wrote out this *vita* on request:

"My health is middling, and I am weak in the head. I was always fond of praying to Our Lady, and of mental prayer once they started me on it, and I am increasingly fonder of mental prayer than of verbal prayer. I have always been fond of sermons, masses and of talking about Our Lord."

A year later, one of his superiors wrote this evaluation of his potential: "He has been occupied with auditing a whole course in theology and in performing minor offices. He is a mediocre preacher and confessor and is not capable of anything more."

Teresa gives no intimation that he was not a mature and considerable person.

At their first meeting he directed her to write out a general confession. She wanted to be understood and she tried to give a balanced picture, but she told the whole truth, not "mightily prettified," and was appalled to see how much the bad outweighed the good.

At least young de Cetina was a good listener—a support for which many of us have gladly paid fifty dollars an hour.

Teresa says, "In talking over my whole soul with that servant of God—for he was that, and very much so, and very prudent—he told me just what was happening, like one who understands that kind of language well and gave me much comfort."

This leads to a record nonstop sentence, even for Teresa, and with even less grammar than I have been forced to lend it:

"He said that it was very definitely the spirit of God, but that it was necessary to go back to the beginning in the matter of prayer because it did not start from a good foundation and I hadn't begun to understand mortification (and that was so for I don't think I even understood what the word meant) and I must on no account give up prayer but strain myself in it greatly since God had shown me such particular mercies; who knew but what the Lord wanted to use me to do good to many people (which seems as if he was prophesying what the Lord has done since then) and I would be much to blame if I didn't respond to the mercies God was showing me.

"In everything he said it seemed to me as if the Holy Spirit was speaking to me through him to heal my soul, it was all impressed on me so deeply."

He filled her with shame, she says, and seemed to lead her into becoming quite a different person. Apparently his teaching, based on what he could grasp in Loyola's *Spiritual Exercises*, was what she had needed: something to trust when she could not trust herself. He told her to base her prayers, each day, on a single incident of the Passion, meditating on its relevance to her own life. He also warned her to fight off those strange states which seemed to be supernatural experience, unless or until he should tell her otherwise.

She admitted that she did not engage in physical penance; her body needed no more pain. De Cetina told her that God gave her pain for penance since she would take none on herself.

"He suggested certain practices which I did not find very savory."

She never would. But during the two months in which de Cetina was allowed to confess her she lashed herself with the discipline as directed in a vain effort to stave off the delights of prayer. But otherwise, she says, he "led [her] soul very, very gently," and made light of a "certain affection" to which she confessed. (Unlike his successor, he saw nothing wrong in the friendship of a Dominican who was *muy, muy principal.*) Still, she admits that the other nuns found her new practice of penance "extreme" though "it still fell far short of what was due her habit and her Order" (hasty, and insincere, addendum made under the same pressure which forced her to expand her finished book).

I suspect that the newly ordained twenty-three-year-old priest got more pleasure than he admitted from his power over his beautiful penitent. Yet those two months actually did deepen Teresa's religious life. Forbidden to seek delight in prayer, and taught that bodily penance alone could increase her gratitude for the sufferings of the Passion, her sense of Christ as a living presence shifted from her times of penance and prayer to the hours she spent in the ordinary necessities of communal living. This happened though she believed that her new sense of Christ's companionship was disobedience to her confessor, and tried to resist it.

Teresa's loss of her first Jesuit confessor and of his successor coincided with two visits to Avila by Francis Borgia. Her book does not mention his second visit, and the Jesuits do not record the first. Years later, in Seville, Teresa told an Inquisitor that she had talked with "Father Francis who had been Duke of Gandía" on two occasions, but not that both were followed by a confessor's being sent away; nor has anyone else, so far as I know, ever pointed out this coincidence. Since Teresa's canonization, few have liked to remember that she had both Jesuit friends and Jesuit enemies — or that Francis Borgia was ever of two minds about her.

The former Duke, who now signed himself Francis the Sinner, had just left the deathbed of Joanna the Mad in Tordesillas and was on his way to visit the Court in Valladolid. Philip II, like his father, had made war on the Papal States, this time avoiding a second Sack of Rome but nonetheless creating both national and ecclesiastical difficulties, including his own excommunication. Borgia, with powerful connections in both Spain and Rome, was engaged in healing the rift. Avila was a natural stopover on the way.

García de Toledo's uncle, the Duke of Alba, had led the Army against the Pope. García, born to the court, would naturally have talked to Borgia about the situation, and would doubtless have mentioned, as a friend, that penances being criticized as "excessive" were being imposed by a young Jesuit on a Carmelite nun, not at all the sort of publicity that the newly established Jesuit College needed.

Teresa — who excludes García from her story until his part in it has become wholly edifying — credits Borgia's visit to *el caballero santo* and her "prudent" confessor. That is possible. At least they would have approved of it; Francisco de Salcedo was surely disappointed in the caliber of the confessor assigned to Teresa, and little de Cetina was surely on the defensive and confident that his penitent would defend him.

Incidentally, Francis Borgia had his own reasons for wanting to avoid bad publicity. The Dominicans set the religious tone in Avila and their approval was important. In another three years the Inquisition — a Dominican institution — would put St. Francis Borgia's *Of Christian Works* on the Index as a temptation to heresy. There were already men in his own Order who called him a Franciscan in Jesuit's clothing and put up with him only because of his ducal influence with the court.

However it came about, he saw Teresa and reassured her greatly. Born to the casual morality of the court he would have felt no guilty, lubricious thrill at hearing her confess her past sins, but only grief for the waste of a soul which, in a healthy Church, would long since have been God's. As for her experiences in prayer, they differed little from those of his own conversion.

He told her that in one sense de Cetina had been right: the joys of prayer should never be consciously sought for their own sake, and that the suspension of the faculties in "the prayer of union" is a gift of which no soul is ever truly worthy. However, to question and reject such blessings because one has been a sinner is not humility, but base ingratitude.

That was the gist of it. One imagines a glance at the hour-glass, the routine priestly words, "Pray for me," and Teresa left greatly comforted until she realized that she had lost her confessor.

It had been inevitable. Borgia knew that his Avilan Jesuits were still on trial, and Doña Teresa was too handsome and emotional to be widely trusted. De Cetina would have to be transferred; as a good administrator, Borgia saw that it had been shortsighted policy to throw such an inexperienced boy to the wolves. But Borgia also had urgent business in Valladolid; he hurried off without mentioning that Teresa might have an older and wiser replacement.

Teresa had come to depend on de Cetina utterly. His apparent understanding had given her trust in his authority; and when he left, all her courage went with him.

The old self-despair came back, intensified. Teresa was convinced that without a Jesuit confessor she would fall back into her weaknesses and sins. Only one thing was clear: she must manage, and immediately, to get away from "that inn just off the road to hell" — the Convent of the Incarnation.

The Incarnation, she discovered, could not have agreed more heartily that Teresa belonged elsewhere. Her current enthusiasms did not fit in with the religious life as the Carmelites so casually conceived it. They let her go for three whole years, a startling fact which nobody later cared to have publicized. Luckily, Teresa knew how to elide: so well, in fact that up to the middle of this century it was taken for granted that almost all of those years were spent at the Incarnation and with a Jesuit confessor — though the wrong Jesuit, as the exchange of her second for a third also had to be elided.

She spent a few days with Francisco de Salcedo and his wife and then moved in with her friend "Yomar," whose given name she never learned to spell other than phonetically. Doña Guiomar de Ulloa was a well-to-do, and truth to tell, somewhat lightheaded young widow who had recently surprised the town by taking up religion and becoming an *aficionada* of the Jesuits.

This is how Teresa covers her loss of de Cetina and the story of those next three years:

"It was as if my soul was left in a desert, so lonely and frightened. I didn't know what would become of me. A relative of mine managed to take me away with her and I began at once to try to take another confessor from the Company. It pleased the Lord that I should begin to have the friendship of a lady of quality and much prayer who had a great deal to do with them." (They were friends of long standing; six years before Yomar had been part of the party that went on pilgrimage to Guadalajara where Teresa prayed for the soul of her brother Antonio, the twice-failed monk, now dead in battle, in Quito.) "She had me confess to her confessor and I stayed in her house many days. I was delighted to be able to have so much to do with [the Jesuits] for simply understanding the holiness of their lives was a great help to me.

"This father began to lead me to greater perfection. . . ."

Juan de Prádanos was, in fact, one of the best confessors Teresa ever had. It's a pity that Francis Borgia had to transfer him, too.

Chapter 11 ❋ Breakdown of Teresa's Health; Living in the House of Yomar (Doña Guiomar de Ulloa); Teresa and Certain Jesuits; The First Rapture

I

Guiomar had been a widow for three years and for one year a patroness of the Jesuits. Like Teresa, she was a striking beauty; unlike Teresa, she had only recently ceased to be careless of her reputation. From evidence given the Inquisition (to show the sort of people Teresa liked) we know that "she went about dressed *de gala* and used much paint on her face," and her manifestations of religious enthusiasm were considered dubious, if not downright farcical.

For example, since churches had no pews, one stood or, if wealthy, had a servant carry a chair. It did not occur to Guiomar that she might stand with the poor, but since her new holy humility forbade her to be followed by a servant, she lugged her own chair to church, there to rest up, panting. Guiomar was absurd, and we know from Teresa's letters that she never developed maturity or commonsense. However, there was no hypocrisy in her overwhelming, though ephemeral, religious enthusiasms. She was overimaginative (as her own florid reminiscences of Teresa betray), but in her own way she was genuine.

Happily we can disregard her report of the years that Teresa spent with her as a penitential recluse, lacerating her flesh with the pronged scourge and receiving floods of supernatural favors. In fact, Teresa's years in Guiomar's house were the only years of almost seven following her conversion in which an ever deepening love of God was permitted to go hand-in-hand with the utmost sanity.

For this we must thank Juan de Prádanos, the brilliant young vice-rector of the College of St. Gil. And for his unimpeded help and Teresa's surprising freedom to visit St. Gil and talk with others about "the things of God," we can thank the fact that the Jesuits lived on false hopes. New foundations need patrons, and Guiomar's wealth was vastly overestimated. Guiomar had no intent to deceive; she was merely a financial ignoramus, and given to promising future benefactions far beyond her actual means.

De Prádanos was no bone thrown to the wolves. Though only twenty-eight he had mature intelligence and percipience joined to true spiritual integrity. He must have found the cure of Guiomar's soul a hard exercise in holy humility. Teresa's quick mind, her wit, her unsparing power of self-analysis and her genuine religious fervor would have come as a vast relief.

Though he was a stern idealist, de Prádanos was also blessed with the sort of human understanding which is both rare and precious in the confessional. He saw that Teresa would never be at peace with herself until she came closer to her own inner self-demands, and that, with her, harsh demands from others did more harm than good. He also saw that little de Cetina had not only

48

prescribed her the wrong spiritual medicine but failed to understand her basic ailment.

She got too fond of men, and not all of them were blameless souls like Francisco de Salcedo. It was as simple as that; she must drop all friendships with those who did not share her real desire to serve God. Until she was stronger, they could only confuse her.

He had the subprior of Santo Tomás particularly in mind; García de Toledo, nephew of a duke, son of a count, handsome, fluent, and vastly indifferent to the Church's need for reform, was no suitable friend for this struggling, waking soul.

Teresa, as she later accidentally betrays, dropped García for almost six years; but here she only tells us this:

"This father . . . told me that to give God full satisfaction I must leave nothing undone. But all the same, he said it with great sweetness and gentleness, for my soul was not at all strong but on the contrary, very sensitive—especially about giving up certain friendships that I had. While I was not sinning against God in them, they did involve much affection and it seemed to me that I would be ungrateful to give them up.

"And so I said, 'If they are no offense against God, why be ungrateful?'

"He told me to commend it to God for a few days, and to recite the *Veni Creator* to help me be given light on what was best. Having spent a day in prayer and begging the Lord to help me, I began the hymn; and while I was reciting it, a rapture came on me, so sudden that it snatched me out of myself—a thing I could not doubt for it was so very consciously experienced" [so unlike those previous states which had been, as one might say, a holy hiatus].

"It was the first time the Lord had given me the grace of raptures. I heard these words: 'Now I want you to talk no longer with men, but with angels.' It threw me into amazement, for that whole movement of the spirit was so great and those words spoken so very much *within* the spirit—and so it frightened me. Yet in another way it brought me comfort that stayed with me after the fear that I suppose was caused by the strangeness had left me."

The proof that it was God-given, she adds, was in the after-effect: she could never again feel a "a particular love" or form a lasting friendship with any man who was not God's loving servant. And, within limits, this was true. Teresa would always idealize men to whom she was instinctively drawn and love those she idealized with an intensity that did not fit her ideal of loving all souls impartially as children of one Father; but nonetheless, the experience had a real and lasting effect. It also gave her total confidence in de Prádanos's guidance.

Those words heard "so very much within the spirit" were the first of Teresa's "locutions"—not, as she often tried to explain, auditory hallucination, but "heard with the ears of the mind."

As to their source, her test was pragmatic: if they came from Christ they set her soul in order. Rebuking, they left her humbled but serene; encouraging, they left her free of vainglory, yet confident that her affairs were in God's hands. At other times, they came from the devil: consequently, while the words themselves might be equally good and holy, when they rebuked she was left discouraged and depressed and when they encouraged she was overconfident, overexcited. The devil, she thought, having seen that she could no longer be tempted in the old ways, had settled for tempting her to spiritual pride or, alternately, to crippling doubts.

It was a good rule of thumb.

The Church calls this first rapture and "locution" Teresa's "spiritual espousal."

II

That Teresa went so often to the College of St. Gil, through those three years, to talk with *letrados* about "the things of God," soon made talk. When her canonization still hung in the balance, it was also claimed that she had gone there *unveiled*, which was anachronistic nit-picking, since Carmelite nuns were not yet required to appear in public with their faces veiled: a point also forgotten by the opposition, which refuted the charge by saying that Teresa had *once* gone to St. Gil unveiled under orders to do so "as a mortification."

But the fact that her frequent visits to St. Gil made talk was what saved her from a danger that can hardly be overestimated. Luckily for her, she enjoyed only the briefest acquaintance with Agustín Cazalla.

Cazalla had gone to Germany as chaplain to Charles V, where he became interested in late fifteenth-century German mysticism. Its insistence on God's nearness to man and man's ability to communicate with Him through prayer appealed not only to the Reformation but to the Counter-Reformation. Cazalla saw himself as a reformer and was so seen in Avila when he came there to preach and teach. He showed keen interest in Teresa and Guiomar until they refused to give up all other spiritual advisers; he insisted that those he taught accept him as their sole guide, and he refused to become one of Guiomar's many enthusiasms. He said that her house "had too many doors."

Just two years later, Cazalla, with forty of his followers, was accused of heresy and condemned at the first *auto de fé* in Valladolid, under the approving eye of Philip II. Cazalla himself recanted, and was mercifully garrotted rather that being burned at the stake with the majority of his followers, but the body of his mother was exhumed and burned, their house burned to the ground, and its ground sown with salt.

By that year, 1559, Teresa would also be inviting the attention of the Inquisition; the last thing she needed was a culminating touch of guilt by association with Cazalla.

She was not yet in that danger, but this is as good a place as any in which to explain it. Ignoring Teresa's Jewish blood for four hundred years has done much to conceal that danger; ignoring the background of Teresa's conversion has done more.

III

In 1557, Calvinism was spreading throughout Catholic France, and our own century has taught us how conflicting faiths and ideologies can lead to wars abroad and suspicions at home. The Inquisition was no longer the financially motivated Jew-hunt that it had been under Torquemada; it was genuinely trying to save Catholic Spain from Protestant and neo-Protestant heresy. In the eyes of the Inquisition, "mystical theology" was a seedbed of such heresy, heresy to which *conversos* were peculiarly prone; and, unfortunately, the Inquisition was right.

A background of forced conversion leaves an emptiness in those who are not naturally irreligious. Alonso had suffered it until Teresa's books (seized by the Inquisition in 1559) taught him that Christian prayer could be more than the recitation of memorized Latin words. His story was typical; books like those that Teresa eventually lent her father gave warmth and immediacy to a faith which many forcibly converted Jews had found alien and tainted with superstition. It was true that more *conversos* embraced "mystical theology" than did those of "pure blood."

Unfortunately for the Jesuits in Spain during Loyola's lifetime, he and his followers pored open scorn on those religious orders which excluded the "impure blood" of Christ, His Mother, and the Apostles. And unfortunately for many others, it was not only the Jewish element in Spanish mysticism that had begun to give it a bad name. Mysticism has always attracted the searchingly religious; and, since they are in greater supply, it has always attracted still greater numbers of crackpots, hysterics, and seekers for a legal, inexpensive high. Of the latter variety there were more than you could shake a stick at, by the time of Teresa's conversion.

All were (inaccurately) classified as *alumbrados*: illuminists. The Inquisition was up against a real problem, because the wholly orthodox, the neo-Protestants, and the simply mad or degenerate were prone to the same symptoms of epidemic hysteria: they saw visions and received revelations; they were seized with raptures in which they swooned or became catatonic. (Incidentally, Loyola's diaries, with their record of his frequent floods of tears, his one great moment of mystic revelation, and his subsequent visions, set him a world apart from his later followers.)

Nor was the Inquisition's problem a mere matter of sorting out divine inspiration from pathological emotionalizing and both from simple fakery. To the mind of the times, such symptoms came from three possible sources: an excess of black bile in the balance of the humors, the devil, or God—with the first two by far the likeliest. To be inspired was rare, but not to run melancholy mad or to be possessed. What's more, the Inquisiton assumed that *conversos* were more prone to demonic possession than those of pure blood, and women more prone than men, and that all thus possessed were a danger to the schism-torn Church. And once again, their judgment was not founded on prejudice alone: the suspected and the oppressed are seldom as emotionally stable as those on top of the heap.

This must be understood if we are to realize that the brief period in Teresa's life for which she is now sanctified was not singular, but part of a nation-wide epidemic, and that it left her permanently endangered. The Inquisition had terrible powers and the strength of a new and terrible integrity. It was no longer out to snatch fortunes with which to back a costly and unpopular war; it was guarding the orthodoxy of the One True Faith, a purpose Teresa always recognized and respected even when she herself was most endangered by the hard fact that its councils were made up of men as capable of mistakes and misjudgements as the rest of the human race.

Since hagiography prefers to overlook this background, we are told that Teresa's danger was only that of being mistaken for a fake, a *burladora* like the notorious Magdalen of the Cross who, ten years before, had enthralled the royal family with her ecstasies and her reception of the stigmata before she was exposed. But suspicion of fakery was a lesser danger: the genuine article, one like Agustín Cazalla, deceived by the devil and become his tool, interested the Inquisition far more.

Once we know this, we can understand the friends who labored to save Teresa from Satan, the Inquisition, or both, in the years just ahead. It was with the best intentions that they came close to driving her hopelessly mad.

IV

De Prádanos, I think, foresaw that danger. After Teresa's first rapture and locution, he introduced old María Diaz into Doña Guiomar's house as a resident *beata* and living example. She was a peasant whose conversion by Pedro de Alcántara left her an ecstatic. In this state, she gave away all she had for Christ, keeping only a blanket. Then she gave that away, too; and the ecstasies stopped. She never again had any comforting sense of God's nearness to her when she prayed.

Nowadays such protracted spiritual aridity is often diagnosed by the sufferer as "loss of faith," and so accepted. Then it was normally seen as a temptation to be overcome.

María Diaz was different.

At first she cried out, "Lord, I gave up everything for You. Will You take Yourself from me, too?" Then she saw that her loss was sent to be the perfection of her poverty. She was uncouth and shabby, and Guiomar's servants considered her a joke. She neither resented their treatment nor gloried in it. Christ had been poor and mocked; and in His goodness, He let her share that expense with Him now. She thanked Him, and lived the stern, unemotional life of prayer to which she thought God had called her.

Once Teresa asked María Diaz if she did not long to die and be in God's presence, His Heaven.

María Diaz said, "Daughter, I'll have eternity for that. I only have a short time to work and suffer for Him here."

Years later, in a time of bitter trial, Teresa wrote of old María Diaz with dry humor, "I love her much more now than I did when she was alive."

But in writing the *Life*, Teresa omits María Diaz. A soul that did so well without the "mercies" that Teresa would soon receive and be unwillingly forced to describe and defend was as unprofitable a subject as Cazalla, dead because his faith in such "mercies" laid insufficient stress on the Sacraments of Holy Church, through which alone man finds grace and salvation.

She also omits the story of how she lost de Prádanos as her confessor. Fortunately her second biographer, Yepes, did not share her belief that it is better to let scandals wear thin and be forgotten than to preserve them under a coat of whitewash.

Chapter 12 ❄ Teresa and Her Confessor, Juan de Prádanos; Visions and Voices

I

De Prádanos fell ill, and went to Doña Guiomar's house for nursing. Both he and his Rector should have known better. Ailing monks are cared for within their own walls by the monastery infirmarian, not in private homes by kind ladies. What's more, the Avilan Jesuits were still on trial, Guiomar was far from universally respected, and Teresa — so discreet throughout her years of sinning — was now compulsively confessing right and left. Nor was she doubted; tales of frail nuns and randy priests have always been popular.

Teresa lacked realism when she believed that "a love in Christ" like hers for de Prádanos could not be misconstrued. So did de Prádanos, that idealist. As for his Rector, Hernando Alvarez, one can only say that he had a strong will to believe; Teresa's uncle had married one of his cousins, Guiomar was seen as a potential benefactress, and de Prádanos had a great name for holy chastity.

Nonetheless, Hernando Alvarez was phenomenally blind, for it was simply the wrong time for such indiscretion. The long quiescent Inquisition was gathering a fresh head of steam, and the chief suspects were religious enthusiasts, especially converted Jews. Teresa was half-Jewish, Guiomar was the widow of a *converso* merchant, and as for the Jesuits, Loyola had recently died and the Jesuits had shown their loyalty to his principles by electing Diego Laínez, a *converso*, to his place as General of the Company. Even Avila was no longer the safe haven that Juan Sánchez had chosen, or the laughing town which declared Alonso Pina to be his step-mother's son and an hereditary knight of Old Castile.

The Jesuits in Rome were more intelligent than Father Hernando Alvarez. True, they had elected Laínez, a *converso*, and a liberal theologian to boot. (Laínez was, as it happens, a friend of Cazalla, so soon to die; they had been fellow-students at the University of Salamanca, where Cazalla graduated first in his class, and Laínez second.) But they understood Spain, and sweetened the dose by naming Father Francis Borgia, the former Duke of Gandía and one of the few grandees of certifiably untainted blood, as "Commissar of Spain, Portugal, and the colonies in the Indies." In this capacity, Father Francis set out on a formal tour of inspection which brought him to Avila.

There he learned that Doña Teresa, young de Cetina's former penitent, had left the convent and lived for almost three years with a lady whose character was described quite differently by the Jesuits and by his own upper-class Avilan friends—and that the ailing vice-rector of St. Gil was living with them!

In time, Teresa's second biographer, Yepes, would present that situation as evidence of the glorious (and nobly born) Mother's holy humility. She "was preparing [de Prádanos's] food for him with her own hands and often sitting up with him at night and doing him every service just as any woman of lowly birth would have served him." Indeed, Yepes says, she "nursed him as tenderly as if he were her own father." (A line which adds a desexualized venerability to that twenty-eight-year-old father of a still-beautiful woman of forty-three.)

The Jesuit chronicler, more discreetly, only says that de Prádanos left Avila "because of heart-trouble, caused by the labor of those early years," with no mention of his nursing home.

What actually happened Teresa so elided in the *Life* that when she next speaks of *mi confesor*, there is no indication that he is another man or that he had not been confessing her continually at the Incarnation throughout those three years—including her visit of "many days" (a month, perhaps?) with "Yomar." She leaves us to wonder why a man she has praised to the skies as one perfectly suited to lead a soul to "perfection" is suddenly shown as a timid, bumbling incompetent. Nor does she mention her second meeting with "Father Francis who was Duke of Gandía."

So far as it concerns Teresa, all Jesuit reports of it are "mightily prettified," to use her own phrase. The records, however, give us its outcome. De Prádanos was transferred to Valladolid. Hernando Alvarez, the Rector, was replaced by Dionisio Vázquez, a man who got on superbly with the Inquisition. (In later years he headed an attempt to make the Spanish Jesuits a separate Order, free from soft-headed interference from Rome.)

It was a showy shake-up. Yomar left town to stay with her mother in Toro, and Teresa went to Alba to stay with her sister Juana. Then, as Martín de Guzmán was once more contesting her father's will, she went to see her Uncle Lorenzo.

Years later, Francisca de Fonseca explained Teresa's two months out of town at that time by saying that she had visited her sister to recuperate from an attack of *gota coral*: epilepsy, that is, which had recently been attributed to droppings of red bile into the brain. The de Prádanos scandal was forgotten by the time Francisca testified for Teresa's beatification; but the symptoms which had soon thereafter made Teresa a likely candidate for the stake and endangered the reputation of a convent which housed an *alumbrada* were not.

II

Teresa was ordered back to the Incarnation. Vázquez, the new Rector, did not feed gossip by denying Teresa a third Jesuit confessor, but he appointed one who could be kept on the leash. Baltasar Alvarez, at twenty-five, was newly ordained, timid, and well-aware of what had happened to de Cetina and to the brilliant vice-Rector, de Prádanos. In maturity he would be Teresa's friend; now he did not dare. Francisco de Salcedo, Hernando Alvarez, the demoted Rector, Master Daza, and their friend Alvaro Alvarez (locally called the Saint) would soon be outdoing him in their concerted attempts to save Teresa from Satan.

In years to come, Teresa wrote, "I am more afraid of people who fear the devil than I am of the devil himself." But that time was still distant, and her next three years demand both pity and a respect generally denied them by believers and unbelievers alike. It is easy to point out Teresa's repressed sexuality and hysteric belief that God and the devil were competing for her soul throughout those next three years—if, that is, one need not write under the *imprimatur*. It is equally easy to treat that same time of visions and public raptures as the crown of Teresa's virgin sanctity, the essence of her sainthood. But the shoe fits just as badly on either foot—unless we prefer to deny the woman she became despite all odds.

Teresa first loved Christ for His forgiveness. As that love matured she came to see that the sins of the Magdalen were not the gravest of those which threatened the health of His Church at the time of the great Schism. But when young Baltasar Alvarez became her confessor, Teresa was only beginning to find her way, and she had to find it alone. Little Father Baltasar was afraid to talk with her "about the things of God." She was no longer welcome to stretch her mind with the *letrados* at St. Gil. For companionship she had only her books, and not even them for long.

In 1557 the Pope put out a new Index of forbidden books; in 1559, the Spanish Inquisition widened it, "since"—its introduction explains-"too many plead ignorance of the Index of 1557." Its scope was astounding: everything written since Luther's break with Rome was examined; all books with mystical overtones were suspect. Francis Borgia's *Of Christian Works* was condemned, and the (now) Blessed Juan de Àvila's *Filia Audi*. So, at long last, was Erasmus's *Echridion*, translated by Teresa's grandmother's kinsman, Archbishop de Fonseca: a book which would live on in Teresa's mind for the clarity with which it distinguished magic—God used—from religion—God served; a distinction which she would try, throughout her last twenty years, to teach the Order she founded.

Convents and monasteries were searched, and all such reading burned. Of this clean sweep, Teresa only says that when "they" took away her books, she heard the Voice say, "Do not grieve. I will be your Living Book . . . but I did not understand, for I had not had any visions yet."

Her visionary period, when it came, could not have been more dangerously timed. 1559 was a year of panic. The first *auto de fe* was held in Valladolid in May, when Cazalla, unlike most of his followers, recanted and was mercifully garrotted; at the second, in October, only twelve accused stood firm and were burned; the remaining thirteen weakened and chose to be strangled. Archbishop Carranza protested the Inquisition's new lease on life, but while archbishops were properly tried in Rome, Philip II got permission to "investigate him" for the next two years, and used that permission, instead, to kidnap and imprison him in a Valladolid dungeon—not for two years but seven.

Since Teresa believed as firmly as any Inquisitor that the devil sends visions oftener than God, and that they invite to heresy—the sure road to hell—we need not wonder that when her visions began she "implored God to lead [her] by another way." Small wonder, too, that she excluded them from the book she brought to its intended end in the June of 1562.

It was at an Inquisitor's orders that Teresa began to expand her book, to satisfy him that no vision had ever tempted her from the purest orthodoxy. She finished the work under anxious pressure from García de Toledo, who insisted that she add certain matters that she had preferred to omit. His motives, as you will see, were not selfless, though they were forgivable under the circumstances. But the effect of this further pressure is to compound the confusion of a narrative already confused enough by its omissions and later unwilling flashbacks.

For example, Teresa described for Inquisitor Soto a period of torments sent from hell which preceded her visions; García demanded that she explain why they had come when they did—in proof, to his mind, of her virtue: a point which her subsequent loss of three other confessors left him anxious for her to stress.

Here, let's take her unwilling addendum first. And before we do, let me point out that men—beginning with the priest of Becedas—had a way of confessing to Teresa. When she was in her sixties and her brother Lorenzo wrote to her about his disturbance over getting an erection when he prayed at night, she told him to ignore it; it was natural for one of his make-up. "The body," she says, "understands only one kind of love."

She had been still far from any such understanding when she acted as Juan de Prádanos's night-nurse, and he made her his own pitiably tormented confession. It is amazing that he could make it; we forget that less than sixty years ago masturbation was referred to in whispers as "self-abuse" and that family physicians told boys—quite sincerely—that it often caused insanity. It was a perversion—and a graver sin than visiting a whorehouse.

Teresa—as we learn from its aftermath—did not belittle that confession. Nor did the fear for de Prádanos's soul that filled her make her love him less or diminish her sense of his importance as "Christ's servant"—which the devil hated and had set himself to destroy through this vile temptation.

Teresa always kept in touch with the confessors she lost during her troubled years. Usually the correspondence had to be secret—their letters forwarded under other cover by a mutual friend. With this in mind, we can understand the passage demanded by García as proof that her period of demonic torments was wholly unrelated to any of the sins that she was so determined to confess—and he to make her "prettify."

This is her account of why the devils came:

"A certain person came to me who had been in mortal sin for a year and a half, one of the most disgusting that I ever heard of, and all that time he never

56

confessed it or cured himself of it but went on saying mass. And though he confessed other sins, he would say to himself, How could he confess such an ugly thing? And he had a great longing to break out of it and hadn't the strength in himself.

"It was such a grief to me that he sinned in such a way that it made me suffer very much. I promised him to pray as much as I could for God to help him and to get other people, better than I am, to pray for him, too."

Thus far we have a priest whose compulsive sin both he and Teresa find more "ugly " than the fornications of the priest in Becedas. Next she lets slip that the priest in question has been sent away and she can only write to him secretly.

"I wrote through a certain person who, he told me, would give him the letters. So that is how he confessed it for the first time. God chose to have mercy on his soul for the sake of all the holy souls who prayed for him . . . and I, wretched creature that I was, had done all I could. He wrote me that he was so much better that he could go for days without falling into it, but that the torment the temptation gave him was so fierce that he felt as if he was already in hell to judge by what he was suffering, — and I should commend him to God."

Next we learn that it was the better nuns at the Incarnation whom she asked to pray for a man struggling with a great temptation, a man they did not know. This would not have seemed strange; she had brothers in Peru, and from one of them she got frequent letters.

"I went back to asking the sisters for prayers that the Lord would grant me this mercy, and they took it to heart. Nobody could have guessed who the person was."

("That the Lord could grant me this mercy." We share the suffering of those we love.)

"I myself begged His Majesty to ease his temptations and torments and to send those demons to torment me instead, just as long as they did not make me sin against God, too. So I went through a month of horrible torture, and that was when those two things happened that I have already told about. The Lord was served and the devils left him, as he wrote me, because of what I had gone through in that month. His soul took strength, and kept completely free from it, and he couldn't give me enough thanks. He said that whenever he felt hard-pressed he would read over my letters, and the temptation would leave him."

Teresa's first mention of her month with demons comes at the point in her book when one would expect her to say of de Prádanos, at the least, "Then he fell ill and had to go away." And her explanation of why the devils came leads to other memories.

After one or two remarks about the impotence of devils if one refuses to fear them, she suddenly urges that we should accept slanders as Christ did, content to have the truth known only to God. But this she follows, as unexpectedly, with a warning that we should distrust our ability to love all souls equally in Christ. Then, as if the context seemed too clear, she mentions her overgreat sympathy for her sister Juana on the visit (or more properly, flight) to Alba, here mentioned by her for the first and only time.

Because Teresa had idealized de Prádanos, she could readily believe that the devil saw him as a particular threat to be destroyed by a compulsion so out of character for him that it was, without doubt, supernaturally imposed. He was also the first priest in that sorry succession to come who was, in her own cautious word, "persecuted," that is, unjustly slandered as having been her lover. We should also realize that while he had not "disturbed her soul" and that although what she felt for him was indeed what she called "a love in Christ," it was also wholly unlike anything she ever felt for a woman. This she knew — and still tried not to know — when her three years as his penitent were ended and she was sent back to the Incarnation.

Her description of what came next fully explains Francesca de Fonseca's loyal attempt to show her as a victim of gota coral.

Chapter 13 ❈ "The Ecstasy of St. Teresa"

I

Teresa's prayer was heard; and the demons tormented her, not de Prádanos. While, with one terrible exception, she saw them only "with the eyes of the mind," she knew that they were all equally real: flights of black imps settling on a book she tried to read, a demon in the form of a hideous little blackamoor dwarf, gibbering in rage when she stole into the chapel and tried to pray. . . . When she threatened them with a crucifix they would only disappear briefly and then come back. Holy water, she discovered, was more effectual.

Her sole "corporal vision" — seen with the eyes of the body — was of Satan himself.

"He appeared to me once in an oratory, on my left side. His face was hideous. I stared at his mouth more than at anything else, for he spoke to me, and it filled me with terror. It seemed that a great flame issued from his body — all light and no darkness."

(She had heard it often: "The devil comes oftenest as an angel of light." He was Lucifer, who fell.)

Three times when Teresa managed to cross herself with a shaking hand, he vanished briefly. Then she reached the holy-water stoop, and got rid of him for good.

Teresa could not conceal it that she saw such sights. Nor could other symptoms be hidden. Sometimes she felt herself being smothered, and collapsed, fighting for breath. She tried to pass it off as heart-trouble; but even so, hoping to sound absurd to the nuns who tried to help her, she sometimes had to gasp out: "If you wouldn't laugh at me, I'd ask for some holy-water."

Once when this happened two nuns refused to be fooled; they detected a strong smell of brimstone. Teresa herself smelled nothing, but she did not doubt that the nuns were telling the truth.

After that, Teresa had a seizure that lasted five hours—pain so excruciating that she lay on the floor "whacking about with arms and legs and head."

Such hysterias were highly contagious. We need not doubt the sincerity of the nuns she cites next:

"Another time in choir I felt a great absorption coming over me, and I went out so that it wouldn't be seen. Those who were nearby heard great blows being struck where I was, and voices agreeing on something. But I did not hear that gross talk, and what's more, I was so deep in prayer that I felt no fear at all. . . ."

Then God put it to an end.

"Then, while I was still in great trouble (I had not yet begun to have any kind of vision)"—holy vision, that is, like those she next described at the Inquisitor's orders—"these words were enough to quiet me and free me from it all: 'Do not be afraid, daughter. It is I, and I will not desert you. Have no fear.'"

She believed. "I took the cross in my hand, and I spoke like this: 'Come on, now all of you! As I am God's servant, I want to see what you can do.'"

The devils are powerless against those whose faith in God delivers them from fear. But the days would soon come of which Teresa says, "I am more afraid of people who fear the devil than I am of the devil himself."

It was Teresa's holy visions which woke that general fear. The devil in his own form can only cause shrinking; but in disguise he can lead many to heresy.

II

The word "visions" commonly suggests the bodily sightings which theologians since Augustine have called "corporal visions"—and considered the most dubious, though surprisingly few Catholics are learned enough to know it. Teresa had only two "corporal visions" in her life, both of angels, and as one of them was of Lucifer who fell, she did not so classify it. Until theologians corrected her, she longed for a "corporal vision" of Christ; but of Him she had only "imaginary visions . . . seen with the eyes of the mind." These, oddly enough, were preceded by her one "intellectual vision" of Christ: theologically, one of the highest order.

Baltasar Alvarez became a noted *letrado*; but he was a late developer, only twenty-five when Teresa tried to tell him about her "intellectual vision."

She had been praying, she said, and suddenly Christ was in the room with her. She saw nothing, heard nothing: she only knew. It was indescribable. Some bodily sense can tell one both blind and deaf that another is in the room with him, and here no bodily sense had been involved. And, no, it had nothing to do with faith, or grace, or the other things that her young confessor tried to suggest. It had been the Living Presence, God made Man.

59

"How did you know it was Christ?"

"He told me so, over and over."

"Then you did hear Him."

"No. He told me, but I can't explain how, or how I knew He was there."

She heard, but not even "with the ears of the mind."

Baltasar was baffled and disturbed. Lives of the saints were full of such visions, but so were case histories of the *alumbrados*, and it put him in a precarious position; the times could not have been worse.

He had already been anxious and tried to have another priest confess her. One can't blame him: Francis Borgia had removed two priests who confessed this beautiful woman with a sinful past. Baltasar knew about her alarming seizures and the stench of brimstone the nuns had smelled in their wake. The substitute Baltasar persuaded to take over was Father Hernando Alvarez — who did not feel bound by the seal of the confessional when the problem was demonic possession, not simple sin. But the new Rector returned poor young Baltasar to his frightening task, which became even more so when Teresa began to see things "with the eyes of the mind."

First she saw only Christ's hands, indescribably beautiful and white with the radiance of the Resurrection Body. Then the face, a holy beauty which surely exceeded her own powers of imagination and was full of light which did not dazzle the eyes, though "it made all other light seem artificial." And after that a vision "which would have made her die for love," if He had not so prepared her for it, little by little. He stood before her, no longer wounded and suffering, but as He is now in Heaven, radiant, the King.

This vision, she tried to explain, was as unlike any product of human imagination as a living man is unlike his portrait. Yet though it came more than once, and though she longed to know "what color his eyes were or how tall He was," she could only know that she had been shown Christ in His glory, a glory "brighter than a thousand suns" yet restful to the eyes as utter darkness.

It was, of course, too much for her frightened young confessor: he was fully convinced that it came from the devil. So were the willing aides he was promptly offered, a holy committee made up of Hernando Alvarez, Master Daza, Francisco de Salcedo and another layman, Alvaro Alvarez, who was called *El Santo* in recognition of his piety. When these all questioned Teresa, she could not deny her Lord, much as she feared their fear and suffered from the mockery of the nuns: "What a St. Paul she is with her revelations! Quite a St. Jerome!"

Sometimes the devil tried to put on the same appearance to deceive her, but he always failed. As she puts it with blunt honesty, "there was no purity" in the love these false visions evoked. But when it was Christ, the love was not only pure but it seemed to release her from all other loves; it was a freedom that had barely begun when she heard the Voice tell her that she must love "not men but angels."

Before those visions of Christ, she says, if she found a man very good and close to her heart, his memory would stay with her so that she found herself dwelling on his graces and virtues in a way that led to perdition as surely as less worthy affection had ever done. But once she had seen the Risen Christ he could have no rival; in body and spirit she could love Christ as perfectly as Mary Magdalen had done when she sat at his feet and looked into His face.

It is not mysticism. It is also painfully frank, and in the long run it was not even wholly true; Teresa was affectionate and far from sexless. Yet it was, at one real level at least, a release; she would never again feel sexual temptation at the conscious level. The loves she felt thereafter would be, to a surprising degree, what she believed: a "pure love in Christ," sprung from shared faith and shared purpose.

III

Teresa's visions, I think, would have shocked others less if they had been more in accord with Spanish tastes: Christ bound to the pillar, lashed and crowned with thorns; Christ on the way to Golgotha bowed by the weight of His cross; Christ crucified in bloody agony. But Teresa only saw Him like this "once or twice" at her own worst times of inner torment. At all other times, He was Christ the King, crowned not with thorns but with the golden crown of His victory over death, royal and radiant: "His Majesty."

This had to be cured. She was forbidden any daytime moments alone, forbidden to pray except for "verbal prayers" — Aves and Paternosters. It was tyranny, she told young Baltasar; but she obeyed.

Yet she understood the fear which led to that tyranny and shared it in part, as children both resent and half-understand the authority that keeps them out of danger. She prayed incessantly "to be led by another way"; and she went about clutching the crucifix that dangled at her side. Then Christ stood before her, took it from her hand, and gave it back with the plain black ebony now jeweled with five precious stones that glowed with their own light, and represented his five wounds. Nobody else could see them, even though, she said, she "always saw it that way."

(*Always* is a long time. Eventually she gave that crucifix to her dear, weak, silly little sister, Juana.)

But in spite of this obedience to "tyranny" the visions still came. Since Baltasar and the holy committee saw so clearly that they were Satan in disguise, they ordered her to "give figs."

For Shakespeare, "Do you make a fig at me, sir?" had the meaning it still retains in Latin countries. The thumb tucked between the first two fingers is no gesture that one would expect from a lady — much less a nun.

But women's virtue was not protected by ignorance. We are in the period when Rosalind, a spotless virgin disguised as "a saucy lackey" in the forest of Arden, is asked the time and makes her little joke: "Even now the bawdy hand of the clock is on the prick of nine." Teresa would not have been shocked at giving figs — or, as we'd say, the finger — to the devil. But to Christ, it was unbearable. She felt that she was being forced to mock Him as he had been mocked by the Jews, and while she obeyed she wept, begging His forgiveness.

Years later her sanest adviser, Domingo Báñez, laughed at this; if those visions came from Satan, he said, they were still beautiful. Does one refuse to be moved by a fine religious picture until one is sure that the painter's private life was admirable? But Teresa had no such comfort then. And, forbidden to pray, she was seized by powerful, trance-like states of prayer. Up to that time these experiences had been brief, and left her quiet in spirit, bettered in daily life: they passed the pragmatic test. Even when part of her remained rapt, she could go about her normal life, as if, she said, Mary and Martha were going about together.

Now that was lost.

IV

What happened was like an unbearable intensity of love which seemed to sweep upon her from outside. At first she did not know whether it came from God or the Tempter, for it involved both body and soul. But finally she came to see it as "the sovereign artifice" by which God released His "wretched slave" from those lingerings of misdirected love which were, she decided, His sole reason for having let her be so tormented in de Prádanos's place. Such experiences, she says, were wholly unlike those tears and tendernesses that can be self-induced by prayer, and for which one simply takes the soul by the hand as if it were a sobbing child whom one quiets "by making him swallow a drink of water."

"These impetuses are utterly different. . . . The soul does not try to suffer from the Lord's absence from it. Instead he thrusts an arrow into the deepest part of the entrails and, at times even to the heart, so that the soul does not know what ails it or what it wants. It only knows that it loves God and . . . would joyfully die for Him. One cannot exaggerate or describe the way God wounds the soul and the exquisite pain it gives; pain that makes it a stranger to itself, but a pain so delicious that no pleasure in this life can give more delight."

Lovers have long cried out that Cupid's arrow has pierced their hearts, and called the pain sweet torment. And men have long accepted Solomon's epithalamion, the Song of Songs, as religious metaphor. Teresa differs only in her honest awareness of how much all loves have in common and in seeing this love as a divine seduction from all earthly loves.

This she describes in obedience to the Inquisitor Soto. A further development she only set down later, in difficult obedience to García, rather more honestly than his tastes required, I suspect.

"Not men but angels," her first locution said. She did not take it literally; but the mind works otherwise at the level of our dreams. Teresa began to have a repeated "corporal vision" — and one which like her only other such vision, of Satan, the angel who fell, also appeared upon her left — the side sinister. It came from God, she was sure, but it was strangely mixed. She describes it with painful honesty; yet an unconscious delicacy reverses the direction of the shaft from that described in those first "impetuses" — from the deepest part of the entrails up to the heart.

"The Lord wanted me to see this vision several times.

"I would see an angel facing me, on my left side; in bodily form, for a wonder,

62

and not as I usually see visions. (Though angels often represent themselves to me, it is without my really seeing them, but in the sort of vision I have described before.)

"He was not tall, but little; very beautiful, his face so flaming that he seemed to be one of those highest angels who are all afire; he must have been one of those they call cherubims."

(The devil's body, too, poured out bright flame.)

"I saw a long old spear in his hand and there seemed to be a little flame at the tip of it. This he seemed to plunge into my heart repeatedly, until it reached into my very entrails. When he drew it out, I thought he would draw them out with it, and it left me utterly afire with a great love for God.

"The pain was so great that it made me moan over and over, and the sweet delight into which that pain threw me was so intense that one could not want it to stop, or the soul be contented with anything but God. It is not bodily pain, but spiritual, though the body does not cease to share in it somewhat — and even very much so.

"Through the days this went on, I acted like someone driven out of her wits. I did not want to see or speak to anyone, but only to hug myself with my pain which, for me, was a greater glory than there is in the whole creation. This happened to me repeatedly when the Lord sent me these raptures — raptures so great that I couldn't hold them off even when I was in company, though it caused me the greatest suffering when they began to be talked about."

Four years earlier, writing willingly as she drew her book to its first-intended conclusion, Teresa described an intense religious experience as unlike the angel vision as can well be imagined. It came when her time of seeing angels, fallen or otherwise, was well behind her, and here she recalls it, as the touch-stone by which her angel-visions should be evaluated.

"Since I had them, I haven't felt their sort of pain again, but the other kind I talked about earlier — I forget in which chapter. The other is unlike it in many ways and is worth more. But before I had experienced that other kind of pain which I am mentioning again now, it was as if the Lord would snatch my soul and throw it into ecstasy so that there was no space left in which to feel pain or suffering because the enjoyment began at the same time."

But before we consider the pain that was "worth more," and which she had described so willingly, one more thing should be considered about the angel's visits. While they went on, Teresa resorted to extreme physical penance for the only time in her life, "to repay," as she puts it, that bodily delight.

"Hoping that it would, at least, give my soul some relief . . . I did myself violence . . . but I might as well have been lashing a dead body." She could feel no pain but the pain that is like delight, the delight that is like pain.

These intensities were followed by a total let-down. Teresa felt "absent from God," her soul a parched garden reverting to desert. It was, she says, the state "in which God seems to be only something about which one has heard rumors from far away." And in this state, Teresa experienced the *arrobamientas* that were "worth far more" than what the angel gave. They came like a rushing wind on which the soul seemed to rise towards God, while at the same time

God had never seemed so far away. Their pain was the spirit's sense of anguished need and of awful solitude.

"It seems as if when one is like that, farthest away from God, He communicates his grandeur in the strangest way imaginable, and I don't know how to express it or believe that anyone will believe me unless he has gone through it himself—for this knowledge is not given to comfort the spirit, but to show how right it is to suffer at being absent from the Good that contains all goods in Itself."

This knowledge is "so exquisite and piercing" that though the soul "has been putting itself in that desert," it is stabbed to life with the knowledge of its own solitude, "like the royal prophet (David) when he said, 'I stood watch and was made like a sparrow on the rooftops.'" (She quotes the psalm in her own approximate Latin.) "And at other times, the soul seems to wander like a starving thing, asking itself aloud, 'Where, then, is thy God?'"

"I remember how St. Paul said he was crucified to the world. . . . I think it is like that with the soul when no comfort comes to it from heaven and it is not there, and it wants nothing from earth and is not there either, but instead it seems to hang crucified between earth and heaven, suffering and with no comfort coming to it from either of them."

To pure mystics, the sense of God transcendent, the Utterly Other, is peace; they are gladly crucified to the world. Teresa was the woman who, years later, would write to John of the Cross, "It would be an expensive business if we could only find God by being dead to the world. It wasn't like that with Mary Magdalen, or the Samaritan woman. . . ." Still, somehow she knew that this pain was worth more than the exquisite piercing of the little angel's lance by which it had seemed as if "her very entrails would be drawn out with it."

In her last year of life, Teresa wrote to a discontented nun that to pray because prayer sometimes brings delight was to be a mercenary, fighting for the sake of one's wages; true love of God makes one "like the grandees, who serve their King for nothing."

It is not a lesson that the prayerful learn easily. These *arrobamientos* expressed Teresa's first unworded struggle towards that knowledge. The knowledge, once gained, brought its own kind of inner peace. When Teresa was forty-nine, and completing her book, on orders that she obeyed unhappily, she was able to say that for three whole years she had not had a visionary experience of any kind.

The Church disagrees not only with Teresa's evaluation of her angel but with her account of him. He came not "many times" but only once, and his lance did not plunge "repeatedly" into her body, but pierced her heart with a single thrust in a physical miracle known as the Transverberation. That heart is in a reliquary in Alba de Tormes; the neat hole with its charred edges made by the flame-tipped lance was first noticed in the eighteenth century. In the nineteenth century, the heart also grew a circlet of thorns like that which surrounds the Sacred Heart of Jesus. This was examined by a committee from the University of Salamanca, who pronounced it "mysterious."

However, it would be a pity if the world had been cheated of Bernini's superb baroque masterpiece, the Ecstasy of St. Teresa: that beautiful and sexually loaded representation of the swooning nun and the little angel with his phallic lance. We can be glad that Bernini lived in a day when the love of lovers was still a reverently accepted analogy for the love that joins the soul to God.

As for the *arrobamientos*, still seen by the Church as of lesser worth, they were at the time they occurred a grave danger. Their outward sign was catatonic trance so rigid that, once it had passed, Teresa says that it felt as if her "bones had been wrenched apart." As they came without warning, could not be controlled or concealed, and were also typical of the seizures undergone by *alumbradas*, they made Teresa, her convent, and even the Jesuits notorious. Unluckily for him, poor young Baltasar Alvarez had begun to trust her, and he was "persecuted" before being removed to Medina del Campo.

The holy committee redoubled their well-meant efforts to drive Teresa mad. She begged to be sent away to hide in the one enclosed Carmelite convent of which she knew, where Francis Borgia's sister was a nun. Her plea was refused. No convent, in conscience, would have wished her on another of its own Order.

By her own admission, Teresa was pushed to the outer edge of sanity. And, as she could not admit without doing harm to her family and to the convent that she founded and in which she wrote the end of this first book, she was a natural suspect for the Inquisition: a visionary, a woman, and of "impure blood."

God alone knows what would have happened to her if Pedro de Alcántara had not happened to come to Avila.

Chapter 14 ❊ *Fray Pedro de Alcántara*

I

Pedro de Alcántara, now a canonized saint, was also a visionary; but his visions inspired the sort of life which most impressed the contemporary Spanish mind. He was a Franciscan, whose Order had degenerated; its men had become the jolly friars of literature, the heavy-drinking lechers who lived by beggary and the sale of fake relics; and Fray Pedro had been one of the first to join the movement which would soon be known in Spain as the King's Reform. The extremes to which he carried asceticism and bodily penance had become a living legend which struck all with awe, and his followers embraced the original, harsh austerities demanded by Francis of Assisi — austerities which are so blurred and softened in *The Little Flowers of St. Francis* and similar writings.

Fray Pedro had known Doña Guiomar's late husband, and he came to Avila to beg for a small, unoccupied country house that she had inherited, which he could convert into one of his reformed monasteries. Yomar immediately invited Teresa to visit her and meet him. Unlike the rest of Teresa's world, she was not upset by her friends "experiences"; in fact, she too, had begun to receive "favors" in prayer which went unrebuked by the Jesuits; she was seen as harmlessly silly — and very rich. The visit was quickly approved; and Teresa went gratefully to stay with the one friend who was not afraid of her or for her.

In the long run, Fray Pedro's reform impressed Teresa far more deeply than did the extremes to which he went in subjugating the flesh. At the time she was awed by the life of self-denial which had made him, at fifty-nine, look closer to eighty and "so fragile that he seemed to be made out of the roots of old trees."

Sleep, he told her, had been the hardest fleshly demand to overcome. It was really nothing to eat only one small meal every other day, once one got used to it; but to overcome sleep he had to use a cubicle so small that he could not lie down or curl up in it, with a rough log set behind him so that if he began to doze he would knock his head on it and wake at once.

He had handled all worldly temptation with equal stringency. He became a monk at sixteen, and for years thereafter shut out the world by keeping his eyes fixed on the ground. Even in his monastery, he could only find his way around by following the feet of one just ahead of him. This finally gained its reward: the lust of the eyes was vanquished. No sight of riches could move him to avarice, no beauty to desire. He saw not only men, but women, as trees walking.

He meant it, and it was a great advantage for Teresa. She says, in her second book, *El Camino de Perfección*, that few of her confessors did not feel, at the start, a distrust of her virtue. It sprang, I feel sure, from distrust of themselves: a disguised hope.

Fray Pedro distrusted neither her post-conversion virtue nor her visions and *arrobamientos*; he had them, too. He had ceased to preach after the first time an *arrobamiento* seized him in the pulpit — ceased not from fear, but distaste at having such a blessing become a vulgar spectacle. As for visions, he saw them more commonly than he saw the world around him. (This was obvious; his bare feet were bruised and scarred with his stumblings over objects in his way.)

His devotion was to Holy Poverty. He kept his needs to bare necessities. The autograph letters from his hand are written on scraps of paper, without margins and in a tiny, cramped script; they give silent confirmation to contemporary descriptions of his way of dress. His one garment, of brown burlap, was so skimpily cut that one wondered how his big-boned frame had struggled into it. This, however, only happened when the last one had worn into indecent rags; bathing, too, is an indulgence of the flesh.

This impressed Teresa, who was ashamed of her own *curiosidad*, or daintiness. (Amazingly, she would outgrow her period's belief that God likes his saints to smell, and wish that laws about clean clothes and clean linens could be written into the Constitutions of her Order.)

Teresa and Fray Pedro talked at length, both in Guiomar's house and in "several churches" where they could have more uninterrupted quiet. He reassured her fervently: all her "mercies" came from God. Those who thought they came from the devil were misled by their own inexperience. He knew good Francisco de Salcedo well: "the best soul who ever wore the cape and sword." He would set him right — and as many others as would hear him out.

This he did. His penitential saintliness was of the kind that Francisco de Salcedo and Master Daza understood. From that time on they trusted his judgment and became Teresa's warm supporters. But as he was not to Dionisio Vazquez's taste, he cut no ice with the Jesuits. Nor did Teresa feel the same degree of inner reassurance once she was back in her "inn on the road to hell," the Incarnation.

Teresa, in fact, would always know swings between inner confidence and deep self-doubt — nor were they dictated solely by her own temperament. The extraordinary thing about this period in her life is that Francisco de Salcedo and Master Daza were so promptly convinced, even by one who filled them with such awe as did Fray Pedro. For it cannot be stressed too often that while Teresa's visions and *arrobamientos* were unusual in such lax convents as the Incarnation, they were epidemic elsewhere, not only among heretical *alumbradas*. For example, the Augustinians in Our Lady of Grace produced a nun who received every "favor" that Teresa described under orders from Inquisitor Soto: visions, *arrobamientos*, prevision of things to come, the whole works — plus a miraculous ability to read Latin.

For that nun, the unquestioned diagnosis was demonic possession.

Furthermore, the most distinguished *letrados*, the intellectuals whom Teresa most trusted, disbelieved in visions *per se*, as one of them said, "even those of St. Brigid herself" (the super-visonary of the Faith).

As Father Ribadeneira wrote at the time, this disorder was like a plague and those most prone to contract it were *mujercillas*: (the scornful diminutive, *little* women). These *mujercillas*, he adds, were much given to setting out on projects of reform. Teresa's work, once she launched it, would not be made easy.

Back at the Incarnation she had problems. Convents known to produce *alumbradas* were being dissolved at the Inquisition's orders. On this point, Teresa's cousin Ana de los Angeles was unusually frank when, in testifying for Teresa's canonization, she described the convent's fears over Teresa's "novelties" (hence possible heresies) and her increasingly dangerous practice of "mental prayer."

And despite Fray Pedro's reassurance, Teresa herself had doubts. They were, indeed, her latent greatness. Something constantly told her that mental prayer could either be a strength to use for the healing of her Church — as Fray Pedro was trying to use it with his Alcantarines — or it could be an intoxication, an escape from the duties of Martha and a substitute for the pre-conversion loves of Mary Magdalen; and of these latter, the first was shabby, the other a temptation of the devil.

But she, a woman, could not take Fray Pedro's way to prove to herself that she had truly been turned to Christ. By their fruits by ye know them — but what fruits were possible for a nun of the Incarnation?

The answer, when it came, was, like so much of Teresa's story, bound up with current events.

II

Philip signed a truce with France and sealed it by marrying Isabel de Valois; France and Spain were joined in armed struggle against the rising threat of Calvinism. A request went to all convents and monasteries for "prayers and processions" to aid the Crown. Teresa knew that souls would not be won by the sword, but she fervently believed that they could be changed by the power of prayer, and she suffered to think of the souls being led unwittingly to hell by those instruments of Satan whom she always sweepingly classifies as "those Lutherans."

It was not for her own sake, she was always convinced, but for the sake of "those Lutherans'" victims that "it pleased the Lord that [she] should see the hell that she had escaped"; and not only see it, but experience it as a reality.

Like all her past visions, this strange waking nightmare came largely from books and pictures that she knew. There was the darkness in which one can still so strangely see. There was the hideous ground: a loathsome slime full of writhing reptiles—our sins perceived at last for what they are in all their ugliness. But for the rest, the vision is her own.

She was there, alone, in an alcove like a closet with no door, unable to move or close her eyes to the awful, lightless view of living, heaving filth before her. She was in such pain as she had never imagined, pain that would go on forever. But the pain was not caused by torturing demons, by flames, by anything external.

Helplessly, endlessly, in her hell's isolation, her "soul was tearing its own self apart."

There had been lonely pain in those "flights of the spirit, *arrobamientos*," that Teresa would always think of as her profoundest visions; but the pain was that of a helpless, earthbound longing for God. The soul forever tearing itself apart in hell knows only itself; it feels horror but no repentence pain, but only the pain of unending self-destruction.

Teresa's first step after this waking nightmare was to take a vow of total perfection. Only a confessor who was a theological illiterate would have permitted it; a broken vow is a grave sin, and to make one humanly unfulfillable is a sin of pride. Nonetheless, Teresa's first biographers, Ribera and Yepes, both cite that vow as saintly and perfectly kept. One would gather from Ribera that thereafter Teresa was never so much as avoidably late for mass.

Actually, within a few years, Teresa came to know some real *letrados*, sound theologians, and had herself formally released from that vow by her Carmelite Superior and her Dominican confessor. But even then, directly after her reaction of self-centered fear had driven her to a vow that only angels could keep, she quickly pushed such narrow concerns aside.

Thousands were being deceived and sent to hell by "those Lutherans." Once God had let her experience hell's hopeless, endless torment, she felt that she "would willingly die a thousand deaths" if it would save only one of those thousands from the eternal exile. Holy wars were futile, and what good could processions do — held in obedience to an earthly king? Or prayers rattled off in houses whose rule was ill-kept and where real devotion was so rare? Surely that nightmare vision had been sent with a purpose; but what could one woman do? A woman so ill thought of, and not even for her sins, but for the first slow workings of God's grace. . . .

The answer did not come in prayer, but from a casual conversation in which Teresa, as usual, passed from gravity into laughter. Teresa's career as founder of a new religious order was born from a casual joke.

Chapter 15 ❈ The Idea of Founding a Reformed, Enclosed Carmelite Convent

I

The *conversos* had strong family feeling; for example, Alonso, at his father's death, did not hesitate to turn to Bishop Juan de Fonseca for help, though the Bishop had nothing to gain by helping him. And Teresa, pen in hand, could warn against the distraction that too much family feeling brought into the religious life — in which, you may remember, she only echoed Christ — but while she could write it, she could not live it. To her last days, Teresa was always up to her ears in family problems.

What's more, her selection of prioresses for the many convents she founded shows a startling degree of nepotism; few of her nieces and cousins were cut out for the work, fewer still were really congenial, but they were family. And it was like that from the start. Once evidence was being gathered for Teresa's canonization, many conveniently remembered being present at the birth of the great plan. Actually, Teresa's loyalists were a handful of nieces and cousins primarily moved by the defensive cohesion of family pride. The nieces were María de Ocampo and Beatriz and Leonor de Cepeda, the cousins Inés and Ana Tapia.

María de Ocampo, who as Mother María Bautista wrote a memoir of Teresa, says that it all began as a joke. Teresa had been wondering if one could live in the Incarnation and still keep the Carmelite rule as it had been in the days before the Mitigation. The talk drifted to the most noted enclosed convent in Spain, the Royal Nunnery of St. Clare in Madrid, or Convent of the Angels, famous for such noble nuns as the Princess of Brazil. (As Teresa eventually discovered, those nuns were the most beservanted and obsequiously addressed Poor Clares who ever embraced Holy Poverty; but their reputation was great for the unusual combination of aristocratic blood and stainless chastity.)

One of them suggested that they form a similar convent of their own. María Bautista offered to start them over with a little contribution — say, a thousand ducats. They were all laughing when Yomar dropped in; and Yomar could never see a joke. According to an inaccurate thirdhand memory—María de San José, quoting Gracián, claiming to quote Teresa—she said, "Mother, I, too, will help with so holy a work."

The tune, if not the words, rings true enough. Guiomar de Ulloa was humorless, unrealistic, and given to promising more than she could perform.

Teresa was swayed from laughter to a sudden hope; but almost at once her realism took over and she let the idea go. As she says, when it came to actually producing cash, "Yomar made difficulties."

But not long after, at communion, Teresa heard the Voice order her to make just such a convent. This upset her painfully. She was forty-five and she knew her world. She could foresee nothing but futile effort and more notoriety, but she could not shake off the conviction that she was under orders from His Majesty. Apparently Yomar had begun to talk, and the word had spread, for a written warning came from little Father Baltasar: a Carmelite reform must have the approval of Carmelite authority.

Antonio de Heredia, the Carmelite Superior in Avila, was a worldly Andalusian aristocrat. Teresa had not thought of him as a helper, for she knew the abuses that he casually countenanced; she saw that warning as a council of despair. What she underrated was Heredia's pragmatism. In the first place, a small, enclosed convent would remove this hysterical nun from the undesired attentions of the Inquisition; and in the second place, the King's most recent hobby was reform of the monastic orders. The Carmelite Provincial for Castile, Angel de Salazar, was a politician; he could readily be shown the advantages to be gained by letting this woman lock herself out of sight—in the increasingly popular name of reform.

Well and good—and overhasty. Avila was a backwater, and both Heredia and Father Angel were men of the great world, far too detached from the local scene. When the news spread that the nun with the seizures, the nun possessed by devils, was about to found her own convent of heretical madwomen, it produced an uproar.

In consequence, Teresa was beset by further doubts. She wrote for advice to the greatest *letrados* whom she believed to have any interest in the spirit of reform.

Pedro de Alcántara (now St. Peter of Alcántara) approved, only warning her to do nothing without the consent of her "spiritual friend." Luis de Beltrán (now also officially a saint) also approved, explaining his long delay in answering by saying that he had made her letter "the subject of much prayer and consideration."

Some Jesuits now claim that St. Francis Borgia also approved, on what evidence I can't discover. Teresa says that the "persecution" was intense. The Jesuits were held responsible for encouraging what they had not encouraged and were warned that "the times were bad," and that the whole idea was "ridiculous."

Ridiculous is hardly the right word. The Jesuit Rector, Dionisio Vazquez, knew that both Teresa and his new General were *conversos*, and that Loyola's

Spiritual Exercises were being examined by the Inquisition. He knew why Francis Borgia had made him rector in Hernando Alvarez's place, and how he would react if a Jesuit College already smeared by the de Prádanos scandal were seen to favor an unpopular project backed by the very women implicated in that scandal—Teresa and Doña Guiomar.

At this juncture, the city began to pressure Guiomar for the payment of her debts; any hope of future benefactions from her that the Jesuits might have entertained was gone for good.

Of all this, Teresa could only say that all but a tiny handful at the Incarnation were enraged that she dared set herself up as a reformer, and that Yomar was refused absolution by her Jesuit confessor unless she would drop the whole thing. She could not say that she herself was threatened with being delated to the Inquisition, or that one faction at the Incarantion favored locking her up in the convent prison, or that the Jesuits would have no more to do with her. She merely begins to talk about "a wise Dominican" who, without explanation, has replaced her third Jesuit.

In fact, the records at Santo Tomás show that she and Yomar simultaneously came to share a Dominican confessor. This is not surprising. The Dominicans were agreed that the Carmelites were in need of reform and they saw the Jesuits as left-wing crackpots who in any matter of judgement were probably wrong. They would have listened even to a silly woman like Yomar if she told them about a nun slandered and cast off by the Jesuits only because she wanted to make a haven in which a few Carmelites might live strictly by their own rule.

Father Pedro Ibáñez listened to Yomar and thought it over. He had been an ordained priest for twenty years, and he was a scholarly intellectual, self-isolated from the ongoing excitement. But he was cautious, and Doña Guiomar hardly seemed objective. He would confess her, but as for the nun who wanted to leave her convent, he would only make up his mind when he met her and heard her out.

Teresa knew the Dominican bias. In stating her case to Pedro Ibáñez she mentioned no orders from His Majesty, but simply urged the grave need for a Carmelite reform. She was impressive, and when Father Ibáñez heard that she had her Provincial's approval, he was satisfied. He still encouraged her when Teresa told him honestly about Guiomar's finances as she was just beginning to understand them. In such a good work, he assured her, God would provide.

García de Toledo was a gentleman. One can imagine him as hearing Ibáñez with a smile, perhaps a shrug, and some words such as, "Let's hope you can live up to her standards, Father. The Jesuits convinced her that I did not." No more than that, I am sure.

But Ibáñez was not left long in his bookish seclusion. "A certain gentleman" —whom Teresa leaves unidentified—came steaming to Santo Tomás to warn the Dominicans against having anything to do with "such women." It seems safe to assume that he told Ibáñez that Father Borgia had found it necessary to transfer two of Teresa's confessors and Vazquez a third, and for reasons to which the nuns at the Incarnation could testify.

Whatever the "certain gentleman" said, Ibáñez was disturbed, and showed signs of withdrawing his support. Teresa decided to risk all, tell Pedro Ibáñez about her visions and locutions, and let him pass judgement on their source.

He asked her to put it in writing that he could discuss with other theologians. The paper Teresa gave him was first published, with other such *cuentas de conciencia*, as an appendix to the *Life*.

It begins: "My way of prayer is this: . . ."

She described the experiences that she saw as supernatural, though she knew that the Dominicans had small stomach for such things. She admitted that she did little in the way of physical penance. But, in better writing than her usual headlong style, she conveyed the intensity of her desire to be and to do good, and her true longing for guidance to safeguard her against error, so that all she believed should be in accord with the teaching of the Church.

Pedro Ibáñez took time to pray over that paper and to discuss it with those whose judgement he most respected. He was moved by Teresa's humble promise that she would abide by his decision, whatever it was.

(In a characteristic flash of honesty, Teresa says, "And it seems to me that I would have done so." *It seems* . . . though I can't be certain. . . .)

Ibáñez's decision was oddly shrewd for one so unworldly; perhaps he foresaw his own danger, for he told her to go ahead, but secretly. Once she had raised enough money for a down-payment, the house she bought should be bought in another's name. Until the convent was an accomplished fact, no one should have a chance to rock the boat.

Teresa says that at this point "they" sent to Rome for the briefs. The likeliest "they" are Pedro Ibáñez and García de Toledo—who had influence with the right people. A request sent from Court to the Vatican and signed by a de Toledo would find its way quickly to an influential Cardinal. (Hagiography prefers it that "they" were St. Peter of Alcántara and St. Francis Borgia.)

II

It took four months to collect the down-payment on a tiny house. The chief contributors were Teresa's nieces, Isabel and Beatriz. Yomar was only able to contribute a jar of salt and a bolt of worsted, but her mother gave thirty ducats.

Juana and her husband came from Alba to make the purchase in their own name, and the papers were ready to be signed when the Provincial, Angel de Salazar, learned for the first time about the furor that this proposed convent had raised in Avila. He withdrew his permission. There were renewed threats of delating Teresa to the Inquisition as an *alumbrada* and warnings, this time to the Dominicans, that "the times were bad, " even though the Inquisition was a Dominican institution.

Teresa says, "And I talked about it with my Dominican, for as I have said, he was such a *letrado* that I could put absolute confidence in what he told me."

However, Angel de Salazar's prohibition was news; the "certain gentleman" who warned the Dominicans against "such women" had spoken for much of the town, and the fury was renewed. "The times were bad" and it did Santo

Tomás no good to have it known that one of its most respected *letrados* was encouraging Teresa to set up a nest of *alumbradas* under the guise of a "barefoot reform." Ibáñez, a man of conscience, would have been the first to see that he should leave Avila, and for a place sufficiently obscure and isolated as to protect not only himself but his monastery from being tarred with the brush that had already been used with such effect on the Jesuits.

Teresa had the counseling and support of her "wise Dominican" for only four months before he became her fourth post-conversion confessor to be transferred from Avila.

De Prádanos, you remember, simply drops from Teresa's narrative; there is no indication that *mi confesor* has become another person. That was Teresa's instinctive way of handling such things, the way that in her sixties she would try in vain to teach the last man to be slandered as her lover; she had neither taste nor talent for explaining-away. But she wrote about Ibáñez at the direction of another Dominican — García de Toledo, back in the picture again and increasingly anxious about his own reputation.

So, she makes it appear that the furor had nothing to do with Ibáñez's departure. She tells of how "a wise Dominican" convinced her that her "experiences" had led her to believe nothing that was not in accord with Holy Writ, and goes on:

"He reassured me greatly; and as I see it, it also did him good, for though he was very good already, from that time on he gave himself more to prayer and took himself off to a monastery of his Order where there is much solitude, so that he could apply himself to prayer better, where he stayed more than two years; and only obedience took him away from that place because he was needed, being the sort of person that he was."

In effect, a two-year retreat. But she has told no literal lies. Two years is less than the rest of his life; and he himself explains a flying visit that he made to Avila four years later "because he was needed." He made it, he says, unwillingly, and only because Teresa's letter had convinced him that "to refuse would be to disobey Christ."

So, as she had done for no other, and never would again, Teresa goes on with it: "In one way, it grieved me when he left because of the lack it caused me, though I would not let that show and hurt him; but I came to understand that it was for his gain, for when I was grieving very much over his departure, the Lord told me to console myself and not feel like that, and that he was making progress, well-guided. As it turned out, his soul was done a great deal of good there, and his spirit made such an advance in growing better that he told me he wouldn't have missed it for anything. I could say the same, for though before he had comforted me with his learning, now he was able to do it with his spiritual experience as well."

It is true that they were not forbidden to correspond. Later in her story she mentions one of his letters — with which she vigorously disagreed — and he speaks of the one from her which brought about his brief, unwilling visit to Avila.

A long-respected myth has it that he went back to Avila to be Prior of Santo

Tomás until his death. Another, more to the point, claims that on his deathbed in Trianos he saw a vision of St. Anthony. St. Anthony, you recall, retained his chastity despite the temptations sent from hell in female form. Clearly, the saint would not have blessed the deathbed of one not equally chaste.

This invention shares its source with Teresa's labored explanation of Pedro Ibáñez's exile; yet surely no other scandal of those that pursued her from her conversion to her canonization, was more groundless. Pedro Ibáñez, a Dominican intellectual, had been able to reassure Teresa that her purposes were good and her "experiences" no flirtation with heresy, and she found it a release from inner conflict: nothing more.

But that in itself was a grave loss, and no loss could have been more cruelly timed. As Teresa says, "for five or six months" she did nothing to further her plans. She felt nothing but a quiet, flat despair. Praying only intensified her sense of being "absent from God," and the Voice that had commanded her to found a convent did not come again.

Help, when it came, came from an unexpected quarter.

Chapter 16 ❈ First Steps toward Establishing a Reformed Convent; Difficulties

I

Dionisio Vazquez made himself disliked at St. Gil. A letter to General Laínez from one of his fellows, Father Vir, is still in the Roman archives of the Company. Vazquez, Vir says, "is excessively opinionated, his ideas are odd, not suited to please the good people of the town" and his "moods of anger and depression" disturb the college itself.

The letter took effect: Vazquez was removed. His successor, Gaspar de Salazar, was no relation to Angel de Salazar, in blood or in spirit. He was a *converso*, a mystic, and by Teresa's account, "receiving many favors from God in prayer." Consequently, he felt no automatic distrust of her. In later years, Teresa would find his friendship more trouble than it was worth but not then, when he first came to Avila.

Teresa, when he came, had hit rock bottom. Towards the end of those "five or six months" of dull despair she suffered a recurrence of the *arrobamientos* that left her racked and enfeebled — and those who witnessed them, afraid. During one such seizure she heard the Voice say, "Your troubles are nearly ended." She took it for a welcome promise that she would soon die; but in retrospect she saw that it had been a promise that she would find Father Gaspar.

Unlike Teresa, Father Gaspar never learned to distinguish between religious experience and religious hysteria. In a letter written when she was in her sixties, Teresa calls his teaching "only suitable for those who are already in the hand of God." But when he came to Avila and promptly offered to confess her, she did not doubt that his unquestioning trust in all the "experiences" she described to him "did her soul much good."

Perhaps it did, in that time of lonely need. However, Father Gaspar was doing his career no good, and for reasons that I have yet to see squarely faced: both Teresa and those who have written about her prefer to look away. The fact remains that Teresa's Provincial, Father Angel, had forbidden Teresa to found a convent, and Father Gaspar encouraged her to disobey him.

The most heavily whitewashed facet of Teresa's story is that her career began with disobeying her Provincial and was nearly brought to an end, fifteen years later, by her disobeying her General. At neither time was she at peace with her conscience; though holy obedience was not part of her native equipment, she saw it as essential to the monastic life. In consequence she developed a gift for making men give her the orders that she wanted to obey, and when that failed she often changed confessors. Confessors can disagree; they still do, and probably always have done.

In this case, one should remember that "for five or six months" she had been in despair. The encouragement of a Jesuit Rector must have seemed godsent, a miracle. And from Father Gaspar's point of view, Teresa was not disobedient. He endorsed a new appeal to Father Angel, and when it was refused — thus invalidating any briefs from Rome that might permit her to found a convent as a Carmelite — he switched horses. By his plan, she should leave the Carmelites and found an independent convent "under the ordinary" — that is, under the jurisdiction of the Bishop.

Teresa was still by holy vow a Carmelite. Her *cuentas de conciencia* (some set down for her confessors, some for her own eyes alone) include a "locution" which assured her that in her proposed convent of the Virgin's Order, the Virgin would guard one door and St. Joseph the other. Teresa believed herself instructed by Christ to restore the Carmelites to their lost perfection, not to abandon them.

Moreover, she knew nothing about the Bishop except that he was one of the powerful Mendozas, a son of the Duke of Infantado. To judge by her only other acquaintance so *muy, muy principal*, García de Toledo, a bishop of ducal family was likely to be of the world worldly, no friend of Christ.

She knew that she was disobeying her Provincial. Was she also disobeying His Majesty? She closed her mind to the question. How could Father Gaspar, so deeply spiritual, so godsent to understand her purpose, counsel a sin? She sent for Juana and Don Juan de Ovalle to reopen negotiation for buying the house. And she had two visions, unlike any others she had except for two that came years later, when she decided to disobey her General.

In the first, St. Clare blessed her determination to found a convent like that which had been its inspiration: the Royal Nunnery of Poor Clares in Madrid. To understand the second, we need its background.

Father Gaspar, never discreet, told his friends about his simple solution to Teresa's problem, and the word spread. This Teresa did not know when, troubled in mind and feeling some inner lack, she went to mass at Santo

Tomás, where she had gone as Pedro Ibáñez's penitent. She took Juana with her, or we would not know the whole story; Juana told it in evidence for her sister's canonization.

The Mass begins with the Liturgy of the Word, which ends with a sermon; after that comes the celebration of the Eucharist. Juana and Teresa heard a furious sermon denouncing runaway nuns who set up convents "under the ordinary" in which they might invent a rule to suit their own sinful, willful natures. Juana says that she could scarcely bear the public shame, though Teresa, sitting beside her, was wholly serene.

Teresa says only that she went to mass at Santo Tomás and could think of nothing but her past, her great sins. She saw herself as fit only for a life of penitence, utterly unworthy to lead others into holy living. Then the vision began.

Our Lady and St. Joseph were beside her. The Virgin took her hand, covered her with a dazzling white garment and told her not to be afraid that she might fall again. And, she continued, even though Teresa felt "obedience to the ordinary" to be " a thing that wasn't to her taste," all would be well. Both she and St. Joseph "would be well served in it. . . ."

"They would take care of us, and her Son had promised to be with us, and for a sign that this was true, she gave me a piece of jewelry." (A gold necklace set with precious stones of supernal beauty.)

The need served by the vision is obvious. The white robe that covered Teresa's sins restates her belief in Christ's forgiveness, and through it, her worthiness to serve Him. And in the pious reading of Teresa's day, female saints incessantly receive gifts from celestial Cartiers — rings, broaches, neck-laces, all set with finer stones than earth provides. The interesting part of this vision is its coda.

When it was over, Teresa says, she realized that she had, in effect, been absent from the mass. Even at the holy moment of the Elevation she was unaware of what was going on: *"which gave me some scruples."*

Scruples? God does not send visions to test our ability to disregard them and attend to holier matters. But daydreaming through mass — yes, even dreaming about Our Lady and St. Joseph — deserves some scruples.

Where God was concerned, Teresa could never tell less than the whole truth.

Father Gaspar's indiscretion provoked more than sermons. Both Heredia and Teresa's Prioress ordered her to leave the Incarnation and go back to Guiomar. At least, it was still believed that Don Juan de Ovalle was renovating the house for his own use, and Teresa could make it seem that her daily calls to oversee the work were calls on Juana, who was in the last weeks of a pregnancy while her little boy, Gonzalo, was constantly underfoot.

Gonzalo, in years to come, would be remembered as one whom Teresa had raised from the dead. One witness had it that he was killed when a wall collapsed, another that he fell from a wall to his death. Juana said that he was killed when a stone fell on his head and came to life when Teresa picked him up and held him in her arms — and belittled the miracle silently, with a smile. But Juana did not explain the favoritism which led Teresa to raise Gonzalo (who never amounted to much) and let his newborn brother die; nor did

Teresa include Gonzalo in her unwilling list of the mercies extended to others because of her prayers.

What Teresa chiefly remembered from that time was her fear that Father Angel would come to Avila, discover the truth about that house she visited — though she was still unreleased from the Carmelites by Rome — and send her to the Incarnation's prison. In December a new-built wall did actually collapse, and she had no money for its rebuilding, and at that black moment a letter came from Lorenzo with two hundred ducats.

"It seemed like a miracle," she wrote him, "for I hadn't a *blanco* left." Not one red cent. And though Doña Guiomar, who promised to help her, is "very spiritual," she is also *sin dineros*. Dead broke. The two nieces' doweries covered the down-payment on the house; nothing more, so it had to bought "secretly and with no means of getting the work done." But it will still be Carmelite — though under the Bishop.

The rest of the letter concerns the family.

De Guzmán got nothing from the lawsuit that was settled just before he dropped dead. María is ill, and de Ovalle threatens a countersuit which "could be the death of her." If Lorenzo sends him that money he wants, it must be with a firm understanding that if he does sue María, he must also give her five hundred ducats — more, that is, than he could hope to gain from a court.

She, Teresa, is so happy that Lorenzo has settled down to marriage at last, and that he and his wife have a baby boy. He must give her particular love to *mi Jerónimo*. (A love they shared for that endearing wastrel; generous Lorenzo married off Jerónimo's illegitimate daughters before they started home for the Indies with poor Pedro still in his care.) There are also oblique references to Agustín, who was currently scheming to keep some money that should have gone to poor María. Womanizing was a de Cepeda trait; but only Agustín was greedy and dishonest, the bad apple in the family basket.

The letter also sends news of Lorenzo's friends, and says that Juana "has grown into a fine woman."

I summarize it at such length because it is both a grateful and generous-hearted letter. Few would say so little about their own problems and give so much thought to those of others. It is also, obviously, a letter from one who writes often, although only one other has survived from Lorenzo's years in the Indies, in contrast to the thick stack that remains of those she wrote him after his homecoming.

The letter is dated December 23. Within a fortnight Teresa, most unexpectedly and against her will, would be living in a ducal palace in Toledo, for which she offers an explanation so thin that only the rules governing hagiography explain why it is never questioned. Simultaneously, Guiomar would leave Avila to live with her mother in Toro, and Father Gaspar would be removed from his Rectorate and sent to Madrid, which Teresa omits as she omitted the loss of de Prádanos. When she wrote, she was under no Dominican pressure to explain away the facts of Jesuits.

Chapter 17 ❁ Teresa Ordered to Toledo as Spiritual Companion to a Widowed Great Lady. Teresa Writes her Life, as Ordered to by García de Toledo

I

Despite the tone of that letter to Lorenzo, Teresa felt danger approaching. As she was ending the *Life*, under orders to list her revelations of things to come along with her other "favors," she gives us this: "Concerning that Rector of the Company of Jesus whom I have mentioned several times . . . a great trouble came to him once, and he was much persecuted. One day as I was hearing mass, Christ told me certain words of comfort that I should say to him, and others to prepare him for what was coming, so as to make him ready to suffer. This gave him much comfort and courage; and it all came out later just as the Lord had told me."

It has been said that Father Gaspar was removed "because of administrative difficulties with the Bishop." This is true, so far as it goes. Few bishops of minor sees visited them often; when Bishop Mendoza came to Avila for his Christmas visit, it was his first since the previous Easter.

At first he was vexed by the situation he found: a Jesuit Rector encouraging a Carmelite nun to defy her Provincial on the assumption that he, Mendoza, would accept her independent convent as his responsibility. The fellow had not ever troubled to tell him what ill-feeling the plans for such a convent were making. Such highhandedness should be handled at once by Francis Borgia — and in his good old ducal style.

But the more Mendoza heard, the more he wondered: not about Gaspar de Salazar, but Teresa. Both, it seemed, were *conversos* — but the Jesuit, it seemed, was in little danger, and the nun was in real peril from the fiercely anti-Semitic Inquisition.

The ducal Mendozas were not fiercely anti-Semitic. Like most noble families, they had Jewish blood, and unlike most they refused to deny it. Bishop Alvaro Mendoza and his brother Pedro Mendoza had been canons of Toledo Cathedral when a commoner named Martínez Silíceo became its archbishop and began his career by refusing to accept a *converso* canon who had been appointed by the Pope himself. The Pope cancelled the appointment when Silíceo wrote him a protest that his Cathedral was becoming "a new synagogue," but Silíceo was still unsatisfied. He chose a time when most of his canons were out of town, called a chapter, and pushed through a decree of *limpieza de sangre*: Toledo should have no more canons of impure blood.

A manuscript which covers the ensuing controversy states that "the Archbishop has discovered that not merely most but nearly all of his priests are of Jewish descent." The Mendoza brothers were furious, though their own appeal to the Pope only served to publicize their bias. The family fought on for *conversos'* rights. In the year that Alvaro Mendoza was named Bishop of Avila, two members of the family were refused admission to the Military Order of Alcántara on grounds of "impure blood." At this, Alvaro's cousin, Cardinal Bobadilla y Mendoza, produced a remarkable piece of scholarship and sent a copy to the King. Torquemada's *Libro Verde* had only traced the Jewish blood in the noble houses of Aragón; the Cardinal's *El Fizón* (the stain) did it for every noble house in Spain.

To this family background one should add that the palace which the Bishop shared with his widowed sister was in Valladolid; he had lived there throughout the recent slaughters.

When he came to Avila in that Christmas season, he was assaulted with tales about a runaway nun, the child of a Jew who passed himself off in Avila as an Old Christian knight: an *alumbrada*, what's more, whose most recent lover, in a rapid succession of five, was the Jesuit Rector. The whole story smelled. The Bishop even forgot his annoyance with Gaspar de Salazar. Of course, for the sake of peace, de Salazar should be transferred, but as pleasantly as possible.

(Father Gaspar's "persecution" resulted in his being received in Madrid, where he became a popular confessor at the Convent of the Angels, with the Princess of Brazil for his most enthusiastic penitent.)

As for the woman, Bishop Mendoza saw no reason to doubt his friend García de Toledo that she was a striking beauty with quite a past, but was now an ultra-repentant Magdalen, much influenced by those puritanical Jesuits. Still, she too should be got out of town until things quieted down. Managing that would take thought. The Bishop decided to turn the problem over to his sister.

Doña María de Mendoza also had quite a past, if we can judge from the correspondence of Philip II. He had blamed the growing inefficiency of his late minister, her late husband, Cobos, on his distress over Doña María's flaunting the jewels given her by other gentlemen. But in widowhood, she, too, had turned religious. She should come on from Valladolid to meet this Doña Teresa, sum her up, and decide what to do with her.

García sent this news to his friend Ibáñez, which I think explains Ibáñez's account of two letters he wrote Teresa, as it seems at his friend's suggestion. In the first he told her that she was about to be visited by a lady, *muy principal*, who had heard of her "experiences" and believed in them. Teresa answered that the idea shocked her, both because she was a "nobody" and because in matters religious she was humble beyond measure.

Teresa had not yet lost the awe she felt for noblewomen, but her friendship with María Mendoza was instant and genuine. And Doña María thought at once of the perfect solution.

Doña Luisa de la Cerda, a daughter of the Duke of Medinaceli, had recently lost her husband and was going in showily for religious consolation. With her current enthusiasm for the Toledan Jesuits, she need only be told that a Jesuit's name was smeared, because he had encouraged a holy Carmelite to leave her sinful convent, to be convinced that both were chaste as the angels. Furthermore, Doña Luisa had been going through a rapid succession of living-in *beatas*: all unattractive. One who was both as holy and as charming as Doña

Teresa de Ahumada could make herself welcome for as long as the Avilan situation made it advisable.

So it was arranged. When Teresa wrote to Lorenzo on the day before Christmas, she knew nothing about the preliminaries which had been carried on through the last weeks of Advent; but by the end of the next fortnight, she was in Toledo. And Angel de Salazar was an ambitious man who saw it as well to agree with what three persons as important as Doña Luisa, Doña María, and Bishop Don Alonso wanted.

Teresa leaves this development unexplained. She merely narrates, without any preparation for such a development:

"In a big city more than twenty leagues away there happened to be a lady who was heartbroken because her husband had died. . . . She learned about this wretched little sinner because it pleased the Lord that they should speak well of me for the sake of the other good things that would come out of it. The lady was well acquainted with the Provincial and knew that I was in a convent that let nuns go away, and the Lord gave her a great desire to see me. . . . The Provincial sent me orders that I should go at once. . . . I learned this on Christmas night."

This left her in turbulent conflict, she goes on, for she knew that she had been misrepresented and felt herself to be "so vile." Then she learned in an *arrobamiento* that it would be for the best if she went away until the briefs came from Rome to legalize her convent. She told "that Rector," who agreed and said that anyone trying to dissuade her would only be trying to get her into further trouble with her Provincial.

That was all she was free to tell. It would be many years before she saw "that Rector" again, but he drops from the story without comment.

On the other hand, García de Toledo—the anxious censor of her expanded book—enters her story for the first time, abruptly and almost as if their renewed friendship was the most significant event of her long, long stay with Doña Luisa. I shall always wonder whether Pedro Ibáñez did not write to persuade her that de Prádanos had been wrong, and she could do García good.

II

Teresa began a chapter with recounting her fears that the Provincial would come to Avila and order the work on her house to be stopped, which "the Lord prevented" because that great lady, twenty leagues distant, desired her presence, and "the Rector" said that she must go. "The Lady" was very fond of her from the start, which caused some petty jealousies in her household, typical of palace life. And that life, with its combination of excessive comforts and restrictions which made the nobility prisoners of their own high place, cured her once and for all of any wish that she had been born a great lady. She also learned that the lady was a faulty human creature like herself, and in consequence she never there-after treated any great lady other than as an equal.

And immediately, she launches into her story of a friendship renewed. Her

80

contemporary biographers, Ribera and Yepes, say that the man was her father's, and her, old confessor, Father Barrón (whom she did see during a later stay in Toledo). For this they had good reason, as Barrón was never (in Teresa's word) "persecuted" for being her friend. But Jerónimo Gracián, writing in fluent self-justification from an exile like that which García de Toledo eventually suffered, gladly identified him — his fellow-victim of baseless slander.

We hardly need Gracián's word for it, when we recall how Teresa's first locution, "not men but angels," made her break off a friendship with a man who was "not God's servant." One should also note, in her story, how things just "happened," as Doña Luisa had "happened" to hear of her. It is a word allied to her impersonal "they": "they" who refused to let her see a priest when she was so near to death in her father's house; "they" who "happened" to give her Augustine's *Confessions*. . . .

"While I was there, a certain monk happened to come, one *muy principal* with whom I had happened to talk several times, many years before; and, happening to be at mass in a monastery near where he was staying, I was given the desire to know how his soul was inclined, for I wanted him to be God's servant very much, and I got up to go to talk with him.

"As I was already very deep in prayer, it came to me next that it would be a waste of time, and who put me up to interfering in something like that? And I sat down again. I think this happened to me three or four times.

"Finally, my good angel was stronger than the bad, and I went and called him to come and talk to me in a confessional. We began to ask each other questions about our lives, for we hadn't seen each other in many years." (Not to talk to, at least.) "I began to tell him that mine had been one of many troubles to my soul. He urged me very much to tell him what these troubles were. I told him they weren't anything for general knowledge or for me to tell him about." (Not the attitude, you note, with which one normally enters a confessional.) "He told me that since he knew the Dominican father I have told about [Pedro Ibáñez] and was his very close friend, he would tell him as soon as he asked, and so I shouldn't think twice about it.

"The fact is, he couldn't help insisting, nor, I think, could I help giving up and telling him: for in spite of all the trouble and shame I used to feel when I talked about these things with him [Pedro Ibáñez, here, one of Teresa's frequent floating pronouns] or with the Rector I have told about, I didn't feel the least bit of pain, but only satisfaction."

(In the strength of this memory she forgets how gladly she let Father Gaspar "understand her soul.")

"I talked with him under the seal of the confessional. He seemed more prudent than he had ever been before, though I had always considered him highly intelligent. I saw what great talents and qualities he had if he would only give himself wholly to God: for I have been like that for some years. Nowadays I can't see anyone who satisfies me very deeply without immediately wanting to see him wholly given to God — along with some anxieties over being worth nothing myself. And while I do wish that everyone would serve Him, where someone who satisfies me like that is concerned the wish becomes a powerful impetus, and so I plead with the Lord for their sakes, very much. It affected me just like that with the monk I am telling about."

(She is trapped in these awkward, labored generalizations; and she needs them both to conceal García's identity at this point and because García would never become quite what she hoped for.)

"He asked me to pray for him a great deal, and he needn't have said it, for I was in a state where I could do nothing else.

"I went off to a place where I could be alone to pray, and began to talk to the Lord in the foolish way I have, without knowing what I am saying because it is love that speaks . . . and the love . . . makes [the soul] forget itself and seem to be in Him and it talks madly, as if they were both the same thing, undivided.

"So, after imploring Him with my tears that a soul like that should be placed very truly in His service (for though I considered him good, I wasn't satisfied and I wanted him to have very much good in him). . . . I said, 'Lord, you can't deny me this mercy! See how well suited he is to be our friend!' "

But Teresa remembered what it had cost her to renounce that friendship which she had seen as "no offence against God" though "it had much affection in it." She remembered the uncompromising Voice, and she knew that García was no angel. And after those prayers and tears she was afraid that they had come from an incurable "enmity to God." Could one ever really know what impulses stirred such prayers, "whether one's soul were alive or dead?" Then — "Oh, the goodness and the humanity of God!" — Christ let her know that "a soul in mortal sin" could not "feel such love for Him" as she had felt in praying for García's soul.

She seemed to hear Christ tell her just what she should tell García, as from Him. But she "hated to take messages to a third person," and she "did not know how [García] would react, or whether he wouldn't make fun of her." So she wrote it out instead.

Even to herself she seemed to be setting down specific facts about him that she had not known. García was startled and moved, and promised "with great sincerity to give himself more to prayer." Then Teresa's compulsive honesty about "the things of God" makes her add, "But he didn't do it right away."

Yet Teresa, "wretched sinner though [she] was," kept on praying that Christ would lead him to Himself and teach him to hate "the satisfactions and affairs" of his worldly life.

To the end of their acquaintance Teresa, in writing to their mutual friend Bishop Mendoza, could never say more for García's soul than that it was "getting better." But she never gave up hope, and she was driven to tell this story — which he would read — if only to remind García of what he could still become.

When she wrote this, García was shortly due to become her sixth confessor to be "persecuted." The coda with which she ends this episode tries to protect his name while it still pleads for his understanding of his own potential as "God's friend."

Learned men, she says, are the only safe guides for the ignorant, even if they are not spiritual themselves; she acknowledges this humbly. But they, too, must be humble and admit that sometimes the Lord can use "a little old woman" to enrich their learning with spirituality. (With García, Teresa carefully made a point of leaning on her years, so much so that in letters she calls him not "father," but "my son.")

It is interesting that Teresa told this story, when she omits so much. As she would, most strikingly, when she told of how her convent was actually founded.

III

Seven months in a palace is an eduaction in practical politics. During that stay, Teresa learned much about the handling of patrons, the fine art of avoiding jealousies, and similar matters which stood her in good stead through the years to come. She also learned that Christianity is egalitarian. In other orders nuns still used their worldly titles, but in hers only two were ever allowed: Sister and Mother.

As Doña Luisa's current holy woman, she was treasued for all that had made her suspect in Avila: her intensities of silent prayer, her eager talk about "the things of God." If this had gone hand in hand with real understanding, it would have been happiness unalloyed, but it did not. Teresa always remembered an occasion when Doña Luisa saw that her spiritual comforter was herself in need of comfort, and gave it according to her lights: she ordered in all her caskets and had her whole magnificent display of court jewelry spread out for Teresa's delectation.

However, Doña Luisa is said during that visit to have taken up almsgiving, which was probably new to her, for unlike most aristocrats she parted with money reluctantly. Teresa would remember that in that palace she first lost her own instinctive shrinking from the rags and stenches of poverty. The contrast between the gloved and scented hands that doled out coppers and the hands that snatched them said much about the accident of birth that separated dwellers in the nobleman's palace from these born to city slums.

One of Doña María's young ladies in waiting was then called María de Salazar, though on later travels as María de San José, Teresa's cleverest prioress, she signed two papers in which she gives herself two different pairs of parents and two different birthplaces. Her memories of Teresa sweeten their relationship in a way that is not borne out by the many letters from Teresa that she saved; but she does say that when, at sixteen, she told Teresa that she would like to be a nun, the Mother said flatly that she was not cut out for it. Her convenient situation in that palace may have been Angel de Salazar's reward for letting Teresa go there, and not, as she had expected, to the Incarnation's prison. Such deals were not unusual in those days.

While Teresa did not find palace life congenial, she nonetheless had much undisturbed leisure there, and in those seven months, it seems, she wrote her book *Concerning God's Mercies*, which she brought to its intended end in June, 1562, the June before she went back to Avila.

She also wrote letters, keeping in touch with everyone who could help her found her convent. When she learned from Fray Pedro de Alcántara that he was coming to Toledo, she told Doña Luisa that it was her chance to meet a living saint. Doña Luisa was properly impressed with the strange old man and offered his Alcantarines a house in her castle-town of Malagón. A letter he wrote the lady, still extant, makes excuses about other foundations to be made first, but his tone is both courtly and warm; he sends his remembrances to her two children.

For Teresa, his visit brought bad news. In taking over the house Doña Guiomar gave him, he had found that her finances were in even more hopeless state than Teresa realized. She had still not relinquished her belief that Yomar would eventually be able to give her convent an income, however small. Nuns, as she saw it, must know at least where their next meal was coming from if their minds were to be free for prayer; poor convents were notorious for their discontent.

But she changed her mind when she met María de Jesús.

IV

María de Jesús, born María Yepes, was a period piece. A native of Granada, widowed in her forties, she joined the Carmelites and left them when Our Lady, in a vision, ordered her to found a convent of her own. She withdrew her dowry, joined a group of *beatas* under Franciscan guidance, and went barefoot to Rome to buy her brief. Cardinal Reinoso, who saw to such matters, received the dowry and gave her the proper Latin papers—which she could not read.

Back in Granada she met a situation much like Teresa's: the Carmelites called her mad and the city denounced her. She set out again, for Madrid, to seek support from the Crown. At Court, she failed to charm, but her connection with the Franciscans got her an invitation to call at the Royal Nunnery, where she met Gaspar de Salazar. And Father Gaspar, ever the enthusiast, sent her to the one person who could best understand her plight and perhaps get Doña Luisa to help her. Doña Luisa was not impressed with María de Jesús; she went back to Madrid and found another patroness. But for Teresa, her visit was an inspiration.

Teresa says that she was "shamed" by the contrast between this woman's response to the Lord's "many mercies" and her own. She stayed in the palace for a fortnight, and they "arranged how these convents should be founded." Carmelite, that is, of the primitive rule; María de Jesús assured her that in the holy past all Carmelite convents had been founded in poverty. Teresa did not doubt her, though she found the idea "astounding." She had believed holy poverty to be an invention of St. Francis, abandoned and now being newly revived by Fray Pedro de Alcántara.

To found in poverty would make the state Yomar's finances irrelevant. Still, Teresa had misgivings. Such a bold plan would stiffen the already powerful opposition—and if no alms came, she would be justly blamed for dragging twelve other souls into penury. (She had decided that her convent should house no more nuns than Christ had chosen to be his apostles.)

"In short, my faith was weak—as that of this servant of God had not been."

She wrote about it to Fray Pedro. His answer (addressed to the Most Magnificent and Religious Lady, Doña Teresa de Ahumada) glowed with enthusiastic support. Her confessor and Doña Luisa's, the Jesuit Rector, Pedro Domenech, on the contrary, was shocked; he told her to forget such a wild notion. She wrote to Pedro Ibáñez, in Trianos. He replied "with two full sheets of contradiction and theology" intended to crush the idea.

"I told him that his theology was no help to me in trying to follow Christ's councils of perfection and embrace my vow of poverty and that his scholarship did me no favor towards reaching that end; and if I found anyone to help me, I would be delighted."

(The memory of her disappointment makes her forget, for once, her need to show herself as always guided by theologians.)

Then, as Teresa tells it, Ibáñez wrote that he had changed his mind. Her Provincial sent word that she "was free to come and go as she liked." "They" (and she simply states it as if it were not odd) warned her that at the forthcoming elections she would be made Prioress: so she wrote at once that all should vote against her. She knew that the briefs for her convent would come soon and asked for guidance. When the Voice said, "You must go at once. If you want a cross, there is one waiting for you in Avila," she assumed that It spoke of the priorate of the Incarnation and tried to ignore the Voice as a figment of her imagination, but Father Domenech insisted that she must believe, and go. Dõna Luisa was grieved, "as she had been to considerable trouble" to get the Provincial's permission for that visit.

She left in a bewildering, simultaneous sensation of joy and grief over the acceptance of His promised cross.

The brief arrived on the day she reached Avila. It was in the hands of the Bishop, Fray Pedro, and "another gentleman." Fray Pedro persuaded the Bishop to let the convent be founded, "which was no small task, but as he was very fond of people whom he saw so determined to serve the Lord, he was soon brought around to favor it." Also, on the day of her arrival, de Ovalle fell ill and took to bed, which gave her an excuse to visit the house and oversee the workmen, and on St. Bartholomew's day she moved in with her nuns.

This is her account. Two months in a nutshell, and with no hint of why the Incarnation, once so glad to be rid of her, suddenly wants her for its Prioress. When she left out so much, why didn't she omit that? Was it because she felt the need to preach the importance of accepting any cross for the sake of Christ's Cross, or because García warned her that things which were common knowledge must be mentioned — but in such a way as to avoid increasing Father Angel's enmity?

At least, the whole story is now well documented; and Fray Pedro can get the credit she longed to give him.

Chapter 18 ❀ Bishop Mendoza; Humble Founding of St. Joseph's Discalced Convent in Avila

I

Fray Pedro had talked warmly about Doña Teresa's inspiration to found in poverty, like his Alcantarines. The news spread fast, and on one point the Bishop and Father Angel were agreed: it was madness that could only discredit the Carmelites and cause the Bishop more trouble. How could she imagine that a city so opposed to her founding a convent decently endowed would give alms to support a nest of beggars?

And here it was late June. The brief would be coming at any time now and Teresa would plunge into action. What could persuade her to stop scandalizing the town and settle down quietly?

Angel de Salazar thought he knew. Teresa was power hungry and wanted recognition; it was as simple as that. And, by great good fortune, the Incarnation was about to hold its triennial election.

Father Angel believed that he could control that election. He was not the last Provincial to make that mistake during Teresa's lifetime, though one would expect any man to have known better. Women had few rights, nuns less than most women, and what they had they clung to. One right of nuns was to hold free elections of their prioresses. Only a man who despised women could have believed that he could control that election — or that any woman would be fool enough to snatch the impossible task of governing a convent that utterly distrusted her.

Father Angel made just that assumption. And Teresa was in a quandary. There was the outside, hideous chance that the nuns could be bullied into obeying their Provincial, and the furor caused by a runaway nun would pale before the furor caused by a runaway prioress. But still, the brief from Rome would come soon, and she should be there to take possession swiftly and secretly.

What happened next we know chiefly from de Ovalle's testimony for his sister-in-law's canonization. When de Guzmán dropped dead, Teresa saw devils fighting for his soul over his coffin, and had a premonition that María might die suddenly, too. As de Guzmán's wife, María had neglected her religious duties and Teresa persuaded her to take them up again. Now she had also dropped dead, and de Ovalle came to Toledo with the bad news, but, also with the consolation that María's priest had told him all was well: María had confessed and taken communion only a day or two before her death.

De Ovalle found Teresa unable to decide whether to stay in Toledo or to go back to Avila. He had left Avila for Alba, himself; Juana was pregnant again and did not want to bear another child in the unfinished house. But, de Ovalle testifies, he had barely got back to Alba when Teresa called him back to Avila. When she made up her mind to leave, Doña Luisa was angry and refused her any escort for the journey. So he came, as Yomar was still in Toro, and Teresa would have to stay at the Incarnation, needing an excuse to see her workmen daily; he also fell ill on the way and took to bed in his supposed future home.

(This Ribera cites as a miracle, adding that on the very day Teresa won the Bishop's permission to use her brief, de Ovalle sprang from his bed exclaiming, "Praise God, lady, there's no need for me to be ill any longer!")

As Teresa says, the brief arrived on the day she reached Avila. That it ever came is largely thanks to Pedro de Alcántara, whose own experience as founder of an order had taught him much. He knew, for example, that a request from a Jesuit for a convent to be directed by a Mendoza would be self-defeating: Cardinal Reinoso, natural son of Pope Paul III and a sound politican, knew that Spanish anti-Semitism must not be allowed to disturb the relationship between the Spanish Crown and the Vatican. Fray Pedro also was heedful of the Gospel warning, "Make ye therefore friends of the mammon of unrightousness." Fray Rodrigo de Cabera, Prior of Mancera, a house of the Military Order of Alcántara, was flagrantly Jew-hating; and his patron was Don Luis de Toledo, Lord of the Five Towns. With García's help he got him to lend his name along with those of two distinguished Toledan clerics, to the project of a noble nun, now living in Toledo: the Most Illustrious and Religious Doña Teresa, who wanted to form an independent convent.

The brief he procured wisely sidesteps all the opposition he himself had faced down in making a "barefoot reform." It permits the Most Illustrious and Religious Doña Teresa to found a convent under the ordinary; its patronesses, Yomar and her mother, are named as "Doña Guiomar de Ulloa and Doña Aldonza de Guzmán, illustrious widows of Avila." This convent should be under the jurisdiction of the Bishop of Avila, but further overseen by the Prior of Mancera and the two Toledan clerics.

As the Most Illustrious Doña Teresa had originally been a Carmelite, the brief further specifies that neither she nor the illustrious widows "be seen as rebels," or disturbed "then or at any other time, publicly or secretly, directly or indirectly, by superiors, friars, reformers or other visitors of the said Order of Santa María del Carmelo or by other ecclesiastics, judges, or persons of whatever title including the apostolic."

(Yes, in founding the Alcantarines Fray Pedro had indeed learned much from experience.)

Teresa, on reaching the Incarnation, sent Gaspar Daza to ask Father Angel for one last time to let her found as a Carmelite. He refused, of course; and since he had been wisely flattered into believing that he had the forthcoming election well in hand, he left town—to indicate that the nuns had been under no pressure. (When the election was held, Teresa did not receive a single vote.)

The brief had been delivered to Fray Pedro, the chief negotiator. He was staying with a friend, Don Francisco Dávila (whose wife, by the way, was a daughter of the late magnificent Moisés Rubén de Bracamonte). Bishop Mendoza, having read the brief and seen with relief that it did not apply to a convent founded in poverty, withdrew to his most remote country villa, El Tiemblo. A pity to disappoint the good old saint, but Avila was currently a madhouse and a man needs peace and quiet.

Pedro de Alcántara was dying. After the Bishop's defection he took to bed in Don Francisco's house. His first letter to Mendoza apologizes for dictating; he was too weak to hold a pen. His next is in his own hand, though a very shaky hand. It begs Mendoza to hear out his messengers, Master Daza, Francisco de Salcedo, and Gonzalo de Aranda: then he will see that even founded in poverty the convent will do good. "The spirit of the Lord will dwell in it," and Mendoza, in protecting it, "will do much for [his] own glory and the benefit of the Church." He also adds that the brief had cost him five thousand reales (approximately 450 ducats).

The messengers brought back word that the Bishop refused to reconsider. Fray Pedro ordered a litter and had himself carried to El Tiemblo. Mendoza saw that the poor old man was near death, and let himself be persuaded to mount a horse and ride back with him to Avila and interview Teresa in person for the first time.

That was that. At once, as it had been with his sister, he and Teresa were friends. No Mendoza ever strove for "perfection" or even "much prayer," but Teresa took the whole family as they were and loved them as they were. Friends, I have often thought, are born, not made. Soon enough Alvaro Mendoza's friendship with Teresa would cost him troubles of the kind he most disliked, but he had no regrets.

His refusal to grant a license had lasted a month and a half. In mid-August of 1562 he gave it, permitting Teresa "to live under the ancient rule of St. Albert," of which he doubtless knew no more than did Teresa — or María de Jesús. The one scholar in his family was Diego de Mendoza, whose library of forbidden books Philip II bought up after Don Diego's death.

But a license was not all Teresa needed.

II

Teresa had a convent but no nuns. Her nieces and cousins who were Carmelites did not dare to run away; those who were not could not get their parents' permission. Fray Pedro had persuaded a de Bracamonte connection, young Doña Isabel de Ortega, to give up her plan to enter the Royal Nunnery in Madrid and join Teresa. According to the process which makes her the Blessed Isabel del Santo Espíritu, she and Teresa then went to mass "in the church of Moisés Rubén de Bracamonte." But that August, her parents were running scared. She had to wait and Teresa had to take what she could get.

Yomar sent her a servant girl María de la Paz. Antonia de Heneo, at twenty-six, was the youngest of the original lot; she remained a problem case until her death, "addicted to doing her body so much violence that her prioress and confessor" had to "amuse her and keep her busy with outside occupations." María de Avila was thirty-six, a sister of the priest who became the convent chaplain; she brought a dowry of 17,000 maravedis (375 maravedis equals one ducat). She was mildly retarded: "talking to her was like talking to a child." The fourth was one of Gaspar Daza's penitents, a lady with a past, aged forty-one. While she is admitted to have been "very gallant" — that is, promiscuous — as

Ursula de los Santos she is said to have become "very recollected." What was more to the immediate point, she brought a dowry of five hundred ducats, without which the Convent of San José de Avila could not have survived its beginnings.

Teresa calls this group "four poor orphans without dowry"; the most tactful way to sum it up is that the convent's beginnings were made on sheer determination and little else. Her own last maravedi went for two statuettes, St. Joseph and Our Lady, to go above the doors to the chapel and to the enclosure, and a three pound bell—bought cheap because it was cracked.

On the eve of St. Bartholomew's day (August 17), Teresa lay awake all night. At dawn she slipped away from the Incarnation, just as twenty-seven years before she had slipped away from her father's house to enter it. She met her "poor orphans," and with them her cousins Inés and Ana Tapia, who had gone home for the night, the more readily to escape undetected.

Gaspar Daza said the first mass and reserved the Host; thereafter the chapel could not be "unmade" without sacrilege. Besides Teresa and her novices, the mass had a congregation of five: Francisco de Salcedo, Gonzalo de Aranda, Juana and her husband de Ovalle, and young Father Julián de Avila, the convent's future chaplin.

Teresa and her postulants took their new habits—of coarse *sayal*, not the Carmelites fine-woven serge. They "discalced"—that is, they took off their shoes and put on hemp-soled *alpargatas*. (The Discalced Carmelites, as Teresa's Order is still called, were not literally "barefoot.") Then since the grilles were still not installed, they withdrew to a temporary enclosure behind loose lumber and straw matting.

It was accomplished, as His Majesty had promised. St. Joseph and Our Lady guarded the doors, the cracked bell had rung to tell Avila that a convent was founded and its first mass about to be celebrated, the mass was said and the Host reserved. Teresa had never felt such exultant happiness. The reaction came, she remembered, three or four hours later when she and her nuns sat down to their first meal together.

What was she doing there, a woman who had broken her holy vow to the Carmelites? What lunacy to think one could lock twelve women away in that tiny house and keep them stable and contented in God's service! Ursula's dowry would soon be spent, and they would have to starve or run away, for who would give alms to these poor souls fooled by her madness, her arrogant disobedience?

The agony was peculiarly lonely, the culmination of six weeks' loneliness, for as she says, "I had nobody to talk to, I had not even been given a confessor." This was true, though three Orders now try to forget it. The Carmelites had disowned her, the Jesuits had a healthy fear of the woman who had cost them three priests and a Rector, and García, not yet "given to prayer" despite his easy promises in Toledo, preferred to stay clear; he disliked unpleasantness. Even Gaspar Daza, though he had said mass and entrusted the penitent Ursula to Teresa's care, did not want to get further into the crossfire of warring opinions.

Teresa went into the chapel and knelt before the Host. But she did not pray; step by step, she reasoned herself out of her anguish of despair. She had asked for trials and got them: "some good ones." She would still meet opposition, and to run a convent well is no easy task; she knew that and had known it all along. So, where was her courage, now that she finally had her chance to repay Christ in some small part for His forgiveness?

Forcing the words out aloud, with an effort, she made her plain and sanely limited vow. She would do all she could do with good conscience to enable these novices to take their final vows under proper authority. She would take care that nothing could be said against them and much in their favor in order that their convent should be fully authorized, even by the Carmelite Provincial, and fully acceptable in the eyes of all who now opposed it.

The effect of that effort startled her. So suddenly that it seemed as if the devil knew that he had lost the game and fled, she was calm and confident. But she had not slept the night before and it had been an exhausting day. She went to her cell, lay down, and immediately fell asleep.

She was not allowed to sleep for long.

Chapter 19 ❀ Saving St. Joseph's from Being Closed by the City Council

I

Teresa leaves out the drama; as she tells it, she was wakened by knocking at the door and received orders to go back to the Incarnation along with Inés and Ana. She went, expecting to be put in its prison and actually looking forward to its solitude after so much coping with people. But she "explained [her] position," and the Prioress was appeased. On the next day, she appeared before the Provincial and did well with him in public, and better thereafter in private, for he said that she might go back to her convent once the city was satisfied. There had already been one council meeting on the matter, and another was being called.

Julián de Avila is one of the two most trustworthy writers who told of their part in Teresa's story. According to him, when the cracked bell rang for the first mass, the city went half-mad: one would have thought that Avila was simultaneously swept "by plague, fire and an invading army" — and all because a handful of women wanted to live a life of seclusion and prayer!

He did not exaggerate the excitement, though he censored its cause. To the public mind, this was no innocent handful of pious ladies. The word had spread that the Jewess, possessed by the devil, was about to set up a nest of *alumbradas* like those in Extremadura, famed for their hellish blend of heresy and sexual excesses. And, as servants in Valladolid had already shown, an investigation by the Inquisition can endanger the innocent along with the guilty.

90

Teresa escaped the convent prison chiefly because the newly elected Prioress was the child of her brother Francisco's second wife; she had an equal dislike for Teresa's enthusiasms and for the dangerous growth of anti-Semitism in Avila.

The city council had also sanely tried to put down Teresa's convent on grounds that would not interest the Inquisition in Avila. At its first meeting, on St. Bartholomew's Day, when Teresa and her "poor orphans" took possession, two men, identified only as Señor Yera and Señor Perálvarez, introduced one Lazarillo Dávila, "a pitcher-vender," who claimed that "Valle [de Ovalle] who bought the house of the defunct cleric," enlarged it in a way that endangered "the fountains" where he drew the water he sold to the neighborhood.

His plea was accepted, and it was moved and seconded that "Valle's" new wing and walls be condemned, and the occupants of the house be evicted.

The Carmelite Prior, Heredia, had the Andalusian aristocrat's native gift for playing both sides of the street. As the Bishop was still in town and was getting on well with Teresa, Heredia went to him and suggested that he go to the convent with the friars to make Teresa's removal as painless as possible. Mendoza did, and his secretary went with him; the secretary's notebook records it that Doña Teresa and her cousins "left behind some others who hid behind boards and mats as they had no other enclosure."

To this María Bautista adds that she was visiting the Incarnation when Teresa came back, "and after she had prostrated herself before the Prioress" she went to her room "and the Prioress sent her up a very nice supper."

Father Angel, hastily recalled to Avila, felt safe in telling Teresa that she might go back to her convent if the city approved. He was sure that it would not, and that its position would be upheld be the Royal Council; for that same day the clerics of Avila had met, and with no pussyfooting about pitcher-venders they convened a junta to be held on the following Sunday at three; and what a junta!

The laity summoned were all the Most Magnificent Dons This-or-that. The clergy were abbots from all parts of the see, priors, dignitaries from the Cathedral and eminent *letrados*. Only one of those present did not fit in; the Jesuits recalled Baltasar Alvarez from Medina — to support Teresa, they now claim, though day after day throughout the lengthy proceedings he never opened his mouth.

García de Toledo was absent, obviously by his own choice since one so *muy principal*, and subprior of Santo Tomás, as well, would not have been overlooked. The prior Serrano came, bringing a Dominican who at thirty-four was already a widely known *letrado*: Domingo Báñez.

(The court clerk set him down as Pedro Ibáñez, a name which had become connected with Teresa's in the public mind, along with those of her other displaced confessors. Down in Seville when Pedro Ibáñez had been dead for ten years, another copyist would made the same slip; Teresa had gained fame, and scandals about her friends died hard.)

Such a junta was not called for small reason; but a runaway nun who was a suspected *alumbrada* and a known *conversa* was no small reason in the Spain

91

of 1562. The sense of the meeting was, overwhelmingly, that a priest be sent to consume the Host and evict the poor orphans.

On the first day, exactly one voice was raised in opposition. Domingo Báñez had not met Teresa, but he had heard enough from Pedro Ibáñez, a brother with a first-rate mind, now stupidly exiled, to be convinced that she was the victim of mass hysteria.

The Carmelite chronicler gave him a long and fiery speech, which pours scorn on all present: it borrows, word for word, from Julián de Avila on the town's reacting as if threatened by "fire, plague, and an invading army." It is far from the unemotional, clear-headed style which eventually won Domingo Báñez the most coveted university position in Spain: the Chair of Prime in Salamanca. Teresa's second-hand report sounds more like him:

"He said that no real reason to dissolve the convent had been given as yet; the matter should be considered carefully, and there was plenty of time for that. Besides, the whole thing was the Bishop's business — or something like that. He did a lot of good, considering the fury, for they determined not to act immediately."

The Bishop's secretary then presented the brief which showed that he was acting under orders from the Vatican; but its flaw was obvious. The "illustrious widows" were now out of the picture; the convent proposed would be "discalced" — i.e., unshod: part of the current dangerous left-wing movement within the Church.

The junta adjourned, first calling for another to be held nine days later. At this second junta, the Bishop presided, and Master Daza was given leave to speak.

"He fought as if it was for his own life and honor," Teresa says. Once again, the meeting voted against sending a priest to consume the Host. "But," Teresa adds, "things had got to such a state that they would have bet their lives, as people say, that [the convent] would be dissolved."

Next the city council turned on Daza. He said that the Host was reserved at the Bishop's orders, which made it none of their business. The city placed constabulary around the building to prevent anyone's going in to celebrate another mass; the constables also tried, once, to break in by force, but the four women inside barricaded the entrances with lumber from the unfinished construction work. Meanwhile the city had appealed to the Royal Council, saying that "the convent, if founded in poverty, would work grave prejudice to the city and to the nation."

This sounds ludicrous, but such an appeal, sent by the junta and not the city council, could have ended Teresa's career before it began. Pope Adrian IV had ceded extraordinary powers to the Spanish Royal Council under Charles V. Thereafter, even Papal Nuncios discovered that they could carry out no directives without the Royal Council's approval; as the saying went, "There is no Pope in Spain." But there was a King; and Philip II was obsessed with certain notions about the monastic Orders.

In particular, he saw all cloistered Orders as a menace: who knew what went on in them? At one point, he threatened that if the Pope did not outlaw the cloisters, he himself would "depopulate the afore-said convents and monasteries, which are full of vicious and scandalous characters." And all unendowed, mendicant Orders "reformed or not, nuns as well as monks, should be reduced to the Observance," (sent back, that is, to their parent Orders).

Luckily, the appeal to the Royal Council went from the city, which Father Angel saw as an impudent interference of the secular arm in ecclesiastical matters. This actually so offended him that he overruled Teresa's prioress and gave her permission to contest the suit. Teresa also got a letter of encouragement from Pedro de Alcántara, now on his deathbed in the house of García de Toledo's half-brother, the Count of Oropesa.

Lawsuits are expensive, and Francesco de Salcedo was frightened and hiding out; but Gonzalo de Aranda was braver and he knew both ecclesiastical and civil law. He went to Madrid, pleaded Teresa's cause before the Royal Council, and managed to impede a settlement until the city was sunk in debt and dropped the case. As Julián de Avila gleefully reports, its investigators, supplied by the Royal Council, had to be paid by the day for eleven months.

But in only five months Teresa would be back in San José.

II

From August to September Teresa was trapped in the Incarnation, forced to breathe its poisonous atmosphere of hate and distrust. She could send no messages to her "poor orphans." She could only pray. Once she heard the Voice: "Why are you discouraged? Don't you know that I have power?" But she was desperately tired.

In November, Bishop Mendoza urged her to give up founding in poverty; he would find her a patroness. Teresa wrote to Fray Pedro that poverty was not essential; she had decided to give it up.

The dying man had himself propped up and wrote her a note in a wavering hand. She must fight it out. God was on her side and with a little patience she would win.

He died four days later. Twice after his death Teresa thought she saw him and heard him remind her gently of their friendship. She was not afraid of ghosts, only happy in Fray Pedro's well earned happiness, for by the light around him she knew that he was now in glory.

Nevertheless, she finally weakened and agreed to accept an endowment. Her decision made, she spent the first half of the night in unhappy prayer, and once more was visited by Fray Pedro's ghost. But now he was stern; he demanded harshly that she keep to her first purpose "and disappeared at once."

Don Francisco Dávila, Mendoza's and Fray Pedro's friend, had arranged for the endowment. Teresa told him that she had changed her mind and was determined to live by Fray Pedro's example. She did not object when the Bishop made himself responsible for their (literal) daily bread, but for the rest she would live on whatever dowries nuns might bring and alms people might give.

She believed that Holy Poverty would be her lifelong rule.

93

What happened next both Teresa and Pedro Ibáñez concealed for the sake of García de Toledo. He had let Teresa down, and did not attend the junta; but now he could be useful. The ducal families resented the Royal Council, which infringed on their ancient powers just as it infringed on those of the Vatican. And, Father Angel bowed to the great nobles. It had made him uneasy to displease a Mendoza; to displease the magnificent de Toledos — a family which included the Duke of Alba, the Marquis of Velada, and Don Luis, Lord of the Five Towns — would be more than he could take. If García's old friend Pedro Ibáñez could shame him for his broken promises, persuade him to rally the clan and take a stand on Teresa's side, however belatedly, all would be well.

By Teresa's account, a priest (like Ibáñez) with the ecclesiastical degree of *presentado*, who had not been in Avila during these troubles, "happened" to turn up and somehow brought it about that the Provincial let her go back to her convent with several nuns from the Incarnation.

Ibáñez, in his defense of Teresa written for Inquisitor Soto, tells of a letter in which she urged him to pass on some words of Christ to "a certain man who had not drawn close to God," though when they had parted he and the "certain man" had agreed together that they would do so (García, it seems, made such promises readily); "and though I had no wish to go back to that place," Ibáñez goes on, "I went to plead with this certain man again."

Pedro Ibáñez' plea was effective. "The man" broke down and wept, though, Ibáñez says, "he was far from being effeminate — indeed, quite the contrary."

Teresa tells one of her literal truths when she says that this *padre presentado* told her that he had "no reason *of his own* for coming," but he knew "in some way" (such as her letter) that the Lord wanted it.

So in a matter of a few days, all was arranged, and she could go back to her convent.

García became Teresa's confessor, and when he oversaw the addendum to the book she had finished in Toledo, he wanted suitable glories to describe her triumphant return to San José de Avila. Teresa could not lie about the things of God. Let me *underline* her modifiers, so unlike any she ever used about the "experiences" she describes in her book as she had first ended it, in Toledo:

"The day we went back gave me the greatest consolation. When I was praying in the chapel I *almost* went into a rapture and saw Christ who *seemed to me* to put a crown on my head and thank me for what I had done for His Mother. . . . Another time, it *seemed as if* I saw Our Lady wearing a white cloak and we were all sheltered under it."

(Dominican influence; by their dearest legend, a newcomer to Heaven sees no Dominicans until She opens her cloak and reveals their hiding-place.)

In worldly matters, however, Teresa does not hesitate to draw a long bow. The town, she says, immediately became devoted to the convent, their former persecutors gave them alms, they took more nuns, and since they will never be more than thirteen, they have all they need. And by a coincidence, María de Jesús, her inspiration in Toledo, founded her own convent at just the same time.

Four strange, wandering chapters follow, full of flashbacks, visions, pre-visions, answers to prayer and the like, including her celebrated angel with the fiery lance.

Then she ends her book on a note of asperity for which one who knows the story behind the story cannot blame her. She and her nuns, she says, have lived "in health and contentment throughout these years," and those who find it hard "can blame their own lack of spirit and take themselves off to another convent where they can save themselves according to what spirit they have."

The untold story begins with the fact that García, shamed into bolder action, did not effect Father Angel's immediate capitulation but only his offer of a compromise: one so distasteful that it is no wonder that Teresa only went "almost" into a rapture. It was the first of many compromises in her remarkable career. Musicians, painters, poets, are not so hampered; but artists in the medium of human life are often faced with a choice between sterile failure and accepting compromise, learning the art of the possible.

Unless or until they abandon the initial vision, which Teresa never did, it is not a happy choice, ever; but it has to be made.

Chapter 20 ❈ *Teresa's Constitutions for Discalced Carmelite Nuns*

I

The story of Teresa's next five years has been richly embroidered: the little convent presented as a shrine to which great ladies thronged to witness the Saint's raptures and levitation — levitation from which she begged her nuns to hold her down in order to prevent such a public show of her sanctity.

The truth, so much of which Teresa was not free to tell, is more edifying.

To begin with, there was Father Angel's compromise.

García's cousins at the Incarnation, Doña Ana and Doña Quiteria, were, you recall, kin to the Marquis of Velada, another de Toledo. Father Angel was only persuaded to let Teresa go back to San José if one of them went with her to be the convent's Prioress, further supported by three other "instructresses" of the lady's own choosing.

Doña Ana consented, but she could not find three nuns who were both unsympathetic to Teresa and willing to leave the Incarnation. She persuaded Ana Gómez and María Ordóñez, but for the third she had to take a cousin of Teresa's, Isabel de la Peña. Isabel had put up a few ducats towards buying the house, but she changed her mind and hung back when the Tapia girls slipped away to join Teresa and the "orphans."

Teresa had ruled against titles, and in San José, Doña Ana became Mother Ana de San Juan. At the Incarnation, this relinquishment of her title was seen as a striking act of humility, but according to evidence gathered at San José, her humility went no further. While she stayed at the convent, her chief business was humiliating Teresa.

Teresa was not only submissive but her face seemed to show some untroubled source of inner happiness. Ana Gómez, who became Ana de los Angeles, quickly shifted her allegiance. She was the most intelligent of the lot; she became Teresa's friend and, in time, one of her most constantly re-elected prioresses. Cousin Isabel de la Peña was unobjectionable and undistinguished. María Ordóñez did not take "a name in religion"; she called herself María Isabel. (No St. Isabel entered the calendar until 1629.) She drops from the convent records after three years.

In a book Teresa wrote just before she left San José for a wider field, *El Camino de Perfección*, she says that she has won permission to extend the novitiate to four years if it seems advisable, and only wishes she could have made it thirteen! I expect María Isabel was a case in point.

In March Bishop Mendoza finally obtained a brief which permitted the convent to be founded in poverty and told Doña Ana that she was now free to return to the more congenial life of the Incarnation. (Five years later, Doña Ana told General Rubeo that she left because of ill-health and her need to procure "fifteen ducats with which to secure the confessor she wanted." Rubeo found her "intelligent.")

Since four "instructresses" from the Incarnation had been ordered by Father Angel, Doña Ana sent Isabel's sister, María de Cepeda, to be her replacement. María was as dim as Isabel; despite Teresa's habit of making prioresses of her nieces and cousins, those two were never advanced, nor do Teresa's letters mention them.

The new brief having released Doña Ana, there could be an election; and Teresa became Prioress of her own convent. She drew up constitutions which specified the way of dress, the hours of the religious offices read in choir, for private prayer and rest, for communal silence — never absolute, but limited to brief, necessary questions and answers — and for recreation, in which all must join. The primitive rule forbade all meat but poultry; Teresa added "except when necessary." Health, she believed, sometimes demands red meat. Similarly, the discipline was not to be leather, but a switch of birch twigs only used on penitential occasions and in view of all, not in private self-torture. All excesses of fasting and bodily penance were outlawed.

The rule stressed "mortification," by which Teresa meant the cultivation of selfless living, each for all, and all for God. It is a rule which couples the highest ideals with the utmost sanity; I have seen no other like it in her time and place.

In August, Father Angel finally gave Teresa permission to stay in her convent permanently, "with Doña María de Cepeda, Ana Gómez, María Ordóñez and Isabel de la Peña as instructresses." (*Sic*: one sister a Doña, the other not.) This made things legal, and within the next four months Teresa gained three more novices. The first of them, María Bautista, brought their number up to nine.

She was the girl who laughingly offered Teresa a thousand ducats to start a second Royal Nunnery. When she entered, a marriage was being arranged for her, but as we have seen, the pickings were poor; she preferred to take her dowry, five hundred ducats, and join Teresa.

According to her own memoirs, she gave Teresa a thousand ducats to found a convent, and was granted a vision of Christ at the pillar: "He was greatly wounded and suffering and He thanked me very much for that almsgiving and asked me to show favor to that convent as its first novice and told me that He would be greatly served in it."

It is typical of María Bautista that she remembers it thus, and especially that Christ thanked her for a round thousand. Her eventual success with the nobility owed nothing to poor-mouthing. She knew instinctively that the big bequests go to the financially solid foundations. She became Teresa's most prosperous prioress. Back then, Teresa saw her ambition as religious ardor.

Isabel Ortega, Pedro de Alcántara's find, came with six hundred ducats from the fortune established by Moisés Rubén de Brancamonte, and would have been worth having without a single maravedi.

To her tenth nun, our gratitude is overdue. Ribera, who was over-credulous of local tales, says that María Dávila came "dressed in fine silks and wearing all the gold jewelry she could beg, accompanied by all the *caballeros* of the city, for she was related to the leading families and all were amazed at the splendid marriages she could have made."

In fact her background was modest and her dowry, two hundred and fifty ducats, would not have gone far in that tight market for husbands; but she brought real value. She took the name of María de San Jerónimo; and Jerónimo, as Teresa always called her, was solidly good, a bulwark in that convent for twenty years. What's more, after Teresa's death she produced a memorial that is remarkable for its dearth of fancy.

Like all of us, she had a few false memories, but she does not over-decorate. Where others reported Teresa's sky-high levitations, San Jerónimo only remembers Teresa's once having told her that at communion she had been so full of joy that she felt as if she were losing weight and being drawn upright, tip-toe; a sensation which she overcame by clutching the altar rail. Instead of marvels, San Jerónimo recalls Teresa's laughter, her courage, her gift for making friends, and her singular lack of resentment when scandals were raised against her.

San Jerónimo's quality is epitomized in her apology for having so few specific anecdotes to offer: "While *La Santa* was alive," she says, "we all took her so much for granted that we didn't think of writing anything down." This nun was blessedly devoid of the "hypocrisy and superstition" against which Teresa waged her lifelong battle.

Such was the group which became the cornerstone of Teresa's Order, the Discalced Carmelites: the four "poor orphans," five blood relations (minus Inés and Ana Tapia, who did not return until better times), plus two more young girls: and all, except for Yomar's servant-girl and her friend Antonia, of "impure blood." They were Teresa's first garrison in the war that the King and the Pope could not win by the sword.

But Teresa called her convents garrisons only when she wrote for her nuns; when she wrote for men's eyes, they were "little dove-cotes of the Lord." That was part of the necessary strategy while, throughout her life, these garrisons were threatened: alternately by the King and the Pope, and continuously by the Inquisition.

II

The convent was founded in the face of public opinion, and public opinion was slow to change. Teresa had eleven nuns, but for five years she could not reach her proposed limit of twelve, and if Bishop Mendoza had not given them "bread and medicines and other charities," they could not have survived, for their supporters were not only few but afraid to make their support conspicuous.

And comprehensibly so. The King's opinion of unendowed and cloistered convents was common knowledge. By 1564 he was increasing his demands that the Pope "reduce to the observance" all such "unchaste and vicious people" rather than force him to "depopulate" their houses and purify Spain.

But the Pope reacted in anger. He sent bulls to the various monastic reforms confirming their right to be considered legitimate members of their parent Orders. These reached Spain in 1565, and while they did not make Teresa more popular, they put her convent legally in the clear.

This also satisfied Isabel Ortega's family: when she professed as Isabel de Santo Domingo in the October of that year, her dowry was raised from six hundred to twelve hundred ducats.

But the city at large remained resentful. Though its first costly *pleito* had been dropped in June of '63, there was still strong feeling about the *alumbrada's* nest of relatives and other riffraff which remained, a public disgrace, "in the center of the city." (A phrase often repeated, as if the convent's central location were the ultimate insult to Avilan probity.) Thriftily, the city waited for some local issue to surface that could be handled by its own legal staff, and at last one came.

Teresa's rule called for periods of solitary prayer. She knew that prayer comes best in a setting made for no other purpose, just as her little oratory in the Incarnation, with its pictures and images, had helped her to center her wandering mind. But for these girls to make similar oratories of their cells would be to break the rule that all things be held in common. Teresa began to make little "hermitages" in the house; one under the stairs, one in a disused winecellar, wherever a quiet nook could be found. They were named for saints — Hilarion, first of the desert fathers, Jerome, the greatest of them and for souls nearer Teresa's own heart, Augustine, Mary Magdalene, "La Samaritana" — the woman at the well.

But in that tiny house they were only token solitudes. Teresa decided to risk a little money on building a few shelters in the garden where her nuns, turn and turn about, could kneel, alone with His Majesty. She had their walls plastered and coaxed a local artist to decorate them with scenes from the Stations of the Cross. Julián de Avila says that the results were quite beautiful and moving.

They were also just what the city wanted. Señor Peralvarez Serrano once more produced Lazarillo, the pitcher-vender. The hermitages cast a shadow on the fountains; in winter, they would make the water freeze.

Teresa, in the name of "the poor sister of San José," wrote her protest to the council: not only could those tiny shelters make no difference to the temperature outside the convent walls, but the prayers offered in them could only benefit the whole city. Her letter was ignored. The legal process began in early January and dragged on into late March. Even before the decision was reached, the city had condemned the garden wall and had it torn down. This they rebuilt at their own expense, but the hermitages were lost.

The Bishop came at Easter, bristling with ducal resentment. In Julián de Avila's name he bought land for more hermitages on the far side of the house. His sister Doña María gave the first of them, and asked that it be dedicated to St. Augustine; and since on that side of the house the convent's scandalous indulgence in "mental prayer" was hidden from the public eye, the matter was finally dropped.

It is customary to write off this trouble over the hermitages as petty spite on the part of a city whose whole objection to Teresa's convent had been irrational. This is grossly unfair to Avila, whose point of view was part of a picture that Spain, with its proud haul of twelve Counter-Reformation saints, still likes to forget. Too many of those in San José were of heretical illuminism, and had "impure blood."

Because of this same will to forget, next to nothing is known of Teresa's visit from Inquisitor Soto, and what is told about it is misleading.

It was nothing that Teresa could report accurately, either.

Chapter 21 ❀ *García de Toledo, Domingo Báñez, and* The Way of Perfection

I

The hermitages had been a flagrant public display of the convent's suspicious addiction to mental prayer. And, as "Jerónimo" tells us with her incurable honesty, there was always "talk about Teresa and friars." Teresa had overcome her compulsive confessing "once [she] had daughters," (as one of her own letters tells us), but the town knew what it knew: four Jesuits and one Dominican already saved from her lusts, and clearly García de Toledo was left equally ensnared only because his Prior was afraid to offend one so *muy principal*!

In another, safer context, Teresa tells of "a great false witness" raised against García. In consequence, his Prior, Serrano, had a problem. He knew that it would be wise to replace García, and he believed that Domingo Báñez could handle the woman. Báñez, it was true, had urged the junta against moving with haste to "depopulate" her convent; but he also had a remarkable knack for getting ahead and taking care of himself. It would be safest, however, to ask an Inquisitor to investigate her convent first. If such an investigation sprang up later, Serrano saw, it would put him in a bad light for not having suggested it himself. True or false, those stories about claiming to see visions, combined with her sexual reputation, could mean only one thing to the public.

It can only be proved that Báñez replaced García after the Inquisitor's visit. But I credit Serrano with that inspection, and I can't blame him.

II

Teresa tries to imply that Inquisitor Soto came to San José at her request. Later writers ignore this, either omitting his inspection totally or explaining it away as a casual visit from an old friend of the family. Teresa's account is part of a statement she gave to a censor from the Seville Inquisition, as a time of a graver peril. The words are hers, though she speaks of herself in the third person.

"Around thirteen years ago, more or less, after the foundation of San José, the man who is now Bishop of Salamanca went there. He was an Inquisitor — I don't know whether from Madrid or Toledo — whose name was Soto. She managed to talk with him in order to reassure herself more and gave him a full account of everything; and he said it did not concern his office, because everything she saw and heard only made her more firm in the Catholic faith, as she always was and always will be ... And ... he also told her to write everything out, for Master Avila was a man who understood much about prayer and she could be contented with what he wrote back to her. And she did that, and wrote him all about her sins and her life."

In the copy of this very lengthy statement that was made for use at Teresa's canonization, all mention of her sins is removed or reworded to sound like saintly scruples over nothing. One hundred and eight words are so deleted; but an addition is also made. García de Toledo's name is inserted in the list of *letrados* whom Teresa mentions as having consulted when she felt the need for guidance as to correct theology.

The passage I cited is Teresa's only published mention of Soto. He was satisfied with what he found in her convent, and further satisfied by a formal defense written, apparently at García's request, by Pedro Ibáñez.

It begins: "In the city of Avila there is a house of Discalced Carmelites founded in poverty ... [by] a Carmelite nun. This lady, now known as Teresa de Jesús, was formerly Doña Teresa de Ahumada."

She has, it states, been accused by numerous responsible clerics of demonic possession on the grounds of certain religious experiences to which she admits. Her orderly convent, in which she, a lady born, shares the housework with her nuns, is clearly no work of the devil. Yet she herself doubted her experiences, for she knew that their like — visions, revelations, ecstasies — "was going on all over the realm" among "women deceived by the devil"; and "since she judged herself to be a sinner" she feared that she was herself so deceived, as her own confessors told her she was. However, there are nine tests by which a theologian can examine her religious experiences, all nine of which she passes perfectly.

The document then goes on to subject Teresa's "experiences" to these nine tests with scholarly thoroughness. It is a typical defense made for the Inquisition, and only for the Inquisition. Since 1972, a sufficient number of Inquisition documents on Teresa—both of attack and defense—have been published, all so similar in tone and technique to this from Ibáñez that its purpose is unmistakable. Its secondary purpose, no doubt, was to protect García from "the great false witness" then rising, which Teresa mentions elsewhere.

Writing it was one of Pedro Ibáñez's last acts of human kindness. He died before Teresa had finished those four strange chapters of flashbacks which fill us in on so much of her immediate post-conversion story. It is not surprising that on hearing of his death, Teresa imagined seeing him in heaven and, like all good Dominicans, under Our Lady's white cloak.

Until the last decade this document was not admitted to have any connection with Inquisitor Soto's visit to San José: it was simply offered (in well-selected part) as a spontaneous appreciation of Teresa by a former confessor. That she ever needed any such defense was inadmissable until she had been dead for nearly four centuries.

One part of Teresa's own brief report of Soto's visit remains a mystery. "Master Avila" was indeed familiar with "experiences" like Teresa's; his *Filia Audi*—taken from her by the Inquisition four years earlier—is dedicated to a lady who often saw the devil, sometimes disguised as a dog and sometimes as a holy friar. But Juan de Avila was more than once in trouble with the Inquisition, a Dominican institution; and Domingo Báñez, once he had become Teresa's confessor, forbade her to send him the book, believing that it could only endanger her.

Did Teresa, after thirteen overcrowded years, have a false memory? Or is it possible that Soto was setting a trap which she never recognized? Or was Soto developing a distaste for the Inquisition, whose councils he deserted to become Bishop of Salamanca? We'll never know. For that matter, was it he or García who ordered her to write the final chapters which transformed *Concerning God's Mercies* into the so-called *Life*?

In *Foundations*, Teresa's later autobiographical book, begun after she had founded seven convents and the first two monasteries of her order, she explains why she leaves out San José: "When I was in Avila in the year 1562, Father-brother García de Toledo, who was my confessor at that time, ordered me to write about founding that convent,—along with many other things that whoever gets around to reading it will see, if it ever gets out into the light."

We know at least that García rushed and pressured her to write much that she preferred to leave unwritten, after Soto made his one brief visit: a visit whose outcome caused considerable disappointment in the city. Typical of this disappointment is the reaction cited by one of Teresa's nuns of "a certain woman." "She only wished she could live to see the end of the Mother because she knew it would be at the stake like Magdalena de la Cruz or that other Fulana de Santo Domingo."

We also know that Teresa herself wanted to send the book to Juan de Avila, though eventually Domingo Báñez forbade it.

Teresa sent the finished manuscript to García with a letter which, like the preface in which she begs the reader to believe in the sins which she is forbidden to describe "clearly and in detail," deserves more attention than it ever gets, hasty and muddled though it is.

"It wouldn't be wrong for me to confront you with this service so as to oblige you to commend me to Our Lord, — for you well should, considering what I have gone through in seeing myself write and bring to memory so many of my wretchednesses: for I can truly say that I suffered more in writing about the mercies that God has done me than about the sins I committed. I have done what you commanded in going on further about myself — on the condition that you will tear up whatever seems bad to you. I hadn't finished writing when you sent for it; some things may be badly said, and others said twice.

"I beg you to correct it and have it copied if it is to be sent to Master Avila, for someone might recognize my handwriting. I very much want you to give the order to let him see it, as that is why I began to write it; and if it seems to him that I am on the right road I will rest easy — since at this point I am not able to do anything but what within me lies . . .

"So in return for this, hurry to serve his Majesty, just for the sake of doing me kindness. For you will see — and by what is going here right now — how well you will be treating yourself if you give yourself to Him who gives Himself to us without measure, — as you have already begun to do. May He be praised forever, and I hope of His pity that we will come to see each other in the place where we will both see what great things He has done with us and praise Him without end."

But I see her lift her pen and stare at what she has just written. Two years before, in Doña Luisa's palace, she had said exactly what she needed to say in proof that no sinner need be shut off, by the way of fear, from his healing discovery of God's limitless forgiveness: the necessary preface to her treatise on mental prayer in its ascending steps from the soul's own conscious effort to its pure reception of God's grace — as a garden receives the life-giving rain.

Now I see her pen come down and write that last firm line, that protest so universally disregarded: "This book was finished in June, 1562."

Finished, as it should have been let stand, before she left Toledo.

García sent back her manuscript. It would still be some time before he was reduced to novice-master and took himself back to the Indies where his churchly career had begun; but he already smelled trouble. He wanted to invite no more, even for one who had entrusted him with her soul.

III

The love Teresa felt for the faulty and weak would always be more stubborn than the love she gave their betters. Teresa never had to question herself as to whether her feeling for Domingo Báñez was a love in Christ; and while he did

102

not "understand her soul" he understood much of her reality that others had failed to appreciate.

He also knew the best medicine for one who had been forced to spoil a book. He encouraged her to start another at once: a handbook for nuns which is, to my way of thinking, the best book she ever wrote. What's more, it is her only public writing that gives us any inkling of what she was up against.

The *Life* shows a convent begun under difficulties but now at peace and comfortably supported since "nobody now thinks it was wrong." In fact, the convent was still regarded with hate and suspicion; few were not determined to starve it out. A postulant who came in 1567 writes: "We seldom had anything to eat but a little bread and cheese and a bite of fruit, and when we had more, perhaps an egg apiece or a sardine." She herself had been warned against joining the convent, for it was the general talk that they were "all running mad from starvation."

María Bautista recalls that on a day when there was nothing to eat but the Bishop's bread, they marched into the chapel carrying a statue of the Infant Jesus and singing *coplas*. Teresa wrote their *coplas*, songs for all sorts of occasions, including one that dealt with an infestation of lice. One verse and the chorus came down to us from the pen of a sister who still dared to remember that "La Santa" liked a little fun:

> Daughters, since you bear the Cross,
> Be valorous.
> Turn to Jesus your own light
> To favor us.
> He will bring defense to us
> In this fix, as in all.

Chorus:

> Since you have clad us new,
> King Celestial,
> Free from bad company
> This *sayal*.

Teresa also wrote seasonal plays whose authorship is generally denied her because, as you might say, they laughed in Church: as when the bumbling shepherds at the Nativity express their bewilderment.

"What's such a fine lady doing out in a stable with her baby? Why, look at her — she must be the mayor's daughter!"

Teresa knew that sanity demands some laughter, and that order demands constant discipline; but this had no place in *The Life*, or in *Fundaciones*, that masterpiece of public relations. In *Fundaciones*, a brief sketch of her first convent shows us a place of unmarred peace in which Teresa found it a living lesson to be among such angelic souls. How selfless they all were! On rare occasion there was not enough to eat, but if she said that the hungriest should get the most, all would insist that they needed nothing. And as for obedience —

"Obedience, that virtue to which I have always been so devoted"—she once handed a girl a wilted cucumber and told her to plant it in the garden. "A fool would have known that it would only rot," but the girl merely asked "whether she should plant it up and down or sideways. . . . Her obedience so blinded her natural reason that she took it for granted."

And their faith! Dowsers reported that a disused well in the garden was permanently dry, but the nuns were so sure that God would fulfill their need that Teresa gave orders to dig, and the water flowed. They thought it was a miracle, "but the real miracle was their faith."

In truth, that faith needed the constant inspiration that Teresa gave it, and Teresa's second book, *El Camino de Perfección*, speaks to that need. In its "unimproved" first version—praise be, still extant and safe in the Escorial—Teresa exclaims, "What would people think of us if this ever got out into strange hands!"

To that, my answer is, "They would find you human and believable."

She began it, she says, "a few days after" she finished "a story of [her] life" which it seemed likely that "her daughters would not be allowed to read," but which had contained "some thoughts about prayer" that she wanted to pass on to them.

IV

Their purpose, she begins, is to save the Church by prayer: prayer given strength through selfless living. The world is on fire; it can understand their purpose no better than it understood Christ. Why should they expect to be better treated than He was?

But it is not their place to preach. If someone brings them a bit of food in exchange for prayers about a business deal, she agrees to the exchange and actually does pray, though quickly, so that she won't have told a lie; but she does it in the knowledge "that God does not hear such prayers."

Some of them object to praying only for all endangered souls alike and not to shorten their own sentences in Purgatory. Well, unselfish prayer may serve that purpose too, —and if not, tough luck.

As a practical matter, they should realize that telling outsiders about their hardships will not make them more eager to give. And their house is small? At least it hasn't the ugliness of magnificent buildings erected with money that should have gone to the poor. "I hope on the day you build such edifices they will fall down and kill you all!"

They must pray that *letrados* will always be willing to guide them, and also that those same priests may truly serve God. Yet they must realize that men live out in the world and are subject to temptations from which they are sheltered by enclosure: so they must forbear to judge erring priests, and only pray "that they may shut their ears to the Sirens' song."

That thought evokes this sudden appeal to Christ:

"Lord, Thou didst not scorn women! . . . We can do nothing in public to serve

Thee and do not dare speak out truths over which we weep in secret. But . . . Thou art not a judge like the judges in this world, who being sons of Adam and, in a word, *manly*, hold every woman's virtue suspect. Yes, but a time will come when all will be known! I am not speaking on my own account; the world knows my sins and I am glad that they should be known. I only speak because I see what the times are like, and because it is not reasonable to belittle strong, virtuous souls even though they are the souls of women!"

She discusses the basics of holy living: love, detachment from worldly desires, and humility. First she warns against the common failings in a community of women: sentimentalizings, partialities, cliques, jealousies, resentments, sulkings. She points out the truth that it is hard for a small group living in close quarters to love the all-too-human neighbor as oneself. Then she comes to their love for their confessors.

One talks with her confessor alone; so it is only natural to get fond of him, and in all human affection, "however spiritual, there is some degree of sensuality." Consequently, the devil turns a whole battery of scruples on nuns over what they feel for their confessors.

Actually, if the man is good, affection can make us try to please him with our own goodness when the desire to please God is not enough. If he is not, there is danger; and for him to suspect that a nun's love for him is less than pure is the greatest danger of all. Yet, alas, that is just what nuns feel most driven to confess. They must not. And if a nun sees that her confessor is "turning towards vanity" (or as we'd say, entertaining notions), she must ask for a new confessor. This convent allows a blessed freedom of choice.

Still, a priest need not be perfect for one to feel an ardent, purely spiritual love that shows itself in anxiety for his soul: she knows what tears, prayers and penances this can bring on. Yet the best loves of all are for those who do not need our prayers: "Love them, sisters, all you want to. Make every effort to keep in touch with them."

On other subjects, Teresa feels no such natural sympathy.

They can give up worldly possessions, she says, but how they treasure every little ache and pain! "Our bodies make fools of us often enough. Let's make fools of them for a change!" By their rule, "nobody need be afraid that we'll kill ourselves with penance here." But how do they follow that rule? By alternating between the desire for violent penance "simply to satisfy their own desires" and soft self-indulgence. Silent times are a good penance, and many can't bear that.

"Going to choir won't kill us, either, but one day we stay away because we have a headache, another because a headache is starting, another because the effort might bring one on." And the prioress must excuse it because she has no way of knowing who is really ill.

"Oh, God help me, that there should be whining like this among nuns! May God forgive it, for I'm afraid it's got to be a habit."

And, oh, their lust for others' approval! "But I'm older than she is, I understand it better. I was right to do that. They had no right to do it! It wasn't right to say that!" Right, right, right!

Postulants with these tendencies should be sent packing. Their prayers will have little effect until they learn to accept the facts of sickness and death and ignore them; and until they break free from all this self-justification. Conquering the body is the first step towards conquering the soul; and after that must come the conquest of pride.

But, right here, what stands in the way is our habit of making excuses for all our faults and errors. There are times when not to explain ourselves would be wrong, — but how rare they are! And how readily we all fool ourselves! All, without exception: "I can always find some reason for seeing it as an act of virtue when I start making excuses for myself." But, did Christ before the Pharisees? Did Mary when Martha blamed her for sitting idle at His feet? Once we learn to follow their example we find that humility is not weakness, but the strongest of the virtues: it is the Queen in the game of chess which can checkmate even our King. It was humility that drew God to the Virgin's womb, "and can draw him to our souls by a single hair."

To learn humility is to begin to understand God's love for all souls, not only those we see as worthy of His love. Only after that can we safely pray as contemplatives: for those who seek contemplation for the pleasure of receiving special "favors" are joining their souls to the devil, not to God. Yet God knows that we can learn this humility that makes mental prayer, contemplation, safe, or He would not have said, "Come ye to the waters."

Then, why do people fear mental prayer, why do they say that it drives women mad, or worse, that reciting their Aves and Paternosters is enough? Well, they would be right, if repeating words were prayer. Christ gave us the Paternoster, but to echo his words with our lips while our hearts wander is worse than no prayer at all.

So Teresa ends her *Camino* by thinking through the Paternoster.

"Our Father who art in Heaven . . . ." Where is Heaven? It is the King's Court, and the Court follows the King wherever he goes. "God is everywhere. We enter His heaven when we pray."

She takes it through to the end: "Forgive us our debts as we forgive. . . ."

God forgives because he loves us. He forgave her when she deserved hell, and we forgive because we love one another. That is what God wants. "Jesus could have said, 'Forgive us because we do many penances, pray much, fast, have given up all we own, would even lose our lives for Thee.' But he only said, 'Because we forgive.'"

V

These boiled-down bones lose the book's flavor. That can't be helped. You see at least it is not addressed to ready-made angels, and that the inspiration Teresa offered them is unlike the religious experiences described in the last chapters of the *Life*. A line omitted from the "improved" version that she was later ordered to make says that she had intended to do for the Ave Maria what she had done for the Paternoster, but decided to leave it out as unnecessary.

106

One who could pray the Paternoster with understanding knew enough to pray all other "vocal prayers." So now, before she gave the book to them, she would submit it for approval "to her confessor, Father *Presentado* Domingo Báñez of the Order of St. Dominic."

Báñez liked the book. Yet Teresa had not written it to please him. She had come a long way since those "experiences" which the final chapters of the *Life* unwillingly describe. As her letter to García states, it was the book as "finished in June, 1562" that she "began" in the hope of having it evaluated by Master Avila.

It is that book, *Concerning God's Mercies*, as finished in Toledo, which is the true precursor of the book she gave Báñez. The confession, necessary to explain the amazement of discovering God's forgiveness even to one who had prayed, with Augustine, "God make me chaste—but not yet"; and thereafter the essay on "mental prayer," from its first laborious beginnings—the soul a garden, the mind a gardener with his clumsy watering-pot—on past the half-way point, the waters now drawn up by a waterwheel—to the blessed rainfall, the quiet soul lying open to God's grace: all this is what led Teresa through much turbulence, much singular self-analysis to that summing up of the Paternoster, —"But he only said, 'because we forgive.'"

And the way was slow, as we know from her young chaplain, Julián de Avila.

Chapter 22 ❋ Enter Rubeo (Father Rossi, New Carmelite General)

I

Julián de Avila writes that when he first became chaplain of San José de Avila he often saw Teresa in a brief but unmistakable ecstasy, her face illuminated, her body immobile, her hands uplifted as one often sees St. Francis of Assisi portrayed. In time he asked her why it never happened any more, and she said that she had learned another, better kind of prayer.

The difference, I think, was much like the difference between a passionate falling in love and an enduring, loving marriage. Mature religion, like mature love, has no illusions. It heightens the awareness of what ought to be, but without denying what is. Lacking either, the spirit of man has no real sense of direction.

Teresa at fifty had both. This gave her, among other things, a gift which her times did not attribute to women: the power of "discerning spirits." While Teresa was at San José she was visited by three men, all with the reputation of holiness. One she saw to be a fraud, one she pitied—and one changed the direction of her life.

Juan Manteca saw visions and had the gift of prophesy. In Avila, crowds flocked to hear his inspired outpourings. Someone sent him to see Teresa, his sister visionary—probably in the hope of getting her into more trouble. Teresa wastes no words on him, but several sisters have witnessed to her reaction. He was possibly mad, she said, but far likelier a fake. Within months the Inquisition confirmed her judgement. Exit Manteca.

Juan Dávila de Cordovilla was a widower who had joined the Alcantarines. He came to ask Teresa to care for his little boy, a child whose addiction to violent penance his father saw as proof of sainthood. Teresa loved children, but as her nuns remembered, she saw that the poor boy was *loco*. She grieved for them both, and kept in touch with them for several years. Then the boy died, and his father set off for North Africa to offer himself in exchange for a Christian captive, any Christian captive; but he drowned in a shipwreck off Gibraltar.

The Mantecas are always with us. Dávila de Cordovilla was a stray from the Middle Ages, and Teresa tells of his death in just that context: "Even in our own times I have known someone like that...."

Stout souls like Fray Alonso Maldonado are rare, but every age produces one or two of them.

The Franciscans in Spain were a shoddy lot, beggars, lechers, and boozers, but South America revived their best qualities. The sight of mass conversions—or annihilations—by the military shocked them into a very different manifestation of Christianity. They became the only true Spanish friends the Indians ever had.

Maldonado was one of our first settlers; he spent his life in founding a chain of monasteries that ran from San Diego up to San Francisco. When he met Teresa, he had come to Spain to beg; his letter from his superior resulted in letters from the King to wealthy nobles, and when he learned from the Mendozas of a Carmelite who had attempted to introduce her Order to Holy Poverty, he went to see her.

They had the same purpose: to save souls, and not by the futile way of the sword. Maldonado left Teresa wishing for once in her life to have been born a man. She prayed about it fervently: not to be made humbly content, but to be given some leeway, some lessening of her woman's impotence to do more for the many who needed salvation through the Faith. She was kneeling in such prayer when she heard her Voice: "Wait a little, daughter, and you will see great things."

She believed that General Rubeo came to Spain in answer to that prayer; and she never came to see him as he was: a limited, thwarted, and resentful man.

But to understand that matters were not as gloriously simple and divinely ordained as Teresa believed, we must go to another part of the forest.

II

Philip II was obsessed with the idea that the Pope did not share his standards of sexual morality for the monastic Orders. He wanted Spanish generals

108

to head Spanish Orders. Pius IV felt that the reforms just passed by the Council of Trent were adequate, and it was only with difficulty that Philip got a compromise offer: the Generals of those Orders whose decay Philip found most disturbing—the Carmelites, Franciscans, and Trinitarians—would visit Spain within the next two years and see to it that such houses as refused to purge themselves were made subject to "the King's reform."

The Carmelite General, Nicholas Audet, saw Philip as muddled by a mixture of puritanism and jingoism. He prepared for his trip in a mood to see no evil; but he died shortly before the promised time for his visit, and was succeeded by Giovanni Battista Rossi—or as the Spaniards all call him, Rubeo.

Rubeo rejoiced in a gratifying self-image. His last will and testament speaks with feeling of his lifelong devotion to Holy Poverty—which he showed in life by travelling with a private cook, barber, valet, two serving men, two letter-carriers and the grooms for his two favorite horses. (Four other entourages were needed for his secretary, his steward, and two assistants in official business, one of whom—a Portuguese named Tostado—would in time loom in Teresa's letters as a figure of fearful menace.)

Rubeo also liked the sound of his own voice. One of his sermons—the recordbreaker, let's hope—went on in Padua for five full hours before he finally ran out of wind.

These, however, are amusing weaknesses. His limitations are better shown by the reforms that he felt impelled to bring into Italy before he could spare the time to go to Spain. At his visits to monasteries, bearded monks were rounded up and shaved in his presence by his own barber. Tassels on birettas and collars on shirts he removed in person with a pair of shears. Thereafter he searched each monastery, cell by cell, for other evidences of sin. Once he caught two monks playing cards, and was proud to report in writing that he "seized their owner and shoved his damned cards down his throat."

Rubeo left for Spain just when Pius IV died. His successor was a Dominican, a former Inquisitor, and a man after Philip's own heart. The King welcomed Rubeo and commissioned him with his blessing. The Vicar-General's attempt to clean up a notorious convent-monastery relationship down in Andalusia had ended in a screaming match with the Prior of Ecija during which they came to blows and the Vicar-General was forcibly ejected. Rubeo intended to begin his work by avenging this humiliation. He was a tall man, powerfully built, and used to seeing Italian friars cower. He had no idea of what he was getting into.

Carmelite Andalusia was run by the Nieto brothers, Gaspar, Melchor and Baltasar, and their crony, Juan de Mora. They were a tough lot. Gaspar, the least violent, was Provincial of Andalusia: when Rubeo asked Vargas (a former ambassador to the Vatican) why the Provincial spent so much time in Ecija, Vargas said, "It must be the nuns." Melchor was currently Prior of Ecija, a position given to compensate him for the time recently spent in the galleys on assorted criminal charges. Baltasar had committed at least one murder, but it was wisely overlooked. He was also a sadist, whose sexual outlet lay in torturing young friars.

Rubeo's visit was a sorry farce. At every Andalusian monastery he heard witnesses to the impeccable government and chastity of their houses. Thereafter, frightened, half-starved, beaten friars would creep to him secretly to spill the beans. But the nuns refused to talk; most prostitutes have a healthy fear of their pimps. The truth about them came out through young friars who did not share the privileges of their betters.

I spare you details. Rubeo had Melchor jailed, and Baltasar exiled from Andalusia; he demoted Gaspar, and appointed a new Provincial. All were excommunicated. Then Rubeo left for Portugal, preached before the King, and headed north to Old Castile. He was in no condition to be shocked by any laxities he found among the Avilan Carmelites. (Years later, in Seville, Teresa said that compared with the Andalusians the friars in Castile had been fairly decent.)

Then Rubeo went to Madrid to give his progress report. Meanwhile Gaspar Nieto and Juan de Mora had enlisted the support of the King's good friend the Conde de Ferria and were coming north to plead their case. Baltasar was visiting the Conde's son and being feted. Rubeo was unable to get an audience with the King, who was otherwise absorbed: there were new uprisings in Flanders and crumbling support from France. So Rubeo went back to Avila for a Carmelite convocation: Angel de Salazar's triennium was ended and an election was due.

This went smoothly. Father Angel's powers were interrupted purely as a matter of form by the election of a frail old man of seventy-eight. For the intendedly brief interim, Father Angel was made Prior of the Carmelite monastery in Avila, and Heredia transferred to Medina de Campo. Bishop Mendoza said mass for the convocation.

Since part of Rubeo's mission had been to examine the suspect claustrals, he was warned about Teresa. She appealed to Bishop Mendoza to set him right by bringing him to visit San José de Avila.

And there you have it. Rubeo was a narrow, self-righteous man. If his visit to Spain had begun with Castile, he would have seen nothing but a runaway nun who had defied her Provincial, left her Order, and set up a convent "under the ordinary." But he had begun in Andalusia; he had seen his own dear-loved self-image damaged. In Madrid the King had no time to hear him out, and he was quickly forced to realize that Andalusia had simply laughed him off. And even at this convocation his fame in the pulpit was disregarded. A fool named de Salazar, not he, was asked to preach — and produced a wretched sermon, barely an hour long.

Rubeo was sadly in need of a build-up when he entered that humble convent and saw it so obviously dedicated to poverty, chastity, and, above all, to reverent obedience. No wonder that he was clay in Teresa's hands.

III

Julián de Avila says that the sight of those quiet nuns in their habits of poor *sayal* moved Rubeo to tears. He came back several times to talk with Teresa in the convent's little parlor with its decent grille between them.

110

Teresa says that she told him "almost" all about her life, expressing her passionate desire that her movement should spread. She was ardent. She was beautiful; at fifty-two she looked like a woman in her thirties. Rubeo called her "my daughter" and Teresa saw him then and always as older, nobler, and more benignant than he was. To her mind, his coming fulfilled the prophesy of her Voice: "Wait, daughter . . . you shall see great things."

Indeed, as she saw it, it had been a miracle. Rubeo gave her patents to found convents anywhere but in Andalusia, and for each of them she might take any two nuns of the Incarnation who would go with her of their own free will. Teresa hadn't a penny, but she had no doubt that the God who had done all this would also provide her with houses.

Rubeo went back to Madrid where the King entertained him with mock courtesy, gave him a banquet in the Escorial, and praised his work in Andalusia. Rubeo knew that he was defeated, he was bitter, and that bitterness, too, worked in Teresa's favor.

She had told him that *mujercillas* could accomplish little alone; a Carmelite reform must have friars, too. He had brushed this off. He was not only soured on Spanish friars but saw that they could become a separatist movement, to his own discredit.

Yet, on that point, Teresa could not give up. Men and only men can get things done. She pursued Rubeo with letters; and in Barcelona, just before he set sail, he capitulated. He sent licences in quadruplicate to Teresa, the Procurador General, the new Provincial, and to Father Angel — still Provincial in all but name. They permitted Teresa to found two monasteries whose monks would thereafter be free to found others. But with one limitation, for the taste of Andalusia was still rancid on Rubeo's tongue.

"Such monks shall live perpetually joined to the Obedience of Castile. . . . If at any time any brothers, on the pretext of desiring to live in greater perfection, and whether or not with the approval of nobles and with briefs and other concessions from Rome, shall attempt to separate themselves from the province, we declare them to be men led by an evil spirit."

Or briefly put, Andalusia must be let go to hell in its own boat. It was a time bomb. But Teresa, reading it with humble gratitude, could not have imagined that one day it would come close to wrecking all she had accomplished, and because she disobeyed.

This disobedience *Fundaciones* does not hint at: nor would one suspect that she only began the book after the foundation of her next five convents and two self-perpetuating monasteries had been followed by another three years' imprisonment in the Incarnation. The epilogue which closes her story of founding her seventh convent lets us know that she intended to end the book there; and the accounts of the six convents that came after it — and after another long, long hiatus which she also leaves unmentioned — give no more hint of why she took up the book again than she gives earlier of when and where and why she began it.

Fundaciones does far better than the *Life* at deceiving by omitting; it has no awkward seams, no confusion of enforced flashbacks; it is lucid, easy reading.

Indeed, if Teresa's letters had not begun to be saved in bulk at the time of her seventh foundation, she would still be a stranger to me, and one about whom I had small curiosity. That they were saved, often for less than admirable reasons, has given my last twelve years a richness, purpose and yes, a singular friendship, for which I am grateful. And as for what I have said about *Fundaciones* — don't blame her for writing it until you know why, God helping her, she could do no other.

Chapter 23 ❀ *House-hunting for a Reformed Convent in Medina del Campo; Heredia; John of the Cross*

I

Medina del Campo was a prosperous market-city only a day's journey from Avila. As Teresa tells it, she wrote the Jesuits there for advice and sent her chaplain to get the city's permission to found. The Carmelite Prior (Heredia) offered to find her a house, and though all Avila thought her mad, she set out, almost penniless, with a handful of nuns. On the way, they learned that Augustinians, next-door to the house they had taken, threatened to make trouble; so she left some of the nuns housed with relatives who lived nearby and went ahead to take possession and install the Host secretly under cover of darkness.

Next, in vivid detail she tells of how she found the house in such wretched condition that the Lord must have struck the good Prior blind when he took it, and of how the Jesuits tried in vain to find her a better, until the kindness of the town and a certain great lady left them well established.

After this she tells of her surprise when Heredia offered to be her first friar, and a young student from Salamanca, Fray Juan de la Cruz, became the second.

II

To begin at the end, when the Procurador General received Rubeo's licences for two monasteries he chose to see them as Rubeo's concession to the King's reform. For popularizing this attitude with the Carmelites, Antonio de Heredia was made to order: an aristocrat, a personal friend of the Duke and Duchess of Alba, and an Andalusian — hence one in a good position to shrug off Rubeo's recent slanders of the Spanish Carmelites, and naturally inclined to do so.

Teresa would find Heredia's offer bewildering on more counts than one. He had never been her friend and was even colder after García's demotion to novice-master and return to Peru: his attachment to the house of de Toledo, from the Duke and Duchess of Alba on down, insured that. Even his offer to find her a house in Medina must have surprised her until she saw the house and could explain his apparent kindness as a bit of spite.

Heredia was, in fact, of two minds about accepting the Procurador General's proposal. When he learned of the excitement rising in Medina over the news that the city was about to be polluted by the *alumbrada* whom two solemn juntas in Avila had failed to quell, Heredia felt that the time for friendly gestures was not yet ripe and took pains to find a house sufficiently ruinous to discourage Teresa and send her home.

Bishop Mendoza surely disbelieved the "great false witness" raised against García and must have pitied the futility of Teresa's letter which tried to convince him that García was demoted to novice-master only because his example was so inspiring to the young—"though it was indeed a lowly position for one of his rank." (Teresa, too, recognized the sorry futility of that letter once she had sent it off. García's departure she mentions only as a loss, without any attempt to explain it away.) However, when Mendoza learned of the excitement in Medina, he urged Teresa to wait for a better time, and was angry when she insisted that since God had brought Rubeo to Avila for His own purpose, she could only obey His will.

This might have caused a permanent rift between them, if the excitement in Medina had not smelled so strongly of the anti-Semitism Bishop Mendoza despised. A visit to his brother Pedro in Guadalajara—the brother with whim he had fought Archbishop Silíceo's claim that his Cathedral was "a new synagogue"—brought his thinking about by one hundred eighty degrees. Since Teresa would need a licence from the abbot who was the town's leading ecclesiastic, he sent him an urgent invitation to visit Guadalajara and talk things over. It worked; the licence was granted.

Teresa only knew that the Bishop had left her in anger. She sent Julián de Avila to ask the abbot and the city for the needed licence, but Julián learned that the abbot had left town and that a junta, then in progress, would settle the issue, so far as a licence from the city went.

It was pretty much the Avilan junta replayed. Domingo Báñez was allowed to sit in, and his memoirs mention the fulminations of Luis de Barrientos, *a gran predicador*, who denounced Teresa as a new Magdalen of the Cross. De Barrientos' opinion of Teresa remained unchanged until the discovery of her miraculous preservation. Another speaker, yet more furious, was Antonio de Sosa—who was also more consistent. Twenty-four years later he was still sending written condemnations of Mother Teresa to the Inquisition, in a last-ditch attempt to prevent her canonization.

Those two expressed the overwhelming sense of the meeting, from the churchly point of view. But three Jesuits spoke up for her: one was Luis de Medina, an Avilan, ex-soldier, and old friend of her brother Lorenzo, another was the Jesuit who had persuaded de Medina to join the Company on his return from the Indies, and the third was the noted scholar, Luis de Santander. Santander was a native of Ecija, the Nieto brothers' pleasure place; he knew why Rubeo desired a Carmelite reform. He was a friend and disciple of Juan de

Avila (once more in trouble with the Inquisition). And finally, like Juan de Avila and Teresa. he too was a *converso*.

However, neither Teresa's churchly attackers or defamers swung the balance, but Simón Ruiz, Spain's sole major figure in the field of international banking. His money talked, and it was Spain's good luck that he had risen from the peasantry—and Teresa's good luck that, in his prosperity, he had outgrown the one vaunted virtue of Sancho Panza. It seemed to him, he said, that this convent of a new Carmelite reform could only do good both to those who entered it and to those who needed encouragement in virtue.

Ruiz's word counted. He was seconded by one wealthy merchant after another. In the plea for Holy Poverty, money won the day: and Julián, with the city's licence, galloped back to Avila, correctly assured that the abbot's licence would soon follow.

Teresa's two nuns allowed her from the Incarnation were the Tapia cousins, Inés and Ana. To them the Prioress—by a somewhat liberal interpretation of Rubeo's stricture that they go willingly—added two more: she found Doña Isabel Arias and Doña Teresa de Quesada a pair of headaches, and so would Teresa before they wangled their way back to the Incarnation. The Prioress, however, released none of their four dowries. Teresa located one modestly dowered novice, and by including María Bautista in the party was able to bring the number, crammed into donkey-carts along with their bedding and the markings of their Order up to seven—with Julián de Avila riding escort.

In Arévalo they were met by a priest who was on his way to stop them from leaving Avila. The Augustinians believed that their proximity "would work them grave prejudice." (One imagines Sosa convincing his monastery that the place would be a second Ecija.)

Teresa left the two already unwilling titled ladies and the two Tapia girls with some Tapia relatives who lived in Arévalo, telling them only that she was going ahead with María Bautista and the little novice to make sure that all would be in comfortable order for their arrival. As the donkey-carts had made a two-days journey of one, Teresa waited for morning. When it came, Heredia and Domingo Báñez turned up, too, both with assurances that the Augustinians would promptly realize that they could not overrule the abbot and the city. Báñez also had a message from the Bishop. He was now at his castle in Olmedo, which was right on her way, and he hoped that she would stop to see him, and his sister, and their youngest brother too.

The visit was a day-long feast of love. Doña María exclaimed that Teresa should have chosen Valladolid for the first of her new convents. Don Bernardino, an endearing young man and a shameless sinner, said that he owned a house which was Teresa's for the taking, since he could use a convent to pray for his soul. The Bishop was appalled by the donkey-carts; Teresa left Olmedo in a ducal coach.

But it was late when they got away, after midnight when Father Julián spurred ahead to knock on the city gates for admission, and two o'clock when the coach arrived.

The delay had been a blessing, for a *corrida* was to be held that day in honor of the Virgin's Assumption, and they had just missed the running of the bulls: no sport for a housebound, rheumatoid, cumbersomely clad nun of fifty-two.

To avoid waking the Augustinians they left the coach at a distance and walked through the streets loaded with the necessities for the first mass. Julián says, "We looked like gypsies who had been robbing a church."

The house was a shock even before dawn revealed its full decay. Outer walls were broken, inner walls shedding their plaster; the roof had gaping holes. A porch, the only covered space large enough to serve as a chapel, was deep in mud; it would have to be shovelled out before it could be enclosed, somehow.

Julián located the owner's steward, who found them some hangings and a big blue bedspread. They pried nails out of the woodwork with which to fasten up the makeshift tent that enclosed the "chapel" from the street, dug out the mud, and Teresa, María Bautista, and the novice entered their "enclosure" and saw the first mass through chinks in the broken woodwork of the door.

But when light came, Teresa saw that she had, in effect, "turned our Lord out into the street"—at the mercy of "those Lutherans, and in times like these!" (She breathed the same air of panic over the Protestant menace, of course, as did her enemies.)

The letdown, the horror at her own headstrong folly was even worse than it had been after she settled her "poor orphans" in San José. She sent for Lorenzo's Jesuit friend, Luis de Medina, who started a vigorous househunt: but he could find nothing for sale or to rent. She sent for Heredia (a fact which she excludes from her book), who responded by sending a notary "to examine a house for religious women"; he reported, in a still extant document, "that it had everything necessary."

For a week Teresa was sleepless. She hired two men to stand guard over the Host by night, but she was afraid that they might doze off and was continually getting up to look out into the broken porch and make sure that the Body of Christ was safe.

The Jesuit, Santander, passed on word of their plight to those who might help, but he was defeated by the romantic appeal that Holy Poverty has for those who need not endure it. The town nobility flocked to see this second Bethlehem and be moved to tears around the humble manger. Finally he managed to interest a rich merchant who was not sentimental. Blas de Medina saw that the place was no fit shelter for women and offered Teresa the top story of his house, a single huge ballroom whose coffered ceiling was covered with gold-leaf. And almost at once help came from another quarter.

Rivalry between the town nobility and the wealthiest merchants was always intense; it would be a constant source of trouble to that convent, for Teresa rarely found a prioress who could handle it tactfully; but for this once, it was a blessing.

Doña Elena de Quiroga was not merely noble and well-to-do; she was a niece of the influential Bishop Quiroga, who in time became Spain's Grand Inquisitor. She was also a social trend-setter, and for a good many years Teresa's problems would be unlike any that had gone before; noble patronesses take delicate handling.

However, Heredia plunged eagerly into the task of endearing himself to Doña Elena. As Ribera has it, "Father Antonio, coming and going, hurried about his work so earnestly . . . that within two months . . . the Mother had a good house in an excellent location."

The convent was not one of which Teresa was ever fond, but it attracted nuns with good dowries and her cousins, Inés and Ana, were steadily reelected its prioress and subprioress for many years.

Then Heredia made his offer. The laxity of the Carmelites, he said, had long made him think of turning Carthusian, but now that the General had made it possible for him to remain within the Virgin's Order and serve her with perfection, he proposed to become Teresa's first friar.

Teresa did not know how to put him off. It was obvious that he intended to use this newly approved branch of the "King's reform" for his own ends, and equally obvious that to offend him would be impolitic to the point of madness. They must wait for a better time to begin, she said. But yet, she would talk with the young friar who wanted to join him, an artist, a recent graduate from the University of Salamanca, just now turned Carmelite: Fray Juan de Matías.

Teresa thought she knew just what to expect. Only a knave or a fool would leave the herd to follow Heredia.

Why Juan de la Cruz so unquestioningly allied himself with worldly, wily Heredia can only be understood once one had grasped the limitations imposed by his very greatness. He was, quite simply, a spirit too pure to be capable of any real human understanding; a great mind — but a mind exclusively occupied with "the things of God." If Heredia cynically interpreted Fray Juan's unquestioning trust in his prior as no more than a convenient simplemindedness, he was absurdly mistaken.

Fray Juan was barely five feet tall, with a handsome, swarthy head that was a little too large for his tiny body. His grandfather, a *converso*, had disinherited his father for marrying a weaver, and as weaving and metalworking were the chief Moorish occupations — and not even Christian *pecheros* equalled *conversos* in their hatred of Moorish blood — it seems likely that Fray Juan was half-Moorish: a social disadvantage which combined with his child-sized body could well have made him retire early to the life of the mind.

Juan de la Cruz — the name he took when he turned Discalced — never understood Teresa, or she him. But he fully understood her ideals, and she at once perceived his singular integrity and his total dedication to the religious life. She could joke about him; she wrote to a friend that her monasteries had already been promised a friar and a half. But when she wrote some months later to prepare Francisco de Salcedo for the sight of that dwarfed body, she said, "He is tiny, but he is tall in the sight of God."

However, the monasteries had to wait. Doña Elena de Quiroga had set a fashion, and the first great lady to jump on her bandwagon was Doña Luisa de la Cerda.

116

Teresa would always try to like Doña Luisa, and try still harder to make Doña Luisa believe that she liked her. However, in the best edition (1968) of Teresa's *Obras Completas*, the founding of Medina gets fourteen double-columned, fine print pages, despite its many omissions; Malagón, Doña Luisa's castle town, rates one — and a short one. It is also worth noting that before Teresa brought herself to give it even that much space, she held up her narrative with five chapters of advice to prioresses about the running of convents and direction of nuns. Malagón always needed straightening out.

Chapter 24 ❀ *Malagón. Trouble Caused by Teresa's Loan of Manuscript of Her* <u>Life</u>

I

The chapters which interrupt Teresa's story deal with a matter that is not touched upon in the *Camino*: the proper treatment of religious hysterics. Why it went on at such length we will only understand when we know when, where and why she wrote that book. What first suggested it to her was probably a letter from Father Daza that Báñez gave her when they met in Alcalá on her way to Malagón. Daza acted as her chaplain at San José de Avila whenever Julián de Avila was escorting her on her travels. Her answer to his letter shows how much she was always needed in the convents that she founded. Once she left them, few did not either relapse into worldliness or embrace what Teresa would come to call "imagination and inventions of the devil."

Daza wrote her at the time a novice called Concepción was briefly tried out. Concepción had to be dropped when she became too occupied with receiving spiritual favors to do her share of the housework. In her five chapters of advice to prioresses, Teresa stresses it that communal work is love in action: "God moves among the cooking-pots." Her letter to Daza — what remains of it — suggests that Concepción be ignored, her work shared by the others, and that above all Daza should not permit any competitive talk about such supernatural "favors."

The first page of her letter was destroyed, and the rest of it censored by much heavy lining-out; but after sympathizing with the convent's continuing need for alms, she says this:

"I was delighted that it made you laugh ... for she could have amused nobody but someone who truly knows how gentle Our Lord is. I beg Him to preserve you for many years for the improvement of those sisters.

"Don't let them talk to each other about prayer, or meddle in that other matter, or talk about Concepción, or everyone will have to add her own piece of foolishness. Let them leave her alone, since when one can't do much work

117

the others are supposed to share it, and God will give her food ... like ... of my ...."

This scrap of a letter and those five chapters contrast sharply with the memories of *La Santa* offered after her death. For one, Alberta Bautista—who treated Teresa like scum in her last days—says that in Medina, Teresa levitated "very commonly," and, in her humility, insisted that all who learned to pray might float aloft just as well. Alberta also said that Teresa further taught humility by waiting on the two titled ladies hand and foot, saying that it was "only right to honor and help them" in view of the rank they had held before they turned Discalced.

But this second lie brushes close to a painful truth. Teresa knew that the beauty of her first convent had been its ability to take no thought for the morrow. The fact that the near-disaster of Medina had been averted by the gift of an unendowed house and the prompt appearance of nuns with adequate dowries she could take as proof that, with faith, the Lord will provide. But should one so soon accept a convent which must be given a regular income in order to exist in that castle-village of Malagón? It was wrong, even though to refuse it would be to invite further trouble by offending the Court.

Teresa says only that "her confessor" stilled her scruples over founding in a place where her convent could not subsist on alms, so she went to Malagón after a brief stopover in Toledo, founded there on Palm Sunday, and left to found another convent in Valladolid: all of this covered, as I say, in a single page.

It is worth filling in.

II

Time heals all wounds. María Mendoza was now on for sixty, and the days when she had received such trophies as "green plumes and gold ornaments from Cortés" were nearly forgotten. Her house had become a little court, even visited by the saintly Doña Leonora de Mascarénas, Philip's revered former governess. And Doña Leonora had a problem, for which María Mendoza could offer the perfect solution.

María de Jesús, you remember, had left Teresa in Doña Luisa's palace and gone back to Madrid. There she met and entranced Doña Leonora, who gave her a convent in the university town of Alcalá—though not in the holy poverty of which María de Jesús had talked so inspiringly to Teresa.

Or, to be accurate, in nothing but appearances. These, indeed, were flamboyant: bare feet in all weathers, habits of rough cloth, scanty commons, and a rule with heavy emphasis on fasting and violent physical penance. Her convent was founded on the day that Teresa was allowed to go back to San José, since when it had remained a nagging mystery that, despite its generous endowment and local alms, it was always in debt. Every inspection made throughout the past six years brought back the same bewildering account. A rule that all funds be kept "in the box with the three keys," and thus never opened except in the presence of two witnesses, changed nothing. Doña Leonora had become sadly disturbed.

María Mendoza told her about Mother Teresa de Jesús. She had founded an unendowed convent in Avila which lived content on next to nothing. She was now performing the same wonder in Medina, and would soon go to Malagón to do it again. What's more, she was also a Discalced Carmelite, like María de Jesús. Doña María and her brother, Don Bernardino, were about to visit the Duchess of Alba at her country place in Ubeda. They could collect Teresa and drop her off in Madrid; then Doña Leonora could take her to Alcalá, where she would quickly set everything in order.

God knows what Teresa thought when she heard that she was to examine the finances of María de Jesús. But she sent for Ana de los Angeles to be her companion and set out in the ducal coach. On the way, Don Bernardino won her assent to found a convent in the house he had offered her, and had the papers notarized before he went on to Ubeda.

Centuries later, the French Bolandists invented scenes in Doña Leonora's house: crowds of court ladies eager to witness miracles and raptures and Teresa putting them off with casual remarks about Madrid's new city-planning, "Such broad streets!"

III

The Convent of the Image got its name from a huge statue of Our Lady, who was the center of María de Jesús's devotions. It is said (in admiration) that on first being called to the religious life she sent her only child, a boy, to live with an aunt, after which she never saw him again. But she liked girls. At the Convent of the Image the records show that one novice was accepted when she was ten, another at twelve. When Teresa got there the youngest nun had turned fourteen; she was the sacristan. Two were older than the rest, one twenty-nine and the other thirty-three. Of the remaining eighteen, none were over twenty. María de Jesús' subprioress and strong right arm was a twenty-year-old named Polonia; she dressed, by preference, as a friar.

Discalced friars who later visited the convent report that the nuns had been shocked by Teresa's cheerfulness. They themselves were never permitted to smile, much less laugh aloud. They were there to suffer, and they boasted at length of their self-torture and anorexia, and of enduring grave accidents and illnesses without asking for help, rather than break their lengthy periods of total silence.

Báñez, then in Alcalá to give a course in theology at the university, persuaded Teresa that she was wasting her time. She was already eager to leave. A letter from Ubeda told her that Don Bernardino Mendoza had suffered a stroke and died unable to confess; and she heard her Voice promise that the founding of his convent would free him from Purgatory.

Báñez was also shocked to learn that Luis de Santander had urged Teresa to send the manuscript of the *Life* to Juan de Avila by way of Doña Luisa, who intended to visit a cure in Andalusia as soon as the Malagón foundation was made. He repeated his warning.

Teresa left a copy of her Constitutions behind her; María de Jesús had learned to read a little, and to sign her name in a large, clumsy hand. But it was clear that the Constitutions would do no good, and what happened to the money remains a mystery.

What Teresa told Doña Leonora about the Convent of the Image is not known. But the least skillful of the Teresian forgeries is a legally impossible document in which Teresa herself releases María de Jesús from a debt of five thousand ducats in view of "the great service she has done Our Lord." Clearly, someone felt a need to square làter reports on María de Jesús with Teresa's account of her visit to Doña Luisa's palace.

IV

Father Julián left Teresa in Toledo with Ana de los Angeles and a second nun from San José de Avila; they waited there until he came back with four from the Incarnation. In Toledo, Doña Luisa's current Jesuit was Pablo Hernández, an upright, fine old man; but in Malagón she had installed her current religious enthusiasm, Bernardino Carleval. When Teresa and her nuns went to Malagón, Hernández led the procession and reserved the Host; but thereafter Carleval took over.

He left Malagón soon, turning over his work to his brother Tomás; he saw no future in that castle-village. While he stayed, the advice he gave Teresa was uniformly bad, but he gave it with the charm for which he later became famous, and she was both tired and badly confused.

She told him of her eagerness to get to Valladolid, and he assured her that she should make every compromise that Doña Luisa wanted, the sooner to be on her way. She told him of a book that she had written in the hope of having it read by Juan de Avila, and that her confessor, a Dominican, forbade her to turn it over to Doña Luisa when she started south; and he assured her that to send it to Master Avila was her holy duty.

Julián de Avila lets us understand part of the weary confusion that made Teresa eager to believe Carleval and get away quickly. The convent, Julián says, was housed on the village square, surrounded by shops; the noise "disturbed all prayer." The nuns he had brought from the Incarnation had been released only on the condition that they should live by the Mitigated Rule; and to this Doña Luisa added conditions of her own.

The convent should eventually hold twenty besides the Prioress, not twelve. They should also take in lay-sisters as servants. The nuns' duties would include the education of the village children: the girls would be taught sewing and religion in the convent—with the aid of a village woman. The boys' education should be in the care of their already ill-paid confessor. He should also say a daily mass—not for the healing of the Church, but specifically to speed up the soul of Doña Luisa's late husband, Arias Pardo, out of Purgatory and into Paradise.

Malagón would have worse problems and invite distressing scandals in the years ahead; but from the start it bore little resemblance to Teresa's conception of twelve nuns and a prioress whose selfless living would strengthen their souls and make their prayers for the healing of the Church a force for good.

One can see why Bernardino Carleval (underpaid and expected to turn schoolmaster as well) quit Malagón so soon for greener pastures. Teresa left shortly thereafter, during a heat wave. She reached Toledo with a fever and spent a week trying to recuperate, but Doña Luisa had so boasted of her holy acquisition that, as Teresa admits in a letter to her, the crowds of noble visitors left her "terribly tired." Still, she tried to be properly flattering and added that for the return trip on muleback (no other conveyance was offered) she had taken a saddle of Doña Luisa's "so that I shall have something of Your Ladyship's with me."

The castle chaplain ("a miserable creature" Teresa's letters to others reveal) was her designated escort to Avila, but he backed out. The village priest took his place. On the way, Teresa made a stopover with García's half-sister, the Marchioness of Velada, who was eager to show the world by that invitation that "the great false witness" raised against him was an absurdity, and disbelieved by all who knew him and Teresa best.

She told Teresa that her friend Don Cristóbal de Moya would gladly become a patron of one of her convents—if she could convince him that rumors he had heard about her troubles with the Jesuits were false, and that her convents were not too austere for his sisters, both *beatas* who lived with him.

At no other time in Teresa's life would she have written the letter that she sent to Don Cristóbal when she got back to Avila. In the 1920's, the eminent Carmelite scholar, Silverio, persuaded himself that it was a forgery. I only wonder that in 1968 the equally eminent Carmelite scholar, Steggink, faced up to its authenticity.

It is a long letter, its tone reminiscent of the state in which some people get too tired to stop talking. She says, among other things, that Don Cristóbal offer chiefly attracts her because she has been told that he and his holy sisters were instructed by the Jesuits — "to whom I owe all the good that is in me and in my Order." Hence, her nuns are more free to talk with Jesuits than nuns of any other Order.

Her Order is also amazingly popular. "Now that the General has given me leave to found convents and monasteries, there is a great rush to join them — even too many friars." (Two, so far.) And Don Cristóbal need not be afraid that her convents are too poor and austere: "If it strikes you that the rule about not eating meat is too strict, we can allow it, as we did in Malagón—and the Council of Trent makes us free to accept endowments."

She ends with a further assurance that the priest who is acting as her messenger will tell him more about the pleasures his sisters would find in his proposed foundation.

No letters remain to tell us how she finally avoided founding a convent for de Moya's sisters. But her letters do tell about the strain caused by her disobedience to Báñez.

Doña Luisa took the manuscript away to Andalusia on April eleventh. A priest who had travelled with her came back to Malagón and reported that in mid-May she still had it with her, and that Mother Teresa's former confessor, Father Gaspar de Salazar, who was Rector of a Jesuit College near Doña Luisa's spa, intended to visit Master Avila soon; he would take him the manuscript, and be glad of the opportunity to read it himself.

Teresa wrote Doña Luisa on May eighteenth: "I can't think why Your Ladyship has put off sending my package to Master Avila. This waiting for Salazar is ridiculous, for if he's the Rector he couldn't go to visit Your Ladyship, much less to see Master Avila." So her ladysip must send it off immediately. "It looks as if the devil is displeased at the thought of that holy man's seeing it. Look, it is more important than you think."

She wrote again from the stopover in Toledo, begging that the manuscript be sent off "this very hour"; it would be terrible if Master Avila died before he read it! (He did die in the following year.) And Doña Luisa can't realize what harm the delay could do. Father Fray Domingo has written her to send him the book as soon as she gets to Avila. Teresa doesn't know what to do, because of the harm it would do if *they* found out what she had done.

She sent off a similar plea when she reached Avila, and twelve days later, a fourth—in which the impersonal "they" is dropped:

"Look at it squarely, my Lady; I have entrusted you with my very soul." What's more, Father Fray Domingo is coming to Avila soon: "I feel so small. He'll catch me out in having stolen it." (In fact, the manuscript had been first García's property and then that of Báñez; never, in the eyes of the Church, Teresa's own.)

How she worked it out with Báñez I don't know. Teresa did not get her manuscript back until November, in Valladolid. Doña Luisa was not responsible for all that seven months' delay, for Juan de Avila apologizes for having been so slow in reading it. The few words of clearance he grants the book are less than enthusiastic; but this may say more about his own delicate position than about his opinions. After one stint in the Inquisition's dungeons he had no desire to invite another, and his health was failing fast.

But Master Avila's delay gave Bernardino Carleval time to visit him, read the book at his leisure, and make a copy of it. This did no immediate harm; but within five years Carleval had developed Messianic pretensions, and aided by Andalusian responsiveness he had been able to use his visions and *arrobamientos* to win himself a considerable cult: in result of which, Teresa's name first appears on the formal records of a trial by the Inquisition in 1572. The trial was Carleval's, and the chief influences cited for his downfall were an Andalusian woman, "the false prophetess, María Mejías," and "the nun, Teresa de Jesús," authoress of a mad and heretical book that he often cited.

Carleval and María Mejías went to the stake; the documentary evidence as to why Teresa did not was first published exactly four hundred years after the trial—a trial still generally excluded from Teresa's story.

We'll come to that. A good deal happened first.

Chapter 25 ❄ A Tiny House for Discalced Carmelite Friars in Duruelo; Labors of John of the Cross; Malaria

I

For almost three months Teresa struggled to pull herself together in Avila, despite her haunting conviction that Bernardino Mendoza would suffer in Purgatory until he had his promised convent to pray him free. She set out with Julián de Avila at the time of the August harvest. On the way they would see Duruelo, where Heredia had been promised his friary.

Duruelo, a village of just under twenty inhabitants except for the migrant labor that came in harvest time, was hard to find. They had travelled in circles for the better part of a day before they found it. The promised house was a tiny, filthy shack for storing grain, surrounded by harvesters hard at their wineskins at the end of their long day. But small as the village was, it had a little church. The exhausted travellers slept on the floor.

Teresa expected shock when she described the place to Heredia, and was amazed when he said that for the sake of her reform he would live in a pigsty. She also tells us that his preparation for entering that first friary—two small rooms and a little loft—consisted of buying five clocks. That was too amusing to leave out. For the rest, she leaves the Duruelo myth undisturbed: the Order's blessed birth in a perfection of Holy Poverty.

It is only in a later chapter that she mentions Heredia's move to Mancera and the patronage of Don Luis de Toledo, Lord of the Five Towns—because he felt that a certain famous painting there "would inspire much devotion." Similarly, she lets the reader think that the offer of Duruelo came out of the blue from a certain "Don Rafael"—surname omitted—whom she had never met.

Heredia had. Don Rafael belonged to the noble branch of the Dávilas, Lords of Lorillana, Condes of Uceda, all intermarried with the de Toledos,—Heredia's friends, who gladly provided him with an initial period of useful, good theater. In Medina Heredia had been distrusted, a suspicious spy for the King's reform. (Or, as Teresa puts it, "he passed through many trials which he bore with great perfection.") A large and prosperous monastery under his leadership would have been seen as a threat to the Mitigation; Father Angel would not have allowed it. But once any Discalced monastery was founded, it would be quite simple to move it to another house, a scant four miles away. Moreover, one sufficiently humble would excite an immediate public reaction like that given by the nobility to Teresa's first "little Bethlehem" in Medina—which had led to her enthusiastic acceptance by nobles and merchants alike.

Duruelo became a legend which still lives despite its brief reality.

Let me add that Heredia never had to cope with Duruelo at its worst. Fray Juan de la Cruz and his mentally retarded brother went there first and worked like slaves for several months to make the place fairly habitable; Fray Juan could see that Heredia was old and not fit for much physical labor.

Fray Juan met Teresa in Medina, where there were nuns to spare. She made her selection while Julián went back to Avila for a few more. She got bad news in Valladolid: the abbot there was strongly pro-Inquisition and anti-Mendoza. He opposed the convent, and the walling-in of Don Bernardino's gardens had to be done in secret.

Don Bernardino's house was large and beautiful, and its view of the river was lovely. There was also a threat of malaria. Bernardino had previously given it to Carmelite friars, whom the "quartan ague" struck down. But Bernardino had been a gambler; he put his money on God to protect the holy Mother Teresa from the night air and its riverside miasmas.

Teresa had Mass said in her proposed chapel even before the walls were built or the licence won, and was overjoyed by an "imaginary vision" in which she saw Don Bernardino ascending heavenward. She had assumed that his release could come, at the earliest, only when the convent was made and the Host reserved upon its altar.

During the wait for her licence, Teresa saw much of Fray Juan and taught him the rules of the Order. She also tried to teach him the necessity of compromise in this so actual and inconvenient world, and did not succeed. Years later she wrote, "I could have learned so much from him then — and I wasted so much time arguing about money."

When the convent was founded in September, Teresa sent Fray Juan to Avila with letters intended to loosen purses and make Duruelo more habitable. Her letter to Francisco de Salcedo says of Fray Juan, "He is brave, but he is so much alone in the world he needs all the courage the Lord gives him [words deleted] he takes it so much to heart."

So much alone. . . . Teresa often unintentionally betrays how little she could ever trust Heredia. Her note ends with the news that the Princess of Eboli wants her to found a convent in Pastrana, his castle town. (The Princess was a Mendoza y Guzmán, and her husband, Ruy Gómez, was Philip's oldest friend and his prime minister. The Princess also had a reputation of which even an innocent like Juan de la Cruz could hardly have been ignorant. This was doubtless one of the matters on which he and Teresa "wasted time" in arguing.)

Teresa's appeal to Francisco de Salcedo did nothing for Duruelo, but he sent Teresa "apples, honey-water and radishes" for which she thanked him for remembering "a poor little nun."

As for founding in Pastrana, it would be some time before Teresa had to decide how God would be best served, for Don Bernardino lost his bet.

The convent was stricken with malaria. Doña María housed the whole community for four months while a new house, her gift, was made ready. Throughout that time, Teresa was ill, for some weeks critically ill with symptoms that suggest typhus, as well as the malaria from which she would always thereafter suffer recurrent attacks of the "quartan ague."

During those four months Teresa considered her next move.

On her way back to Avila from Malagón she had seen good old Father Hernández and told him how badly things had turned out. When she wrote him about her offer from the Princess of Eboli — an offer so unwise to refuse and one so likely to be even worse than Malagón — Father Hernández gave it serious thought. One of his penitents, a *converso* merchant, was near death; very likely he could be persuaded to make a will that would enable Teresa to found a convent in accord with her ideals.

Before Teresa fell ill, Father Hernández was able to write her that Señor Ramírez would leave her twenty thousand ducats. Ramírez died on the last day of October — the day that Teresa and her stricken nuns were taken from the house by the river. In November, her manuscript came back at last from Master Avila, and Teresa, almost too weak to hold a pen, wrote at once to Doña Luisa. She realized how important that lady's friendship would be if she founded a convent in Toledo — one so much better endowed than Malagón and under so much lowlier patronage.

Father Avila, she said, had found no fault with the *Life*, though some things had to be better explained and others reworded. And "Your Ladyship managed about the book so well that it couldn't have been done better, and so I have forgotten all the ravings I got myself into." Thereafter, praise for the Malagón convent and regrets to hear that Father Hernández has left Her Ladyship's service. "I should like to write him myself, but can't without doing myself harm." (Too ill, that is.) She wants to come back to Toledo where she can be near Doña Luisa and in that warm climate which always improves her health. She loves to talk with Doña María about her Ladyship's kindness. And finally: "You can tell Father Velasco whatever you like and leave him to God." (A wise thought; the priest to whom she had first entrusted the manuscript could get all the blame for the long delay which caused those "ravings.")

It was the best Teresa could do to ease Doña Luisa's shock if she learned that the soul of a merchant Jew was due to receive care equal to that being given to the soul of her late husband, Arias Pardo.

Teresa wrote again in mid-December. Though she "still hasn't the strength to write much," she knows she'll soon be well in Doña Luisa's company, so isn't it splendid that the Lord is bringing it about? Her Ladyship must keep trying to get her a licence. (A letter now missing must have told of her intention to found another convent in Toledo.)

These letters are baffling until we know about a current situation in Toledo, one that made Teresa fiercely determined to accept *converso* merchant patronage even while it showed her the near impossibility of getting a licence without the backing of a grandee.

Chapter 26 ❀ Convents in Valladolid and Toledo

I

María Mendoza romanticized Holy Poverty: but she could not help drowning it in generosity. Teresa tried to choose nuns for Valladolid who could keep their simplicity despite the Mendozas' smothering over-kindness. She had left María Bautista behind in Medina; but, alas, Doña María missed that witty, charming young cousin, and persuaded Teresa to send for her when they moved into their new house. As Teresa had foreseen, Valladolid was María Bautista's native element; she became prioress at the second election and remained so lifelong. And living in plenty never made her love money less.

From the time Teresa heard from Father Hernández about a patron who was, as she discreetly puts it, "neither distinguished or well-born," she had been eager to try again. Her illness caused a delay that was peculiarly unfortunate. Nobles, Teresa had learned, had many ways of being difficult patrons. In the best of circumstances it would have been daring to put off the Princess of Eboli for the sake of an offer from the Jewish middle class, but between October and January it also became clear that she had taken the worst possible time to do it.

A Moorish revolt broke out in Granada, and the King sent the military to put it down. Toledo still had a large population of Moorish weavers, potters, and metalworkers; and in times of trouble with the Andalusian Moors, Toledo became a hotbed of distrust for all of "impure blood." In a similar climate of opinion, Juan Sánchez and his sons had gone before the Toledo Inquisition. Furthermore, claustral Orders were still on the King's black list. A *converso* might will hesitate to patronize a convent of a new enclosed Order.

In view of this, Teresa wrote to Alonso Ramírez, his late brother's executor: "When they stone you and your son, you will know that you will have lost nothing by founding this convent."

It was her call to battle: God rewards the brave. However, facts are facts; Teresa also knew that as things were in Toledo, *converso* patrons could not hope to get a licence. That was up to her. And if Doña Luisa were allowed to believe for a time that Teresa hoped to found without patrons, as she had in Avila, she might help. No outright lie would be necessary.

II

By mid-January, Teresa was well enough to leave Valladolid. There was much that always saddened her about that convent, so smothered in love and wealth; but for the sake of her friends the Mendozas she wanted her account of it to shine. So, when she came to write about its founding, she expanded the account to include the stories of two nuns who came there much later. One was a runaway heiress of twelve who fled to the convent to escape from an unconsummated marriage with her uncle, — and if Teresa had known how that story would end, she would not have set down its beginning.

The other concerned a gentle creature, Beatriz de la Encarnación, who bargained with God when the Inquisition held an *auto de fe* in Valladolid. She would give her life if any one of the condemned would repent, confess his heresies, and escape the stake — and hell. Apparently her prayer was granted; for she fell ill and died, joyfully.

Medina, on learning of the luxuries allowed to Malagón, had written to Rubeo, protesting that their rule was too strict. Teresa found a letter from him waiting there for her to read aloud: all convents must accept her as their director for she "was the precious stone upon which their Order was founded." (Rubeo's style was always florid.)

He also asked to hear about his two Discalced monasteries, which he assumed to be already founded.

Teresa herself was eager to see Duruelo. Two merchants, en route to Avila, offered her escort. I daresay Heredia had heard visitors approaching, for they found him sweeping the porch.

Teresa laughed: "Father, what has become of your honor!"

"I curse the day that I ever had any!"

The friary held three: Heredia, Fray Juan, and his retarded brother. It was theatrically poor; they slept on straw and went barefoot even through snow. (Which Teresa outlawed as unhealthy.) The merchants wept: "So many skulls, so many crosses!"

Do you know that drawing by John of the Cross which Dalí adapted and vulgarized: the cross that seems to lean forward as if seen by one staring up at the tortured, dying Christ? Teresa says:

"I shall never forget a cross made of two sticks over the holy-water stoup; a piece of paper was tacked onto it with a sketch of Christ which seemed to stir more devotion than a thing of the finest workmanship."

When she wrote that, she prepared her reader for further information which she would give without comment. Don Luis de Toledo had moved her first friar to a fine house where, as she put it, Heredia went because he felt that a famous painting from Flanders could inspire much devotion.

III

Teresa and a handful of nuns made their rough, perilous journey to Toledo on muleback. She had wangled an invitation to visit Doña Luisa, and her one letter from that stay in Toledo tells Doña María Mendoza that they had been given a room where they could be "as quiet as if they were in their own convent."

(This was only too true; once Teresa's new patronage was known, Doña Luisa and her circle withdrew.)

She also says, "These founders of mine are full of tricks." That, too, was true. Alonso Ramírez had turned the business of administering his late brother's affairs over to his son, Diego Ortiz, and Ortiz, by objecting to Teresa's Constitutions at every point, was doing his best to make her drop the whole thing, and save him twenty thousand ducats.

Teresa also adds — with as little explanation — that the Dominican Provincial is in town and preaching to large congregations, but she "has had no talk with him." The Provincial, Hontiveros, loved the Inquisition and hated Jews. Teresa's honest nun "Jerónimo" says that "Hontiveros was always glad to believe any talk about Teresa and friars."

That letter also contains a sentence which is the mirror image of one in a recent letter to Doña Luisa: It is pleasant, Teresa says, to hear Doña Luisa sing Doña María's praises, but, Oh, it is such a trial to be down here, away from her Ladyship.

Alas, all great ladies, even Doña María, needed flattery.

Weeks dragged on, and it seemed increasingly impossible to get a licence. Father Hernández could not help her. But a certain young Jesuit gave Teresa courage. As she says, she sometimes went to Mass at the house of the Company to meet "with others."

"Others" (for a tragic reason still to come) is the closest she can come to naming Martín Gutiérrez. In time he became Rector of Salamanca and persuaded her to found there. Now he only "understood her soul" and gave her courage to found in Holy Poverty, as she had in Avila, without help from either grandees or rich *conversos*.

The licence she needed would, in the proper course of things, have come from Archbishop Carranza; but he had been kidnapped and imprisoned for criticizing the mass executions in Valladolid. His place was held by the ecclesiastical governor of Toledo, one Girón, who knew that the city council opposed Teresa's convent as strongly as those of Avila and Medina had done — and this time with no opposition from the nobility.

Teresa decided that she would try to work through channels no more; she would see Girón herself. And encouraged by Father Martín — himself a *converso* — she told Diego Ortiz to keep his money; though after two months' struggle she had exactly three ducats left.

Girón's house was near a church. Teresa went into it and sent a messenger to beg for only a few brief words with him. The result is less surprising when we remember her meetings with Soto and General Rubeo; she always did best in face-to-face encounter.

"When I found myself with him, I told him what a miserable thing it was that when women wanted to live in such perfection and so strictly enclosed, they could do nothing about it simply because those who like to make spoiled pets of themselves objected to any works in the Lord's service. I said this with a great determination that the Lord gave me, and in such a way that he gave me a licence before he left."

Teresa had a licence, but she had no house.

She was assured right and left that no houses were available to rent or to buy. A merchant friend from Avila offered to help her and then sent word that he was taken ill. A Franciscan who came to the palace begging offered to help; he was leaving town, but he would send someone to meet her in the Jesuits' church.

The help that appeared was a youth named Andrada, in appearance wholly disreputable and reeking of poverty. When he assured her that nothing would be easier, her nuns enjoyed a laugh at her expense.

He appeared at the church the next morning, keys in hand. He had found just the place, and it was being vacated that very day. Would they come and look? There would have to be a small downpayment on the rent, but he would gladly help with moving in their furniture.

Teresa laughed at herself as she told him what the moving would amount to. Immediately upon getting the licence she had spent her last penny on two straw mattresses, one blanket, and two pictures — for something to put behind the altar, once an altar of sorts was made. Her nuns assured her that she would never see the boy again; clearly one so poor was only hoping for pay.

He was back after nightfall at the palace door as he had promised, along with two laborers who offered to help her with whatever had to be done before she had her first Mass said in the morning. Teresa borrowed the first month's rent from Doña Luisa's butler's daughter (which we only know from nuns less careful of Doña Luisa's feelings than Teresa felt forced to be in her book). Martín Gutiérrez lent her all that she would need to have things ready for the first Mass. They could not afford even a cracked bell to hang outside; but Teresa took along a second little bell like the one used at the Elevation, for a nun to ring at the door.

Two old women who rented a wing of the house were wakened in the night by the laborer's hammers; they took the noise of constructing a makeshift chapel for the racketing of vandals and became hysterical. But, Teresa says, "the Lord calmed them," the priest came, the first Mass was said; and as it had been in Avila and Medina, the convent could not be "unmade" without sacrilege.

By a later claim of the Toledan Carmelites, that Mass was celebrated by their Prior, Juan de la Magdalena, and "Doña Luisa heard it reverently." Juan de la Magdalena, in fact, was Teresa's lifelong enemy; but his surname conveniently was Gutiérrez. Juan de la Magdalena was thus named for the same reason that Teresa left Father Martín Gutiérrez unnamed: because of "a great false witness" in Salamanca that ended in tragedy. As for Doña Luisa, Teresa did her clumsy best. It may seem strange, she wrote, that a lady so fond of her should have let her and her nuns go off to suffer cold and hunger — "but perhaps she did not think of it."

They tried to keep warm by using their mantles for blankets. "We did not have so much as a twig to broil a sardine on," Teresa says. Then a neighbor dropped off a bundle of faggots which they lit and huddled over gratefully. Next, a few scraps of food began to appear. And within some days old Alonso Ramírez heard of the city council's fury over the new convent — which should have been his dead brother's. Pride and shame overcame his caution: he began at once to see that they got food and fuel and a little furniture; and Teresa could send north for more nuns.

She was hanging curtains with them and making the place more habitable when a coach drew up at the door. The Princess of Eboli had dispatched a manservant with a demand that Teresa come at once.

Teresa explained that it was impossible. The convent was not yet organized, and some of the nuns had just come to it from a convent of the Mitigation and did not even understand her Order's rule. She would see that the man was given a meal, and he could come back in a week or two.

The man was frightened. The Princess, he said, had already left Madrid and gone to Pastrana to wait for Mother Teresa; he could not go back without her.

The Princess, clearly, was a terror. But she was also the wife of Ruy Gómez, in whom Philip II, slightly paranoid in most of his relationships, had absolute faith. If Teresa angered the Princess and she, in turn, led her husband to sour the King, Duruelo-Mancera would turn out to be Teresa's first and last monastery; and in the man's world on which she depended, all future convents, too, would be doomed.

But how could she leave these nuns, all disorganized, some still uninstructed — and even, through Alonso Ramírez's belated kindness, robbed of that first sense of drama and holy daring which had held them together? One of them had looked downcast when the food and fuel began to come from Ramírez, and said, "Oh, Mother, now we can't feel poor any more!"

Teresa went into the chapel to pray before the Host. The Voice spoke: She must go and take a copy of her Constitutions with her; more was at stake than a single convent in Pastrana.

This was not what she had expected and she doubted its source.

As she says, though she heard the Voice and saw great reason for going, she still "did not dare." She sent for her confessor (Father Martín) and put the situation to him, but without mentioning the Voice: "For I am always better satisfied if I leave this out, only asking the Lord to give them light according to what they can know by their own human natures; and if the Lord really wants it done, he will put it into their hearts."

Her confessor told her to go, and she went. But for once Teresa would have done better to ignore her Voice and seek no further council.

Chapter 27 ❀ The Princess of Eboli

I

The appearance of the Princess's coach put Teresa in a new light. The Carmelites rushed over with a friar to go as her Pastrana chaplain. For her nuns, Teresa took Isabel de Santo Domingo (Old Fray Pedro's find, Isabel Ortega y Bracamonte) and a little lady from the Incarnation who had not yet chosen a name in religion. Their first stopover was in Madrid with Doña Leonora de

Mascarénas. Doña Leonora was also entertaining two other Eboli protegés: hermits, she explained, who had been given a hermitage in Pastrana though they were now living with her while the younger of them studied painting at her expense. This unusual way of being hermits goes unexplained, like most tales about this singular pair.

Mariano Azzaro was fifty-nine. Teresa did not doubt it that he was, as he said, an Italian knight who had, among other things, been governor of the palace of the Queen of Poland, and falsely accused of murder but cleared, like Susannah in the Bible, by witnesses who contradicted each other on cross-examination; witnesses whom he then saved from suffering any penalty for their perjury—though how he managed that also goes unexplained.

All accounts of his life are equally showy, but they vary. And those who claim that he was influential in the Council of Trent confuse Mariano with Maranini, an Italian Carmelite theologian.

But at least Mariano actually was an amateur engineer with a gift for selling his dubious schemes in high places. He had felt his call to the religious life when a plan sold to Philip for canalizing the Guadalquivir failed. He then, briefly, became a hermit in an illegitimate colony of holy men who all lived apart in the desert near Córdoba, praying—and spinning. (One account claims that Mariano could spin finer thread than any woman.)

There he met Juan Narduch, whom Teresa describes as "very simple." To judge from the autobiography he wrote in his old age, he was quite mad. Until he met Mariano he was often transported from place to place by invisible hands. He had joined the Franciscans, but they turned him out because of the racket made by the devils who tormented him. He also created miracle-working statues—in places where no such statue has been recorded. Then he met Mariano, and they became inseparable.

But they were restless hermits, and went to Seville, where Nicholas Doria, a son of the great Genoese banking family, first met them. Doria tells a story of Narduch's brief disappearance, Mariano's hysterical search for him, and their joyful reuniting, which indicates that Mariano told the truth when he assured Teresa that he had never been tempted to have anything to do with women.

It was also in Seville that Mariano met Ruy Gómez, who was there to size up the Moorish uprising from a safe distance. When Mariano told him that he had left his colony of hermits on hearing that it was opposed by the Council of Trent, Gómez—who felt that the Council opposed the King's Reform—invited him to Pastrana, which was full of caves, ideal natural hermitages. Mariano thanked him, but put off taking up residence there.

One popular tale about Mariano is worth considering before we limit ourselves to facts. At one time in his career—sometimes placed in the desert hermitage, sometimes Pastrana—Narduch found a rare pearl in his cell and took it to a Madrid broker who recognized it as property lost by the Princess of Brazil—or alternatively the Queen of Portugal. Narduch was jailed, but Mariano came and returned the jewel to the Queen, or Princess, who tried to give him a hundred ducats which he refused, saying that the gift would make him "a poor orphan."

No version explains how the pearl got into Narduch's cell; the fact that the devil planted it there is considered too obvious to mention.

At least one fact about Mariano is obvious: he throve on the credulity of a society in which few ever made Teresa's attempt to disentangle religion from superstition, let alone legend from history.

He also possessed an indisputable genius for selling himself. When Teresa showed him her Constitutions, he declared that he had never lived otherwise than in accordance with them, simply by instinct. When she told him of her need for a second monastery of her new Order, he told her that he had been given the perfect place for it in Pastrana, where she was going.

But he also knew enough to play hard to get. Despite his devotion to Holy Church, he told her, he had always avoided entering a religious Order; all were tainted with greed and worldliness, which shocked him.

She begged him to think about it for one night in prayer, and was overjoyed when he told her in the morning that he had been led to join her holy enterprise; he and his innocent brother Narduch would be her friars, like the two who had begun the work in Old Castile. Teresa could hardly wait to send the necessary letters to the present and past Provincials and the Bishop.

Teresa had been going through an extremely difficult time, and she deeply wanted to believe in the Voice she heard as she knelt before the Host in her unsettled new convent. This appearance of two friars, one so gifted and led by her own love for Holy Poverty, and the other so simple, must surely have seemed like a blessed proof that she had not been cowardly to obey the Princess, but truly, truly acting under divine guidance.

And let him who was never fooled by wishful thinking cast the first stone.

II

As page and prince, Ruy Gómez and the King had been boyhood playmates, and the friendship endured. The King had made Gómez Prince of Eboli and given him his Princess, Ana, when she was twelve years old. Her brother was Diego Mendoza, the brilliant humanist, and her grandfather had been the great Cardinal Mendoza, throughout his lifetime the most powerful man in Spain; on her mother's side she was a Medinaceli. She and Doña Luisa were first cousins.

For seventeen years there had been small love between the Prince and the Princess, so neither suffered from that marriage as much as might have been expected. The Prince loved the King, the Princess loved herself and, from time to time, the Prince's secretaries, in consequence of which she had eleven children — all promptly put out to nurse at hired breasts.

Despite these numerous inconvenient pregnancies, the Princess retained a strange, ethereal beauty to her last days; even allowing for the gross flattery of court painters, her portraits have a compelling loveliness which is only given piquancy because in childhood she had lost an eye, and wore a black patch.

She was oftenest referred to by her contemporaries as mad or "a terrible woman.' She was prone to rages in which she used her fists as often as her tongue; they could be triggered by the most trivial annoyances. Yet she also had periods, equally startling, when she was all gentleness, sweetness and light. She also alternated between her shameless infidelities and periods of prissy pietism.

The Prince was admitted, even by his worst enemies, to have a perfect disposition, charming manners, and a most delightful gaiety. He was handsome, small boned, and wore his blue-black, crisp-curled hair and pointed beard cut neatly close.

A contemporary who disliked him said that next to his God, he loved— in order—the King, cards, masquerades, jousts, tournaments, and banquets. This was unfair; he did much to further Spanish industry and exports, and he was a first-rate diplomat and peacemaker in times of domestic turbulence. The Spanish Moors and Jews had reason to be fond of him; he disliked unpleasantness.

In military and international affairs, however, the King leaned on his opposite number, the Duke of Alba, a man so unlike the Prince that the saying went, "To like the Duke is to hate Ruy Gómez and vice versa."

Pastrana was the Princess's Malagón, but she disliked the fortress castle and that year had built herself a palace set in gardens full of little artificial waterfalls and similar fancies, and now needed only a convent like those of her cousins María and Luisa.

This is the setting to which Teresa went, and to which she granted three paragraphs and part of another in her book, though she remembered her stay, from early June to mid-July, as three months. It must have felt endless at the time. There were, she says, many trials to bear and she would have left if she had not felt the overriding importance of founding that second monastery— though Ruy Gómez did his best to handle the Princess.

Eventually, it was opened, by Heredia, her first friar, as was proper. He came in the company of a new postulant, a famous preacher, for which she thanked God. That is all *Fundaciones* tells about Pastrana.

III

Despite La Eboli's demand that Teresa come at once, the house was not ready. Teresa and her nuns were penned in a single room of the palace for weeks. The finished house turned out to be minuscular, and its later improvements, according to Isabel de Santo Domingo, were not extra rooms, but "too many things" crammed into what space there was. They would live without income, the Princess told them; it would "show more perfection." However, if the villagers could not spare sufficient alms, she would eke them out. Which meant, they soon learned, that things could be run to suit the Princess or they would starve.

Early on, the Princess demanded that the convent admit a friend of hers, an Augustinian nun who did not like her convent in Segovia. Teresa doubted that such transfers were possible. She wrote to Báñez, who was in Alcalá, only a half-day's trip away and got his firm answer: "To receive nuns from other Orders is improper without mature and lengthy consideration."

The Princess was furious; but in her role as patroness of a convent she could not ignore a noted theologian's opinion.

This sort of thing Teresa could have put up with. The acid test of how much she wanted her second monastery—which would be free of female interference even from a Princess—was still to come.

Doña Luisa had probably complained of the inconvenience it had cost her to get a book, that Teresa called her "soul," to Juan de Avila and back to her again. The Princess asked to see it. When Teresa tried to explain why that was impossible, there were tantrums which finally became unbearable. The Princess read it, laughed herself sick, and circulated it among her ladies-in-waiting, who also found it hilarious. She also wrote to Madrid about it, with liberal quotes and witticisms. I suspect that the famous angel gave her the most fun.

Far too many vouch for this for me to doubt it; but it is such clear proof of mental instability that it leaves one pitying the creature with her rages and need for constant drama. To found a convent of Teresa's Order while simultaneously making her a laughing-stock leads one to think that the many who called the Princess insane did not much overstate her condition. She was, let us remember, a self-willed and virtually powerless person—a woman with no outlet but her tantrums and extravagances—who had been forced when she was twelve into marriage with one wholly indifferent and probably homosexual. Because of her rank, Teresa saw her as rather stronger than she was.

But Teresa meant it when she called that book her soul. Despite its censorings and unwilling additions, it was Teresa's confession in both senses of the word: her confession of sin and her confession of faith. When it was made the butt of lewd laughter, she could not have stayed in Pastrana if it had not been for her second, promised monastery.

While she waited, she made habits and mantles for Mariano and Juan Narduch, as she had for little Fray Juan—her one true follower in that first strange Company. She "had everything ready so that they could take the habit at once." Even before her own house was completed she sent to Medina for more nuns and waited for Heredia to bring them. He came at last with the "famous preacher" who would become prior of Pastrana: by name, Father Baltasar de Jesús.

Baltasar Nieto, exiled from Andalusia by Rubeo. Baltasar, the most violent of the three Nieto brothers.

Rubeo had told Teresa nothing about his stay in Andalusia; she knew that it was forbidden territory to her Discalced, but that was all, nothing more specific. When she went back to Toledo to finish all that the Princess had commanded her to leave undone, she still believed that the Voice which told her to go had come from God. An unsatisfactory convent had been made, but she had seen Heredia place the Host upon the altar of her second monastery.

She would be some months in coming to doubt the perfection of that monastery; the Princess could not disturb the work of men. But she had a clear moment of foresight about the convent. Before she left she instructed the Prioress, Mother Isabel, to keep a notarized inventory of everything that the Princess had given them or would give them.

That foresight and Isabel's following it to the letter was something they could both thank God for when it was needed, five years later.

Chapter 28 ❊ *A Year in Toledo; Inquisitor Soto*

It was one thing for Diego Ortiz to see Teresa as a liability forced on him by his late uncle's deathbed folly, and quite another to see her a treasure considered worth snatching from his family by the Princess of Eboli and the great Ruy Gómez. At her return he could hardly wait to set her up in the best part of town, in a convent whose splendid chapel would dazzle Toledo — a monument to *converso* piety and munificence.

Teresa understood him all too well. She intended to stay in the house that she had founded in poverty; but Doña Luisa's circle learned of Ortiz's offer — a fine house and a chapel to which the body of her merchant patron would be moved, with daily masses said there for his soul. Their furious protests soon changed her mind. Teresa recalls their effect in one of her private *cuentas de conciencia*:

"When I was in the Toledo convent and people were warning me not to permit a person who was not gentry to be buried there, the Lord said to me, 'You will make a great fool of yourself, daughter, if you attend to the rules of this world. Keep your eyes on Me, poor and despised by it. Perhaps the great of this world are great in My sight? Should you and yours be judged for their family origins, or for their virtues?'"

Teresa knew that an ostentatious merchant could upset a convent as well as any grandee. She insisted that the chapel and its masses were to be wholly Ortiz's concern and her nuns not required to attend them as part of the daily show. After ten months of arguing she hoped that it was so settled, but the nuns continued to be disturbed by that chapel until the year she died. It remained what it was, a splendid, over-decorated nuisance with eight (yes, eight) chaplains, continual crowds and loud singing — though at least the nuns did not have to perform.

Of that undesired munificence, over which she was forced to struggle nearly a year, her *Fundaciones* gives a glowing report: "The house alone cost twelve thousand ducats" and the chapel's many masses "are a great consolation to the nuns." But when her brother Lorenzo sent her two thousand ducats, she wrote him that it would leave her more free to speak her mind to her patrons, who constantly gave her money to turn their convent into a show-place and her into a business woman.

It is only from her letters to Lorenzo and her *cuentas* that we know the truth, and what the Voice meant when it had asked, "Should you and yours be judged for their family origins?"

Teresa had family loyalty, and Toledo was full of her relations. Uncle Rodrigo, who after the trial for false *hidalguía* went back to Toledo as plain Ruy Sánchez, had left a needy son and a daughter, for whom Teresa sent begging letters to Lorenzo — which were never ignored. While she was in Toledo her sister María's son joined the Alcantarines, and was made the friary's overworked courier, and Teresa wrote to his superior, de Segura, that she had not thought Pedro de Alcántara's Order "would forget Teresa de Jesús so soon." If the boy is not given more time to pray, she will "write to Doña María Mendoza and a few more of that kind."

She knew where power lay, and was willing to use it for a nephew's sake.

She also tells in a *cuenta* of complaining to God of Ortiz's burdensome munificence, and hearing the answer: "There can be no less of it, daughter. Try through it all to act with the right detachment and look to Me."

But the strain was hard and she was lonely. Martín Gutiérrez had been transferred to Salamanca, and Báñez suggested that she take Vincente Barrón, her father's former confessor, in his place; Barrón had been made a confessor to the Inquisition which might be useful.

Politically, Báñez was right; but Teresa's writings mention Barrón's name only once, in a list of useful names to drop when, seven years later, she was being tried by the Seville Inquisition. I doubt that Barrón ever really trusted her.

His connection with the Inquisition may account for her second visit from Inquisitor Soto. She showed him her *Camino*, and he suggested that she re-write it under sound guidance and appointed Dr. Ortiz (no relation to her patron) to oversee it; Ortiz was dean of theology at the University of Alcalá. The visit was pleasant, and Soto was surely delighted with what Teresa told him about Pastrana; he was strongly one of the Alba faction. Indeed he was on his way to visit the Duchess of Alba, where his visit resulted in a counter-invitation for Teresa to found a convent there. (Teresa asked Soto to take a note to her little nephew Gonzalo which, we gather from one of her letters to Juana, he forgot to deliver.)

Inevitably, a visit from an Inquisitor made talk. There are many reports of Teresa's *arrobamientos* during that stay in Toledo. But we also have her *cuenta* for the same time in which she tells of asking God why she has been spared those *arrobamientos* for so many years, and of being answered: "It would serve no good purpose. Now people trust you enough for what I am trying to do. After all, think of malicious people's failings!"

God, as usual, had put his finger on it. During her lifetime the raptures of the Saint of Raptures were reported only by the malicious, as evidence that Teresa, like so many women of impure blood, was an *alumbrada*.

Towards the end of that year in Toledo, Teresa wrote to Lorenzo that she was anxious to get back to Avila where her convent needed her and her long delay was vexing Bishop Mendoza, to whom she owed so much. Besides, she had another foundation in mind: "They have found me a house in Salamanca."

Nobody had found her a house in Salamanca, though Martín Gutiérrez had asked her to come; and after that confused, crowded, yet somehow empty year she longed to go and be with someone who "understood her soul." But that was something she did not want to write about in a letter that others would read.

So she opened a door to a tragedy at which *Fundaciones* does not hint.

Chapter 29 ❀ *Founding in Salamanca;* *the Bad Friars at Pastrana; The Book* *of the Foundations*

I

Teresa's foundations in Salamanca and Alba de Tormes led to three years of house arrest in the Incarnation. She believed that they would be her last foundations, and abandoned the book.

Luis de León, the great descendant of *conversos* and scholar who eventually became Teresa's first editor, had been imprisoned by the Inquisition during her stay in Salamanca. He knew the circumstances under which she was forced to write her belated chapters on Salamanca and Alba, and wisely decided that the book should not be published. Too many people knew too many facts. Poor Martín Gutiérrez was dead, the scandal on its way to oblivion, and those chapters she had written so much against her will only seemed to confirm, by their wild omissions and additions, what they tried to deny. And Teresa had known it, poor woman. Small wonder she had to give the book a new preface — simply to avoid blasphemy!

De León died believing that he had blocked the publication of *Fundaciones* forever. Consequently, he did not hesitate to publish Teresa's original preface as one of her *cuentas*, though it seemed to show that one of her manuscripts had been lost.

She was in Malagón, it said "in the last week of Lent" — that is, just after its Palm Sunday founding — when she saw Christ, "in an imaginary vision, as usual." A golden crown hid His wounded forehead and He told her that she must not grieve for His sufferings on earth but for those He was given now; and that she must go on making foundations and write about them as she had for San José de Avila.

She protested, and He pointed out that the founding in Medina had been a miracle: "I mean that only He did it when there seemed to be no way to go on. And so I determined to see the whole thing as good as done." Teresa wrote as naturally as she talked. In the 1968 edition of her *Obras Completas* the output of her last twenty years comes to over eleven hundred double-columned pages of fine print, and her letters show that several times as much again is lost. It is impossible to believe that she put off obeying Christ for four years and eleven months — though she asks us to in the preface to that book as it was first published, in Flanders, twenty-two years after the others.

137

She begins this preface with a prayer to be strengthened in holy obedience, a virtue not native to her, for the sake of the painful task before her. Back in 1562, in the Convent of San José de Avila, her then confessor, Father Fray García de Toledo, commanded her to write an account of that convent's founding, "along with much else." Now, "eleven years later" she is in Salamanca, it is 1573, and her confessor, the Father Rector of the Company of Jesús, Master Ripalda, has ordered her to write about the seven convents she had founded since, as well as about the beginnings of the Discalced Fathers of the Primitive Rule.

With so much other pressing business, this seems almost impossible, but God has taught her that obedience gives strength. She hopes that her readers will not think that in writing this she seeks any advantage for herself; her nuns know how little they owe her and how much to God, and she asks one Ave Maria from every reader to help her out of Purgatory.

She must also warn her readers that as she has such a poor memory, many important things will be left out—and her poor judgment may lead her to include things that had been better left out.

Teresa was too wise to hope that many would not shake their heads over all that was left out about the founding of the Salamanca Convent or the nonsense that had to be substituted for fact in the story of Alba de Tormes. But she was under orders, and she can only plead that she writes in unwilling obedience, not in cowardly self-service. She also needed that new preface, for her orders from Father Ripalda would not have come from Christ.

This is not to say that Ripalda was not a good man with a good purpose. He was trying to protect the reputation of the Company. Teresa would have chosen the wiser way of silence, through which in time all scandals are forgotten. Yet she obeyed and was rewarded in after years by being able to offer the Seville Inquisition the name of Ripalda along with those of the numerous other *letrados* who had given her their approval—though, she would add, Ripalda "had begun by thinking much ill of her."

It is a tragedy of the absurd that the two great scandals which both threatened and interrupted Teresa's career concerned her fondness for Martín Gutiérrez, when she was fifty-five, and for Jerónimo Gracián, when she was sixty. She loved them as she never loved a woman; but one could say the same for her love of her father and three of her brothers. It was a pattern that began in childhood, as blameless as the contrast between her love for Christ and her respect for His Virgin Mother.

True enough, her desire to found in Salamanca sprang in large part from what she found in Martín Gutiérrez; his many friends have described him as gracious, laughter-loving, idealistic, and dedicated to monastic reform. He was also a scholar with such a verbal memory that he seemed to have Aquinas by heart, a gift that offered Teresa protection from heresy incurred through her woman's ignorance. She had surely missed him.

But what he offered her in Salamanca mattered much more. She had founded five convents which all, in their varying ways, hampered her nuns when they tried to live the life that she had described in her Constitutions and the

Camino. In Salamanca she could found as she had founded in Avila and set out to found in Medina—in poverty, and strengthened by sheer faith.

She snatched at that hope for her convents yet to come, while she prayed for those now made. Yet the news from Pastrana made her more often wonder if she had been wise to ask for friars; if they went wrong no woman could set them right, and she heard no praise of the Pastrana friary that did not fill her with dread.

It was rising to fame in ways that are not surprising when one knows the whole picture, as Teresa did not: beginning with the identity of Prior Baltasar, the Nieto sadist. Simple Juan Narduch, who took the name of Juan de la Miseria, saw only through Mariano's eyes; Mariano knew what sold best in the holiness line; and the Prince was awed by the holiness inflicted on Baltasar's novice-boys by torture and near starvation.

Teresa heard enough to persuade Heredia to visit the place before she left Toledo, but he spent the visit with their Highnesses and managed to see nothing amiss. She went to Avila convinced that if Pastrana were not set to rights it would destroy all she had set out to build.

As, indeed, it nearly did—though the denouement was still some years away. Ruy Gómez was not one to act in haste, but he laid far-sighted plans and he knew that a nation-wide extension of the Pastrana movement could be shown to Philip as gratifying proof of the righteous power of the King's Reform.

As a first step, he wrote a humble letter to Rubeo. There was need for a Carmelite college in Alcalá, not technically Discalced, but true in spirit to Rubeo's ideals. That done, Pastrana would be enabled to found as many monasteries as Rubeo could desire, all filled with the same perfection for which Pastrana had gained such fame.

Rubeo, as ever obsessed with trivia, did not know that the Nieto whom he had exiled was Prior of Pastrana. Vargas, Nieto's friend and Philip's former ambassador to the Vatican, was now Apostolic Visitor to Andalusia, and in Granada the Duke of Medina Sidonia was kin to the Princess of Eboli and, like her husband, saw the political advantage to a nation-wide expansion of the Pastrana movement; but Rubeo, dead in love with Rubeo, did not dream that anyone would ever dare to ignore his strictures against founding in Andalusia.

Nor did Teresa. She was in Avila when Heredia sent Fray Juan to Alcalá as his emissary; the college was almost ready for occupancy by its staff and first eighteen students. He approved what he saw and went to Pastrana, where—unlike Heredia—he was shocked by what he would always call "the penances of beasts." He blamed the ugliness on the novice-master and replaced him with one Gabriel de la Asunción, a man whom he saw at once and rightly as capable of combining firm discipline with gentle persuasion. In consequence, what he told Teresa when he saw her in Avila on his way back sounded almost too good to be true. And it was.

Nieto and Mariano had shortened Fray Juan's visit by letting him think that he had some authority. When he left, they simply restored the status quo. They knew that Teresa could make no trouble; the Princess disliked her, and better yet, she was going to Salamanca.

Bishop Mendoza understood Teresa's long absence. He was sympathetic, not annoyed. He stressed the importance of the Duchess of Alba's invitation; in that polarized Court she needed the approval of both factions. Yet what she told him of the Princess and Diego Ortiz showed him her immediate, pressing need to found once more in poverty. But in Salamanca, and at a Jesuit's invitation? He had to warn her.

His brother Pedro had recently become Bishop of Salamanca and was already unhappy with his see. The dominant force in the University was Bartolomé de Medina, who held the Dominican Chair of Prime. He held enclosed convents suspect, loved the Inquisition, and disliked Jesuits — all Jesuits, but particularly those who, like their General, were of "impure blood." Pure blood was his obsession, and a number of the University's most distinguished professors felt distinctly threatened by their Jewish ancestry.

Pedro, the Bishop knew, would grant Teresa a licence all the more willingly because she was asked there by a Jesuit *converso*, but she should know that she was walking into the lion's mouth. Did she really want to risk it?

Teresa loved challenge. Even so she would have done better to recall de Prádanos, Ibáñez, Father Gaspar, García de Toledo — all demoted and sent away. Father Martín's situation was more precarious than theirs had been. His college was newly founded, in that very mid-October while she was in Avila; it was the crown of his career, a Jesuit college in Spain's greatest university; but it was won against opposition, and only a little "persecution" could harm it and him. But Teresa shut her mind to that already too-familiar word.

Or, almost. Though she says in her book, "To judge by the ease with which I got the licence it seemed to me that the convent was already as good as founded," she showed caution. She made sure that the de Ovalle niece who found her a house let nobody know its intended purpose, and she entered it first by night and with only one nun to bear her company; she intended that the Host be reserved and her "church" made before any others came to Salamanca.

That was on Halloween. By the following May, Teresa was grounded in the Incarnation, forbidden to found any more convents, ever. Everything had worked out according to Mariano's happiest expectations, and he even had a substitute "foundress" ready to present at court. It would take a miraculous preservation to recreate Teresa as a saint wholly to the King's taste — but Catalina de Cardona came ready-made and gift-wrapped for the purpose, as you will see in time.

Teresa had begged Rubeo for friars to give her order strength; she got what she asked for, but it was a strength over which she had no control and one which her growing multitude of friars used to serve ideals that were wholly alien to her conception of the religious life. To this she would find one exception, and believe for many gently deluded years that she had found two. In that lies this book's real story, to which all I have had to tell so far is prelude.

It had just begun when she was released to revisit Salamanca briefly, before she went on to found in Segovia. Martín Gutiérrez was dead, murdered in exile by Huguenots. Ripalda knew of the book that she had begun and ordered her to correct and continue it in a way that should deny the "great false witness" which had caused his friend's fall and tragic death.

Teresa obeyed; but Salamanca gets two chapters, for Teresa had barely begun the first when her pen ran away in a spate of words that you will understand once you know about the growth of the Pastrana movement, which had been so nourished by her ill-fated decision to found in Salamanca. There was nothing that she could do about the friaries — Altomira, La Roda (blessedly by the holy presence of its "friar", Catalina de Cardona), La Peñuela (of which it was said that in their excesses of penitential fervor none of the others even "reached to the foot of La Peñuela"), and Granada — in Andalusia, on forbidden ground. But she could at least struggle to save her nuns.

When you know the facts, I hope you will look back in pity at all that her "poor memory" omitted from the story of Salamanca and her "poor judgment" included in her account of Alba de Tormes; and that you will see her chapter of self-interruption for what it is: her never-cited reason for disobeying General Rubeo and going to Andalusia. You will also see why Teresa, in Segovia where she wrote these chapters, also eliminated whatever she had originally told about Malagón except that it was founded on Palm Sunday, and made her more obviously necessary censorings of the Toledo-Pastrana story.

Others have always interwoven the few facts in her Salamanca and Alba chapters with much that can be known from other sources. Those chapters tell more, you will see in time, as they stand: more of the tragedy that they try to conceal, its aftermath, the grim obedience in which they were written, and the equally grim determination with which they reinforce the unspoken appeal of her preface, an appeal to be questioned and disbelieved.

Chapter 30 ❄ *Teresa's Very Partial Account of the Foundings in Salamanca and Alba de Tormes*

I

She had, Teresa begins, returned to her Toledo foundation from Pastrana and was getting it in order when she received an invitation from the Rector of the Company of Jesus in Salamanca to found there. She hesitated, because the city is "very poor" (which it definitely was not), but she considered that Avila was just as poor, and on reaching Avila wrote for a licence "from the one who was then Bishop." This was promptly granted, and a lady she knew rented her a house, taking care that its purpose not be known. For greater secrecy, she went with only one nun, arriving after a long, cold journey on which she had been very ill.

Then, her pen runs away.

She will say nothing, she begins, about those journeys through snow, through fierce summer heat, in illnesss and crippling pain — and then says much about them, and how they could not deter her from their purpose: the creation of one more "church" when so many were being destroyed by "those Lutherans."

At which point she plunges abruptly into her plea for gentleness and human understanding in the religious life: "Though I may be going far from the foundation I started to tell about, certain things about mortification occur to me here and now." (Mortification: in Teresa's vocabulary, the practice of love in action, freed from self-centered desires and self-righteousness.)

We all have different talents and virtues. No prioress must try to force her own on those with other gifts. One given to penance must not drive her nuns to penitential lives; one much given to prayer must not keep nuns on their knees when they would be better off abed and asleep. When a prioress "gets drunk on her virtues," her "poor lambs of the Virgin" are forced to obey until they are empty of all real virtue, all inner life: they are only "flayed lamb-skins." For even holy obedience becomes temptation if it leaves a nun so "drunk with God" that she endangers her health and her sanity.

That happens. A prioress in Malagón had made such an idol of blind obedience that when a nun showed her an enormous worm that she had dug up in the garden and the Prioress said, "Well, go eat it," the girl went directly for the frying-pan. Amusing, perhaps; but not the case of the prioress who, in boasting of the state to which her nuns were reduced, said of one that she would obey if she were ordered to throw herself down the well. The girl had to be rescued from drowning, for the poor creature took it as a command, though it was a command to suicide, a mortal sin.

Obedience is necessary if there is to be order, peace; but until a nun has learned obedience, a prioress must never, never try "to improve her by brute force . . . but dissemble and go on gently, little by little, until the Lord can do what is needed . . . for to disturb her spirt and burden her with affliction is a terrible thing."

Teresa had learned much since she praised the girl who planted the wilted cucumber because "obedience had so blinded her natural reason." That girl is said to have been María Bautista, — perhaps because Teresa wrote to her years later, "You must realize that I no longer govern as I used to. Love does it all."

It was dangerous to say even so much about the Pastrana disease. One known to have seen visions could not safely attack the only way of life which — to the mind of Teresa's world — cleared them of being visions sent from hell. But it had to be said, and for the whole chapter which I have here condensed, Teresa's pen ran away.

II

"I have gone far astray," her next chapter begins, "but when I am reminded of something that the Lord has taught me through experience, it seems wrong not to point it out."

Then she tells what she may about Salamanca.

When she reached the city, she was *bien mala*—good and sick. She sent for Nicolás Gutiérrez, "a good man who had lost a fortune but bore the loss cheerfully." He "worked on the foundation with great willingness and devotion." The previous tenants had been students who left the house filthy. They worked all night to have it ready for the first Mass, but the Host could not be reserved; the place was still too dirty.

The next night they slept on straw under borrowed blankets. Her companion, old María del Sacramento, made her laugh with her fears of ghosts, of lurking students, and of what the poor Mother would do if she, María, died in the night. Next day a nearby convent sent them bedclothes, and she sent to Medina for more nuns. The community stayed in that house three or four years, she forgets which, as "they" sent her back to the Incarnation. (No comment or explanation . . .)

She hated to leave the house unsettled, though during her absence she managed to arrange for its support. But the nuns were often ill because the house was unhealthy, and worst of all they could not have the Host reserved. (Again, no comment; we are left to think that the dirt left by the students defeated three or four years of housecleaning.)

Finally a superior (unidentified) took pity on the nuns and brought her back. She bought them another house, "though without the King's licence," so they had their own chapel at last. The roof leaked and she feared it would rain in on their installation Mass; but Nicolás Gutiérrez reassured her, and sure enough, the sun came out and all went well.

So much and no more for Salamanca.

III

Alba de Tormes presented a problem that could not be handled by omissions alone. Why Teresa de Laiz, not the Duchess of Alba, was made its nominal patroness, called for decoration.

Luckily, Señora de Laiz herself was highly imaginative, and in the most popular contemporary vein. So, in a startling flashback of almost "three or four years," Teresa begins.

She had been in Salamanca less than two months when the wife of the Duke's steward invited her to found in Alba. She hesitated, because in a castle-village she would have to accept an endowment, but her "confessor, Father-Master Domingo Báñez, who happened to be there," insisted that she accept.

Señora de Laiz's parents were "very much children of somebody" and "of pure blood," but they were poor, so the lady had "'no education.'" Because she was the fifth girl in a row, she was forgotten for three days after birth. Then "the woman who took care of her" suddenly remembered the child and hurried to the cradle, expecting to find her dead. She snatched her up, saying, "How now, child, crying because you are not a Christian?" At this, the baby lifted her head and said, "Yes, I am." Since there were "several witnesses" to this wonder (after that empty room of the past three days!) the child "was brought up in the ways of chastity and virtue," and when her parents found her "a rich and virtuous husband" she went with him to Alba. There he had to share a house with a man who lusted after her, so she persuaded her husband to leave for Salamanca and work as an accountant at the University.

They had no children, and when she prayed for them, St. Anthony granted her a vision. She saw him standing beside a well, and beyond it was a field of white flowers. The Duke then rehired her husband, "at a smaller salary" but in a house he need not share; and to her amazement, the house, the well, and the field were those in the vision, lacking only the white flowers.

This she saw as a sign that she found a convent, but when all, including her confessor, dissuaded her, she and her husband decided that they would instead arrange a marriage between her nephew and his niece and give them their property. (The "rich and virtuous" husband's wealth disappears and reappears in this tale without comment.) But God showed his disapproval, for the boy dropped dead, and the confessor—a Franciscan—changed his mind, and told the lady about Teresa's convents.

Having thus set down Teresa de Laiz's tale in its undoctored implausibility, Teresa slips into her own voice:

"Her confessor suggested that she talk it over with me. We had great trouble in coming to an agreement. Finally they came to see reason and gave enough for that number [as in Malagón it was to be twenty from the start] and what vexed them most, was giving up their house for it and having to move to another which was in very bad condition.

"The foundation was made and the Holy Sacrament reserved on the Feast of St. Paul to the honor and glory of God, where—so it seems—His Majesty is much served. May it please Him to lead it further forward."

IV

Think about it.

First the Señora's tale, then a hassle with her husband, the Duke's steward, over money, and the lady's unwillingness to leave the house for the purpose shown in her vision by St. Anthony: what is this but a deliberate plea for disbelief? And as if to make assurance doubly sure, Teresa adds that she has decided to tell no more stories like the one about the nun who died in Valladolid after bargaining her life for a heretic's confession and repentance, since such tales might be seen as miraculous; also, "In the account of the years that these Foundations were made I suspect that sometimes I have been inaccurate, though I have tried as hard as I could to remember. But since that doesn't matter much, seeing that it can be corrected later, I tell about them in what I can take notice of in my memories. It will make little difference if I have been incorrect."

We know that the chapter gave her troubles because, years later, when she

144

had the story of another convent to tell, or rather, to avoid telling, by the same distasteful method (this time, the yarns about Catalina de Cardona) she wrote to Avila for the original version of the Alba story (now destroyed). Only three convents out of fifteen gave her similar trouble; for the others, simple omission was enough.

Now we can grant her the grace of a few facts about Salamanca and Alba de Tormes.

Chapter 31 ❀ *Cause of the Delay in Salamanca; What Happened in Alba de Tormes*

Ribera, Father Martín's fellow Jesuit and Teresa's first biographer, did better with the Salamanca story. He stressed Teresa's spiritual debt to Martín Gutiérrez and quoted her as saying that his death was the hardest loss she had ever borne. (Though, as with the supposed drowning of her brother Rodrigo, he adds that she "was comforted because he died a martyr.")

When Teresa came to Salamanca, Father Martín was forty-six. He had only with difficulty persuaded Borgia that it was wise to found a Jesuit college in a university that was becoming so virulently pro-Inquisition and right wing, and Borgia had been wise to hesitate. In a few years time, General Laínez would be replaced by Francis Borgia and the latter by Mercurian, a man remarkably unlike Ignatius Loyola or his first successor, and the Spanish Jesuits could begin to feel secure. But now they were still on trial, and suspected of the one vice of which no enemy has ever since accused them—excessive mysticism and visionary delusions. (Loyola's diaries, which describe the great mystic experience of his conversion and his subsequent visions and frequent floods of tears, come to most of his readers as a surprise.)

The college was not yet a month old when Teresa arrived. Martín knew that opinion on her was divided, and that the approval of two Mendoza bishops cut no ice with the Inquisition. She was suspected of illuminism, heresy, and known without question to be a nun who disregarded her own rule of enclosure. As the Dominican Antonio Laredo put it, "If she had been a man who had to preach and travel, it might have done them [her nuns] some good. But a woman who should have stayed enclosed—what would she do for them?"

From the start Martín must have wondered if his invitation had been wise. Then just before her arrival his newborn college got a letter from the Jesuit Rector in Avila, warning all Jesuits against her.

Julián de Avila, who dropped her off at the inn and left at once for Medina, found the city well stirred up on his return. "None of them" he writes, "understood what she said or felt, though most of those who slandered her were important and highly learned."

One can see why Father Martín sent his brother Nicolás to meet Teresa when she arrived at high noon and why Nicolás sent Julián back to Medina at once. The nuns, at least, were veiled, but Teresa's chaplain might be recognized.

Father Martín came to the inn after nightfall along with two friars and a carpenter, who remembered that night for Teresa's beatification process. It was eight o'clock, the carpenter says, and he was tired from a long day's work, but he could not resist Father Martín's "determination." All four men worked until four in the morning, "shutting some doors and opening up others and making a window into what would be the chapel." Father Martín also got a carter to fetch lumber for what would be a rough altar, as well as two benches, two blankets, and some straw to serve as beds, though the nuns got no rest that night. They spent it in sweeping and cleaning. Then, before dawn, one of the friars went for the vestments and vessels and Father Martín said Mass. (To this Mass, one of the friars, Bartolomé de Pérez Núñez, also testifies.)

But no bell announced the Mass to the outside world, for Teresa had made no "church." After that only Mass ever offered in the house, Father Martín consumed the Host. He had urged Teresa to come to Salamanca, but now she had come he dared not make the public gesture of granting her a chapel which housed the Body of Christ.

Salamanca was a painful chapter in Teresa's life, for cowardice was a fault that she found it hardest to condone. Teresa reached Salamanca on the last of October and left it for good in the following May, but as *Fundaciones* admits, that convent had no "church" for "three or four years." But sadly for her, flaws in the men Teresa loved never made her love them less.

Before she came, Martín had learned enough from the Rector of Avila and from his brother Nicolás, who lived there, to be wary. There is no reason to doubt the beatification testimony of Fray Bartolomé de Pérez Núñez that he invariably chaperoned Martín's visits to the convent, though he overstated it when he said that he always remained within earshot — since one cannot evesdrop on the confessional. Fray Bartolomé can also be believed when he says that "they only talked about the things of God." It is even possible, in view of two tragic *cuentas* which Luis de León salvaged from Martín's papers after his death, that as Fray Bartolomé says, Teresa "told of many visits from the Lord," though we may hope that he embroidered when he adds that she "described her many bodily penances and fierce austerities." Still even that is possible, for at the end of that stay Teresa was less emotionally stable than she had been since the loss of de Prádanos, which had made her, for a time, a conspicuous danger to the Incarnation.

This fact, plus the "great false witness," are Ripalda's excuse for bungling things so badly and demanding an account of Salamanca, Alba, Salamanca, the house arrest in the Incarnation, and Salamanca again, an account so full of omissions that even to a reader partially informed it seemed to cry aloud that there was much to hide.

Take, for example, the contrast between Teresa's story of how she was forced to desert Toledo temporarily by the Princess of Eboli and how the same thing happened when an order — in more humiliating form — came from the Princess's opposite number, the Duchess of Alba, and at a still worse time: for the convent she had to leave was not only unsettled but "unmade"; its altar was bare, and it could be "depopulated" at any time without sacrilege.

For Pastrana she could tell of prayers, her Voice, and, despite Its orders, her lingering doubts. For Alba she could only say that she hesitated to found for the steward's wife because a convent in that place would need an endowment, but that this hesitation was overcome by "[her] confessor, Father Fray Domingo Báñez."

Báñez knew the situation. In September, when Teresa decided to accept Father Martín's invitation, Báñez had gone to Salamanca to give a lecture. (For which he was paid one ducat; it's on the books of the Dominican college.) He had seen how Melchor Cano (who played a key part in the Inquisition's imprisonment of Archbishop Carranza and his like-minded fellow-Dominican Bartolomé de Medina) had begun to terrorize the University. He could see that it would have been the wrong time for Teresa to go there at the invitation of a Jesuit *converso* and on a licence granted by the notorious Jew-lover Bishop Pedro de Mendoza, even if it had not been planned as the next step before giving the Duchess her convent in Alba de Tormes. And as such it was madness, for Alba is near Salamanca, and Bartolomé de Medina was the Duchess's confessor.

What Báñez expected, of course, was that the Duchess would simply withdraw her offer on de Medina's advice. As it turned out, she could not make up her mind. Teresa had been vouched for by Inquisitor Soto, and by that keen-minded friend of the de Toledos', Heredia — not to mention her several noble patronesses. Still, de Medina did seem to know that Teresa might have trouble with the Inquisition. Ruy Gómez could weasel out of such an embarrassment if he found he'd made a mistake in his work for the King's Reform. But could she afford such trouble? Ruy Gómez was making Philip increasingly dissatisfied with the Duke's firm way of quelling unrest in Flanders; there were even more rumors that the Duke might be recalled. Furthermore, wasn't it a sin to offer a religious Order a convent and then renege? The Duchess was hesitant.

She was also rather a fool; and it finally came to her that she could put the convent in her steward's name, or his wife's if the patronage had to be that of a woman. Her friends need not know, and if trouble ever developed she could produce a documented disclaimer.

It was an insult. Teresa's angry report of it brought Báñez back to Salamanca. The Duchess was a fool, but Teresa must not let herself be angered: she needed the support of both wings of that polarized Court. That's life, in this Spain of ours. To do any good one must accept the world as it is.

As Teresa says, they "quarrelled" when he "happened" to be there, but she gave in. He "happened" to do more. He went to Alba, persuaded the Duchess that de Medina did not represent the whole body of Dominican opinion, and offered to take the business out of her hands by staying inconspicuously in Teresa's sister's house and acting as Teresa's representative, while the Duke's noble and respected secretary, Albornoz, should act for her.

So Teresa left her disorganized "unmade" convent, hoping against hope that the Duchess's cautious loophole need not become known and reflect on her Order's honor or that of Father Martín, who already saw that he should not have brought her to Salamanca.

She signed the preliminary papers on December third, a month and three days after she got to Salamanca. Juan de Ovalle signed for the steward's wife, who could not write: he makes her name Teresa de la Iz.

But the Alba foundation, too, was interrupted. Teresa's cousins Inés and Ana came to fetch her post-haste to Medina to oversee an election which threatened them with trouble. Inés had just finished her triennium, and in the natural course of things would be reelected, but she had angered Angel de Salazar, and he intended to make Doña Teresa de Quesada their prioress, as he had made her sister, Doña Ana, the first prioress of San José de Avila.

The situation involved the fortune of Simón Ruiz's niece, Isabel de los Angeles. It was large, and her uncle had expected it to pass at her death to his children; family fortunes should be kept intact. But Isabel was determined to give it all to the Discalced, and Father Angel, who respected great fortunes, sided with the family. There had been scenes. During one session in which he tried to shame Isabel for her disloyalty to her kith and kin, she tore off her Carmelite scapular and stamped on it.

Eventually, the family offered a compromise: Isabel might give the Discalced her money if it were used to build a magnificent chapel and her family recognized as its patrons. Teresa was fresh from Toledo and Diego Ortiz's chapel with its eight chaplains and constant holy racketing; she knew how such a gift can disturb convent life, and refused. Inés and Ana, moved by their own family pride, backed their foundress cousin's refusal, and Father Angel was furious.

So Inés and Ana hurried to Alba. Teresa must get to Medina before Father Angel could push the election through, and encourage the nuns to assert their own right of choice.

Inés never much liked Teresa, but she saw her as her only hope. Teresa had strong family loyalty and she was grateful to Inés for backing her opposition to that chapel. She explained the situation to Báñez, took cousin Ana de la Encarnación to Salamanca, hastily installed her as Prioress of the disorganized, "unmade" little convent she had been forced to desert, and went off in a rush to Medina, where she called for an immediate election.

Inés won by a landslide. The Carmelite friars got the news, misinterpreted it, and spread it about that Father Angel had changed sides, hoping to gain more, in the long run, from the stubborn heiress than from her family. This slander, of course, threw Father Angel into a blind rage. He galloped to the convent, pronounced the election void, Doña Teresa de Quesada Prioress, and Teresa excommunicated. He then ordered Teresa to leave at once.

It was night, Teresa was ill, and the only conveyance that could be found was a water-carrier's cart too small to hold the required companion for a travelling nun: but the order was "out!" The winter cold had brought on one of Teresa's rheumatoid seizures of near-paralysis, but she was half-lifted, half-shoved into the cart and shipped off. By the convent records, this happened on December twelfth.

Teresa rested for a day in Avila, hired a wider cart, and went back to Alba with a young novice as her companion. That novice would become the Venerable Ana de Jesús, largely on the strength of her highly imaginative memoirs of "La Santa." Of this journey she writes (incorrectly) that they made a side trip to visit the Bishop of Salamanca at his country place in Aldarrubias, where they got a license for the convent in Alba. Actually, Teresa—defeated, ill, and shocked by her excommunication—only wanted to get back to her sister's house in Alba as soon as possible.

The excommunication was invalid, Báñez assured her; the General had specifically laid it down that her convents should be subject to no interference from those of the Observance, their Provincial included. The new Apostolic Visitor, Báñez's friend Pedro Fernández, would overrule it at once.

Báñez writes that he reminded Teresa of how this same Fernández, at the Medina junta, had told "a monk of a certain Order"—that is, the Augustinian, Sosa—"who spoke much evil of the Mother and called her a Magdalena de la Cruz," to drop his baseless, vicious talk or get out of the assembly.

But at this, Báñez adds, Mother Teresa cried, "Oh, sinner that I am, they didn't know me. If that Father had really known me he could have said much worse things about me—but not that I am a fraud!"

Then she ran from the room with her eyes shut and gave her head such a whack on the door as might have knocked her unconscious. Her sister, running to help her, found her sitting on the floor, laughing. "Oh, sister, what they are saying about me now is like this bump—I know where it hurts. The other things they said back there—I didn't even know where they hit me."

Apparently, the "great false witness" had already begun to stir in Salamanca, for in the context that Báñez gives these words, Teresa means "Slanders that falsely impugn my confessors hurt; those that impugn my unwavering Catholic faith only glance off, not worth a second thought." Báñez at least wrote this account with the Salamanca scandal in mind.

Báñez and the steward, Señor Velázquez, had done much of their haggling over the Duke's money in Teresa's absence. Báñez had won an agreement for a generous yearly income for the twenty nuns specified by the Duchess. That income, it should be noted, was one-third again that of the steward's recorded salary as accountant for the University, though that (according to his wife) had been more than he had earned in Alba.

These arrangements made, the house had to be readied; and since Teresa could not yet leave for Salamanca, her mind turned back to the Pastrana movement. Fray Juan de la Cruz should still be in Alcalá. Báñez could persuade Heredia that the Duchess could use Fray Juan's help with her new convent; and thereafter, that sending him back to Alcalá as his representative would show that Heredia's friends, the ducal de Toledos, were as close to the King's Reform as the Princess of Eboli. Báñez, his friend, the new Apostolic Visitor, could see to it.

This worked out fairly well. Though Fray Juan had no interest in Court politics and spent most of his time out-of-doors, helping the laborers wall in the convent grounds, he shared Teresa's unhappiness over the Pastrana movement, and his subsequent talk with the Visitor, Fernández, resulted in his becoming, for a time, once more Rector of the Carmelite College of Alcalá.

At last the convent was ready for occupancy. The Bishop's license, issued on December twentieth, ends its general approval with the words "especially as we are assured that Francisco Velázquez, steward of the Duchess of Alba, agrees to give the convent its proper benefactions and estate." Nicely put, capable at need of either interpretation: Velázquez the patron or Velázquez the steward. But his wife, Teresa de Laiz, rates no mention.

Rather than come himself, the Bishop sent a representative to lead the procession which bore the Host from the ducal Church of San Pedro to the convent altar. Nonetheless, the foundation ceremony was magnificent. The local monasteries, Franciscan and Jeronimite, sent all their nuns to swell the procession, following Teresa and her nuns — almost all of whom were chosen by the Duchess.

Teresa's sister and brother-in-law attended the Mass, as did the "foundress" and one of her brothers; but her husband, Velázquez, stayed away (a show of resentment, perhaps, at his eviction to a house which, as Teresa says, was *muy ruin*). These lesser figures, however, are overlooked in the account written by the Duchess's son-in-law, the future Bishop of Jaen. He names only the Duchess; her daughter Doña Juana de Toledo; the dowager Marchioness of Velada; and their cousins, the Count and Countess of Monterrey. These he mentions with family pride to show the occasion for what, in truth, it had been: de Toledo support of "La Santa" long before her sanctity was generally recognized.

Teresa liked to name her convents for St. Joseph; Teresa de Laiz would doubtless have preferred St. Andrew. But the choice was the Duchess's, who named it for Our Lady of the Conception.

How Teresa felt about it all we know from a letter she wrote just before she left Alba. In Toledo, a lawsuit was going on between the convent's eight chaplains and the priest of the church in which Martín Ramírez was buried; so Ramírez was still having his disruptive masses said for him *in absentia*. Teresa wrote to Diego Ortiz that despite such difficulties, God only knows how she wishes that she had never left Toledo. "I tell you, I don't recall a day I've had without many, many troubles since I left it. I have founded two more convents; this is the least of them. Pray God it may be of some service to Him!"

It remained of depressingly little service by Teresa's standards, but Báñez had meant well, and he meant well by his attempt to keep her from going back to Salamanca. He travelled with her, and persuaded her to spend some time with their travelling companions, the Count and Countess of Monterrey.

After Báñez's death, the Venerable Ana de Jesús would cite him as witness to a miracle there, which he himself forgot. A daughter of the house, a very young girl, was dying. Teresa touched her, she was healed, and Báñez, who had seen St. Catherine and St. Dominic presiding over the miracle, suggested that the girl, in gratitude, should take the Dominican habit for a year.

This story is weakened by the fact that the girl whom Ana de Jesús names was at that time thirty and married to the future Duke of Olivares. Perhaps this explains why two slightly later accounts of this miracle make the girl an unidentified small child, and alternatively, a servant — the latter edifying as an instance of La Santa's indifference to worldly rank.

However, one fact about that visit is certain. The Condes de Monterrey became Teresa's warm friends, though they could do nothing to help her in the immediate future.

Chapter 32 ❀ *Teresa and Martín de Gutiérrez; Climate of Fear*

Teresa, back from two months of conflict and compromise, found her convent in a bad way. The house stood beside an open sewer, and the nuns ran constant fevers. Even in Medina, when the "church" was a tumbledown porch walled in with curtains and a bedspread, there had been the comforting presence of the Host. At one unwilling level she must have known that it would be best to call Julián de Avila to take those girls back to their own convents; but she could not give up.

She now knew fully what she and her Jesuit confessors, with their Jewish blood, were up against. De Medina and Melchor Cano were powerful, and on the prowl for *converso* heresy. But she tried not to know why Martín came to the convent so seldom and stayed so briefly. Teresa loved him too much to face his lack of faith in God's power to protect those who set out to heal His Church; and too much not to suffer an intensely personal sense of loss that she blamed herself for as an "imperfection." Out of that sense of loss and the shame it brought, she wrote this *cuenta*:

"One day the Lord said to me, 'You are always desiring trials with one part of yourself and refusing them with another. I arrange things to conform to your will, not to conform to your sensuality and frailties of the flesh. Strengthen yourself, for you must see that I do it to help you; I have wanted you to win this crown. In your own day you will see the Virgin's Order greatly advanced.' I heard this from the Lord in the middle of February, 1571."

She believed that promise and she wanted, God knows, to want her crown of thorns; but wanting it grew increasingly hard. Instead she could only feel, more and more, the aridity that she called "being absent from God."

Martín Gutiérrez cannot be blamed. The Jesuits in Spain still had to be careful. In December, when Teresa was gone to Alba — and, Martín may have hoped, gone for good — he wrote to Francis Borgia. The Jesuits, he said, had been in Spain for twenty-three years and though they had finally got a college accepted in Salamanca they still had no church as the other Orders had. One room set apart for Masses was not enough: "We even have no place to hear confessions, and if something is not done it will go on like this year after year."

It is a useful sidelight on his situation. In Salamanca the Jesuits were still clinging to the outer edge. Moreover, Teresa was being denounced from the most influential pulpits—Dominican, Augustinian; and such news travels. Francis Borgia certainly remembered Teresa; one did not forget her—and no administrator would have forgotten having to remove the able subrector, de Prádanos, from Avila.

But in all Orders there was fear in the air. *Conversos* thought twice about what they said from the rostrum and what they published; there was danger from the Inquisition in words they would have spoken and books they would have published in confident hope of advancement a year or two earlier. We need not wonder that the Jesuit Provincial, Gil González, wrote several times to Borgia about the new Rector. His disposition, he said, had changed. From being trustful and outgoing, he was becoming ever more rigid and withdrawn.

Yet, during that period, Martín did commit one indiscretion. He lent Teresa Luis de León's recent translation of the *Song of Songs*. Within the year this translation would land de León in a dungeon of the Inquisition, since it might lead the ignorant to read it as secular writing, an epithalamion, not a prophetic work on the love between Christ and his Church. At least Gutiérrez did not encourage this error, for when Teresa, back in the Incarnation, wrote her *Meditaciones sobre los Cantares*, she did not even grasp that it was a duet—either sacred or profane. She expounds, for example, "Let him kiss me with the kisses of his mouth, for thy breasts are sweeter than wine," is the soul's response to God's tenderness, like a woman's yearning for her lover, or a child for its mother's breast.

Teresa was ordered to burn that book. If she had obeyed—as she only appeared to—religious literature would not have been greatly impoverished. Needless to say, it was not published during de León's lifetime. And before that, Yepes countered rumors that Teresa had read the Bible, and in particular, the Song of Songs, with an anecdote. (Yepes, who transformed Teresa's acting as night-nurse to a priest in a private home from scandal to evidence of the nobly born Santa's holy humility.) In Toledo, he says, a young lady applied for admission to Teresa's convent, saying that she owned a Bible and would bring it with her. Teresa responded as a saint should: "Bible, daughter? We want neither you nor your Bible! We are ignorant women who only know how to spin and to follow orders." The girl, Yepes adds, died thrée years later, at the stake as she deserved.

On being released from the Inquisition's dungeon, de León returned to the podium years later and began his lecture: "As I was saying yesterday. . . ." Then, in going through his dead friend's papers, he found some of Teresa's. Among them was a collection of seventeen prayers, or rather, outpourings of her troubled soul to God. These he copied and misdated, 1569, destroying the original. (His copy is still in the University of Salamanca.) They begin, "Oh, life, life, how can you sustain yourself when you are making yourself absent from your Life?"

Why are we so brave, another asks, in fighting off God but never in fighting off the devil? Oh, if it were not a sin to end this life and be done with it!

And, last of all, comes her tragic doubt of the freedom to know "a love in Christ" with men: the freedom from earthly loves that she had belived to be the gift of the glorious Rival. "Oh, free will to please yourself, so enslaved by your own freedom if you do not live enslaved by God!"

These passionate self-searchings and appeals to Christ are profound and moving. De León published them as "Exclamations and Meditations on the Soul's Way to God, by Mother Teresa." He also found two letters to Martín which he published among the *cuentas* which made an appendix to his edition of the *Life*. One could wish that he had not, if they did not explain so much about the end of the Salamanca story.

Ten days before she wrote these two letters, she wrote a letter to Diego Ortiz, so suave, so tactful that one can hardly believe that they came from the same pen. She is in a hurry to get her Salamanca nuns well housed so that she can get back to Toledo. And who wouldn't be in a hurry to see your dear old father-in-law, Ramírez, once again? Etc.

De León doubtless found those letters to Martín reminiscent in quality to his favorite parts of the *Life*: his — like ours — were those of his times. They were written when Teresa could no longer say anything to Martín that was not also for Fray Bartolomé de Pérez Núñez's ears; for the whisperings had made Teresa see that it was kindest and best for her to take a Carmelite confessor so that it might be known that they did not even share the privacy of the confessional.

Palm Sunday always meant much to Teresa: the day when all Jerusalem crowded to hail their Messiah, only to turn against him when they realized that His Kingdom was not of this world. That year, Palm Sunday fell on April eighth. Teresa went to Mass, and a few days later sent Martín this letter:

"On Palm Sunday, after I received communion I stayed in such a state of suspension that I could not swallow the Form. When I came back to myself a little with it still in my mouth it really seemed to me that my mouth was full of blood; and then it seemed as if my face and my whole body were covered with it, as if the Lord poured it out. It felt warm to me, a sensation of exquisite sweetness, and the Lord said to me, 'Daughter, I want my blood to do you good. I poured it out in great suffering and you enjoy it in great delight. You see, I repay you well for the invitation you have always given me this day'."

For thirty Palm Sundays past, she goes on, she had gone to communion and tried to prepare her soul to receive Christ, "though in a terribly bad inn"; and so she trusts this vision more than any other she ever had. (One may add that except for her angel she records no other vision — if one may call tactile experience a vision — that is so typically Spanish baroque.)

Next she gives this experience its background: "Before this I had been in that state of being absent from God that I feel more at some times than at others, and this time it had been so painful that it seemed as if I could not bear it. I was so exhausted by it that I could not eat . . . and the vomitings it brings on when I can't [eat] before [I go to bed] leave me very weak." (Even the physical symptoms of that worst post-conversion time in Avila have recurred.)

153

She tried to force herself to eat some bread: "And at once Christ showed Himself to be there. It seemed to me that He broke the bread and put it in my mouth and said, 'Eat, daughter, and do what you can. It weighs Me down that you are suffering, but it is right for you to suffer now.'"

This comforted her, she goes on, all through the next day; but then she had an afterthought: "That 'weighs me down' made me reconsider, because it has occurred to me strongly that now He cannot be weighed down by anything."

I am glad that de León did not leave this out. Too many dislike the honest critical analysis with which Teresa compulsively examined what she saw and heard with "the eyes and ears of the mind."

Her second letter to Martín is best considered in connection with Luis de León's description of her pre-conversion life in the Incarnation: "The devil put before her those persons most sympathetic to her nature, and God came and in the midst of those conversations he would show himself aggrieved and sorrowful. The devil delighted in those conversations, but when she turned her back on them, God redoubled his delights and favors. . . . And as rivals in love make every effort to estrange the desire of those they love from strangers and draws it to themselves, so it seemed while the world and the devil entangled her still more, God made every effort to show himself to her more abundantly."

Until Salamanca Teresa had seen it so, too, and believed that through the Rival's triumph she had won an innocent freedom to love any priest who truly loved Christ. As she explains in her *Camino*, she could only feel a tolerant amusement for the confessors who began by distrusting the quality of her love for them; they did not know how hopelessly they were outclassed by the perfect beauty of His Majesty.

But a habit of love formed in childhood for a tender father, a dreamlogged older brother, is hard to break. Teresa was fifty-six when she wrote this letter to Martín: but only the very young think that the "freedom" it speaks of has become, by that age, a fact of life, inevitable.

"All yesterday [April 15] I found myself in such great loneliness that except for the time when I was receiving communion nothing whatever stirred any feeling in me that it was the day of the Resurrection. Tonight, when I was with the others, one of them sang a little song about how hard it is to bear living without God. Since I was already in just that suffering, the effect of it on me was so great that my hands began to go numb, and I was not strong enough to hold it off, but just as it is when I go into an *arrobamiento* of contentment, my soul was suspended in the same way, but in the greatest possible pain, and up to now I have not understood it.

"Even a few days ago it would have seemed imposssible to me that I should ever have those great impetuses again as I used to. I don't know if this is possible: I mean that before this time it never reached the point of my going wholly out of myself, and because I was conscious, I would cry out. But this time, as if it had intensified, it reached the end in this piercing, and in my understanding of what Our Lady bore, for up to that time, as I have told you, I did not know what piercing was."

(He had read the *Life;* here we see that she had told him how the piercing delight of the angel's lance was not true suffering, as in those impetuses, "visions of greater worth," in which the soul hung alone, between earth and heaven, longing to die and be with God Whose presence it could not feel.)

"Tell me when you see me if this madness of pain is a possible thing or if I am deceiving myself. I am so battered in body that I can scarcely write. That pain lasted until this morning when I was praying and had a great *arrobamiento,* and it seemed as if the Lord lifted me up to his Father and said, 'I give you her whom You gave to Me,' and it seemed as if He [the Father] drew me to Himself. This was nothing visualized but on the contrary a great inner certainty so spiritual that I don't know how to express it at all. He said some words that I do not remember, something about giving me grace. He held me within Him for a long time."

But now she spells out the cause of her self-doubt. It was not only the nun's "little song" or the pain of being "absent from God" which precipitated a seizure like those she had known in the Incarnation, even to the post-convulsive pain.

"As you left me so quickly yesterday — and I do know that you have too many occupations to let me console myself with you even though I need it, for I can see that those occupations are more necessary for you — I was pained and sad for a while. Since I was in that state of loneliness, your being there had been helping me; and since it does not seem right that any earthly creature should hold me so bound, I began to have scruples, afraid of that freedom's being lost to me." (That treasured freedom to love "in Christ," without temptation.)

"That was last night. Today the Lord answered and told me not to wonder, that just as mortals need companions in their sensual pleasures, so the soul — when there is anyone who can understand it — desires one to whom it can communicate its delights and sufferings, and grows sad when there is nobody with whom it can speak. He said to me, 'He is making good progress now. His works please Me.'

"I remembered how I had told you yesterday that these visions pass away quickly. He told me that this experience [the morning's *arrobamiento*] was different from imaginary visions, and that there was no fixed rule about His mercies. Sometimes one way was right, sometimes another."

She laid the paper aside and did not send it off for another week. On that Easter Eve when Martín left too soon she had believed that her piercing pain was like that which Simeon had foretold to Mary. Now she knew better, and she finished what she had written and sent it off.

"After I took communion, I began to have a clear consciousness of the Lord within me." It was not an imaginary vision, but she knew, as clearly as if He had taken her hands and laid them on His wounded side, how little she had really suffered in spirit. How had she dared to compare that sense of piercing pain with that of the Virgin? "I know how different, how wholly unlike hers, my piercing was. Oh, how much greater hers must have been, compared to that!" Teresa, unlike most people who think they want to be understood, really did want to be.

155

She wanted understanding, that is, from people she believed capable of helping her to understand herself. But it was in Salamanca that Teresa first fully realized that for the sake of her work she must be seen as good in the eyes of the world, whatever her past or whatever her present self-doubts and self-accusations. Even with confessors, who by Church teaching stand in the place of God, there would only be three in the eleven years that still remained to her with whom she allowed herself the luxury of opening her soul—eleven years of travels and trials when she often longed for it.

We have these somewhat painful writings to Martín because with him she was largely denied that luxury. There was much that she could have said to him alone that she could not say when he came safeguarded by young Bartolomé de Pérez Núñez. But de León gave us more than he intended when he let us hear that human, tormented voice: "Tell me if I am deceiving myself. . . . It does not seem right that any human creature should hold me so bound . . ."

Facts for the end of the Salamanca story are missing. We only know that with her convent still "unmade" she left abruptly, at Father Angel's command. We are often told that he recalled her to Avila for a meeting with the Apostolic Visitor; but she had been in Avila at least five weeks before that meeting took place.

Similarly, we do not know precisely when Martín learned that he must leave his newly-founded college and go to Rome with a fellow Jesuit, Suárez—one of Teresa's arch-enemies for years to come. On the return trip, made overland, he was killed by Huguenots. Only the silence lets us know that there was scandal, slanders; and a later, equally undeserved scandal will let us know in still-recorded specifics the quality of such slanders—described by her nuns as "unfit for chaste ears."

But at least we do know what Father Angel was up to by early May, a fortnight or so after Teresa wrote Martín the letter which de León, in time, would publish as "a meditation of the holy Mother," dating it at around the time she was founding in Pastrana.

Father Angel had a plan.

Chapter 33 ❀ The Carmelite Provincial's Plan to Sidetrack Teresa

I

The plan as originally conceived looked simple.

Fernández the Visitor, was going to Salamanca. There Bartolomé de Medina and Melchor Cano would be happy to persuade him that Teresa, far from deserving his support, was a blot on the King's reform and should be separated from the Discalced whose true spirit was so perfectly expressed in the Pastrana movement. She should be retired to the Incarnation—to which, as an added fillip, Doña Teresa de Quesada should be brought back as her Prioress.

Father Angel, for a first step, visited the Incarnation; it was well to prepare the female mind tactfully for accepting a Prioress of his choice, though he did not doubt that the place would prefer a cousin of the Marquis of Velada to one of Teresa's cousins. He closed that visit with a written statement that the convent met his full approval; nothing had needed his correction.

Next, he visited Medina del Campo. It was imperative that Doña Teresa should leave as one treasured by all but a handful of rebels, chiefly family connections of Teresa de Jesús. This, he found, would be easily arranged; the nuns who had resented Doña Teresa's being forced on them as Prioress were glad to be rid of her at any price, including perjury.

Doña Teresa's departure should come only when Father Angel sent the word, but preparations for it—along with her only two loyalists—were promptly made and paid for, by the convent. Fine leather slippers to replace their alpargatas and a large box of "candied lemon peel, sweetmeats and dates for the road: 11 reales and 22 maravedis," plus "40 reales for travel expense"—and as a final token of affection and respect, a parting gift to each of "4 ducats: sum total, 2, 992 maravedis."

The same account book records a more typical day: "4 reales, 11 maravedis for bread and oil; alms received, nothing." Teresa's refusal of the Ruiz chapel had offended the town's most dependable almsgivers, the *converso* merchants. Still, Father Angel had laid it down that Doña Teresa de Quesada would leave in style or not at all, and as the saying goes, "Needs must, when the devil drives."

But the plan had to be altered after all.

Fernández, the Apostolic Visitor, did hear things in Salamanca that made him wonder whether he had not been too quick to defend Teresa at the Medina junta; but Báñez saw him too, and assured him that Teresa was only a victim of those now attempting to control the University by means of false accusations and delations to the Inquisition. Fernández was far from wholly reassured; he was, as Báñez put it, "a very legalistic theologian and wary of false spirits."

Fernández also visited Teresa's Salamanca convent; her cousin-Prioress Ana remembered sensing his distrust and telling him that when he saw Teresa, he should express it to her openly, "as that was what she liked best." Then he went on to Avila, where Teresa was waiting for further orders in San José.

"So," Báñez testified, "he began to examine her, and in the end she won him over, and he told this witness that Teresa de Jesús was a good woman, whose convents let the world see that it was possible for women to live within the evangelical rules of perfection."

A contemporary tale has it that the Visitor said to Báñez. "You told me that she was a woman, and I found a bearded man." (Referring not to her complexion but to the fact that real men, not timid friars, wore beards.)

Of their talks, Teresa wrote to María Mendoza, "The Father Visitor gave me new life again." He understood her, she said, without illusions. "It is a great thing to be able to talk frankly with one who stands in the place of God."

This turn of events gave Father Angel pause, but only briefly. Teresa, he saw, should not be sent back to the Incarnation in disgrace, a blot on the King's Reform, but as the reform's worthy instrument: as Prioress of a convent in sorry need of her proven ability to direct, to organize, and to inspire. He need only deny the Incarnation its right to a free election to insure a rebellion which could be used to discredit her utterly; and Mariano was now ready and waiting for the right moment at which to produce his Order's true saint, La Cardona. Though she would never enter Teresa's story directly, she demands an interruption that has to be made sooner or later. It may as well be now.

II

Mariano had found Catalina de Cardona ready-made for his purpose; but her background as eventually unearthed by an honest and disillusioned friar, Juan de Jesús Roca, is a period piece worth considering. She was the illegitimate child of a Barcelona physician, whose father placed her, at puberty, in a Capucine convent in Naples, where Italian became her second language. In time she ran away from this convent and attached herself to the household of the Princess of Salerno. As the Princess was born a Cardona, Catalina was able to persuade her that they were distantly related; and Catalina, even at the height of her religious fervor, continued to pass for an Italian noblewoman.

The Princess was a Princess by marriage, and the Prince, not a Prince by birth, was deprived of his title shortly before his death. The Princess believed that this could be rectified by a court in Valladolid. While living there, she and her household became devotees of Agustín Cazalla—the same who had said that Yomar's house had too many doors. By sheer luck, the Princess and her protégée were in Toledo when so many of his followers died in that first great *auto de fe* in Valladolid. La Cardona, in a revelation, saw that the Inquisition was right and that Cazalla, unchecked, would have led her to hell with his heresies. Her conversion was genuine, and a stunning tribute to "the way of fear."

She plunged into excesses of self-mutilation. Her face and body became a mass of scar-tissue. She saw visions: not held suspect when granted to lives of such conspicuous holiness. She became a self-ordained Franciscan, wearing a friar's habit. Finally, the Princess of Salerno passed her on to the Princess of Eboli and went back to Italy.

When Mariano first saw Catalina she had simply been wandering about in Ruy Gómez's Madrid palace: an adjunct to court life like that which Yomar had aped with her inferior, unmutilated María Díaz. But the Princess soon found her a bore and turned her over to a retired chaplain who lived in a village called La Roda. He found her a cave in which she lived on roots and berries and offerings from the awed peasantry.

As the hermitess of La Roda, Mariano perceived her enhanced publicity value. Teresa tried to interfere with Pastrana; but if rumor was true, a moment would come when Teresa could be replaced with a Foundress figure more to the Royal taste, and hence to that of Ruy Gómez.

When the moment came, it exceeded Mariano's wildest hopes. Teresa was grounded in the Incarnation, and he moved to consolidate his gains. His letter to La Cardona begins, "I don't know if you will remember me." They had met when "a certain prelate" sent him to court as his emissary to the Prince of Eboli; shortly thereafter he had been called to the religious life, and now felt that her inspiring presence was much needed in Pastrana. "We" — yes, "we" — had founded two monasteries and six convents "like those of the Capucins but in greater poverty." Her presence would further the expansion of the Order.

Catalina left her cave. Her appearance, gaunt, scarred, dressed as a friar and carrying her instruments of self-torture — a horsewhip, a knotted rope, and the hair shirt — "caused great devotion," according to the monastery's records. Baltasar Nieto gave her the habit of a Discalced friar; and, with Mariano, Juan de la Miseria, and Pedro de los Angeles, he carried her off to court along with a chest in which to bear back the harvest. In Madrid alone this came to over a *fanega* — fifty-five and a half liters — of gold and silver coins, plus a heap of court jewelry.

From Madrid they went to the Escorial, where La Cardona embraced the King and called him "Don." One look at her had assured Philip that his reform was blessed with a living saint. Back in Madrid, they also met Don John of Austria. After the battle of Lepanto he recalled La Cardona's blessing with emotion, and spoke of her as "my mother." Father Angel also found her inspiring — even before he shared Mariano's hopes of putting her to practical use. He wrote: "She looked more like a once robust friar wasted and weakened by fierce penances than a woman, the delicate and beautiful woman she once had been, according to what the Princess told us."

Mariano, though an Italian, knew what would sell best in Spain. La Cardona gave the Pastrana movement superb publicity. The foundation on the craggy heights of Altomira embodied La Cardona's highest ideals, and inspired others that strove to outdo it. Of La Peñuela, the chronicler says, "Duruelo, Altomira, Pastrana, even in their most flaming fervors barely reached that monastery's foot." But in many ways, La Roda outclassed them all.

Mariano spent wildly on La Roda, constructing a tunnel by which La Cardona might go from her cave to Mass in holy seclusion; it collapsed repeatedly, demanding reconstruction and decoration, and the friars felt the pinch and resented it. But eventually their discontent died, they felt holier than all other houses of the Order, and continued to call themselves "the monks of the Good Woman" long after Teresa had become La Santa.

The expansion into Andalusia ("led by an evil spirit" Rubeo had warned) began before Teresa was released from the Priorate of the Incarnation; and it is against this background that she unwillingly picked up *Fundaciones*, laid aside for three years, told what little she could about Salamanca and Alba de Tormes and Segovia, and then laid the book aside again—until a man less selflessly motivated than Ripalda forced her to take it up again.

III

Father Angel told Fernández that only Teresa could rectify the shocking conditions which he had recently discovered on an inspection of the Incarnation: conditions which could only "give scandal" and harm the monastic orders if they became known. Fernández believed him, and Teresa was trapped. To reveal Father Angel's true opinion of her was only too likely to make Fernández rethink his own. She could only plead that those of the Mitigation hated her reform and would use her return to keep her a prisoner, unable to live by Primitive Rule.

Fernández reassured her. He would call a convocation at which Teresa should sign a formal declaration of her right, as given by their General, to live by the rules of the Discalced; and since some opposition might be based on her own convent's being "under the ordinary" and hence not truly Carmelite, he himself would pronounce her Prioress of Salamanca.

And since Father Angel had so recently seemed to belittle her authority, she should go first to Medina, send Doña Teresa de Quesada back to the Incarnation, and as acting Prioress let the nuns call a free election, reinstating the prioress they preferred.

There was no arguing with such respect, such kindness; nor could it have come at a worse time.

IV

We know about it only from *cuentas* that she set down for her own eyes alone. She doubted all that she had felt for Martín and she longed for death. She tried to feel a loathing of the flesh like that so praised in La Cardona, and when the Voice told her that It valued her obedience more, she questioned the reality of that obedience. Whom had she chosen to obey? Then, in an extension of her self-despair she began to feel that she was wrong "in clinging only to Jesus Christ" and struggled to get away from "bodily images." But Teresa had no mind for abstractions, and a brief "intellectual vision of the Trinity" would not hold. The Holy Spirit became once more a fluttering dove, the Father a baffling, bodiless Presence whose speech "was like thunder" but incomprehensible.

Teresa could only find God as God made man, and she desperately needed the strength of Love given for love. She was about to be torn from her work and exiled in the Incarnation, and Martín was going into an exile far worse. It was mid-July when she heard that he would eventually be sent from Rome to France, and she wrote this *cuenta*:

"A day after the Octave of the Visitation I was . . . commending one, my brother, to God, and I said—I don't know if it was aloud or only in my thoughts— 'Why is this person, my brother, gone where there is danger of his

160

salvation? If I saw a brother of yours, Lord, in this danger, what wouldn't I do to help him! It seems to me that there is nothing I would leave undone.'

"The Lord said to me, 'Oh, daughter, daughter, these women in the Incarnation are My sisters. Come, take heart! See, I desire it, and where you think that those other houses will lose, both they and the other will gain.'"

It marks a turning point; the tone has grown stronger in the few days since God had told her that if she could make herself understand the Trinity, then He, in each of His Three Persons, "would enable [her] to suffer in Christian love and feel that love like a fire in [her] soul," — and hearing, she had remembered hopelessly, how many past mercies He had shown her, "only to have [her] drop His hand." Twelve days later, as she set out for Medina, Teresa could write that her release had begun, though only just begun:

"The longing and the so-great impetus to die have left me, especially since the feast of the Magdalen when I determined to live for the sake of doing God some service — except for some times, for however much I try to throw off the desire to see Him, I cannot. . . ."

Men who write about Teresa always say that "a certain person, my brother," is her brother Agustín. Admittedly, six years later, Teresa did write to Lorenzo that she was glad that Agustín "was no longer mixed up in that business," ending wearily, "Pray for him as I do." And Agustín was a crook right up to his deathbed, which he occupied free of charge and hovered over by the Sisters of Charity, by whose report we know that he claimed to have been La Santa's favorite brother and showed them his silver-framed bit of her miraculously preserved flesh which was not, as the honest Ribera describes it, "brown and shrivelled like a walnut," but according to the sisters, "so white that it might have been made of wax."

But for the Agustíns of this world, Teresa knew, one place is as spiritually safe, or dangerous, as another. Martín was going where his soul would be endangered by "those Lutherans," the Huguenots. Her fears for his soul would be worse, poor woman, when she finally learned that he died under torture and unconfessed. His gravest fault, she knew, was a lack of courage. Had he tried to win mercy by professing the heresy of his torturers with his dying breath? She could never be sure.

Many years later, Teresa wrote a letter to Velázquez, the Bishop of Osma. He had been her confessor when, past sixty, she suffered *arrobamientos* for the third and last time in her life. She had made him a general confession, and he knew how, in Salamanca, she had read the Song of Songs: "Oh that thou wert my brother who had sucked the breasts of my mother!" If Martín had been her brother by birth, there would have been no scandal, no flight into Egypt — the pagan exile.

Teresa wrote to Velázquez that the *arrobamientos* have long since ceased. Her sole supernatural experience nowadays comes as an assurance that all whom she has loved and lost are now safe in heaven — with one exception:

"The loneliness makes me think that it is impossible to give that sense to 'him who sucked the breasts of my mother'; the flight into Egypt . . ." (remainder of sentence blacked out by a later hand). The *loneliness* after many years the thought of Martín brought back, and in a way that she could never feel for those she believed to be now released from all pain and temptation, safe with God.

Gil González, Martín's Provincial, told Teresa's biographer, Ribera, that she was comforted for Martín's death by a vision in which she saw him wearing the martyr's crown, and Ribera was glad to believe it. I wish for her sake that it had been so.

But on the Day of the Magdalen in 1571, Teresa put her loneliness and tragic self-questionings behind her. She set out for three hardworking months in Medina.

Those months were a blessing. Teresa was too busy to hear "locutions" nor did she need them. She readjusted Doña Teresa de Quesada's travel allowance from forty reales to the twenty-seven needed for a comfortable trip. She checked and signed the convent's account-book daily, and set herself to mending fences with previous almsgivers whom Cousin Inés and Doña Teresa had offended.

She also repaid Domingo Báñez's kindnesses; she wrote to María Mendoza that he had been offered a priorate in Trujillo, not much of a place, and was also considering a post in Salamanca: "I don't know what he'll do. That place is very bad for his health."

She needed to say no more; Doña María knew enough about Salamanca from her brother, Bishop Pedro Mendoza. Teresa only indicated in one more laughing line where the Mendoza influence should be used: "Your Ladyship should scold the Dominican Provincial for not coming to call on me while I was in Salamanca for such a long time. True, I don't like him much."

No more direct request was necesary or advisable. Shortly thereafter, Domingo Báñez became Rector of the Dominican College of San Gregorio in Valladolid, a pleasant prominence in which he continued to gain scholarly distinction until, at the height of his career, he replaced Bartolomé de Medina in the Chair of Prime, the most coveted academic post in Spain.

As much as anything, that generous gesture shows Teresa calmed and restored to herself when she went back to Avila: so much so that she could see that the Incarnation faced problems as bad as her own through Father Angel's decision. Waiting in San José, she learned what she could, and thought ahead.

Chapter 34 ❈ *Her Return to the Incarnation as Prioress*

I

Father Angel had expected Teresa to be badly received; how badly he had underestimated. Nine years before, Teresa had made Avila a battleground, and she was still a reimflammable issue. The news that she was now appointed reformer-Prioress at the Incarnation came close to producing mass hysteria. Teresa tried to see it from the point of view of that unfortunate convent.

The city was blindly angry over her appointment, but the nuns had good reason to fear it. For some time the Incarnation's prestige, and in consequence its alms, had been dwindling. Most of the nuns had taken up dining at home daily, simply from hunger. Their number had only shrunk from a hundred and fifty to a hundred and thirty, but they took in so many boarders as to make control impossible: boarders who had taken no vows and were only happy to be free of parental oversight. Teresa saw that simply as long-term economy her first step would have to be unpopular. Immediately on getting back to San José she issued her first order: all boarders must be sent home before her installation.

Parents felt that their judgment had been maligned, and by this woman who tried to better her own reputation by maligning a convent supposedly in need of her, *her* reform! The nuns saw it as robbery. They needed the boarders' rent. Their fury was equally visited upon Father Angel; none of them believed that Teresa's coming had been forced upon him by the Visitor (a claim to which he stuck until Teresa's imminent canonization made it less profitable).

Father Angel had expected Teresa to meet with a revolt which would gradually discredit her as one unable to handle any nuns but her own hand-picked groups of the mentally unstable and readily cowed. He had not expected such a widespread storm, or that he, not the Visitor, would get the blame. He tried a last minute retreat, sending a messenger to tell the Visitor that the plan must be abandoned since the nuns were determined to risk their souls and defy his apostolic authority.

The Visitor only sent back word that the installation should go on as originally planned. Father Angel should escort Teresa to the convent himself, along with an excellent subprioress whom he was sending from Valladolid: Isabel de la Cruz, highly recommended by Doña María Mendoza herself.

This order upset Father Angel badly. Having learned that the nuns "had called many gentlemen of the town to their defence," he alerted the guard to prevent bloodshed, and for a personal escort to that installation he collected two popular and well-connected Carmelite friars, the chief magistrate of the city, and a second judge—whose son, Don Luis de Espinosa, observed the scene and reported it for the canonization process.

It was dusk when they walked through the shouting, menacing crowds. Teresa carried a statute of St. Joseph. At the door of the Incarnation, a group of armed gentlemen granted permission to Father Angel and the magistrates. Father Angel tried to go through the church and open the door of the lower choir to Teresa and the friars, but a mob of nuns and their sympathizers blocked his way.

Teresa sat on a step and waited. A few supporters who had walked behind her for the greater part of the way now hung back in a park called the Little Meadow. One lady among them, Mencía Roberto, reports that "even from that distance the uproar was so loud that you would have said it was all the devils in hell screaming."

The friars eventually managed to force the doors of the *coro bajo* and push Teresa through a crowd of nuns, some weeping and the rest shrieking. Then, as one of them recalls, "they took her and put her in the Prioress's seat and read the patent."

The reading could not be heard. The nuns remained standing as they shouted Father Angel down. According to one of them, "They made a terrible bellowing with many revilings of La Santa, objecting with the utmost violence to her staying in that house." Others witness that the language the nuns used was "most foul," "shameful and ignominious," "lewd and licentious," and the like. One Doña Teodora is said to have startled even that group of nuns turned foul-mouthed harridans with her gift for obscene denunciation.

While those testifying for the canonization avoid such specific terms as Jew and whore, their combined testimony does not leave the gist of their argument in doubt. Some nuns fainted during the excitement, but the majority screamed on. Father Angel's response was quaint. He shouted above the uproar, "In effect, you ladies do not want to accept Mother Teresa de Jesús?"

Unexpectedly, one Doña Catalina Castro y Pinel pushed forward and shouted, "We accept her and love her! Glory be to God!"

Two or three more raised their hands and nodded in timid agreement. And, abruptly, all seemed to feel screamed out. The hysteria lapsed into a grim, defeated silence. According to María Bautista, Teresa told her that it was as if they had suddenly decided to accept the worst and bear their cross.

Throughout all this, Teresa sat still, holding the statue of St. Joseph and showing a quiet face. With no intent to detract from La Santa's own quality, this calm was afterwards credited by one witness to her having had a fragment of the True Cross with her. Whatever its source, her poise made an impression. She was allowed to go to the Prioress's cell for the night; and when, next morning, she received communion without having gone to confession some saw it as a proof of remarkable virtue. How otherwise would she have dared?

Teresa knew that despite the weary quiet all was far from well. (Indeed one nun, María Yerro, later testified that she had been far from alone in her determination to go to Father Angel, renounce the habit, and return to secular life.) For that first day, Teresa let things rest. On the next, she and her cousin Isabel de la Cruz waited for the afternoon's siesta, and during it set the stage for her first chapter meeting.

All came, some tearful, but the others, the "valiant," prepared to disrupt proceedings as before. They entered the chapel and froze, staring.

The convent's fine statue of Our Lady of Mercy stood on the Prioress's chair; the convent's keys, symbol of prioral authority, hung from her hand. Teresa sat on the step of the dais at its feet. On the subprioress's chair, beside it, stood the statue of St. Joseph; Isabel de la Cruz was sitting in one of the seats appointed for the nuns.

It was inspired theater. When all had entered and seated themselves, still staring, Teresa got to her feet and spoke.

She was there, she said, in obedience to orders; but they must know that such orders could only make her the vicar of their true Prioress there before them, the one Prioress of whom no man could rob them. She herself would live by the rule of the Discalced while she was among them, but they need only follow their own rule, as they had promised to do when they took Our Lady's habit. She herself would do what she could to ease their lot, so that they might serve Our Lady and Her Son more gladly every day.

The effect was remarkable; to this day Our Lady occupies the chair of the Prioress while the Prioress sits were Teresa had placed St. Joseph. But Teresa knew that one moment of good theater was not enough. She had, as she says of her stay in Our Lady of Grace, "the gift of making herself liked wherever she was," and she set herself to use it unflaggingly. Unflaggingly, but not effortlessly; and while it is the custom to show her next years in that place as an unbroken triumph, her letters tell another story.

II

At the end of the first month, Teresa answered a long, complaining letter from Doña Luisa de la Cerda who was, as so often, nursing her health in a spa. After the proper expressions of sympathy and pious encouragement, Teresa allows herself a little complaining of her own.

She is not asking God for trials, these days; she has enough already, thanks. Little by little she is managing to cut down on the girls' less suitable pastimes, and their freedom to come and go, "but chanigng your habits is death, as the saying goes." They treat her with respect, but with a hundred and thirty of them it is hard to get things "within reason." And she worries about her own convents which she must leave unvisited. Still, by God's mercy, her spirit is not disturbed "in all this Babylon." And her body's weariness is a small price to pay for all the times she has offended God.

There are letters to Juana: de Ovalle and his brother will not let the Alba convent cut a lane to their door through a field they own; such indifference to her affairs makes her feel "terribly alone." And can Juana get her "a few reales since she takes nothing from the convent but bread."

Begging from poverty-stricken Juana? Where are friends like Francisco de Salcedo? It is plain that things are going none too well.

Entries also appear in the little notebook which she had not used since going to reorganize Medina. She had an "imaginary vision" of Our Lady, which looked like a picture given her by the Countess of Monterrey; but words came with it that haunted her, the only comprehensible words that she had ever seemed to receive from God the Father: "I gave you this Virgin and My Son. What can you give me?"

What could she give, in this Babylon's futility? Once more she had an "intellectual vision of the Trinity" — and with it a line came back from the Song of Songs: "Let my beloved come into my garden and eat." It was, she told herself, an invitation to the soul in grace, and at once, it seemed, God "let her see" the soul in sin, blindfolded, confused, wandering.

(Remember this when the metaphor of the garden comes back to her in an "imaginary vision" concerning the last of her "loves in Christ" and she does not fumble for a metaphor but lets herself say honestly, "I am afraid that it is temptation.")

She was lonely, and it came back to her ever more strongly that for Martín's sake she should not have gone to Salamanca. In March, after four months in that Babylon, she wrote to María Mendoza.

There is so much to be done here, she says, that she laughs when she thinks of St. Paul's saying, "I can do anything in God," and considers the bad health He gives her to work with. What's more, she has to do everything herself. "For I have no confessor, and I am so much alone here. There is nobody to whom I can unburden my heart, but everything has to be said with caution."

And the convent remains poor, though the nuns have changed: "When I see them so patient and good, I hate to see how they have to suffer. The change in them is something to thank God for. The roughest of them are now the gentlest and get on with me best." They are even observing a strict Lent, something quite new to them, yet they put up with it: "My Prioress has done it all."

It is not surprising that Teresa has no confessor, nobody with whom she can talk openly; but the rest of this letter throws light on a situation that is both surprising and shocking: it can only be called a form of blackmail.

III

Teresa's opinion of Carmelite confessors was unchanged. The Dominicans at Santo Tomás were in awe of Bartolomé de Medina and Melchor Cano, and doubtless thanked God that Báñez was now safely out of town. And while Teresa pitied Master Daza for his "way of fear" and even felt a certain fondness for him, she had long since learned that one could talk with him only cautiously, never openly. As for the Jesuits, who had lost an able rector and a subrector on her account, it is not surprising that their current Rector, Antonio Lárez, having denounced her to Salamanca before she got there, could now say, "I told you so." It was natural that Teresa had "no confessor."

The Valladolid situation was another matter.

The convent, known to be wealthy, was being pressured by two Salamanca Jesuits to accept two novices, their protégées. María Bautista wanted to accept them rather than risk displeasing the Valladolid Jesuits, who disputed her right to the fortune of Casilda de Padilla, the little runaway from marrying her uncle. Teresa had made inquiries about these Salamanca girls and rejected them; but María Bautista had convinced Doña María that Teresa was wrong.

One of the girls was badly disfigured. Whether this would lead to her being shunned or to having undue allowances made for her failings, it was undesirable. The other was simply a girl with a thoroughly bad reputation. Their sponsors were Father Alvarez and Father Ripalda; Ripalda who at that time (as Teresa later told the Seville Inquisition) "thought much evil of her." And why one who "thought much evil of her" wanted to put a girl in one of her convents has a simple answer: he had precedent.

Juan de la Magdalena Gutiérrez and Martín had both been natives of Valladolid, and distantly related. As Prior of the Toledan Carmelites, El Magdaleno had distrusted Teresa's friendship with his kinsman Martín; after Salamanca he hated her, consistently and lifelong, as we'll see. In Toledo, Teresa had hoped to weaken his opposition to that friendship by letting her Valladolid convent thus provide for his daughter. It had been an error, as she soon discovered; and now she would not yield to Martín's friend, Ripalda, or Ripalda's friend, Alvarez, when they tried to follow suit. It could no longer do Martín any good, and it could do the convent much harm.

Currently, María Bautista had talked the Duchess of Osma into taking the deformed girl into her household; and what her next step would be, only God knew. Doña María could be persuaded that Ripalda, angry, would air the Salamanca scandal in such a way as to discredit her Bishop brothers and herself as well: Jew-loving Bishops and a woman with a past.

Isn't it a fact, Teresa's letter asks, that Doña María wants to accept those girls "only to be rid of those two men?"

"If that should be it, it would be a great relief to me, for I know how to deal with those Fathers of the Company, seeing how little they would accept anyone unsuitable to their Order for the sake of doing me a kindness!"

She protests at length and ends, "For the love of Our Lord, Your Ladyship, think it over well and realize that one must consider the good of the whole community." Did Doña María want to risk giving her convent a bad name at this time, "and when, so near to that beginning of doing so, one has to be careful not to tarnish the reputation of the house?"

But Teresa hated to displease a Mendoza, and the next day she got letters which made a compromise possible. Ripalda's girl herself refused to enter the convent when she learned that it was enclosed and the enclosure strictly enforced. And the Duchess of Osma, her chaplain, and a Valladolid Jesuit had all written her that the deformed girl had a fine character. She withdrew her objections.

She ended with a paragraph that she could have written to no other patroness: "When shall I see you more free? Please God that if I do see you I'll find you in more control of yourself, because you have courage enough to be. I think it would do you good to have me near you, just as it does me good to be with the Father Visitor, for he, as my superior, can tell me home truths and I—impudent and already shown how much you will put up with from me— can do the same for you. Commend me to the Duchess's prayers."

She has indicated that she is pleasing the Duchess, not placating the Jesuits, and has affectionately rebuked Doña María's weakness. But having signed the letter, she looks back and adds a postscript, a joke on herself for having been the first to be so weak: "You never tell me how you get on with Fray Juan Gutiérrez. Someday, I'll tell *you!* Give him my regards. I haven't heard whether his niece has made her profession yet."

IV

Such problems intensified Teresa's need for a confessor with whom she could talk openly. She also was troubled in spirit for the nuns in her care, with confessors who had assured her for so long that her mortal sins were only venial, and her venial sins no sin at all. Since God had surely sent her to that Babylon with some purpose, it was her duty to find it a confessor worth having.

It was necessary, with the girls' confessors undoing all that she tried to do. Could she possibly bring Juan de la Cruz to the Incarnation? He, if anybody, could teach them what it should mean to be a Carmelite. And he would see it selflessly, as an opportunity; he had been discouraged by the little he had done in Alcalá. But how could she bring it about? How?

Chapter 35 ❃ *John of the Cross at the Incarnation as Its Vicar and Confessor to the Nuns*

I

Teresa could not have handled it alone. As witnesses for the beatification of John of the Cross said, Teresa could teach, preach and inspire for days on end, and in minutes a Carmelite friar could undo all she had done. Such rules as she could enforce were not enough, nor were those newly imposed by the Council of Trent. The grille which now separated visitors from nuns in the parlors could not block out whispered assignations, and the convent was as popular as ever with bored young married men.

Teresa did what she could. She ordered the porteress to refuse certain men admission. With one persistent Don Juan she waved the porteress aside and threatened him in the name of the King's Reform: "Come here once more, and the King will have your head." We are told that he transferred his attentions to another convent, saying, "There's no fooling Mother Teresa."

But she could not order off the friars, though she remembered that some had not only belittled sins but invited them. She had come there in late September, and in late May she wrote, "In the Octave of Pentecost the Lord did me mercy and gave me hope that this house would get better—the souls in it, I mean."

After eight months, she found it a mercy worth recording that she could so much as hope.

There were also painful interruptions to what little she could do. First, her cousin Leonor's madness became too much for San José to handle and she was sent back to the Incarnation to die. There the nuns saw the poor thing as possessed by devils, and it took an exhausting struggle to get her buried in the convent's crypt. Then Yomar, who became more trying through the years, tried to force a marriage on a daughter who was in love with another man, and failing, got Teresa to accept the girl as a novice. Teresa believed that the unfortunate creature would at least be happier in the convent than at home; but she had been there only briefly when Teresa, coming out of her cell, met the girl, who went rigid, staring, and collapsed, seemingly dead. It must have been a cerebral hemorrhage, for she never recovered the power of speech, though she lived for nearly a year and was able to scrawl a brief deathbed confession.

II

We do not know when Teresa learned of Martín's death. In March, her sworn enemy, the Jesuit Suárez, still a captive of the Huguenots, managed to write about it to Baltasar Alvarez and to Father Gaspar, both now in touch with Teresa, but letters from abroad were months in transit. At least, she knew by July. And she wrote, "On the day of the Magdalen, the Lord turned me back in order to confirm a mercy that he had done in a certain person's absence from Toledo lifting me up to act in his place."

Coming back from Pastrana to Toledo she had prayed for strength of her own, in Martín's absence. Now he was dead, and on the day of the Magdalen she prayed once more for strength to do what should be done. It was a day or two at most after she wrote this *cuenta* that she took her own first step to bring Fray Juan—John of the Cross—to the Incarnation. She called for Julián de Avila, and sent him to Salamanca.

III

Salamanca was the stronghold of the enemy. The Visitor, Fernández, was staying in the Dominican College of the University, and Julián's mission was to persuade him that Fray Juan could do more good as a confessor to *mujercillas*, "little women," than he could as Rector of Alcalá. The Carmelites would see Fray Juan's presence in Avila as a reflection on their honor; the Discalced would be angered that one of their number was so demoted. Both, Fernández would know, could only hate him for such a decision.

Still, Father Angel had made Fernández believe the worst about the convent he had sent her to reform; Teresa, she knew, could plead her own helplessness. She could also plead that Fray Juan's gentle conception of the religious life made him ill-suited to prepare men for the rigors of the Pastrana movement. But could that outweigh Fernández's natural instinct of self-preservation, let alone his true desire to keep the peace between those of the Observance and the reform? And for that matter, could Julián, fluent, earnest, but not over intelligent, be adequately persuasive?

Julián had a good memory, as his memoirs show. He was also disarmingly simple and unpretentious. Teresa coached him thoroughly, and Fernández listened. Fernández, in turn, was a diplomat. He saw all the right people, beginning with Ruy Gómez, and he did not forbid the Carmelite friars to confess any nuns who preferred to keep them on. And by September, Juan de la Cruz came to the Incarnation as its Vicar and confessor, and Fray Gabriel de la Asunción was made Rector of Alcalá.

IV

Nuns who had once confessed to Fray Juan de la Cruz were willing to confess to no other, except for his assistant, Fray Germán — as a second best. They had been apprehensive when Teresa told them that she was bringing them *un varón santo*, a holy strong-man; but the tiny man who came among them was unlike anyone they had ever known. Men found it easy to ignore or belittle John of the Cross during his lifetime; women, never. I have wondered if this phenomenon did not spring in part from his curious sexlessness. Since he saw only souls, he treated them all with the same grave respect, and women were not used to respect.

He pleased but without trying to please. He smiled, but rarely laughed, and his gentle perceptivity went hand in hand with an utter otherworldliness, and an almost inhuman lack of inner conflict. A nun remembered how his unexpected ease of manner made her ask him, "Are you really one of the Discalced?" Smiling, he had covered his feet with the hem of his habit: "There, daughter! Safely shod."

A young nun who had earned herself the nickname of Robert the Devil recalled, in later years, her first confession to him. She had put it off, after hearing the others praise him, sure that he would be shocked and put her to shame. She seemed to think he was some kind of saint, he told her. That was nonsense, but if she had been right she would have less cause for confusion and fear, "for the more saintly they were, the more they could understand the human condition . . . even though it sometimes moved them to tears."

Yet it never occurred to him to talk down to simpler minds. As one who has always found him a writer both difficult and inspiring, I like the evidence of several nuns who said that when he talked, their minds could not understand him, yet somehow they always left him more conscious of God than they had ever been, and more eager to do His will.

If there had been an ounce of false pride in Teresa she could not have loved him as she did; for he had greater hopes for her than for all the others, and hence less tolerance of her complexity. They had identical religious values and wholly antithetical personalities. Fray Juan, more angel than saint, lived without effort that "freedom" of which Augustine said, "Love God and do what you will." At one level, Teresa would always feel that he lacked any real contact with the living world, while he, in turn, longed to teach her a greater detachment, a more unencumbered spirit. Yet he wholly trusted her purpose and she his goodness. She said, "All that I have learned from other *letrados* bit by bit, I find

170

complete in *mi Senequita*." My little Seneca, accepted in her day as the type of all wisdom and virtue.

Yet the nuns remembered how he often went out of his way "to mortify the Mother." He shrank from her overflowing emotionalism; when she said that she almost loved him too much to respect him, he said, "You must cure that, daughter." Young as he was, she could never have called him "my son," as she had García de Toledo and would in time Jerónimo Gracián.

Above all, he could not tolerate her instinctive charm. He once said to her nuns and in her hearing, "When the Mother confesses, you can't think how sweetly she excuses her sins."

It was teasing, but he hoped that it conveyed a medicinal grain of truth, and it came from a nature that was both a little more and a little less than human. Perhaps in that moment now called the Spiritual Betrothal, Teresa had done well not to take literally the command from the Voice that she talk thenceforth "not with men but angels." Angels and people don't really understand each other well.

As I see it, it was the act of an intellectual angel which brought about the experience now celebrated by the Church as Teresa's Spiritual Marriage. She had once remarked that she loved it when the communion wafers were large — a mouthful of God. This John of the Cross found not only bad theology but distastefully carnal. Here is Teresa's own account of what happened:

"When I was in my second year as Prioress of the Incarnation, on the Octave of St. Martín as I was receiving communion, Fray Juan de la Cruz broke the Form in two, so as to give half of the Holy Sacrament to me and half to another sister. I thought that he did it not because he was running short, but to mortify me because I had told him that I enjoyed it so much when the Form was a big one — and that was not because I thought there was less of the Lord than in a small one, for I know that He is entire in even a tiny crumb.

"His Majesty said to me, 'Do not fear, daughter, that anyone should allow himself to separate you from Me,' making me understand that it did not matter. Then He showed Himself to me in an imaginary vision — like the other times, very much within me; and He gave me His hand and said, 'Take this nail, for it is the sign that you shall be my espoused bride from this day on. Up to now you did not deserve it. From now on, think of my honor not only as that of your Creator, or of your God and King, but as if you had truly become My bride. My honor is yours, and yours, mine.'

"This mercy had such effect on me that I could not collect myself. I was left like one witless, and I said to the Lord, 'Either stretch up my lowliness or do not do me such mercy.' For truly, it seemed as if my flesh could not bear it. For the rest of the day, I was much intoxicated.

"Since then I have felt a great benefit, and a greater confusion and grief at seeing that I do nothing in the service of such great mercies."

Still, Teresa thought it through. And there was no "intoxication" in how she continued, on the same page:

"But on another day, the Lord said to me, 'Do you think, daughter, that there is any merit in spiritual enjoyment? There is not, but only in work, and in enduring, and in love. Haven't you heard that St. Paul enjoyed the delight of heaven only once?... The great saints who lived in the desert—as they were guided by God to do, and to great penances without which they would have had grave battles with the devil and with their own selves—those saints spent most of their time with no spiritual consolation at all'

"Believe me, daughter, the Father gives the greatest trials to those He loves, and it is to those trials that true love for Him responds."

Juan de la Cruz, that purest of contemplatives, could never wholly convince Teresa that the "locutions" that she—and countless others—were currently receiving should always be distrusted; but he tried, and only learned years later that he had failed. He also tried to teach her the vast difference between the *arrobamientos* of the ecstatic and "the prayer of union," that total, painless renunciation of self and acceptance of God in which the spirit finds the peace that passeth all understanding.

She tried to write out her own thoughts for him to read, for with all but the shy and inarticulate he was a better teacher than listener. In the last decade, one page of what she wrote has been accepted for publication among her writings. The first page is gone; the second begins by quoting a locution of which Fray Juan could have approved if he had not been convinced that all locutions should be treated as deceits of the devil or one's own imaginings. In fact, the Voice echoes his own teaching:

"'Do not think, daughter, that it is union to be closely bound to me, for even the souls who sin against me are so bound, and even though they do not want to be. Nor is union in the regalements and delights of prayer, even though they are of the highest kind. Though these may be Mine, they are only a device for saving souls—one used over and over even though the souls are not in a state of grace.'"

These words, she goes on fumblingly, seemed to explain the first words of the Magnificat to her *Exultavit spiritus meus*—meaning, to her, that the spirit is master of the will. So, in union the spirit is so detached from earthly desires that "spirit and will are in such accord with each other, so detached from earth and concerned only with God, that there can be no memory of love in this state, nor any lingering trace of the servant girl."

Such brief moments of union as she has known, she says, are "gone in a flash." She can go on acting "justly and worthily and willingly," but one "cannot call it going on in unity of soul. . . ."

"I went on thinking . . . that there is so much dust of our wretchedness and shortcomings and hindrances into which we are always going back to plunge ourselves that it may not be possible to stay in that purity of spirit that is joined to God, and . . . if union is the state in which the spirit is made one with God, it is not possible that one should have it who is not already in a state of grace. . . . So it seems to me that it will be pretty hard to know when union exists—unless through some particular grace of God—since it is not possible for us, by ourselves, to know when we are in it.

"Write me about how you see it and where I am talking nonsense and send me back this paper."

She is incoherent, but not talking nonsense. She should not, from her own experience, understand a life like Fray Juan's—free from inner conflict. She could still, though rarely, have "intoxicating" visions and thereafter subject them to moral criticism. In moments "gone in a flash" she could know the peace which says, "Thy will be done," without regrets for the self-will renounced; but she knew that for herself such moments could not last. She could only try to go on, often despite herself, in the way that her Voice had summed up in three words: "Work, enduring, love."

Teresa trusted the utter purity of Fray Juan's spirit; she always saw that tiny man as "tall in the eyes of God." Fray Juan felt equal trust in her vision of a Church brought back to Christ by the example of selfless living and the power of selfless prayer. This trust, this shared purpose was a blood-bond between them, a familial love, no less genuine for being devoid of personal understanding.

Nonetheless, Teresa burned to be out and about her own work again; and that longing increased for a double reason. She saw that the Incarnation needed her less for every day that it had the guidance of John of the Cross; yet it is equally true that letters she had begun to receive from a young man in Pastrana spoke to a wholly different side of her complex personality.

Fray Juan was more angel than man; Gracián was a weak man, no more. But for years to come, Teresa would not perceive that contrast; she saw the one as he was, but she idealized the other.

Chapter 36 ❀ Enter Gracián; a Letter from Teresa to King Philip

I

Jerónimo Gracián kept all of Teresa's letters, but the hundred and eight that have survived date from a time when they had been corresponding for three years. Those that dim the glory of Pastrana and those which concern his decision to expand the Order to Andalusia in defiance of his General's orders were suppressed. Teresa herself saved no letters except for one or two from old Peter of Alcántara and Juan de Avila's response to her *Life*. But we cannot doubt that Gracián wrote a lovely letter; the books of sugared self-justification that he wrote when he was expelled from the Order after Teresa's death are proof of that.

He first began to write her from Pastrana. He had gone there from Alcalá because, as Ruy Gómez's foundation, it held promise for a young man with

Court connections; Gracián's father and brother were both *hidalgos* who served as secretaries to Philip II. In Alcalá, Gracián heard much about the founding of the Order and the ideals of Mother Teresa from Juan de la Cruz. What he found in Pastrana we know about from its proud chronicler, who shared the current admiration for "the penances of beasts."

Baltasar Nieto's sadism was not modified by the cooler air of Castile. As the Discalced chronicler boasts, the novices who lived in the caves of Pastrana subsisted on a starvation diet and let their bare flesh be lashed until it was torn and bleeding. One of them, who died of such penitential excesses, had been permitted to keep his eyes on the ground while he walked, but otherwise ordered to keep them shut to exclude worldly temptation. On his deathbed he humbly asked permission to open them for one last glimpse of the world he was leaving.

Since tales like his are recorded to the greater glory of God and the Prince of Eboli, one can see why Teresa's comments on them have not survived. And one also sees why Gracián's soft, sentimental letters made her feel that he was sent by God to give spiritual council to her nuns in Pastrana.

Gracián, though he sentimentalized himself too much to know it, was ambitious. He saw that Pastrana was a blind alley, and it was proved that Teresa had influence when the Visitor sent the Rector of Alcalá to the Incarnation at her request. Even from Teresa's first answer to his first letter he would have caught the right tone with which to charm her: idealistic, warm, sometimes indignant, sometimes gently humorous. He told her that he had formed a little group that practiced her own rules of "mortification" despite his Prior's predilection for brutal penances. As a result, we have our only surviving sample of their friendship-by-letter for the next three years. This is the so-called *Vejamen:* the challenge. In fun, Teresa and twenty-two of her nuns challenged "the cave man," Gracián, and his group to a tournament of competitive "mortification."

One sample from the nuns will indicate the tone throughout: "Sister Ana de Vargas says that if the knights and said brothers will pray the Lord to cure her of her innate distaste for humility, she will give them all the merit she gains by it — if the Lord gives her any." So twenty-one more, and finally:

"Teresa de Jesús says that to any knight of the Virgin who can make every day a great act of determination to suffer lifelong from a superior who is very stupid, vicious, greedy, and evil-tempered, she will give him one-half of the merit she earns on the same day, both in communion and in the heavy griefs she bears — small enough, when one thinks of Our Lord's humility before his judges and his obedience even to death on the cross. This contract is to last a month and a half."

That's a paragraph full of Teresa. As she sees it, Nieto and Father Angel have her and Gracián both trapped, unable to serve the reform as it should be served. Yet they must not indulge in self-pity (Gracián's unconcealable weakness) for their obedience is trifling compared with their great Example. Then — in one of her typical leaps from high seriousness to laughter — the offer, which teasingly values Gracián's troubles as worth half of hers, also sets a time limit: six weeks.

At this point Teresa did not know of the plan Gracián had made with Mariano to break away—in the General's words, "led by an evil spirit." And a sense of her own impending escape from the Incarnation was lifting her spirits high.

II

The Visitor came to Avila and was impressed by what she and Fray Juan had accomplished between them. He wrote about it to the Duchess of Alba; they were friends and he understood the political ins and outs which had made her the actual, but not the nominal, patroness of "her" convent. The hundred and thirty at the Incarnation, he said, "live together in the same quiet and holiness" that existed in the tiny convent of San José. It had inspired him to bring "several Discalced to the friars, not to turn their monastery Discalced but simply so that it may be governed by its own laws."

Fernández, Apostolic Visitor, was in fact pulling wires to help Teresa. She had convinced him that her convents were suffering through her virtual imprisonment; but his own situation was chancy. Pius V, who had appointed him, had died; and Gregory XIII was showing himself no friend to the King's Reform. But there were times when one could be glad of that saying, "There is no Pope in Spain." The King talked with his Court; and the King liked his own way. He also liked what Ruy Gómez told him about the Discalced, so ardent for his reform. Too bad the Princess of Eboli and Teresa seemed not to hit it off, but perhaps the Duchess of Alba . . . ?

A first step would be to have Teresa visit the Duchess, just unofficially, in a way that could be managed without the exercise of papal authority. "So," Fernández's letter to the Duchess goes on, "you see that if she does not get away from here, two or more of her convents will be destroyed."

One of those two which would be "destroyed" if Teresa were not free to cope with its troubles was Pastrana; the Duchess, Fernández knew, would be glad to hear that the Princess's convent was being ill-used by its patroness. The other was Salamanca, concerning which he had now convinced the Duchess that she had been given false information. Fernández, himself a Dominican, had also worked hard at changing de Medina's opinion of Teresa—sufficiently, at least, to make him safeguard his friendship with the Duchess by telling her that apparently he had been deceived by hysterical Jesuits. Fernández's letter was written on February twenty-seventh, and it worked so well that a document Teresa signed in Alba is dated April eighth.

Unfortunately, Fernández overstepped himself in his attempt to see that the Carmelites "lived by their own laws." He not only replaced all authorities at the Avilan priory, from the Prior down to the porter and the procurer of supplies, but he had a shack built against the walls of the Incarnation to house Fray Juan and his companion, Fray Germán, the better to insure the nuns against any interference with their Discalced confessors. An undated letter from the Papal

Nuncio, Ormaneto, to Gracián—with whom he got on well—says that it was an arrangement which only invited scandal. And these improvements were indeed a time-bomb, though they were some years at ticking off before the final explosion.

III

But Teresa would be freed; and the first step towards that end went well. She and Heredia—ever eager to please the Duchess—went to Alba in the ducal coach with a companion, Doña Quiteria de Avila. In Salamanca they were joined by a priest, and a seminarian who later described Teresa's welcome at the castle.

"The Lady Duchess received her with downright incredible love, and the Mother, with a face as composed and with words so politically smooth as to show her quite able to deal with such talk and such excessive fervor, had to stay . . . in her company until after midnight without anything to eat or even a glass of water, though the tables were set and everyone had finished eating."

This is only too likely when one knows why the Duchess wanted the "spiritual comfort" usually given as the reason for this visit. Her husband was in trouble. Ruy Gómez had finally persuaded Philip that a crusader saint can be a bad politician and that Alba's Court of Blood in the Lowlands (which tried eighteen thousand "heretics and rebels," executing all found guilty) was creating not unity, but a constant threat of desperate rebellion.

Philip sent Luisa de la Cerda's brother, the Duke of Medinaceli, to replace him; Alba would send him back with his tail between his legs, but the Duchess did not yet know that. But she did know that Medinaceli's close-fisted sister and Ruy Gómez's licentious wife must be irksome patronesses. Teresa, she could hope, would sympathize when she learned that the Ebolis and Medinacelis were plotting against her husband—and on the grounds that he was treating "those Lutherans" with a firm hand.

Furthermore, the Duchess now regretted her cowardly foolishness and pretense about the steward's wife; the Dominican Visitor, Fernández, had always believed in Teresa's purity and her value to the King's Reform, and de Medina now admitted to having been deceived. The Dominicans, who had been the Duke's strong supporters ever since he had brought the Inquisition to the Lowlands, favored Teresa; and the Dominicans had influence with the King. Yes, yes, Teresa must be made to see that she, the Duchess, not an Eboli or a Medinaceli, was her true friend! We need not wonder that she showed "downright incredible love." Or, that she talked nonstop until midnight, forgetting to eat or to offer food. She was not only a silly woman, but a worried one.

Teresa was politic. During that visit she told de Ovalle that if he did not drop his lawsuit and allow the lane to the convent to be made, he could expect not one maravedi more from her brother Lorenzo. She also took her niece Beatriz, then a pretty child of ten, to the castle to kiss the Duchess's hands. Beatriz, years later, remembered that the glamor of the occasion was spoiled for her because of her embarrassment over the darns and patches of her Aunt Teresa's habit.

How Teresa felt about that visit we'll never know. She did not mention it in a letter she wrote to Father Gaspar on her return to the Incarnation. She only apologizes for her long delay in answering his last and says that things will go better now in Malagón as she has made their mutual friend Brianda its prioress. And she adds, without comment, "I am confessing with Father Lárez."

Lárez, the Jesuit Rector of Avila, Father Gaspar knew, was a dangerous enemy. Teresa made great efforts to meet such enemies in the confessional, but this time she failed. As we learn from her Jesuit biographer Ribera, she managed to see him only once or twice, and then never saw him again.

Nonetheless, things moved on; and in this Gracián managed more than he commonly gets credit for.

IV

As Gracián knew, Ruy Gómez was in failing health; Pastrana would lose its importance when he died, and when that happened, even Mariano would see that Teresa, free, active, and with impressive support among the nobility, could be far more useful than the legendary Cardona in her cave. The King should be made more aware of Teresa—as Foundress of Ruy Gómez's Discalced. Thanks to those royal secretaries, his father and brother, Gracián knew an ideal go-between, Juan de Padilla, a cleric who enjoyed making himself useful to Church and Crown. Gracián's friend, the Papal Nuncio Ormaneto, arranged for de Padilla to have an audience with the King, and in June, Gracián sent him to Teresa for coaching. Gracián also knew that the King had a taste for secrets; consequently, the letter that Teresa sent to the King through Padilla stresses secrecy.

Her convents pray for His Majesty continually; his aid will mean more convents to increase that flow of prayer. So she dares ask him to favor them in certain matters which the Licentiate, Juan de Padilla, will describe to him. It should not be set down in black and white, but "seeing his great zeal has convinced me that I might entrust him with this business, for if it became known the very thing it attempts would be injured—a thing which is wholly to the honor and glory of God." May God protect His Majesty. "In the trials and persecutions it suffers now it is a great comfort that the Lord has a help and defender of his Church as great as Your Majesty." It was well put. At fifty-eight Teresa knew that in this world good seldom triumphs on its merits alone. Padilla delivered her letter and spoke her piece about the need for freedom in mid-June. By July, Teresa got back to Salamanca.

A biographer of Juan de la Cruz attributes this change in Teresa's fortunes to a miracle: both learned that it was about to occur in a revelation sent while Fray Juan was hearing her confession, and in holy joy they floated up to the ceiling. The convent was awed to see them kneeling on air, unaware of their elevation, while Fray Juan heard Teresa's whispered confession of her sinless sins. Which brings up a reflection on the tastes of the times: it is just as well that Philip never met Teresa. Compared to La Cardona, she would have struck him as hopelessly inferior.

Ana de Jesús explains the return to Salamanca more simply: Teresa told Báñez that the Incarnation no longer needed her, Báñez told the Visitor, and that was that. This makes for easy reading, but while history often clutters a story, its omission distorts it. What's more, Teresa's life was full of clutter.

For instance, just before she left for Salamanca and after she got there, Teresa was doing her best to warn Medina against a plan of Doña Elena's for a young ladies' boarding school to be taught by her Discalced and the Jesuits in conjunction. It could only make trouble for both Orders, her letter insists; Father Baltasar Alvarez will tell them why they must not think of such a thing without getting the approval of their new Provincial, Suárez. (Gil González's health had failed, and Suárez, recently ransomed from the captivity in which Martín had died, had been named Provincial in his place.)

It was one of Teresa's problems that while it was often best to keep her patronesses from understanding a situation, this same lack of information could lead them to make trouble quite innocently.

Chapter 37 ❀ The House at Salamanca, Father Baltasar Alvarez, and the Widowed Princess of Eboli as a Nun

I

It was an exhausting journey to Salamanca, three days and part of a fourth on donkey-back over mountain trails. Julián de Avila makes it amusing with the story of how they first lost and recovered the donkey that bore Ana de Jesús's dowry, in golden ducats, and then Teresa herself—the party having got separated in the dark and each part of it thinking she was with the other.

The nuns in Salamanca had bought a house from one Pedro de Bando, described as "of a most indigestible temper." He was also dishonest, and made years of trouble by selling without admitting that the house was entailed upon his wife, and at her death to go to a kinsman in Peru. It took six weeks for the papers—supposedly legal—to be signed and the necessary labor to begin. After which Teresa had to keep the workers working on a vague hope of being paid sooner or later. That she did so led future witnesses to credit her with a second miracle of Cana: she kept their spirits up with a wineskin which proved miraculously inexhaustible.

As Teresa says in *Fundaciones*, the roof still leaked when they moved in, but the sun came out and the Sacrament was brought from a nearby church "with much music and singing." Thereafter, as she does not add, they were left to starve. A workman witnessed that he saw them at dinner, saying grace over "a jug of water, a piece of bread about the size of two fingers, and some greens." Two nuns died that year, one of them Isabel de los Angeles, the heiress to the Ruiz fortune, which she left to Medina.

But the workmen were paid. The seminarian, tells how: "She told me that she must have that money and by means of my own words to others, and that I must not fail. She put it as if her very food and her peace of mind depended on me alone. I was appalled at her thinking that a student like me—for I was that—could find two hundred ducats for her. Yet it is the truth that within three or four days I had collected a considerable sum for her, and two days after that, without my even trying, I received an alms that brought it up to the exact sum that she needed."

Teresa's new preface to *Fundaciones* is dated nearly a month after she reached Salamanca. The orders, you remember came from her "confessor, the Father Rector of the Company of Jesús, by name Master Ripalda." We know, from her comment made down in Seville, that at the time he "thought much evil of her." We know, from her letter to Doña María Mendoza about this girl who would "tarnish the reputation" of her convent, that Teresa thought no better of him. When Ripalda's opinion of Teresa improved we do not know. Nine years later, she planned to found in Burgos, and she identifies him in a letter to Gracián as "a friend" who may be helpful there. She had clearly not ever mentioned him to Gracián before, since he needs this identification—so Gracián had apparently only seen the original preface, or none, when he ordered her to go on with the book which she had laid aside once she wrote about Segovia and Alba de Tormes (laid aside, I may add, for the same reasons that Gracián demanded that she continue and "prettify" it).

The Jesuits now like to remember Teresa's relationship with their order as an unbroken love-affair. This is sadly untrue, but for a time Teresa's connection with the Jesuits did promise to be a story with a happy ending. Four months after she gave *Fundaciones* its new preface, Baltasar Alvarez replaced Ripalda as Rector of Salamanca, and Teresa's confessor.

II

Baltasar had never doubted the falsity of that "great false witness." He remembered how de Prádanos, Father Gaspar, and even he—young and overcautious as he had been—were "persecuted." Moreover, Martín had long been one of his dearest friends. It was he who raised the money that would have bought both Martín's and Suárez's release if Martín had not died; and one who knew Baltasar well has written that Martín's death left him literally ill, prostrated with grief.

Baltasar, though still in his thirties, had become a widely recognized scholar; his appointment restored to the College in Salamanca what it had lost in scholarly reputation by losing Martín Gutiérrez; and Suárez—so deeply in Baltasar's debt, was now the Jesuit Provincial. It seemed during her last month in Salamanca Teresa would have a confessor who need not hesitate to show how much he liked and trusted her. He came often to talk with her about "the things of God." He spent time generously on instructing her nuns and novices. He did not doubt Suárez's gratitude, since Suárez owed him his freedom and perhaps his very life.

He did not know Suárez. Whatever gratitude Suárez may have felt showed itself only in a determination to separate Baltasar from the Jewish whore whose affair with Martín had brought about his own captivity.

Teresa had left Salamanca shortly before General Mercurian, the Jesuits' fourth — and first anti-Semitic — leader, received Suárez's letter. Baltasar, he read, was overwhelmed with Teresa de Jesús's convent. "It is known that he takes the care of nuns in hand far more than our Order permits, examining those who want to enter that Order and solving the problem of their administration." Thereafter, Suárez warmed to the work until, with Mercurian's blessing, he could issue his final order that all Jesuits, and Baltasar in particular, "must spend no more time with women, especially Carmelite nuns, but be suavely and efficiently removed from them."

From that time on, letters passing between Teresa and Baltasar had to be delivered secretly by mutual friends; and we know of them only because she speaks of them in letters to others. She was sixty-five when she enclosed one in a letter to Gracián which said, "He is one of the best friends I have . . . a saint. Do manage to put this letter into his own hand." It was her last to him, for within a fortnight, Baltasar had died, at forty-six.

Ruy Gómez died, too. The Princess, to the general amusement of the Court, flung herself into the role of grief-stricken widow. Standing beside her husband's deathbed she demanded that Mariano, then and there, give her the habit. When Isabel de Santo Domingo heard the news, she is said to have cried, "The Princess a nun! That will be the death of us!"

It nearly was. The Princess entered the convent along with two ladies-in-waiting who also had to be given the habit. She insisted on taking her meals in the lowliest place, with the novices and lay-sisters; but she opened the parlors to her friends, making the convent into a cramped and noisy court. When the Prioress tried to protest, the Princess flew into one of her rages and moved to a hermitage in the garden, to which her waiting-women brought their meals and her many guests. And when this became a bore, she went back to the palace and expressed herself by cutting off the convent's funds.

This would have meant starvation for thirteen women if the Prioress, old Pedro de Alcántara's gift to the order, had not been born Isabel Ortega y de Bracamonte. Avila and Segovia were the de Bracamonte strongholds. Mother Isabel wrote to her Segovian cousins, and Ana de Ximena promptly offered a house to which they could all be moved, only asking in return that her daughter, María de Bracamonte, be Mother Isabel's first novice. First, of course, Teresa would have to go to Segovia and make the foundation to which they would escape. But she could not leave at once. Still another situation had risen to demonstrate how much "such things" as family "mattered in religion. . . ."

The situation, left unexplained by hagiographers, is best clarified by the Duke of Alba's friend and first biographer, Osorios. Alba's son, Don Fadrique, Duke of

Huesca, seduced a Mendoza niece, Magdalena de Guzmán, and jilted her in order to marry his cousin, María de Toledo. Magdalena's mother, Beatriz de Sarmiento, appealed to the King, who might well have yawned it off if he had not at the time been infuriated by his first failed attempt to remove Alba from the Lowlands. As it was, he took pleasure in putting Fadrique under house-arrest in Ubeda, and appointing Bishop Alvaro Mendoza, the girl's uncle, to pronounce Fadrique and Magdalena betrothed and insist that the marriage take place as the price of his release. Fadrique said he'd die in prison first. The Duchess blamed the whole situation on the Mendozas in general and the Bishop in particular. The Mendozas were justly angry, since the King had put them helplessly on the spot. And the girl's mother, Doña Beatriz, exacerbated the situation by shuttling between Alba and Valladolid, alternately berating the Duchess and the Bishop for their inability to control Fadrique.

Báñez, the most useful friend Teresa ever had — and the most fortunate — saw that a rift between the ducal houses of Mendoza and de Toledo could cost her the patronage of the one or the other. Teresa loved and needed the Mendozas; but to lose the friendship of the Duchess of Alba would be to lose such highly conditional tolerance as Teresa now enjoyed from the most powerful Dominicans in Spain, de Medina and Cano — tamed only because it was to their advantage to please the Duchess. In consequence, Báñez took it upon himself to pacify the mother, Doña Beatriz, while Teresa should go to Alba and do all she could to endear herself to the Duchess while assuring her that the Bishop and Doña María were thoroughly wretched over the King's senseless spite. It would delay the foundation in Segovia; but that, too, could be used to advantage, since the Duchess would so relish all Teresa could bring herself to tell about her hated rival, the Princess. His plan worked well. Teresa was able to write to Bishop Mendoza from Alba that she had shown the Duchess that none of the wretched business was his fault. "But I had rather congratulate you and Doña María and [your sister] the Countess on anything rather than the betrothal!"

On that same visit, the Duchess demanded a copy of the *Life* — which, she'd been told, the Princess was too shallow and impious to understand: her confessor, Father de Medina would have it made for her. How de Medina felt about that order either then or when the book was eventually impounded by the Inquisition, I have often wondered. At least, as a friend of the Duke and Duchess, he never admitted to the existence of that sole, illicit copy.

When the Duchess sent a fine trout to the convent, Teresa had it taken to her cousin Ana in Salamanca with directions to sniff and make sure that it was still perfectly fresh before it went to Father Medina with her compliments. By the time Teresa got back to Salamanca, Báñez had tamed Doña Beatriz. And, sensibly, he asked a favor in return.

Chapter 38 ❀ Father Domingo Báñez, Gracián, Nieto, and Mariano

I

Báñez was a man of conscience. Some eight years back he had become over-fond of a blackamoor slave girl, who gave him a son. Few men of his day would have given the situation such responsible care as he did, putting the child in a foster home and placing the girl as a servant and nurse for old María Díaz in her declining years. Then, before Teresa went to Alba, María Díaz died. In Andalusia, slave-girls were admitted to convents as dusky lay-sisters, but not in Castile. The girl had turned out well; Teresa, he believed, would like her and accept her as a lay-sister in Salamanca if she would consent to give her a trial admission, only a trial, in return for all he was attempting: the taming of Magdalena de Guzmán's mother, Doña Beatriz, and the healing of the rift be-tween Teresa's so greatly needed patrons, the Duchess and Bishop Mendoza.

But along with Teresa's consent, he would need that of the Visitor. The rule against dusky lay-sisters in Castile was only an unwritten law, but without the highest authority for its infringement, there could be repercussions.

He sent Teresa some of his correspondence with Fernández just before she left for Alba, and she answered it in a letter that might safely be read by anyone. "Those letters between you and the Visitor made me laugh, for though he is as holy as his friend — more than he knows how to show openly — and though his words may sometimes be at odds with his acts, he won't fail to admit her, because there is a lot of difference between some employers than others." (This, as a later letter clarifies, means, "He knows that old María Díaz would not have approved of anyone unfit for convent life.")

She mentions other matters on her mind. "The Princess as a nun was enough to make you cry." And Báñez should see that María Bautista's greed for little Casilda's fortune only promises more trouble with the Jesuits. And "I am mak-ing some progress with Father Medina, though he is so busy that I can hardly ever see him. Doña María Costán says that I shouldn't love him as much as I love you!" (Rest of this passage censored.)

Then, safely separated from the beginning of the letter, comes praise of his handling of Magdalena's mother, who is briefly visiting her home in Salamanca: "Doña Beatriz is behaving well." Teresa had been "terrible worried," but now, thank God, she will need to do nothing about that herself — though "if some-one hadn't kept her in line, the whole business would have slipped off into utter ruin." The tone is casual. Teresa was fond of Domingo Báñez and trusted him to send her nothing like Ripalda's attempted offering to Valladolid.

She was right, and Báñez also showed his unfailing prudence. While Teresa was in Alba he corralled, albeit unwillingly on her part, a nun of the right hue, sending her to Salamanca along with a dusky lay-sister, supposedly the white girl's slave, in Doña Beatriz's care. (Furthermore, Báñez had taken care of all his responsibilities; Doña Beatriz now had a charming little page boy.)

Teresa, child of the double standard though she was, felt in the end that sin must get some gentle rebuke. Her letter dated February 28, 1574, begins: "The grace of the Holy Spirit be with you—and with my own soul! It's no wonder what people will do for the love of God when the love of Fray Domingo has such effect that what seems good to him seems good to me, and what he wants I want!

"*La su Parda* (your brown girl) had won us over. She is so beside herself with happiness since she got here that it's something to thank God for. I don't think I'll have the heart to let her stay a lay-sister, since you have set yourself to bettering her state in life, so I have decided that they'll teach her to read, and we'll see how it all works out." (The girl professed a year and half later under the name of María Parda de Cifuentes: for surnames her nickname plus the name of Báñez's mother—a double jest, since her son was Báñez's "nephew.")

It gave her joy, Teresa goes on, that God has shown Báñez mercy by making him merciful, a help to the helpless. "Oh, but the wailings of the one that brought her! I thought they'd never stop! I don't know why you wished her on me here." Still, if Báñez likes, she can take the *lloraduelos* (mourner) to Segovia, for though there are already too many who'll be going there, Salamanca has enough trouble without this wailer. "La Parda has a good father in you. She says she still can't believe that she's in a convent. I myself praised God when I saw your little nephew; he came here with Doña Beatriz. Why didn't you ever tell me about that?"

But now she worries about a problem of her own; after Segovia, she will need the Visitor's permission to make a foundation in an obscure village near the Andalusian border, and Báñez should have pleaded for it in her behalf. (It is too bad that Gracián could write such plausible letters.)

"Why don't you tell me what you have got done? God make you as holy as I wish you were! I keep wanting to tell you about those fears of yours, for they don't accomplish anything but make you waste time." Why even Melchor Cano's son, who has taken his father's name, shows a braver spirit than Báñez and more trust in her work: "That comforts me, more or less.

"Well, I don't seem to have anything better to do than to tell you about spirits unlike ours. Stay with God—and pray that He inspires me to do nothing that departs from His will."

Báñez was braver than Teresa knew; prudence is not pusillanimity. He would not hesitate in time to defend her before the Inquisiton. But he knew that a convent on the Andalusian border could only invite trouble: trouble involved with those men whom her General had denounced, long before the act, as "men led by an evil spirit."

II

Teresa never fully understood the situation, but we should.

Vargas, the Apostolic Visitor to Andalusia, wrote letters to Rome which are in full agreement with Rubeo's report on the deplorable state of the Andalusian Carmelites; but he wrote them in order to get papal backing for the expansion of the Discalced which Rubeo had forbidden. This, he believed, would please the King and profit his own career. He trumped up excuses to get his Andalusian friends, Heredia and Nieto, over the border, deceiving Father Angel—who did not want to see the Discalced flourish anywhere, north or south.

Both were so furiously opposed by the Calced that they soon went back to Castile—Heredia deserting the famous monastery of San Juan del Puerto, made Discalced by *fiat* to receive him, and Nieto fleeing from Vargas's attempt to make him Apostolic Visitor in his place—in a panic effort to escape the consequences of the storm he had aroused. Shortly before Teresa was released from the Incarnation, the Duke of Medina Sidonia persuaded Heredia to slip back as if on a visit to Granada. Nieto knew better than go back to be Vargas's scapegoat; as a traitor to his Order and his family he would have been inviting sudden death at the dinner table. Instead, he offered to send Jerónimo Gracián, a man with valuable Court connections.

To do so, Nieto had to befuddle Father Angel once again. Luckily, Mariano had not taken holy orders; he could ask as a simple friar for permission to go to Granada on business for the Princess's brother, the Duke of Medina Sidonia, with some other friar to bear him company: the other friar being Gracián, left unnamed, as Father Angel would have smelled a rat at the mention of one so close to the Court.

Mariano, who had ambitions of his own, foresightedly had himself ordained a sub-deacon just before he left, a deacon when he reached Córdoba, and a priest when he got to Seville. Vargas, who had begun to regret his involvement, warned the pair to keep a low profile for the time being and gave Gracián the position that Nieto had rejected, issuing two patents, one making him Visitor to the Andalusian Discalced and the other—to be kept secret until the right time came—to the Calced.

Gracián's first act was to give San Juan del Puerto back to the Calced; Heredia could visit the nobility and bide his time. In Seville the Calced grudgingly consented to house Gracián, Mariano, and Juan de la Miseria in an attic of the Casa Grande, that greatest of the Carmelite priories. Then Vargas had a word with the Archbishop, who gave them a splendid monastery: Los Remedios, overlooking the Guadalquivir and named for its famous statue, Our Lady of Refuge; galleons returning from the Indies fired their guns in Her honor as they passed.

This generosity made the Carmelites furious again. Gracián showed them his patent for the Discalced, pointed out that the Calced had not questioned his right to give them back San Juan del Puerto, and that Los Remedios had always been in the gift of the man who became Archbishop of Seville, to bestow as he wished.

Teresa saw it as God's will that Andalusia should be healed by one so gentle, so free of the Pastrana malady. She was also grateful that Gracián wanted to meet her on the Andalusian border and learn more about her beliefs and purposes than any letter could convey. She had hoped that Báñez could get her a licence from the Visitor; and Báñez found this increasingly unwise as he began to see the whole picture. Teresa herself knew only what Gracián chose to tell her; but this is as good a place as any for us to learn more, though much of the picture only developed after Teresa had gone to Segovia.

The Calced appealed to the Pope, and the Pope revoked the patents which made Gracián Apostolic Visitor. Vargas sent de Padilla, Gracián's ever-useful go-between, to protest to the King. The Visitors had first been appointed at royal request, and the King let the Pope feel his anger. The Pope replied that he would announce his decision at the General Chapter of the Carmelites, to be held in Italy within the coming year. In time the Nuncio Ormaneto, the previous Pope's appointee, decided that it was still in his powers to renew the Visitors' rights and restore the status quo; but about this he was still in some doubt when Teresa left Segovia and headed for the border. Gracián's appointment was still illegal. But Teresa quite genuinely believed what she was told: that the village of Beas was north, not south of the border, and that the Pope had extended the rights of her friars to found monasteries in Andalusia, under Gracián's rule.

There is a plethora of contradictory evidence on Gracián. Much of it was written to justify his expulsion from Teresa's Order after her death; much is luminous whitewash, in full accord with his own biography, written in exile. Gracián saw himself as having been, like Christ, persecuted without a cause, and he did not hesitate to draw the analogy in just so many words: an estimate with which Teresa's canonization forced all to agree.

At least the sexual slanders on him were undeserved. Gracián was a sentimental capon whose chief fault was an unhappy blend of ambition and cowardice; he could neither fight for power nor relinquish it, and like many so afflicted he saw his cowardice as gentleness. Teresa would share his belief for years to come.

The Visitor Fernández himself came to Salamanca just as Teresa was about to leave for Segovia. When she showed him the invitation from Beas, Fernández told her to waste no time on it. Convents in those parts could only be founded with licence from the Military Order of Santiago, which would refuse her both because she was of impure blood and because the convent she intended would be enclosed.

Teresa trusted Fernández, and saw clearly that he was glad to believe a foundation in Beas to be impossible. Teresa herself knew that Beas could only give her an isolated, necessarily endowed convent, lacking even the justification of a useful patroness, as promised by Malagón and Alba and, alas, even Pastrana. It also weighed heavy on her that the friars' work in Andalusia, however good, however needful, had been forbidden by Rubeo — to whom everything was due. And after Teresa had talked with Fernández, she tried to put all thought of Beas aside.

Years later, when Teresa was under house arrest in Toledo, with her work once more, it seemed, brought to an end, she began to write about Segovia — at Gracián's order. She told no more than the truth when she said that she went there "in great darkness and dryness of soul."

Chapter 39 ✿ Founding a Convent in Segovia

I

Fernández did at least agree wholeheartedly that the Pastrana convent should be moved. He may have seen a letter to the Duchess in which Heredia describes a visit to Pastrana, where he stopped off to consult with Nieto on his final trip south. The Princess, it says, is being a nun *con brío*, though, as often, she is noticeably pregnant and still orders the other nuns around like servants. (The Duchess would have enjoyed that letter and passed it around; the Princess's highly fertile liaisons amused the Court.)

The Duchess, we are told by the Alba nuns, persuaded Teresa to visit her on the way back to the Incarnation and gave her a thousand ducats to spend on its needs; this sounds likely, for she would have loved to shine in contrast to La Eboli. The nuns also say that Teresa spent some time with a visitor to the castle, Don Teutonio de Braganza, a member of the Royal house of Portugal who had recently taken holy orders. This too seems likely, though Teresa had met him first through Baltasar Alvarez, who housed him in Salamanca. Don Teutonio was a rather bumbling fellow, but endearing, and he wished that he were more religious than he was; he found Teresa inspiring, she found him a dear, and their friendship flourished on letters from that time on.

The journey from Alba was made in the Duchess's coach: first to Medina, where affairs constantly needed straightening out, then to the Incarnation with the ducats from the Duchess, a visit to San José, and on to Segovia. Antonio Gaitán, a young widower from Alba, rode armed guard. Julián de Avila and Juan de la Cruz went, too, and since the foundation must seem like any other from the start, the caravan included a nun and a novice (*la lloraduelos*) from Salamanca, and one each from Alba, Medina, and Avila. *Fundaciones* makes no mention of the Pastrana nuns, who were the reason for that foundation; when Teresa wrote the Segovia chapter, almost three years later, the Princess could still be a dangerous enemy. Indeed, what she tells about Segovia is not much.

The Lord told her to found there, and the Visitor consented, though her triennium at the Incarnation was not yet ended. A lady, Doña Ana de Jimena (*sic*), offered a house and all they would need for a "church." But she set out for Segovia running a fever and with "the greatest possible evils of darkness and dryness in [her] soul . . . and for the half year [she] stayed [she] was always ill."

They reserved the Sacrament on St. Joseph's day, having entered secretly the night before. It had not seemed important to get the Bishop's licence in writing: "And I was mistaken because when it was brought to the Provisor's attention that a convent was made, he came at once, and very angry, and would not let Mass be said there any more and wanted to put the one who had said it in prison—a Discalced friar who had come with Father Julián and another servant of God named Antonio Gaitán." (She dates the writing of this chapter by praising Gaitán, for his help on her journey to found in Seville, as well as by the unexpected anonymity she gives Juan de la Cruz.)

The Provisor posted an armed constable at the door, which frightened the nuns; but she sent for "some people" considered *muy principal* in that place, and they talked the Provisor into letting them stay in that house, which was rented, until they had one of their own. Getting one made trouble with the Franciscans and the Mercedarians. A nephew of the Bishop and a Licentiate named Herrera helped them, but they still had to go into their permanent home "very, very secretly," just before Michaelmas. And less than a week later she had to leave, in order to be present when the Incarnation elected a new Prioress.

Teresa would tell no more about Segovia.

II

The Bishop was Covarrubias, President of the Royal Council, who lived in Madrid. The Provisor, Hernando Martínez de Hiniesta, who acted for the Bishop, was notorious for his uncontrollable temper: the Cathedral's records show him as so often defiant of the Bishop and the King in all matters which favored the reform that one wonders why he was tolerated.

The Bishop's nephew, Don Juan de Orozco y Covarrubias, tells in a letter of having seen a cross on a house, gone in, and on finding a Mass being celebrated without his uncle's licence, told the Provisor, whose response was violent. To this Julián de Avila adds color: he recalls hearing de Hiniesta's screams even before he burst in on the Mass, raging and calling the guard before he rushed off again, leaving young Don Juan behind, deeply embarrassed. Then Teresa in talking with Don Juan discovered that her late Uncle Pedro's wife, the pious Doña Mencía, was his mother's cousin; this put things on a family footing, though he could do little but sympathize.

Don Juan had just left when the Provisor returned with a lesser priest in tow and ordered him to consume the Host — as if he were a hired taster at a suspect feast — after which he gave himself the unaided pleasure of overturning the altar, smashing the breakable vessels, and flinging the rest of them about.

Teresa knew that she had one friend in town, albeit a Jesuit and a *converso*. Luis de Santander, who had defended her before the Medina junta, was now Rector in Segovia: a city which, to the Provisor's unending fury, was still in de Bracamonte hands. The Provisor was still throwing crucifix, chalice, and such about when Teresa sent Julián to find Santander, who came with their patroness's brother, Andrés — the Regidor of the city. The Bishop had given Andrés his casual word of mouth consent to a convent his sister wanted to found for herself and her daughter, María de Bracamonte. According to Julián, Santander and the Regidor told the Provisor that he was defying his Bishop and interfering not only with women's business but with God's, so the Provisor allowed it that a priest might come to say Mass for them, and that once they had their promised house they might have the Host reserved.

He could not have done less, and he knew it. The de Bracamontes (or as Teresa calls them "some people") were indeed "*muy principal* in that place"; the Cathedral depended on their benevolence. When the city council met four days later, it moved that as a Discalced convent had come to Segovia "the city would do well to visit it and see to its welfare."

Julián went to Pastrana, had a secret night meeting with the Prioress, and on the following day's midnight got Mother Isabel, her nuns, and their belongings into five carts—without taking a single item on their notarized list of the Princess's gifts, as she learned when she tried to sue. After that, the small house was crowded. Nuns were constantly ill, and Teresa, ill herself, took care of them—though she had, as she once said in a letter, neither patience nor talent for nursing. It is not surprising that only one of her letters from those first three months has survived.

But those of the last three months tell much that is worth knowing.

III

Teresa went to Segovia in "dryness and darkness of soul." By mid-May she saw that depression as having been purely physical. She wrote to María Bautista that the syrup Báñez recommended did her worlds of good; it lessened the fevers of her quartan ague and "the torment of melancholy" was wholly cured.

She gave the syrup too much credit. The same letter goes on:

"Oh, if you only knew the excitement over what's happening—secretly, of course—in favor of the Discalced! It's something to praise God for, and those two who went to Andalusia, Gracián and Mariano, started it all. The grief it must give our Father General chills my pleasure badly, for I love him much; but on the other hand I see the ruined state we are keeping ourselves back in. Commend it to God." Báñez will tell María Bautista more, she adds, but she must mention none of it in her letters unless she can find a wholly reliable messenger, for secrecy is essential.

Secrecy was impossible. The news that Teresa would be granted her licence for Beas leaked; Mariano, at one point in his varied career, had been a member of the Military Order of St. John and seems to have known how to talk to its brother Order of Santiago. Báñez and the Visitor, Fernández, were distressed, and Bartolomé de Medina was noisily appalled: the Duchess's protégée turned *romera*, holy tramp, to please some obscure nobody in Andalusia! What a mockery of her rule of enclosure!

This meant trouble, but Teresa shrugged off María Bautista's warnings: "As for that thing about Father Medina, you needn't be afraid it will upset me. On the contrary, it just made me laugh. If Fray Domingo said only half as much, I'd feel it more—for that other one owes me nothing, and it really matters little to him whether I keep that rule or not. He doesn't know anything about these convents, he doesn't know what they are like, and he has no reason to love them as Fray Domingo does—and he's certainly keeping it up!"

The ambivalence is clear. Báñez did love her convents, and he owed her his place at San Gregorio in Valladolid as well as her kindness to "*la su Parda*," his dark girl; yet he was "keeping it up" with his objections to Beas, and talking about them with María Bautista.

(And, I repeat, Gracián could write a lovely letter.)

Teresa wrote to tell Antonio Gaitán, the young widower in Alba, that another, longer journey lay before him. Gaitán had begun to wonder if prayer was not a better way to save his soul, and Teresa reassured him: "Don't tire yourself with trying to think or pay attention at all to meditation, for . . . I have told you again and again what you should do and how your doing it is a greater mercy from God. . . . Please the Lord, you and I will both find a way to repay some part of what we owe Him — even if it should be with fleas, ghosts, and the road."

But he still worried. He sent her a book on prayer and asked if the sort of religious experience it described was common; his own was so inferior to it. Shouldn't he just stay at home and try to pray better? As to whether he should make the trip, she said, she couldn't advise him, being "the most interested party." For the rest, his book described a perfection only known to rare contemplatives.

"I have told you over and over, but you forget. Grasp it that in this life there are all kinds of weather, and it is just the same in the inner life, too, and can't possibly be otherwise. Don't brood over it, it is not your fault." Teresa was not talking down to this young man; she wrote the same advice to Don Teutonio, the royal activist who had quickly involved himself in all the secret dealings of the Discalced in Andalusia.

"About that thing you have about wanting to escape from prayer, don't give it a second thought. Just thank the Lord for such desire to pray as you have . . . and so try, sometimes when you feel that kind of pressure, to go outdoors where you can see the sky, and take a walk. Doing that won't be deserting prayer. Sometimes it is necessary to lead the soul gently, so that the body won't cramp it in."

She advised them both to talk with Baltasar Alvarez. But she expressed relief when she found a way to send her letters directly to Don Teutonio. The Jesuit Francisco de Olea, who had been delivering them, was not a reliable messenger. Teresa had to walk delicately among her once idolized Jesuits: men like Santander and Father Baltasar were the exception, not the rule.

IV

María Bautista knew Teresa's pattern: the loss of one confessor who "understood her soul" left her hungry for another. She was disturbed by Teresa's accounts of Gracián's perfections and achievements, and above all by her determination to go to Beas. She wrote a letter that let Teresa know it.

Teresa's answer begins with describing the death of a nun in Salamanca, while she herself "still lives on, made useless"; *made* useless by other cautions and hamperings. Then she bursts out: "What a fool you are to send me those self-satisfied remarks about the commands and in . . ." She crossed out the last words, and ends the sentence, "and about the rest of it. Until I see you, I do not dare tell you in full the plan I have. But know that every day I am more free, and more safe from offending God by way of that person — for I myself fear nothing else, and I have seen great falls and dangers from that sort of thing —

189

and I love that soul very much, and it seems as if God has given me that concern [for him] and I am delighted that he delights to be in a [spiritually] safe place, though truly in this world there is no such thing, nor is it well that we should feel safe, for we are surrounded by enemies." This is not Teresa's last defensive letter to María Bautista concerning what she feels for Gracián.

Teresa had acquired two troublesome nuns with her convent. One of them, a dear friend of her patroness, is described by Colomares, in his *Historia de la Ciudad de Segovia*, as "a woman of much gallantry, beauty, and willfulness." She and her husband had separated, he to enter the Franciscans and she the Mercedarians, the Orders which, along with the Carmelites, topped the King's list of those in need of reform. Now, at fifty-six, she had decided to move to her friend Doña Ana de Jimena's convent — and she had to be put up with. Of Doña Ana's daughter, María de Bracamonte, the same historian says that she, too, was a famous beauty, but so given to bodily penances tht she became a lifelong invalid. A convent record sets down Teresa's rebuke: "Daughter, to serve God well you must care for your health." (Though witnesses from that convent thirty-seven years later portray a Teresa in continual ecstasies of bloody penance, while the walls of her cell dripped gore.)

We can be glad that Mother Isabel de Santo Domingo told of Teresa's two favorites in Segovia. One, a Portuguese girl, Teresa called *Maríabobales* — Crazy Mary. Once, while she was dancing with a basketful of dishes, Teresa said, "Maríabobales, you laugh loud enough to pierce high heaven!" To which Maríabobales said, "Well, if something about me gets into heaven I'd better keep it up." Teresa was delighted, and equally so with Ana de la Trinidad, the convent comedian. Once Teresa was gravely explaining the importance of Ana's chosen name in religion: "You know, daughter, those Three Persons are always within you." "Aha," said Ana; "So that's why I always feel like eating for three extra!" Teresa, passing it on to Mother Isabel said, "Every convent ought to have one like her!"

She needed those girls' laughter. The Mercedarians, irked by the loss of a nun so wealthy and *muy principal*, sued for the ground rent of the first house they tried to buy. Santander found them another, for six thousand ducats plus six hundred for the city council's permission to cancel the first deal. Immediately, the Franciscans (who had also hoped to inherit, since the lady and her husband had not bought an annulment of their marriage) claimed that the second house was on their land, and sued again. Such troubles dragged on into mid-July.

Then, in Andalusia, the Order of Santiago heard news which led them to send Teresa's licence, finally granted, not to her but to the Apostolic Visitor to Castile — which would shift the blame if their decision to grant it turned out as mistaken as rumor had it to be. Fernández came to Segovia, tried once more to dissuade Teresa, failed, and left without telling her that he had the licence with him. Instead, he took it to Valladolid and gave it to Báñez with the order that he investigate the rumors and then summon Teresa to Valladolid. There, if the facts warranted it, Báñez could tell her more than could be safely put in a letter, and as her confessor, order her to keep out of danger.

Fernández was not being an alarmist. Beas is not far from Córdoba; and the rumors concerned the Córdoba Inquisition.

Chapter 40 ❀ The Spanish Inquisition

I

The rumors concerned a heresy hunt. It was headed by Alonso López, a man of fixed mind who would still be sending his written denunciations of Teresa to the Inquisition years after all others were resigned to her canonization as inevitable. Thus far it was only known that López's chief target was Carleval, illuminist and *converso* Jesuit, who claimed as his twin inspirations "the false Andalusian prophetess, María Mejías," and "the nun, Teresa de Jesús," whose book which he frequently cited was clearly the work of an *alumbrada*.

The book was in Carleval's possession only because Teresa had disobeyed Báñez. Báñez mentioned the rumors in his letter directing Teresa to come to Valladolid. Teresa discounted the rumors, read anger between the lines in what he said, and turned defensive. She refused to come, and in a letter to María Bautista she sent a warning: "Don't stop talking to the Jesuit Rector. He may turn out to be the best friend you have." (Jesuits did, at least, see the Inquisition as the enemy; and from their own experiences, justly so.)

María Bautista took Báñez's side and added her own insistence that Teresa obey his summons. Teresa replied that such anger made her laugh, since she would have been only too glad to visit Valladolid if it were not necessary for her to leave for Beas directly from Avila. But for this, she must have her licence, and Báñez will only send her exaggerated warnings. "Oh, what a gloomy letter our father sent me! If you can, get him to send it [the licence] to me at once, if he doesn't want me to die here."

By mid-September, Báñez washed his hands of the Visitor's responsibility and sent on the licence. Meanwhile Don Teutonio, unwise and overkind, tried to override the Visitor's opposition and get Teresa to Beas by special permission from the Nuncio. The Visitor learned of this through Gracián's friend, the Prior of Atocha. He wrote about it angrily to Teresa, who saw that her friend must have some unspoken warning that he was endangering his own hopes of a bishopric. It had to be put obliquely, for her letters were still too often read in transit. "The Visitor did not tell me to tell you this because he thought you already knew it from the Nuncio." But while the Nuncio will licence the Beas foundation, *if Don Teutonio thinks best*, he can still tell her to refuse the Nuncio's offer. (He was inept at reading between the lines, and it cost him the bishopric.)

The Segovia foundation had cost twice what Ana de Jimena expected, and Teresa found two well-dowered novices to cover the debt, though she had to ask María Bautista for "a few reales" so that she would not have to go to Avila "like a beggar." Then a delay occurred: further letters from Valladolid made it plain that the rumors had enough substance to call for a certain sacrifice. Bishop Mendoza wrote for her copy of the *Life*; Báñez should read it and prepare a defense, if one were needed down in Córdoba. Teresa sent for it from Baltasar Alvarez, who had kept it with him to read and think about. She also released one of her wealthy novices; Bartolomé de Medina, too, had wanted that dowry for a Dominican convent, and one threatened by the Inquisition could not afford to vex him.

María Bautista, edgy on many points, took this bit of news as a snide rebuke to her own determination to keep little Casilda's fortune from the Jesuits. Teresa tried to soothe her in a note written on the eve of her leaving Segovia. She "can't give her reasons for not wanting to get into Master Medina's bad graces" as "there is so much that can't be explained in a letter," but it looks as if the Lord wants them to have humbly dowered novices, and dowered or no, "little Casilda is worth all the money in the world." As for Master Medina, "I am sick and tired of talking about that blessed soul!" At least she has one novice with money, so she is on her way, to Avila and then to Beas.

"Don't worry about it! God reward you for your advice. I know quite well where the border is. Do grasp the fact that it [Beas] is five leagues on this side and I already know that I can't found in Andalusia! I am taking Ana de Jesús with me, and be informed that they speak marvels of the holiness and humility of one of the ladies, and both of them are good, and that it is essential not to take anyone along who will smear her faults on them. . . . I say this about that nun of yours. Another convent may be made, please God — though a nun you can't put up with would be a bad founder for any convent, much as I'd like to take her off your hands."

(A rejected deal? Take her, and I won't air my views to Fray Domingo?)

"You think, daughter, that you do me great honor by insisting that I should not go. I will be there this winter, as the Lord had brought it about. I don't know how I stood the winter in these parts. What it was like was something I don't think even you could have wanted me to go through. It may be as . . ." (final page missing). María Bautista and Teresa did not feel for each other that mutual enduring devotion which is part of the legend; but Teresa would not have told María Bautista an outright lie. Gracián had said that Beas was north of the border and Teresa believed him.

Father Angel wanted to see Teresa re-elected at the Incarnation, and permanently grounded. This, the Visitor saw, could make trouble for Calced and Discalced alike if what was now brewing down in Córdoba actually ended as López seemed to hope. He ordered her instead to San José. Doña Isabel Arias was elected on October sixth, and on October seventh, Carleval was brought to trial. Suárez, the Jesuit Provincial, heard the good news and rushed in for the kill, denouncing Baltasar Alvarez to his General for his ties with Teresa and all her works. She could no longer write to him, she had no friends among the Avilan *letrados*, and Juan de la Cruz would only tell her that her stubborn determination to go to Beas was a sin against holy humility as well as a danger: a danger that even she was eventually forced to recognize.

Teresa spent two months in Avila, her eager expectation of soon meeting with Gracián reduced to a hopeless longing, and the convent she had loved become her prison. Báñez wrote to her. He had been her confessor in those troubled days when Soto inspected San José, and García unwisely urged her to add so much to the *Life* that had better been left unwritten. Surely she had found him a good confessor then? Why would she not come to Valladolid and take him for her confessor now?

Teresa's answer did not come from a quiet mind. "Jesus be with you. I tell you father, that my pleasures, so it seems to me, are definitely not in this kingdom, for what I want I haven't got, and I don't want what I have." (Castile, Andalusia, León, andso on were "kingdoms," the word a holdover from the days before the unification of Spain.) "The trouble is that what used to give me ease with my confessors no linger does; one has to be more than a confessor. Less than something which can respond through its own likeness to the soul does not draw out its desires. It certainly gave me ease to write you this: may God always give it to you through your loving Him.

"Tell that little person of yours who is so greatly absorbed in whether the sisters will vote her in again or not that she meddles too much and shows too little humility, and what seems best to you and the rest of the house will be done — not what seems good to one single nun. It is necessary for you to make the nuns understand things like that. . . . I believe that it is the third of December, and that I am your daughter and servant, Teresa de Jesús." In sum: You do not understand my soul; Gracián does. You and María Bautista are a pair!

Within the year there had been Báñez's successful effort to heal the Mendoza-*Toledo rift for her sake; and for his, a place made in Salamanca for la su Parda.* He would write her defense for the Madrid — yes, Madrid, not Córdoba — Inquisition. But something was changed by that letter. One more she wrote him, well over four years later, still exists — its tone overappreciative, overwarm, reminiscent of those she sometimes wrote to useful acquaintances in need of a little sweetening. Teresa was at her lowest ebb. She was ripe, as events would show in another month, to be used, deceived.

Still, three weeks after she wrote that letter she was in Valladolid to see María Bautista re-elected, and Casilda de Padilla take the habit. Casilda would witness in time that on that Christmas Eve La Santa preached a sermon "so moving and saintly that all of us said that it was the most learned sermon ever preached in the whole world, and so saintly I can't describe the wonderful things she let us hear." When Teresa spoke from inner joy or from darkness and dryness of spirit, she could always inspire her nuns.

It is also possible that she had learned that within three weeks she could dare to set out for Beas. Let me explain this, as I think, for the first time. The Spanish Church so dislikes the idea that a Spanish Saint was ever endangered by the Spanish Inquisition that the necessary documentation which explains the removal of Teresa's trial from Córdoba to Madrid, and its being, in consequence, dropped, has only been made available in bits and pieces over the past dozen years—and those bits and pieces never yet put together.

II

For a sound, compact, superbly documented study of the Spanish Inquisition none is more useful than that of the Oxonian Henry Kamen. The Inquisition's initial anti-Semitic passion, never lost, and its subsequent anti-Jesuit activities give us Teresa's historical background. Almost every notable mentioned in her books and letters appears in its pages, from her de Fonseca ancestors on through her lifetime of distinguished friends and enemies, ducal nobility, bishops, writers. Page after page of those which deal with the Inquisition's activities throughout her lifetime are loaded with familiar names: the Mendozas, Luis de León and "that blessed soul" de Medina—on and on.

I cannot recommend it too highly to one about to read Steggink and Efrén's equally scholarly, eight-hundred-page biography, *Tiempos y Vida de Sta. Teresa de Avila*. (*Times and Life*, to distinguish it from Efrén's less informed and informative *Life and Times*, its predecessor.) The text tells us about her grandfather's conversion and bought title; the footnotes, in themselves and as guides to further reading, give us the family history, and countless characters, who without Kamen's material might be confusing, are made comprehensible.

This book's chief oddity is its delicate treatment of Teresa *vis à vis* the Inquisition. Soto's visit to the Incarnation is given her own preferred treatment: omission. He appears only once, in a footnote on Malagón: "Years before, the Inquisitor Francisco de Soto advised her that she consult on her spirit with Master Avila. Perhaps on setting out for Medina del Campo she took the book with her, with that intention. But without doubt the presence of Dr. Bernardino Carleval, an intimate of Father Avila, brought her to the point of decision." Further information on Carleval is limited to the footnote information that he was succeeded in Malagón "by his brother, Tomás Carleval, also an excellent confessor of Discalced."

Information on Córdoba comes in connection with the Seville trial. Steggink cites a request to Madrid for a copy of the *Life*, "which had been remanded to Madrid from Córdoba"—minus any explanation of why it was in Córdoba to begin with.

The Seville trial, discussed by too many previous writers to be thus treated, is treated lightly: the result of false accusations by a disgruntled *beata*—which caused Teresa no anxiety since she so trusted the purpose and integrity of the Holy Office. After that, one gathers, the Inquisition and Teresa were hand in glove.

That part of the story is straightened out by Emilio de Llamas Martínez, from Inquisition records. Read in conjunction with the *Tiempos y Vida*, footnotes and all, which in turn has been read in conjunction with Kamen's *The Spanish Inquisition*, it gives as much as we can get of the whole story; read by itself it tells us as little as the first, which does not mention Teresa, or the second, which barely mentions the Inquisition, for it says — in one single throw-away line — that the Inquisition concentrated largely on *conversos*; but it never once hints that La Santa was not an Old Christian, of pure blood. The three books together, along with such other source-material as is available to a layman, become a passionately absorbing puzzle.

But to understand the situation as Teresa found it on reaching Valladolid, one must also understand what it meant to have powerful friends. Teresa had "impure blood," but so had thousands. Teresa had shown symptoms of illuminism, and so had countless others. As one *letrado* described that epidemic: "It is a grievous thing, the multitudes of deceived women one meets in many of the most important cities of Spain who with their *arrobamientos*, their revelations, and other afflictions have so stirred up the general public with their talk of prayer and other spiritual matters that it seems one can find nobody who does not experience raptures and extraordinary favors from God" (Father Ribadeneira).

From Spain's embarrassment of riches in *alumbrados* the Inquisition had to pick and choose. Carleval, *converso* and ecstatic, would have been safe enough if he had not become the Messianic leader of a cult. Teresa had been safe enough when, as Prioress of a tiny independent convent, some unknown person delated her to the Inquisition. A visit of inspection by an Inquisitor was enough. But Teresa, claimed as Carleval's twin inspiration along with the false prophetess, María Mejías, was another matter. She had founded a rapidly growing left-wing Order which taught the crypto-Protestant practice of mental prayer. Its growth had spread from Castile to Andalusia. She was no nonentity.

And, in consequence, it was her great good fortune that Diego Mendoza, son of the Duke of Infantado, grandee of the grandees, was also swept up in Alonso López's net. Diego Mendoza had to be handled with care, or the King and the Court would not like it. In such cases an order to the Inquisition to call off its dogs was unthinkable; however, a seemly argument could be made that certain of those cases be remanded to the Central Committee in Madrid: cases believed to be of unusual significance.

The significance did not have to be spelled out. "The nun Teresa de Jesús" was a protégée of another son and daughter to the Duke. The son, a bishop, headed her first convent; the daughter was patroness of another. The Duchess of Alba and a sister of the Duke of Medinaceli were the patronesses of yet another two. It was a foregone conclusion that no action would be taken against Don Diego or Mother Teresa when their cases were considered in Madrid — though, despite Domingo Báñez's splendid defense of the *Life*, it remained impounded (along with such other shockers as St. Francis Borgia's *On Christian Works*), since as Báñez himself admitted as its sole fault, "it said too much about visions."

It was also a foregone conclusion that Carleval and the false prophetess María Mejías would go to the stake in Andalusia. One following the first three months of the Córdoba trial, however, could not have guessed that another Andalusian woman, an obscure village eccentric also delated by López — rather mysteriously in view of her limited appeal to the public — would not go to the stake, but quite the contrary, would have her case also remanded to Madrid, and tactfully dropped. Her name, with Teresa's, was removed from the Córdoba records. Madrid identifies her as "Catalina Godóñez, resident of Beas, who claims to talk very intimately with the Lord and to have been shut up for twenty-four hours with a sweating Ecce Homo, and thus cured of an ailment that she had, as if by a miracle." López, it appears, had known more about the plans to get Teresa into Andalusia than Teresa had herself.

Llamas Martínez thinks that Teresa knew nothing of all this, since her letters do not mention it. He forgets that the Inquisition was not a safe subject to discuss in a letter, or one that would have moved others to save that letter for posterity. I cannot doubt that she knew of her delation to Córdoba, or that she and one of her prospective patronesses were safe once the Mendoza influence had moved their trial to Madrid. After all, she set out for Beas less than a week after that glad news came, though the formal proceedings would take another two months—and all that had gone before had held her back from early October to mid-January. But I am equally sure that she did not know that Beas was in Andalusia or that the lady of whom "they spoke marvels of her holiness and humility" made such claims for herself. She believed, I am convinced, only what Gracián saw fit to tell her. And it made a chill in her relationship with Báñez.

III

Just before Teresa left Valladolid she wrote two letters. One was to a woman who would have known the whole story from the Mendoza point of view. Doña Ana Enríquez, their intimate friend, had not gone to the stake with Cazalla in that great *auto de fe* in Valladolid. As the daughter of the Marquis of Alcañices, she had only been paraded in the *sambenitillo con sus cruces*. She was currently out-of-town on her parents' estate, and Teresa thanks her for having Baltasar Alvarez there to visit. It is long, she says, since she had heard from him directly. (Doña Ana would have known why.) And though she recently heard Fray Domingo preach brilliantly, she has seen little of him here: "He is always busy." (Báñez was loyal, but we need not wonder that the letter which called him, in effect, an inadequate confessor, created a strain, and especially in the face of Teresa's determination to go to Beas whatever he might urge to the contrary.)

The other letter was to Don Teutonio. He had learned enough about the Visitor's objections to Beas to find her two alternate foundations, and she wrote to refuse them. She also tries to encourage his failing hopes of a bishopric; with the Marquis on his side, she says, things will straighten out in Rome. But he and Father Baltasar must drop their plan to move her convent out of Salamanca. For their own sakes, they "must put things off, one way or another, so as not to make talk." She herself will come and see to it in April if she can.

Apparently, Don Teutonio still feared that Teresa's letters to him might go astray and their warmth be misinterpreted, for she says, quite out of context with anything she herself has said before: "I had grasped something like that, but your great zeal and my grateful nature give me the appearance of being very different from what I really am. Still, I'll be careful."

She promises to write him often from her long journey, but her only other extant letter to Don Teutonio, written three years later, congratulates him on getting his long desired bishopric, in Portugal to which he had soon returned. Indeed, once Teresa reached Beas, nobody heard from her until late May. Beas was on the road to nowhere, it had no messenger service, and Gracián carried those first letters from Beas to Madrid. Sadly revealing letters they are, too.

Beas had been a set-up; having founded there, she could be persuaded to found in Seville. In for a penny, in for a pound. And as another proverb has it, love is blind.

Chapter 41 ❁ *Founding a Convent at Beas; Teresa's Blind Faith in Gracián*

I

Teresa was under house-arrest in Toledo when Gracián ordered her to do for him what Ripalda had ordered her to do for Martín Gutiérrez: pick up the book, abandoned for the second time after her account of Alba de Tormes, and carry it on for Segovia, Beas, and its apparent end in Seville. Segovia presented no problems. But when she wrote to Lorenzo, now home from the Indies, to send her the manuscript of *Fundaciones* "as the Father Visitor [Gracián] has commanded me to go on with it," she asked him to go through her papers and find, as well, the alternate chapter on Alba that she had discarded.

It did not help. For Alba she had, at least, dealt with fact enough to mention the financial arrangements and describe the placing of the Sacrament on the altar. But about the actual founding of Beas she could tell only this: She had been sent from the Incarnation to Salamanca when she received an invitation to found in Beas from a lady who was well spoken of. The Visitor Fernández said that she might accept it if she got permission from the Order of Santiago. This he believed to be impossible, but God willed it otherwise, and so the convent was founded on St. Matthew's day, in 1575.

That is all. Thereafter she simply set down Catalina Godónez's story in Catalina's own version. How she felt about it we know from a letter she wrote not long after to María Bautista. A nun had died in Valladolid and she warned María Bautista not to let El Magdaleno's daughter write her obituary, for "that stuff she wrote about Estefanía was so full of nonsense and exaggeration that it was unbearable!" (Estefanía, too had died.)

Catalina, at fourteen, refused any marriage proposed for her "because of her high opinion of herself"; but one day, as she looked at a crucifix and read the words above it, "she underwent a change of heart," despised herself, desired martyrdom, and vowed her life to God. This occasioned "such a noise that it

197

seemed as if the house was being turned upside down." Her father rushed in, sword in hand, but found only Catalina on her knees.

For three years she begged her parents in vain to let her enter a convent. To avoid their anger, she only prayed from bedtime to dawn, occasionally interrupting herself to steal about and kiss the servants' feet. Throughout one Lent she wore her father's chain-mail next to her skin, which "caused the devil to play strange tricks on her." But God was good and after four years "He granted her the suffering she desired by afflicting her with fever, consumption, gout, sciatica, and a burning in the liver which could not only be felt through the bedclothes but which burned a hole in her nightgown."

At her parents' death she said that if she were healed, it would prove God's will that she should found a convent. At once she recovered, leaving all greatly astonished as she had suffered these simultaneous ailments for seventeen years—though rejoicing in them, and in having salt rubbed into her cuts after bleedings, and in the cauterizings of her cancer. (Another malady, unfortunately not in her self-cauterizing liver.) So she went to Madrid and the King gave her a licence when he heard that it was to be in favor of the Discalced. She knew about the Discalced from a vision granted her twenty years earlier, in which a friar described them and showed her Teresa's Constitutions.

And who was this friar who showed Catalina the Constitutions years before they were written? Teresa tells us, as her own voice breaks through at the end of this story which I have drastically reduced:

"While I was in Beas, a Discalced friar came there—actually a lay-brother named Juan de la Miseria—and she said he was the very one who had appeared to her in a vision. . . .

"Certainly all this seems impossible. If the doctor and people who lived in the house had not also so informed me, I am so wicked that it would not have taken much more to make me believe that it was somewhat exaggerated."

She had to allow herself that identification of the "friar," that "much more," that "somewhat." But she makes a firm restatement of Catalina's piety and chastity and ends with a prayer: "May it please His Majesty to keep her in His hand and increase the virtues and graces He has given her for the sake of His greater service and honor. Amen."

Alba de Tormes, you recall, was also finished off with a prayer that it get better. Still, whitewashing the Duchess was an incomparably easier job than whitewashing a man in whom one still longed to believe.

II

It was part of the plan that Teresa, in all innocence, come prepared to make not one convent but two. To this end, an offer must be found which could not be accepted for a year or so; this would make the substitution of Seville easy to urge once Teresa discovered that she had already founded in Andalusia. Mariano located such a prospective convent, and, I think, with double purpose. He had come to want Teresa out of the picture even more than he had when the picture only involved Castile and he had found the Order its Cardona. He was unhappy when he learned of the likely end of the Córdoba trial, but a study of its cast of characters gave him a further inspiration.

He foresaw that Seville would be a disaster, one that he could readily compound without alienating Gracián. Teresa would gladly leave it for Caravaca: and Caravaca would be a disaster too—one involving no inconvenient Mendozas. I have no proof of this. If I wrong him, you will at least admit that Caravaca was an odd choice under the circumstances.

Caravaca has dwindled. In those days it was sizeable and flooded with a constant stream of pilgrims, for it housed the True Cross, from which the tiny crosses sold from its splinterings guaranteed protection from lightning and fire. (Remarkably for relics so precious, no other claims were advertised.) However, its chief attraction to Mariano would have been that it had housed for four years a group of Andalusian Jesuits whose Rector, Diego de Salazar Marañón, a disciple of Master Avila, was a close friend of Carleval. Whether he blamed Teresa for his friends' now certain end at the stake or defended her as the blameless inspiration of a blameless soul, he would talk about her incessantly, and from that pilgrimage-center, talk would spread fast and far. Either way, his presence promised to make Teresa further trouble with the Inquisition.

She would go to Seville first, because it would soon be discovered that the donors, Rodrigo Moya and his wife, wanted the convent for two nieces, discontented Franciscans; which meant that a licence could only be obtained through the Council of Orders, a lengthy process.

(Teresa herself never saw Caravaca, though she did send nuns there before she left Seville. She explains her hesitations over accepting the offer by saying that getting a licence was "complicated." But a further difficulty was removed when, after she reached Seville, Diego Marañón was eliminated by the Inquisition. He is also, like Carleval, erased from Teresa's story for the next four hundred years.)

Caravaca (or any such encumbered offer) had been an afterthought of Gracián which he left to Mariano to carry out. Ribera says that Teresa got her offer from de Moya through a certain Father Leida (otherwise unidentified) who happened to hear of Teresa's coming south just in time for Señor Moya to catch her in Avila with his invitation. The offer, as Teresa received it, was for a second convent to be made on her homeward way. She assumed that it had been arranged for by Gracián, and was grateful and unsuspecting.

There was, as it happens, much else that she did not suspect.

On April 26, 1574, while Teresa was in Segovia, General Rubeo wrote to Gracián about the Andalusian expansion: "Presumably your intentions were godly, but since you acted against obedience and under censures and expressions of disapproval which must have disturbed your conscience, it does not seem to me that you acted in God's service." Consequently, Rubeo went on, a papal counterbrief was being drawn up which annulled Gracián's office as Apostolic Visitor.

This was not the sort of thing that Gracián told Teresa. According to his own account, however, he kept her fully informed of everything that was going on in Andalusia, "which gave her great joy." They planned, he says, to meet in Beas after Easter, following which he would go to Madrid "to confer with the Nuncio." This last is true. Gracián hoped that Ormaneto, appointed by Gregory XIII's predecessor, could win an extension of his powers by which he could cancel the counterbrief; and this actually happened, though not until long after Teresa had gone to Seville.

Still, Gracián feared that a leakage of such information, plus her troubles with the Inquisition, might make Teresa change her mind. Hence, when she made her stopover in Medina to see Doña Elena de Quiroga's daughter take the veil, she found Juan de Padilla waiting to make sure that she would definitely go to Beas, prepared to found two convents, and stay there until Gracián arrived. This we know only from Padilla's own account; after his arrest and imprisonment by the Inquisition, five years later, he was more willing to record his services to the Discalced than they to recall them. In consequence he remains a shadowy figure of whom one can only say that one who bore the same name as that unforgotten leader of "the Jewish revolt" — the War of the Comuneros — was ill advised to get into ecclesiastical quarrels.

Gracián need not have worried. Teresa, all blind faith in him, walked into the trap.

III

What we know of the journey comes from convent records and the writings of Julián de Avila, Ana de Jesús, whom Antonio Gaitán brought on from Salamanca, and María de San José, who left from Malagón — to become the Prioress of Seville.

Collecting enough nuns for two convents was not easy. Only one of the four Teresa had expected from Segovia came; María Bautista offered none she could accept; and since in Medina, cousin-Mother Inés always saw eye to eye with María Bautista, Teresa found it wise to relieve her of Isabel de San Jerónimo, the nun diagnosed by Juan de la Cruz as only mad, not possessed by the devil. One of those she took from Toledo turned out to be well worth having, a future prioress, Isabel de San Francisco, as did two of those from Malagón, very unlike one another. Leonor de San Gabriel was an endearing, tiny creature; one would not have guessed that in her middle-age she would become the remarkably competent prioress of a difficult convent; but María de San José was a handsome, brilliant woman with a will of her own. Years before, Teresa had known her as one of Doña Luisa's waiting women, and called her unfit for the religious life. But, as Teresa remarked of her bitterly in a letter written some years later, she was indubitably well fit to handle Andalusians. They were also joined there by a priest, Gregorio Nanciano, who had decided to turn Discalced.

It would be a two-month journey, and on the night they left Malagón, Teresa, in a note to Diego Ortiz, apologized for dictating; the bleeding she had just undergone to bring her fever down "has left her too weak to hold a pen." On that journey the men rode mules: no horse could have crossed the sierras that lay before them. The women, to prevent criticism of nuns who broke enclosure, went in covered carts like prairie schooners; portable convents in which they observed the hours of convent life. Teresa rewarded the muleteers for being silent during their times of prayer with a bite to eat and a passing of the wineskin, after which they were free to begin their cheerful cursing and singing and general racketing once again.

The first intended stopover south of Malagón had been Dalmiel, a town of two thousand. Julián and María de San José (an even more gifted writer of memoirs) leave out Dalmiel. Ana de Jesús, as usual, prettified it. There was no food there, she says, though she did manage to wheedle two eggs from the mother — and later the innkeeper sent food to Beas. Less cautious nuns witnessed to a likelier story: their appearance started a riot, and La Santa said, "We must shake the dust of the place off our feet and pass on." The incident, like two later, more graphically recorded, is not surprising. South of Toledo the Córdoba trial had become bad publicity. Someone had identified "the nun Teresa de Jesús," that tool of Satan, carting her *alumbradas* from place to place.

By doing their planned first two days' travel in one, they reached Montezares, the home of a member of the de Bracamonte y Jimena clan where, as Julián happily reports they "feasted on partridges." That was the one easy rest on a journey of which Teresa leaves no word except to call it, years later, the journey she most wondered over having survived, fevered and crippled with pain as she had been on all the way.

Day after day they pushed on through withered fields, bare olive groves, with the snowy peaks rising higher before them at every mile. In a town at the foot of the sierra they asked directions for Beas and found them useless. A mounted man who knew his way could have crossed the gap in a day; their muleteers got lost repeatedly, and their carts skirted gorges six hundred feet deep.

Once as they were about to round a corner, sheer cliffs to one side and sheer drop on the other, they heard an old man screaming from a cliff top: "Stop! Stop! Push back and find a place where you can turn around!" A rockslide had now so narrowed the way that the fearless mules would surely have pulled the foremost wagon to destruction, with no survivors. Once they had reflected, the nuns knew who had saved them. Who but St. Joseph?

The final stopover on that two-month journey was first revealed in 1963, when Efrén de la Madre de Dios worked out Teresa's only possible route to Beas — though he did not see its inescapable conclusion. La Peñuela, the Discalced monastery taken over from the illegal colony of hermits in which Mariano had once stayed, lies in wild country at the southern foot of the sierra, just before one reaches Beas. On their journeys, Julián was always overjoyed to find a chapel or a shrine in which he could say Mass. It is unthinkable that he passed La Peñuela by, or that Teresa saw the habits of Discalced friars without asking questions and learning that she had reached the border of Andalusia.

Beas, to the south on the road to nowhere, was conveniently placed for friars seeking alms in the nearest village; Catalina Godóñez had considerable wealth for one in such a place, and inquiries sent to La Peñuela about some possible patroness who lived not too far south of the boundary of New Castile would have got a ready answer. Catalina was a perfect prospect. Better still, Juan de la Miseria, who grew up in those parts, could serve as guide to that isolated spot. (As Gracián mentions, Juan de la Miseria guided him.)

Beas was, after all, in Andalusia!

But what could Teresa do but go on to Beas for a resting place? She could find something wrong with the place, refuse to found there without telling her nuns the true reason, and then take them to Caravaca which she believed to be nearby, though luckily it was over yet another border in the "kingdom" of Murcia. The sole alternative was to drag those bewildered women back again to their own convents and without explanation — another two-month haul.

Teresa went on.

IV

She went on, and met with a welcome that could only have taken some hours to prepare. Beas could not have known by precognition just when her long journey would end; but a friar on muleback could reach Beas from La Peñuela in a third the speed of her wagons, and carry the word. María de San José, like Teresa, was too shrewd to report that welcome; Julián, the guileless, and Ana de Jesús with her love of drama, gave it the works.

As soon as the wagons came in sight of the village they were met by two men in armor who galloped up to them, and reined in, *hacienda gentilezas*, as Ana puts it: dismounting, removing their helmets, and bowing low. They were led into the village, where everyone from tottering old men to babes in arms were gathered, "all crying out praises to God." At the church, a procession had already formed amd was waiting to bear the Host to the altar of Teresa's sole instant foundation.

What could she do but get out and follow with her nuns through the crowds that wept, cheered, and demanded her blessing? At the house, Julián says, "those ladies were waiting to receive them." Their self-imposed rule of enclosure had kept them from joining the crowd.

Except for its startling readiness, the welcome is not surprising. Catalina's imagination, so congenial to Andalusian tastes, gained further credibility from the ample alms from which she gave to the poor — which, by definition, meant almost the whole village. Furthermore, a wealthy hysteric in the right setting can believe a lot of remarkable things about herself and have them believed; in that time and setting one could even believe that Catalina had suffered a fire in her liver that burned holes in linen. God knows what they were willing to believe of her imported saint.

María de San José says that Catalina, then thirty-five, was unusually handsome and graceful. This is also striking, since that grace and beauty had survived seventeen years of simultaneous cancer, heart-disease, consumption, gout, sciatica and a fiery liver. Ana de Jesús says that just after that overwhelming welcome and instant foundation, Teresa said, doubtless in jest: "And what would you two do now if I refused to admit you?" To which Catalina replied, "We would serve you humbly as lay-sisters, fetching and carrying and living on alms."

That's as may be. But the evidence shows Teresa determined to get out of Andalusia as soon as possible. In her Caravaca chapter, written after four long chapters on Seville, she says that as soon as the convent was founded, she dispatched Father Julián and Antonio Gaitán to make sure that all would be ready when she and her nuns arrived. Anxiety made her merciless to that faithful pair, and she drove them off before they had caught their breath after two months of hard travelling. Andalusia was forbidden ground, Caravaca was over the border.

From the report they brought back, Teresa realized that she could not send word from Caravaca to Gracián that she would wait for him there. She would have to wait in Beas. Mercifully, during that time, she had Julián to make her laugh. He was an inadequate confessor, which her letters often deplore, but he had high spirits and a sense of humor. Let me give you a bit of his account of his trip back over the mountains to find Caravaca. (As it lay on the main highway from Seville to Madrid, they had bypassed it to reach Beas.)

He will skip, he writes, their struggles through the snow and such other adventures "or [he'd] never be finished" and begin when they were only a short way from their destination. That night, thoroughly done in, they reached a place called Moretalla and found the *posada* so packed "that there wasn't room to turn around in." Since Caravaca was said to be only a couple of leagues further on, they decided to push ahead, and they found a guide who said that they could make it in two hours.

"We were going along at top speed when we saw the man rolling down what was nearly a precipice, and we called out, 'Brother, have we lost our way?'

"'Sí,' said the man, with the utmost calm. 'Sí, Señor.'

"Well, I won't repeat what I said when I heard that."

While they tried to haul their guide up to the road, Gaitán was blaming Julián. He'd confused the poor man's mind "with all that talk about contemplation!" Nothing of the sort, Julián insisted; he'd only been telling him what commandments he should follow if he wanted to get to heaven. Still quarreling, they dragged the fellow back and set him on what they could only hope was the path — at which point they discovered the senselessness of their argument. Their guide had started out with a keg lashed to his back, and while Julián had been trying to show him the way to heaven, his pupil had been steadily and quietly getting dead drunk.

"So we left him and went on with no more notion of where we were going than as if we were blind." They saw a shepherd's fire on a rise above their path and called out for directions. The shepherd refused to come down and only shouted, 'This way! No, I mean that way!'"

They were down on their hands and knees, feeling about for some sort of path when they saw the dim shape of a man before them. Wild hope — until it turned out to be the guide they'd deserted, still up on his legs but as drunk as ever. They took the opposite direction from what seemed to be the general intent of his waverings and floundered on through the snow until they heard dogs barking.

"And once we had convinced ourselves that it really was just that, we listened as if it had been the sweetest music in the world."

They followed the sound, came to a house, woke a sleeping man and asked him where they were. He said, "Caravaca."

And, Julián ends the saga, "Once we really began to feel back in our own bodies once more, we began to laugh and said it certainly had been a *cara vaca*: a costly cow."

He did not, of course, record his findings, but he and Antonio Gaitán reported to Teresa on their return. They had learned enough to keep her immobilized.

It was almost two months before Gracián came. Teresa was sixty, far from well, and tragically confused. She had come to Beas in defiance of two men she admired and trusted, Fernández and Báñez. She had felt "absent from God" since she left the Incarnation and John of the Cross. But Gracián would come in April, and she had a desperate need to believe that if he had indeed used her—as all evidence seemed to indicate—it had been for reasons that she would be able to accept as holy, sprung from their mutual "love in Christ." She had to believe (as she had tried to write in her tactless letter to Báñez) that Gracián's spirit was enough like her own to help her own reach out to God again.

Try to see that. It explains a good deal about how things went after Gracián came.

Chapter 42 ❧ *Teresa's Love for Gracián, and Her Vow to Him*

Seville gets three long chapters in *Fundaciones*. The first of these begins, "While I was in Beas waiting for the licence from Caravaca, a Father of the Order came to see me, by name Father-Master Jerónimo Gracián, who had taken the habit a few years back while he was in Alcalá."

The rest of the chapter celebrates his virtues. It describes his distinguished family, his perfect disposition, "sweet but firm," and his lifelong devotion to Our Lady, whom he calls "My Beloved." Next it details the happy accidents by which he was persuaded to join the Order despite the brilliant future his parents had planned for him; his sufferings under a novice-master "without education or experience," his consequent temptation to leave the Order, and "other temptations not fit to write about" (these, we know from Gracián's own pen, he held off by sleeping with a statuette of his Beloved inside his nighty).

"It may seem uncalled for that he told me so many intimate particulars about his soul. Perhaps the Lord desired it so that I might set it down here in order that He might be praised through His creatures, . . . for I know he never told so much to a confessor or to anybody else . . . but it seemed to him that I was so old and had so much experience."

His self-mastery, his great gifts, and above all, his humility show him for one predestined to serve the Order. "I have certainly kept myself in hand in describing all this, for if it ever fell into his hands it would grieve him." (*If* it ever fell into his hands. . . . A neat touch. Nobody must suspect that these chapters are written at Gracián's orders and not, as her preface now indicates, in continuing obedience to Ripalda.)

And, she says, without Gracián her Order would have fallen into decay: "For there came a time when I should have been sorry that I had ever begun it, if it had not been for God's mercy. I am speaking of the friaries, for the convents, through His goodness, have always gone well — and the friaries had not become really bad, but they were on their way to falling very soon. This God prevented by making Gracián head of all the Discalced, both in Andalusia and in Castile."

So may Our Lady and Her Son be praised!

The chapter is long and fulsome, and at one deep level it is self-justification. Teresa would always be burdened by the knowledge that she had forfeited General Rubeo's faith in her. But it also has a pitiable sincerity; no girl swept away by the illusions of first love, no mother doting on an idolized only son, ever so overestimated a man as Teresa did when she first knew Gracián. However, he was almost a month in persuading her to that disobedience. And even a vision, her first since her final days with Martín in Salamanca, was not accepted without some difficulty. She described this in a *cuenta* for Dr. Velázquez, who became her confessor at a time when "feeling so bound" to Gracián had begun to cause her increasingly disturbing inner doubts.

"I was in the foundation of Beas in April of 1575 when Father-Master Gracián happened to come there and I confessed to him several times, though I did not put him above other confessors I had, so as to be ruled by him in everything. Then I was eating dinner, without the least spiritual recollectedness, when my soul seemed to be suspended and drawn in on itself so that it seemed to want to bring some sort of *arrobamiento* on me, and it showed me this vision — short as a flash of lightning, as they usually are.

"My Lord Jesus Christ seemed to be at my side, in the way His Majesty usually shows Himself to me, and He had me on His left side and this same Master Gracián on his right. The Lord took our right hands and joined them, and He told me that this man was to be accepted in His place as long as he lived, and that there should be total agreement between us in everything, because it was right that it should be so.

"A great certainty that this came from God remained in me, although two confessors whom I had followed and greatly depended on set themselves in my mind in a way that caused great resistance in me."(Báñez scorned visions; Juan de la Cruz saw them as almost invariably sent by the devil to confuse the soul.)

"The confidence that this was right persisted in me, and so did the relief from that feeling that I was shifting from side to side which goes with seeing things from different points of view, as they were given me by certain men who made me suffer a great deal through not understanding me — though I would never desert a confessor until he finally went his way and I went mine." (As she felt Báñez to have done, in Valladolid.)

"And that same confidence came back to me at two other times, along with the Lord's telling me not to fear it, because He gave it to me." (He used other words.)

"So I determined to do nothing else, and set myself to carry it out for the rest of my life — so long as he does not act perceptibly against God's will, which I am certain he will never do. . . . And I still remain possessed of a sense of peace and relief that has astounded me and seems to prove that this is what the Lord wants, for I am sure that such comfort and peace of soul could not have been put there by the devil."

Velázquez had not raised such a possibility; Teresa was refuting Teresa. But her second Seville chapter, written on Gracián's orders that she protect Gracián, is more pitiable. To begin with, she must underline it that Gracián's coming to Beas was unplanned.

"We had never met, though I had written to him: yes, several times. I was delighted, extremely so, when I learned that he was there, for I greatly wanted to meet him on account of the good reports of him others had given him of me, and I was happier still when he began to talk to me. . . ."

He had, she says, a commission from the Nuncio to govern the Discalced and was going to Madrid where the Nuncio extended it to the Calced, "which gave [her] great joy." The license for Caravaca was unsatisfactory, so she wanted to go back to Castile, but Gracián insisted that she found in Seville, to which the Archbishop had agreed.

(A slip, accidentally showing that Gracián had planned the move in advance.)

This is followed by the supreme example of those tangled non-sentences into which Teresa falls when she tries to explain away rather than omit:

"I, though I had always objected strongly to making monasteries of those men in Andalusia, and when I went to Beas I certainly would not have gone if I had known that it was in Andalusia, and I was deceived for I believed it was some five or six miles before the boundary begins, but, yes, it was in the province, and seeing my Superior so determined I gave in at once, for the Lord does me the mercy of feeling that my superiors are right in everything though I was already determined upon the other foundation and there were also other reasons, very grave reasons that I had for not going to Seville"(she leaves them unmentioned).

Teresa made her vow to obey Gracián because of the first "imaginary vision" she had experienced since she had felt "so bound" to Martín Gutiérrez. But the vision did not let her go to Seville with a clear conscience or a light heart. Because of that I choose to leave her tangled non-sentence as she wrote it. Others, through four centuries, have preferred to clear Teresa of disobedience and Gracián of dishonesty by ignoring it. (Though in the 1940's E. Allison Peers smoothed it into comprehensible — and misleading English prose.) Teresa deserves to have it known that she was far from casual about the Seville foundation, which through four long years she would believe to have ended her service to the Church. (This is why her epilogue to *Fundaciones* comes before the story of her last four foundations; for she died just before she could make the one she intended to be her last — after which she could put the epilogue where it belonged.)

II

Gracián wrote about his first meeting with Teresa when he had been cast out of the Order, and she was on her assured way to sainthood. There was no further need to present it as accidental, and he did not. By his account it was planned well in advance, and to guide him to a place so far off the beaten track he enlisted a friar born in those parts — one, he adds, who had previously acted as his messenger to arrange for her coming: Juan de la Miseria.

"We talked over all the affairs of the Order, both past and future. Still more, we talked about the way the spiritual life should proceed and how it must be sustained for both nuns and friars. This went on for many days, and all day long was spent in it except for Mass and our meals. . . .

"She opened her soul to me without concealing anything, and in the same way, I told her all of my own inner life. And then and there we agreed to be at one with each other in all our affairs; she, over and above her vows in religion, made a particular vow to obey me for all the rest of her life."

Teresa wrote at a time when her post-conversion life was being slandered, in lubricious exaggerations of the past from which she had been released by Augustine. The records of the Seville Inquisition have apparently been destroyed, but the dirty stories poured into its ears still exist in the form of several sheets of retractions — highly specific, though each ends "which was a big lie." Hence, while she lets us know that much of Gracián's "own inner life" was "not fit to write about," she explains that he so opened his heart because she "was old."

This necessity was heightened by the vivid beauty which remained hers so dangerously long. But no such danger existed when Gracián wrote. Teresa's death and miraculous preservation disproved all scandals concerning her relationships with her confessors. Gracián could write, "She looked more like a girl"; and, without hesitation, claim: "I loved her more than any creature on earth, and she loved me."

This was not wholly true, for Gracián indubitably loved Gracián more than any creature on earth. However, he loved Teresa's love for him until it became inconvenient; and when he wrote his masterpiece of self-love, the *Peregrinaciones de Anastasio*, his memory had become conveniently exclusive.

In Beas, he persuaded Teresa to go to Seville; and we have three of the letters that she gave him to post in Madrid.

The first was to Bishop Mendoza. Every day, it says, we learn how undependable our pleasures are. She had been hurrying with her foundation so that she could be in Avila or Valladolid by April when Father-Master Gracián arrived. "He is Provincial of Andalusia by commission of the Nuncio, who sent his there after the counter-brief" (of which she appears to have heard from the Visitor when the Bishop did, shortly before she set out from Valladolid). She has been much gratified to find a man of his quality in her Order and is eager for the Bishop to meet him so that he can tell her "whether [she] is deceiving [herself]."

Then, abruptly and without explanation: "So it seems that we are leaving for those parts on next Monday. I really believe that he wouldn't have forced me to go, but he wanted it so much that I would have had some scruples about obedience if I hadn't complied . . . though I take no pleasure in the thought of living through a fiery hot Seville summer. Please give me your blessing, your Lordship, and don't forget to commend me to Our Lord. . . . May this be to Our Lord's service, and may He take better care of Your Lordship than of me.

"Tell me whether I am deceiving myself. . . . May this be to Our Lord's service. Though, admittedly, I am obeying a Provincial's order to disobey my General, please see that I am only trying to do what seems right, and not indulging my own desires. . . ."

It was surely no easy letter to write and the next was harder.

While Teresa was still at the Incarnation, not yet released to go to Salamanca, Gracián visited Heredia in Medina. Heredia took him to call at the convent, and Inés thought little of him. She thought still less of him when María Bautista told her that he was luring Teresa to Andalusia in defiance of their General's orders. Teresa did what she could to sweeten Inés; she took poor mad Isabel de San Jerónimo away with her; but it was not enough.

I will boil her letter down; we often write too much when we had rather not write at all. Inés's letters have finally reached her, Teresa says. Having waited for them so anxiously made her realize how much more she loves Inés than all her other close relations. How sorry she is to hear about her ailments and troubles. Then: "Oh, Mother, how much I have wished that you were with me during these days! Father-Master Gracián has been here for more than twenty days, and I assure you that even with all the talk I've had with him I haven't completely grasped that man's worth. In my eyes he is perfect and more suited to us than anyone we would have known how to pray God for." So Inés must pray that God will give them Gracián for their superior. If that happened, Teresa could take a rest from having to oversee all her convents. (Inés would like that!)

Teresa has never seen anyone who is at once so perfect in the religious life and so gentle. She "would not have missed seeing and talking to him for anything." He has been waiting here for Mariano, who "to the delight of all" was slow in coming. Father Julián de Avila and the nuns are lost in admiration for him. He preaches superbly. "I truly believe that he must have improved greatly since you saw him. The great trials he has been through must have improved him very much." (The relative she "loves best" had not shown poor judgment. Oh, no! It is only that Gracián is changed so much for the better — to the admiration of all.)

This done, she breaks the news: "God has brought it about that I am leaving for Seville next Monday, God willing. I am writing to Don Diego" (Doña Elena's

Dominican son) "to explain it all. Briefly, it turned out that this house is in Andalusia after all, and as Father-Master Gracián is Provincial of Andalusia, I found myself his subject without realizing it, and as such he has power to command me."

So, since the licence for Caravaca was "all wrong" and she had come prepared to make two convents, it has been decided that she should make one in Seville at once. She only wishes that she could have Inés for its prioress, except that she sees how necessary Inés is to Medina. She hopes that Inés will see Father-Master Gracián before he goes back to Andalusia from Madrid, where he is going now to visit the Nuncio. And, oh, how much rather she would have spent a summer in Medina than in "the fire of Seville." That does it, except for messages from several nuns to friends in Medina, and her own regards to the Jesuit Rector.

Yes, it's regrettable. And inconsistent with the other in everything but her complaint over spending a summer in Seville rather than in Avila or Valladolid (the Bishop's see and home) or in Medina (with Inés). She wishes that the Bishop could meet Gracián and tell her whether he has the fine qualities she sees in him, or if she is deceiving herself. She tells Inés that, in her eyes and those of all with her, Gracián "is perfect" — so he must have changed greatly for the better after Inés saw him.

She tells the Bishop of her doubts about the move to Seville; her scruples may have led her astray. "Pray God it may be to His service." To Inés she simply says that God has brought it about. Saddest of all, perhaps, she feels no need to express the affection for the Bishop that she truly feels, — but Inés is the dearest member of her family and the one she would long to have as prioress of Seville if she were not so indispensible where she now is.

The letter, of course, was saved and served its purpose while it was read only as one from a saint, not from a woman, troubled and human. Whatever she wrote to María Bautista must somehow have failed even that test. Teresa doubtless spent nights before Gracián's departure in a spate of letter writing, but only one other remains. Until 1968, it was saved but confusingly misdated, for good and sufficient reason.

Don Teutonio, having lost his bishopric and been accused, with Baltasar Alvarez, of overkindness to Teresa's Salamanca convent as well as unseemly meddling in her affairs, started back to Portugal. In Seville, he met Gracián and gave him a farewell letter to Teresa and a parting gift: his treasured copy of Luis de Granada's *Guía de Pecadores*, which had gone on the Inquisition's Index of '58. De Granada, a Dominican, had also gone to Portugal to avoid continuing friction with the Inquisition. Apparently Don Teutonio's farewell letter suggested that Teresa ask de Granada the truth of whatever mangled story had reached him about their friendship.

Teresa had once owned and loved de Granada's *Guide for Sinners*. She wrote to him willingly, and far more honestly than she had to Cousin Inés. She is one of many, she begins, who loves de Granada in the Lord "for the great and universal good he has been to many souls, of whom [she is] one." She had longed to meet him while he lived in Spain, though it had not been possible for her, an enclosed nun: "For whenever these circumstances have not held me back, I have tried to seek out people like you to reassure my soul against the terrors it has lived in for so many years."

Don Teutonio has told her to write and ask him to pray for her, "for I need it badly." De Granada will understand why: she is a public figure who lacks the inner means to live up to what the good people believe of her, and she has, as he knows by now, a past to outlive. "If you understand this, it will be enough for you to do me this great mercy and charity—for you understand what the situation is, and the great trouble it presents to one who has led a very wicked life..." She asks him to see Don Teutonio, though he is one of those mistaken about her worth: "Do not think that there is no reason for you to do this."

De Granada had influence in Portugal; he should hear Don Teutonio clear himself of the whispering with which he and Baltasar, like so many before them, were being "persecuted." But it was not a letter written only out of a sense of duty. Teresa believed that she was going to Seville in much need of prayer. "Obedience" was not the matter over which her conscience was most tormented. It was the fear out of which she had written in Salamanca to Martín: "It does not seem right that any human creature should hold me so bound." She had not thought that any man would again threaten the "freedom" which had been the gift of the Rival.

But now one had; and Teresa, as I've said often before, had next to no native gift for self-deceit. Indeed, if we exclude her usual success at face-to-face charm, especially with men, the whole field of deceit found her limited: consider her compulsive, repetitious pleas of climate, too hot or too cold, to prove her need to move or her preference to stay here or there; her expressions of affection for women in need of sweetening, more extreme and less convincing in their degree of truth—until Inés becomes the dearest of her relatives. Most of all, I ask you to reread the non-sentence which tries to explain that founding in Seville —a subject on which simple omission was most painfully inadequate.

But at least, where politics demanded it with others, she tried. Not with herself. That in her eyes would have been not only a futility, but a shameful futility—the closest we ever come to committing the sin against the Holy Ghost. With only a little more gift for self-deceit Teresa could have set out for Seville with no need to be reassured "at two other times" by her Voice that her vision had justified her vow.

She did love Gracián, and for a long time she believed in him. But from start to finish, that was never quite enough.

Chapter 43 ❀ The Journey to Seville

It was an eight-day journey to Seville. Teresa described it at unusual length, and so did Julián.

The heat was intense. The covered carts were little ovens in which the nuns comforted themselves by thinking of hell—which, unlike their journey, would have no end. Teresa found their courage amazing. With that group, she said she would have dared to make a foundation in the country of the Turks.

The inns on the way were unfortunately bad. After a day in which Teresa's fever had shot up and she lay on the floor of the cart in a stupor, unrevived by the warm water her nuns splashed on her face, they found an inn in which their room was a windowless shed. If they opened the door for air, the blazing sun made it even worse, and the one bed was so full of jagged ups and downs that the sick woman was more comfortable on the floor. In another town they slept in a church, grateful for the coolness of the stone floor they lay on.

As they ferried across the Guadalquivir, the raft broke loose from the ropes by which it was hauled from side to side. The nuns prayed. Teresa says that her own chief feeling was pity for the ferryman, who had no oars aboard, and for his little son—both wretched with the fear of losing their livelihood. Luckily the ferry grounded on a sandbar, and onlookers from a castle sent help to get them to the other shore. Yet, except for the one day when she could not stir, Julián says that Teresa managed to keep them laughing with funny stories and "witty sayings" and *coplas*—little songs that she ad-libbed about their various adventures and misadventures.

They would, of course, have been wise to bypass Córdoba. Well before the Inquisition had remanded her case to Madrid, "the nun, Teresa de Jesús" had gained local fame. Julián should have been warned by that small-town riot in the posada at Dalmiel; but it was Pentecost, and he was determined to say Mass. He was not even made wary when they were stopped at the gates of the bridge which led into town and were told that they could not go on without a licence from the governor. Gaitán, a well-dressed layman, was allowed to cross the bridge and somehow managed to procure it. Then they found that their wagons were too wide for the gate. Gaitán went for a saw and cut the protruding axles from the wheels.

All this had cost a three-hour wait under the windows of the Alcazar, seat of the Inquisition: long enough for them to be identified and the word to spread. In town they found the streets filled with holy processions and the churches packed with crowds intent on celebrating the Pentecost fiesta with its usual mixture of worship and merrymaking. "Never since Córdoba was Córdoba," Julián wrote, "could there have been such a celebration as was being held that day."

They entered a church where Julián hoped to get leave to say a Mass and let his nuns receive communion. Their distinctive habits and veiled faces sent the church into a frenzy. Both Teresa and Julián leave the reaction unexplained — and indeed it was inexplicable without explaining too much, since so many other nuns as well as monks, priests and laymen were joining the celebration. Teresa only says, "It was one of the worst moments I ever went through because the wild uproar of the people was just as if so many bulls had come in." A kind man, she adds, managed to get them into a little side-chapel from which they could slip away and get out of town, taking their siesta under another bridge.

It hadn't been that simple. The man who helped them was the sacristan. He had brought the needed vessels to a side altar, and Julián had just begun to say Mass with the sacristan acting as his altar-boy when a priest rushed up, dragged the sacristan down from the altar and began to beat him up. They slipped away while the fight was going on. Julián mentions it only as an amusing oddity — those excitable Córdobans. It was, however, a promise of things to come, and the priest had only been doing his holy duty. The Mass was being said for "the nun, Teresa de Jesús," so recently denounced to the Holy Office. What priest with conscience and courage could have let such a sacrilege go on?

So much for the whole flavor of that eight-day journey. In *Fundaciones*, Teresa makes it sound like an adventure. Only her private writings let us know that throughout she was more troubled over an "obedience" which was in fact disobedience than she could ever admit: a disobedience which, in Rubeo's words, declared her to be led by an evil spirit. Thus, *Fundaciones* passes abruptly from the siesta under the bridge to, "We arrived at the house that Father Mariano had found for us."

Only a *cuenta* describes the stopover in Ecija.

II

The Ecija *cuenta*, along with twenty-one others, makes up the emotional background of the whole Seville story. At no other time in her active career did Teresa so often find reassurance from the Voice, or find it so fleeting. In Ecija, she went to a hermitage shrine, a holy grotto, to rethink her vow of obedience to Gracián. She was torn between a belief that she was acting in accordance with God's will and a terrible reluctance which, she says, "was almost exactly what I felt when I left my father's house to become a nun." (Disobeying her father, as she was now disobeying her father-figure, Rubeo).

Had she ever been obedient, she asked herself, and would this vow to obey Father-Master Gracián help her to become obedient by nature? She was obeying an order to disobey. And confessors can change; if Gracián changed, she was vowed not to take another. Her spiritual life would have no more freedom of choice. She fought the doubt off. If Gracián was right, and she was right in her evaluation of him, to obey Rubeo would be to run away from God. "And that was why I did not hold back for thinking of how much I loved him [Rubeo] as

I did with that other [her father], but only if it was a good thing for the Holy Spirit."

She told herself that the vow need not apply to trifles but only to major issues, and she renewed it. She still does not know, her *cuenta* goes on, but it seemed to her then that she had indeed done a great thing for the Holy Spirit. Then, startlingly, she pushed doubt aside and ends, "Blessed be He who created someone who satisfies me so completely that I could dare to do this!"

But throughout that year the doubts remained. One *cuenta* tells of praying with particular ardor on the feast of the Magdalene; and her letters tell us that on that same day she received two bitter letters from General Rubeo, denouncing Gracián: letters so long in coming that when he wrote he had not known that she, too, had gone to Andalusia.

And much as she needed her Voice, it rarely spoke plain. One brief *cuenta* says only, "I was commending my Eliseo to God when I heard, 'He is truly My son, I will not fail to help him' — or something like that which I couldn't remember clearly afterwards."

Gracián was long in returning, and as it had been when she left Salamanca and Martín, she was haunted by the Song of Songs. Words came back: "I am black, but I am beautiful, Oh daughters of Zion." And a vision came, a flowering orchard. "There I saw my Eliseo, not at all black but strangely beautiful, his head circled by a garland." He was surrounded by maidens singing praises to God and making celestial music, and the Voice spoke: "You have deserved to have this man among you, and this fiesta will take place on the day appointed for him to lead it in praise of My Mother." (The day, that is, when the Nuncio should gain an extension of his powers and give Gracián the Visitorship over the Discalced).

But twenty years earlier Teresa had distinguished between the visions of Jesus Christ and those in which the devil took on his appearance and roused a love "that had no purity in it." So, she continues: "All this went on for an hour and a half, for I could not distract myself from it. It was all delight, and a very different sort of thing from other visions that I have had. What I got from it was only more love for Eliseo, not for Him. I am afraid that it is temptation, for its having been only imagination is not possible." Too vivid, too intense for a daydream, it could not have been imagination. And since the only love it left was for Eliseo, it had not come from God. *Lead us not into temptation...*

Teresa, for the last time, was in love. But above all, she truly wanted to serve God and his ailing Church. She had taken a move that left her full of doubts; and far more than any but a handful on this earth at any given time, she wanted to know the truth about her duty and about herself. Do not smile at these *cuentas*; just bear them in mind as the background music to the rest of her life, a life in which she would continue to learn and grow.

III

By the time Teresa wrote about her year in Seville, Mariano was aligning himself against Gracián; she could express some bitterness against him for the situation she found there. Though he had "sent [her] three letters which all expressed the utmost love," the house she found still unfurnished, there was no licence from the Archbishop as she had been led to expect, and Mariano refused to let her write to him. She could tell that, and of how the Calced came in rage, demanding that she get out of town, and of how the Archbishop only came after long, long delay.

"I told him all the trouble he had made, and finally he said that I might do what I liked and as I liked. After that he showed us kindness and favor whenever the opportunity offered." (This, the convent records show, was three ducats a month to prevent their eviction and an allowance of wheat to grind for their bread.)

The third Seville chapter covers eleven months of hardship, of danger, by telling next to nothing. The city, she says, was rich, but she never found it so hard to provide a convent with bare necessities. Of the many novices promised them, only one came, "of whom I will tell you later." (For reasons always piously avoided, that novice would get a chapter of herself.) "They say that the devil finds the climate of Seville congenial and advantageous." She knew at least that while she was there she "had never found herself so cowardly and pusillanimous."

Julián and Antonio Gaitán had to get back to Castile on borrowed money. She herself would have left with them for Caravaca "if she had not known that it would grieve the Visitor." (Not yet Visitor, nor had she as yet a licence for Caravaca.) But fortunately her brother Lorenzo returned from the Indies. He got them a house, after troubles like those she had met in Segovia. An Augustinian prior persuaded the Archbishop that the foundation should be made in proper Sevillian style, and so there were processions, fireworks, and a fountain that played perfumed water. A flame from the fireworks blackened a wall of the house but missed the borrowed decorations, and "the nuns praised the Lord that they did not have to buy any more taffetas." As it seemed, the devil had wanted to spoil the celebration, "but God prevented him."

End of Seville, chapter three.

But Teresa's task was not yet done. Though the convent had survived its trial by the Inquisition, Gracián was afraid of a woman who threatened to stir up new trouble; and at his order, Teresa wrote the strangest chapter in the book. As with Teresa de Laiz and Catalina Godóñez, she gave Beatriz Chávez's own account of her life — plus praise of her virtues (which I shall omit) and one further "though": Beatriz, though thirty-seven, is called throughout "the girl." Beatriz was the novice who actually came to the convent, unlike those others who had promised to come as soon as it was founded. She had been besotted on Gracián from the time she first heard him preach and rushed up to embrace his knees and kiss his feet. It was chiefly through jealousy of Teresa and María de San José that she had turned dangerous.

Herewith the skeleton of the story Teresa told: The girl had noble, wealthy and Christian parents. (Perhaps they actually were Christian, but no more.) At seven her parents, who had six other offspring, gave her to an aunt. In her adolescence, three relatives who feared she would inherit the aunt's money accused her of buying corrosive sublimate with which to murder the aunt. (Before a will was made, hence without motive?) Her parents took her home and made her sleep on the floor for a year, beating and torturing her daily in hope of extracting a confession. They also "tried to strangle her." (Their failure in this goes unexplained.) At this point they decided to marry her off instead, but she refused because, at twelve, she had learned of how St. Anne, the Virgin's mother, used to visit a Carmelite convent; consequently "the girl" remained determined to become a Carmelite too.

When she heard Gracián preach, she recognized his habit from a vision she had seen fourteen years earlier in which the same habit was worn by an old man with a white beard—obviously St. Joseph. So, on having learned of Carmelite convents like those St. Anne used to visit, she ran away to San José de Sevilla as soon as it was founded. The convent notified her mother, who arrived furious, but was soon soothed, gave alms, and at her husband's death, entered the Order herself and "gave it all that she possessed" (by the convent records, very little).

Satan tempted the girl to leave the convent, but the Lord vanquished him three days before her profession, and the girl and her mother now live there, praising God for His mercy to them. (And no hard feelings about the attempted strangulation.) Teresa is careful to avoid all likelihood; she knew that the other nuns had heard these yarns and would vouch for Beatriz's having told them. If worst came to worst, they would show the Inquisition that the woman was either a phenomenally unconvincing liar or simply mad.

As things would turn out, the chapter was not needed. When Beatriz finally did go into action, it was in concert with a lay-sister whose imagination was still more fanciful; and while the Inquisition was willing to believe much, it could not believe that a man as ambitious as Gracián would have risked his career by frequently stripping and dancing naked before the nuns as a preliminary to retiring to Teresa's cell for the night. Since the Inquisition's records of the Seville trial have been apparently destroyed, we are fortunate to have the notarized retraction of this charge and others like it as proof that Teresa suffered accusations which her nuns describe as "unfit for chaste ears."

For the facts of that year we have two mutually self-corrective books: Gracián's *Peregrinaciones* and María de San José's *Libro de Recreaciones*. Both had different things that they chose to hide or to reveal. Legal documents, convent records, and Teresa's letters do the rest. Those letters are often longer than any of her chapters on Seville. Read in context and unsweetened by translation, those letters often tell more than she intended.

Chapter 44 ❀ Teresa in Seville; Her Letters to Her General, Rubeo

I

Seville was the richest city in Spain and, despite its Inquisition, the least pious. Teresa's contemporary, Alonso de Mogador, dwells at length on the charms of its women, their scents, their seductive curls, their dress; even mantles for the street were of silks and satins in brilliant hues, with matching silk parasols to guard their complexions. They walked with head held high, shoulders back, but taking tiny, rapid steps: the effect at once proud and disarmingly feminine. They also "took many baths."

As a girl, Teresa would have found it paradise. Seville was as alien to Avila as Stockholm to Naples, and its wealth made it truly the needle's eye. The Inquisition disturbed few of its citizens, since few did not take it easily for granted that the good things of the next world, as of this, were for sale by its appointed shopkeeper, the Church.

There were, of course, exceptions. In the year Teresa came there the Inquisition had to burn a previously unexceptionable merchant who had taken to seeing visions, receiving revelations and otherwise endangering the Faith; and the year before an *alumbrada* had collected a following of *beatas* who similarly had to be done away with. But on the whole, Sevillians were not drawn to heresy and the Inquisition was more or less resting on its laurels. It was even employing Jesuit *letrados* to do the dog-work when suspects had to be investigated on purely theological grounds, as Sevillian Dominicans were no bookworms.

In fact, the Archbishop rather outdid them in their own line of work. He was Don Cristóbal Rojas y Sandoval, a natural son of the Marquis of Denia. He had served Charles V as his chaplain in Flanders, got his first bishopric at forty-six, and had recently left his third, Córdoba, to be Archbishop of Seville. He had served at the Council of Trent and was strong on reform, especially as it concerned keeping the litany uncorrupted with Spanish words: a sign of creeping Protestantism. His devotion to the Inquisition was intense; in both Baeza and Córdoba he had brought groups of *alumbradas* to justice and the stake.

With this background, there can be no doubt that he had received advance information on the nun, Teresa de Jesús, and her most recent patroness, a suspected *alumbrada*, Catalina Godónez. Nonetheless, Gracián had reason to believe that once Teresa was in Seville, the Archbishop would accept her convent as a *fait accompli*. In the first place, he was of noble if illegitimate blood, and the aristocracy stuck together; the Discalced in Andalusia were approved by the Duke of Medina-Sidonia and the Count of Tendilla, both connections by marriage of the Archbishop's late father. More important still, Mariano had been able to do the Archbishop a remarkable service.

Don Cristóbal had come to Seville saddled with a typically noble debt of one hundred thousand ducats. But Mariano's good friend Nicholas Doria belonged to the prominent Genoese banking family of that name. Doria had powerful connections in the world of high finance — and he took the long view. In Genoa, as a younger son, he was somewhat crowded out; in Seville, he found Spanish finance hazardous. On the other hand, sufficient business sense could get one a long way in the Spanish Church. Doria had been thinking about that. And Mariano had convinced him that the Discalced were the coming thing: an act that made them grateful could open up a better future for him than he could find in any other Order. Doria played the hunch, but cautiously. The Archbishop learned that Doria had consolidated his debts and at vastly reduced interest to please a Discalced friar who was the Archbishop's admirer. However, Doria wanted to see a good many hands played out before he joined the Discalced. He always hedged his bets.

Gracián was less cautious. When he went to Beas, he assumed that Mariano had the Archbishop in his pocket. He also believed that the many girls who, like Beatriz Chávez, had responded so ardently to his preaching would swarm to any convent that he would be visiting often. Gracián never really understood Seville; nor did he understand Mariano who, on his departure, took pains to find just the right house for Teresa — tiny, damp, but on the Calle de las Armas, a house which would sound first-rate on paper if Gracián read those letters which, as Teresa says, "showed the utmost love." Mariano even found two patronesses who could be counted on to meet the arriving nuns in his company, and then vanish, never to reappear. He did not expect an Archbishop so lately from Córdoba to approve "the nun, Teresa de Jesús"; but if the Archbishop turned sufficiently unpleasant, she could be explained as Gracián's innocent mistake — not that of the Order, whose true inspiration (and that of the King) was La Cardona.

Finally, by refusing to let Teresa write to the Archbishop, Mariano could keep her from learning that he had made no request for her licence — at least until she lost heart and headed north, for Caravaca, he could still hope, and certain trouble. But Mariano did not know of Teresa's vow of obedience to Gracián.

Gracián had sent her to found in Seville, and there she would found, come hell or high water.

II

María de San José tells about the disappearing patronesses who "did not give [them] so much as a jar of water." She also lists Mariano's benefactions: "six straw mattresses and some old blankets, not good ones, a straw mat, a weak little table, a frying-pan, a candle or two, a few mugs and plates, and things like that." Sometimes after dark neighbors left them "something to put in the frying pan and then left, flying like ghosts," but most commonly their diet was "bread and water or weak camomile tea" with "a handful of greens or a few dried peas" as an occasional treat.

Isabel de San Francisco and Leonor de San Gabriel agree that they "hadn't a *blanco*" once they got to Seville — not a farthing; and to all intents and purposes this was true, though Avila and Malagón had contributed enough for their first month's rent with a bit left over. Teresa, despite phantom patronesses and no prospective dowries, knew the importance of putting up a good front, and the convent records show that an otherwise unbroachable little fund provided that their visitors — angry Carmelites, the Archbishop's succession of underlings sent in his place, and the Archbishop when he came at last — were entertained with food and wine that the nuns must have longed to snatch from them and gulp down their own hungry throats.

How Mariano explained to the Archbishop that Teresa and five nuns had come to Seville believing that he had granted them a licence, we'll never know. But when one of the Archbishop's canons gave permission for a single Mass to be said in their house on Trinity Sunday, the Calced heard of it and took it for evidence that the Archbishop was aligning himself with the King, against the Pope and against them.

The Calced of Seville not only possessed the Casa Grande, the finest monastery in Spain, but three overflow monasteries, three convents, and three houses for *beatas* — all of which were sources of income, not expense. But this had not lessened their rage over the Archbishop's giving the Discalced Los Remedios, with its famous statue of Our Lady, lighted by night with five silver lamps: a beacon for returning voyagers and second only in their hearts to Our Lady of Guadalupe, the shrine at which one sought the Virgin's blessing on the outward voyage.

At word of that Trinity Mass, the Calced came in fury, demanding that Teresa get out of town. She only plied them with wine and sweetmeats and showed them their General's permission to found convents. It was in Latin, and since they were not scholars, they left — sufficiently checked by the sight of Rubeo's signature and his seal.

There is doubt as to when that dubious blessing, Beatriz Chávez, entered the convent. Some say it was in June, but the convent records make it in September. At least we can trust the report that having heard Gracián preach she wept, embraced his knees, kissed his feet and implored him to accept her as a novice in the convent he had planned. Many women were susceptible to Gracián's charm and grew jealous of Teresa and "San José" — who, truth to tell, became increasingly jealous of each other before Teresa left Seville.

Teresa blamed their bad housing and long-delayed licence on Mariano. So did San José, when she wrote about it in Lisbon, years later; but at the time I suspect that she chewed her handsome, clear-cut lips a good deal in private, remembering how she had seen Gracián sweep Teresa off her feet in Beas.

But the situation was hardest for Teresa. Only she knew that they had come to Seville in flagrant disobedience to their General, and she was self-convicted of the two sins which she felt, by instinct, to be more base than any others: disloyalty and ingratitude. It haunted her that without Rubeo she could have founded only one tiny convent "under the ordinary," and the Voice could not make her forget that the Order owed him everything.

When she had been in Seville a little over a week, Teresa wrote Rubeo two letters in virtual duplicate — one sent to Rome, the other to Palencia, his home as well as the meeting place of Carmelite General Councils—to make sure that one of them would reach him as quickly as possible. Those letters are lost, but a third, which she wrote on July eighteenth, begins by summing up the gist of the two written a week before; so we know that they improved on the facts by saying that she had been in Beas for over a month before she knew that it was in Andalusia, and that when the proposed convent in Caravaca was delayed she came to Seville because "having found [herself] in Andalusia, the sin was already committed" and she "wanted to get the tangle about these fathers straightened out."

On the seventeenth, the Feast of the Magdalen, two letters from Rubeo had finally reached her. One had been written in the past October while she was in Segovia, the other in January, just after she left Valladolid. The first, that is, was written at the same time as his rebuke to Gracián which I have quoted; the second when, that rebuke having gone unacknowledged, he ordered Father Angel to pronounce Gracián and Mariano excommunicated and expelled from the Carmelites as disobedient sons.

In Beas, while "opening his heart," Gracián, by his own admission, had let Teresa know that the General was "displeased"—but not much else. Rubeo's long-delayed letters told Teresa all that she had not known before. We need not wonder that they drove her to "ardent prayer" concerning the vow that she had taken in Beas.

She had also just heard from Gracián: so her third letter to Rubeo summarizes the two that are lost and goes on to give him the news from Madrid. Gracián, she reports, first tried to see Father Angel, who refused to receive an excommunicated priest, so he went to stay with his father and brother, both royal secretaries. When the Nuncio heard of this he called for Father Angel, rebuked him harshly, and said that if anyone else called Gracián excommunicated, he would be punished. "And he sent him back to the monastery and he is there now, preaching to the court." This is the only note of defiance in her letter; the rest of it, page after page, is all humility.

Rubeo must know that he is in the daily prayers of every one of her nuns— the father to whom they owe their whole way of life. As for Gracián and Mariano, they now realize that they should have explained Andalusia's need for reform to him and won his permission before they came here "at the orders of Fray Baltasar, who was then Prior of Pastrana." Their misunderstanding with the General is all hot-tempered Mariano's fault. She herself has quarrelled with him, but Gracián "is like an angel. . . . If Your Reverence knew him I am sure that you would rejoice to have him for a son—and even Mariano, too."

For Mariano, she believes, is not ambitious, only moved by zeal for the Order. "But as you said, the devil gets a second chance in this business, and Mariano does say many things he doesn't really mean . . . and because I see that he is virtuous, I let it pass. If you could hear the excuses he makes you would be satisfied, because he told me that he would not rest until he had thrown himself at your feet." So, for this third time, she is conveying to him, their General, their apologies and pleas for his forgiveness "because they begged [her] to, not daring to do it for themselves."

None of this is true. In time Mariano would write the General an insulting letter of sheer defiance, but Gracián, despite Teresa's many pleadings throughout the years to come, refused to write to him at all, let alone write — as one of her letters to him begs — "putting in every sort of compliment that [he] can think of."

Teresa's letter goes on and on. She urges the virtues of the Discalced and their ever-increasing favor with the King. (True: on that issue Philip would soon split with the Pope.) She describes the desperate need for reform in Andalusia. Since she wrote Rubeo last, two Carmelite friars were arrested in a bawdyhouse at high noon and dragged off for all the world to see. "The frailties of the flesh don't shock me, but. . . ." But, at noon? They should at least have thought of the honor of their Order! And then the Calced superiors go to the Archbishop and say that they don't dare to punish erring friars because their General will object!

The lady doth protest too much. . . . At one point she tells of having shown the Calced her patents from Rubeo, saying that while she cannot read Latin, *letrados* have assured her that the patents mention no particular kingdom and allow her "to found anywhere." This comes close to hysteria; calmer, she would not have tried to make Rubeo think she believed that his written prohibition to the friars did not extend to the nuns.

So she goes on until she comes to her final plea: Can't he forgive the past, like a good father? Surely the Virgin will grieve if he rejects these men who have labored so greatly in Her service!

That long, long letter is often less than honest; but Teresa's love for Rubeo was real. She could no more have told him the whole truth about her own knowing disobedience than she had been able, as a girl, to tell her father the truth about the love that ended with her immurement in Our Lady of Grace, or told him at the Incarnation that she had ceased to pray because her sins made her unworthy to seek Christ's company. At one unwilling level she would always see her vow to Gracián as somehow sinful — and in a way that she could not admit, let alone repent of.

It was an exhausting letter to have written. But on the very next day she sent a note to Doña Inés Nieto, the wife of Alba's secretary, Albornoz. Doña Inés would mention it to the Duchess, and the Duchess would probably mention it to the King. It was well that the Court get the right picture of affairs in Seville.

While Teresa was in Valladolid Doña Inés had tried to give her a fine statue of the Virgin which her husband had rescued from "those Lutherans" in Flanders. Doña Inés hoped that María Bautista would accept an undowered niece of hers as a novice, at Teresa's request; and Teresa had seen that it was no time to vex María Bautista. Since the deal was not one a lady would make explicit, Teresa simply refused the gift on the grounds that she was about to do much travelling.

Now, she wrote, she had just the place for that statue, and Father Gracián, who was at Court, would arrange for having it brought to her. It must be lovely indeed, since her Ladyship's husband liked it so much. Then this — and, mind you, the Archbishop had not yet made his first call, they were unlicenced, hungry and ill-housed; "I am very well, thank God, and everything is going nicely in this land to which the Lord has sent me." She hopes that Doña Inés is well, too, and won't have to stay long in the hubbub of the Court, "though nothing is really tiresome to those who love the Lord. It is June 19 in this house of the glorious San José de Seville."

Just the right, casual tone. Mission accomplished. It took a strong heart to recapture such political acumen after sitting up all night over that anguished, interminable letter to Rubeo.

Eventually, the Archbishop came. The civil arm of the Government was headed by the Count of Barajas, who never left his palace without an honor guard of twenty-one men who rode before him in seven ranks, three abreast. This gave the Archbishop something to live up to, and he had not failed it, even while he was still saddled with excessive interest on a debt of a hundred thousand ducats. His honor guard wore capes, not armor, and rode mules, not horses, but he was always preceded by a youth who carried the archepiscopal mitre on a green velvet cushion.

While the handling of his debts had predisposed him to Teresa's friars, the Córdoba Inquisition had definitely not done the same for Teresa. However, Teresa did best at face-to-face encounters, and the Mendozas, as the Archbishop was beginning to learn from Madrid, were not her only noble *aficionados*. He granted the licence, and added three ducats a month for rent until the nuns should have found a house of their own, plus a monthly allowance of wheat for their bread.

So three weeks after her letter to Doña Inés, one went to Antonio Gaitán. Things are going splendidly! Such a shame that he and Julián had to leave at the only time they were hard up! The ducat enclosed is to pay the messenger who is bearing her letter. They still haven't quite decided on a house to buy, but it will all work out well. Antonio mustn't worry about them at all.

Teresa was Juan Sánchez's granddaughter. Like every successful businessman she knew that next to success, nothing succeeds like the appearance of it. She was fond of Antonio Gaitán, but she could not trust his discretion. If his sympathies were aroused, the word would spread all over Alba de Tormes; and if she asked him not to mention her troubles, he would only start praising her courage.

At least, she had won her licence from the Archbishop.

Nine days later she began a campaign that went on for years. She wrote to the King.

Chapter 45 ✻ Teresa's Appeal to King Philip;
Her Strangely Unadmirable, Self-justifying Letter
to a Prioress

I

Over the years, Teresa wrote four letters to the King: unusual letters from her pen, short and carefully composed.

His Majesty's help is needed, this one begins, if the Order of Our Lady is not to decay. Its Discalced, if they survive, will strengthen the Calced by their example. Having herself lived among the Calced for many years, she knows the need for this and believes that the Discalced will be powerless to effect any real reform until they are made into a separate province.

It would be much to the good if their first Provincial could be a man she has recently met. This Father Gracián is young, but his spiritual gifts have helped so many that God seems to have chosen him for the good of the Order.

She thanks His Majesty for a licence he has just granted for Caravaca, and apologizes for her boldness in writing to him. She dared only because the Lord hears the poor, and the King, in his care for the Church, acts in his place. It is her prayer that he may live long, for the sake of Christendom.

The letter was not answered and doubtless had no effect; but two months later the Nuncio appointed Gracián Visitor to the Discalced of Andalusia and Castile, and—to Teresa's consternation and Mariano's delight—Visitor to the Calced of Andalusia.

Gracián nervously delayed any exercise of his latter function by setting out on a protracted inspection of the Discalced foundations in Castile. It was makework; the convents were in no trouble, and power had shifted from the Castilian monasteries to Andalusia. (Indeed, Nieto, barred from Andalusia, had returned to the Calced, seeing Pastrana as now a dead-end.) It would be mid-November before Gracián came back to Seville, and Teresa had expected him to be gone for a few weeks, not six months.

At least she was relieved to hear that she was in no bodily danger from the Madrid Inquisition. Báñez's defense of her book had also defended her. Teresa's works, his defense says, are good and remarkable; and while her book says "too much about visions, which are always to be mistrusted, and especially in women," it is clear that "while she may be deceived she is at least no deceiver," for one less honest would not have told the facts of her life so plainly, "both the evil and the good." And, while the book should not be shown to all and sundry, educated men would find it of help in understanding women's confessions. This measured judgment was wisely put; it was not of the kind that stirs active opposition. However, the Inquisition did impound the book, thus protecting even "educated men."

In mid-August, Teresa's brother Lorenzo came home from the Indies. He had wound up his affairs, found husbands for Jerónimo's illegitimate daughters and started out with him and the ever-dependent Pedro; but Jerónimo contracted a fever in Panama and died there. Three of Lorenzo's sons had died soon after the death of his wife, but three children came with him: young Lorenzo, now fifteen, Francisco, two years younger, and little Teresa, "Teresica," just turned eight.

Lorenzo learned that Teresa was in Seville from letters being held there for the next sailing. He was shocked to find her ill-housed, ill-fed, and cold-shouldered by the great, rich city that lay around her. He was fifty-six, and aged by his long service in the Indies, and he had to be off at once for Madrid to collect a large pension due him from the Crown; but he swore angrily that Teresa would have a good house when he returned, and meantime, thank God, they would have enough to eat.

Teresa would have felt no less joy if Lorenzo had come back penniless. Rodrigo had been the brother who had shared her dreams; Jerónimo she had loved more like a mother than a sister; but Lorenzo was her twin in temperament. In the psychomedical jargon of the day, they were both "of the sanguine humor," warm and outgoing. Teresa did not hesitate to write at once to her poor baby sister Juana to tell her that her money troubles would soon be over.

Lorenzo went alone to Madrid. The boys were housed in Los Remedios and little Teresica in the convent. The Council of Trent had forbidden the habit to children under twelve, but Teresa made her a little habit in which she could play at being a novice. The child was precocious, amusing, and like her aunt, a talker. María de San José calls Teresica their "enchanting little elf," and Lorenzo their "second founder." (The first having been one of the vanishing patronesses who did not give them so much as a jar of water?)

Lorenzo was gone for three months on what he expected to be a routine matter. As a last resort he offered a paper which gave detailed legal proof of his service to the Crown. It reports his struggles to aid Pizarro through thirty-four years of "attempting to pacify the Indians," first in battle and then as "corregidor of several cities in Peru." The document is dated November 12, 1575; he got it back exactly five days later, with three words and a date written at its foot: *No hay lugar.* English needs only one word for the message: *disallowed.* He had won what almost all retired officers did at the time: exactly nothing. Philip, twice bankrupt and always overextended, had no money to waste on past services.

He got back to Seville on the last day of November, tired and ill. He would still be decently well-off once his affairs in the Indies were settled; but he had three children, a dependent brother and a needy married sister to care for as well as his dear Teresa.

II

During those three months, Teresa had other things on her mind. Gracián reached Valladolid at the time Lorenzo set out for Madrid. María Bautista was not predisposed to like him. She was a hard-headed, unemotional young woman, in some ways incapable of understanding Teresa, and in others of understanding her only too well. She knew about Teresa's succession of "persecuted" confessors and Teresa's need for one who "understood her soul." That need had first taken Teresa to Salamanca, with its aftermath; and as she saw it, Teresa was about to revive an old play with a new male lead.

There could have been no more unfortunate time for Teresa to ask her to accept Martín Gutiérrez's daughter Bernarda as a novice. Martín had been a physician in Valladolid. He had placed the child in a foster home, headed up by a peasant whom Teresa's letters refer to simply as "Pedro"; and when he underwent his conversion and joined the Jesuits, he deeded her his money. When the girl came of age, Olea and Ripalda, who had been his friends, accepted the duty of placing her in a convent where no questions would be asked.

Olea, you remember, had already succeeded in so placing one such responsibility of his own, in a way that smelled unpleasantly of blackmail. (When he attempted a repeat performance in the wake of the Gracián-Seville scandal, yet to come, Teresa could not be intimidated.) But though Bernarda was well-dowered, always a strong consideration with María Bautista, she not only refused to accept her, but made sure that Mother Inés in Medina would understand why she, too, must refuse.

Months later, as a last resort, Bernarda was brought to Seville. The convent records are fudged: Bernarda Gutiérrez, they say, is the daughter of a Corsican, Pedro Matías, resident of Trianos—the suburb surrounding Los Remedios. This would have been convincing if the girl had arrived at a better time; but she came in March, while the Inquisition, far from secretly, was examining Teresa and her convent on charges of heresy and whoring. Even a Corsican would have thought twice about putting his daughter in such danger of the stake, if not of eternal damnation as well.

(Incidentally, the Inquisition and the subsequent Gracián scandal worked to Pedro's advantage. Since it left the convent in no position to risk a lawsuit over Gutiérrez money, he kept it, saying that he would leave the convent its equivalent in his will—a purely verbal offer so transparent that the record of Bernarda's profession, a year later, is followed by the words *no dowry*.)

Bernarda was gentle and lovable: María de San José describes her sweet, pious nature and her early death in the *Libro de Recreaciones*. But she gives her a name not on the convent records: Bernarda Ramírez. The name apparently suggested itself in connection with Margarita Ramírez, who reported Gracián's dancing in the nude: one of Teresa's supposed love-affairs making a subconscious link with the other.

To return to that November: in refusing the girl, María Bautista apparently wrote Teresa quite a letter. Much of what she had to say comes clear in Teresa's answer; though one more clue is needed. Teresa had asked Gracián to give Báñez her *Meditaciones sobre los Cantares*. Báñez (as Teresa had not yet learned when she wrote back) wisely refused to receive it: a book inspired by de León's translation of the Song of Songs was best ignored for Teresa's own

224

sake. Any comment on it could too readily go astray. He had already warned Teresa not to write to him, since her letters were sometimes intercepted, and it was well that his defense of the *Life* not be seen as a favor to a friend.

Teresa's letter to María Bautista is distressingly revelatory. In its original form it was considered so much so that it first received unusually frequent censorings, and later it was copied, with further omissions, and the name of Fray Domingo changed to a nonexistent Fray Damiel—after which the autograph was sent as a holy relic to the Cathedral in Lima, Peru. This original was not published until 1963, though its censorings had long made it quite adequately confusing when denied the light of its background.

It begins with its sole attempt to disarm. María Bautista's letters are never tiring, like those from others, and answering them is a "restful occupation." But once she has forced out a little casual family news, Teresa forgets that opening. She is "worn out" with answering letters, but she'll "try to answer" this one. As follows: The Medina convent is her constant torment. What a coincidence that Inés, just now, finds herself so overcrowded! And "Though you say so much about your own convent I'd have you know that if the nun you say so much about were settled on you there, you couldn't avoid taking her, and you needn't be so sharp. Believe me, to send her off where nobody knew her would be the death of her, and many houses would have no convents at all if everyone dared to pick and choose like you."

Much more of this is followed by a confused alternation of thin excuses and angry protests. Teresa wouldn't have accepted the girl if she'd known who she was, but María Bautista had no right to warn other prioresses without telling her first; and this girl wasn't the one Teresa originally intended to send to Valladolid, but a relative of Olea's who now does not want to go, and María Bautista's behavior is outrageous . . .

"No other prioress ever dared to set herself up against me like that, or any other nun. Keep on that way and you may lose my friendship. Let me tell you that the way you see things displeases me, and there is nobody else who sees things the way you do. And it isn't enough for you to feel free" (that loaded word, free to love in all innocence as the Rival's gift) "but you think you have to teach the rest of us how to be, too. Perhaps you think you are holier than anyone else. I can't think where so much spirituality comes from, to make you so vain. . . ."

She shifts back to apology again, with an irrelevant half-truth: "I take all the blame for not finding out first who she was; since he [Olea] had given the other one who turned out to be so unobjectionable [the disfigured girl] I thought this would be the same sort of thing."

Thus far the letter, given its blacked out censorings, was obscure enough to suit the copyist: what concerned Báñez's reaction to her having entrusted to Gracián's care anything so dangerous as a book about the Song of Songs—in condemned translation—had to be cut, as well as any defensive remarks she had made about going to Seville at his orders. The cuts get larger, and Fray Domingo becomes "Fray Damiel." Even the original in Peru gives us only this: "As to what concerns [deleted] Father Gracián [deleted] that what happened would shock you [deleted]. I have been unable to do anything else and I do not repent it. If you find faults in him it is only because you have him with you so little, up there, and talk with him so little. I tell you, he is holy and not at all rash or imprudent, and more important things than books could be trusted to him safely!

"You say that the way I feel about him shows that I have forgotten Fray Domingo. You only think that because they are so different that it amazes me, for the friendship that he has with me is untouched by anything that isn't completely spiritual. I don't see where the 'temptation' could have been, for it is a wholly different sort of thing."

Next comes an angry *tu quoque*: is María Bautista sure that she herself is free from human bondage in what she feels for Báñez? "Oh, what a life that nun of yours must be leading you, the one you say is 'even worse' than I am!" (One Catalina de Jesús had proved susceptible to Gracián's charm.) "Though I fully understand that she sums up all my fears—fear that you may lose your own holy freedom; for if I were sure of that, nothing else would seem important to me—except ingratitude—just as I can't give a second thought to that nun up there."

But this brings her back to the "temptation" that she has already denied: "Look, when I was up there I came away with more confidence that you held nothing against me, and it did me good; and in the same way [deleted, the words "Father Gracián" and letters which fit the phrase "servant of God" alone left legible] as the other friendship, as I keep telling you, gave freedom before" (Martín, whom she could also "love in Christ").

Has she said too much? She drops it. Why doesn't María Bautista tell her if Báñez liked the "little book"? "I would be very glad not to have burned it." Also, not yet knowing of the final decision to keep the *Life* impounded, she hopes that its confession will not be censored: "I should be very glad if the big book was allowed to stand as it is so that when [deletion] tear it up [deletion] because of my [deletion] do good to many souls. I want God to be glorified, and I want others to praise him, so I certainly want others to know of my wretched doings."

(The copyist omits her fear that the "little book" may be burned or the big one censored so as to destroy its central message of God's forgiveness. But he does let one sentence stand, as evidence of the well-known saintly incapacity for distinguishing between grave sins and trifling faults: "And one of the things that comforts me down here and will have to go on comforting me is that there is no memory of that farce about my holiness that I had to bear up there, and so I am at liberty to live and act without fear of having that tower of hot air fall in on me.")

She asks to be remembered to Báñez: "I tell you, it weighs heavy on me that I can't write to him. There is no fear that anyone will break up that friendship which has cost so much." (Even you, his "little thing.")

She comes back to Catalina de Jesús, the nun who seems overfond of Gracián. She has already written to Gracián about her, and she hopes that María Bautista has written about her to him too. She is "glad he is there because of . . . [thirteen lines obliterated except for their final, telling words]: Today is St. Augustine's day. I repeat that—so you won't have to look up the date." (*I repeat that*, to remind you of how I discovered Augustine and through him of God's unending forgiveness.)

Then, to give María Bautista something to read aloud, she tries to end on the easy note with which she began. The nuns in Seville do embroidery, very fine. . . . A rich novice is coming to them soon, and they'll be buying a house. . . . *et cetera.*

But all of Teresa's other letters to prioresses end with the equivalent of our English, "Your faithful servant": *Servidora de Vuestra Reverencia.* This one, as if the word *servant* clogged on her pen, is signed, *de V.R., Teresa de Jesús.*

There is also a postscript: Casilda de Padilla should read the notebooks she sent north with Gracián along with the "little book." What they say about temptations can help her—when so many oppose her ever taking her final vows.

Also—largely obliterated—there is one more message to Báñez: a plea, it seems, for him to understand the obedience to Gracián which brought her to Seville: "Tell him [*deleted*] afraid to know it [deleted]. One way or another I'll manage to get away from here, though I can't convince myself of [deleted] and my subjection does not come from affection, but from an understanding that God has brought about—as I have told you."

It is a strange, sad, unadmirable letter. But though it is inspiring to know that we can put our sins behind us, I find it still more so to find evidence that we can blunder into a morass of moral confusion and self-justification, and then be once more back on our way—as Teresa would be. Augustine confessed to nothing like that; nor did Teresa, other than thus, inadvertently. But she did so suffer and eventually overcome—and, to my mind, giving up fornication at forty is by comparison no great effort.

What is more to our immediate point, you can see from this letter that Teresa was not thinking straight when the rich novice she mentions in its labored closing turned up, strangely attended.

Chapter 46 ✽ *María del Corro; General Rubeo's Condemnation of Teresa; His Authority versus that of Gracián as Apostolic Visitor*

I

That letter to María Bautista conveys the quality of the time for which Teresa would condemn herself for being "so cowardly and pusillanimous." Her strength always came from her belief that she was doing God's will, and about that she was now cruelly of two minds. In consequence, her judgment was disturbed when she admitted "the rich lady," her *beata*, and the servant-girls whom they left behind at their departure.

Doña Ventura's last name is unknown for a double reason: along with that of her *beata*, María del Corro, it was stricken from the convent records; and it also failed to enter those of the Inquisition, as shortly after leaving she entered another convent, went quite mad, and was too incoherent to be of use to Teresa's enemies. *Ventura* means *luck*, and years later a nun witnessed that Teresa said, "Ah, Ventura, Ventura, you bring no *ventura*—and Margarita, too!"

While we may doubt this burst of prophesy, it pretty well sums things up, since Ventura also brought—or was brought by—her *beata*, along with Margarita Ramírez, of the creative imagination. Of the four, only the other lay-sister, Ana Sánchez, remained harmless.

Their admission is revelatory, for Ventura was clearly "melancholy," María del Corro embodied all that Teresa most despised in the religious life, and thanks to Lorenzo, the convent was no longer on the brink of starvation.

San José calls María del Corro a "gran beata" who was "canonized by the whole city" and says that they were "importuned to take her in by many important, nobly-born people and spiritual authorities." Since the convent had no such backing or approval, I have wondered if the Archbishop did not engineer it for the very purpose it so nearly served. He wanted to be at peace with the Calced but without displeasing his recent benefactors, Doria's friends.

Teresa in her usual form would not have put up with María Corro for a week; but San José would have thought twice about how it would look if they dismissed this local saint, unwilling though she was to accept the rule of enclosure. Sometimes she left the convent for days "because she was ill" and found the diet inadequate; she often insisted on visiting distant churches to confess to her favorite priests. So did Doña Ventura. Once the date of their entry and departure was expunged from the records, we have only San José's vague information that they were in the convent "for a short time."

We do know, however, that María del Corro's first accusations were nothing to those she made subsequently. Yet even then, she had to say something; she could not have it thought that enclosure and lean commons were a strain on her sanctity. Instead, she claimed that Teresa acted as the nuns' confessor, refusing to let them see a priest. For penance, she suspended them by their hands and feet while she lashed them, thus dangling, with a leather whip. Worse still, she taught strange Jewish customs, such as praying face to the wall. (For this last, there was a grain of truth; the nuns received communion through a grille let into the chapel from the patio, and afterwards knelt facing the wall to shield their eyes from the Andalusian sun.)

The strange pair seems to have left them and made these accusations in late November. It created murmurings, but the Inquisition paid scant attention. For those who "canonized" María del Corro there were as many who thought her a fraud who wanted more attention. It is less noteworthy that she found the Inquisition indifferent at this point than it is that Teresa put up with her for two or three months.

Throughout that time Gracián was in Castile, Lorenzo in Madrid, and sister

Juana and her husband Don Juan de Ovalle in Seville, anxiously awaiting Lorenzo's return with money to give them; and Teresa was preoccupied with the situation that Gracián would meet when he came back as Apostolic Visitor to the unwilling Calced.

In mid-October, a month before his return, she had written him sound advice: If he goes slowly at first, playing down his authority and only criticizing the most flagrant abuses (whoring at noon?) he can win the Calced over bit by bit. But caution, tact, a light touch are of the essence. Even up there in Castile he must realize his delicate position; they write her from Toledo that "Macario is terrible" and "going back to his lair" to avoid meeting "mi Eliseo." May he stay there until he cools off! (Heredia, angry that Gracián, not he, had been given authority by the Nuncio, had made a brief return to Mancera.)

Then the politician gives place to the mother: are Gracián's clothes warm enough, now that the weather is changing? Ten leagues a day on a pack-saddle? That's suicidal! And why does he keep falling off his donkey? He should tie himself on! (Gracián was on the soft, plump side, and a notoriously bad horseman.) "Laurencia" tells her that no confessor satisfies her after having had one so perfect; and she fears it will always be like that since Eliseo is "such a busy man." Nonetheless, he should spend at least a week at the Incarnation and make sure that John of the Cross will be there permanently, and he must not be discouraged by the way the nuns regressed once they found themselves under the Carmelites again: "They will settle right down, once they know that someone will be in firm authority over them." (Fray Juan had been ousted briefly but Fernández got him back again.)

The de Ovalles, as usual, lived in their private dream. A fortnight before Gracián got back they pressured Teresa to write to Doña Inés Nieto asking her to persuade her husband, Albornoz, to persuade the Duchess of Alba to accept their son Gonzalo as a page, though he was much too old for it. (After this embarrassing exercise in futility, Gonzalo became a monk to avoid military service. He wasn't much good at that, either, and when in time his body, like Teresa's, was found to be miraculously preserved—withered and dehydrated—the miracle was soon hushed up, as more hindrance than help to her canonization.)

Then six months after they had parted in Beas, Gracián came back, and Teresa had no more time to waste on side-issues. Her unequal contest with Mariano had begun.

II

Gracián brought nuns for Teresa to take to Caravaca, and Heredia to be Prior of Los Remedios—a sop to his pride, it could be hoped. The Calced, as Teresa had tried to warn Gracián, were up in arms and sure of their rights. At the Council of Palencia, Rubeo had read out the counter brief by which the Pope abolished the office of Apostolic Visitor; could Ormaneto defy his Pope on the authority of a Pope now dead? In Castile, Angel de Salazar was visiting convents to make sure that the nuns understood that his orders, not Gracián's, were valid. Even the Andalusian Discalced showed signs of rejecting Gracián's authority.

Gracián, in Los Remedios, was lapping up Mariano's bad advice when Teresa sent him a letter. The Bishop of Columbria, she said, had just called and tried to persuade her that the Calced would submit once Gracián let them know that their disobedience would only earn them excommunication and a public scandal, but he was dead wrong. Strong-arm tactics would only make them feel cornered and increase their resistance, while a tentative, gentle approach had a good chance of bringing them around. Surely the way those two friars the Calced sent to represent them in Rome had avoided the Nuncio when they made their stopover in Madrid showed that they felt the weakness of their position? Of course, Gracián and those advising him would know best, but . . . . (*But* . . . . Even with Gracián it was bad policy to forget the woman's humble role.)

She ended with one more plea that he write to Rubeo: "And pay him as many compliments as you can. . . . It's bad enough that we acted against his will, without our refusing to say a few courteous words or pay any attention to him. Only think about it, Father; we promised him obedience, and you can't lose anything by doing just that much." A postscript saying that this convent has given her more troubles than all the others combined ends, helplessly, "And I always say more than I mean to and nothing I'm trying to say."

Mariano suffered no such difficulties. The words put in his mouth by the chronicler are literary invention, and the gist of them is only too trustworthy: "Let them subject themselves to the Nuncio and the King! After that you can deal gently with anyone who truly deserves it. If the Father General calls us contumacious and rebellious, we aren't the first to endure such insults nor will we be the last. . . . Choose the day, prepare the Archbishop and the head of the civil government and other ministers of the law, and then let the Calced know you as their Visitor and reformer, and every one of them will obey you!"

Heredia agreed. Teresa, he pointed out, was getting her advice from the Calced subprior, Juan Evangelista—the one fool in the Casa Grande, and she called him "reasonable"!

Gracián believed them.

On the twenty-first of November he went to the Casa Grande with Heredia and read the Nuncio's brief in Latin. The Prior requested that he read it again in Spanish so that all present could understand the grounds on which it should be declared invalid. Gracián refused, and a riot broke out. The doors were barred from within against the dignitaries and men-at-arms who were gathered outside to support him if support should be needed.

Gracián wrote later that his life was saved only by Teresa's prayers. Whether or no, he was terrified, and read the brief out in Spanish, but only Juan Evangelista tried to listen. All the rest screamed him down with threats and curses, making such a noise that, to those outside, the walls of the Casa Grande seemed to be paper-thin. One of them rushed to the convent to tell Teresa that Gracián had been assassinated. She tells in a *cuenta* that as she prayed, the Voice spoke "Oh, ye of little faith! Be quiet, it will all come out well."

In fact, Gracián, Heredia and their novice-secretary—brought with them to take notes on the meeting—were merely ejected, Gracián somewhat battered but nothing worse. He sent off a report to the Nuncio, and the Nuncio sent back orders to the Casa Grande that the Calced obey, and submit to his appointed Visitor, Gracián. These orders the Prior read out with a smile, saying that they could be ignored as their emissaries would shortly be back from the Vatican with orders to the contrary. The Prior had some reason to be confident. One of his emissaries to the Vatican was Fray Pedro de Cota, from Córdoba, who had much to tell, not only about the Discalced in Andalusia, but their Mother Foundress who had now joined them after a trial by the Córdoba Inquisition on charges grave enough to have been sent on for consideration by the Central Council in Madrid.

However, the Pope was inclined to bide his time, Ormaneto was old, ailing, and it would not be long before his death would make it easy to replace him with a right-minded man in a way that would seem natural and avoid unpleasantness with the Spanish Crown.

General Rubeo did not take Cota's report so calmly. His orders went direct to Father Angel in Madrid: it was to be published that Teresa de Jesús was "apostate and excommunicated." She must return at once to Castile and live hereafter under house-arrest in whichever convent should be agreed upon. Those convents she had already founded need not be depopulated, but she was hereby forbidden to found another. Father Angel published as ordered and thereafter sent an underling, Michael de Ulloa, to inform Teresa.

San José says that all were shocked "that such a holy old man should do such a thing." Little Leonor de San Gabriel remembered the moment more vividly. When she heard out Fray Michael, she says, "the Mother turned gray and went to her cell without saying a word."

The news spread fast. María del Corro was finally able to get the ear of the Inquisition, and with tales which would leave Gracián wallowing in self-pity for years. Gracián himself first heard the inside story from a friend of Doria's, Fernando de Aranda, who was the Inquisition's Prosecutor. The word, in essence, was that Teresa was a whore and a whoremonger, and Gracián her most recent lover, who had discredited his whole Order, the Reform and the Mitigation alike, by his affair with a woman not only notorious for her sexual excesses but as an *alumbrada*, a heretic.

In Gracián's version: "They were saying as much in grave and passionate discredit of the Mother Teresa de Jesús as it was possible to say. All these words drove me nearly out of my mind." But, he adds, Teresa rebuked him: "Quiet, Father; no more words against the Inquisition, which only tries to guard our Holy Faith." And when he could not be quiet, she laughed at him saying that pleasant as it would be to die for God, he needn't fear that their work would be crowned with martyrdom until God saw it as properly completed.

That last touch sounds like her; she could always find her courage and laughter in a crisis. But she was eager to obey the General and leave Seville at once. Gracián forbade it; as he saw things, the Inquisition would see her departure as flight, and evidence of guilt—his own included.

María de San José admits to having agreed with Gracián, and adds that once the trial was behind them Teresa laughed and said, "What marvelous comfort you gave me when we were all so afflicted—assuring me that whatever I did, I'd still be found and carted off by the Inquisition!" María de San José, however, does not tell the sorry truth that she thereupon separated herself from Teresa as pointedly as possible, or that she was joined in this disloyalty by her friend from Malagón, Ana de San Alberto, whom Gracián had brought on for the Caravaca foundation; or that Teresa broke up this dangerous alliance by sending San Alberto and her nuns to Caravaca, with San Alberto to act as Prioress—assuring her that she would be out of Andalusia, that her escort would be a friar from Almodovar, not one of these excommunicated Discalced, and that the licence from the Council of Orders, as procured at the King's word, made the convent not even properly Carmelite, let alone Discalced—and so not under Rubeo's authority.

Caravaca, then, was founded on December 18, 1575, under conditions concealed for centuries; concealed along with the fact that Teresa, ordered to house-arrest in early December, took six months to obey—though, God knows, not by her own desire. I was glad to find that the evidence from letters and legal documents was not destroyed, only ignored.

III

Gracián, confused by his unfortunate blend of ambition and cowardice, was running scared in a way that made him senselessly bold. He had to prove that he was the Apostolic Visitor, so appointed in August by the Nuncio Ormaneto; and, on Christmas Eve—the only day of the year, with the exception of Easter Eve, which could have disturbed as many communicants—he excommunicated the entire Casa Grande, posting on the door of its church a list of every one of its friars, lest one should dare to celebrate the Eucharist. The many who routinely went to Casa Grande's midnight Mass got a shock.

This, in the Catholic phrase, "gave scandal" with a vengeance. Gracián himself found his bold gesture so overexciting that he quite forgot to send a friar to the Convent of San José to hold a midnight Mass for its nuns. A priest, Garciá Alvarez, on his way to celebrate the midnight Mass in his own church passed the convent and saw its chapel dark and empty. He blamed it on the Calced, who to his mind feared reform more than they feared the devil. The convent, he believed, was being outcast and victimized because it tried to serve its God. He stormed to his own church, mounted the pulpit, and persuaded the congregation to follow him, candles in hand and singing, to a midnight Mass in a place as holy, humble, and neglected as the manger had been before the shepherds had heard the heavenly host.

So, for that year, at least, García Alvarez—whose name Teresa always runs into one word, Garcíalvarez—was all that the convent could have wanted from a chaplain and a friend. Even Teresa, usually so shrewd in her estimates of character, did not see until she had left Seville behind that this impulsive and dramatic act of kindness had indicated an emotionalism and love of excitement which could become at best a mixed blessing and at worst a renewed danger from the Inquisition. However, during her forthcoming trial "Garcíalvarez" did no harm, for luckily he was not the sort of person with whom Teresa cared to discuss her past or her visions.

Chapter 47 ❀ A Letter from Teresa to General Rubeo; the Inquisition Comes to Seville to Question Her

I

It is pleasant to feel justified by events and able to say directly or by smiling implication, "I told you so." María Bautista's Christmas letter mentioned, among other things, the holiday *coplas* that were surely being written and sung to celebrate Gracián's return to Seville. That was pure malice.

Another point in that letter deserves more sympathy. Gracián, in collecting Doña Ana Enríquez's statue, had led her to believe that in return María Bautista would accept young Doña Mariana as a novice. This she had already refused to do, and it was no time for Teresa to be highhanded.

A third point she made for Báñez, who felt that as Teresa's defender in Madrid before the Central Council his interest would show as more impersonal, unbiased, if they broke off all direct communication. Teresa's letters to María Bautista were less likely to be intercepted. Báñez had another "nephew" from an earlier time: a boy too old to become a lady's plaything, like La Parda's child, but well suited to be a page for Lorenzo's boys. (The boy had a sister, too, but that could wait.)

Teresa wrote her answer on the last day of December. "I had to laugh when you said that some day you'd tell me about certain things. As usual, you have advice to give!" She has already written to the General out of a love that she only wishes were mutual, and Gracián does nothing to discourage that love, though he well might. But, oh, the troubles that Gracián's reforms have made! "We have nobody to confess to, he has excommunicated them all. I tell you I've had much more pain than comfort since he got down here. It was much better before."

She only wishes she could be in Valladolid, out of all this "hubbub of reform," but "the Father Visitor" will not let her leave until summer. And as things now stand, she could not make Doña Mariana happy there — quite aside from the discouraging things she hears about her. (A much censored letter to Doña Ana Enríquez written on the following day is evasive and apologetic about this Doña Mariana, of whom little is known. This letter was sent to Naples as a holy relic, and like the letter in Lima it was not published until 1963. Apparently it was not wise at one time to say too much about this Doña Mariana, for the few

233

other references to her that exist are similarly veiled in mystery. Could Doña Ana have had a little accident to repent of, back in the days when she became the unlucky Cazalla's convert?)

About the boy, however, Teresa'll only have to ask Lorenzo, and he'll agree at once, since "they need a page—and it's excessive!" (This apparent self-contradiction is the first of her protests, this time a laughing shrug, over the nouveau-riche pretensions of all who had lived in the Indies—even her dear Lorenzo.) She interrupts her letter to ask Lorenzo, and he agrees as she had expected, saying that the boy can study with his sons at St. Gil, the school they'll be entering.

Then, after a little more carefully casual talk, Teresa breaks down. "I hope to God He'll grant a year or two more of life to the Pope, the King and the Nuncio, and our father [Gracián] . . . for if any one of them were lacking, we'd be lost, with our Most Reverend being the way he is. I think I'll write to him now—and serve him better than I did before, for I love him very much and owe it to him. It weighs heavy on me to see what he has done because of misinformation."

The letter has reached its moment of truth. Teresa could imagine María Bautista's smile when she asked about the holiday *coplas* that Seville must be enjoying this year. "We aren't fit for *coplas*! Do you think that things are going like that? You should be commending our father to God. Just today an important person told the Archbishop that they're planning to kill him. Things are in a state that ought to make you grieve, and you'd grieve more if you saw the offenses that go on here between monks and nuns. May His Majesty cure it . . . and may he keep me from getting involved in anything, for down here [censored] to visit our Father Gracián [censored]. But if it serves God at all, my life counts for little. I wish I had many lives. . . ."

A postscript tries to lighten the tone of that last passage with remarks about the pleasant weather, the cool nights, the beneficial winter climate—and the news that Pedro's attempt to join the Jesuits had been rejected.

II

On January 28th, the Seville Inquisition applied to the Central Council for its directions. Much of their information came from poor mad Isabel de San Jerónimo, of whom Teresa had relieved cousin Inés. Since Teresa always forbade her nuns to discuss their life of prayer with any but their confessors or to listen to any nuns who disobeyed, San Jerónimo must have been enraptured with the audience given her by Doña Ventura and María del Corro.

Hence the request begins: "We have received testimony against Teresa de Jesús and Isabel de San Jerónimo in a convent recently founded in this city; and apparently false doctrines, deceits and superstitions go on there like those of the *alumbradas* of Estremadura." (The group Teresa's letters mention with horror as "those of Llerenos," noted as much for their sexual excesses as their heresies.)

The information, this document goes on, came "not only from a holy lady, María Corro, and her confessor, but also from many others over a considerable

234

number of days." Hence, as further evidence, the Seville chapter requests a book "written by the said Teresa de Jesús, a woman whose tricks and deceits are highly prejudicial to the Christian republic." The book, they are told, is held by Fray Domingo Báñez. Their information against these women should be presented to the Grand Inquisitor, "who will tell us how to proceed against them." Carleval and María Mejías were ashes; but Teresa's case had been remanded to the Central Council. Hence only the Grand Inquisitor was qualified to weigh God's cause against whatever political considerations had left Teresa de Jesús alive and free to come to Seville with her sister *alumbrada*, Isabel de San Jerónimo.

On February 3rd, the Grand Inquisitor decided for God; the pressures to which he had been subjected over the Córdoba trial had hurt his dignity. The book, he ruled, must stay where it was, but Seville should know that though it was unfit for circulation, it had been found to contain no heresy. However, on the grounds of their new information, Seville was authorized to examine Teresa de Jesús, Isabel de San Jerónimo, and their convent, and proceed in accordance with their own judgment.

III

Teresa had put off writing a fourth letter to Rubeo. What more could she say? Gracián refused to write him a single word, Mariano had sent him a letter of defiance, and to plead for the one she must plead for both. She did not write until the day that the Grand Inquisitor sent Seville his answer. The Inquisition's treasurer, Aranda, had doubtless known what was in the works and told Gracián, who told her: but of that, she knew, she must appear ignorant.

Whatever she said must help the cause whether her letter reached Rubeo or was intercepted. (A sane precaution; three of the five letters she tells of sending him from Seville did not get to Rome.) She begins with Caravaca: one more convent of Rubeo's reform. Next, she assures him that while others tell him lies about Gracián and Mariano, she herself would hold it treachery not only to him but to God to deceive him about them. This is the truth of it: The Nuncio forced the Visitorship on Gracián. She urged him to be patient in exercising it, "for there are more learned Calced in Andalusia than in Castile"—but others persuaded him that he must use his authority. That was wrong, but the harm is done. Won't Rubeo forgive him? He longs to have Rubeo understand how this all came about and will soon be writing him in the hope that the General will see that he is still an obedient, humble son.

As for Mariano, what he says always comes out the opposite of what he means and the devil seizes on this ineptitude to create worse confusion. This is pitiful, for like Gracián, he longs to throw himself at his General's feet and beg for pardon. Heredia, too, is here now, and will write to him more convincingly than she, an ignorant woman, can. But Gracián's gifts are needed above all, for no other friar understands the General's reform so well. She begs him, for the sake of Calced and Discalced alike, to let this work continue to be carried out by his subject and son.

Next, without implicating Gracián she must explain why she is still in Seville. . . . If the General had sent her his orders directly, she would have seen it as his kindness "in granting her a much needed rest." Loving him as she does, she was hurt by the way she did receive them. Father Angel even said that she might appeal to the Pope if she liked—as if she would ever disregard her General's wishes! She wanted to leave at once, but "they" were sure that the General would not want her to, though she herself is eager to get away. "There's no making myself understand these Andalusians!"

There is also trouble in Avila. The Calced Prior, Valdemoro, is making the nuns at the Incarnation confess to his friars, and in result they are losing both honor and alms. Oh, if Rubeo would only come back to Spain! "But the journey is hard, so my soul will have to wait for Eternity to gain that relief. Pray God that I may deserve it." She constantly asks the priests of his Order, Calced and Discalced alike, to pray for him, and she and her daughters beg him for his blessing.

It was the best she could do—a letter that would do no harm if it were intercepted. No more talk of whoring friars, but praise of Andalusian scholarship—at low ebb among the Carmelites of that time and place, though her belief in it could be laid to her ignorance and gratify whoever read it. No more presenting Gracián as an "angel"— only the man most capable of carrying out Rubeo's wishes, despite what he may have heard to the contrary. And no mention of any troubles nearer than the Incarnation. Nothing like her incautious New Year's Eve letter to María Bautista: no hint of plots against Gracián's life, much less of any current danger from the Inquisition.

IV

Yet Teresa knew her present danger. Gracián recalls her rebuke, when, as he says, the talk against her "had [him] nearly driven out of [his] mind": "Quiet, Father. Not a word against the Inquisition. . . ." Though he cites it to prove her faith, her orthodoxy, she may well have said just that—as a caution that he badly needed.

It was mid-February, as Gracián recalls it—ten days or so after Teresa wrote that letter—when he went to visit the convent and found the whole broad Calle de las Armas blocked by the horses and mules of the Inquisition, those unmounted held by their still-mounted guard, and all surrounded by a fascinated crowd of townspeople. He had, he says, been waiting for just that "through many days in which [he] could neither eat nor sleep."

I don't doubt it. Nor do I doubt his description of Teresa's calm, and her laughter at his anxieties throughout the days that followed. It was never in times of crisis, of open battle, that Teresa found herself "cowardly and pusillanimous."

236

Chapter 48 ❀ Teresa's Superb Successful Defense; the Convent at Caravaca; Letters of this Time

I

Once Teresa had left Seville, María de San Jose' was slandered in turn as Gracián's bedfellow. Rather than refresh this in her readers' memories she chose to remember the investigation as concerned only with heresy. In this she is alone. San Gabriel, San Francisco and numerous others recall endless accusations that were "unfit for chaste ears." Little Teresica heard it all. She was nine, but a precocious nine in a period which did not confuse innocence with ignorance. After the trial she took it upon herself to write an account of it to Juan de Padilla, up in Valladolid. She must have been graphic, for María Bautista saw the letter and was enraged with Teresa for having allowed it to be sent off along with her own correspondence.

We still have Teresica's adult memories of that grilling, which went on, day after day, from morning until night: "They were accused with the vilest testimony raised against them of things so foul and unimaginable that they are not fit to write down. The Mother suffered less for herself than for her nuns and the prelate [Gracián], but at the same time she preserved such heavenly calm and vast serenity that they were all struck with admiration."

Father Garcia Alvarez, in witnessing for the canonization process, also says that throughout the ordeal, Teresa conducted herself "like a saint." In evaluat-this evidence one should remember that he was not present, and that it was with his advice and consent that Beatriz Chávez and Margarita Ramírez made their highly creative accusations, two years later. He was, as you might say, changeable. We may be sure, however, that from the start, reports of Teresa's love-life were quickly seized upon and given Andalusian embellishments. While Gracián was named as the current star-performer, Mother Isabel de San Domingo, up in Segovia, was told that people down there were even saying that to satisfy her lusts Mother Teresa had to take both black and white men to her bed.

Luckily—and to give credit where credit is due—the Inquisitors quickly saw eye to eye with Juan de la Cruz on poor San Jerónimo. She was mad, nothing more. Furthermore, Teresa carried herself with dignity, and that year of strain and illness had not left her looking her best at sixty-one. In a matter of days she had managed to make the sexual angle appear ludicrous, to the Inquisitors, at least. Only her orthodoxy appeared in doubt.

She was ordered to prepare a written defense of this to be judged by three independent censors, all Jesuits. If the Inquisition knew that her Jesuit friends were few and far between, their hopes, in this instance, were ill-founded. One of the three, Enrico Enríquez, cleared her at once. She had aided him in tactfully discouraging her brother Pedro's attempt to join the Company, and in gratitude he had given a formal permission for Teresica to live in the convent.

Jorge Alvarez, the second censor, simply turned the work over to his more scholarly brother, Rodrigo.

What Teresa wrote for Rodrigo Alvarez became the first in a series of undated *cuentas* which form the appendix to Luis de León's edition of the *Life*. He worked from a manuscript beginning with a note in Teresa's own hand which explains that what follows is a copy made without additions or subtractions by her confessor, as she herself has kept the original. Needless to say, de León did not publish it as a defense written under orders from the Holy Office. Nor did he publish it intact; but the over three hundred and fifty words which he lined out for the printer to omit are all left legible. It is curious that he used it at all, especially as an appendix to the *Life*, with which its narrative does not always agree.

With one or two lapses, she uses the third person throughout, beginning, "It is forty years since this nun took the habit." "This nun" said her Rosary and meditated daily on the Passion, but for almost twenty years she had no true conception of God's glory. (A passage omitted by de León explains that she was held back by "the way of fear" and thought of prayer only as a means of shortening her stay in Purgatory.) In this aridity, "it never occurred to her to want more"; but during the last three of those twenty years, pictures would flash into her mind and endure in memory more vividly than as if she had seen them with her eyes. This disturbed her, as did the idea of founding a convent like those of her Order's earliest days, and she sought Jesuit advice for fear she was being deceived by the devil.

Of these, she "talked once with Father Araoz, the Commissary, and on two separate occasions with Father Francis who was Duke of Gandía"; "also with a certain Provincial, Gil González, who is now in Rome and with the present Provincial, though with him very little" (Suárez, left unnamed), and to Baltasar Alvarez, "her confessor for many years." She also confessed to the Rectors of Cuenca, of Segovia, and of Burgos, Gaspar de Salazar, Santander, and Ripalda, though Ripalda "had a bad opinion of her until we talked together." In Toledo she talked with Pablo Hernández, who was a confessor to the Inquisition, and to an unnamed Rector of Avila who happened to be in that place. And finally, "to the Rector who was in Salamanca when I talked to him, Dr. Gutiérrez, and to other fathers of the Company whom I managed to talk with while I was there because they were said to be spiritual." (De León omits this carefully casual afterthought, which Teresa had decided to include since any Jesuit would note the omission with raised eyebrows.)

Next she mentions Pedro de Alcántara: "He was a holy man, a Discalced Franciscan." (Also omitted by de León; opinions on Peter of Alcántara varied, and he would not be canonized for another ninety-five years.)

These listed, "this nun" gets back to her story. For six years she prayed to be led by another way, for while she could not help seeing that her life was improved, she was ashamed to be thought a visionary because of her (*great:* deleted) sins and her fear of being laughed at "for the sort of silly women's talk that I have always had a horror of listening to" (also deleted). A talk about this with Inquisitor Soto reassured her, since he found that her "imaginary visions" only strengthened her faith in the Church, but he suggested that she write it out for Master Avila. "And she did, and also wrote him an account of her sins and her life" (once more, deleted).

Master Avila's response brought her only partial belief since she knew that such spiritual people as he can be misled, so she decided to consult with Dominicans. (The Inquisition is Dominican and its opinion of "such spiritual people" as Master Avila was unfavorable. Teresa has introduced her list of Dominicans most aptly.) She confessed "for a year and a half" with Vincente Barrón, who is confessor to the Inquisition in Toledo. (She did confess to him briefly when she returned from Pastrana and Martín had gone to Salamanca; and perhaps she forgot that the "year and a half" includes the ten months after her father's death when she put off confessing to him.) She also confessed for six years to Domingo Báñez, who is President of the College of San Gregorio in Valladolid; and to Master Chávez, and to Bartolomé de Medina, "because he had a bad opinion of her and so could see better whether or not she was deceived": and "after two years" (that is, after Fernández released her from the Incarnation) "he became and remained *muy su amigo.*"

Besides these, Father de Meneses once came to Avila to see if she was suffering from delusions, and she talked to a former Provincial, Salinas, and to Luna, a Prior of Avila, and Yanguas, in Segovia. "And there were others, in various places she has been." (In listing her Jesuits, Teresa had finally seen that the Salamanca scandal necessitated her mention of "Dr. Gutiérrez and other Fathers of the Company," whom de León preferred to omit. But the whisperings about Pedro Ibáñez and García de Toledo were almost forgotten; she herself decided to leave them out. However, though left unnamed in the *Life*, both could readily be identified, and de León inserts them — between Chávez and de Medina, as good a place to stick them in as any.)

But note: Teresa has protected only her active, post-conversion life. She wanted what went before to glorify God's forgiveness. De León, who wanted to prove that He had nothing to forgive, omits her plea that her sins have at least saved her from vainglory, as the memory of that evil past "is always in her nostrils like a stinking ooze"; and her protest that while in prayer she now seems to forget her body and lose all fear of it, since her whole being is occupied with God, she still fears sin, prays constantly to avoid it, "and would do anything that her confessors directed, believing that to be God's will, as confessors who have known her for the past twenty years will confirm." Twenty of those forty years since "this nun took the habit." No danger could make Teresa belittle God's mercy by denying a past which "is always in her nostrils like a stinking ooze." And her final statement is both honest and moving to any who have ever shared it: though she cannot explain her recurrent sense of God's presence, "or how it comes," when it does come, "she cannot doubt it."

Rodrigo Alvarez declared Teresa free from heresy. At his request she also wrote him a long *cuenta* in which, as in the *Life*, she describes the developing stages of "mental prayer." She kept a copy and used it as the ground plan of her last book, *Moradas* — written when she believed that her last foundations were made, and their story told at Gracián's orders; told in a way that would relieve his anxiety.

But Gracián, at this time, was showing his anxiety in another way. He put Teresa through a singular torment that neither he nor she would ever mention. We know about it only from San José.

II

Gracián does not exaggerate when he says that the slanderous accusations nearly drove him mad; they involved him, and, unlike Teresa, he was at his worst in times of crisis.

After its intensive grilling of Teresa and her nuns, the Inquisition was satisfied that the "vile accusations . . . unfit for chaste ears" were flowers of María Corro's imagination. The past she had long since fled was merely typical of the Carmelite nuns they knew, and the scholarly Rodrigo Alvarez had cleared her of heresy. Yet for the Holy Office to make a formal statement of this decision without any show of giving the evidence its due consideration would have been unsatisfactory to both the excitable city of Seville and to the Central Council's Grand Inquisitor. Consequently, Teresa de Jesús and Isabel de San Jerónimo were not pronounced innocent for another six weeks; and throughout those six weeks, Gracián subjected Teresa to a general confession which went on, San José tells us, "for a month and a half, every day and for several hours of each day."

A general confession, a review of a penitent's whole lifetime of sin, is of limited application. It is expected of a convert; it would have been properly demanded of Teresa's grandfather when he confessed to a lifetime of nominal Catholicism which was actually stained with "grave crimes of apostasy and heresy." Possibly Gracián found his theological excuse in Teresa's having been declared apostate by her General. However, such a confession can be made in hours, at most; hours in one meeting. A confession that took hours of the day for seven days a week over a stretch of six weeks has only one explanation: Gracián, in blind panic, was determined to show himself as on the side of the right and ready to abandon Teresa if he found himself deceived in her.

Teresa believed that her sins were forgiven by God, but she could not forgive herself for that past that was "always in her nostrils like a stinking ooze." Week by week, Gracián dragged her through an agony of which she was not theologian enough to doubt the propriety, nor if she had been, could she have borne the pain of facing her confessor's underlying motive: self-defense, engendered by panic fear.

Love clings to its illusions. Almost to the end Teresa turned her eyes away from Gracián's ambition and his cowardice.

III

Two of Teresa's letters — or more accurately a letter and a half — date from the time when she had just finished her written defense for the Inquisition's censors, and that protracted torment of her general confession had begun. At the same time, María de San José was giving Teresa the cold shoulder even more firmly than she had since the past December when María Corro's departure first promised trouble with the Inquisition. This hardly eased the loneliness and strain.

Yet Teresa's letter to Rodrigo de Moya, patron of Caravaca, is wholly upbeat, sane and unflustered; encouragement given, one would say, by a woman who had not a care in the world. Caravaca, de Moya felt, was in real trouble. Teresa had assumed that its double license, from the Council of Orders and from the King, put it "under the ordinary" and thus made it exempt from Rubeo's prohibition that any more Discalced convents be founded. However, our troubles never come singly. The Bishop of Cartagena, doubtless inspired by the news from Seville, was demanding that the convent be dissolved.

De Moya's letter is a relief, Teresa tells him. She is sorry that the Prioress is in such a state, though she has written to reassure her. They need not worry about the Bishop's threat. Convents are not so easily dissolved, and she has written to certain people whose influence will bring him around. As for the price of the house, it is not too much for one with a perfect location, as all agree this one has. When a house is so perfectly situated, she never hesitates to pay a third to a half again as much as it is worth; a few more dowries will take care of that.

The half-letter to María Bautista is much longer, though Teresa says that she's worn out with "all the reading and writing" that she's having to do. Are they "out of their heads" to think she'll come to Valladolid? She'll have to go wherever she's sent. The Nuncio wants her to found more convents, but she will do nothing and go nowhere except at the General's orders.

There is talk (largely blacked out) about *lo de Agustín.* One gathers that the girl Agustín left behind him is trying to force her daughter on the Discalced against the girl's will. "May God give them light" on how to handle it!

One illegitimate child leads her pen to another: If Báñez's pains in his joints come from his sleeping on the floor in Lenten penance as he did last Advent, María Bautista must insist that at least he cover his feet. And she hadn't realized that the page-boy was so young, just turned eleven; he'll have to learn to read, or he'll wander off while Lorenzo's boys are in school. "But my brother says they'll have to take him even if they have no use for him, because it concerns Fray Domingo. The good thing is. . . ."

A long, obliterated passage is followed by a last plea for María Bautista or Inés to take in Bernarda Gutiérrez, who is still unnamed, but readily placed by later references, "they say, a little saint." If María Bautista will change her mind, Teresa will find a place "for that one of our Father's," the page's sister, though she had rather provide for one of Gracián's sisters. (He was eldest of thirteen children, mostly girls.)

I have summarized tightly; even without its missing page or pages, the letter is very long, though she had "hoped to make it short." Long or short it would have been futile where the "little saint" was concerned. Even before the Inquisition formally cleared Teresa of all charges, the convent had accepted a

241

novice: "Bernarda Gutiérrez, child of Pedro Matías, a Corsican resident of (the suburb of) Trianos."

The Inquisition's pronouncement, as one might say, took Teresa out of the headlines for a bit. The volatile city of Seville looked for new excitements. In that comparative calm, the Carthusian Prior, a good old man identified as "a member of the Pantoja family from Avila," now felt free to help Teresa; he had influential friends, and used them to urge Teresa's interests on the Archbishop. And Lorenzo, at last, could start househunting, for Teresa's most earnest wish was to get away.

IV

He found a house which Teresa describes as ideal, its white stucco walls "like sugar frosting" and its windows looking out over the Guadalquivir, with the galleons setting out for the Indies and returning. Beatriz Chávez's mother and Pedro Matías promised a hundred ducats each for the downpayment, and Lorenzo gave all he could outright, the remainder as a loan made in his name. He discovered too late that he was also responsible for the *aecabala*, the notorious sales tax. As he had failed to collect from the crown and no money had reached him from Peru, he had to hide out in Los Remedios to avoid debtor's prison.

On the last night of April, Teresa, San José, and two of the nuns slipped into the house by dark to take possession before the Franciscans, next door and spoiling for trouble, could prevent it. García Alvarez said the Mass and reserved the Host. The Archbishop's fireworks, described in *Fundaciones*, would not come for a month more.

Just before she left the Calle de las Armas, Teresa sent a letter to María Bautista which enclosed one—no longer extant—to be forwarded to Inés. They may be worried, she says, though she has told "little enough about their troubles." "Grasp it that all the troubles I have gone through since the founding of San José are exactly nothing compared to what I went through here. Some day you'll know how true that is and that we could only have got out of it by the grace of God...." The lies and double-dealing and injustice that go on in this place, and the things they were accused of! One could only wish that the nun who left them had said nothing worse than that Teresa hung nuns up by their hands and feet and beat them! But now it is cleared up, and the next-door Franciscans seem to be lying low.

Now the letter shifts abruptly to another subject. The question of "pure blood" came up whenever a junta or the Inquisition moved against Teresa. She also knew that while it was dangerous to have Jewish blood, it was still more dangerous to try to hide it: a false title of *hidalguía* invited all too many to unmask the deceiver and punish the lie. Even Avila was not any longer the smiling town that Lorenzo remembered. Moreover, pretense was pretense: the boys should grow up wth better standards. On Lorenzo's return, Teresa had persuaded him to go back to Avila as plain Señor de Cepeda. María Bautista, a realist, had been pleased and relieved. Unfortunately, Don Juan and Doña

Juana de Ovalle were both shocked at the notion. Lorenzo changed his mind, and when María Bautista heard of it, she blamed Teresa. Strangely enough, Teresa's response was published some fifty years before any doubt was cast on her own *hidalguía*: perhaps as evidence that she saw *all* titles as worldly vanity.

"To begin with, about *dons*. Everyone in the Indies gives himself a title as soon as he can afford servants, but when the boys came back I asked their father not to let it go on, and I gave him the reasons. So he agreed, and it was all perfectly straightforward. But then the de Ovalles came here, and they said so much about it to him that I could do nothing . . . And it certainly gave me one in the eye because of the way it can affect them." (As she had known that Lorenzo would agree to a page for them, if only because it was "excessive.") "As for myself, I don't believe that anyone will connect it with me enough for you to worry about — and compared with the other things they say, it's nothing, anyway. I'll try to take it up again with their father for your sake, but I don't think there'll be any chance of bettering things with the boys' aunt and uncle, for they're dead set on it — so much so that I have to hold myself in by force every time I hear it."

She ends wearily with saying that she doesn't expect to be believed. María Bautista will never get over the notion that Teresa changed her mind to humor Lorenzo because she loved him.

If she had chosen, Teresa could have written about far more disturbing matters.

Chapter 49 ❀ *The Vicar-General, Tostado; Teresa's Flight from Seville to Malagón; Financial Problems of the Convents*

I

As the saying went, "There is no Pope in Spain." Rubeo, on his own visit, had got a taste of the King's dislike of foreign interference, but I doubt that he realized what Jerónimo Tostado, his companion on that visit, would be up against when he sent him back as Vicar-General. Tostado faced a hard job, for Rubeo was equally bitter against the Andalusian Calced and their disobedient would-be reformers, now become the King's pets.

Tostado landed in Barcelona in March, found little support in Madrid, and reached Andalusia just as Teresa was slipping by night into her new house. Mariano had left for Madrid when the first whisperings about Teresa and Gracián promised the Inquisition's visit. His excuse was impeccable: the brewing trouble made it imperative that the Discalced have a representative in Madrid. And for Gracián to go was as unwise as it would have been for Teresa to obey the General's command to leave Andalusia at once: flight was evidence of guilt, and simply staying put evidence of innocence.

243

But now the situation was changed, and Tostado was staying with the right friends for his purpose, only thirty-five miles away. Tostado's strongest ally was Cota, Prior of Córdoba. He had done well in Rome with his story of Gracián's bringing "the nun, Teresa de Jesús" to Seville when her trial by the Córdoba Inquisition was still undergoing further examination in Madrid. Now Cota, as Rubeo's sympathizer, guided Tostado to the right, understanding friends. The Prior of Carmona received him with open arms. His sympathy overflowed for the excommunicated friars of the Casa Grande, and he was fervent in declaring that Tostado would have been Visitor to the Carmelites if the King and his senile friend, the Nuncio Ormaneto, had not outwitted the Pope.

In Andalusia, a current method of simplifying such disagreements was poisoning. The Archbishop and the Count of Barajas, having decided to place their bets on the King, urged Gracián to disappear, for a time at least — simply as preventative medicine. A Carmelite chapter was due to be held at Morejas at which his right to be Visitor to the Calced would be tried; and if that attempt to discredit him failed, the next step might well be to "give him something to eat," as the popular phrase put it.

Teresa sent the news to Mariano. "You left us in a mess" she says. They now have a house worth twenty thousand ducats, though it keeps her brother in hiding to avoid debtor's prison; but Tostado is in Carmona, and Cota is coming from Carmona to stir up trouble in Seville. The Calced will hold their chapter in three days. If they fail to discredit Gracián's Visitorship, the battle will be half-won. Still, some plot is afoot and Tostado is still to be feared, for Cota does not know that Gracián has slipped away, and he would not dare come to Seville if he believed that Gracián would retain any real power.

Mariano must have liked the ida; he saved the letter.

II

Mariano had finally deserted his Juan de la Miseria. Gracián, on leaving, gave the unhappy creature a parting order to decorate the chapel of Teresa's new house and to paint her portrait. San José says that the portrait was ordered "to mortify the Mother," and calls it a good likeness. San Francisco and San Gabriel found it ludicrous and said that when Teresa looked at it, she said "God forgive you, Fray Juan, you've made me look like a bleary-eyed old hag!" Gracián calls it a bad likeness and adds that the Mother looked far younger. Since no other portraits of Teresa were done from the life, one can't judge the resemblance; but it does prove that Juan de la Miseria was not a gifted painter. His murals, mercifully, have all peeled away, but the portrait remains — now touched up with a halo and a hovering dove, the Holy Spirit.

It was early May before the house was made into a workable convent. Teresa asked that the move from the Calle las Armas be effected quietly. The convent had been "made" when the Archbishop issued its licence, and once it became plain that the Franciscans were not going to bring a lawsuit after all, the Host was consumed in the new chapel and the altar had only waited for moving day to be blessed once more with the Presence.

The move could not be made quietly. The Archbishop and the Count of Barajas were too eager to show themselves on the King's side, not the Pope's, in this business of the Discalced. So all went off as Teresa describes it: processions, artillery, fireworks, and the fountain that played perfumed water. There could not be a Mass since to celebrate it fasting would have deprived the Archbishop of his fireworks, but once the Host was installed, he came down from the altar, knelt at Teresa's feet and asked her blessing. San José had told nothing in her *Libro de Recreaciones* that makes the gesture seem anything less than suitable. Teresa could not have brought herself to mention such a nauseating display of insincerity.

It was two in the morning before Lorenzo could safely creep out of hiding and let them be on their way, a safe three hours before dawn. After those thirteen months in Seville, it would have meant much to Teresa to kneel at that altar on the following day and receive communion in company with the nuns whose convent had cost them so much privation and so much public shame, but that was not the sort of thing one told in *Fundaciones*. That chapter ends with the devil's failure to profit by the fireworks and the nun's thankfulness "that they did not have to buy more taffetas."

Still, that secret, hasty flight had surprised many. And as she began that unwilling chapter on Beatriz Chávez which Gracián found, she set down a few preliminary sentences which attempt to explain it away.

III

The sisters, she says, were full of joy on the day she left, and so was she, in the knowledge that she was living in such a fine, well-located house and that the convent was so well known that when it came time to make up their number, they would be able to live there free of debt. And best of all, she had shared the trials that made this possible. (They had gained only two novices to go with the five original nuns—Beatriz and Bernarda, and when she wrote, Teresa had discovered María de San José's sublime indifference to debt, native to one who had grown up in a palace.) "Since it was now possible for [her] to get some rest," she went away. The fiesta was held on the Sunday before Pentecost, so she left "on the following Monday." The summer heat was beginning, and she wanted to avoid the crowds that would be on the road during the Pentecost holidays, and she also wanted to get to Malagón in time to spend some days there. "That is why I made such haste."

So she "never heard a single Mass in [her] convent"—a deep sorrow to her and to her nuns. After the trials they had lived through together "for more than a year"—greater than any since she had left Avila: "Though I shall not set them down here" she adds, and hastily describes her own as having been chiefly "interior," that is, in her frequent usage, spiritual. Malagón? It is not mentioned again in the book. And a fear of oncoming hot weather and holiday travellers her sole excuse for causing not only herself but her nuns a sorrow that marred their day of joy? To know her is to disbelieve her. But it was the best she could do to please Gracián.

Gracián had seen the King and the Nuncio. Both assured him that the Carmelite chapter could not discredit him; he was still Visitor to the Andalusian Calced and must go back at once to Seville. But Gracián wanted no more scandalous talk. He let Teresa know that she should leave as soon as possible and that they would not meet on the road to Toledo, since he was coming back by way of Almodóvar. Teresa got to Almodóvar as quickly as she could and waited. Quickly, for fear she should miss him on the road: waiting in the hope that she could persuade him to go with her to Malagón. She could not safely explain why he was needed there in a letter, nor would she have known of it herself if Antonio Ruiz had been less her friend.

Ruiz belongs to the Malagón picture as Antonio Gaitán to that of Alba. Both were local residents, widowed, untitled, fond of travel, and instinctively drawn to Teresa from the time she had founded in their castle-villages under patronesses with nothing more to recommend them than their ducal blood. On a trip to Seville, Ruiz had heard enough slander to convince him that Teresa could not afford another convent that was earning a bad name. When he learned that she and her brother would soon be leaving for Avila, he told her why she must first stop over in Malagón — and in company with a trustworthy friar who could handle that part of the situation which she, in propriety, could not handle herself. He was glad to learn that Gregorio Nanciano already planned to go as far as Toledo with them as he wanted to revisit Malagón, the home he had left to go with Teresa to Beas and Seville.

As Teresa saw it, the presence of the Visitor himself was necessary. He alone could persuade Doña Luisa that her convent must be moved to her other country residence in Paracuellos, at a safe remove from the Alcantarine friars whose friendship with the nuns had become a scandal. From the start, their shared task of educating the village children had thrown them too much together; the result, Teresa felt, was only what one might expect when young girls are subjected to constant temptation. Nor had it helped things to give them Brianda for their new Prioress: she was a Mendoza, with all that family's tolerant warmth and predisposition to think no evil. Moreover, Ruiz told Teresa, Brianda's devotion to her confessor, the young Licentiate, Gaspar de Villanueva, was also making talk— and in a way that Teresa could understand all too well. Gracián, she was sure, would give it the same understanding, and not misjudge Brianda.

That is why her rush to be off lest she miss catching Gracián in Almadóvar could not be easily explained, either to the nuns she left behind at the first possible moment — or to those who eventually would read her twice-abandoned book, *Fundaciones*. All subsequent writers have also avoided mentioning that stopover in Almodóvar, with one exception: Efrén de la Madre de Dios, who traced her only possible way to Beas — past La Peñuela, which he ignored — admitted and tried to explain her visit to Almodóvar.

She went there, he says, to talk with the monk who took her nuns to Caravaca, and she lingered because all the best families there were so anxious to meet her. Moreover, he points out, she was drawn to the place because

Master Avila and Master Martín Gutiérrez were born there, both "deeply loved friends of La Santa." Efrén enriches his account of that stay with an anecdote from the beatification process of the Blessed Juan de la Concepción. Teresa, it is claimed, visited his house and singled him out from his seven siblings for a life of holiness, saying that her prophesy would be proved true when one of his sisters died. A sister who died thereafter was later exhumed and found to be miraculously preserved. It is odd that this was seen as reflecting no glory on the deceased, but only on her brother and La Santa. Many contemporary non-Spanish Catholics would also find it odd that Fray Efrén found it worth citing for the same purpose in 1968 A.D.

How things actually went after her five days' wait for Gracián we only know from the two letters Fray Gregorio took back to Seville from Malagón. From the first, to San José, we gather that Gracián did not want that meeting known. Of the journey, Teresa only says, "We came by way of Almodóvar," and the rest is news, highly selective news, of San José's first convent, Malagón. From the second, to Gracián, we gather that he wanted as few as possible to know of that brief meeting—even in Almodóvar.

As so often, Teresa tries to begin lightly. On the way to Malagón, she tells him, they were lunching in a field when a salamander ran up her sleeve. Horror! But Lorenzo caught it by the tail, flung it away, "and it caught Antonio Ruiz square in the mouth!"

But then she speaks of "the joy of seeing you the other day," and her grief "that you were in such a hurry to get to Seville. . . ." "But I will never be sorry that you would not come here, for the same *disparates* would have gone right on, regardless of your person or your office." (*Disparates*, with Teresa, was a strong word: "terrible things.")

Gracián, after hearing Antonio Ruiz's report, had wanted to replace Brianda at once. In time he did, though Teresa would always defend her. In this letter she only says, "She has learned so much from sad experience growing out of the faults she had—according to what they say—that nothing must be done without taking time to think it over. I am very fond of her, and it holds me back still more to see how fond she is of you, and how whe worries over your health."

Even with a messenger as reliable as Fray Gregorio she still found it best not to spell out the health problem which soon had her begging Gracián to eat nothing but hard boiled eggs, served in the shell, when he had to eat with the Calced. Still, as though it concerned only his convenience, she here goes on at once to beg him to take all his meals at the convent when he must be away from Los Remedios. He must not worry about the expense to the nuns; she herself will raise the money for his food elsewhere.

But this must apply to him alone: "For the nuns are all young, and believe me, Father, it is the safest thing for them to have no dealings with friars. Nothing else makes me fear for our convents so much as that." So, she hopes against hope that she can persuade Doña Luisa to move them to Paracuellos, "for as things are now, it's impossible to handle matters as we did with

Pastrana." If the lady won't look at the facts and spend the money, it's hopeless — made hopeless by the General's decree. (This passage was omitted from Teresa's published letters until the 1960's. Teresa's realistic struggles to save young nuns from needless temptation have always lacked popular appeal; in the preferred version, she went about creating convents of impermeable chastity and obedience.)

Let me add that while Brianda may have been overfond of her confessor, and certainly lacked the art of government, she was Teresa's sole truly congenial prioress. Her letters say of Brianda often, as they do of no other woman, "I love to talk with her." With Brianda Teresa could be open, for breaking confidences was not among her faults. Their correspondence would have been invaluable; but only one heavily censored first page of a letter from Teresa to Brianda — a confidential, spontaneous letter which is already one of many — was allowed to survive.

I should add that Teresa's letter to San José, written at the beginning of this friendship with Brianda, ends with an order: "Tell Sister San Francisco that she must send me an honest account of what goes on with those friars. When I got to this house, I felt I had made a change for the worse." (Even Discalced friars, it seems, could get too friendly.) Still, she goes on, she greatly enjoys Brianda's company: "Pray God she won't prove somewhat lacking." That half-expressed doubt is the sole criticism of Brianda in Teresa's letters; nor does she ever again mention the friars in Malagón. She worries only over the convent's poverty, for Doña Luisa was so in love with holy poverty for others that she gave her nuns what Teresa saw as exactly half of what they needed for food and medicine. (Despite which, this letter encloses money from Brianda as a first installment on Gracián's meals. The Mendozas were all compulsive givers.)

About Brianda herself, Teresa thereafter would mention only one worry: her delicate health. She coughs until she brings up blood, and the doctors have given her up as consumptive. Brianda lived to be ninety; the doctors were wrong, but their diagnosis eventually proved convenient. She could be removed to Toledo without scandal, as one needing care because of her fatal illness. And there Teresa, through the last years of her house-arrest, had her "to talk with." There are few blessings greater than having a friend with whom one can be wholly open.

But saintwatchers have never liked Brianda. They divide her place in Teresa's heart between those two highly dissimilar prioresses, María Bautista and María de San José.

IV

Teresa got a letter from San José three days after Fray Gregorio took these two letters back to Seville. The Archbishop's fireworks had attracted no novices — with their much needed dowries; and the debt which had kept Lorenzo hiding had now gone to court. The nuns were in danger of being evicted. San José asked permission to accept her sole finding, a girl who was not yet fourteen. Teresa's rule set a minimum age for novices at seventeen, with nineteen the lowest age for taking the final vows — before which a dowry could be reclaimed by the family. But in answer to this letter she not only gave permission for San José to accept the thirteen-year-old novice, but to profess Beatriz Chávez, who was illiterate and as such ineligible. For, she wrote, "It would put an end to her temptations."

Beatriz's chief temptation at that time was to take herself and her dowry away, as had María Corro and Doña Ventura. Later Beatriz would swear that she had been professed against her will. Perhaps; but Teresa had much to swallow down as well. In her convents, you may remember, she had won the right to extend the Carmelite novitiate two years and "only wished that she could have made it four." Beatriz, by the earliest of the two contradictory convent records, had taken the habit only nine months ago, and her illiteracy would have kept her a lay-sister like her friend Margarita if her newly widowed mother had not supposedly been rich. Two months later, when Beatriz's mother also joined the convent "and gave it all she had," that turned out to be fifteen hundred ducats. Malagón, rent free but receiving no alms, was struggling to survive on two thousand a year, which Teresa was trying to get doubled. Seville got no alms either, other than the Archbishop's three ducats a month and grain for its bread; and Teresa could not bear to see that agonizing year ended, put to waste with an ignominious eviction.

Indeed, Teresa faced constant monetary problems. Sentimentalizings of holy poverty obscure the hard fact that with two exceptions — Valladolid and Toledo — none of her convents could have survived if she had not inherited the financial intelligence of her grandfather, Juan Sánchez. All her other convents were constantly threatened by inadequate alms, indifferent patronesses, prioresses with no ability to handle money, or all three at once. Teresa's constant work and watchfulness on this score deserves more credit than it ever gets. At the same time, one should remember that she only wanted her convents to be free of actual need and its distracting anxieties. She was repelled by María Bautista's greed, and would soon be by her discovery of María de San José's palace-bred indifference to one's honest debts.

V

Teresa also deserves more credit than men like to give her for the fact that within her lifetime the Discalced became a separate province — their first step towards becoming the separate order that they are now. Early on she saw that Calced Provincials would repeatedly destroy whatever her Priors and Prioresses built up, and that a visitorship which depended on an old and ailing Nuncio could not change the future. It was now almost a year since she had written to beg the King that he urge on the Pope a separate province for the Discalced, under Gracián's leadership.

Teresa still saw Gracián as the only fit Provincial to the Discalced, and still could not believe that Rubeo, properly approached, would refuse to forgive him. Yet she saw quite as clearly that there could be no such forgiveness and no separate province while Gracián's Visitorship gave him power over the

249

Andalusian Calced. She also saw that she was powerless. Quite aside from her holy vow to obey him, she knew that whatever she, a woman, said to him would be outweighed by the contrary advice he got from men.

Then a man's misjudgement of her led to a stirring of hope. It came before she had ended her month-long, unaided, and seemingly fruitless struggle to better the state of affairs in Malagón.

Any hope, however brief, gives the spirit some rest.

Chapter 50 ❦ *Some of Teresa's Troubles with Gracián*

I

The Prior of Carmona, Cota's friend and Tostado's supporter, was shocked by the mass excommunication of the Casa Grande. He was sure that he could, at least, persuade the Nuncio that only the ringleaders of the revolt against their Visitor should be punished; and he dared hope that he could further persuade him to rid Andalusia of Gracián. If the old man insisted on a Visitor allied to the King's Reform, Heredia would be no trouble — an Andalusian and a gentleman who knew how to get along. It might also help if he could see the woman in the case and manage to modify her ambitions for her lover with fears for his safety.

He went to Seville, discovered her whereabouts, and stopped off in Malagón, on the way to Madrid. To his amazement, he met only with encouragement and gratitude. Teresa wrote about the meeting to Gracián: "I have been wondering if it wouldn't be a good thing for you to ask just that of the King and Nuncio yourself, explaining that since they are to totally obstinate and feel so much enmity towards you, you can do little with them." (A blacked out passage leaves enough words legible to fill out her floating pronouns in the sentence that follows.) "And even if [the King and the Nuncio] don't like it, it would be a consolation to think that you had done what you could to get rid of [the Calced]. It is simply death to me to think that they will be forced to obey you again and the whole thing will start over. Consider it seriously, my Father. If you can do nothing else, at least you will have the strength that comes from obedience, and the Lord will take it in hand." (A direct order from the Nuncio, that is, would overrule any from the General, for so long as Gracián had been free to refuse the Visitorship he had disobeyed, and was still disobeying.) "They say that they should have their province left to them and Tostado will manage it. May God manage it, for it will be good for Him to manage such desperate people by some means, once you have given up trying to put it in order. Oh, Jesus, what a thing it is to have to be so far away from you, in the face of all these things! I tell you, it is a great, great cross to bear."

250

It was indeed, and Teresa was determined to get no further from the center of things than Toledo, where Lorenzo had waited out the last month still expecting to take her back to Avila. Teresa used the importance of moving the Malagón convent as her excuse. This letter says that she has got Doña Luisa "to send some official or other" to look into it, "but she says it with great lukewarmness."

In hard fact, Doña Luisa's contract to build a house that would give her a convent outside the village — though not in Paracuellos — was signed that very week, and Antonio Ruiz was prepared to take care of all business in Teresa's absence. But this she preferred to conceal, for Rubeo expected for her to go to Avila and Fernández, the Visitor to Castile, expected her to go to Salamanca. (Technically she was still its Prioress, with cousin Ana only acting for her in her absence.) For staying in Toledo she needed an excuse.

Ruiz had already lent María de San José money that he could ill afford. In Toledo, Teresa found that Lorenzo had arranged with his bankers for another loan which he, in turn, could lend San José, to pay off the *alcabala* in Seville. Teresa, herself, did not yet fully realize that those who lend to the palace-bred do well to kiss their money good-bye.

Lorenzo, indeed, was both generous and extravagant: in money matters much his father's son. Teresa's letters after his return to Avila try to warn him that "if he begins wrong, the damage will be done before he knows it." But they did not deter him from buying La Serna, a *término redondo*: that is a country estate which made its owner not only Lord of the Manor, but judge and jury when judgment was needed on any crime from petty thievery to murder. Teresa protested: he "thinks too much of honor." At least, he must buy an all purpose farm horse, not a high-bred creature to ride about in style, and as for the boys, "it will do them good to walk."

But a good education for them is not display. "One of Rodrigo's daughter's children is a boy, luckily for him" and is now a student at Salamanca, along with a son of that noble Avilan, Don Alonso del Aguila; and his sons may go there, too, "if they keep at their books." Such letters often included some cutting remark about Don Juan de Ovalle; Teresa's hope that Lorenzo would eventually see reason and drop that *don* for himself and his boys died hard.

II

For months San José let Teresa believe that the *alcabala* was paid and the lawsuit dropped. Her letter of thanks received Teresa's assurance that she loved San José as much as San José "said she loved" her, and none of her apologies for past unpleasantness were necessary; "I see perfectly well that it was not your fault. I said just that to the Prioress of Malagón. On the contrary, since the Lord wanted me to have so many trials down there, he ordained that you take yourself off."

It was essential for Gracián's sake that San José feel no lingering resentment and no guilt which might feed that resentment. Gracián had gone to Madrid, but only to complain of Calced intransigence. The King told him to talk with the President of the Royal Council and the Grand Inquisitor and take their advice. Since both disliked interference from the Vatican as much as the King himself did, their advice was simple: face Tostado down.

Gracián took his time going back to Seville. Mariano involved him in grandiose, ill-timed plans for a Discalced monastery in Madrid. It was asking for trouble, but Gracián did not see that. However, he did see other sources of trouble. Teresa was a woman in her sixties, weakened by years with the quartan ague and God knew what other ailments. When she died her papers would be read. During that six-week general confession he had learned of the chapters she added to *Fundaciones* for the sake of Martín Gutiérrez's memory and her abandonment of the book thereafter. He sent her a direct command: the book must have its final chapters.

Teresa wrote to Avila for the manuscript of *Fundaciones*. "The Father Visitor," she told Lorenzo, "has commanded it." Lorenzo must also go through all her papers and find an alternate chapter which she had written about Alba de Tormes and decided not to use. But when the chapter came, it showed her no way to avoid using Catalina Godóñez as she had used Teresa de Laiz. If she omitted none of the implausibilies, she could hope that the few who understood her would understand.

But she put off the task. And no letter that she wrote Gracián from that mid-June until the very end of August has been saved. Letters that repeatedly urge him to renounce the Visitorship, beg his General's forgiveness, and stay out of Andalusia were too out of key with the letters in which, as Angela or Laurentia, she sends messages to her Eliseo, her Paul.

III

The way from Madrid goes through Toledo. Gracián took it at least twice, perhaps oftener, without seeing Teresa. His caution is comprehensible; as he himself complains in his *Peregrinaciones*, from the past December until Teresa's death the Calced never ceased to trade on his supposed liasion with La Santa. After that meeting in Almodóvar from which he hurried away, Teresa did not see him until the end of August—in a meeting still briefer, and this time not even in private.

He had gone to Madrid at the Nuncio's orders. The Nuncio had been spurred to a decision after a face-to-face clash with Tostado. In his first open display of the authority he still claimed, despite the obvious wishes of the new Pope, he instructed Gracián to call a Discalced Chapter in Almodóvar—a Chapter which should boldly counter that held by the Calced in Morajales at which he had once more been proclaimed a rebel, apostate, and excommunicated.

In this the Nuncio clearly had the King's backing; and Tostado, unsure of his ground, withdrew to Portugal to await further directions from Rome. He left on the day that Gracián passed through Toledo on his way to Almodóvar. The meeting was so short and so thoroughly chaperoned that all Teresa had wanted to say went into a pair of letters that reached Gracián in Almodóvar before the chapter opened. As we know from their identical dating, she had folded one of them inside the other, one to be read aloud and the other for his eyes only. However, both could have gone astray, so the inner letter concerned their mutual friends, Angela, Paul—and *Joseph*. Even Jesus needed a pseudonym.

An old friend of Angela's, the Rector of Cuenca (Gaspar de Salazar), had been in Toledo and persuaded the King's confessor, Yepes, to be her confessor; but Yepes "hardly ever" turned up, and though Angela dislikes changing confessors, Joseph advised it, and, as Paul knows, Joseph is "a very important person" whose advice Angela respects. The Rector agreed that Joseph was right, and sent her a great *letrado* in Yepes' place, Dr. Velázquez, who said that he had rather confess her once a week than be made Archbishop—"not that he'd want to be an Archbishop, he's too good."

Now that Angela has changed confessors rather than "vex Joseph," she says that it is the first time any other confessor has eased her soul since she first met Paul, so she hopes that Paul will be glad for her, as she has suffered from losing him as a confessor. She also hopes that Paul will tell her that she may obey Dr. Velázquez's orders if they came from him, for while "this woman can't do great things," her desire to serve God is overwhelming.

Under the circumstances, Gracián might well have felt it inadvisable for Teresa to exchange the King's confessor for another. Luckily, he had much else on his mind and gave it little thought, for "Joseph's" advice was sound. Velázquez saw her without telling Yepes, and though Yepes continued to see her "hardly ever," he was delighted to write a reverent and wonder-laden life of La Santa, once it turned out to be to his advantage and the King's.

The other letter of this pair was the first of many that Teresa wrote in a futile attempt to make that Discalced Chapter deal with the most immediate and pressing issues. A Mendoza who was a canon of the Toledo Cathedral had friends on the Royal Council, and she learned from him that the Nuncio's hands were politically tied. Since he could not even licence a monastery for the Discalced in Madrid without great personal inconvenience, Teresa says, the Chapter must see how important it is for them to send their own representatives to Rome—and meanwhile get in closer touch with the right people at Court: "the Duke and others."

Perhaps the men who ignored this practical and often-repeated advice saw it, correctly, as locking the stable after the horse was stolen. Perhaps they did not give it even that much thought, for as the records of that useless Chapter show, their minds were exclusively on higher things.

IV

The Chapter spent much time on a discussion of whether contemplatives should also be preachers. Juan de la Cruz, who urged the undistracted contemplative life, was finally overruled. Then Roca (in religion, Juan de Jesús) urged more stringent asceticism. As Prior of La Roda he had become a passionate *aficionado* of La Cardona, but he insisted that the Mother Foundress herself had intended them to go barefoot, and he drew up a proposed rule, with heavy stress on fasting and physical penance. Mariano forwarded this to Teresa, who wrote back that it gave her a headache even to read it. As for going barefoot, nothing looked sillier than a barefoot friar on horseback. "There is too much of this going barefoot already!"

Except for this outburst, Teresa forced herself to be tentative, humble; a woman must not presume to teach men. But it was hard sledding. She could persuade nobody to put first things first, hurry to let Rome hear their side of the story, and move their General to forgiveness. Gracián was the most baffling of them all, for though he headed that Chapter, and time was of the essence, he chiefly gave belated, ludicrously irrelevant thought to Malagón. Brianda, he wrote to Teresa, should be replaced with a nun he had found for the purpose. Teresa protested this unknown, saying that she herself had thought of sending her cousin Ana from Salamanca, as over-strict as Brianda was overlenient, until she realized that it would only result in Ana's becoming self-important, and also leave the General still more displeased with them, since he had forbidden them to move nuns from one convent to another.

To this, Gracián replied that Teresa should go herself. That was too much. Her pen runs away. Didn't he know that she refused to go when Brianda was too ill to say a word, and simply told them to have Brianda appoint her best nun to act for her until she recovered? She had even told Antonio Ruiz that he, not she, should see to their moving day—if it ever came. "I was shocked at your leaving the business on my hands. . . .For one thing I am not well enough myself to care for sick nuns or charitable enough to deal with the convent—the work, I mean. . . .I have an odd nature; when I see that you don't care whether I want to be here or not—not even enough to give me direct orders—it gives me the greatest freedom and satisfaction to speak my mind and express my own wishes—just from knowing that my opinions mean nothing to you."

She catches herself up, tries to change her tone with talk about a visit from his mother, about his little sister, Isabelita, who replaced Teresica as the convent pet when Teresica went to Avila; but soon she was hammering again on the central issue. "I implore you to hurry on the Roman business. Don't wait for next summer, the weather is good now. And do believe that it is the right thing to do!" Before he received that letter, Gracián's attention had wandered from Malagón and did not come back to it for another eight months. She need not have written about it; and, like her other letters, it accomplished nothing else.

V

Oddly enough, it was only Roca who gave the main issues any thought—Roca, obsessed with the sins of the flesh and producing the rules that it gave Teresa a headache to read. Roca, like the Calced, overestimated Teresa's influence on Gracián; and as Gracián had read none of her letters aloud, Roca believed that she did not know the facts. So once back in La Roda, he wrote her a letter.

They had, he told her, frittered away two weeks on arguments about contemplation and preaching, and given so little attention to their need for greater austerity that a former Jerónomite had left both the Chapter and the Order in disgust. Worse still, nothing whatever was done about sending friars to Rome to deny the lies being told by the Calced. His own protests went unheard; Teresa must make herself grasp the importance of its being done immediately and urge it on Gracián. If Teresa laughed when she read that letter, she laughed at herself. About the Jerónomite, she could be casual: she's heard that "he suffers from melancholy" . . .which might have got worse on our diet"; so, "please God he'll go back to his own Order and his leaving won't hurt ours." But for the rest nothing would serve but bare, tragic honesty.

"Don't you realize that I can do next to nothing about the matter of going to Rome? I have begged for it days on end, and I have not been able to get a single letter written to the one whom there is so much reason to write, since all we are we owe to him. And nothing will come of it by way of our Father Visitor, for however much I urge him, there are so many to urge him differently that I count for very little. I am deeply grieved that I can do no more. I believed they still meant to make that journey; they told me so. May God bring it about, and you, Your Reverence, keep urging it on them. You can do more than I can."

Mary, pity women! Teresa had not only been thinking of Malagón when she told Gracián that she knew her opinions mattered nothing to him. Even Roca, whose proposed rules "gave her a headache," could be more convincing, simply as a man. Still, she clung to her belief that Gracián's sole faults, a certain timidity and overcredulity, were the tragic side-effect of his gentle, trustful nature. What he did wrong, he did only because he was ill advised. Yes, too trustful. And perhaps not only of men. . . .Teresa worried. Women can be deceivers, too. Could Gracián, so pure and holy—yes, and gullible—really direct those convents from which she was now cut off? Seville, for instance. So much could go wrong in Seville. . . .

San José was not honest. She had twice accepted Teresa's glad congratulations on having paid off the *alcabala* with Lorenzo's money, and only God knew what she had actually used it for. She remained equally indifferent to debts she had incurred at usurious interest rates and to her interest-free loans from Antonio Ruiz—money he really could not spare—and from Lorenzo, now spending far beyond his means.

Teresa also worried because San Francisco had let her know that San José was drinking sarsaparilla—that aphrodisiac from the Indies. Her repeated warnings against it were futile: "I must warn you again not to drink sarsaparilla. . . .I don't care if people do say it is good for the womb."

But, for Gracián's safety, it was necessary that he and San José be on the best of terms. . . .

Teresa prayed about it. She pushed away her task of making a *sabrosa cosa*, "a savory thing," of *Fundaciones'* final chapters. She wrote a little book.

Chapter 51 ❀ Teresa's New Book, *The Visitation of Convents*; Letters She Wrote During a Year in Toledo

I

The Visitation of Convents — so sane, so practical, and to pious eyes the least inspired of all Teresa's writings — is the only book for which she ever claimed divine inspiration. She sent it to Gracián, with a double-columned paper of questions and answers: Laurentia's answers to questions supposedly raised by Eliseo. (Until recently, some of these selected answers, copied out of context, were presented as a letter to Gracián with intent to prove that she wrote the book at his orders, like a proper nun.) The little book, though written for Gracián's guidance, was one which she hoped, in time, would guide others. The paper of questions and answers concerned a problem which she did not care to hand down to posterity. She begins it with generalizations. Laurentia cannot agree with Eliseo that all unendowed nuns should be rejected, though she does believe that sometimes a lawsuit over a dowry promised and then withheld is justified. However, a certain large dowry now being offered is insufficient reason for accepting the girl who will bring it.

Gracián understood what she was talking about. The Jesuit, Olea, encouraged by Teresa's troubles, was attempting to rid himself of a girl for whom he claimed "to care no more than for any he might pass in the street." (Teresa's own bitter, twice-repeated quote after Olea decided to shift his pressure from the Segovia convent to Seville, as the more vulnerable.) At this time, Olea, wanting to avoid the trouble of a trip to Andalusia, had increased his offered dowry to Segovia.

"Eliseo" wanted to accept. "Laurentia" protests. Segovia, she says, needs the money, and so do many other convents "in which they have more holiness than clothes on their backs . . . ," but if dowries are made a main concern, "things will go from bad to worse." And if Laurentia took any confessor at his word and believed "that any girl who confessed to them a couple of times was thereby sanctified forever," it could do great harm. "Good hopes are better than evil possessions."

Laurentia has already done more than she should by permitting this girl a trial novitiate and then asking Segovia to extend the novitiate a little longer. If Laurentia goes to Salamanca, she will look into the matter further. (She was under Fernández's orders to be in Salamanca, you remember, or if that could still be allowed, in Avila.) But having said so much, Teresa recalls her unending need to be disarming.

"But how I'm trying to justify myself! The worst of it is that I find the man I'm talking about [Olea] so extremely vexing." And Eliseo will find all his other questions answered in the little book she has sent him: "It seems to have been given me by God." She would be glad of the General's orders which keep her

256

from attending to such trying matters directly "if [she] weren't afraid that [prioresses] would manage to fool [Eliseo] even worse than they do [her]."

God had given Teresa extremely practical advice. Let me boil it down to the essentials, and you will see what I mean.

II

A Visitor must be above all an authority figure: "Nothing can be worse for the nuns than to think they can treat him like an equal." They must see him as "a merciful, loving father," but a father whose word is law. At a first visit he can correct faults gently, but not if he finds them unchanged a year later: disregard for the Constitutions can become second nature, taken for granted. And sometimes even a saintly prioress must be replaced, for not all saints know how to govern.

Finances must be scrutinized: nuns must share what they earn by spinning and plain sewing—no waste must be allowed, nor may patronesses be wooed with expensive presents. Where there is poverty, the Visitor must see to it that those who are well sacrifice for the needs of the sick. Above all, no house should be too large or costly to maintain. If the Visitor insists on all this, even a poor convent can get on well enough.

A Visitor must inspect the whole house, including the parts normally kept enclosed: there must be no corners that invite occasions of sin; all must be open, all separated from visitors by proper grilles. He must also make sure that those who come to hear confessions keep them brief and to the point. However, when the Visitor interviews the nuns separately, he must realize that some will exaggerate their temptations and opportunities to sin, and with such "melancholy" nuns he must show himself firmly on the prioress's side.

He must also balance his careful watch for favoritism with a recognition of the fact that we all enjoy helping some more than others and get more pleasure from their company: this is not sin, just a fact of human life.

His instructions must be kept simple and based on the Constitutions. "Improvements will only be confusing." With one exception: whenever possible, nuns should be permitted a secret ballot on whether any novice should be professed; it is the only way to make sure that she will fit in harmoniously. Also, the number of novices must be kept below the permitted maximum so that there will always be room for another if an unusually promising girl shows up; and prioresses must not be allowed to take as many lay-sisters as they are beginning to feel that they need.

When the Visitor finds a prioress too strict, demanding fasts, penances, and hours of work that can injure her daughters' health, he must—in her hearing—instruct some nun to write him, under obedience, if this is not changed. This will make him, in effect, always present. And in convents where the prioress seems too lax, he should make a little speech to assure the nuns that they are not disloyal in reporting her faults to him. But in this case, he must take care not to seem on such good terms with the prioress that the nuns are afraid to speak up; and while he must never act on accusations brought by only one or two, he must also remember that the nuns have only one chance to say their say, while the prioress has all the time she wants to explain their statements away and justify herself.

Indeed, she, Teresa, has often been taken in like this until she has spent weeks in a convent—and discovered that the nuns were right. So, the Visitor, who lacks such opportunities, must take all a prioress says with a grain of salt. This is so even though few would deliberately try to deceive him. "It frightens me to see how sly the devil is, and how he makes every one of us think she is the most honest soul on earth. . . .So, may the Lord always send us a cautious and holy Visitor. . . .His Majesty will give him light so that he may understand us women and lead us to greater perfection."

Every point is well and fully argued, but I have given you the gist of them all. Teresa believed that Gracián was the friar by far the most fit to be Visitor to the Discalced; but she had been forced to realize that he was not a good judge of character. To advise him in his dealings with men was obviously futile; where women were concerned, it might not be hopeless. If only because she loved him and believed without question in his love of God, she had to try.

III

The eighty-nine letters still saved from the year that Teresa managed to stay on in Toledo prove chiefly that she could have been extremely useful to the Discalced if anyone had listened to her.

They also prove that politics, like necessity, knows no law. While the Chapter in Almodóvar was still in session, Doria offered the Seville convent a novice and Garcia Alvarez offered two. She refused them when she found that Doria's offering was only too like Olea's and that, of García Alvarez's cousins, one was "melancholy" and the other said to be quite mad. But before the year was over, Teresa was saying that she had never positively refused Doria's girl, and that García Alvarez's cousins were probably good enough. Her reasons for that change of mind were not financial.

This is not to say that María de San José's finances were sound. By October, Teresa congratulated her prematurely for the third time running on the payment of the *alcabala*, and made the first of what would become her unending requests that some part of Lorenzo's loan be repaid. The estate he had bought for fourteen thousand ducats, La Serna, gave Lorenzo status—and it cost far more than he could afford.

But money was the least of that year's problems. At the end of Angel de Salazar's term the Calced elected the one Provincial who could be counted on to oppose Teresa and all her works still more hotly: El Magdaleno, Juan Gutiérrez, had hated her since she first founded in Toledo with Martín's help. Tostado, working through El Magdaleno, was continually strengthening his support in the Court circles where Teresa had urged Gracián to strengthen his own.

258

The Calced, playing for time, were waiting for Tostado to act as their executioner. Their hopes were heightened by events in other Orders plagued by reform. In Córdoba, for example, Franciscans in revolt against Peter of Alcántara's movement had gone into armed battle and literally demolished the largest and most thriving Alcantarine monastery in Spain. (Yes, Franciscans with drawn swords! Sixteenth-century Spain provided many oddities which religious Orders prefer to forget.)

Valdemoro, the Prior of Avila, having managed a brief removal of John of the Cross from Avila, was bitter when Teresa persuaded the Visitor Fernández to bring him back. In consequence, he began to cultivate Mariano's friendship — with devious intent. He would have preferred Heredia, equally jealous of Gracián's ascendance, if Heredia had not been too clever to turn traitor before the time was ripe. He encouraged Mariano in his project of a Discalced monastery in Madrid, and Gracián joined Mariano there, both ignoring all that Teresa had written them about their need to have the Nuncio on their side. Mariano brought a flock of friars with him, and a friend offered them temporary lodging, but he proudly refused it, demanding that they be given their own house at once.

Teresa wrote to him in near despair: "Oh, Jesus, what things Thou dost consent to! I very much want to see that little house taken. The other can be founded if God wants it to be . . .though you shouldn't want to see it granted from people who love us so little. I have told you that a single letter to the Nuncio will settle it all. Let us hurry, Father, and if you can, talk to him about the separate Province. You can lose nothing by doing this."

It was useless. The Nuncio was ignored, and the need for a separate Province was forgotten. Gracián returned to Seville with nothing accomplished. But the Chapter had given him a false sense of security, and to Teresa's terror he took up making visits to the Casa Grande and dining there.

Moreover, new danger threatened from the Inquisition. Isabel de San Jerónimo was seized with a fresh wave of visions and revelations, and Beatriz Chávez — now professed as Beatriz de Jesús — had become her competitor. San Jerónimo had been cleared by the Inquisition as deranged; Beatriz could be another matter. Teresa sent warnings to both San José and Gracián to say nothing about it to Rodrigo Alvarez. Why, I don't know, nor why she felt that they might safely confide in another Jesuit, Father Acosta: her fear of the one and her confidence in the other were equally misplaced. But her judgment was better in urging both Gracián and San José to ingratiate themselves with the Company by asking them to hear their confessions, "And think up a lot of questions for them to answer. They like that."

But that late October brought worse dangers: dangers to which Teresa's friars were strangely blind, and she most uncomfortably farsighted.

IV

Once he had made the right friends, Tostado had not done badly in Spain until he had a bad clash with the Nuncio. The King had liked his notion that the pack be shuffled and Discalced monks be placed in Calced monasteries to teach virtue by example. It was old Ormaneto who had seen that it was a plan to divide and conquer. Tostado withdrew for a time to Portugal. There he looked for allies among the royal family—and managed to win the confidence of poor, well-meaning Don Teutonio de Braganza.

Don Teutonio had much to tell him about the injustice Teresa had met in Salamanca, and the city's need for reform. It was true, of course, that university towns were the ideal base for prostitutes, but Don Teutonio's disproportionate distress over this fact of life combined with his glowing report of the chastity of all Discalced friars—as inspired by their Foundress—suggested to Tostado a tidy side-play, a flank attack. As Tostado had observed before he left Spain that Mariano combined a distaste for women with a notable lack of political acumen, Don Teutonio could doubtless be encouraged to sell him, in all innocence, an idea delightfully sure to make trouble. Roca, from what he had heard, would embrace it with ardor; with luck it could even draw in Gracián. As he put it to Don Teutonio, it is useless to preach chastity to hot-blooded young men; but a Discalced mission to the whores of Salamanca could do vast good, indirectly, to those young men. The ideal base for such a mission would be the Hospital of St. Lazarus, which specialized in the pox. From such a base they would quickly find the whores most easily converted—frightened women, near death as wages of their sins. These in gratitude would lead still others to hear the Discalced and find salvation. And Don Teutonio should describe this holy plan to Roca and Mariano and help with the necessary arrangements.

But, Tostado warned, he should do it without mentioning him; for though he had come to Spain as a peacemaker, ardently desiring reform among the Calced through the aid of the Discalced, the Nuncio Ormaneto had so poisoned minds against him that they saw him as the enemy, not their friend.

Incredible though it seems that any men, however detached from reality, should have bought it, Mariano, Gracián and Roca all did. Teresa first learned of it in a letter from Mariano, who urged as a preliminary measure that the Salamancan Jesuits' attitude towards the Discalced be improved by Teresa's accepting Olea's girl as a nun—if not in Segovia, then in Seville. Roca, the letter went on, had fallen ill. To his grave disappointment he would be unable to begin this noble work; but with Gracián's help a worthy substitute for Roca could be found—once Gracián had overseen the beginning of the blessed enterprise.

Roca's illness and his disappointment, I am sure, were genuine. Whether Mariano was fooled, or consciously out to get Gracián, is anyone's guess. His letter reached Teresa on October twenty-first, and she sent him an immediate answer as long as any chapter in *Fundaciones*. She begins with an attempt to shake his self-confidence: whatever he says, Seville cannot accept Olea's girl. Segovia had found her impossible, though they needed her dowry, and had been persuaded to extend her trial novitiate. As with Gracián she repeats, "If I go to Salamanca I will look into the whole thing." And Mariano's saying that he could sum the girl up at a glance if he went to Salamanca only makes her laugh: "We women aren't so easily understood!" As for Doria's girl, "Don't say any more about it, for the love of God!"

Mariano's behavior in Madrid also makes her laugh—bringing a crowd of friars there and preparing a church just as if he had a right to do it! "You didn't even get the Bishop's permission, and you know what it cost us in Seville when I hadn't done that." Mariano must calm down, approach their friends at Court, see the Nuncio—and learn whom to distrust. Can't he see that Valdemoro is no friend? And "God keep the old Nuncio alive, for Tostado is only waiting for him to die!"

Then, having done what she can to prepare his mind, she gets down to the real issue: a group of Discalced in the hospital of St. Lazarus. By God's mercy Roca's illness had delayed this madness, and she had to prevent it if she could, by spelling it out as bluntly as possible. She is personally acquainted with the new Bishop of Salamanca, Soto, an Inquisitioner. She can assure Mariano that he would be wholly alienated by friars who engaged in work that should only be handled by nuns, if indeed it should be handled by any religious at all. Women, at least, would not have their work seen as confirmation of the tales spread by the Calced about Discalced hypocrisy and lechery.

"I tell you that whatever we hope to gain from it will result in our being almost certainly lost: and it does nothing for the authority of our Order to act as [the Calced's] puppets, for that is exactly what [Tostado] wants. It is not work for people who should show themselves as hermits, contemplatives, however carefully they are scrutinized—not as the sort of men who would go off to be associated with women like that; for even if one of them actually was snatched from her evil way of life, I cannot believe that it would look good for us."

At the end, she tries to tone it down, to sound tentative enough to prevent Mariano's falling into a stubborn rage. She suggests that he read her letter over and discuss it with friends. He should also consider the unlikelihood that he can get a licence. "Quite apart from the Bishop, I have very small confidence in Don Teutonio as a good negotiator. Great goodwill, yes; capability, little." But, on the other hand, they do need a Discalced monastery that will provide their Salamancan nuns with confessors. "I've been waiting to get to Salamanca myself and boil things up. I'm a great hand at bargaining. Think not? Tell that to my friend Valdemoro!" (Who would know better, after failing to rid himself of Juan de la Cruz?)

Teresa forwarded Mariano's letter to Gracián; her own restates the same objections. She also repeats once more her weary wish that Gracián would rid himself of authority over the Calced and reminds him that since he has not had the Nuncio's *motu* confirming his Visitorship read out in the Casa Grande, its friars do not even know that they have any right to obey him, their own desires aside.

With both men, Teresa might as well have saved her ink and paper. The enterprise as spelled out to Mariano is deleted from all editions of Teresa's letters until 1963; but Gracián writes at length in his *Peregrinaciones* of the work done by the Discalced to save the "fallen women" (*sic*) of Salamanca. The repercussions which Teresa had foreseen, he mentions only as part of an ever-continued campaign of sexual scandal from which he so unjustly suffered.

Yet Teresa could only see Gracián as Mariano's victim, innocently misled. She can warn him, but her tone remains tender, protective. It was her misfortune to love Gracián; and I ask anyone who doubts that such love is blind to visit a juvenile court and hear a mother explain how her boy got into trouble only because he never saw through the delinquents who pretended to be his friends.

But, for a time at least, Salamanca was forgotten. Gracián began to have trouble enough in Seville.

Chapter 52 ❀ Teresa's Fears for Gracián

I

Only the bare bones of the situation can now be recovered. In part, this is because Teresa's unending danger from the Inquisition was admitted and documented only in the past decade. In part, it is because Elías de San Martín was the first General elected by the Discalced Carmelites when, after Teresa's death, they became not only a separate province, but an independent Order. Fray Elías, with Heredia, Doria, and Mariano, made up the gang of four who expelled Gracián from the new Order; and hagiographers find it so distasteful that the first General of Teresa's Order was the first to turn traitor to the man for whom she had such holy love that even her most scholarly biography to date mentions him only in a footnote.

Three *beatas*, friends of María Corro, had a revelation which they were advised to report to Elías de San Martín, the likeliest to believe it since Gracián—motivated as many thought by cronyism—had robbed him of his priorate and replaced him with Heredia. As they reported it to Fray Elías, Christ had told them how Teresa fooled the Inquisition into disbelieving María Corro, when shock at the evil she found in that unholy convent caused her to flee and drove poor Doña Ventura mad. They also had Christ's word that nothing had been changed by Teresa's absence, except that Gracián had transferred his lusts to María de San José.

Fray Elías, acting in haste on the belief that what was bad for Gracián was good for him, went to the Casa Grande and reported as fact what had been told to him as revelation. Almost at once Heredia realized that questions about his source of information could be dangerous. The truth would show itself as an instance of the Discalced's encouragement of women given to visions and revelations—*alumbradas*. Heredia took action. God, he explained, had let the shock of hearing such tales addle Fray Elías's wits. Indeed, it had left him ill in both body and mind, and while he had now begun to recover it was the general belief at Los Remedios that he had better convalesce quietly in Granada.

Gracián made a flying trip to Madrid to set the rumors at rest with the King, the Nuncio, and the Grand Inquisitor. He was back in Seville before Teresa learned the whole story from Fray Alonso, a friar who served as messenger for Gracián and San José. Their two letters were folded together, for Gracián had decided that, for the time being, he and Teresa should not be widely known to correspond. Letters to and from her prioress would excite less interest.

It was probably San José's letter that disturbed Teresa most. As one might have expected, the excitement had set Isabel de San Jerónimo off with a fresh spate of supernatural experience; but that would be discounted by the Inquisition. However, Beatriz had joined the act, and Gracián thought he "understood her soul." Apparently, he saw her "experiences" as a reward of that humble piety which she showed by embracing his knees and kissing his feet. But, as San José knew, Beatriz was jealous, and could turn dangerous.

Worse still, Gracián had been frightened into a sorry repeat performance; he was now demanding a general confession from San José, as he had from Teresa — since surely no lover would force a general confession from his mistress; and similarly, San José was repeating herself by an attempted withdrawal. She no longer wanted Gracián to take his meals at the convent.

Teresa's covering letter to San José would have to be read aloud to the nuns. Hence one comment on the situation has to be carefully casual: The convent should pray for Brianda's health, since her great sins make her own prayers count for little. She envies San José the general confession she is making to Gracián, so easy, surely, compared with her own, since San José "has so much less to confess."

But, on the other point, she is reduced to begging. She "worries terribly" about Gracián's eating at the Casa Grande; and — as if for the first time — she reiterates the promises made months before. His food, and even the price of the water he drinks, will be paid for with money that she herself borrows — and if she only could, she would manage to give even more than that as the price of this kindness.

The letter to Gracián is singular. For the first time she must warn him — somehow, somehow — against his willingness to "understand souls," against his own spirituality. She works up to it slowly: "I was horrified by the things that Fray Alonso tells me they were saying about you. God help me, how necessary it was for you to make that trip! I don't see how they can make such false accusations. God give them light. . . ."

She points out the folly of Heredia's advice that they try to placate the Casa Grande by removing Juan Evangelista, the one friar there who does not hate the Discalced, since no substitute would satisfy them but a prior who could see no fault in them, "which isn't surprising." "The surprising thing is that Paul can talk with Joseph so peacefully." But on this point, Gracián must give Paul some advice: Paul should be content with prayer as it comes and not seek holy "favors."

"The truth of it is that in spiritual matters the most trustworthy and acceptable prayer is simply that which leaves us with good desires." All other prayer brings "pleasures which only please ourselves." The prayers born of "inner dryness, a troubled spirit, great temptations" are far better, for they give us the strength of real humility. Such prayer, felt in the heart as one goes about his daily business, is true prayer — not that in which "one goes apart, smashes his head over it, and thinks he is praying if he manages to squeeze out a few tears."

If Gracián agrees, he should pass this on to Paul, who would not resent such advice if it came from him, not from her; and she thinks that Paul should hear it and realize that, in the religious life, "nothing matters but our works and good conscience" (the least quoted words of the saint of raptures). As for their other friends, Father Johannes (Gracián overcredulous) can get his friend Eliseo (Gracián again) into trouble. Eliseo must warn Johannes not to believe that Joseph (their mutual Friend) told Clemente (Fray Elías) anything, or that He "told all that . . . to *beatas* . . . Joseph doesn't tell secrets. He is very discreet."

The fact of it is, people are trying to make trouble for Laurentia again. Gracián must keep himself out of it — rest assured that "those three [beatas] will soon be punished" — and, above all, get the Angel's [the Grand Inquisitor's] approval before he tries to help Clemente. As for the convent, he must make Isabel de San Jerónimo eat meat and give up prayer, all prayer, for a while, and consider seriously whether that would not also be best for Beatriz. For the rest, she can say that she is grieved by his intention to go to Granada.

Gracián reacted badly to advice. He suggested that Teresa expand the story of Seville with an account of its chief treasure, the wonderfully devout Beatriz de Jesús. There was only one way it could be handled: set down Beatriz's own story. The other nuns had heard her yarns and would vouch for it that Beatriz herself had told them. Then, if worst came to worst, they would show the Inquisition that the girl was either a liar or mad. She was blessedly unconvincing, like Catalina of the flaming liver. Since Gracián was not thinking well, he would be satisfied if one added enough praise of her piety and reduced her thirty-seven years by referring to her throughout as "the girl." Herewith, in capsule, Beatriz's story, which we already know.

At least it did not take long to write the chapter. The plot was provided. Teresa wrote to Gracián. She has nearly finished *Fundaciones;* he will be set at ease to see what she has done; it is a *sabrosa cosa.* A savory thing. "See how obedient I am! . . . When I'm only ordered in jest to do something, I do it in earnest." (In case he comes to his senses about that final order, she has let him off the hook.) She also takes care to give no more advice, other than to suggest that he "make up something nice" as a message to Heredia from her and not to let him know that she writes him so often. She saves any warnings about his news that he is keeping the long fast from September to Christmas for her covering letter to San José, though it troubles her, as you'll see shortly. She only replies that she is keeping it herself. "It doesn't do me as much harm in a cool climate as it does in other places."

The rest of the letter is about Santelmo (Father Olea) and his girl. He has "terrified" Mariano into urging her to accept the girl in Seville. "And with all this he says that he doesn't care any more for her than he would for any he passes in the street. What a life! And what would he do if he *did?* I'm afraid we would have to take his article."

"This is All Hallows Eve. I took the habit on All Souls Day. Pray God, father, that he will make me a true nun of the Carmen; better late than never. Regards to the Prosecutor [of the Inquisition] and Father Acosta, the Rector. Your true subject and servant—blessed be God I will be that always, come what may."

Her covering letter to San José begins with saying that she knows from Gracián's letter that he is not receiving some of hers. "For the love of God, your Reverence, find out when he gets mine. . . ." (Let his failure to get them seem to be the porteress's fault; to make any open accusations would do no good.) She is glad that San José gets on well with Nicholas (Doria) and that he now hears her confessions. San José must write her how things are going, "and no dodging around, but the truth." Then three apparently disconnected sentences sum up her anxiety: "I must warn you again not to drink sarsaparilla. I have written to García Alvarez and brought him strongly to our father's attention. Write me in detail just how things are and why you don't make our father eat meat for a while."

Actually they all bear on the subject just mentioned: Gracián's decision that for the time being it would be best if San José had Doria take his place as her confessor, a suggestion which came, I suspect, from San José herself. Gracián had managed to discredit the *beatas'* revelations to Fray Elías in Madrid, but they were still remembered in Seville. Similarly, García Alvarez was now confessing Beatriz; her dangerous jealousy of both San José and Teresa was now apparent to San José, at least.

Unfortunately, García Alvarez was credulous; eventually he believed not only Beatriz's stories, but their enrichments as added by her friend Margarita Ramírez. Consequently, Teresa has warned him not to believe all he hears and brought his credulity to Gracián's attention. (This, at the time, she thought to be enough; she was slow to suspect García Alvarez of ill will.)

For the rest, we need only remember that sexual depravity and illuministic heresy were close-coupled in the Inquisition mind. Whether or no San José drank sarsaparilla only for the relief of some menopausal discomfort, she did not drink it in secret—and its aphrodisiac quality was known. And Gracián was fasting—a practice which invited "favors," and of a kind which even Teresa was coming more and more to see as "pleasures which only please ourselves." A visionary Visitor and a Prioress who drank sarsaparilla could well be perceived as confirmation of the three *beatas'* accusations.

Teresa had tried, only once, to describe a better and worthier kind of prayer to Gracián. She could tell him directly to make Isabel de San Jerónimo "give up all prayer and eat meat," and suggest that it would be good for Beatriz, too. But after her vision in Beas and her vow of obedience, she could give no such orders to him. San José, with her keen sense of self-preservation, could handle the situation, give up her sarsaparilla and "make him eat meat for a while." Why didn't she, especially with García Alvarez now confessing Beatriz and ready to believe anything?

Teresa had cause for worry. And bad news travels fast. Within two days she was writing to María Bautista. Things are going splendidly, both in Toledo and Seville. Why should María Bautista have imagined that they weren't? Gracián keeps her in constant touch with all that goes on in Seville, and in Madrid. María Bautista's notions only come from "imagination and a bad humor." For the latter she should try a syrup called King of the Medes. "It has put new life in me." Still, the devil can use such ailments for his own purposes. "So manage to get well, for God's sake. Eat hearty meals and don't think about anything."

María Bautista saved letters, and other prioresses did not. Teresa doubtless wrote to many assuring them that the rumors they heard were nonsense, and all the affairs of the Order were going well. But she knew that a net was closing in on Gracián, and that his enemies were not all among the Calced. Elías de San Martín was not the only friar to be treated warily. Heredia was greedy for power and and far from stupid; and it was becoming increasingly plain that even Mariano was not the headstrong fool he appeared to be. There was trouble ahead, and it was not limited to the real and present dangers in Seville.

Chapter 53 ❄ *New Problems; María de San José; More Letters to Gracián*

I

Valdemoro was devious and persistent. When the General issued an edict that the Carmelites accept friars from no other orders, and Valdemoro's brother, a failed Dominican, had to be expelled from the Carmelite priory, Valdemoro set out from Madrid. Mariano, he was sure, would be delighted to defy Rubeo, accept an ex-Dominican among the Discalced — and thereby compound the reform's difficulties with Rome.

He met disappointment. Mariano, set on procuring his priory in Madrid, had turned unexpectedly cautious, playing both sides of the fence. Valdemoro left for Toledo — to beg Teresa to intercede with Mariano on his brother's behalf. To Teresa's amusement, he put on quite an act. Paul, he said, had persecuted the Christians before he saw the light on the road to Damascus. Just so, God had opened his eyes and changed his heart. What greater proof could he offer than his eagerness to further his own brother's earnest desire to turn Discalced? Surely Teresa would write to Mariano and urge him to accept this humble soul who had fallen so in love with her reform? One letter from her could do so much!

Indeed it would, Teresa knew. It would travel far and end up in the General's hands, one more proof that the Discalced were set on defying his every command. She listened gravely, assured Valdemoro that his words had brought her fresh understanding and gave her word that she would write to Mariano that very day. Gave it, and kept it: she wrote Mariano a stern reminder of the General's orders plus a hope that he would do nothing that he did not truly believe to be in God's service. Then she wrote to Gracián, describing that visit. "Oh, what a great friend to me Valdemoro always remains! God help us all!"

That story is the light touch in a serious letter. When Ormaneto died, Teresa knew, the Pope would appoint a Nuncio who would strip Gracián of his limited authority. Fernández, Visitor to the Castilian Carmelites, was annoyed at her extended leave of absence from her priorate in Salamanca. Gracián, as Visitor to all the Discalced, had said that she might retire to Avila, instead. But Ormaneto's death would bring back Tostado as Vicar-General. He would surely accuse her of a year of illicit wanderings after she had received her General's orders in Seville; for that, he could well see house-arrest as insufficient punishment and expel her from her own order. And this, not Valdemoro's nonsense, was what had to be said in a letter only too likely to go astray.

And she sums it up: "Mathusalah" is in precarious health. In consequence, Gracián must decide whether to send Laurentia to Salamanca or send Angela to Avila. Joseph himself told Angela that Paul stood to lose much if Gracián did not make his decision promptly.

II

The letter was one that Gracián chose to ignore. He had come to realize that Teresa was most useful in Toledo, the ideal listening-post, but this was not a decision which he cared to publicize with a formal order. Consequently, he gave no orders at all—which made a bad beginning to a month in which Teresa felt pressures mounting from all sides.

In Seville, it was essential to insure San José's loyalty and antagonize as few others as possible. This took a letter full of compromises. She had never positively refused admission to García Alvarez's cousins. And San José can accept Doria's girl "even if she isn't quite right." But in return, San José must not try to get Bernarda Gutiérrez's money away from Pablo Matías—"for reasons I am not free to write about." Seville spelt danger, and Teresa could neither be sure that Gracián would protect himself or that San José would protect him.

Medina was also a problem, as she knew from the letters delivered to her secretly from Baltasar Alvarez. Transferred from Salamanca and censured for overkindness to Discalced nuns, Alvarez now found himself between two fires. His Provincial, Suárez, wanted him to have nothing to do with the Discalced; but Doña Elena de Quiroga insisted that he, such an old friend of the Mother Foundress, be her confessor and approve her own entrance into the Order—

with the stipulation that her fortune be used to found a girl's school under Discalced supervision. This, he knew, Teresa would oppose as hotly, if not as dangerously, as Suárez. On the other hand, Doña Elena was the niece of the Grand Inquisitor, who might well resent her rejection. Poor Baltasar felt that he was being given a choice between making Teresa further trouble with the Jesuits or with the Inquisition, and doing himself no good either way.

Malagón, too, was going from bad to worse. Brianda had responded to the suggestion that she appoint an acting prioress while she was ill by choosing Teresa's youngest brother's child, Beatriz de Ahumada—who in religion was one of the five—yes five—nuns called Beatriz de Jesús in Teresa's convents. This appointment had effected exactly one change: as a side diversion (or as Sister Beatriz chose to see it a "mortification") the nuns had taken up slapping and pinching one another.

Teresa felt increasingly frustrated, impotent. When San José wrote Mariano a letter full of Latin quotations and sent a copy of it to Teresa, she let it make her disproportionately angry. There was no level at which Teresa felt any sexual jealousy of San José; her utter faith in Gracián's purity was equalled by her faith in San José's cold heart. Teresa envied San José's position in Seville, where she felt herself to be most needed; she envied her strong body, just approaching middle-age, her handsome, unfaded face, but only as a house-bound, aging mother might envy a vigorous, fortunate, and basically uncongenial daughter, nothing more. She also tried to deny that envy, knowing it for a sin. Moreover, Teresa was not petty. It is sad and absurd that San José's Latin should have unlocked, as it did, her own bitter sense of inadequacy and all that pent up anger that it bred. Teresa stared at those Latin phrases and wholly forgot the grave importance of handling San José with care. She seized her pen:

Her daughters should not parade their education. She would have expected Gracián to teach San José more humility; he was "good at that!" Just the other day she had made what was, in effect, a general confession to Dr. Velázquez, and it had not "cost a twentieth part of the pain" it cost to confess the same sins to Gracián, and San José should tell him so! Back in Seville, a confessor like Dr. Velázquez could have given her more comfort than God saw fit. "And when I saw what trouble our father was in and you could have said something to me if you had wanted to—for you can always amuse me—you didn't want to. I am glad that you understand my affection for him now. As for the other one in Caravaca [Ana de San Alberto, San José's angry supporter] she grieves over it, too. This very day she sent me a serge habit. . . mine was full of holes."

She has caught herself up, sweeping bitterness back where it belongs, under the rug. But in so doing, she has also let us know that María Bautista was not the only Prioress who doubted the quality of Teresa's "affection" for Gracián. We can only wonder whether the more recent slanderings of San José had persuaded her, and San Alberto, "too," to change their tune and defend Gracián as a means of self-defense.

As that year edged towards winter, Teresa had only one source of unforced pleasure. From her many messages to children in her letters we know that she loved them, not sentimentally and *en masse*, but as individuals. She would have been a good mother, and Gracián's little sister, Isabelita, was loveable. Teresa gave her a "hermitage" of her own — in effect a private play-corner where she happily spent hours at making new arrangements of the little crèche Teresa bought her — Holy Family, angels, shepherds, the Three Kings.

The child had a thin-lipped little mouth, and Teresa tried to teach her to smile in a way that would do her justice: but lips closed or parted, nothing worked. "She says it's her mouth's fault, not hers," Teresa wrote, "and she's quite right." She also had a loud, harsh laugh, and was "always laughing," but Teresa delighted in her and often quoted her — as when she bit into a sliver of Seville melon chilled in a wintry well and said, "Oh, it's so cold it makes my throat deaf!"

The affection was mutual. Teresa now often broke her own rule and stayed in her cell at recreation time, writing her endless letters, but when she did not, Isabelita was delighted; and she wrote a poem:

> When Mother Foundress joins
> Our recreation joys
> We start to dance and sing
> And make a noise.

I think I am the first to translate this unconscious tribute to Teresa's capacity for keeping her troubles to herself. It was hard, in that November, and it would be harder.

Angela's advice to Paul only made Paul feel rather unappreciated and see Angela's spirituality as somewhat on the wane. In fact, Gracián showed himself incapable of learning from experience. Incredible as it seems in the light of his narrow escape from the three *beatas* who had set themselves to outdo María Corro, he had begun to receive inspiration from and give guidance to a lady known to be on such intimate terms with Joseph as to excite the interest of the Angels. It was unthinkable folly at a time when women who boasted of "favors" from Christ were promptly suspected of bestowing favors of an earthier variety on their confessors; and Seville was already only too well prepared to believe Gracián receptive to favors of both kinds. Teresa would always confuse Gracián's sentimentality with angelic innocence, but she saw such innocence as a danger in itself, since it bred incautious trust in all who claimed supernatural experience.

The news left her desperate. She wasted no time on further messages to

Paul, but found a messenger who could be trusted to put a letter into Gracián's own hand and warned him bluntly: "Drop that woman if you do not want to suffer the fate of Santa Marina." Santa Marina — now dropped from the calendar — so fell in love with holy chastity that she disguised herself as a boy and, like La Cardona, became a friar. As such, she was accused of begetting a village bastard and suffered from this false witness until she died and the friars appointed to wash her body and prepare it for burial found that the charge had been a physical impossibility.

Gracián had not needed Teresa's letter. It reached him at a time when there was already so much talk about his taste for *alumbradas* that he had decided to get out of town, briefly at least, and with an excuse that would be widely approved. Tostado's idea of sending Discalced reformers to Calced foundations could now be put to good use, as even the Calced admitted that one of their convents needed reforming. The convent that Teresa emptied in Pastrana had been refilled with Calced nuns. Their bad name may have been no more than a side-effect of the fact that the Princess of Eboli was now living openly with her late husband's secretary, Pérez, in Madrid, but it was enough; it served.

One of the nuns Gracián took from Seville for this noble purpose was poor, mad San Jerónimo; I expect he thought he was killing two birds with one stone. The other was San Francisco, on whose letters Teresa had depended to get the whole truth from Seville. Teresa allowed herself no comment on their choice beyond saying that she envied them their chance to do good as she, in her enforced inactivity, no longer could. Gracián dropped them off to accomplish their reform, sent Teresa a note to tell her how much they had been needed, and went on to visit the Marquis and Marchioness of Villena.

Teresa wrote to him there: he must be glad "to get out of all that *hubbub* in Seville," though Angela wants him to tell Paul that it doesn't sound as bad as the trouble they had with the Angels. She herself hopes that Gracián, at least, learned something from it. "Now you see what a cause for grief the 'spiritual' people are in those parts." She was also glad that he went so quickly to visit the Marquis and Marchioness; a longer stay in Pastrana could have evoked yet further slanders.

"What were the grounds of that indecent story [from Pastrana] about the virgin nun who had the baby? It strikes me as the utmost foolishness to bring up a thing like that! But nothing even approaches the thing you wrote me about the other time. Do you think it was a small mercy of God that you carried off these things the way you did? I tell you, you'll go on paying for those services you did down there. That woman won't be the only one."

Still, Teresa could only feel the anger of a loving mother. She is scolding the son let into folly by his sweet, trustful nature, his innocence.

V

Someone told Mariano that the President of the Royal Council had issued an edict barring Tostado from Spain. He believed it, and passed on the news to Teresa as fact. Almost simultaneously, Catalina de Tolosa, a wealthy widow whom she had known and liked in Valladolid, wrote that she was returning to Burgos and wanted Teresa to found a convent there. Teresa wrote to Gracián. It was perfect, she said: a house and garden in Old Castile, the northern "kingdom" where alms would be assured plus an estate which would give six hundred a year in interest or thousands to spend on needier convents at once. Better still, the Jesuit rector there is Father Ripalda, who has become her "great friend." Juan de Avila and Antonio Gaitán will take the nuns there as soon as Gracián gives the word. But he must do it quickly, for when the Nuncio dies he may lose his Visitorship and the authority to permit a new foundation.

Gracián preferred to do nothing. The Bishop of Caragena was still denying the Caragena nuns permission to have Mass said in their convent, and the Bishop of Burgos was reputed to be a cut from the same bolt. Nor was María Bautista pleased by that offer. The Valladolid Jesuits had hoped for a tidy slice of Catalina de Tolosa's husband's fortune, and to lose it to the Discalced would only heighten their determination to get what they had expected from the de Padillas before little Casilda refused to stay decently married to her Uncle Pedro and ran off with her money to be a nun.

Casilda's annulment had finally come from Rome. She could now be professed on the day she came of age, and the Jesuits, strongly backed by Uncle Pedro, were making a last-ditch stand to get their just due. Casilda's profession would mean their legal defeat; the money would go to María Mendoza's convent, where it couldn't be needed less!

Brianda, as a Mendoza cousin, knew all about it. Teresa could write about it to her, and did—in the sole letter which has been saved, or rather, saved in part, out of all those she wrote to the prioress with whom she "loved to talk." It was a Christmas letter. It went with a hundred ducats scraped up somewhere in the hope that Brianda would not have to take another novice into that problem convent. (On this point, a long passage is blacked out.) There are Christmas greetings, warnings that Brianda should stay abed in such cold weather, another gap, and then: "A great hubbub is going on over making Casilda give it up. My confessor Dr. Velázquez says they can't make her give it up against her will. I finally left it up to Don Pedro's conscience. They want to give her fifty ducats plus the expense of her taking the veil. Just think, what a hideous expense for him to have to face!... Out of pity for the child and because I would like to have the whole thing dropped, I wrote her not to care if they gave her nothing." Since the rest of the letter concerns Malagón, only a few words are left legible after the opening comment that Beatriz says she is not worried, "which she would say anyhow." One can decipher only, "I never saw anything like what the poor Licentiate said to [long gap] to the other nun ... nightmare, now ...."

Malagón was one kind of trouble, Valladolid another. María Bautista's love of money could make more trouble than any dowry was worth, now that the Jesuits' Provincial, Suárez, was obsessed with hatred for all Discalced nuns,

—not only those of Salamanca, as poor Baltasar Alvarez was painfully discovering. A few similarly censored sentences from Teresa's letter to María Bautista tries to make this plain: "I find it funny that D. Velázquez thinks that Don Pedro will only have to settle it with his own conscience, considering who will tell him how to see it." (His Jesuit confessor.) "What seems so bad about it all to him is the general belief that the Fathers of the Company have such an interest in it and feel, just for the sake of that interest, that Don Pedro should act like this. But it's for that very reason that it concerns my reputation more than yours, now that you are turning the whole thing loose on me. God forgive you — and give you many years."

That was too much; María Bautista must not be antagonized. Teresa quickly goes on to say that she has sent on one of María Bautista's letters to Suárez: the one that said that the girl's mother had wanted her to renounce her whole fortune to the convent "before all this came up." And María Bautista must be careful not to anger the lady, whatever happens.

Next comes a sentence which she would repeat almost word for word in the year she died, though about other Jesuits and their greed for Catalina de Tolosa's money. "I myself don't know what to say about this, for once they have financial interests at stake there is no sanctity left in them, and it gets me into such a state that I want to hate the whole lot of them. I can't think why you chose a Jesuit to handle these negotiations — that is what Casilda wrote me this Mercado is — when you know how they come into it."

But she makes one exception for the whole Valladolid lot: "Prádano" is not like the rest. "I believe that man has great perfection. God give us some of it, — and let them keep their money." "Prádano" — Juan de Prádanos, taken from her so long ago, after he fell ill and was nursed in Yomar's house. De Prádanos, whose confession of compulsive masturbation had led to her sorry bargain with the devil, so long ago.

Since then, Teresa had come a long way. But this is one scrap of the bountiful evidence that she never lost touch with any soul she loved. And after this outburst against the rest of the Company in Valladolid, she asks María Bautista to discount her "disgust" for what it is, emotional and onesided, and instead to write to Báñez for advice; and meanwhile, somehow, to put poor little Casilda's mind at rest. (Báñez had taken a professorship at Salamanca.) The final page of the letter is missing. If it made any further plea to let Casilda's money go, the words were wasted. María Bautista always knew what she wanted.

VI

Teresa, for her part, always wanted to believe that she loved María Bautista. She did have intense family loyalty — and it was an unending burden, for in truth she could love only one surviving member of her family without effort or reservations. Teresa loved Lorenzo as he was, and felt no need to idealize him. Luckily for us, Lorenzo's trusted messenger and servant was illiterate; Teresa could write to Lorenzo as openly as she could have talked with him alone. In consequence, as more than one baffled churchly scholar has learned, most of her letters to him are still under lock and key in Avila; but the few that we have tell us much about her feeling for a man whom she not only loved but understood.

The letters she would soon be writing to him contrast strangely with letters she would soon be writing to Gracián: letters from Teresa who loved her faulty Lorenzo as he was, and from Angela, struggling not to wake from a dream about her Paul.

Chapter 54 ❀ *Teresa and Her Brother Lorenzo*

I

Lorenzo gave little thought to religion until dear, faulty Jerónimo died in Panama and, on reaching Seville, he found his long-loved Teresa so faultless, it seemed, so perfect in a life of penitence, so unlike the Teresa he had left in the Incarnation. Teresa, for her own part, had assumed that she and Lorenzo, so alike in temperament, had found a like faith, though he by an easier path, blessedly uncrippled by "the way of fear."

But in truth, Lorenzo went back to Avila trembling on the verge of a conversion like that she herself had undergone twenty years before: a conversion which Francisco de Salcedo had done his well-meaning best to make a living hell—and de Salcedo, poor soul, was still more capable of such efforts now. The latter had made bad investments, lost money, and seen it as a warning of yet worse to come in eternity. He began to shower Teresa with letters about the sorry state of his soul—and then of his fears for that of his sin-stained friend, Lorenzo.

Teresa wrote letters intended to humor him as well as to comfort him; she knew that anything else would only exacerbate his "melancholy." And she did her best to protect Lorenzo from his attentions. But it was not easy.

He had overspent on La Serna, Lorenzo wrote. He would take Francisco's advice, sell it, and reinvest in city real-estate, and there in Avila, with Francisco's help, he would save his soul. He had taken a vow that he would never sin again in any way, but he was still frightened. At night the devil made him sin in his dreams, by day he had sudden, evil imaginings about women, and worst of all, when he prayed to feel more love for God, the sensations of love that surged through him were far from spiritual. Teresa knew that he would have written so to nobody else. She would have to free him from Francisco de Salcedo, but gently, hurting neither.

Lorenzo must keep La Serna, she began; he hasn't the temperament for collecting rents or forcing victims. Besides, his sons would marry better if their father was owner of this estate.

Will Lorenzo send on all her papers? The Nuncio wants a full list of her nuns, perhaps because he's begun to think about the separate province, but far likelier only because he wants to see how many can be sent to Calced convents, like those two now in Pastrana. And she wants her old seal with the IHS; she hates sealing letters with this death's head.

Which reminds her: he must never read any of the letters she sends to Francisco de Salcedo, and if Francisco tries to talk religion, Lorenzo should change the subject; the poor soul has gone melancholy. Lorenzo would do better to read the passage on *Thy Kingdom come* in her *Camino*.

As for that vow he took, whatever possessed him? We all sin sometimes, but a broken vow is a serious matter. Luckily, it's a jubilee year, with dispensations going cheap; he must get himself released from it at once! Love to all, and "tell Teresica there's no danger I'll ever love any girl the way I do her!"

She had tried to be casual, and saw that she had overdone it. It could not end there; Lorenzo needed more, and she wrote on: It is good to want to love God, but not to pray for it; God knows when our power to love should be given and when withheld. And why should Lorenzo want to fear hell? God is leading him in a far better way than the way of fear. And while it's all right for him to sit up in bed for a little when he gets those "surging desires," he would not be afraid to sleep if he had heard what old Peter of Alcántara had told her about dreaming — or even afraid "of the sort of dream that comes when one is wide awake."

She loves Lorenzo's letters, she goes on, and did not hesitate to answer this one in a time alloted to prayer. And she's enclosing some *coplas* that her nuns made up; little Francisco will enjoy singing them, "though they have neither head nor feet."

"Just now, I thought of one I made myself when I was deep in prayer. It goes something like this." She gives three stanzas and breaks off abruptly: "I can't remember the rest. What a head for a Foundress! But I tell you I thought I had a great head when I said it." And New Year's greetings to all . . . .

II

The poem is one that Angela sent to her Paul. We will never know the end, which Teresa suddenly chose to forget, for Gracián's copy is lost. But his response to it drew an answer from her which makes its meaning clear, and suggests its proper title: *The Knot.*

> O beauty that excells
> all beauties else!
> Unwounding, you make pain
> and painlessly unmake
> the loves of earth.
> O knot that thus has bound
> two things so unalike!

Why should you be unbound
since binding gives both strength
to see all ills as good?
You bind the beingless
to Being without end.
Unending, they end all,
unforced to love they love;
our nothing will grow great.

Whatever its last stanza, Gracián would have understood that poem. When he heard Teresa confess, every day and for several hours a day through six long weeks, he surely heard of how she wrote to Martín Gutiérrez, "It does not seem right that any human creature should hold me so bound." He knew, as well, that Teresa's "imaginary vision" in Beas had seemed to bless just such a bondage to him, a spiritual marriage in which the knot was tied by Christ.

But Gracián, alas, also knew how six of his predecessors had been "persecuted." He valued his career, which was endangered, as theirs had been, by slander. We need not wonder that the poem made him suggest that her bondage to him was an "imperfection." He wrote her a letter about other business and enclosed what he had to say about the poem on a separate sheet of paper. He had, his letter said, got as far back as Granada, confessing Calced nuns on the way, all in bad taste like those in Pastrana, and was staying a few days with the Count of Tendilla, to strengthen his ties to their Order.

Teresa's letter gives the praise his asks for, with a warning: "But we mustn't ask God for miracles, and you must stop and think how many Jesuits have lost their minds from overwork. Still, I have wept for days over the damnation of those poor souls who entered religion only to please God." And, putting Discalced nuns into Calced convents can do no good; they need good confessors, as she knows from what Juan de la Cruz accomplished at the Incarnation.

Then she comes to "Angela." Angela wishes that she were good enough to deserve that her prayers be answered; but at least they have saved her from cowardice, "except about Paul's affairs. Oh, how comforted Angela was with the feeling he showed on the separate page he enclosed in the letter he sent her! Tell him that she longs to thank him many times, and that he can be wholly untroubled—for the match-maker [Christ] was such a person and the knot he tied was so firm that only death will loosen it— and even after death it will grow still firmer. So Paul needn't go on so much about 'perfection' for the memory [of] that vision helps her to praise God—while the freedom she used to have only made war on her. Now it seems to her that her subjection to that man is better and more pleasing to God, for she has found someone to help her lead souls to praise Him—and this is such a relief to her that part of it catches me up, too! May He be forever blessed! Your Reverence's" and so forth.

How deeply she could still make herself believe it, God only knows.

On the same day, she wrote to Mariano. He wanted Doria to come to Madrid, but Doria was trying to interest a widow in entering the Seville convent. The widow was newly back from the Indies, her fortune compactly stored in gold ingots, and Teresa asked Mariano to leave Doria undisturbed until the widow's ingots were secured. That done, she wrote about it to San José in a tone of lighthearted teasing. How proud San José must be now, a "semi-Provincial" with both Seville and Pastrana in her charge! And as for her complaint that nobody in Seville will point out her faults, she needn't worry; they'll do that for her in Toledo! "I'm laughing at myself for taking time to write all this non-sense . . . and I'll wholly forgive you for singing praises to yourself once you have carried off all her gold ingots!"

Few could have written those three letters on the same day. Teresa kept her life rigidly compartmentalized. How rigidly, we know from a fragment of a letter to Gracián written shortly thereafter, when he got back to Seville. And what she paid for that overcontrol we also know, from a letter to Lorenzo.

III

"Angela" had written her last message to "Paul." The fragmentary page, halfway through a letter, clearly came down to us past opposition, for it disappeared, reappeared, disappeared, and after its final disappearance in 1939 its sole photocopy also vanished. There seems to have been a recurrent hope that without the evidence of Teresa's handwriting, it could be proved a forgery. It is what remains of her only letter to Gracián that survived from the next half-year. It was saved, I suppose, for the very reason that led Gracián to read Angela's letters aloud to others: to emphasize the spirituality of their relationship. And I suppose that those who kept making off with it in the hope that it could be considered a forgery simply saw, like Teresa, that Angela's letters could be otherwise interpreted, and that scandals are better ignored than denied.

Gracián lacked discretion; and Teresa, not Angela, sent him this warning: " . . . In time you will lose a little of that openness which I certainly realize to be that of a saint; but the devil doesn't want all of us to be saints, so nuns who are wicked and malicious — like me! — would like to take away others' chance of it.

"I can talk with you and love you very much for many reasons — and the others cannot. Nor will all priests be like my father, who lets himself to be so open with them . . . and I tell you frankly, I am more afraid of seeing you robbed by men than by the devil.

"And what the nuns see me as saying and doing — only me, because I know the one I am dealing with, and at my age I can — will seem to them something they can do themselves — and they'd have a point.

"To see this is not to love them less, but to love them more. However vile I have been, it is the truth that since I began to have daughters I have so constrained myself — seeing how the devil could tempt them through me — that I think there are very few such things that they could have seen. . . . For, I confess, that though my faults have been glaring, I have always managed to keep them hidden from them—and my love for Paul, and my worries over him.

"And so, because you understand how much I love you, you can do me the mercy of not reading my letters to you aloud to them. Realize that they can be understood in more than one way—and that a father superior has to be so transparent about certain things. And whether I write you in the third person or my own it will never be good for them to know anything about it at all, for there is a great difference between the way I talk to myself or to you, and the way I talk to anyone else, even my own sister. And just as I would not want anyone to hear what I say when I talk to God, or to keep me from being alone with Him, so with Paul it is the very same way that . . . ."

The danger was real; but since the first and last page are lost we do not know who warned her that Gracián read her letters aloud. We do know that it drove her to self-questionings even more intense and agonized than those which produced the many "locutions" which I have called the background music to the Seville story.

Two weeks after Angela had written to Paul about the knot that the marriage-maker tied in Beas, she got a letter from Lorenzo. She tried, at first, to keep her answer casual.

The sweets and sardines came, bless him. She does hope that the winter house he still wants to buy in their old neighborhood is in better condition than people tell her it is. And Dr. Velázquez says he needn't worry about what vow he took; in the eyes of the Church it wasn't valid. It's good that Lorenzo can talk with Juan de la Cruz. The little religious experience Francisco de Salcedo has is not of the kind that God wants to give Lorenzo. "He seems to delight in lifting up wretched sinners . . . and with such favors . . . ."

Then, as if in mid-sentence her voice had broken, she goes on: ". . . for I don't know anyone else as wretched as we two are. I must tell you—for more than a week I have been in such a state that if it was to go on I could only attend badly to so much business. Since I wrote you last, the *arrobamientos* have come back on me—and in public. It happened at Matins today, and it has several times. Trying to hold it off doesn't work and no pretence can hide it. It leaves me so terribly ashamed that I want to go away I don't know where!

"I pray to God to free me from this in public. You must pray for it, too, because it can cause very serious difficulties—and it doesn't seem to me to be any deeper prayer. I go around like a drunkard, more or less. At the very least, one should be able to understand that the soul is left willingly disposed! But this way, since none of my faculties are free, it is hard to understand anything more than that my soul wants something.

"For almost a week before that I had been in such a state that I could not even think a good thought—and without any let-up that would have let me have one, but only the greatest possible dryness of spirit."

Still, she adds, in that earlier state the soul can at least stand apart and know that our own efforts can have no effect on either our spiritual aridities or on states like the one she is suffering now. So, "May He be blessed Who does, everything, amen! I have said too much. The rest isn't fit to put in a letter or even to talk about."

The date of the letter tells more than she told Lorenzo. The week in which she could not so much as think a single good thought began on the day that Angela wrote to Paul that her bondage to him was better than the once-treasured freedom which had only made war on her. The date of Gracián's return to Seville lets us know that the *arrobamientos* began shortly after she wrote him her appeal not to read her letters aloud.

Teresa had suffered *arrobamientos* after de Prádanos was transferred from Avila and she was sent back from Yomar's house to the Incarnation; they only came again when, in Salamanca, she felt "so bound" to Martín—and, for the last time, now. Years later she was able to write to Dr. Velázquez, then become Bishop of Osma, that they never came again.

Lorenzo knew at least about the ones that had come in Avila. He also knew the temper of the times, and why Teresa needed his prayers. In this letter, read by generations of pietists as a saint's humble desire to conceal her divine favors (read so, despite her calling them a drunken state that was not even "deeper prayer") he could read her fear of the dungeon or the stake.

But more than that, she had met him on his own ground, one equally "wretched," asking his prayers in response to a letter full of fear that his prayers led only to sin. And that done, she lays her own doubts aside to deal with his, so like those she had suffered twenty years ago. Somehow, she says, she must make him understand that his "experiences"—his moments of ecstasy in prayer—amount to more than he thinks. They can be a great beginning, if he does not lose them "by his own fault." (*Su culpa*, with its overtones to Catholic ears: "By my fault, by my own fault, by my own most grievous fault," as the closed hand strikes three times above the penitent heart.) She, too, has experienced such prayer as he describes, in which the soul alternates between peace and a consuming desire to do penance for the love with which God has touched it—the touch that is unthinkable delight and pain, both felt at once, and felt both in the body and the soul.

That is what she meant by the *coplas* he had not understood, "for though what is happening is really a wound of love that God gives the soul, we do not know where it comes from or how it comes. And so I said, 'Unwounding, you make pain, and painlessly unmake the loves of earth,' because when this love of God touches the soul it loses its love of human creatures without pain."

(But has she lost that love so painlessly? She makes herself go on.)

"I am talking about the way the soul is not bound to any love—no love, I mean, that sets it apart from the love of God: for whatever hurts His creatures will hurt us if we love them very much, and still more if we are separated from them." Yet Lorenzo must realize that this touch leaves us changed:

"And even when He takes away His pleasures and joy (which is what you were complaining about, as if you had experienced nothing but those sensual pleasures which God saw fit to allow their part in your soul's delight) He is not

278

abandoning the soul or failing to leave it rich in mercies, as you will know by their effects as time goes by." Thus far, she has only talked about the Love that draws the heart from lesser loves. But Lorenzo was a man, affected in a way hard to ignore.

"About those lascivious feelings you get afterwards, pay them absolutely no attention at all, for though I haven't had them myself—as God in his mercy has left me free from your bondage to those passions—I think it must be that because the soul's delight is so great it brings on some stirring in the flesh. It will pass away, all spent, if by the grace of God you do nothing about it. Certain persons have talked that over with me." (De Prádanos, but who else? Gracián, one remembers, slept with a statuette of Our Lady in his nighty to ward off that least mature of fleshly temptations, and in Beas described his temptations with an intimacy which she defends as proper because he saw her as "so old.")

Teresa gives Lorenzo her final reassurance: the tremblings and the waves of sweaty heat will go away, too; they have nothing to do with prayer. And his feeling afterwards as if nothing had really happened is a common experience. It was St. Augustine, she thinks, who says that the arrow of God passes and leaves no trace, just as an arrow passes through the air.

Abruptly, she draws down the curtain. Has she told him that line of Augustine's before? She writes so many letters she can't remember. Lorenzo would find letter-writing easier if he did as she does and just put down the first thing that came into his head; the general idea will be clear enough, and "corrections are just a waste of time."

She's sending the hair-shirt he wanted, but he must never, never wear it under his clothes or sleep in it, but just use it occasionally in his own room while the weather stays cold. Come summer, he "can think of some other little thing to do." And the pastilles sent along with it give a nice scent when they're thrown on a fire. He needn't be afraid they're a luxury; her nuns make them from dried herbs and petals.

Oh, and a rich woman is planning to enter "his" convent in Seville, so his loan will be paid back at last. (It never was.) And Gracián is about to visit the Calced houses in Andalusia, which seems wonderfully calm. No wonder, after all the prayers said for him! (It was the calm before the storm, and Teresa had written to San José to delay Gracián's setting out as long as she could.)

There is also a postscript. Will Lorenzo ask Bishop Mendoza to send back the *Life?* She wants to fill it out with all the Lord taught her in later years — enough to make another book, and a big one if He "should care to guide it straight. If not, it's no great loss." And she is sending brother Pedro a *bolillo* (a ball-shaped metal container for hot coals, wrapped in a padded case for use as a handwarmer) to keep his hands warm now that he's taken to spending so much time in church.

IV

Male fornication was a little sin, unremarkable in the priesthood and only to

279

be expected in the laity. Teresa, newly converted, had written Lorenzo of this when, in his forties, he married and settled down. Nowadays, she only teased him about such things, saying in one letter that as "it would kill him" to give up being a *galán*, a womanizer, it was nice that his fancy had settled on such holy ladies as the nuns of Seville.

Masturbation was another matter. We tend to forget how recently it was mentioned in whispers, as "self-abuse." Lorenzo was troubled because, as Teresa told him in another letter, "the body only understands one kind of love." And she could help him by making him see that the temptation was simply a side effect of his emotion when he prayed, not its source.

Undeniably, in helping him she helped herself to analyze the inner conflict which had brought back those *arrobamientos* which she now saw to be not only dangerous, but worthless to her soul and to her God. But few would have taken so generous and painful a way to think things through, and fewer still would have combined those words of grave encouragement and blunt honesty with practical warnings about the danger of hair-shirts to those "of the sanguine humor" — as they two were — or have thought at such a time of sending poor, neurotic Pedro a handwarmer.

I offer that letter as evidence of a faith deeper than the ecstasies for which she became the saint of raptures.

Mendoza, of course, could not release the *Life*, which had been impounded by the Inquisition; and her last book, one almost as long, was written in the year that lay ahead: a year so devoid of leisure, of inner peace that its writing stands as a minor miracle. Neither her nuns nor her friars now like to remember how much she had to cope with in that year, and against what odds.

Chapter 55 ❄ *Things Go from Bad to Worse for Teresa, Gracián, and the Discalced*

I

San José spent money like a proper courtier. By the end of January she was showering Teresa and Gracián's mother, Doña Juana, with expensive presents. Teresa could not help ending her thanks with a dry "How rich you are!" The widow with the gold ingots was soon forgotten: a pleasant dream.

María Bautista, on the other hand, was merchant to the bone. She took money seriously. San José was the prioress who knew how to deal with Andalusians — as Teresa once put it in a two-edged compliment. But María Bautista, surrounded by influential nobles in Valladolid, was as important to the Order in the north as San José in the south; and her initial prejudice against Gracián had not weakened. It made a delicate problem when Gracián, out of a clear sky, rethought Catalina de Tolosa's offer and decided that a convent in Burgos was highly desirable.

María Bautista was now passionately embroiled in her struggle to secure Casilda de Padilla's fortune. To accept another on which the Valladolid Jesuits had long had an eye would upset her considerably; and Teresa wanted no difficulties with María Bautista. She tried to broach the subject in a note that congratulated María Bautista on securing yet another dowry against some difficulties.

"Our Father Visitor is so set on our taking that house that *if you would agree to it* [italics mine] I would send for Antonio Gaitán at once to draw up the papers. Once it is ordered, you will have to find your way to put up with that woman [Catalina], who is old and ill, and give up something for the sake of the souls up there who are in great need. God direct it and watch over you for me. You got out of things well with your own business. May He be blessed Who does everything, for you are thoroughly mean. Your servant. . . ."

Perhaps Teresa flattered herself that the tone was light.

María Bautista did not "agree to it," but in another fortnight the whole question of further foundations would be irrelevant.

II

The Pope's nephew, Cardinal Buencampo, Protector of the Carmelites, knew only what he was told; and neither Teresa nor Roca could get anyone sent to Rome to tell him another story. For over two years Buencampo had urged Ormaneto to discipline Gracián. Ormaneto only answered by stressing the need for a Carmelite reform, which Buencampo shrugged off as the rantings of an old fool who should have lost his Nunciate with the death of Pope Gregory's predecessor.

Ormaneto, in fact, had ideals much like Teresa's. He detested greed, lived as simply as was consistent with the dignity of his office, and scorned its opportunities for self-enrichment. Indeed, he would soon be discovered to have died penniless; the King paid for his funeral. That death was near; but Gracián continued to act as if the old man were immortal.

Ormaneto was not blindly in love with reformers. When Buenaventura showed himself bloody-minded in his attempt to reform the Franciscans, Ormaneto got rid of him; but Gracián he saw as a potential peacemaker for the divided Carmelites. Ormaneto had rejoiced when Tostado, rebuffed by the King and Royal Council, left for Portugal; and when he learned that the Pope had ordered him back, he saw red. On February fifth he wrote to a friend in Rome: "Tostado is coming back, Vicar-General of all the Discalced; and so far as I can see he is coming with no purpose other than to humiliate the Discalced, particularly those in Andalusia."

Canon González y Mendoza got the news on the same day and told Teresa, who wrote about it to Mariano. It was tragic, she said, about "those knifings" in Andalusia, and God's mercy that Gracián knew how to handle things peacefully.

He's been taking the waters at a cure in Lejos and couldn't come when the Nuncio sent for him. The Calced thought he was hiding and planned to bring him to Madrid by force, believing that the Nuncio would unseat him as he had Buenaventura: "Good luck may that bring them!" But the real threat was that Ormaneto's days were clearly numbered. The plans to replace him were already laid; the Canon had learned about it from a friend in the Vatican. He advised that the Discalced do all they could to appease Tostado unless he gave orders directly counter to those of the Apostolic Visitors, Fernández and Gracián. And he clearly was right. Mariano must see that this is no time to go on making a noise about getting that priory in Madrid. For the time being, at least, he should lie low.

The letter is strikingly sane, though Mariano disregarded it. It is also striking that Teresa could find time on the same day to write a long letter to Lorenzo, reassuring him about his religious life and urging him to forget bodily penance—as his patience with poor brother Pedro was penance enough. And as for Lorenzo's current aridity, he's been needing it! "It can be useful in many ways."

Another such letter begins with bits of good news. The Grand Inquisitor has got around to reading the *Life* and says that it could have done Doña Luisa no harm when she read it in Malagón; indeed some things in it could have done her good. He seems to be favoring the Discalced. And, she hears from the Indies that Agustín isn't going to take that position that had them so worried, after all (dishonest Agustín, their constant embarrassment).

But then comes a sentence which only a letter to Mariano, written the same day, clarifies: "Now that Tostado is coming back—if we went by what people say—the urgent thing is to make the world understand all our private affairs—which strikes me as nothing but a comedy."

It was the right attitude, and one that Teresa could sell to neither Mariano or Gracián. The news that Tostado was returning had been the clue for the Calced to revive as many scandals as possible. The project for reforming the Salamancan whores already had the Court laughing and the pious discussing it in shocked whispers. This was now outclassed, for the Calced published a scurrilous broadsheet founded, it seems, in large part on the *beatas'* yarns as passed onto them by Elías de San Martín.

Even with the first sniggerings about the Salamancan whores, Mariano had withdrawn to Alcalá, on grounds of ill-health. Don Teutonio, told that his noble plan for saving souls had misfired, rushed all the way from Portugal to make sure that the Nuncio "understood the business" and the Nuncio expressed a wish to keep in touch with Teresa, inconspicuously, through their mutual friend Canon González y Mendoza. Then the broadsheet was circulated, which accused Gracián of choosing his bedfellows from ecstatics in general, and Teresa in particular—though this did not exclude San José and her subprioress from also receiving his tireless attentions.

Mariano, Teresa wrote, must come back from Alcalá at once. He must not seem disobedient in any way at such a time. None of this is the Nuncio's fault.

The devil has been bringing up his heavy artillery, but God will see to it that the Nuncio hears Mariano out about the Salamancan business—if he will only keep his temper, and not start in again about that Discalced Madrid priory. The Royal Council were only playing for time when they asked to see his licence; as the Canon knows, they have had their own copy of it for months. As for the scurrilous broadsheet, it must be ignored.

What Teresa says about it to Mariano leaves one regretting intensely that a half-year's letters to Gracián were destroyed.: "What do you think of the way they tried to oppose us with that paper? I don't know why people try to disprove such things. Our father acted very badly; it was the utmost grovelling! For the love of God, Your Reverence, don't you take that attitude to anybody. You will be handling things with very little prudence if you notice such things or talk about them. I consider doing that a grave imperfection. Just laugh at them instead. . . . As for your managing to tell the King about it, don't give that a second thought until you have stopped and looked at things squarely; for, as I see it, your doing that would only lose us the great respect he has for us—and the other way, God will guarantee the outcome."

She was even more cool with San José and her subprioress. She saved any word about their disturbance for the end of a letter which dealt briskly with other and indifferent things: "As for the things they said about us, especially such low things, I was thoroughly displeased that our father tried to prove that they are nonsense. The best thing to do is to laugh at them and let people talk. Where I was concerned, in a way, they pleased me." (It isn't the false prophets who get stoned.) "I am writing to the subprioress. Her moanings made me laugh."

The whole of that letter had been sharp, with good reason. San José used Pastrana as a convenient dumping-ground for her problems. Having packed off San Jerónimo, she followed up with Margarita Ramírez, whose odd, malicious hobby was getting the convent's hysterics still further disturbed. Bad as she'd been for Beatriz Chávez, she was far worse for San Jerónimo. She had now worked her up into having more visions and revelations, and in enemy country. The Calced were all too likely to report San Jerónimo, their supposed reformer, to the Toledo Inquisition, and the Inquisition had no rules about double jeopardy.

Teresa had only learned about it from San Francisco. San José, fearing that, wrote her a letter that was defensively self-congratulatory. Things were going well for her in both this world and the next; the widow's gold ingots would soon pay off the convent's debts (hope springs eternal) and she had also been receiving great favors in prayer. This letter came with presents again, too many and too fine, including an expensive reliquary. For once, Teresa could not even say thank you: "Please God my prayers for you are heard, for what with your riches and your position and everything going so well you will need help very badly to keep you humble."

As for San Jerónimo, "That woman really makes me suffer. She should never have been left out of my care or gone where she wasn't kept in fear." (The universally accepted way of handling the mad.) San José must tell San Francisco not to "let her write as much as one letter of the alphabet" and warn her that San Jerónimo "is in the grip of a very bad humor—and if not that, then it's something worse!" (Either melancholy-mad or at long last truly possessed, Satan's instrument.)

But Teresa could not afford to anger San José. The next day she sent her belated thanks for the presents—so useful for her to pass on to Doña Luisa and others. The drinking-cup, the prettiest she ever saw, went to the majordomo in Malagón. "You must have thought that drinking from anything so elegant couldn't hurt someone who wears serge [the serge habit with which San Alberto had replaced the one of rough sayal that was "full of holes"]."

It was only with San José's boasts of religious growth that Teresa could not be less than sincere. "It shows no lack of humility to know that God is giving you mercies, so long as you realize that what He makes of you is not of your own making; and this always happens when the prayer comes from God. I give Him praise that you are coming along so well—and I will try to give you the congratulations you ask for."

She adds further warnings about Beatriz, and says that at Gracián's orders she is writing San Francisco a stern letter about keeping San Jerónimo in order. It is enclosed, and San José must forward it, *"if* [she] thinks it is the right thing to do." Again, I italicize—as with the Burgos arrangement that Gracián wanted, for which the papers should be signed *"if* [María Bautista] *would agree to it."* María Bautista was anti-Gracián from the start and San José had twice shown a tendency to withdraw when scandals raged and the Inquisition threatened.

I have read often in the last fourteen years, and in three languages, that Teresa had two favorite prioresses, but never that she showed such deference to their wishes as to place them above those of the Father Visitor. Neither of those prioresses, I am sure, suspected Teresa and Gracián of being lovers; but they did believe that she idolized him blindly to their common danger. Teresa knew it, and tried to deny it in the only way she could: indirectly, by such deferrings to their judgements, whatever Gracián's wishes.

But Beatriz Chávez was danger of another kind, and about that Teresa could be direct. "Heaven knows what she means by God's exerting such force on her! Consider the trouble it can make when the others see her crying and writing at every step of the way! Get hold of what she writes and send it to me, and take away all hope she has of talking to any confessor but our father; for the others are destroying her. You must realize that they understand that kind of talk down there even less than you think. . . . I know very well that [confession] does her less good than it could do anyone else!" It was sound advice. If Beatriz only confessed her jealous suspicions of Teresa and San José to the object of her affections, it would get no further.

San José ignored it. She felt herself to be above suspicion with any but the ignorant and powerless, and she knew that the same was not true of Gracián— or of Teresa. She was an ambitious woman, and her hopes were pinned to Heredia and Mariano.

Teresa knew Gracián's enemies. Once, swept away by shock and disappointment, she said her say to San José and Mariano about Gracián's "grovelling," but that was her only such slip. Though she despised cowardice, her loyalties were strong. And she would always say more face-to-face with one who disillusioned her than she would say behind his back.

Yet, in one strange way, that disillusion brought relief. The *arrobamientos* ceased, so suddenly and completely that—as she wrote to Lorenzo—she could hardly believe that she had ever had such an experience. Teresa would always love Gracián, with the yearning love that a mother never ceases to feel for a disappointing son; yet from that time on, it was a love increasingly free from illusions. And as such it made no inner struggle, demanded no justification.

To the news that the Pope had ordered Tostado back to Spain, Ormaneto responded by reissuing his counterbrief: Gracián was Apostolic Visitor by the authority of the late Pope Pius. Tostado, assuming that Ormaneto acted in response to the will of the King and the Royal Council, decided to wait. Ormaneto would soon be dead, and Tostado's own first cousin, Sega, was already chosen as the Vatican's new Nuncio to the Court of Spain.

Teresa saw the delay for what it was: a breathing-space. Her friars mistook it for a triumph. Even Doria, no man's fool, made his final decision and took the Discalced habit on the twenty-fourth of March. Mariano became so swaggering that Teresa had to warn him to spend Lent in a monastery; it was essential that the King, the Council, and the Nuncio all see her friars as humbly obedient.

Mariano spent his penitential season with the Madrid Calced. Rumor had it that he had changed sides, and Tostado wrote to him, asking that he persuade the Nuncio to receive him favorably. This Mariano reported to Teresa, along with a request that she write nicely to Baltasar Nieto, who was wondering whether he should go back to the Discalced.

Teresa answered briefly. She had just been bled, she said, and was too weak for more than a few words. In the past she had written to Fray Baltasar more than once, and that was enough. As for Tostado's request, "I never heard of anything so funny!" She is glad that Mariano gets on peaceably with the Calced; "but for the love of God, father, deal very cautiously with them and watch your words."

In other letters, she mentions having sent the same warnings to Gracián, along with a suggestion that his letters be carried only by a convent servant, Juanico, since Juan de Padilla is in danger.

(De Padilla would not be arrested by the Inquisition for another seven months, but his name, unfortunately identical with that of the Jew and traitor who led the War of the Comuneros, had already led to mutterings that blood will tell.)

In hard fact, things were slipping from bad to worse; and Teresa saw everyone willing to face it except for her most influential friars.

Chapter 56 ❦ More Letters; Writing *The Interior Castle;* Death of the Friendly Papal Nuncio

I

The plague swept Seville. María de San José was dangerously ill, the sub-prioress was not expected to live, and Bernarda died. Teresa suggested that Doria might pressure Pablo Matías for some part of her money. Since the letter was meant to be read aloud, she refers to him for once as "Bernarda's relative." It would have to be read aloud, for Bernarda's death had touched off a wave of seeing visions. Teresa wrote that Bernarda, "that angel," had doubtless bypassed Purgatory, but as for the nuns' imaginings: "Do realize that they are nothing but frenzied raving! Pay no attention to them—and pay just as little to anything Beatriz says."

She sends news from Gracián. In Caravaca he found the nuns still denied Mass in their convent, and those in Beas engaged in a lawsuit with the church next door. He expects to reach Toledo by Pentecost: "Just think, what happiness for me!" And Brianda, now moved to Toledo for better care, is given no hope by the doctors, but is nonetheless "wonderful company." And it looks as if Ana de la Madre de Dios, now sent to Malagón to act as President in Brianda's absence, will straighten things out.

Teresa needed Brianda's company. Nagging worries seemed endless. Father Angel not only wrote Bishop Soto—quite needlessly—that he must not license a ministry to the whores of Salamanca, but also started a lawsuit against the hospital which had offered to house it. The plan, Teresa wrote wearily to Mariano, "did nothing but hurt the friars' good names. God reward you for the respect you pay my opinions!" She added none of her customary sweeteners, *but she did write on the outside of the letter: To be delivered into his own hand.*

A note to San José thanked her for still more lavish gifts, urged her to pay off at least debts which were running on at ruinous interest, and to do what she could, with Doria's help, to get at least a little of Bernarda's money. "Leave 'perfection' behind you, for whatever we do, it won't make people say we aren't covetous." It was one thing to consider the lilies, quite another to ignore one's debts. If only San José could make that distinction!

Gracián reached Toledo a leisurely three weeks after he received the Nuncio's summons. Tostado got to Madrid on the same day. Of Gracián's visit, Teresa's letters say only that he is "fat and well." Gracián, in his *Peregrinaciones*, makes it the occasion of his ordering her to write her last book *Las Moradas (The Dwelling or The Interior Castle).*

Yepes, the confessor whom Teresa had gently eased out for Dr. Velázquez, beat Gracián to print with his own claim of having fathered the *Moradas.* He had, he says, no sooner commanded her to write it than its whole allegorical scheme came to her in a vision: the religious life like a castle carved from a single crystal in which the soul progresses through its seven "mansions" to find the King of Glory in the last of them "illuminating and beautifying them all." But, he adds, her vision ended with all going dark, and the venomous reptiles in the courtyard penetrating and defiling the whole castle—from which she learned how terrible it is for a soul that has once found God to fall back into sin. This, says Yepes, she told him in confidence, making him promise to keep the end of her vision secret until after her death.

The apparent purpose of Yepes' invention is to reassure the reader that, once converted, Teresa never relapsed into the sins described in the *Life*, whatever scandalmongers might persist in saying. (It took yet another generation for that whole confession to be reverently disbelieved.) Yepes excelled at such touches, as when he described the *hidalga*, Doña Teresa, nursing de Prádanos with all the humble services one would expect only of a woman of lowly birth.

Gracián, for once, told the truth. Teresa, he says, was talking about prayer with him when she suddenly exclaimed, "Oh, how much better I said that in my book!" at which he ordered her to write another. He wanted one quickly: one that could be published with no trouble from the Inquisition; one free from autobiographical material, one that did not invite comparisons with known fact as he now saw that the unwillingly completed *Fundaciones* might. He demanded it though her many current problems were now complicated by a new and tiring ailment: she had developed an inner-ear trouble which became chronic, resulting in some loss of the sense of balance and constant, distracting head-noises, sometimes like twittering birds, and sometimes like the sound of rushing water.

This Teresa reflects in her preface; she had intended to write the book, but to do it once God gave her a little leisure and better health—meanwhile, little by little, taking time to think it out. So she mentions the order with such utter impersonality that Yepes' claim might well have been believed if he had not so overdecorated it. "Few orders that obedience has imposed on me have been as hard as that I should write here and now on matters of prayer. For one thing, it does not seem to me that the Lord has given me the spirit or the wish to do it. For another, through the last three months I have had noises in my head and been so weak that I even wrote the business letters enforced on me with great difficulty. But knowing that the power of obedience often makes things easy that seem impossible, my will is determined to do it gladly, though my body rejects it as pure suffering—for the Lord has not given me so much virtue that I can fight constant illness and carry on many kinds of business without resentment.

"May He who accomplished harder things with me do me the mercy to accomplish this, too. I trust in His pity."

The best she can do, she goes on, is to repeat things she has said so often that she feels like a parrot repeating words it has been taught without understanding them. She can only trust God to stir up her memory and give her a few insights. She was ordered to write because nuns need such a book and women understand other women's language best. (That is, no Inquisitor need think she fancies herself capable of teaching men.)

Teresa first mentions working on the book a week after she dated that preface. Except for the final, expanded version of the *Life*, it is her longest book and by many her most admired. None of her other books attempt the "good writing" by which it is often marred, with the faults of her period, which ran to the ornate and rarely made a plain statement where a metaphor would do, or still better, several of them well mixed. But the book's virtues are her own, showing oftenest in bursts of direct, spontaneous insight for which she often apologizes as self-interruptions. These are most powerful when they touch her central theme: that we can most truly evaluate our love for God by observing how truly we love our neighbor — flawed, faulty, all too human, like ourselves, and like ourselves, a child of God.

Through the half-year to come she worked at it steadily, and usually — against her doctor's orders — between midnight and two in the morning. If it sometimes sounds forced, artificial, unlike her, we need not wonder; the wonder is that it so often comes startlingly alive, ringing so true.

II

Gracián got to Madrid at a bad time.

In Ávila, Valdemoro had once more sent John of the Cross and his companion friar packing, restoring the Incarnation to Calced authority. Ormaneto, on learning of it, excommunicated him and all his friars, in an act of blind anger directed as much at his own approaching death as at anything else; younger and stronger by even a little he would have seen that to excommunicate innocent friars along with their Prior was not only unjust but highly impolitic.

All the Calced were up in arms. Mariano's ill-timed attempts to found a Discalced priory in Madrid became overnight no mere show of ludicrous arrogance, but a *casus belli.* In that atmosphere, it was apparent that the Nuncio's public blessing and confirmation of Gracián as Visitor to the Andalusian Calced would only serve to intensify his troubles. He put their meeting off from day to day.

Teresa was humiliated by his weakness, and a letter from Seville exacerbated her sense of impotence, of imprisonment. San José was dead broke and being sued for payment of the *alcabala* which she had so often led Teresa to believe paid up. It was now a matter of payment plus legal expenses or eviction. Lorenzo, still unpaid for all he had lent, offered to find enough money to procure a two-month stay in the court proceedings.

The half-year's gap in Teresa's letters to Gracián is at last broken by one brief note, preserved I daresay because one who did not know a good many facts could make no sense of it. She begins by saying that his letter from Madrid has "somewhat eased the pain" caused by letters from "those others."

The "others" were Gracián's friends among "the Angels" — their prosecutor, "the Fiscal" — and Juan Evangelista. When the *beata* had gone to Fray Elías with her scandalous tales of Gracián and the Seville convent, Teresa, as you recall, had urged Gracián to keep away from Granada and Fray Elías, and to disregard Heredia and leave their friend Juan Evangelista in his place as prior of the Case Grande — all of which Gracián ignored. The Fiscal, thinking more as Angel than friend, interpreted Gracián's hurry to see Fray Elías, and to bring him back to Seville, as evidence of a guilty conscience, an attempted hush-up. And Fray Elías, on his return to Seville, persuaded Juan Evangelista that Gracián had feared and victimized them both, seing them as true reformers. This made Juan Evangelista "Elías's friend."

Teresa, having mentioned the pain their letters caused her, briefly changed the subject: Gracián must *command* San José to pay up the current installment on the *alcabala* — and see to it that the money being sent her for the purpose goes directly into the lawyer's hands. Then she comes back to her relief that one scandal at least is fading: "I am delighted that Elías's friend is beginning to grasp the truth at last. Let me tell you that a long time ago I made a great effort to get the Fiscal to understand it and to send you word that you should not go [to Granada]. I did it. I don't know if they showed you the letters. I can say no more. Your unworthy servant, Teresa de Jesús."

Yo lo hice. I did it.

When Teresa worked behind the scenes, she preferred to keep it secret and especially from those she tried to help. To me, those three proud reproachful words tell much about the half-year's letters to Gracián that nobody wanted to save — including those in which she kept urging Gracián to see the Nuncio while there was still time.

Ormaneto died on June eighteenth, five days after that note was sent off. Gracián, on hearing that he had only hours to live, rushed to his bedside, frantic to pour out excuses for his long delay, pleas for his forgiveness, anything which would bring a few words to show those around the deathbed that he, Gracián, was still the appointed Visitor over whom Tostado had no power.

Ormaneto had slipped too far away; apparently he could neither see nor hear. In letters now preserved among Rubeo's papers, Tostado declares that Ormaneto revoked Gracián's Visitorship with his dying breath. This Gracián calls "a big lie," and I believe him. One can imagine that, disappointed by Gracián's dilatory response to his summons, Ormaneto might have transferred the Visitorship to Heredia, though it can be proved that he did not. But it is unthinkable that the dying man's proud anger against the Calced, let alone his sense of right and wrong, would have let him play directly into their hands and simply revoke the Visitorship, as his final act.

Either way, it would hardly have mattered. Ormaneto was dead, and his successor would be Tostado's cousin Sega. He was dead before the Discalced had sent their own friars to Rome, dead before Gracián had so much as written one letter to beg Rubeo's forgiveness for having gone to Andalusia — led by an evil spirit," in Rubeo's words.

Teresa knew that her Discalced faced chaos. It was not in her to admit defeat; she was right when she said that her year in Seville was the only time in which she had ever been weak and pusillanimous. Had her courage failed even briefly, she might have found relief in tears or prayer. She could only feel anger: anger that she was barred alike by love and pride from venting where it belonged, on Gracián.

San José served a blessed purpose when she chose that time to announce that she was accepting two blackamoor slave-girls for extra convent servants and intending to sell the frosting-white house with its view of the galleons outgoing and returning for one still finer, found for her by Fray Gregorio Nanciano. The letters Teresa wrote them both must have been scorchers. They were destroyed, of course, but the one to Fray Gregorio worked promptly, and Teresa changed her tune with San José.

Of course, she wrote, they needed extra help after all that illness, and perhaps the slave-girls will improve themselves in San José's care. At least, they can work, and doubtless God will make them good if San José doesn't demand too much perfection. She herself is much better: nothing left of her recent illness but dizzy spells. And: "Oh, what letters I wrote you and Fray Gregorio! And how that stopped whoever got the idea of moving that convent! Remember me to *those friends*—and to my daughters." (The friends are *esos amigos:* unidentified men). San José should let her girls wear linen "and forget austerity in a time of need." Then, "God keep you, I don't know why I love you as much as I do. Brianda wants to be remembered to you. Even ill, she is wonderful company for me." There is also a postscript. "Have them try to borrow money for your food. Don't go hungry, that makes me very unhappy, and we'll try to borrow some for you up here, too. God will provide, sooner or later."

One gathers that San José's reply to that first—unpreserved—letter must have contained an excessive amount of poor-mouthing. At least she put off buying a still finer house for quite some time. So, for Teresa, the next task immediately at hand was to undo the troubles that Gracián had caused while he visited convents rather than go in time to see the Nuncio.

Chapter 57 ❀ War between Calced and Discalced Carmelites; Teresa's Effort to Overcome Effects of Gracián's Inactivity; an Imbroglio and Violence at the Incarnation

I

It was back in the June of '76 that Teresa had written Gracián her plea for Brianda—not a wise prioress, perhaps, but one learning from her errors. Teresa knew that to demote her would only make more talk; and that to replace her with a nun from another convent would be an act of disobedience to the General—besides which she knew nothing about Gracián's intended replacement. He seemed to forget it, until May of the next year. Then he did exactly what he had first proposed.

Brianda had been sent to Toledo—on grounds of ill-health, which Teresa, who loved her, never failed to stress; and her replacement, as threatened, was Ana de la Madre de Dios, an inexperienced nun whom Gracián had met when she took the veil in '75. Since Brianda's removal had to appear temporary, Sister Ana's new title was President, not Prioress.

This was all done by letter; by the time Gracián had finally got as far on his visits as Toledo, he was too busy to drop in and see how things were going in Malagón. It would have been as well if he had also missed going to Caravaca as he headed reluctantly towards Madrid and the dying Nuncio after his visit to Beas. Ana de San Alberto was prioress of Caravaca only because she and San José had seen so dangerously eye-to-eye on Gracián in Seville, and she had not increased in her warmth towards him through an unhappy year in which she was continually harrassed by the Bishop of Cartagena. She gave Gracián an icy reception, to which he responded unwisely.

He deplored the laxities that she allowed: serge habits (her patron's gift), not the coarse *sayal* demanded by the Constitutions, duck served in place of fish (though cost-free, from the duck pond beside the convent). He let her know that he was quite capable of removing a prioress who permitted such laxities, and ordered her since she was so rich with her serge and her duck dinners — to send a good stout present to the President with whom he had replaced Brianda. Then he topped it all by hearing out a complaint of their patron, Don Rodrigo de Moya, and insisting that San Alberto satisfy him at once.

Don Rodrigo's sister had been placed in the convent; but after a brief trial, San Alberto had sent her home. It had been a wise move: the woman was unmanageable, and nearly mad if not wholly so, but Gracián did not question Don Rodrigo's belief that his sister was a model of holiness whom San Alberto was incapable of appreciating.

San Alberto, anti-Gracián from the start, could be a dangerous enemy if she reverted to the Calced. Teresa knew that she must be handled gently — and still without overt criticism of Gracián. Teresa's letter to her begins with talking of the convent's isolation (which made it utterly dependent on its patrons) as a delight — so cool and quiet, with that lovely duck pond! How she wishes that she might visit them where they live like hermits, safe from the world! Gracián told her that San Alberto was one of his best prioresses; his visit there left him very happy.

As for the money he asked them to send the President of Malagón, San Alberto must only send *what* she feels she can and *when* she can. About the serge habits, perhaps the best thing to do would be to replace them with *sayal*, just one by one as those they had wore out. It was not a matter into which they should plunge as a needless expense, made in the name of holy poverty; and the same went for buying fish when duck is free! (Men, she implies, are impractical.) But as for their patron's sister, it does look as if they will have to put up with her. "Treat her as if she were ill." And don't expect much of her in the way of improvement. Just try to remember that all foundations have much to bear at the start — and that all souls, even hers, are God's dwellings. . . . There is also news; though the Nuncio is dead it seems that Gracián is still Visitor; at least Tostado hasn't started making visitations.

I give you only the main points of this anxious exercise in tact. It was hard to write, under the circumstances. But a letter from the Licentiate Villanueva in

Malagón called for no tact at all, and I think it must have been a relief at that time, with so much inevitably about to go so wrong, to snatch up a pen and put a man, any man, in his place. And, clearly, the Licentiate Villanueva asked for it. The nuns in Malagón wanted Brianda back; so did the Licentiate. He did nothing to ease their resentment of their new President, or to quiet niece Beatriz, who had much enjoyed the authority unwisely delegated to her by Brianda when her health was at its worst.

Teresa said just what she meant: "Your letter pained me deeply, for to think that worse things go on in that house than do among the Calced is death to me. I have got little happiness from that house. I don't know what evils the President perpetrated to get them into the state you describe, but it would only have taken a director like our father to quiet them down. . . . I can't help blaming you, because I know that if you made as much effort as you did while Mother Brianda was with you it would be a different story.

"What they will get out of this is simply that they won't see her again even if God restores her health, and they'll be left without you, too, for that is how God pays back people who serve Him badly—and you'll find out what happens to such unmanageable people who lead me such a life all the time! And I ask you to say that from me to that Beatriz! I am in such a state I don't want to hear her very name! I beg you to tell her that if she starts to interfere or to oppose the President in any way at all, it will cost her very dear!

"For the love of God, teach them the way you used to—to hold Him close and not keep up such disturbances if they desire His peace."

Her pen is flying: the berating and warnings go on.

The Discalced friar whom Gracián sent to be the convent's confessor gave up at once and left. He has been replaced with a priest who needs watching: his intentions are dubious. Villanueva himself is being too hard on a mentally disturbed nun. He complains that the President is not being frank with him about the poor creature's case; she returns the favor, saying that he is not frank with her. If they can't talk plainly to each other, "this snarl the devil has made will only go from bad to worse"; and he, not the President, will be the one who has to leave: a solution he shouldn't object to since his letter makes it plain that he cares more about preserving his own peace of mind than anyone else's, including hers, Teresa's.

"May the Lord give us all peace, as He surely can." Then an odd, abrupt ending, which apprarently answers greetings sent on by the majordomo of the castle and Antonio Ruiz, and some comment of Villanueva's about the Nuncio's death as it may affect Gracian: "I kiss those gentlemen's hands many times. People say that although the Nuncio is dead, his commission is not terminated—for which, in a way I am very sorry."

It is equally likely, of course, that Villanueva fortified his complaints with saying that Ruiz and the majordomo, like him, blamed the current situation on Gracián: in which case that final sentence would have meant, "Much as he's needed, I should like to see him freed from work which will always inspire unjust criticism." She would surely have implied no more to Villanueva.

But she had other reasons to regret that Gracián was still Visitor. He, and all

292

other writers after him, mention only her fear that he would be poisoned. True, she did fear it; but it is also true that one can love a son dearly and still perceive that he is no fit head for the family firm.

For over a year Teresa had tried to make Gracián see it as imperative that he beg the General's forgiveness, send Discalced emissaries to Rome, come promptly when the Nuncio summoned him and, while he still could, give orders as to where she should live out her enforced inactivity. In fact, Teresa's stay in Toledo was now indefensible; in January of that year '77, the General had issued orders that no Discalced nun leave her own proper house for any reason whatsoever; orders which he ended with special reference to Teresa de Jesús—who had still not obeyed the order she had received from him in the December of '75, thirteen months ago. Gracián had moved Brianda to Toledo and Ana de la Madre de Dios to Malagón in a gesture of superior authority which could only increase the General's anger over Teresa's long loiterings in Toledo. She knew it and had begged him to order her to her "proper house" while he still could.

However, it took the Nuncio's death to frighten Gracián into action. Her letter to Caravaca says of Gracián, "I think he is now in Palencia." He was there with good purpose, though she does not say so.

II

Much has been said about the tact with which Teresa removed San José de Avila from Bishop Mendoza's authority and put it under the Carmelites. In fact, no tact was necessary. Bishops only govern in their own sees, and Mendoza was about to be transferred to Palencia. Mendoza's formal installation would not take place for another four months; when Gracián met him, he was only there to inspect his future see. But the move returned San José de Avila to Carmelite jurisdiction, and Gracián could express Teresa's grief that only this turn of events had made it possible for her to return legally to her first, best-loved convent which owed its existence—as did her whole Order—to Bishop Mendoza.

Teresa's regrets were real, though they were mixed with relief since otherwise she should have had to go to Salamanca, trouble-beset even before her friars had alienated Bishop Soto with their plan to save the town's "fallen women."

Gracián took her to Avila a week later. She wrote to San José in Seville on the eve of her departure: The coconuts, San José's most recent gift, were "a grand sight." She continues to hope that San José will take that really good novice despite her smallish dowry, and that she will manage to refuse the *beata* being urged on her by the Archbishop. If Doria can't persuade him that they've suffered enough from *beatas*, San José will just have to invent excuses and keep putting it off indefinitely. Gracián, she adds, insists that someone else go to Pastrana and bring back their poor exiles. (San Francisco, San Jerónimo and Margarita,—the two latter enough in themselves to leave San Francisco helpless.) He says that the Calced no longer consider him their Visitor, and his going there would only intensify the confusion. And—since the enclosed letter to Fray Gregorio is now outdated — San José should keep it and read it over the next time anyone tempts her with the foolish notion of moving to another house.

So Teresa went to Avila, and Mendoza to his castle in Olmedo. Teresa wrote to him there. He must not worry over leaving them without his support, for her convents all help one another, though the nuns will miss him and always think of themselves as his servants. She is well, "except for these noises in the head."

Then in carefully veiled language she sympathizes with his current personal problem: a young niece, pregnant by a count in Valladolid, was having the marriage blocked by certain members of the Count's family. She hopes that the Bishop need not get involved as he had with that other kinswoman, Magdalena and Don Fadrique. And she asks a favor: since Mendoza will be technically Bishop of Avila until his installation in Palencia, can't he still give poor old Gaspar Daza a canonry in the Cathedral here? It was like her to ask it, and like Mendoza to give it at once.

III

As September began, Teresa was frightened by rumors that Father Angel hoped to put her back into the Incarnation. By mid-month, this had become unlikely, for reasons still more disturbing.

With Tostado back in Spain and his cousin Sega the new Nuncio, Baltasar Nieto hoped to profit by their enmity to Gracián. He drew up a set of papers to present to the King. They prove that while he had the soul of an opportunist, he lacked the mind to go with it. A better intelligence, on reflecting that Philip considered Tostado and Sega Roman insults to his power, the Gracián family all admirable civil servants, and the Discalced a useful element in the King's Reform, would have realized that a broadside of sexual slanders on Gracián, Teresa, and her nuns would not endear him to the Crown of Spain.

Fortunately for Nieto, the King was preoccupied. He believed that his illegitimate half-brother, Don Juan de Austria, still flushed with his victory at Lepanto, dreamed of invading England by way of Scotland; he would then assassinate Elizabeth and crown Mary Stuart, in gratitude for which she would doubtless make Don Juan her Prince Consort and Philip's most powerful rival. Philip had sent him to Flanders, where he hoped that the current troubles would keep his mind off such dangerous ambitions; but it was rumored that Don Juan was using this move as an opportunity to win over a force of underpaid, discontented mercenaries with promises of English plunder. Such worries left Philip no time to waste on a friar's obscene nonsense.

Nieto's "memorials" did, however, get the full, lubricious attention of the Royal Council, and Teresa, on hearing that they were addressed to the King, wrote to him a letter that was, for once, not neat and studied like the others she sent him.

"The Grace of the Holy Spirit be with Your Majesty, amen.

"A memorial against our Father Gracián which was given to Your Majesty has been brought to my attention, and I am horrified at the wiles of the devil and of these Calced fathers; for not content with smearing that servant of God, — as he truly is and such a holy lesson to us all that they always write me from convents he has visited to say that he has left them with a renewed spirit — they now try to defame those convents in which the Lord is truly served."

These mad accusations, she goes on, could only amuse her if it were not that the devil could use them to do harm which would be "a monstrous thing" for her nuns.

"I beg Your Majesty not to let these accusations go before the tribunals. because it is the way of the world that some suspicion would remain, however thoroughly such charges were disproved . . . and it will not help your Reform to befoul what is, by God's goodness, already so reformed, as Your Majestry will see by the document that Father Gracián ordered to be drawn up and signed by grave and holy people who have dealings with these nuns." (Yes, the very document she had denounced as "grovelling.")

This matter, she goes on, touches the King's own honor and glory, for he is known to favor Gracián and his family; and if it is not checked, this attack will go on from accusations of sexual licence to accusations of heresy in a man "sent [her] by God" after she "had suffered seventeen years from these fathers of the Calced"; suffered helplessly, since her "own weak powers were not enough." His Majesty must forgive her for writing at such length, but love for him has made her bold, and her Order prays for him constantly, "since he is their only protection in this world."

Having brought this letter to it formal conclusion, she gives it a postscript in a torrential nonstop sentence full of pronouns with shifting references (she even writes Calced for Discalced unless by now she herself was confused as to where Nieto actually stood): "I suspect that while Tostado is the way he is now his visits will do the Order no good but much harm, especially as he has been reached by that preácher [Nieto] who used to be a Calced friar concerning whose life I beg Your Majesty to inform himself; and if it is necessary all the Discalced nuns will swear that we never saw a thing or heard a word about him [Gracian] that was not for the sake of our edification, and as for his not entering our convents, he has always carried it to such great extremes that he even held the Chapters — at which it would seem that he had to come in — through a screen, usually."

Grecián's father made a copy of this letter for his files, but I doubt that he showed it to the King. Excited women tired His Majesty; and in any event Tomás Gracián knew that it would be unnecessary — as Nieto himself learned when the matter came up before the Royal Council. It looks as if the shrewder Calced had known it, too, for Nieto's sole fellow-signer was a retarded lay-brother, who broke down as a witness. According to records of the Royal Council, Fray Miguel wept, swore that these "memorials" hadn't even been read out to him, and that he had only signed after awful threats and beatings. (Probably true; it was Nieto's preferred means of persuasion.) Once the Council had weighed the evidence, Nieto retired to a Portuguese monastery for life.

As for Teresa's letter, one should realize that it sprang from a justified terror.

If the King had taken those "memorials" seriously, it would have been a bad business; his Reform meant much to him, and especially as it embodied the ideal of holy chastity for priests, friars and nuns.

But our troubles and blessings often come strangely intermixed. Nieto's scurrilous broadside did, in fact, give Teresa such a black eye at the time that her most dreaded fate — that of being sent back again to the Incarnation — was averted, and not by her friends but her worst enemies. Father Angel believed all he heard, and he convinced many that no Carmelite convent should be so befouled.

IV

The Incarnation wanted Teresa back. During her last stay she had bettered its reputation and brought it, in consequence, a material prosperity that it had not known since. The nuns assumed that the scandals they heard repeated were Valdemoro's invention, dreamed up for the purpose of ridding himself once more of their good little John of the Cross.

Father Angel knew this, and warned Tostado. Tostado instructed the new Provincial, El Magdaleno, to open the election with a solemn warning that a vote for Teresa de Jesús would mean excommunication; nor would voting be secret. All ballots must be signed and presented by the signer, one by one.

Teresa passed on the story of what happened to San José. Fifty-five nuns came forward "as if they hadn't heard a single word he said to them . . . and at each vote the Provincial cursed them and excommunicated them and pounded the notes with his fist and whacked the nuns and burned the votes up." Then, on the day after "that smashing-election," El Magdaleno came back, saying that they were forgiven and might vote again, properly. The Prioress told him that another election was pointless; no minds were changed. So "he excommunicated them all over again," dragged out a nun from the forty-four who had voted for somebody else, declared her Prioress, and sent to Tostado to have his choice confirmed.

The fifty-four announced that they would only accept her as Teresa's Vicar until they were assured that Tostado would honor their right to free election. Tostado sent word that they might receive Teresa as a penitent, but as Prioress, never! So — Teresa ends her tale — the nuns are not only excommunicated but have been held incommunicado for the past two weeks, not even allowed to speak to their parents or to a confessor. The *letrados* say that they are not excommunicated and that the Calced have defied the Council by making a Prioress of one who got the least votes. It is all mad, for the nuns surely know that they were trying to get her, Teresa, back against her will: "But I could forgive them, and willingly, if they would only leave me in peace, for I have no wish to go back to that Babylon. May God give them what will serve them best — and keep me free from them!"

The letter was written to be read aloud. The situation was worse than it indicates. Heredia, returning from a visit to Mancera, was captured and imprisoned by the Calced (though later he was allowed to "escape"). Mariano was put under house arrest in Madrid. Gracián hid out in the caves of Pastrana.

Teresa forced herself to write letters and mention none of this. She tells about Teresica, growing up and getting still prettier. She expresses hope that San José can lure back the widow with the gold ingots. She makes small-talk, to be read aloud at recreation-time, saying nothing that could foster self-fulfilling prophesies of defeat, either in the convent parlor in Seville or among those who might intercept her letters on the way.

She also concerned herself with a family problem in Alba. Juana's daughter Beatriz—a third problem Beatriz—was seventeen and overblessed with what Teresa, in writing to Bishop Mendoza about his own niece, called "the gift of making herself loved." Since her parents could not afford to marry her off, they could only hope to get her into a convent; but the girl had a fixed horror of the poverty and strict enclosure of San José de Avila, and those among Teresa's prioresses who were not too poor to accept an unendowered nun knew too much about her to admit her. Teresa had one hope: if Brianda could write a sufficiently persuasive letter to the President of Malagón—who now had hopes of a better house and income—it might work.

Don Juan de Ovalle should "happen" to be in Toledo. With Brianda, alone of her prioresses, he could be wholly honest about Beatriz and move her to write an adequately compelling letter to Malagón. Teresa thought everything out, down to advising Don Juan to come on a humble mount, not one of the showy creatures he liked to hire for effect. It was important that the President in Malagón should not take him for a rich man who preferred to save money by trading on his family connection with the Foundress.

It did not work. Ana de la Madre de Dios, already unhappy in Malagón, sensed that she was being used. Teresa wrote de Ovalle that she was sorry he had spent so much to no purpose. She urged him to move to a little country place he owned where Beatriz would be out of temptation's way: "I can't see why you think that's so terrible; many *hidalgos* live on their country estates." But Don Juan stayed in Alba. Eventually Beatriz became involved with a married man, creating a scandal which did no good to Teresa's convent in that gossip-ridden village. But at the time, Teresa had only wanted to do for a wayward girl what her father had done for her: to shut her away until the talk died down and Beatriz, God willing, should learn a little sense.

She made time for this even while she was consumed by anxiety for her threatened Order and for Gracián in hiding, and by her growing fear that Valdemoro would use the disobedience at the Incarnation as his excuse to rid Avila of Juan de la Cruz, once and for all. At the same time, sick or well, weary, anxious or no, Teresa worked away at writing the *Moradas*, each night, from midnight until two.

I

From the start, the Avilan Calced had felt Fray Juan's presence as an insult to their whole Order. When Valdemoro's third attempt to get rid of him only resulted in his getting himself and his friars excommunicated, the scandal had been great. All over Castile the Calced rallied behind their Andalusian brothers, equally determined to be rid of the dying Nuncio's puppet, Gracián.

Sega had reached Madrid on the last day of September, and Gracián came out of hiding, moved by a panic impulse to resign his Visitorship. Covarrubias, speaking for the Royal Council, told him that to do so would be to defy his God and his King. Sega demanded Gracián's patents, so that he might judge of their legitimacy. Gracián refused to show them; he feared that the gesture might offend the King, since Sega had refused to present his own authorization to the Crown, saying that the Pope's orders were not Philip's concern.

Sega was enraged and, in Teresa's eyes, justifiably so. Gracián began to doubt his own judgment and consulted Quiroga, who told him to go directly to the King. Since Nieto's "memorials" were still in the hands of the Royal Council and Gracián did not know that the King had ignored them, he felt it was no time to visit the Escorial. Quiroga, according to Teresa, "told him he had no more courage than a fly, and made him go." The King ordered him to go into retirement until he had studied the case—and promptly forgot it. Gracián went back to his caves, and the Calced smiled.

It was against this background that Teresa had feared for Juan de la Cruz once the rebellion at the Incarnation gave Valdemoro his excuse for action. If Fray Juan were represented to Sega as Teresa's tool and the fomenter of those nun's intransigence, Sega would believe it. Teresa wrote letters to everyone who might have influence in Madrid: "For the love of charity find out if there is any way to get Tostado or the Provincial to absolve those nuns, for if this goes on it will be bad business. They must be made to obey Mother Ana!"

She had Lorenzo set up a guard of armed friends to stand nightly watch over Fray Juan's shack outside the castle walls. The Calced laughed, set half the town to laughing, and made Lorenzo's friends feel like fools. As Valdemoro had expected, they disbanded.

Teresa finished her book in the first hours of the last day of December. Two nights later a mob of friars armed with cudgels broke into the shack and seized Fray Juan and his companion, Fray Germán. As they were being dragged off to the priory, Fray Juan, tiny and wiry, broke from his captors and got back to his shack under cover of darkness. Before he was recaptured he had torn all his writings to shreds and trampled them into the mud, an illegible mass. In the priory they were flogged so violently that when Fray Germán was removed to Medina the next day, he was seen to be vomiting blood. John of the Cross simply vanished. Seven months later Teresa still believed the rumor that he had been carried off to Rome.

Actually he was imprisoned in Toledo. Heredia and Mariano had been "treated affectionately by the Calced"—as Gracián would write of his own eventual imprisonment. Not Juan de la Cruz. He spent nine months in a stone-walled closet so small that, tiny as he was, he could not lie at full length on the floor. His only light came from a narrow air-hole near the roof. The straw underfoot was occasionally cleared of his excrement, but throughout that imprisonment his only garment was the under-tunic in which he had been captured.

He kept himself sane by alternating prayer and contemplation with composing and memorizing lyric poetry. His best known book, *The Dark Night of the Soul*, was written in response to a lady's request that he explain one of those poems to her; knowing him, she knew that it must concern more than a young girl's memory of a summer night when she slipped from her sleeping parents' house to a gentle assignation with her lover.

Juan de la Cruz was a pure mystic, an artist, an intellectual, and wholly devoid of worldly ambition; yet he was far worse treated by the Calced than were any of their most dangerous enemies. And while the century that canonized Teresa in 1622 also canonized those two vastly dissimilar souls, Francis Borgia (in 1670) and Peter of Alcántara (in 1669), John of the Cross was not canonized until 1726, in a wave of Papal reaction against eighteenth-century rationalism. In his lifetime only Teresa spoke of him as a saint.

We may be sure on the evidence of all he wrote later that the work Juan de la Cruz destroyed on the night he was captured was consistently first-rate writing, with none of the flaws in the book that Teresa had finished two nights before; and also with none of her sudden, live perceptions of the world as it is, and people as they are.

II

As I said before, the flaws in *Moradas* are obvious. It so runs to metaphor that within the space of a single short chapter the soul is a castle, a tree, a beehive, a silkworm that becomes a butterfly, a dove, and even an artichoke through which we nibble at the bases of its leaves until we get to its heart. Yet that same chapter talks about the timidity that checks religious development through our fear of appearing "different" or holier-than-thou; and its ugly, then all-too-prevalent opposite, the excesses of self-isolating prayer and brutal penance which cut one off from the basic human virtue: the love of God that is inseparable from love of our fellowmen.

That love Teresa makes the test of all supernatural experience; locution, visions, raptures may come from God, the devil, or our own imaginations, but we need no aid from *letrados* to sort them out: those sent by God leave us kinder, braver and humbler in our daily lives than we were before.

Las Moradas recalls conversion experiences from the *Life*, but as experiences described to Teresa by a friend—and with amendments. No little angel wielded the arrow—or flame-tipped lance—of God; and she stresses it that the pain and delight of that wound are not physical. (She is not writing for beginners like Lorenzo or her own past self.) But she leaves unchanged her description of those terrible impetuses in which "that person's" soul hangs between earth and heaven, longing for God and feeling the hopelessness of its earth-bound nature; and above all else, *alone*. The soul's final earthly dwelling, the seventh, she does not yet know, she says, by experience. It is the place where Mary and Martha come together in perfect harmony, free of *arrobamientos* and *abobamientos* too (one of her nicer coinages: the *bobo* is the fool).

None of us ever find that inner peace consistently and permanently; but even the bare knowledge of what it should be is a source of strength. (The strength, I think, that enabled Teresa to write this book when she did. And it is not surprising that sometimes she gets off the track and writes, "I forget what I was going to say!" or interrupts a passage with complaints about the noises in her head, like twitterings and the sounds of rushing water.)

On the night she finished the book, she only feared that John of the Cross would be put under house arrest, as she was, and Heredia and Mariano—since he would never run away and hide, like Gracián.

Four days later she was at work on yet another letter to the King. It was a stronger and far more dignified letter than that in which she tried to refute Nieto's "memorials." The Calced were wrong, she said, in thinking that she wanted to be Prioress of the Incarnation; in a previous stay she had seen that its sole need was for good confessors and had persuaded the Visitor Fernández to appoint two Discalced friars for that purpose. The city had found the change Fray Juan de la Cruz made in that convent's religious life so remarkable that Avila now thought of him as a saint.

So had the late Nuncio; but after his death the Calced had sent back their own confessors, leaving the nuns confused as to whom they should obey; and the friar who was sent to absolve them after their misguided election refused; instead he only confirmed it that they were excommunicated and denied them any confessors whatsoever. The city is now scandalized by the arrest of their Discalced confessors, and she herself had rather see them in the hands of the Moors, who might well show them more pity. Fray Juan is already frail, weakened by suffering that he has endured for the sake of the King's Reform. She implores the King that he be released at once and tormented no more. In the previous summer, the Calced had granted such a release to "a good old man, Fray Antonio de Jesús—Heredia—who was similarly imprisoned without cause: hence, they can be persuaded.

And may God grant His Majesty many years, since he seems to stand alone in his desire to do Him honor.

It is unlikely that the King saw that letter, either. It is one that Covarrubias, the President of the Royal Council, would have brought to the King's attention; but Covarrubias had died suddenly, outliving Ormaneto by little over three months.

III

It was a time when indiscreet friends could be as dangerous as enemies. Down in Granada, Gaspar de Salazar had not learned of the arrests, but he was enraged to hear of Nieto's "memorials" and was ready to spring to Teresa's defense against his Provincial, Suárez, and the Grand Inquisitor. He wrote her a frighteningly emotional letter. He was only too likely to compound her troubles.

Teresa's answer avoided all current news. The memorials, she said, had been withdrawn, and their signers' fate was being considered by the Royal Council. Father Gaspar must also tell his friend Carillo that Peralta's relative appreciates his loyalty to her and that "the piece of jewelry" now in the hands of "that person in Toledo" is one of which "that person" speaks highly. Peralta's relative now has another, just completed; the gold is of better grade and the enamelling more delicate, though the jewels in it do not stand out as well as in the other. (As good an evaluation as one could expect from the writer of a book on whose last pages the ink was barely dry.) Teresa could only hope that her cool tone, coupled with the pseudonyms which said, in effect, "Take care, my phone is tapped," would quiet Father Gaspar down.

The news of Nieto's accusations of Gracián, Teresa, and her nuns had even reached Portugal. Good Don Teutonio's response posed no threat and was rather touching. He had finally gained his bishopric and offered Teresa a convent in Evora—safe in Portugal, out of the wind and the world's eye. (The same that San José would accept, after Teresa's death and Gracián's expulsion from her Order.)

As Don Teutonio was safely remote and busied with his new office, Teresa could tell him more: Gracián in hiding, friars imprisoned, including "that saint, Fray Juan de la Cruz." But the King has got the Royal Council to cancel Tostado's authority in Spain. (A false rumor; the struggle between the Crown and the Vatican still went on—though it continued to put the King even more firmly on the side of the Discalced.) As for the convent in Evora, she is confined to Avila by the General, but possibly Don Teutonio could get a patent from the Pope which would let her found *in absentia* if he asked the Cardinal Protector of the Carmelites, "who is, they say, the Pope's nephew." (He couldn't.)

She had told Don Teutonio so much, the letter ends, because Tostado might soon be back in Portugal with a far different story to tell. God only knew how this all would end!

It had hardly begun.

IV

De Ovalle would not go to his country place in Galinduste, or even send Juana there with her daughter, "the Lady Doña Beatriz." Teresa began to speak of her mockingly. Don Juan was sure that though the convent in Malagón was closed to Beatriz, Teresa could get Doña Luisa to accept her as a lady-in-waiting. Teresa bitterly suggested that Don Juan ease that request by making

Doña Luisa's brother, the Duke of Medinaceli, a present: "as that lot never see their way to doing anything unless they can get something out of it."

Seville was equally stubborn. A Calced revolt had started in Pastrana, but San José was too absorbed in her plan to buy a new house to think about bringing back her nuns. In Teresa's letter to her, the news about the arrest of Fray Juan and Fray Germán is sandwiched between urgings that the Paterna exiles be rescued, and protests over the still-intended move: "I haven't yet managed to grasp what money you expect to use to buy the house you want. . . . If you are so rich, don't forget what you owe my brother!" "Even two hundred ducats" out of all San José owes him would be a help; money he'd depended on from the Indies hasn't come . . . . San José's reply came in the form of Christmas presents. Teresa said thanks, but no more presents, please! The porterage she had to pay on them "hurt her conscience."

Then, on Christmas Eve, Teresa tripped at the top of a flight of stairs, fell headlong and broke her arm at the shoulder joint. Her good old cousin, Mariá de San Jerónimo — as sane as the other San Jerónimo was mad — saw it happen and remembered Teresa's words: "Glory be to God, *he* tried to kill me." As things were going, it is small wonder that she blamed the devil rather than the inner-ear trouble that made for dizziness and noises in the head.

A *curandera*, finally brought in to break and reset the shoulder-joint, finished the devil's job. Thereafter, Teresa could only get dressed and undressed with another's help. Luckily, she said more than once, it was only her left arm and shoulder; she could still write letters.

V

The last thing Teresa needed at that juncture was to have Gaspar de Salazar abandon his Jesuit rectorate and turn Discalced. She learned about his intention from others; he had wanted to save it for her happy surprise. Teresa, appalled, wrote to Father Gaspar to dissuade him. His Provincial, Suárez, heard of it at the same time, and sent Teresa a furious letter, in care of the Rector of Avila, Father Dávila, who passed it on with a stinger of his own.

Teresa wrote to Suárez: she had just got the news herself. She was ill when it came, and it made her worse. Not having heard about it from Father Gaspar she knows nothing about his purported "revelation" and if she herself had received the "develation" (her own coinage) Father Suárez mentions, she certainly would not have told anyone about it. "Thank God [I] know enough to doubt such things!" She would have thought that Father Salazar did, too; he has "always seemed quite sensible" to her. Suárez is wise to order an investigation; Salazar would certainly not disobey his superiors' orders.

True, she goes on, they are old friends, though for years at a time they have not written to each other; but in view of that old friendship she can only say that he'd have done better to change Orders when her own consisted of exactly two friars! And as for her having said that Suárez stood in Salazar's way, spiritually, "May God never write my name in His book if such a thought ever crossed my mind!"

For the rest, she would do anything for the Company that did not involve opposing the will of God; she would even lay down her life, for their purposes are hers; they serve the same King. "May He and His Blessed Mother grant that we may always serve under the same banner."

It is an effective letter, though it had little effect. Her letter to the Rector of Avila simply released her anger.

Each time she rereads Suárez's letter, she says, she is more stunned by its lack of simple honesty and its assumptions that she had done things she would never dream of doing. He should have dealt with Father Salazar directly, and as for the "truths" he wants her to write him, she can hardly say more than she already has, short of telling him that she has received direct word from God on the subject! As for Suárez's saying that she should tell the world "the whole story," can't he realize that she owes Salazar some loyalty? Why should she defame him by spreading reports of his disobedience? It is his Provincial's task to see that he obeys. If she let it be known that Suárez had told her to do such a thing, he would be more blamed for giving the order than she for disregarding it! Finally, if she had actually been party to this business, it would have merited no such tongue-lashing since whatever Salazar does or doesn't do can't hurt the Company all that much! "May it please God to show me His will—and may He do the same for you!"

It was not a good letter to have passed around. A rift was irrevocably widened, more's the pity—for as Teresa had truly said, she and the Jesuits were fighting the same battle to save their Church from within. Young de Cetina, de Prádanos, Father Gaspar, poor Martín Gutiérrez, and eventually even Baltasar Alvarez were taken from her, but Teresa never forgot what she owed the Company, her first understanding counsellors in the time when she had most needed understanding (as the Company would love to recall, after her death).

But now Teresa's sense of outraged justice, the pain of her broken shoulder, her fears for her work, and her utter weariness had finished what Father Gaspar began. Suárez had long detested her, and once that letter to Father Dávila had passed from hand to hand, few Jesuits would not see eye to eye with him about her while she still lived.

Chapter 59 ✤ *Beginning of a Year of Crisis; Idea of Making the Discalced a Separate Order*

Teresa's angry letter to Father Dávila was the last impulsive act she would allow herself for a long time. The year between that Christmas and the next was the year of crisis. All she had worked for since Rubeo empowered her to launch a Carmelite reform came close to destruction. Left to her friars, it would have been destroyed, and Teresa knew it. And while it may sound odd to say that a woman who had lived so deeply, done so much, and developed such a sense of religious values gained a new maturity at sixty-three, there is no other way to put it.

How she managed to temper the hostility of the Valladolid Jesuits we don't know, though a letter to Gracián reports in late March that she had done it. In Avila, she persuaded the Rector to be her confessor, and took pains to be the humblest penitent imaginable. His house had a clogged spring for which she offered to get the services of that brilliant engineer, Mariano; and for months on end her letters to him urge the importance of his coming to see it. Things like that count, and she refused to give up until it was done, though her friars must have thought her mad to insist on such trivia while the sky was falling.

De Salazar's case continued to disturb her. She warned Gracián that the Discalced had no right to take him from the Jesuits and that his notion that the Pope would grant him special permission to join the Discalced was lunatic. Still, if they were only rejecting him through fear, that, too, was wrong. Might God make it plain! Worse still, Catalina Godóñez of the flaming liver, now Catalina de Jesús, had somehow heard about it and written Father Gaspar a letter that welcomed him to the Order, thanking God for his "revelation." If he showed it about, it could get not only Beas but the entire Order into further trouble with the Inquisition. The whole de Salazar business, Teresa said, made her sometimes feel that she should be thrown overboard, like Jonah, to quiet the storm — on the chance that her sins were the ship's real peril.

But she does say *sometimes, on the chance*. While slanders raged, she knew that she was the storm-center, the *converso* woman with an evil past. But she also knew that she had built the ship and that it was her responsibility. There are times when the greatest sin is to whisper *mea culpa*, and withdrew.

II

In early March, Gracián emerged from hiding and went about preaching sermons. Teresa wrote that she envied him, since she can only "eat, sleep, and cope with these Fathers " — the Jesuits. But isn't his zeal a subtle temptation? Isn't he putting them all in danger? For he is still their Visitor; de Padilla tells her that Sega has decided to accept the Royal Council's decision on that, rather than show himself for an enemy of the King's Reform . . . .

And de Salazar is still calling them cowards, while the Jesuits act as if his leaving them would start a mass defection of every Jesuit in Andalusia. Now he seems to have persuaded the Count of Tendilla to get the Pope's permission for him to switch Orders. May the Count fail in that, please God! But his going to Rome gives them a blessed chance to send friars in his entourage to present their counter evidence to the Cats' lies. (The Cats are the Calced; the Jesuits, often the Crows.)

It was a year and five months since Teresa had written Roca about her futile urgings that this be done. And her current moment of hope was fleeting; for the Count of Tendilla, Governor of the Alhambra, did not go to Rome after all, nor is it likely that anyone would have got around to sending friars with him if he had.

Luckily Bishop Mendoza could help Teresa to meet and cultivate the friendship of others who had influence in Spanish politics. The Very Magnificent Roque de Huerta, honorary Keeper of the King's Forests and Secretary to the Royal Council would be most useful in the growing storm.

Without de Huerta Teresa could not have kept in touch with Gracián, for Juan de Padilla's uses came to an abrupt end three months after the arrest of Juan de la Cruz. He came to Avila with a letter from Gracián, and was persuaded to carry a message from the Incarnation to the Royal Council: the nuns' protest against being robbed of the right to free election and thereafter of the only confessor who took their vocation seriously.

El Magdaleno learned of that errand, announced that de Padilla would be imprisoned if he ever set foot in Avila again, and came back to the Incarnation itself, where he and Valdemoro spent ten days in browbeating the rebellious fifty-five and convincing the weaker faction that only a formal retraction of their complaint to the Council could keep the whole convent from permanent excommunication and imprisonment, cut off forever from friends and family.

Teresa let Roque de Huerta know how that retraction was gained, expressing only sympathy for the rebels. But she wrote to Gracián that rebellion at the Incarnation, blamed on the Discalced, had lost them their Dominican support, and that even El Magdaleno and Valdemoro could have accomplished nothing if she, fed up with the nuns' clamor, had not sent them word to have done with it.

The Incarnation soon regressed to the state which had first shown Teresa the need for a Carmelite reform, but she saw that she could no longer help it without hurting her Discalced. As it was, her friars were hurting themselves enough. Far from trying to win their General's forgiveness and regain his support, they had set themselves on a course which could only bring down the lightning.

305

Gracián, Mariano, Heredia and Doria met in Alcalá and worked out a plan. Roca heard of it and was appalled. He rushed to Avila. He assumed that Teresa was privy to it and could never believe how little she could influence Gracián. He begged her to stop the folly before it was too late. Teresa had known nothing, and was as dismayed as Roca could have hoped.

The plan was to establish a separate province—which she and Roca both ardently desired—but to do so by a foredoomed short-cut. They would call a second chapter, but this time without the consent of either the General or the Nuncio, and at it they would declare themselves separate from the Calced, under their own Provincial. After this they would send their long-delayed messengers to Rome, not to beg forgiveness but to make their proud announcement of a *fait accompli.*

It was open rebellion and could lead to no good. When Roca left for Alcalá to make his own last-ditch attempt at discussion, he carried a letter from Teresa to Chávez, the King's confessor. It begged him to impress his royal penitent with the need to establish a separate province by means not open to dispute, preferably by sending Gracián to Rome with a request written and signed in the King's own hand.

Before she wrote to Gracián himself, she laid the case before Gaspar Daza and Dr. Rueda, a local specialist in canon law. Their backing, she hoped, would keep her appeal from being discounted as the emotionalizings of an unlettered woman. Both assured her that such a Chapter could make no decisions that were ecclesiastically valid unless, before it was held, the Pope himself were to give the Discalced written permission to bypass their General. To accomplish that, Rueda said, someone must persuade the King to put the matter in the hands of his ambassador to the Vatican; and even with the Papal permission granted, the Chapter should be held under some respected outside authority, such as that of Fernández, the Visitor to Castile, who was a Dominican. No loophole should be left for a Calced claim that the separation was made illegally.

Teresa's letter to Gracián spelled it out, point by point. She said, "I cower at the thought that you may be blamed with some justice. When they blame you for something you haven't done, it only gives strength to my wings."

Gracián must stop and think. It might be best if he, not Roca, delivered the letter to Master Chávez, whose advice the King takes very seriously. Then he could also talk it up with his friends at Court, and Heredia could use his friendship with the Duke and Duchess of Alba to get them enthused and talking with their own circle: the King listens to them all. Mariano should join in, too—and all of them must remember to remind the King that their little saint, Fray Juan de la Cruz, is still in prison.

It would be good if, on the way, Gracián stoped off in Toledo and asked the Grand Inquisitor for his approval; Quiroga would warm to being asked humbly and in advance of everyone else. It would be wise, as well, "to give something to the Nuncio." (Few churchmen were like Ormaneto in scorning cash tokens of respect.) This done, she ends, their friars could go to Rome as bearers of the King's letter to the Vatican; so armed, they could not be denied audience.

It is well thought out; too much so, Teresa realizes. She has forgotten her woman's place and the reaction that such forgetfulness inevitably earns. "But what a lot of talk I've made and what foolishness I'm writing to you, father! And you put up with it in me. . . ."

She plunges into general news, then sees that what she has dashed off in defense of the Prioress of Alba against some current criticisms may be taken as a backhanded slap at Gracián's interference in Malagón, and covers it quickly: "Oh, what a big thing the Malagón nuns are making over Brianda! But I laugh at the very idea of her ever going back!" And, oh, how Teresa looks forward to seeing Gracián's mother and sister when they stop off on their way to Valladolid! Her letter crossed with one of his: plans for the Chapter were progressing well, and when he took his mother and sister to Valladolid he would stop off to see her before he went to reorganize Alba.

The news of the proposed Chapter had already leaked, and the Calced were up in arms. It was no time for Gracián to make any journey, least of all one that would take him to Avila—or to Alba, which had to be reached through Salamanca. Teresa made Gracián's messenger wait for a letter that urged him not to take that trip, and repeated her previous advice as tactfully as possible.

Only her warnings against travel had any effect, and they had too much. Gracián did not go to see the King, or Quiroga, or the Nuncio; and, of course, no friars went to Rome. However, he expressed his disgust at Teresa in the unwomanly role of counsellor in a letter which his mother dropped off on her way to Valladolid. Teresa wrote back: "Jesus be with you, my 'Father and Superior' as you called yourself, which made me laugh a good deal and without discomfort; on the contrary, all your warnings that I must not judge my superiors amuse me. Oh, father, how little need there was for you to swear, and not even like a holy soul but like a muleteer, considering how well I understand you! Anyone God has given such an earnest desire to do souls good shouldn't rob his own soul for the sake of others! Now I want to drop all that—with a reminder that you gave me leave to judge you and think about you as I like."

Something had changed, and permanently. Teresa would always love Gracián, always believe him the one friar capable of both understanding her rule and purpose and doing them public service. And she would always suffer a mother's vulnerability to the slights of a self-centered child. But Angela's belief in her God-given spiritual marriage to her Paul was outgrown.

Chapter 60 ✸ Teresa's Attempts to Influence the New Nuncio, Sega, who is Hostile to Reform

I

It would be midsummer before Teresa relinquished her last hope that the Chapter would not be held, but throughout the intervening months the Calced grew ever more united, and the Discalced seemed to feel less and less need for common loyalty.

Take, for example, Heredia and Malagón. Its state still had Teresa protesting to the Licentiate in defense of Ana de la Madre de Dios, "That woman isn't killing them!" and saying of the nuns, "How they even adore the things they found unbearable in [Brianda] when she was there." But Heredia found it useful. Conditions in Malagón, if publicized, could be made to discredit Teresa's witless Gracián, who had edged him, Heredia, out of his proper place as head of the Order. He went to Malagón, exacerbated the discontent, drank up all the local talk about the nuns and the too-friendly neighborhood friars—and spread the word wherever he hoped it would do him the most good.

At first Teresa tried to excuse what she heard; she "loved" Heredia, he was "good and holy"; it was only that God had given him a gift for administration. But as it got worse, she had to alert Gracián. What Heredia said about her, she wrote, did not matter; in this world of men, the fate of the Discalced was not in her hands. But what he said about Gracián could be used by the Calced to destroy them all. Her letter ends, "Tear this up as soon as you read it."

As the Calced fury grew, Teresa pressed Gracián more and more strongly to see the King. Instead, he took off for such remote spots as Guadalajara, where his preaching, he reported, moved many to tears. "This is no time for sermons," Teresa wrote back; but her words were wasted.

As an added exacerbation, the strain caused by Gaspar de Salazar continued, all the more burdensome because she could not square her attempts to put him off and placate the Jesuits with her haunting sense that she had denied the poor man the right to act in accord with his own convictions.

"I am so tired," she wrote to Gracián. "You'd think he was about to commit heresy. As I told them, what they really worry about is that it became public knowledge—and the fact is, father, that we ourselves clung as hard and as fast to the world's opinions as they did, throughout this whole business."

Next, Sega ordered Gracián to retire to Los Remedios and the King countermanded the order, saying that Gracián should go back to his visitation of convents. He obeyed the King and began with Valladolid, but in a state of such nervous anxiety to prove his "perfection" that María Bautista was justly angry for once, and Teresa agreed: "It's enough if they simply obey the Constitutions."

Aggrieved, he would hear no more urgings that they send friars to Rome, or even that he urge Mariano to repair the Jesuits' water supply in Avila. Nor would he go to Pastrana to bring back the exiled nuns, though that had now become imperative; San Jerónimo's revelations had begun to be accompanied by screaming fits.

Teresa wrote to San José. She must send someone else for them, as Gracián would not reach Seville until September. San Jerónimo could then be kept isolated and two nuns with the steadiest nerves detailed to care for her. If all else failed, she had read that St. Euphrasia had cured such a problem nun by whipping. Please God she won't tell Father Acosta too much about her reve—lations!

II

Gaps in Teresa's steady flow of letters from Toledo and Avila always coincide with scandals later suppressed or troubles with the Inquisition. A two-month gap at this point is punctuated only by a note to Domingo Báñez. The Inquisition had finally imprisoned Juan de Padilla, and Báñez offered to come from Salamanca and do what he could. That would be useless, Teresa told him. Gracián had already gone back to Valladolid to the Inquisition there. They could only pray that when de Padilla came to trial he could defend himself. "We all run the same risk. I tell you, everything is going into an utter muddle."

It was indeed. Sega issued a brief revoking Gracián's Visitorship. Gracián went back into hiding, this time in the palace of Don Luis de Toledo in Mancera, where Roca was currently Prior of the monastery. The King published an edict revoking Sega's brief, a royal defiance of the Vatican wisely ignored by all but a handful of hotheads in Granada, who nailed copies of it up on the doors of the Cathedral and several churches, thus precipitating bloody riots, armed friars against armed friars.

Teresa got word of this from Roque de Huerta and wrote to Gracián by way of Roca. The riots, she said, were all to the good; now the Nuncio would not dare anger the King by giving "those wolves," the Calced, all they wanted. At the same time, Sega's brief leaves Gracián free from his dangerous responsibilities until the Discalced get their separate province and peace at last. And Roque de Huerta is right: at this juncture all, without exception, must let the Nuncio know that they accept his authority.

At that point, her letter was interrupted; the rest of it describes the inter-ruption and her own immediate action. Rioja, one of the Avilan Calced, hammered at the convent door and delivered a copy of Sega's brief. "God forgive me, I can't believe that the Nuncio gave such an order—I mean, one written in such a style!"

It was violent invective, aimed at Gracián. Teresa immediately wrote Sega a formal assurance that she and her nuns were his subjects. She sent for Julián de Avila to deliver it in person, and "to make a great show of the humility and gratitude" with which they received Sega as "their protector," while he also begged him not to let them be subject to the Calced. After that, she wrote letters to everyone she knew who might influence Sega, asking them to tell him that Gracián had laid aside his duties as Visitor when Sega came to Spain, and only resumed them at the orders of the Royal Council, and even then "only because of Tostado's intention to destroy them."

309

One of these letters still exists. It went to Bartolomé de Medina, *muy su amigo*, if only through a wish not to displease the Duchess of Alba. It is a calm, well-reasoned letter, clear about the legalities as she had learned them from Dr. Rueda, and stressing Gracián's position as one who was getting contradictory orders from the Crown and the Vatican. Unless or until her friars got to Rome and received direct orders from above to hold their proposed Chapter, Teresa, at least, knew that there must be peace with Sega.

She was in the midst of this effort when Juana wrote her a letter, not about Beatriz but about Gonzalo: Teresa must keep him from running off to the Indies with young Lorenzo. This was nonsense; young Lorenzo considered Gonzalo a dolt, and nobody would have bought him the captaincy Gonzalo expected. Still, Teresa wrote a kindly, reassuring letter to Juana, too.

We often preach best what we practice worst. Teresa wrote convincingly about the need for those in the religious life to free themselves from the "particular loves" imposed by the bonds of blood-kinship, family loyalty; but few ever gained so little of that freedom.

III

The King found Sega vexing. The Royal Council issued a pronouncement: the Discalced were not subject to the Nuncio. Gracián was sufficiently emboldened to slip away from Mancera, go to the Escorial, and see the King. His way led through Avila, and under cover of dark he made a brief stop at Teresa's convent. All she had lacked time and privacy to say to him went in a letter to his father's house in Madrid.

She had not really suffered for him, she said, until she saw him "hiding like a criminal and afraid every step of the way." Now he must proceed carefully, ignore Mariano's advice, and so far as possible "keep out of this fire" — the contention between the Crown and the Vatican. The Calced hoped for some false step on his part which they could use to win direct orders from the Pope to put him down, along with the Discalced.

He should pray that the King will not make him keep on with his visitations, but he should express this to the King as a fear of opposing God's will and leave any direct reference to the Pope out of it. At the same time he should urge the need for a separate province on the King and on Sega as well; yes, and on Quiroga, too, the Grand Inquisitor, and on the new President of the Royal Council, showing them that nothing else will avoid more scandalous conflict within the Carmelite Order, since the Andalusian Calced now have no Visitor and can't be called to account for anything they do.

But above all, before he says a word that might raise any difference between them, he must beg the King to order that Fray Juan de la Cruz be set free.

As for her own news, Doña Quiteria had just come from the Incarnation to show her a letter from the General. On the grounds of Quiteria's reports, he now ruled that the Medina convent could no longer be Discalced; it needed strong Calced supervision. He had bitter words to say against Teresa, and praise for Doña Quiteria's having returned to the fold. "God forgive those who give him false information," Teresa wrote.

Fray Juan had escaped on the day Teresa sent off that letter, and was hidden, for the time being, by Toledan nuns. In the eighteenth century the credit for his escape was taken from his pitying jailer and given to the Virgin, who also supported him in a leap from the castle wall which would otherwise have killed him. There were no such tales at the time. Only Teresa had troubled over his captivity. Her pleas to Gracián, Heredia and Mariano, that they beg the King for Fray Juan's release, had been futile; their own affairs left them no time to waste on minor matters.

The nuns in Toledo wrote to her, describing Fray Juan's physical condition: about what one would expect after the nine months just past. When he was smuggled away to Almodóvar, Teresa sent a begging letter to Gracián: "See to it that they take good care of him there. . . . You will not find many like him if he dies."

IV

The Count of Tendilla was at Court, and Teresa wrote to Roque de Huerta, urging him to make sure that the Count went with Gracián to the Escorial. Since the King was hearing so many conflicting stories, he would be likeliest to believe a courtier whom he took to be objective. How that meeting went we can only guess from the fact that it changed Teresa's mind about Gracián's seeing Sega, too. He must "wait, wait, and not meet trouble halfway."

In Seville it was also important not to meet trouble halfway. García Alvarez had offered dangerous encouragement to Beatriz, and now he was giving it to the returned exiles—especially to Beatriz's friend Margarita. San José threatened to dismiss him. Teresa knew that Seville could not afford even one more enemy, and she dared hope that García Alvarez, unangered, would at least observe the secrecy of the confessional. "For the love of God," she pleaded, "I beg you to suffer and be silent, and do not let anyone else talk about getting rid of that father. . . ."

Concerning the proposed Chapter, Teresa's friars did their best to keep her in the dark. As her sole hope for the Order, she went on urging that friars be sent to plead their case before the General before the Chapter was held; afterwards would be too late. In later years, that Chapter would need so much defense that only the last page of Teresa's final plea was saved—a relic whose relevance, it could be hoped, was sufficiently obscure: ". . . which would be a great thing; or at least one of them. Both are well thought of by the Company, which would be far from unimportant for the sake of our business. In any case, father, write to me at once. Everyone is shocked that we have nobody there to negotiate for us, and so those others have it all their own way. It is necessary for us to act quickly, right here and now! There is so little time left, as you must see! You can let me know from there if it is already too late, for however much hurry you give yourself, it will still take the rest of this coming month."

311

But once more she sees that the tone is wrong; it will only annoy him. "I am laughing at myself, as if you had them all ready to go and the means to do it with! But if we don't start it will never be done, and we should have begun right after we obeyed his counterbrief."

Heredia, she goes on, is furious because nobody told him of Sega's decree, and he has gone on giving orders in Andalusia as if Gracián were still Visitor. No wonder he's angry. How could Roque de Huerta have forgotten to tell him? (Yes, Teresa, blame anyone but Gracián himself.) Heredia has a point, with Andalusia so unsafe anyway! The Calced have already arrested Juan de la Miseria. (So it was believed for a time; but actually Juan de la Miseria, deserted at last by his Mariano, had run away to Italy, begged forgiveness, and joined the Calced.)

Gracián, she ends, can read Mariano as much of this letter as he sees fit. She herself has just learned that a Jesuit who is really her friend is going to Madrid to see de Pazo, the new President of the Royal Council, and luckily de Pazo is an old friend of his, they are both Gallicians; so she'll write to him at once.

Even in Avila, Teresa managed to keep her ear to the ground. The friendly Jesuit with the right connections was Doña Luisa's former confessor, Pablo Hernández, and we still have the letter that Julián de Avila took to him. When she heard he was in Madrid, she says, she felt as if God must have sent him there. It would be a blessed relief if she could tell him all that has happened since their last meeting, but Father Julián can at least describe the present situation. He can be trusted.

In brief, the devil hates her friars. They now have nine priories, but they are not yet a separate province, and they suffer much from the Calced. Their future is in the Nuncio's hands, but his mind has been so poisoned with lies about them that there's no telling where it will end. They tell him that she is a restless tramp who founds convents without the consent of her General or the Pope. Damning enough — but they invent still worse things: "These blessed souls say things about me that are not fit to repeat; and about Father Gracián, who was their Visitor, the unbearable accusations are something to weep over, for I swear to you that he is one of God's greatest servants, of the utmost chastity and purity of conscience, and you must believe that I am telling you the truth. In fact, his whole life was bred and formed by the Company." (He had indeed received a certain amount of Jesuit education.)

Moreover, they have never questioned the Nuncio's authority, and she herself answered his brief with all the humility that she could express. It must be God's will that they learn from suffering, for she cannot find anyone who will say a word for her, and the devil is doing his best to discredit her and her friars. "Oh, father, how few friends there are in a time of need!" So she is sending him copies of her patents to found convents. She is told that he and the President of the Royal Council are old friends. It would help greatly if Father Hernández would show him those patents and say something to undeceive him: "For you can see into my very soul."

The Nuncio must also be made to understand that the Order is simply a return to the primitive rule of the Carmelites. Perhaps Father Hernández can explain this to the Nuncio's confessor and urge him to learn the facts before he spreads these filthy inventions any further. "And tell him that however vile I am, I am not bad enough to do the things they tell about me. Say this, I mean, if it seems to you like the right thing to do, and if not, don't." He owes it to her affection for him to stand up for the truth in whatever way he finds best. God will surely reward him. And he must tell her if he is well. May God take care of him!

Teresa badly needed a good word from a Jesuit, and despite his lack of proper anti-Semitism the Very Magnificent and Reverened Pablo Hernández was an ideal spokesman: a noble, of "pure blood" and—unlike Gaspar de Salazar—not suspected of "enthusiasm," no mystic. Teresa had stretched truth when she said that he could see into her very soul.

But Teresa could keep in touch with almost everyone else better than she now could with her own friars. Within five days from the time she wrote it, they would have made her letter to Hernández one more futility.

Chapter 61 ❃ Teresa's Advice to Gracián on an Appeal to Rome

I

The Discalced convened their second Chapter in Almodóvar without Teresa's knowledge. Only two dissidents raised their voices: Roca and Juan de la Cruz both called it an act of open rebellion, saying flatly that in casting off their General they were not creating a separate province, but attempting to create a separate Order without the necessary papal authority.

They were ignored.

This Chapter, unlike the first, immediately attacked the matter of selecting friars to go to Rome, to announce the separation. Almost two years before, Teresa had suggested the two who should go to seek forgiveness: Pedro de los Angeles, because he was the General's long-time personal friend, and Mariano, who was at least an experienced traveller and fluent in Italian. This choice was once more under consideration when a rumor from Madrid threw the proceedings into panic. Gracián left Almodóvar abruptly, rushed to Madrid where he claimed that the Chapter had been called against his advice and his will, and then fled back to hiding in Pastrana. And Mariano wrote for help—to Teresa.

Sega had reacted to the Chapter as she had foreseen. He pronounced the Discalced all subject to their Calced Provincials and demanded that the ringleaders of the revolt be banished: whether by exile or imprisonment, Gracián, Heredia, Mariano, and Doria were to be put out of circulation.

Teresa's Dr. Velázquez had just been named Bishop of Osma, and the new President of the Royal Council, Pazo, was also his old friend. Since sending friars to Rome would mean defying Sega, Mariano wrote, it was important that they go with the approval of the President. Clearly, he himself could no longer be an emissary, but Teresa should urge Dr. Velázquez to urge President Pazo to approve their sending Pedro de los Angeles, with some other friar for his companion.

Teresa did write Velázquez, though not as Mariano had hoped. The scheme, she said, was madness, and one with which her friends should have nothing to do.

Then the news came: General Rubeo was dead.

It was Rubeo's belief in Teresa that had fathered the Discalced. She had always been sure that if Gracián begged forgiveness, Rubeo would forgive.

She had written her own first plea for that forgiveness three years and three months ago, and through all that intervening time she had implored Gracián to write him at least one such letter of his own and to send his representatives to describe the need for Discalced reform in Andalusia and to counter the lies of their enemies.

Gracián's letter from Pastrana was all self-pity. Teresa had much to say in reply, but little in the way of flattery or comfort. "Insofar as I see you freed from that hubbub I am freed from pain; for the rest, what happens will happen. But the pain it gave me when they wrote me about our Father General was very great. I am completely shattered, and the whole first day I cried as you should be crying for the unhappiness we gave him, which he certainly did not deserve—and if we had only gone to him, it would all have been made plain. God forgive the one who has always been holding you back, for left to myself I could have done something with you, though you put so little faith in me about it.

"May the Lord make it turn out well. . . . what you wrote me in that first letter of the two that you wrote after you spoke to the Nuncio was like gulps of death. Let me tell you, father, I was completely undone because you did not turn those papers over to him. . . . I am glad that you are now left thoroughly taught by experience, so that you will go by the road that must be taken and not go against the tide, as I always kept saying.

"Well, after all, there always were questions they could use to hold up everything, and there is no need to talk about it any more, for God ordains things for his servants to endure."

But the past is past; she must spell out their course for the immediate present. He and Mariano must agree to send a messenger to Almodóvar, where the consultations are still going on, and tell them that the friars must not go: it is madness. "And especially since our Father General is dead, and for these reasons: First, it cannot be done secretly and the Calced might capture them, which would simply be putting them to death. Second, they would lose their papers and money. Third, they are quite inexperienced in negotiating with Rome. Fourth, they would surely be arrested as fugitives, for they would find themselves wandering through the streets with no place to go, as I have written to Father Mariano. When we could do nothing to help Fray Juan here, what could we do for them there?"

This is not despair; it is clearing the decks for action. She urges something that she has clearly urged before, in one of those missing letters, since she leaves unnamed the churchly gun for hire whom she proposes: "It seems to me that the one who is soliciting the business should go. Father Rueda has such confidence in him that he thinks nobody else would be necessary. This man, who would go from here, is very, very good, except that he is more expensive; but if it is provided for now, all the convents will give the money later. It could be borrowed from that money that was willed to Alcalá, and paid back afterwards — since as far as my borrowing it here goes, I couldn't raise anything like that."

"This man" was Canon Montoya, of Madrid, a representative to the Roman Inquisition, and an agent frequently used by the King. He had gone to Avila and met Teresa as an investigator for the King's Reform. Like many in the Church that Teresa longed to purge from greed, Montoya was not in business for his health, but the skill with which he had gained all the right connections shows that he would have been a bargain at any price. Teresa knew it, and she knew that the current crisis was too grave for overnice scupling about ends and means. Bumbling friars could do nothing to save the situation. Montoya could.

That Montoya was for sale or that Teresa advocated his purchase is side-stepped by saintwatchers. This letter caused her pious translator Peers much trouble. By substituting "the friar" for her simple "he" and changing "the one who is soliciting our business" to "someone who knows how to present our case" he does what he can — though he raises a question as to why a friar from Avila could cost so much more than two from Almodóvar. And in this letter's final, urgent sentence: "The whole thing should be undertaken by this man I have already written you about," Peers changes *undertaken by* to *entrusted to*, with a footnote that Teresa refers to Father Hernández — as a general adviser, of course, not an emissary.

Before Teresa died, no need was felt to hide either her practical intelligence or Montoya's offer to use his political skill and useful connections for a fair recompense; and we can be grateful, for Teresa is worth understanding, and cannot be understood unless we know what she was up against. It is harder to work for the glory of God in the world as it is than it is, as she put it, "to seek God in corners." Teresa knew her world.

She also knew her woman's place in it, and having finished this letter she saw that once more it would only put Gracián's back up. She added a postcript, blaming everything on the devil, the death of Covarrubias, and on his replacement, "El Pausado" — who did not know whether to blame or praise the friars in order to please the King.

So, she goes on, Gracián has been martyred by those who led him in the wrong direction. When she wrote Heredia to protest holding that Chapter, he said that it could not be avoided without pain of sin, and she had not dared to contradict him. . . . She adds several more such gentle touches, begs Gracián to keep her informed, and signs the postscript, "Your unworthy subject and daughter." She never signed any other postscript, and the letter itself had been signed, "Your unworthy servant" — the equivalent of our "Yours truly." She had once laughed out of turn when Gracián rebuked her as her "Father and Superior" for daring—a woman and his subject—to criticize her betters. She knew better now.

Think about it, brothers, and try to be tolerant of women who make so much humorless noise about being fully human. After so many centuries we have a lot to work out.

II

Neither the letter nor its postscript worked. It was Pedro de los Angeles who went to Rome, as Mariano had written her that he would shortly before she heard of the General's death. Teresa had written to Fray Pedro at once, in the hope that he would be conciliatory with his old friend. Above all, that letter had said, he must persuade the General of her love for him and her willingness to do any penance, reminding him that fathers forgive their erring children. He should ask this of Rubeo for the sake of her nuns, now suffering for her sins, not for their own. Then, since the Visitorship has been abolished, he should beg the General to appoint some authority who will permit them to live by the Primitive Rule. He should hint that without this the Calced might force them into rebellion, which would be tragic, since Rubeo would no longer be their General. He should also stress it that they are not a begging Order or in financial need; once made a separate province, their annual dues will of course continue to go to him as they do now.

And, while her own first choice for their Provincial is Gracián, if the General is displeased with him, he should appoint another, preferably one of her two first friars, Fray Juan de la Cruz and Fray Antonio de Jesús—and if he objects to them, too, let him name anyone he pleases, so long as he is not an Andalusian. (Any inquiries about her first friars would reveal that Heredia was an Andalusian. Rubeo might assume that she had not known it because they met in Castile and his upper-class voice concealed his origins; put thus, she could tell Heredia that she had named him without actually telling a lie.) This done, she ends, the General will surely see that they should get back their right to form new houses of his Order, as they had before he was given so much false information.

It was well thought out, and thought wasted. We have the letter because Fray Pedro left it behind in Alcalá. We may doubt that he even bothered to read it; he had already decided upon his course of action. Once properly financed, he would go to Rome, beg forgiveness for having joined the Discalced, turn over his papers and money, and be readmitted to the fold.

Some weeks would pass before he left, and months before the word of his defection got back to Spain. Meanwhile, the four who had a choice between exile or imprisonment attempted instead to hide out in Pastrana.

Chapter 62 ❊ Gracián, King Philip, and the Nuncio

I

Pastrana offered safety from either exile or imprisonment. When Mariano had got "letters of provision" from the Royal Council and turned them over to the Governor of the Eboli lands, it insured that none of the four "ringleaders" could be seized. The Nuncio, still dim on Spanish law, sent two representatives, Coria and Juárez, with a band of bullies to raid Pastrana — instead of which they fought a losing battle with the Governor's constabulary and an armed rabble of local citizens.

Gracián was almost pathologically indecisive, and this violence exacerbated his doubts. Was it truly God's will that he stand by the Discalced and the King, or that he yield to the Nuncio who, after all, acted for the Pope?

He found his answer in a way that must have shocked Teresa to the core. A friar then resident in Pastrana was noted for a singular gift. When such doubts as Gracián's were laid before him, he could fall into a rapture at a moment's notice and discern the will of God, thus insuring a decision upon which one could act with total confidence in His protection. God's word was to yield to the Nuncio. Gracián acted on it, and all but Doria were immediately imprisoned, though under comfortable conditions, since the Calced so approved their decision. As I've mentioned before, Gracián would write of his time under house-arrest in Madrid that he "was treated with the utmost affection." If he gave Teresa his reason for turning himself and the others over to the Nuncio, her answer would not have survived. For her sake, I hope to God that he did not. To Roque de Huerta she wrote simply, "They should not have gone."

None of the three arrested could now receive or send letters. Teresa was dependent upon de Huerta to know how things stood. The Calced, she told him, were in the saddle. They had come to San José de Avila along with a crowd of justices, lawyers, and other gentlemen to issue Sega's latest pronouncement "with so little air of religion that it was shocking." Lorenzo had complicated matters by coming too, and bringing armed constables with him. It was being said that she was about to be moved to a Calced convent where she would be treated no better than Juan de la Cruz had been. She sent Roque de Huerta a letter for Chávez, the King's confessor; he must talk to him, too, telling about her frightened nuns "and what those blessed souls are putting them through." That would reinforce the effect of her letter, which simply spelled out what it had been like to be a nun under the Calced.

Teresa had an instinct for those she could trust and those she could not. De Huerta knew the facts and knew how to use them. In payment, she pours out her gratitude: May God forgive those who give de Huerta such trouble! Where does he find such strength? And what a burden it must be, collecting money to send to "those fathers in Rome." (Fray Pedro, — and Canon Montoya, by her decision. Somehow, her convents would manage to pay him back.)

317

Montoya backed out for a time, when he learned of Fray Pedro's defection: it implied complications that he had not foreseen. But the letter is important for what it shows about Teresa. A morning which would have reduced most people to hysteria or despair had sent her into action with further efforts to influence the King's confessor and to buy Montoya if possible. She dealt with the world as it is; she knew that the King was a Puritan (hence that account of life under the Calced), and she knew that money talks.

It had already talked effectively for Doria. A Genoese gentleman who knew the Nuncio explained to him why Doria should not be confined, and the Nuncio agreed. It was expensive to live as a Nuncio in proper style, and the report of what Doria had done for the Archbishop of Seville was impressive. The best that has been done in explaining away this exception made by Sega in favor of one of the four "ringleaders" originally named as heading the revolt is the suggestion that Sega kindly allowed Doria to return to Seville to help his brother Horatio with some unspecified family business. Like the often witnessed levitations of Teresa and Juan de la Cruz, this can't be disproved.

II

The two dissidents in that Chapter, John of the Cross and Roca, were at first left free. Roca made the mistake of going to Madrid to plead unselfishly for those he had opposed, and was jailed. Teresa quickly arranged for John of the Cross to go to Beas, the least and most isolated of all her convents. This served a double purpose: it gave Fray Juan shelter in a situation which could excite no dangerous envy, and it promised some control on the imagination and ambition of Ana de Jesús. She had formed a dangerous friendship-by-letter with Father Gaspar in the hope of getting away to Granada and a wider stage.

Ana became the Blessed Ana de Jesús on the strength of her inspired writings about La Santa and Fray Juan, once both were dead. Consequently only one of Teresa's letters to her survived, by accident; as you will eventually see, it is a scorcher. However, one small fragment of another saw the light when John of the Cross began to get his overdue recognition in the eighteenth century. It shows that the Blessed Ana was slow to appreciate the qualities which she would so fluently celebrate in her later years. "I have to laugh, daughter, that you complain so unreasonably of having Fray Juan de la Cruz with you, for he is a divine and heavenly man. Since he left these parts, I have found nobody like him in all Castile, nor one with such fervor on the road to Heaven. You can't imagine how lonely it makes me feel to be without him."

It is to be hoped that the Blessed Ana herself was not the author of a now admitted forgery that was used for her canonization. Unlike the rest of Teresa's letters, it does not begin "Jesus be with you," or "The grace of the Holy Spirit be with you," but, "My daughter and my crown!", going on to liken Ana to the pillar of cloud by day and of fire by night that led the children of Israel through the wilderness. Oddly enough, this "fragment" was not explained as an appreciation of Ana's soul, but as appreciation for money sent to repay Roque de Huerta's fund-raising for "the fathers who went to Rome." Its style contrasts

318

sharply with that of an invention offered by María de San José, who had the instincts of a good novelist. San José's bit sounds so like Teresa that if the content were not so far from the realities, one could accept it even though San José had, atypically, failed to save the original. It urges San José and her nuns to remain worthy of the high opinion that the whole city holds of them. San José's writings never make Gracián's mistake of "grovelling" or refuting slanders.

She would have been spared the worst of those slanders if the King had been on better terms with the Pope.

Teresa lost one source of influence at Court when the Duke of Alba got tired of blackmail by his son's ex-fiancée and the poor young man's senseless imprisonment. He collected a small armed force, set Don Fadrique free, and had him married quickly and secretly to his cousin Mariá de Toledo, as Fadrique had demanded all along. Teresa wrote the Duchess a letter of warm congratulations. It also gives thanks for all that the Duke and the Duchess have done for her Order and still try to do in a time that leaves the Discalced feeling like the Hebrews when they were slaves in Egypt (a line which may have inspired the simile of the Blessed Ana as the pillar of cloud by day and fire by night).

The Duke, of course, was immediately imprisoned, along with Albornoz, his powerful secretary, who had signed the papers for Alba to which Teresa de Laiz appended her mark. (The Duke was imprisoned for only a year and a half, as Philip needed him to head an invasion of Portugal in the war of succession which followed the death of King Sebastián. Alba is quoted as saying that it was the first time in history that a general went into battle dragging his chains.)

Such scraps of history are the background music to Teresa's story. Another of them is the convenient murder which freed Philip's attention from its absorption with Don Juan de Austria. The murder was that of Escobedo, a former secretary to Ruy Gómez and former lover of the Princess of Eboli, now attached to Don Juan de Austria, and as Philip believed, handling the logistics for Don Juan's proposed invasion of Scotland. Escobedo came to Madrid, and Pérez — Ruy Gómez's secretary at the time of his death and thereafter a brilliant confidential adviser to the King — obliged his Majesty by hiring assassins to relieve that worry.

Pérez was currently the Princess's lover, lovers exchange confidences, and the Princess enjoyed making trouble. Philip saw his indiscretion, but he worried about it for a year and four months before he took action, accused Pérez of the murder, named the Princess as his accomplice, and had them imprisoned. The delay was like Philip, and so was his having one long last discussion of foreign affairs with Pérez before he had him seized on his way home.

A friend who witnessed the seizure hurried to his house, where the Princess, as often, was spending the night, and warned her to get back quickly to Pastrana; but on the way, she was snatched from her coach. She got brutal treatment in her first place of detention, and Philip, genuinely shocked to learn of it, had her sent to house-arrest in her Pastrana palace. That, too, was like him.

Against this background music I may say that Teresa would have fared better if the whole Court had been equally distracted from the current problems of the King's Reform—and particularly, Don Luis Hurtado de Mendoza, Count of Tendilla and Governor of the Alhambra. The Count is said to have sold his diamond vest-buttons to aid Teresa's cause. I doubt it, as nobles did not raise money that way, and the Discalced accounts show no such gift from him. However, he liked both Gracián and Heredia, he saw the King's Reform as an overdue answer to Papal indifference to the decay of the monastic Orders, and his Valladolid cousins were devoted to Teresa de Jesús. Furthermore, in his eyes Ormaneto had been a gentleman, Tostado and Sega were beneath contempt, living insults to the King's integrity and authority—and the Count himself, as eldest son of a Marquis, was unused to being pushed around.

Above all, he had the Spanish noble's hatred for high-handed Italian churchmen. He felt Sega's imprisonment of Gracián and Heredia as an insult to the Spanish Faith, and he stormed up to confront Sega eye-to-eye and demand that he hear out those supposed rebels, respect what they had to say in their own defense, and withdraw his brief against them from further circulation until that was done. The Nuncio's jaw must have dropped at such effrontery. He refused, the Count lost all self-control, was violently insulting in the presence of witnesses, and steamed off to his friend Chimacero, Fiscal of the Royal Council, to get a warrant forbidding any further publications of the Nuncio's brief—which thus far had only reached the top: the Discalced priors and the Mother Foundress.

The Nuncio demanded that Philip reprimand Tendilla and send him down from Court. The King assured him that the Count should be reproved and made to write a retraction to the Royal Council and—as if in kindly warning— remarked that he heard of an enthusiasm for Sega among the Calced which could be more unfortunately misinterpreted. "See that you favor virtue," he is reported to have said in closing the interview, "for people are saying that you are no friend to my reform." With which, he walked away.

However, the King kept his word. He asked Tendilla to go back to Granada for a little, and to retract his request to the Royal Council. Tendilla complied, ending his letter with a strong defense of the Discalced. This the President sent to the King, and the King, as always with documents he studied, filled its margins with comments in his maddeningly illegible hand, all endorsing the Count's defense of the Discalced. And having kept his word, he called Tendilla back to Court.

Tendilla then told Sega that his demands had the King's written endorsement. Sega meanwhile had sent a protest to the Pope—though he expected (and would get) only a cautiously waffling reply. He also tried to enlist the support of the Grand Inquisitor—and got the cold shoulder. Quiroga, too, was a Spanish nobleman; and the Spanish Inquisition was just that—Spanish.

Sega played his last card. Baltazar Nieto told him which Andalusians would gladly swear again to all previous defamatory evidence against Gracián. He then assured the Count that he favored the reform but not the ex-Visitor. He would gladly consent to an investigation of certain charges against Gracián made by clerics of the King's own choosing. Once vice was exposed and punished, the matter of a separate province could be settled properly in Rome.

Tendilla told the King, and the King appointed a judiciary committee of four to examine the Andalusian evidence: Fernández, the Visitor to Castile; his friend and fellow Dominican, Hernando de Castilla; Don Luis Manrique, the King's almoner; and an Augustinian scholar, Lorenzo de Villavicenzo. They studied the matter of a separate province and agreed unanimously that it should be granted. Then they came to the charges against Gracián and laid the matter before him as they saw it.

The charges they pointed out, were false; but it would do him and his Order no good if he chose to have them publicly aired and tried to defend himself. The world loves to see hypocrites exposed, and particularly those who set themselves up as reformers. Moreover, the scandal would have particular appeal because it concerned enclosed nuns—ostensibly the most chaste and dedicated brides of Christ—as well as the Foundress, old enough to be his mother, and, in her absence, the handsome Mother María de San José.

The devil would win that trial, for even if Gracián were proved innocent, the verdict would be happily disbelieved; it would only be said that the King's examiners had decided not to "give scandal." But if Gracián waived trial, and let himself be punished for crimes unspecified, he would be seen, in Castile at least, as a blameless victim of the Nuncio, a man who had few friends. As for the punishment, it would be hardly more than a normal Lent, prolonged until the Pope saw that Sega was doing him no good in Spain: that is, house-arrest in Alcalá with Monday, Wednesday, and Friday observed as fast-days, and "the discipline" taken twice a week—by his own hand and in private.

Gracián, needless to say, decided wisely.

Of all this, Teresa only knew that on December third the King ordered certain charges against Gracián to be examined and that on the twentieth he was condemned—as scapegoat for those who had first persuaded him to hold that rebellious Chapter, Heredia and Mariano.

In San José de Avila that Christmas there was no play with comic shepherds clowning before the manger, no merriment. According to Teresica, Teresa spent Christmas Day kneeling before the altar in tears. If she did indeed break down, for once, at others' expense, and I can believe it, within two days she had herself in hand again. On the twenty-seventh, a letter came from Roque de Huerta which explained the whole situation. Her answer expressed all confidence that sooner or later, God's cause would triumph and they would have their separate province.

She wrote in the same vein to Gracián's mother; he has always prayed for trials, and these will so strengthen his soul that he will hardly know himself. And since Heredia and Mariano are soon to be set free, everything will work out. The sisters miss Gracián's letters, but they won't have to miss them long: "Though the devil wants to take that from us. God is over all."

However, though the devil had run into difficulties at Court, he was about to have a field-day in Seville. When the tales, refreshed for Sega, reached the convent by way of muted rumors, they proved a source of inspiration to jealous Beatriz and malicious Margarita.

Chapter 63 ❀ *Accusations at the Seville Convent; Teresa and Doria*

I

San José saw to it that Teresa knew as little as possible. When the Calced Provincial wrote her about the accusations brought by two sisters in Seville, Teresa assumed that they were Beatriz and San Jerónimo. Months later she wrote to San José, "But even at that, I never imagined that Margarita was in it." Yet in her *Libro de Recreaciones*, San José claims that throughout the trouble Teresa ordered her to suffer García Alvarez in silence "since it was the devil's work" and that her complaints of "a certain nun" only brought the response, "Don't be a fool, daughter. That So-and-so [she used the right name] will come to her senses."

San José was eager to clear herself of blame; and admittedly, she had been up against a bad situation. San Jerónimo came back from Pastrana too mad to be interesting to any confessor, however misguided, but Margarita Ramírez came back ripe for deviltry, and found such amusement in acting the part of the visionary St. Beatriz Chávez's sole true believer that the pair became García Alvarez's holy obsession. As San José says, he spent three months in confessing them "from morning to night, sometimes separately and sometimes together" — and less as his penitents than as his twin inspirations.

When San José tried to stop this, "he went to all the other convents in Seville" and was assured that she had no right to interfere. Since she persisted, "he appealed to *letrados*" (the Jesuits Acosta and de Hoja) and passed on so many lies told by his inspired pair that when San José tried to explain the situation to Acosta, he accused her of being dishonest and secretive. When she still refused to be intimidated, since Beatriz and Margarita were disrupting the whole convent with their hysteria, García Alvarez complained of her interference to the Carmelite Provincial, Cárdenas — who warned her to keep in her place.

At this point, the convent learned of Sega's search for Andalusian witnesses against Gracián; and Margarita was inspired to encourage Beatriz along new lines. Beatriz ceased to stress the supernatural favors showered on her by Christ and Our Lady, and confessed to a grave sin: out of cowardice she had long kept secret her ugly knowledge of Gracián's sexual misbehavior with the Mother Foundress and San José. Since the same tales were being newly refreshed among the Calced, García Alvarez gladly believed her; it justified his struggles to protect the saintly pair from their enemy, the Prioress.

García Alvarez was a small man with a great need for appreciation. Such men often attach themselves to unpopular causes and give them ardent service; but if that service is repaid with less than humble gratitude, let those so served beware! A small man can contain a mighty rage.

García Alvarez saw his duty and took Beatriz and Margarita before the Inquisition. Margarita was delighted at this opportunity to use her creative imagination. While the documents containing their detailed, lengthy accusations have vanished, we know that they existed from the covering letter with which they were sent on to the Madrid Chapter, fifteen years after Teresa's death — as part of an attempt to block her beatification.

The Inquisition preferred to shift the responsibility, not only because they had heard much the same stuff before, but because the Grand Inquisitor was presently known to be on the King's side against the Nuncio, and hence on the side of the Discalced against the Calced. Consequently, the investigation was turned over to the Provincial Cárdenas, a select group of friars, and the Jesuits Acosta and de Hoja. The examination was a nightmare. The Provincial and his assistants questioned the nuns day after day, never less than six hours at a time. They worked from a copy of the accusations taken down from Beatriz and Margarita. Nuns who tried to deny them were bullied, cursed, and threatened with excommunication. Finally, all were forced to sign their names to the whole list of obscenities. Tiny Leonor de San Gabriel held out the longest. "I hoped," she testified later, "that some friar would come from Los Remedios and tell me what to do, but at last I did sign my name, in very great sorrow."

Doria was then in Seville, but he preferred to play it safe. When San José was deposed as Prioress and Beatriz made Vicar-Prioress in her place, he saw it best to distance himself from the convent, and went back to Madrid. The examiners told the city all they knew and a bit extra. Petronila, a nun who in later years became Prioress, witnessed to this for Teresa's beatification: "The good name of the Holy Mother suffered so greatly that there was no lack in Seville of those willing to say that she had sent several of her sons to live with her brothers in the Indies. . . . And she also took young girls from place to place, for her friars' pleasure." To this, Isabel de Santo Domingo added: "It was said that though such an old woman, she still took both white men and black to her bed to satisfy her lusts."

San José, it seemed, only enjoyed sex with Gracián; but her mind was so perverted by reading forbidden books that "in one single sentence she was heard to pronounce three heresies." La Santa was no such scholar, but she confessed the nuns herself, saying that they needed no priest, belittled their fleshly sins, encouraged them to eat before communion, and said that the Lutherans were right to rid themselves of holy pictures and statues. Such accusations, recalled after long years and in part gained by hearsay, are not hard evidence. But by some oversight of censorship, we also have Margarita's eventual retractions, properly signed and notarized, each tidbit ending, *"which is a big lie."*

Gracián, she had stated, "lay on embroidered cushions and ate turkey" whenever he came to the convent. His sexual appetites were phenomenal; not content with the Mother Foundress and San José, he enjoyed all the others, warning them that they must never confess what they did with him. He even attempted the seduction of a child of eight, and had her between his legs when Mother Teresa came upon them and said, "Teresica, what are you doing?" He roused the nuns' jealousy by making Teresa strip before them so that all might see "how fat and white she was." And, as I have mentioned before, he himself "often stripped down to his bare skin and danced naked before them all" before engaging in deeper pleasures. (When one thinks of Gracián, so afraid of scandal, excessively ambitious, somewhat overweight, and so clumsy that he even kept falling off his donkey, this particular fancy outshines all the rest.)

San José, witnessing for Teresa's canonization, said that Beatriz outdid Margarita in her "unchaste" accusations; but what she actually said is lost, for seven months later she refused to dictate any such retraction. She preferred to imply that she herself was too chaste to have understood any such goings-on other than the rampant heresy which made Father Acosta cry out, "This is my Father's house, and ye have made it a den of lions." On this, in effect at least, Beatriz told the truth; for while Acosta said *ladrones*, not *leones*, this Gospel denunciation is also credited to him by San José, San Gabriel, and Mariana de los Santos — though as evidence that the world always bears false witness against its saints and stones the prophets.

Beatriz enjoyed her power while it lasted. She made Sister Mariana her sacristan, telling her of the enforced profession at which she lay on the floor and wept over being imprisoned in that den of lions. The convent, she said, would soon be put under the Calced and saved from damnation, and then she would have San José, San Francisco and San Gabriel all sent to house-arrest in Castile; but meanwhile they must be kept in their cells and not allowed to see one another. And, to make their enclosure perfect, the porteress must accept no letters at the turn.

Before Beatriz had thought to pass that rule, but after the Provincial had ordered that all letters from Teresa to her Seville convent be sent instead to the Nuncio, she wrote a letter to her embattled nuns; wrote it, as she herself said later, in the hope that it would go to the Nuncio instead. She sent it in care of the old Prior of Las Cuevas, with a note which says that the Prioress had not dared tell him of the convent's troubles and that she herself cannot tell of them in a letter. She can only beg him not to distrust her nuns and to realize that what they signed was under duress.

To her convent she says that the Calced have taken pains to let her know all that has happened to her daughters, and she has never loved them as much as she does now. They must see their trials as a chance to gain riches of the spirit; God is giving them treasures for which they need not voyage to the Indies. "Courage, courage, my daughters! Remember that God gives us no more than we can bear, and He is with us in our tribulations. Prayer, prayer, daughters! Let your humility shine out, and let nobody be less obedient to your Vicar-Prioress than your Mother-Prioress will surely be." (A wise warning to San José.)

She hopes that the false accusations of which the Provincial has told her are all Calced inventions. "But, for the love of God, think whether any one of you said a thing out of fear or confusion, for as long as there has been no sin against God, the rest is nothing; but lies told with intent to do harm would give me much to grieve over." This would be true even if they said things that they knew nobody would believe, since Gracián's "virtue and his purity" in dealing with them are so well known. So they must all question themselves, and ask the Holy Trinity to guide them.

She especially wants to comfort little Leonor, for she knows she must have grieved over seeing her Prioress used so. She does not grieve over San Jerónimo (whom Teresa still believed to be one of the accusers) if she meant well, and was merely deluded by her madness; but if not, she grieves over her more than all the rest. (The devil can use madness for his means of capturing a soul.) But for a letter with that brave—and studied—beginning, she ends oddly: "I had much rather talk to Señor [not father] García Alvarez than write to him, so since I can't put what I want to say to him in writing, I am not writing to him at all. Remember me to such of the sisters as you dare mention this letter to."

It is as if she forgot that the letter was addressed to them all and meant, if it did not miscarry, to be read aloud. But Teresa did not, in fact, know whom she could trust, and this fact directed her pen. Indeed, she had sent the letter in care of the old Prior of Las Cuevas because he was inclined to believe what he heard—for which Teresa in time forgave him, though San José did not.

Actually, Teresa's sole defender in Seville during that time was Rodrigo Alvarez—whom she had warned San José to keep away from Beatriz and San Jerónimo. Alvarez had courage, and Teresa had impressed him more powerfully than she knew. In later years his Rector would prefer to forget how Alvarez had stood alone, and he testified ardently for Teresa's canonization, as did García Alvarez. Rodrigo Alvarez would have smiled tight-lipped to hear them, if he had lived.

II

The news of Pedro de los Angeles' defection came with the return of the ship that took him to Italy; he had wasted no time. Doria planned to go in his place, and Teresa protested. He must not go! He was needed in Spain, the only leader of the Discalced who was still free.

She protested it as well to Roque de Huerta: the Nuncio will see the truth in time: "The end hasn't come yet!" Dr. Rueda has got a number of influential people to write in her favor, and de Huerta must put the packet of letters into Tendilla's hands for him to give the King—except for the one from the Augustinian Prior and the Franciscan; Roque must find some way for those two letters to be delivered without its being known that they were forwarded by her.

It is all highly Byzantine. It had to be, and nobody else was willing or able to take on her burden of political complexities: above all, not Gracián, that credulous soul. Her letter to Roque ends with a hope that Gracián will never be Visitor again; she had rather see anyone else in that place, except for one of the Calced.

That was in March. Things were getting better than Teresa let herself hope. Her letters to those in power kept their feeling for her warm, and Sega had badly overstepped himself. Like the imprisonment of the "ringleaders" the Seville story worked against him; many who had merely disliked him were now outraged, and the Pope began to see that a Nuncio so universally detested did him no long-term good. Spain might be slow to rally its armies to aid the Papal States the next time they were needed. He recalled Sega on April Fool's Day.

Sega, after due thought, made Angel de Salazar his Vicar before he left. Father Angel, after all, was Teresa's long-term enemy. Teresa was pleased. It was, as she said, only a temporary arrangement and as things now stood, Father Angel would do small harm because he would not want to offend the King. In this she was right. Sega had moved Gracián from the "affectionate" Calced in Madrid and given him Elías de San Martín for a jailer in Alcalá—the one Discalced friar sure to enjoy making his life painful. Father Angel put a stop to that, allowed Gracián to live comfortably, and to correspond with his friends.

Teresa wrote to him, a letter full of hope. Perhaps he could soon visit Avila and, more important still, get San José reinstated. And best of all, Roca was going to Rome. He was now in Avila, and the more she talked with him, the more convinced she was that he would be effective. However, they were having an argument. She wanted to have duplicates made of the King's letter and all other important documents and have them sent to Canon Montoya by his mother. (That lady was glad to help, for she and Teresa had many mutual friends in Valladolid, and nobody would think to intercept her letters to her son.) This was important, since journeys are hazardous. And besides, now that the Canon is willing to serve them again, he can take up their business with the Vatican in a way that would show him as a disinterested friend. Then Roca could go directly to the General, who wouldn't like it if he heard that Roca was going to first one and then another before he went to him. But Roca keeps saying that he can't see why he should go at all if the negotiations are to be carried on by somebody else. That is like him, but she will have to make him see that both he and Montoya are necessary.

For a wonder, Teresa did manage to do just that. She got her own way with one of her friars. The event would show how wisely she had planned, with a diplomat to handle such key figures as the Pope's Cardinal-nephew, and Roca to go straight to the General, all sincerity and simplicity.

Roca and his companion, Diego de la Trinidad, travelled as two merchants, José Bullón and Diego Heredia. Caution was still necessary. In writing about it to Roque de Huerta, Teresa addressed her letter to his friend Cassademonte, who would pass it on to him secretly; and she could only make oblique reference to the glad news that the charges for which Gracián had let himself be imprisoned without trial were due to be dismissed. "Rest assured," she wrote, "that with those two gentlemen [the travellers] and the Dominican fathers [Gracián's judges] to help out, I have no further worries about this part of our business. The ones I worry about now are the Mitigated fathers, as such ugly things can cause great sorrow to those who wear our habit." The "ugly things" ("not fit for chaste ears") would not be forgotten during Teresa's lifetime; and they had thrown a comprehensible scare into Gracián. He was in no hurry to go to Avila—though he wrote Teresa that now his trials were ending, he longed for more.

Teresa was not impressed: "I had to laugh at your saying that you want trials all over again! Leave us alone, for the love of God, for you aren't the only one who has to bear them! Give us a few days' rest."

It was Doria who came to Avila. The wind was changing, and he knew it. Teresa's gift for making the right friends had largely brought it about, and he knew that, too. Doria saw that Teresa should be respected; it would pay off.

III

Doria, Heredia, and Mariano all saw Gracián as a stumbling-block to their ambitions, but Doria was the most farsighted of the three, Mariano the least. Doria had got out of Seville when the trouble started; scandals can do no good; and least said, soonest mended. Mariano, on learning of the upheaval—through the Calced, as Teresa had—wrote letters and preached sermons in García Alvarez's praise; thus showing himself, he hoped, on the side of the reform where it was needed—even if the need concerned degenerate convents of his own Order. When Teresa, enraged, and Doria, cool-headed, urged him to visit Seville and see for himself that he was deceived, he did—and corrected matters by replacing Beatriz with poor, mad San Jerónimo. If the slanders that destroyed Gracián also destroyed a convent, it was worth it; women were creatures Mariano could not take seriously. He also called on the Prior of Las Cuevas and confirmed his suspicion that where there was smoke there was fire. Things had not been as bad, perhaps, as the Calced believed, but good little García Alvarez's work in that place had been sadly needed.

In contrast, Doria's first act of self-service was to tell the Archbishop that he had long been distressed by García Alvarez and his two lunatic penitents. The man was a dangerous fool who should be forbidden entrance to any convent. The Archbishop found the benevolent son of a great banking house more credible than a failed engineer turned religious as last resort, or a senile prior who lived out of touch with the world. He forbade García Alvarez to go near the convent, and when Mariano and the Prior pleaded for him, he shrugged them off. Doria saw to it that Teresa knew what he had done. He also saw to it that Teresa could once more hear from Seville directly and send back a long, long letter expressing her trust: "For though I know my daughter Josefa is very wicked indeed, she could never have deserved such punishment."

She asks if they got the letter sent them through the Prior of Las Cuevas. Doria tells her how he tried in vain to write them through his brother Horatio. San José owes Doria much: "You have him fooled better than you fooled García Alvarez!" She continues in the same ironic vein: too bad they've lost García Alvarez, "though it's only the convent's loss since he found it so much trouble before he left. We certainly owe him a lot!" But if the Archbishop won't let Mariano or the Prior of Las Cuevas bring him back, who can?

327

A more serious sentence begins, "It's as if the devil were trying to put us down in every way, especially in this thing they are doing about [deleted]." (The irony had to stand as straightforward praise once the letters were published. García Alvarez, who witnessed for Teresa's canonization and Mariano, a founding father, could have no stain upon their shining garments.) But Beatriz and Margarita have Teresa "completely worn out." When she first tried to warn San José, she "hadn't realized that Margarita was in it," but now both women must be handled carefully. Beatriz is a type whom the devil finds it easy to use—and San Jerónimo probably believes that she actually saw all that those two invented. They must all be treated gently, San Jerónimo not allowed to talk with outsiders, and Beatriz and Margarita kept separate as far as possible. Father Nicoleo (Doria) will talk it all over with her; he's going back to Seville on business; but, "for the love of charity, do what I'm telling you *now!*"

And she makes a suggestion which is highly practical but far from saintly: it would be best if San José could trick Beatriz and Margarita into a quarrel about something. There are times when the vision of what ought to be can only be served by a straight look at things as they are.

Chapter 64 ❄ *Teresa's Travels Resumed*

I

Some things had to be kept top secret. Raising the money to pay Montoya had to be done without spreading the news of Fray Pedro's defection, which in turn could have led to the discovery of Roca's secret mission. It was one of those jobs of which Teresa has said, "Sometimes one must dissemble a little."

Fray Pedro needs more money, Teresa wrote to María Bautista, and Ana de Jesús (of whom she knew María Bautista to be jealous) has contributed a hundred and fifty ducats. She is sorry to learn that María Bautista demanded four hundred ducats for receiving Gracián's sister, since his family has so little to spare. She addressed the letter to the Prioress and Nuns of the Convent of Valladolid, to make sure that it would be read aloud, and ended it, "I beg the Mother-Prioress that what her daughters want to do may not fail on her account." It was hitting below the belt, for María Bautista was as proud as she was tight-fisted, but it had to be done. A dream that had once seemed to need for its fulfillment only lives of prayer, harmoniously lived, had turned out to need hard cash as well.

Incidentally, the generosity of the Blessed Ana de Jesús—which produced that supposed fragment beginning "My daughter and my crown!"—was not spontaneous. It resulted from the insistence of John of the Cross, as we know from a letter to Gracián: he, like Roca, had always seen the importance of sending Discalced representatives to Rome.

Alvaro and María Mendoza wanted a visit from Teresa. They told Father Angel that they needed spiritual comfort for the death of their brother, the Duke of Sesa. Father Angel saw that to keep Teresa confined would offend many, but he still hoped to destroy her. Malagón was in notoriously bad condition, and Salamanca had the added advantage of being in enemy country; either might discredit her. He replied that visits to both were urgent, but she might make a brief stopover en route "to comfort those lords" in Valladolid.

Heredia had a notion of the same kind. A group of *beatas* in Villaneuva de la Jara could be made into a convent, and one likely to make trouble; better still, it was in a part of the world where the Seville scandal was well known. Teresa was frightened, especially as Father Angel—now Vicar-General—had recognized Heredia as her Provincial. She wrote for advice to Fernández, who was clearing away the tag-ends of the troubles which had imprisoned the friars. He told her to put Heredia off as best she could; if word of her founding a new convent got to Rome, Sega would use it as an excuse for making trouble for Roca, both with the new General and with the Vatican.

So Teresa told Heredia that Father Angel's orders must come first, and wrote to María Bautista: "Now look at the poor old hag, off again!" She describes her plans as she sees them, but at the bottom of the page are a few words about Casilda de Padilla's disputed fortune: "I tell you, it will end with their giving you nothing. . . . What good does all this hubbub do? There was never so much turmoil stirred up over so little." The rest of the letter is missing. Unsurprisingly so. Money to buy a separate province was one thing in Teresa's eyes; to satisfy greed it was quite another. She would have said more about that than María Bautista cared to see.

Father Angel arranged and rearranged his plans. Teresa's final sailing orders came on the eighth of June. She should go to Medina, accompanied by Valdemoro, of all people, straighten out some business there, spend a day or two in Valladolid, go to Salamanca, and then to Malagón. Just before she left she wrote to San José, who was at odds with Doria and putting on an act about not wanting to be Prioress again. Doria deserves their gratitude, and as for San José's not "feeling worthy," well, *"for want of good men, as they say."* It's a proverb: "For want of good men, my husband is mayor."

Furthermore, Gracián took a notion to go to Rome himself. In writing to dissuade him, Teresa urged that he was now no longer alone. Heredia and Mariano, to her grief, had always misled him for their own ends, but in Doria he now has a true friend. There had been a time when Teresa could smell out ambition a mile away, but now she was tired—and Doria was a very clever man.

Valladolid offered no rest. The nobles, quickly recovered from the Duke of Sesa, could not do enough to entertain her, and the convent, not to be outdone, was equally overattentive. Teresa was worn out when she left them and went on to Alba—where yet another nun had gone mad. Only a wise prioress could keep an enclosed convent from breeding hysterics, the Prioress of Alba was a problem-case herself, the convent was always at its worst when the Duchess was away (as now, with her imprisoned husband in Ubeda), and Teresa de Laiz seized the opportunity to make herself felt as its patroness.

The Alba problems dragged on for a month. Teresa got to Salamanca in mid-August, and found it in still worse state. Pedro de Banda's house was falling apart, the nuns were ill and demoralized, Cousin Ana as acting Prioress was making things worse with her growing taste for fasts and penances, and Father Angel demanded that the convent be set to rights or dissolved. No one was willing to sell them a better house. By October, Teresa was still struggling to find one, and to calm the nuns. In June, Gracián had let her hope that she would meet him there, but now he had even ceased to write to her. It was the wrong time to get news that San José, having used her act of "unworthiness" to fine effect, had gone back to house-hunting — actually encouraged by Heredia to buy a house that would impress Seville in the way he best understood. Was he grooming her to take Teresa's place when she died? Had he persuaded Gracián that after the most recent scandals he would do better to ease himself away from the Mother-Foundress to her handsome, clever, obvious successor?

Teresa wrote Gracían a letter which was destroyed; he answered it, and she wrote another which was saved and published — perhaps because it mentions Angela — though not the Angela who had once had such God-given trust in her Paul: "The grace of the Holy Spirit be with Your Reverence, though Angela has not got over the suspicions she was entertaining. And no wonder, for according to what she says, she has nothing else to comfort her and no wish to give herself leeway to find anything else and — according to what she says — the flesh is weak and she suffers when she feels herself badly repaid. You must tell that gentleman, for the love of charity, that he should not be careless with her, for love cannot sleep so long."

She drops Angela, sympathizes with his various excuses for not writing to her, starts to tell of her past month's troubles — and is swept off into open bitterness. "It's the tragic fact that I can't find a house in Salamanca that is worth anything. Certainly if these sisters here had that house in Seville, they would think they were in Heaven. The folly that Prioress is showing pains me greatly, and I have lost much of my faith in her. I'm afraid the devil has got a start in that house and means to destroy it completely. . . . I see a rapacity there that I can't stand, and that Prioress is more knowing than one in her position should be, and so I'm afraid that it will end with her winning nothing; and as I said to her when I was down there, she never dealt with me straightforwardly. She has much [deletion] of law [deletion].

"I tell you I went through with a lot with her, down there. Seeing that she had written me often with a great show of penitence, I thought she had changed for the better and come to understand herself. This telling the poor nuns how bad for them the house is, is enough to make them all believe they're sick. I have written her terrible letters, and she gives way no more than steel."

Teresa ends with asking Gracián to ask Doria to make Heredia "stop encouraging her." Why she didn't simply write about it to Doria scarcely seems worth asking. San José was at least sixteen years younger than Teresa; she was strong, handsome, clever, ambitious, and Teresa knew it. She also knew her own weariness, and Gracián, in his time of approaching triumph, seemed to have forgotten her.

As Angela asked Gracián to remind "that gentleman," the flesh is weak.

II

Teresa had to leave Salamanca much as she had found it. She got back to Avila in early November. She was in such bad physical condition that her nuns tried to keep her from going on, but she was under orders. She had to leave, without rest, for Malagón.

A lay-sister, who in time and deservedly would get papal recognition as the Venerable Ana de San Bartolomé, became, in those final years, first the servant who helped Teresa dress and undress, then her nurse, and finally her amanuensis. Unusually, for one of her background, she could read, and Teresa taught her to write. This made her eligible to become a choir-nun, but she refused; she wanted no position that would separate her even briefly from the Mother who needed her care and gave her in return a friendship like none she had ever imagined. We can be glad of that, for San Bartolomé was as frank as Teresa's old cousin, San Jerónimo the sane — but unlike San Jerónimo, she did not "take her so much for granted" that she forgot her quality or their shared adventures.

This is how she describes the endless journeys of Teresa's last two years: "There were times when we followed the road all day through rain or snow without finding a single village or any shelter to keep us from getting wet through. At night we would come to an inn where they had no fire or anything to eat and the cracks in the wall let the rain in on the bed, and often our clothes would be soaked. I remember how we got to an inn like that one night, in bad need of shelter, and our clothes were drenched and it had given her a sore throat; and I was with her and seeing her shake with cold I went to get fire to warm a little bread. When a rich man who was in the inn found out who was there he began to say foul, insulting things...." But Teresa, she says, never complained.

The sore throat developed in the following year, but not from wettings; it was cancer. The "foul insulting things" were commonplace from the time of that second Seville investigation to the end. The Calced had felt that Beatriz's and Margarita's tales were too good to keep; they spread fast, and a wide audience enjoyed them. Gracián's caution is not unforgivable.

Teresa reached Toledo after such a journey as San Bartolomé describes; she was fevered, crippled, and had to spend her four days there in bed. Gracián wrote the Duchess of Alba about his anxiety over hearing of it; Teresa would have found that anxiety a pleasant surprise.

As soon as the weather cleared, she was off to Malagón. Leaning on her stick she managed the walk to the long-promised, almost-completed convent just outside the village, where she hurried the workmen along and directed them to set up a temporary enclosure so that the move could be made before the work was done. She oversaw them daily, and the wine with which she cheered them on became, after her canonization, a miraculous wineskin which could never be drained dry. (Her second such recorded miracle.)

She had come prepared for difficulties; she brought the best of the Salamanca nuns, Jerónima del Santo Espíritu, to be prioress; and she had Doria choose her a strong-minded, dependable friar to be the nun's sole confessor. She had got there by the end of November, and by the second week of December the nuns went in procession to their new house, looking, she said, "like little lizards creeping out into the sun."

When she met with the Licentiate with whom she had quarreled so much by letter, she forgave him. He was young and had doubtless been overfond of Brianda; but he lacked authority, and she believed him when he told her that he could not check those wilful girls who were so friendly with the Alcantarine friars, and that he worried when the convent also produced its own visionary — another Ana de Jesús (surnamed Contreras).

Moving the convent helped to correct much without wounding the pride of any but the visionary nun, who luckily had not been popular with the others. Teresa had dreaded that visit, but once there and in the new convent, so pleasantly remote from the village, so quiet, she wanted to stay as long as she could.

Doria wrote her that he planned to get her a convent in Madrid; he had found a wealthy young girl whose family would endow it if the city refused to let her found in poverty. She embraced the thought; a convent in Madrid to crown her work! Simultaneously, Heredia was directing her to found in Antoca, down on the Portuguese border, while Father Angel, having considered Heredia's original idea, now demanded a convent for the *beatas* of Villaneuva de la Jara. Teresa could hardly tell which prospect she dreaded most.

Fray Germán, so promptly released after his arrest with Fray Juan de la Cruz, died, and Teresa wrote to Gracián: "God have Fray Germán in heaven, for there were good things about him though his intelligence didn't go so far as to let him understand much about the ideal of perfection." It is an interesting sidelight on the helper chosen by the Discalced for the companion to St. John of the Cross.

Gracián, now cleared by his judges, was preaching in Alcalá with great success. Apparently he apologized for the satisfaction it gave him, for Teresa wrote back, "I had to laugh at Paul's pride! About time! Don't be afraid it could grieve me or do him any harm, for he'd be very foolish — which he isn't — if he doesn't remind himself of the water-wheel whose buckets fill up as soon as they're emptied. Happiness is a great thing, so his letter gave me a rest from my own troubles. Tell him so."

But she thought it over, and her Christmas letter contained a warning. The Licentiate had just preached them a sermon: "He's a good creature and would never have put anyone's good name in doubt intentionally, but it makes me realize that even if preachers are saints, they should have as little to do with nuns in these convents as possible.... Even if it was Paul, I believe that the sight of him having so much talk with their like can do him no good, but real harm instead, and some loss of the good reputation that people like him ought to have." It is clumsy; but it is hard to say, "Please try not to get yourself talked about again."

Then, suddenly, she comes out with it: "Oh, father, what suffering I have gone through over this at certain times in the past! And how Christmas Eve reminds me of the days when your letter made me suffer so much, just a year ago! That letter was certainly one of the kind that I will never forget as long as I live." That letter about the slanders he was suffering . . . . He is cautious about seeing her now, but has he forgotten that the slanders also concerned San José and all the nuns in Seville?

Three days later, she wrote to Doria: Now the Malagón nuns understand how the devil used Brianda's faults to leave them all blundering, and even Brianda's own sister does not want her to go back. But this may not last, if San José's nuns keep on writing to tell them to demand Brianda's return, as if their case had been like San José's replacement by Beatriz. If they did get her back, things would be as bad as ever, here, and San José surely realized that she would never have let Brianda be sent away "without grave cause." Doria must rebuke San José for allowing them to send such letters, "and give her a good penance!" (Teresa is too disturbed to remember that she has never mentioned any problem other than Brianda's health.)

Her letter to San José, written on the same day, begins sweetly: she is "touched" because San José's most recent letter is "so good and humble." She hopes that her own letters have not distressed her. "You must forgive me, as I am unbearable with people I really love. I can't stand seeing them go wrong in anything. It affected me like that with Mother Brianda. I wrote her terrible letters, but it did small good."

But she can't leave it there. She has heard that San José has been entertaining a Jesuit in the convent. Can't she realize that it could make fresh scandal? God knows they went through enough with Acosta! And how can she think that Doria is against her, or that she, Teresa, resents having her advice ignored? "I tell you truly that I don't care whether or not people attend to me, so long as they are seen to be living up to their obligations." What hurts is not having her judgment disregarded, but having that disregard "covered up by deceit."

She hears that San José is expecting money from the Indies. Why doesn't she use it to pay off her debts in Seville, where the interest on them is so high? And she also hears she's expecting money from Toledo: "I wish you would use it to pay my brother some part of what you owe him; he really needs it." He is having to sell off property at a loss; perhaps San José can send him "some part of what [she] owes, if not all at once."

She wishes that Beatriz would retract all those lies she told, though it seems likely that only God could make her do it. And now that Doria has told San José the whole Malagón story, she will doubtless be sorry that she and San Francisco wrote all that stuff to the sisters about getting their Prioress back. "Oh, God help me, what nonsense there was in that letter, just to get your own way!" Abruptly she realizes how the letter has strayed from its intended tone. She ends abruptly, "Well, we learn by our mistakes. I can't go on with this any further. God take care of you."

Teresa kept few illusions, but it must often have struck her hard that so little she had accomplished had much to do with the dream as it was first embodied in San José de Avila: twelve nuns and a prioress, learning to love God through learning to love one's neighbor as oneself, and using that love in prayer that should bring about the healing of His Church.

San Jerónimo sent her a letter signed "Manure Pile." Teresa did not let herself laugh at the poor creature: she only wrote back gravely that she would be glad to believe her contrition more than a matter of empty words. And she wrote to Doria that he had better leave Andalusia again. He should keep free of the plotting and planning that seemed to go on there incessantly and realize that it might be better for his friend Gracián if Heredia, not he, were to head the new province once it was established. Better not only for Gracián himself, but for the whole Order, since it would do away with much jealousy and mean-spirited snipings.

It was mid-January in 1580 when she wrote that letter. Before the month was over, and before she was wholly sure that the separate province would be granted her Discalced, let alone sure which of her friars would head it if it were indeed granted, Teresa was on her way to make the first of her last four foundations. The chapter that she had written as an epilogue to *Fundaciones* still stands displaced, no epilogue after all.

Chapter 65 ✳ *A Foundation at Villanueva de la Jara; a Threat of Violence to Teresa in Montalbán*

I

No chapter in *Fundaciones* could have been more painful to write than that on Villanueva de la Jara, including those on Alba, Beas, and the strange chapter which appears to celebrate Beatriz Chávez.

It begins by explaining the four year "persecution" which brought the work of the Order to a standstill. This was caused by malicious misinformation which the Calced gave their General, and grew worse when a good Nuncio died and was replaced by one who imprisoned all who disagreed with him. The two who suffered most were Fray Antonio de Jesús (Heredia) and Fray Jerónimo Gracián, though the new Nuncio was also greatly displeased with Father Mariano de San Benito. However, this was all straightened out when the King "learned what was happening" and took matters into his own hands.

(You'll admit, that's compact. Next, for the new foundation . . . :)

She was in Toledo, to which she had gone from Seville in 1576, when a certain Dr. Augustín de Ervias invited her to found a convent for nine women who were living together as hermits. He had heard of her from Fray Antonio de Jesús and also from the Prior of Our Lady of Succour, Fray Gabriel de la

Asunción, whose priory was in La Roda, only three miles away. For various reasons (Teresa gives five, none much to the point) the place seemed unsuitable, and at the advice of her confessor she gave an evasive answer — though Fray Antonio and the Prior so urged it on her that she wrote Father Angel, asking him to refuse her permission, and from his answer she believed that he agreed.

But she was wrong; and while she was staying in Malagón the Lord told her to make that foundation, so Fray Antonio de Jesús and Fray Gabriel came to Malagón to take her and four nuns away.

II

Here let me interrupt Teresa. Fray Gabriel replaced Roca as Prior of La Roda when Roca went to Mancera to replace Heredia. Fray Gabriel shared Heredia's hatred of Gracián and his fear that Teresa could win him too much powerful support among the nobility. Their first attempt to give her a convent of nine *beatas* was inspired by the twice-demonstrated happy tendency of *beatas* to delate Teresa to the Inquisition. Heredia soon gave up on the idea and returned to it only later at Father Angel's urging.

But why did Teresa give in?

To begin with, even after Teresa's death one branch of her faction-torn Order still hailed La Cardona as their true founding saint, as Mariano had once planned; they called themselves the Monks of the Good Woman. Roca had become disillusioned with La Cardona even before his discovery that though a genuine masochist she was a fake aristocrat, but Gabriel de la Asunción remained faithful to her glorious memory.

La Cardona lived for only a year after Fray Gabriel came to her holy place as its Prior, and was two years and nine months dead when Teresa consented to found in nearby Villanueva — largely in the hope that her compliance would soothe Heredia's jealousy and in some measure quiet the growing factionalism in her Order. If to this end she also had to approve the late La Cardona, she would do that, too; there was no danger that Heredia would emulate her austerities as poor Roca once had, and the Constitutions would always safeguard her nuns.

And who was to say that La Cardona had not served God in her own misguided but ardent way?

Teresa chose four nuns, and after some hesitation decided to take along her niece, Beatriz de Jesús, née de Ahumada. Beatriz resented her loss of authority, disliked the President, and was a disruptive element in Malagón. Better not leave her behind, unwatched. One could pray that the attention would do her good.

The night before she left, Teresa wrote to Gracián. Doria was seeing friends who would urge Quiroga to grant the Madrid convent a licence. Would Gracián urge it, too? Then she could found there on the way back from Villanueva.

Teresa also knew that Gracián might fear that Heredia was winning her over, and she goes on to describe a conversation just held with the Prior of Almodóvar concerning the factional disputes among the Calced:

"He strikes me as an intelligent, well-meaning man; not that I opened up to him about anything, important or unimportant. On the contrary, I skirted everything with the utmost caution, neither agreeing nor disagreeing. But I tell you, I was delighted to hear that those cliques that even he believed to exist—if they really do—are beginning to fall apart. As for Fray Juan de la Cruz, I swear to you that such a thought never entered his head, but he helped the ones who went to Rome in every way he could, and he'd die for you if he had to. This is absolutely true."

She wrote a follow-up note the next day. She had not expected Heredia to go with her, but he had turned up "fat and well." "Commend it to the Lord! Now good Fray Antonio can't deny that he loves me since, old as he is, he has come all this way. I wish I didn't have to go; I have already written you why."

Fundaciones passes immediately from their setting out to their arrival in La Roda: "It is in a desert solitude, very sweet, and when we drew near the monks came out to greet their Prior, all in close accord. Since they went barefoot, wearing mantles of coarse sayal, it filled us all with devotion." ("There is enough of this going barefoot around already!" her angry letter had said of this same place.) "I was greatly moved, as I seemed to be back in the flowering time of our holy fathers. In that field they seemed to be white, sweet-scented flowers, and so I believe they are, in God's eye. . . ." (One is oddly reminded of the vision granted by St. Anthony to Teresa de Laiz.)

She describes the underground entrance to the church, grieves that the Lord had not found her worthy to meet the holy woman for whom it was made and follows it with a life of La Cardona in the vein of her tales of Teresa de Laiz and Catalina Godóñez—and equally reminiscent of the nun whose "nonsense and exaggerations" she had found "unbearable." With a further touch: the thought of La Cardona "taught [her] to hate [herself] as she should" and know that she "deserved to be in hell."

On a subsequent day, she adds, she went back there to receive communion and was "seized with a suspension that left her *enajenada*," in which she saw La Cardona glorified and surrounded by angels. *Enajenada*, which can mean alienated from herself or driven mad, is a word she uses to describe no other mystical experience. I don't deny that it happened. Teresa was unsure of the rights and wrongs involved in making her first foundation since Seville and grimly aware that La Cardona—in whose pure blood and masochism she had equal faith—needed to be approached with reverence in this chapter if a rift in her Order were to be healed. It was a disturbing business at both the conscious and unconscious levels.

Years before she had made her only other known reference to La Cardona in a *cuenta:* "Once, when I was thinking of the great penances that Doña Catalina de Cardona was doing, and how I might have done more—according to the wishes the Lord sometimes gave me to do it, if it hadn't been for obeying my confessors. . . . He said to me, not that, daughter. You take the good, safe road. You see all the penance she does? I hold your obedience to be worth more."

Once La Roda and La Cardona are taken care of, Teresa's description of the actual foundation comes as a blessed relief. The village gave them a welcome.

They were escorted to the church "with crosses and banners...and bells ringing," all singing the Te Deum; and after a solemn high Mass they met the nine *beatas* who were weeping for joy, as they had longed to be nuns for years only to be refused, even by the Franciscans. They were dressed oddly, "though modestly." They were poor, ill-housed, ill-fed, and afraid that when real nuns saw them they would run away. They had got some religious instruction from the Franciscans (of whom Teresa had said in a letter, "They can teach our nuns how to beg!"). They owned a manual of prayer by Peter of Alcántara, one by Luis de Granada, and some breviaries.

"Most of the time they spent in reading the Divine Office—though few knew how to read and only one could read at all well and not one of the breviaries agreed with another. Some priests had given them the outdated Roman texts they could not use any more, and others they had come by as they could, and since they couldn't read anyway, this 'reading' took them many hours. They did not recite the Office where anybody from outside could hear them. God must have had to accept their intentions and hard work, for they could have said very few of the real words."

Still, they baked bread well, in a little oven, and they lived in surprising unanimity for a group that had nobody to direct them. "All this made me praise God, and the more trouble it cost, the more I was glad I had come.... And those of my company who stayed with them told me that though they resented it at first, once they got to know them better and understand their good qualities, they were very happy and got fond of them." And, she adds, God will surely see to it that their living conditions get better.

He did not, in her lifetime. Once Teresa had done what she could, she got word to Heredia, and five weeks from the day they left Malagón, he came to take her back. She had to abandon four resentful nuns, but at least she spared them Beatriz de Jesús; to leave her there, she saw, would be cruelty to all.

Beatriz persuaded them to go back through Montalbán, the town to which her father, Francisco, had moved so long ago—when his young wife's reputation made things unpleasant in Avila. Teresa had not been there since she went through it on the way to Guadalajara from the Incarnation—to pray for Antonio, the brother who left his second monastery for the Army and died in battle, unconfessed. But her fame was known there: too well known. Small towns love scandals connected with their leading citizens. Nobody in Montalbán would have been surprised to learn that the sister of the *converso* merchant who called himself *Don* Francisco was as whorish as his wife—and heretical, like "those of Llerenos" whose vileness was the Church's living shame.

Teresa had planned to stay with relatives overnight, but the town was holding a fiesta in honor of Our Lady, so along with Heredia, Beatriz and San Bartolomé, she went first to the church. Their garments caught attention, someone recognized Beatriz, and the word spread through the congregation. The woman with the cane was Teresa de Jesús, repeatedly escaped from the hands of the Holy Inquisition through the devil's arts. Teresa ignored the threatening murmur and went forward to kneel at the altar rail. Such a bold insult to God and His Blessed Mother was too much; the entire congregation closed in upon her, venting their holy outrage in a roar of curses and obscenities.

The priest behind the rail tried to plead; there should be no bodily violence. It would serve to keep her prisoner in Montalbán until her sins were finally laid bare, once and for all. His words were drowned out, but somehow Heredia, an impressive figure, managed to fight through the crowd, mount the pulpit, and convince a sufficient number that it was a case of mistaken identity, thus letting Teresa escape to her coach and be off to Toledo.

Fundaciones describes, without explanation, the near-riot in Córdoba when a congregation reacted as if she and her nuns were stampeding bulls, but we know of this Montalbán incident only from Teresa's faithful nurse-amanuensis, San Bartolomé. *Fundaciones* passes from a description of Villanueva and the poor *beatas* to the setting-out for Pastrana, six months later. But that chapter — in which the La Cardona passage contrasts so sharply with the good-natured realism which describes the poor *beatas* — covers a time of strain which ended, in Montalbán, with a bad shock. Teresa reached Toledo played out and extremely ill. It was, she wrote to San José, as bad an attack as she could remember: high fever, bad heart, rheumatoid crippling. Though no longer bedfast, it was still hard to get to the grille and talk with Doria, glad as she'd been to have him there for the past two days.

She did not exaggerate her condition. She was in no state to be writing letters; but that particular letter had to be written, and without delay.

Chapter 66 ❀ *Orders to Visit Valladolid and Segovia and to Found in Palencia; John of the Cross, a Saint*

I

To begin with, Gracián had been elected Prior of Los Remedios. He was naturally leery of Seville, and went first to Madrid to talk it over with Mariano and Doria. Heading south, he stopped in Toledo for a brief and, he hoped, secret word with Teresa. Then Doria came. He had recently been back to Seville himself, and he brought her the written retractions just made by nuns who had lied or signed false statements during their examination. Beatriz, disturbingly, had retracted next to nothing.

Gracián would now be visiting that convent again, and often. San José was waiting. It called for warnings, but lightly, lightly given. San José did not take suggestions well.

Teresa began with a little teasing. Doria was all praise for San José. "I'm shocked at how well you've deceived him. I helped with it, because as I see it, it will do that house no harm for him to be deceived. The worst of it is that some of his deception seems to be sticking to me, too. Please God, daughter, that you don't do anything to take it away, and may He keep you in His hand. . . .

"I was delighted to hear how well everything is going . . . and now that Father Gracián is going there you will need nothing else. Take care, daughter, that you put an end to all *occasions*—for you have someone there who will tell more than the facts. Frankly, I believe that she has it much on her mind.

"Some things that Father Nicoleo told me about the nuns were shocking. He gave me the papers and I am reading them little by little. That soul leaves me terribly frightened. May God make things better. The way you take to cope with her seems right. Never get careless about the other one, either."

Having placed all possible blame for future troubles on Beatriz and Margarita, she goes on to discuss San José's new house as if it had never been a matter of dispute. Doria praises her choice, but San José must examine it very thoroughly before she puts down her first payment. And Doria will see to collecting on the promissory note from Toledo which San José has sent Lorenzo in part-payment of her debt. (It was worthless, Doria discovered—and as San José already had, before she relinquished it.)

She has just learned that as soon as she gets well (Teresa ends) she is to go back to Segovia, then to Valladolid, and after that to found a convent in Palencia. But now since she is too ill to write any more, Beatriz de Jesús will tell her about Brianda.

Why Beatriz, not San Bartolomé, as usual? Quite simply, it was a "mortification." Beatriz still resented Gracián's interference in Malagón. Beatriz, of course, stressed Brianda's most recent severe illness. How shocking it would have been to take her back to Malagón, where the house is so poor! then: "Our Mother found Father Gracián here; he is well. That little stove we found out about isn't worth anything. It cost almost a hundred reales and we took it apart because it burned more wood than did us any good." Teresa had not mentioned Gracián's brief, secret visit, and because she believed that a show of trust is good for blundering souls, she would not have read what Beatriz wrote.

But when Beatriz had finished, Teresa dictated further to San Bartolomé; only this page of the letter was saved, but the long unfinished sentence with which it ends urges San José to be very attentive to the old Prior of Las Cuevas, who had not been reelected, "so that it won't look as if we forgot him now that he no longer holds an office in which he could do us any good, because it would look bad if. . . ."

II

The orders to go to Valladolid and Segovia came from Father Angel. Now that a separate province for the Discalced seemed assured, he was eager to please the King and the Court. María Mendoza wanted a longer visit from Teresa, and the Bishop wanted to give her a convent in his new see, Palencia.

Segovia was another matter. Juan de Velasco, Doria's close friend, had daughters to provide for. On the strength of his promise to raise five hundred ducats to repay San José de Avila for what it had sacrificed to send Montoya to

Rome, Teresa persuaded the prioress of Toledo to accept de Velasco's daughter Inéz without dowry; but her sister Juana was harder to place. She could not be taught to read, and was apparently retarded. Only one convent would accept her: Segovia, whose de Bracamonte Prioress, Isabel de Santo Domingo, understood the importance of de Velasco's friendship—since he was among the Grand Inquisitor Quiroga's circle of intimate friends.

Still, Teresa hesitated to force the girl on Mother Isabel. She had urged San José to profess Beatriz Chávez, another illiterate, against the Order's rule, and with what result? God is not mocked. For matter of that, why had she weakly founded that incredible convent in Villanueva? And, to go back to Segovia, where things first began to go wrong? Segovia, where she had written those letters insisting that Beas was not, not in Andalusia. . . .

Teresa was almost glad of the illness which let her put off the decision, though as Doria made it clear, she would have to provide for Velasco's Juana if Velasco were to urge Quiroga to grant a licence for her convent in Madrid, and if Doña Isabel Osorio's Jesuit confessor, Valentín López, made no trouble about its necessary endowment. The Jesuits were angry about the threat to the de Padilla fortune and still angrier at the prospect of losing that of Catalina de Tolosa, now gone to Burgos.

Then, astoundingly, the picture promised to change. Suárez's triennium ended, and it had been one that gained the Jesuits little popularity with the other Orders. Baltasar Alvarez was now a noted scholar, and he had suffered much from Suárez; what way to disclaim Suárez could be more striking than to elect Father Baltasar in his place?

There was much that Teresa and Baltasar had never been free to discuss in letters; though friends had made their correspondence possible, her letters were too often intercepted. It would still be unwise to flaunt their continued friendship; the election had been close, and a Suárez faction could still make trouble. But Teresa made a secret visit to Gracián's parents in Madrid, who in turn arranged a secret visit from Baltasar—after so many years. During it, they made a wise compact. Baltasar would criticize the greed in Valladolid so openly and strongly that Doña Isabel's confessor would be ashamed to follow suit. But this should seem to spring from gratitude for a favor that Teresa did the Company—to which, as she often said, she "owed everything."

The Marquis of Alcazán was a relative and close friend of the Duke of Alba; and at present he was Viceroy of Navarre. Up there, in the town of Pamplona, the citizens were trying to drive out a new house of the Company, on various unfounded false charges. Teresa should write to the Duchess asking her to ask the Marquis to intercede for these beleagured holy souls—and say that if the Duke were not now leading the war in Portugal he would surely do so himself. Teresa did so gladly. It meant that a dangerous secret meeting with Baltasar (and what secrets are ever safe?) would be seen as one that he, not she, had sought, and for one purpose that Suárez himself would feel forced to approve.

She went back to Toledo and the unending clutter of irrelevant problems: convents whose financial affairs needed constant straightening out by borrowing from Peter to pay Paul; family problems, now centering on Pedro, Lorenzo's burden, who suddenly turned up, mad as a hatter and insisting that he was going to live in Seville. (Teresa persuaded Juana—for a sum that Lorenzo could ill afford—to take Pedro in for a little, and give Lorenzo a much needed rest.)

A letter came from Rome; once the brief for the separate province was granted, Gracián not Heredia would head it, thanks to Montoya's advice. This news was supposed to be kept secret until the brief arrived, but Father Angel immediately told Gracián that as Commissary he should set off at once on official visitations to Andalusia. His order may have been founded on a malign hope: an epidemic known to history as the universal catarrh had just reached southern Spain by way of Seville. It had already decimated Northern Europe.

Hypochondria was not among Gracián's failings. As he hurried from one highly contagious deathbed to another, his sole fear was that he could not grant valid absolution to those who died without forgiving their enemies. *Letrados* assured him that such forgiveness was not necessary, but he disagreed. For once, Teresa sent Gracián a plea to show less courage, not more. And she told him of a letter that she had written to Juan de la Cruz.

Fray Juan was so removed from the tangle of politics, so lost in contemplation, that his fellow friars forgot him. Teresa did not, and the news from Rome forced her to face a hard reality. Her Order had grown from her belief that the Church could be healed from within by selfless prayer. Fray Juan's whole life was that prayer, offered in perfection, but she had put all her faith in Montoya's bought services.

One would give much to see the letter that she wrote him. Her letters continually mention their correspondence, but exactly one taste of it remains, by accident, in the so-called *Vejámen:* the Judgment. It belongs to the period when she was fighting off her last *arrobamientos* and reassuring Lorenzo, disturbed in his prayer because "the body only understands one kind of love." In one of those letters to Lorenzo—now lost or made unavailable—she told him of words that had come to her in prayer:

> Lord, I must find myself in Thee
> And Thou must find Thyself in me.

The meaning of the last line had baffled her. Lorenzo discussed it with Francisco de Salcedo, Father Julián, and John of the Cross. They mentioned it to Bishop Mendoza, who was in Avila for the twelve days of Christmas, and he suggested that each write out his own explanation, give them to him, and let him send them to Teresa for her decision as to which had done best at explaining it.

Her letter begins with telling "His Lordship"—that is, the Bishop—that she will obey his orders, though her head is in such a state with the business and letter writing she's had to do that she only hopes she'll say nothing to endanger her with the Inquisition. Then, forcing a light-hearted tone, she answers each—pointing out, primarily, their irrelevance to her own central question, and ending by telling His Lordship that since all have their faults and their good points, she cannot decide.

To Francisco de Salcedo she says that since he follows quotations from St. Paul and the Holy Spirit and says that he has signed his name to nonsense, she will have to denounce him to the Inquisition unless he corrects himself.

Julian de Avila's critique ends, "However I forgive him, since he didn't go on at such length as Father Fray Juan de la Cruz."

And to him, with the same rebukes for irrelevance that the other three get, we have her words, so relevant to her own current spiritual problem: "It would be a bad business if he could only seek God once we were dead to the world. It wasn't like that with Mary Magdalen, or the Samaritan, or the Cananite woman" (the much married woman at the well, and the bride at her earthly marriage feast). "God save me from people who are so spiritual that they want to turn everything into a perfect contemplation, come what may!"

She could write to him like that, not because she belittled him, but as she had said long ago, "He is tall in the eyes of God." She could because she spoke of him often as "that saint"; because she warned, "Take care of him. If he dies you will not find many like him"; because she expressed her shock that Ana de Jesús could find any fault in "that divine, heavenly man." Juan de la Cruz would never disillusion her; and one does not "dissemble a little" with a saint.

Try to remember this when we come to their final meeting and parting. It explains a tragedy which saintwatchers handle by Teresa's own chosen means, omission. It is also one possible explanation of three—one of them favored by saintwatchers—as to why no letters from Teresa the Saint of Raptures to Juan de la Cruz have survived. The one of those three which I pray is correct is simply that he, like Teresa, never kept letters that had been answered.

Let the third wait. It is enough to say here that Teresa wrote at once to tell him that their separate province was assured.

Chapter 67 ❀ Teresa's _Meditations; Death of Her Brother Lorenzo_

I

Promised brief or no, they still lived in an atmosphere of suspicion. Gracián felt it, and though on hearing that Teresa was dangerously ill he made a timid, tentative offer to see her if she felt it necessary, he was doubtless relieved by her answer. He must not come, she said: "Much as it would comfort me, I am afraid that these brothers would take note of it."

She hoped to get "a little stronger" and talk with Quiroga about the Madrid foundation; but Father Angel's orders for her to make the Palencia foundation with no more delay "gives [her] scruples." So, if Gracián thinks she should, she will write to Segovia now about Velasco's daughter—though Madrid would be the perfect place for her; and he should write, too, telling Mother Isabel how much it would please him if she took the girl. "And tell her how much we owe Velasco, because he has just paid the five hundred ducats . . . for San José de Avila." Yet, Gracián should know that she herself does not want to send the girl to Segovia until she has talked with Quiroga about Madrid.

That hope died hard, but Quiroga granted Teresa no audience. At the end of two months, she wrote Gracián that Mother Isabel was taking in the retarded illiterate. "After all I wrote her, she could hardly have done anything else. Thank God I'm through with all I had to do to manage this. I tell you, father, it took plenty of hard work with every prioress wanting so much for her own house that she feels that all the others must agree with her."

Juana would bring nothing, not even her trousseau and bedding. Perhaps Gracián could beg or borrow that much in Madrid, now he was there again. As for Doria's wanting him to go back to Seville where the epidemic raged, it would be the death of him "quite apart from the other unsuitable angles," though "the Beatriz business" did now seem to be under control. It would really make no more talk if he came to Toledo, ostensibly to see Quiroga, and then went on to Segovia with her in a covered cart. Heredia had offered to do that, though he was still weak after his own bout with the disease and would be more care than help.

Four days later she wrote again. She has given up hope of seeing him, or Quiroga, and Heredia is far too ill to travel. "I held back this long in hope of the comfort of seeing you, for I can never manage to see why it is that whenever I want any happiness in this life, everything seems to go the other way." But she catches the whine in her tone, and changes it. Brianda is well; Cassademonte will pay for Juana de Velasco's trousseau, for Doria has the money and will pay him back promptly. And finally, apropos of nothing, "They were saying that the Princess of Pastrana was being kept under arrest in her house in Madrid; now they say it's in Pastrana. Either one would be too good for her."

Hope deferred is, among other things, a drain on one's charity.

II

Before that letter could have reached him, Gracián appeared. From his *Peregrinaciones* one does not gather that Teresa ever doubted he would come. He tells of taking her to see Quiroga and quotes, as if verbatim, a lengthy speech that Quiroga made in praise of the *Life*, a speech thereafter plagarized by Teresa's first biographer, Ribera, and in time by many others. (We tend to forget how recently historians renounced the techniques of fiction for their present-day limitations.) What Quiroga had to say about the Madrid foundation Gracián did not quote, and no letter of Teresa's mentions that meeting at all. In truth, her long-sought encounter with the Great Angel was fruitless.

Teresa went to Madrid with Ana de San Bartolomé in a covered cart, to pick up Velasco's Juana. Heredia had decided that he was well enough to accompany Gracián, and Father Angel suddenly announced that he wished to travel with them. They stayed with Gracián's parents for three days, waiting for him.

Of that stay, Tomás Gracián wrote to a friend that one morning Teresa and his wife came back from Mass laughing themselves weak. In the church, Teresa had accidentally trodden on a woman's foot, and the woman promptly kicked her, first with one foot and then with the other, and what's more, she was wearing clogs. That Teresa found it hilarious is doubtless one reason that she held up so long.

She needed that spririt for the journey. She had not really been well enough to make it, and she reached Segovia in bad shape. Luckily, Juana de Velasco was endearing, despite her handicap. Her childlike obedience became one of the convent's legends. This was fortunate, for before Teresa left she gave her the black veil of a choir nun saying that it should never be taken from her. The girl had not been there a month, the shortest novitiate allowed by the Constitutions was two years, and Beatriz Chávez was the only other nun who could not read. But Teresa had promised Velasco that the child would become a nun, not a permanent lay-sister, and she could be sure of it in no other way.

Juana, it seems, deserved her legend, though it was also convenient, explaining as it did La Santa's having ignored the Constitutions to make her a nun. Nor was this the only other incident of that time in Segovia to need, and in time, receive its touch of legend.

While Teresa's previous confessor in Segovia had been Luis de Santander, she had also found it wise to confess occasionally to the Dominican, Diego de Yanguas. He had been a twenty-three-year-old friar at Santo Tomás when Pedro Ibáñez was sent away to Trianos shortly after de Prádanos left for Valladolid and shortly before Father Gaspar lost his Avilan restorate. Despite the Salamanca story, Teresa had made at least enough of an impression on Yanguas to win her the benefit of the doubt. This mattered, for Yanguas, now in his forties, had become a respected scholar and was a member of the local Inquisition.

On her return to Segovia, it also mattered much to Gracián. As he saw it, Yanguas' formal approval of Teresa's new book, the *Moradas*, would carry weight at future need; ideally so, since his acquaintance with Teresa had been brief and slight. (Incidentally, that acquaintance so grew in Yanguas' memory that when he testified for her canonization it was as one who had been her "chief confessor for her final eight years"!) Gracián took the book to Yanguas, and with it — at Teresa's suggestion — he took her *Meditaciones sobre los Cantares:* the convent copy, for as with her *Camino*, Teresa had arranged for copies to be made and distributed as aids to her nuns' life of prayer.

Yanguas read both, and called for Teresa and Gracián. He objected to a passage or two in the *Moradas* which she readily promised to delete. The *Meditaciones* he ordered her to burn at once. It was shocking that a woman had dared to expound Holy Writ, and above all that her inspiration had been that translation of the *Song of Songs* for which Luis de León was condemned to the Inquisition's dungeons.

In *Peregrinaciones* Gracián tells about that judgment and Teresa's humble acquiescence, burning it over the brazier in Yanguas' presence. He wrote before the long-delayed publication of that book necessitated the explanatory legend. Teresa, the story runs, believed that the sole copy was destroyed; but it was not. A nun had watched her writing it, by night—always on her knees, and oftenest hovering, kneeling on the air. We need not wonder that this inspired her to read it and copy it in secret, bit by bit, each night when Teresa returned to ground level and slept. In consequence, the precious work was saved, and God's will that it finally be published prevailed.

Teresa says nothing about meeting with Yanguas or about giving Juana the black veil of a professed nun. Indeed, one would gather from her letters that her month in Segovia was wholly occupied by family affairs.

III

Young Lorenzo went back to Quito; like a true de Cepeda, he left a baby girl behind for Teresa to worry over. His father, so newly obsessed with the sins of the flesh, was anxious to see Francisco, the younger brother, married early. He negotiated with a Segovian caballero for his daughter's hand. Within two days of her arrival, Teresa wrote him that this was not working out, though she'd see what she could do. Heredia, who left Segovia shortly for Valladolid, carried her letter. Lorenzo answered it promptly, and Teresa had time to answer his answer just a week before he died.

The beginning of her letter is full of gaps and now exists only in copy, so one cannot tell how much was obliterated in the autograph: "Jesus be with you. They told me about that messenger, at a time like this . . . it would make me very unhappy if . . . hide . . . for the love of God . . . .

"I don't know where you get the notion that you'll soon be dead, or why you have these crazy ideas and depress yourself with what isn't going to happen. Trust in God, who is a true friend and will not fail you, or your sons, either.

"I wish with all my heart that you could come here, since I can't go there. At least you are doing yourself a bad turn to go so long without calling at San José. The exercise would do you good, not harm, and it's so near, and you wouldn't be staying alone. For the love of charity, don't act like this, and let me know how you are.

"I am a lot better now that I'm finally in this place, and I have got over the little fever-spells I was having . . . I haven't been too worried over the business you wrote me about, though I won't be able to do anything about it until Father Angel leaves, and he'll be here for a week . . . .

"Mother-Prioress and Father Gracián and San Bartolomé all send you their best, and so do I, and to Don Francisco. Tell me how you are, for the love of charity, and stay with God, for there's no room for anything more. This is June 19. Perhaps I'll have to send you a messenger soon, because one point has been won in that business and it didn't come out badly. I myself can't do anything until Father Angel goes."

A sentimentalist would have felt that the news of Lorenzo's death should go in one letter and the necessary business matters of the day in another. Not

Teresa. She had loved him, and now she must care for his affairs, and for those of her convents. So, she wrote to María de San José in Seville: Lorenzo's death was sudden; there was a rushing of blood from his throat, and he was dead in six hours. He'd taken communion two days before, and he died fully conscious, commending himself to God. "Prayer was part of his daily life, and he did more penance than I would have liked him to. . . . He always told me everything, and it was strange how much faith in me he had. It grew out of the great love he came to feel for me, somehow. I repay it by being glad that he is out of this miserable world and safe. And that isn't just a way of talking but it really gives me joy to think of it. I grieve for his children, but I think that God will show them mercy for their father's sake."

That was it; the rest is business. Gracián and Father Angel intend to stay together until the brief comes; in a day or two they will be taking her back to Avila where she will have to stay as executor of Lorenzo's will until she finds what money will come to Teresica, poor child. That is uncertain. For example, the promissory notes that San José sent are worthless; even the one on some Toledan property won't be paid for a long time, "and God grant that it ever will be."

As for news, it is shocking that Beatriz is trying to put the blame for all she did on García Alvarez and that San José can't see that she should be forced to retract her lies, just as Margarita did. If she says any more, Rodrigo Alvarez must get a full written retraction, signed with her name.

The best thing for San José's urinary infection is an infusion of rose-hips. The nuns in Segovia envy them down there "with all the flags and hubbub" — troops leaving for Portugal. And Doria must let her know as soon as the fleet comes in with Lorenzo's money and see to it that the man in Lima who owns the house in Salamanca, that the nuns need so badly, gets the papers about it notarized and sent back to Spain.

Lorenzo might be free of this miserable life, but while one lives, its affairs still need attention. No administrator can afford that peculiar grace granted to Juan de la Cruz — a one-track mind.

IV

Gracián and Father Angel had both left Segovia well before Lorenzo's death; they came back on learning of it. Few did not overestimate Lorenzo's wealth and feel a keen interest in its disposal. They took her to Avila, where Teresa found the seal broken on Lorenzo's will. On its last page he had written, "I opened this after it was sealed to see if I should put something in or take something out. I say and declare that though it was opened, it should be seen as valid and complete." But the law ruled otherwise; because of the broken seal, the will would have to go through chancery in Valladolid before it was validated.

It provided Pedro with a yearly allowance to be paid from a sum held in trust. The remaining property, including La Serna, was to be liquidated and divided equally among the three children. As Teresica, now thirteen, had become a novice, her share would go to her convent, earmarked for building a chapel to which the remains of the deceased should eventually be moved. The work on this chapel should begin at once with four hundred and thirty ducats owed him by the Discalced convent in Seville. (That is, what still remained of San José's debt minus the amount to be collected—supposedly—in Toledo.) If this payment were delayed, the same amount could be borrowed from what was due the eldest son, now in Peru, and reimbursed to him later.

Teresa understood Lorenzo's insistence that the chapel be built with no delay. Though she had no anxiety for his good, loving soul, she had not been able to free him from "the way of fear." Francisco de Salcedo had taught him too well concerning the sins of the flesh. It filled her with pity, and a determination that he should have his chapel—his bribe to the Judge—as promptly as if it were really needed.

She would still be fighting for it until she died.

She also understood why he had so reduced the sum owing to him from Seville: loans for which he had been forced to hide from debtor's prison and loans made thereafter—to pay the debts that were never paid. It was like him to credit María de San José with a conscience like his own and to let her ease it by buying him—at cut rates—out of Purgatory, or Hell. God rest his dear soul, now released from fear and safe in God's love!

Chapter 68 ❀ Teresa's Brush with Death; Deaths of Friends

I

Teresa would always feel Lorenzo's chapel as a trust laid upon her, a demand of love. Francisco's marriage was another matter. Lorenzo's obsession with St. Paul's warning, "It is better to marry than burn," was one she had pitied but could not share. Men will be men, good husbands are twice the age of their virgin brides, and Francisco was too childish for the marriage his father had been trying to arrange. Indeed, one could doubt that the boy would ever have the makings of a good husband. But he did seem to have a genuine piety. She could take him to Valladolid and let Gracián show him where his best future lay. As a friar, his weak will might be all to the good. . . .

July was three-quarters gone when Teresa made her stopover in Medina. Doña Elena de Quiroga was newly widowed, and cousin-Prioress Inés was persuading her to take the habit. This was likely to prejudice Quiroga against the Madrid convent, but Teresa did nothing to dissuade her. Her mind was distracted, for the universal catarrh had reached Castile. A friend of Lorenzo's died in Avila, and Teresa had just sent off her letter of condolence when she learned that Baltasar Alvarez was dead.

He was forty-six. They were worlds apart in temperament, and their friendship had grown slowly, but it had deep roots. He had gained a place from which he might have taught many that their Orders, far from being enemies, were comrades-in-arms. Four months ago they had promised to help each other as they could, and he would have kept that promise; but if he had still been powerless, still the friend to whom she was forced by Suárez to write in secret through trusted mutual friends, she would have felt that loss no less.

Inés de Jesús had never seen Teresa weep. She was not one in whose company Teresa cared to show emotion. Years later, Inés testified that she was "amazed" that when Teresa "heard the news, she cried for a whole hour without being able to control herself."

Baltasar had become a man with a vision which his world did not widely share. His last words are quoted as evidence of his serenity: "I have no particular wish to live and no grief at dying. If it must be sometime, why not now?" But to me, these words echo those that Teresa wrote to Gracián after founding her strange convent in Villanueva and escaping the ugly riot in Montalbán: "I cannot make myself care whether I live or die."

She wept for an hour in public, despite herself; but she did not mention that death in any letters. She talked about the difficulties of settling Lorenzo's will, the necessity of finding out exactly what money had come for Lorenzo with the fleet—and the need for San José to pay up the amount Lorenzo had named. "As executor I have to collect this money, though I don't like to—so you must get it straightened out. To make up for this and the money you gave the Order [to pay Montoya], it wouldn't be bad for you to take in another nun if you can find one."

Teresa had forbidden just that not long before, as San José's convent had reached its outer limit of twenty, not counting lay-sisters, both black and white; but Lorenzo's chapel must be built. This is so important that she gives only one sentence to the news that the separate province has been granted, the brief sent off by the Ambassador to the Vatican's own courier, "so now it is in the King's own hand." That said, she inquires after Gregorio Nanciano, who had come near to death, sends "regards to Beatriz—and to all the sisters," and gets back at once to the main issue: "I need you very much in this business about the Indies, which I trust you'll be able to take care of in all particulars. About the other money, write me how much you can send at once, and how much you can collect until I send for it." Teresa had dreamed of the separate province for years, worked for it, planned for it, fought for it. But it was not the matter in hand. Nor was her part in winning it to be mentioned; it had been men's work.

But she had a more important letter to write. In Segovia, Teresa had found yet another nun gone mad, and now in Avila a nun was either faking, going mad, or possibly, undergoing some genuine mystical experience. Teresica, just entering puberty, was overresponding. When she thought the nun a fake, she tried to tell herself that she was unjust, fooled by her own lack of spirituality. When she trusted instead, she found herself filled with shame at her lack of similar ardor, her worldling's heart. She had not been able to talk about that while Teresa was there, but once she was gone she could write to her, confessing her fears for herself; she felt no sense of God's reality when she prayed, but instead she often found herself lost in sinful imaginings.

Teresa answered at once. Of the many letters she wrote the girl, this alone was saved, which is surprising in view of its content. Few women so pressured by life would have found time for it—and few nuns of her day would have said what it says. "Your letter was a joy to me, and it makes me happy that you like mine so much. About that matter of your aridities, it seems to me that the Lord is treating you like one who is strong, so He wants to try you out and see if you understand that His love for you is just the same in the dry times as in the times that are full of delights. I see that as a very great mercy of God. Don't let it make you sad, because perfection doesn't lie in that sort of thing, but in the virtues. Your feelings of devotion will come back when you least expect it.

"As for what you say about that sister, try not to think about her. Just turn your mind to something else. And don't be so quick to think that it is bad when some distracting thought comes into your head, even if it should be a really bad one, for that isn't anything. I wish that sister had some aridity herself—for I don't believe she understands herself, so we can wish that for her own good.

"Whenever a bad thought comes to you, just bless yourself and say a paternoster, or strike your breast and try to think about something else, and then it will count to your merit because you are resisting it.

"I would like to answer Isabel de San Pablo [the subprioress] but I haven't got the time. Give her my best wishes. You already know that you are my dearest. . . . Don Francisco is an angel and getting on well; he and his servants took communion today. Tomorrow we're going to Valladolid and he'll write you from there because I didn't tell him about this messenger." (Or he'd have asked to see his sister's letter.) "God take care of you, daughter, and make you as holy as I pray for you."

There you have it once more: the faith of Teresa, still called the Saint of Raptures, set down for a girl of thirteen to understand. Thoughts are not sins, and religious emotion is no virtue. What matters is how we live and what we do.

It took two months for the will to be probated. Gracián stayed on in Valladolid, waiting word from the King about the brief, but the King's mind was on the war in Portugal. Juan de Ovalle turned up with Pedro, in hope of a piece of the pie, but at the end Lorenzo had forgotten Juana's need. Teresa could only send her word that she would do her best to make the boys remember her. And Juana must pray that God will tell her what is right about arranging a marriage for Francisco; it does not seem right, though people all tell her she should follow out the wishes "of him who is now in Heaven."

Towards the end of August, Diego de Mendoza offered the convent his young ex-mistress, amply dowered. María Bautista was highly gratified, and Teresa did not want to displease her. Furthermore, Teresa was fond of Don Diego; he was charming, brilliant, civilized—and enviably so, a law unto himself: at his death Philip bought his superb library of forbidden books.

Still, Teresa was firm: if the girl was not convent material, she would have to be rejected. Teresa wrote Don Diego a letter which allows itself only one naughty touch. The girl had been introduced to the convent as Don Diego's goddaughter, and as if by a slip of the pen, Teresa twice calls her *su comadre:* literally, "your fellow-godmother," but a word avoided in polite speech since *comadre* more commonly meant midwife, gossip, and even whore. Teresa hopes, she says, that "his little *comadre*" will win the convent over. Several nuns have written him letters about her, and she is sending them on, "bad spelling, foolishness and all, to test [his] humility." She adds a gentle rebuke to a noble who is also, somewhat casually, a priest. Gracián, she says, tells her that he is not contented with Don Diego's simply being a good man; he wants him to be very holy, too. But: "My ideas are more down to earth. It would satisfy me if you, your Grace, satisfied your own needs and didn't overextend your charity by arranging for the needs of others. And it strikes me that if you would only consider your own inner rest, you could have had it already and been busy with gaining eternal wellbeing by serving the One who always has to keep you with Him—and without getting tired out by doing good." In other words, "Since the girl seems a born *comadre*, you could have saved us the trouble of easing *your* conscience, dear man."

A girl's past meant nothing to Teresa, but her present did, when the good of the convent was at stake. And this girl, she saw, was not convent material, despite her useful family connections (Velasco and de Salazar, as it happened; hence worth considering not only for Don Diego's sake but for her own), and despite the fact that her acceptance would have pleased all the Mendozas, whom Teresa loved.

The decision angered María Bautista, but she did not venture to give the girl the veil until Teresa was dead; then she became the convent's second good Magdalen, under the name of Magdalena de Jesús.

As the epidemic intensified, Teresa thought about Francisco de Salcedo, aging, not strong, and worn down by worry over his worsening finances. He would have been told, she wrote him, why she was in Valladolid. "I only want to know about the state of your health and your business. I have more time to pray for you here. Please God it will do some good."

He was dying when she wrote it. None of her letters mention his death; after all, she would only have talked about it with Lorenzo. But another death in that month concerned many, and Teresa doubtless learned of it with feelings too mixed to be edifying. She had reason to write about it to a good many, but those letters are all among the missing.

II

The brief from Rome, it turned out, did not mention Gracián. The separate province should be planned and its leadership determined by free election held under two overseers: the Archbishop of Seville for Andalusia, and the Visitor Fernández for Castile.

The Archbishop, one more victim of the epidemic, died in September. Gracián, on hearing the news—and at long last, the contents of the brief— decided to consult with Doria in Alcalá and then go to Seville. He had charmed young Francisco into a decision to turn Discalced, and they left together. He first made a stopover in Medina, with intent to aid cousin Inés further in persuading the Grand Inquisitor's widowed niece to take the habit.

Teresa wrote to him there on a matter she found more urgent. Pedro has moved back into La Serna—the *estate* valued at fourteen thousand ducats. He is in a rage at its intended sale and a greater rage that any part of the proceeds will go towards building Lorenzo's chapel. He plans to get to Medina and have it all out with Francisco. If he comes, they must keep Lorenzo's horse and send Pedro back on a hired mule; a horse only helps him to rush about and spend other people's money. He has already told Teresica such a hard-luck story that she sent a hundred reales to La Serna, where he has no right to be. They must pay no attention to any such tales, for he'll always get the yearly allowance Lorenzo left him. And he quarrels with Lorenzo's old soldier-servant, who knew more about running a farm than Lorenzo did. If he does come, Francisco must tell him to stop that, too.

Above all, Francisco must drop this pointless effort to keep Pedro from knowing that he intends to become a friar. His page has already told so many people about it that a Valladolid priest just told her he had learned about it from the corregidor of Avila! And if Pedro comes on that horse, Gracián should sell it and buy himself a mule. After all, if Francisco kept the horse, he'd only have to give it to the monastery in Pastrana when he entered. But, on the other hand, perhaps Gracián's donkey was best—he could hurt himself worse, falling off a mule.

That's it. No word to Francisco about the religious life he was about to enter. No word to Gracián about the problems raised by the death of the Archbishop of Seville. It is also the last letter of any length that Teresa would ever write in her own hand; thereafter, she would dictate, sign, and sometimes scrawl a postscript. As for this letter, she was already down with the universal catarrh when she wrote it, though she did not think to mention that. Three days later she was not expected to live.

III

Told that she was near death, Teresa dictated what was, in effect, her will. She directed that it be read aloud to the nuns in Avila and then placed in "the box with the three keys."

The money left to Teresica was now legally hers: "God alone knows what it cost me to get it to that point." Her brother's papers are in the box with the three keys in Valladolid; at her death, they must be transferred to Avila. When Don Francisco is professed, his monastery should get a yearly allowance like that paid out to Pedro, but the actual capital is to be divided between Teresica and young Lorenzo. Teresica's money will go to the convent when she takes her final vows, but meantime she must remember that her Aunt Juana is in real need and help her out as she can.

The building of Lorenzo's chapel must be started at once—with the use of young Lorenzo's inheritance, which María de San José will repay when she can; and on that chapel there must be no scrimping. The first four hundred ducats will pay for a reredos behind the altar, grilles wide enough to let the nuns see Mass celebrated without crowding each other, and an arch like the one which Lorenzo himself drew on the paper herewith enclosed. And, if young Don Lorenzo dies without legal issue, his share of the inheritance must be used to enlarge the chapel's nave.

At present, the nuns should have a priest inspect La Serna regularly until it is sold, since it would lose market value rapidly if it were allowed to get run down.

"Oh, sisters, what weariness these temporal possessions bring with them! I have always thought so, but now I have learned it by experience. It almost seems as if all the cares I've borne with all the foundations never left me as broken and tired as this business has. I don't know whether it's just my being so ill that has increased this feeling."

Teresa survived. She would found three more convents in the next two years, but she never wholly recovered. Luckily, San Bartolomé was competent, strong, and utterly devoted.

Three weeks after Teresa had been given up for dying, she was able to dictate a letter to Seville, though it was more expressive of post-influenza depression than of Teresa. All the deaths and grave illnesses around them fill her with a weary wonder over why God kept her alive. She "felt no sorrow" on learning that Father Soto had died (an unfriendly Jesuit who aided Acosta's persecution of their convent), but she is truly sorry to hear that the poor old former Prior of Las Cuevas has been stricken; San José must make up a message from her, as she's too weak to invent one, "and make up something particularly nice" for Rodrigo Alvarez.

It's a good thing that San José found and burned the fresh list of accusations that Beatriz wrote. If, please God, the separate province is ever actually established, Beatriz can safely be punished, but not now. And the fleet brought nothing at all for Lorenzo? Doria's brother Horatio should see to all that; he has many business contacts in Peru.

There had been many deaths in Los Remedios which San José surely reported, and a final line in Teresa's own weak, uneven scrawl says, "Tell them that God makes saints that way, and tell yourself, too. I can't write that sort of thing unless I write it in my own hand."

The letter is dated October twenty-fifth; on the same date, Doria also wrote to Seville, asking the nuns to pray that Fernández, near death from the epidemic, would live, since "only the Virgin can save him," and her Order is now in such desperate need of his influence.

The separate province, as Teresa, too, had hinted, once more seemed uncertain.

Chapter 69 ❈ An Unopposed Founding In Palencia

I

The brief, as Teresa knew from Roca, had been obtained in a last-minute struggle. Caffardo, the new General, furiously opposed a separate province headed by "inexperienced, headstrong men all under forty." (His written protest is still in the Vatican archives.) The Pope's young Cardinal-nephew, Buencampi, "Protector of the Carmel," sided with him. Together they might have prevailed if one of Roca's friends had not, by happy chance, been a close friend of Cardinal Sforza.

Sforza was the most powerful figure in the College of Cardinals. He saw Buencampi as a vexatious accident: Popes will have nephews, but the Counter-Reformation must go on. This placed Sforza for once on the side of His Most Catholic Majesty of Spain, and with his backing, the King's party won, though General Caffardo still hoped for a compromise: alternate three-year periods in which the Discalced should be ruled by a Calced Provincial and by one of their own.

This suggested compromise made Teresa for the first time afraid, not hopeful, that Gracián would lose out, and Heredia be named head of the Discalced. Caffardo lacked Rubeo's bias against Andalusians, and Heredia was not "under forty" but a good quarter-century older than Gracián. Nor was he "headstrong"; indeed his inbred aptitude for playing both sides of the street would make a province under his leadership one separate in name only.

Gracián himself learned of Pedro Fernández's slim hold on life when he reached Pastrana. He abandoned Francisco with barely a word of introduction to the friars and rushed to Salamanca, much as he had made his belated rush to Ormaneto's deathbed, on the chance that the dying man would confirm his right to lead the Discalced, — confirm it in the presence of witnesses.

He found Fernández in coma with apparently only a few more hours to live. The King was in Badajoz, near Seville, interviewing generals on the progress of the Portuguese war. Gracián left the useless deathbed and hurried south in a vain hope that the King would forget the war long enough to write to Rome for an authorization to replace the dead men mentioned in the brief.

Fernández, in fact, lived four weeks longer. When Philip heard of his death, he did write to Rome and ask that two Dominicans be appointed to fill his place and that of the late Archbishop. He wrote the letter on the day his queen died, weakened by the birth of their fifth child when the epidemic took her as one of its victims.

It was like Philip to carry on business as usual. And Gracián's account of all this in his *Peregrinaciones* is regrettably like Gracián. It was midwinter, he says, when Fernández was stricken. (October; but midwinter removes him from Teresa when she was founding in Palencia.) He was with Teresa in Valladolid when the news came, and he left at once for Salamanca; but finding the Visitor at the point of death he hastened, of necessity, to Badajoz "without going back to tell the Mother." The queen died at the same time, and he was asked to be a pall-bearer, but refused "because he had to be in Seville on the King's business."

The Chronicler of the Order improves on this still further. Gracián reached Fernández in time to hear his last words: "Tell the King that I am setting out for Heaven where I will aid him with my intercessions, for I am of no further use on earth." Then Gracián conveyed these words to the King and returned to take Teresa to Palencia.

Gracián, in fact, did see Palencia before Teresa went there. He made a flying visit from Segovia to rent her a house before Lorenzo's death, the troublesome probating of the will, and her near-fatal illness delayed her plans. As it was, he stayed in Seville from late October until the following March.

Two days before Fernández died, Teresa wrote to Gracián in Seville. One brief sentence, unconnected with anything that goes before or comes after, says, "Father Fray Pedro Fernández is not dead, but he is gravely ill."

It is an unhappy letter. Francisco de Cepeda, deserted in Pastrana, had promptly fled and hid out with his Uncle Pedro in La Serna. He seems, Teresa says, to have become a totally different person. Why had God let him out of his hand so quickly? Now he wants to marry, but only with some girl of his own choosing. "He will surely make a bad match so that he won't run out of troubles." It would not have happened if Gracián had not abandoned him so abruptly and he had not found the friars in Pastrana "so greedy for his whole inheritance."

But greed for Lorenzo's money is everywhere! The nuns in Avila refuse to spend the money they have received on Lorenzo's chapel, and Father Angel supports their refusal. He has left Avila, but he did not go to Madrid as he had promised, and he says that he has instructions from General Caffardo as to how the Chapter should be held once the replacements for the Visitor and the Archbishop are settled upon, if both need to be replaced. Today, she ends, is the Eve of the Presentation. On that same day Gracián had tried to present Ormaneto's brief to the Casa Grande, as she will never forget.

On the next day Teresa added a postcript. Francisco had come to talk with her. "God help him and guard you. As I see it, with the holy he would have been holy. . . . I hope to God he will manage to save his soul somehow." And San Bartolomé wants to send him her affectionate greetings.

The letter went off with one to San José: Teresa is sorry to insist, but she must have that money; the man in Toledo is not going to pay up on the promissory note San José sent instead. There's no way out of it: San José must take another postulant and send on her dowry. She adds a warning intended for both San José and Gracián: "For the love of charity, you must all act with the utmost caution for you have somebody in that convent who can make nothing look like a great deal. Tell me how the poor thing is."

By the end of November Teresa felt strong enough to make the Palencia foundation; she planned to set out before New Year's Day.

Just before Christmas, Francisco married as badly as Teresa could have feared. He went to Madrid with his cousin, Diego de Guzmán, and was snatched by the mother of a girl who was not only penniless but had an ancestry to live up to, a mother determined to get her child every ducat of Lorenzo's supposed wealth by hook or by crook.

Three days after Christmas Teresa wrote a letter to young Lorenzo to go off with the next fleet, her first opportunity in six months to tell him of his father's death. He could take comfort that the blessed soul would have to spend little time in Purgatory, or perhaps none at all: "But for me it has meant great loneliness, more than I've known for anyone else." Teresica is a good nun and happy, and Francisco is married. The bride, Doña Orofrisia de Mendoza, is not yet fifteen, "a great beauty and very discreet"; and her mother is a cousin of the Duke of Alburquerque and a niece of the Duke of Infantazgo "and other high grandees" and in Avila she is related to the wife of Don Luis de Bracamonte. And, if the brother of the bride should die, "she might inherit something. . . ."

"I can't see anything else wrong except that Don Francisco has so little and the whole estate is so heavily mortgaged. If they don't send over what they owe him soon from your part of the world, I don't see how he will manage. Try to see to this, for the love of God. Since God has given him so much honor, he'll need the wherewithal to keep it up." Loyalty kept Teresa from saying in so many words that Francisco had made a fool's bargain. It also kept her from mentioning Francisco's so-brief dip into the religious life. But she trembled for the prospects of Lorenzo's chapel; and she knew that this splendid marriage was a calamity that could have been avoided if Lorenzo had not been overpersuaded to ignore her advice to go back to Avila free of the family's false titles of *hidalguía*.

She mentions the financial straits of the others, Pedro, Juana, her children, and ends with an unexpected rebuke — apropos of money, or rather, the lack of it. Gonzalo, Juana's son, had called on her. "He is very fond of you, like the others you left behind who were fooled into a high opinion of you, and I wish I could see you in a better light myself. Please God he will give you the holiness I beg him to, amen." She rebuked what was in her eyes a real sin: the boy's irresponsibility towards the baby girl he left behind him. His father would have spent as much on the child as he did on his legitimate offspring, and as he had on his brother Jerónimo's illegitimate daughters; but in this virtue, young Lorenzo was not his father's son. It is her first and least specific mention of the subject, but it would not be her last.

The letter went off with one sending Christmas greetings to San José — and a warning that any money from the Indies must go to her directly, as Francisco "would only spend it on something else." As for Beatriz, "I can't bear to hear her promises. They don't fool God." But she expresses relief at hearing that

San José is being nicer to the Prior of Las Cuevas. It is wise to let bygones be bygones.

Gracián had brought back a discouraging report from his flying visit to Palencia. The town was proverty-stricken, it already had five convents founded in poverty, and resented them. It resented still more its non-resident bishops, who appointed all members of the civil government as well as maintaining a cathedral staff of eighty, what with canons and assorted underlings, all fed at the town's expense.

Teresa loved Bishop Mendoza, and he wanted that convent. Yet even before her near brush with death, Teresa had put off her departure. Now weakened by illness, she dreaded it still more. And Burgos? Baltasar Alvarez had warned her that she must not try to crown her work with the convent in Madrid until the separate province was an accomplished fact, so Burgos came next. But Ripalda was about to lose his Rectorate and be transferred, and she had little doubt that this was somehow connected with her supposed fortune-snatching from the Jesuits.

He called on her in Valladolid. Neither talked openly about the situation, but Teresa made excuses, and he was proudly, stubbornly determined that despite his own fortunes she should go; and to make sure that she would still come, Catalina de Tolosa had sent two of her daughters with him, each dowered with eight hundred ducats with which she could buy a house in Palencia, to speed things up. Teresa pleaded illness, the Burgos climate, the anger of the Jesuits in Valladolid, but Ripalda only said, "You're getting old. The years have drained off your courage." It rang true. When he left, Teresa knelt, berating herself for her weakness and once more she heard her Voice: "Why should you fear? When have I ever failed you?"

So she laid her plans. She could be finished with both houses before the Chapter on the separate province was over. And it was also an opportunity to straighten out things in Medina. The place would do better without Inés's incessant lawsuits, her inability to make both nobles and merchants happy at once, and without her blatant pressuring of Doña Elena de Quiroga, which was far from affecting Quiroga as she and Gracián believed. Inés would snatch at the idea of being a Mendoza prioress, like María Bautista, Palencia would give her a fresh start, and Alberta Bautista, born and bred in Medina, was well suited to take her place.

By Holy Innocent's Day, December twenty-eighth, the party was collected and set out for Palencia. Teresa, San Bartolomé, Inés, the de Tolosa girls and a nun apiece from Avila, Segovia, and Valladolid were jammed together in a covered cart with a secular priest and a local gentleman, Señor Vitoria, for their escort. By travelling from one dawn to the next, they reached Palencia before it was full day, entered their house secretly, and heard their first Mass.

The secrecy had not been needed. When the convent bell rang, it woke a magnificent welcome. At Mendoza's orders, Canon Reinoso had spread the word that Palencia was to be honored by the presence of a noted holy woman, one greatly esteemed by both the King and the Pope. Furthermore, the house itself was immaculate and well furnished, even to the freshly made-up beds. As Teresa wrote Roca at the end of the week, she could almost take such smooth sailing as a bad sign in view of all the devil commonly did to keep her from making a new foundation.

Only Roca had seen the importance of making peace with General Rubeo. It was Roca who had enlisted Cardinal Sforza when it was necessary to counter General Caffardo. Teresa was grateful, but the letter she answered made two requests that she had to refuse. Roca had ideas about how the forthcoming Chapter should be run, and to support them he wanted Quiroga's backing. He had already persuaded her to write to Quiroga directly—a letter Quiroga ignored. Now he asked her to write to Quiroga's sister, Doña Elena's mother, in the hope that she would pressure her brother. Teresa had to refuse. She had never met the lady: "And I hate tiring people where it will do no good, especially as I'll soon have to be begging him for the Madrid licence." Nor can she make a place in Villanueva de la Jara for the poor girl whose family Roca had come to know while he was Prior of La Roda: they are too poor there already, and she has already given in once and told Fray Gabriel de la Asunción that he might place a poor relation there. (Roca would see why Heredia's old crony, Fray Gabriel, had to be so favored.)

Palencia was the only sizeable city in which Teresa had not met with widespread distrust, enmity, or double dealing. She never ceased to be amazed by the straightforward friendliness of the townspeople. It was not their fault that it took her five months to find a house, when it turned out that the one she was renting was not for sale.

The Cathedral Chapter met on January second. Its archives report, "A certain Lady of the Order of Discalced Carmelites is here because His Lordship the Bishop greatly desired it." Hence the Provisor, Canon Tamayo, has found them a pair of houses next to the Church of Our Lady of the Street into which a grille may be opened so that the nuns can hear Mass and take communion. "A vote was taken, thirty in favor, two opposed."

The opposing votes were cast in Teresa's favor. Canon Reinoso and Canon Salinas had met her on previous visits to Valladolid, and wanted something better for her than the houses which Tamayo had, for excellent reason, been long unable to sell.

Teresa went to Palencia believing that it would be found quickly, along with Burgos, so that she might celebrate the conclusion of the Chapter which made the Discalced a separate province with her last foundation in Madrid.

It did not work out like that. Her chapter on Palencia tells of the joy it gave her to found on "St. David's day"—by which she meant a feast, now lapsed, which commemorated King David—December 29. Along with Mary Magdalene and St. Augustine, "St. David" shared her particular devotion—the three who taught her that a sinful past may be forgiven. It is five months and a day from December 29th to the Feast of the Most Holy Sacrament, on which Bishop Mendoza came from Valladolid to install her formally in Tamayo's long rejected houses, with "much music" and ceremony—leaving her free to depart from Palencia at last.

In February Mendoza had paid his first brief visit to his undesired see—of which the previous bishop had been dead for two years. Quite naturally, he had no desire to quarrel with a thirty-to-two vote of his new Chapter. Teresa says nothing about that visit, and only by a few veiled hints lets fall what was wrong with Tamayo's houses. (One throwaway line, late in her chapter, admits that the vigils kept in Our Lady of the Street "were not all for purposes of devotion.") Actually, as Reinoso warned her, the church at night became a brothel, and the couples who used it liked to make obscene sport of its purpose, leaving the statue of Our Lady toppled on her back with her embroidered dress pulled up waist high.

Teresa says that she preferred another house until the Voice directed her to take Tamayo's, but not that she negotiated for three others before the Voice spoke, or that it delayed speaking for five months. Towards the end of the chapter she justifies the Voice by saying that nowadays "fewer" sins are committed in the Church; she also justifies Mendoza's protracted (but unmentioned) delay by saying that "of his own initiative" he has now built the nuns a chapel of their own.

We know from her letters, however, that throughout those months, Palencia was not her chief concern. The Chapter that would decide the fate of her Order was about to meet. It was all arranged a fortnight after her convent bell sounded to announce the first Mass. The Chapter would be held in Alcalá, and this time with the blessing of both King and Pope. The Dominican, Juan de las Cuevas, was appointed to fill Fernández's place, and a separate voice for Andalusia was ruled unnecessary. The elections would come first, and thereafter the business of unifying the Order's Constitutions in a manner which should clarify their points of difference from those of the Mitigation.

Throughout that time, Teresa did all that a woman can do; she prayed and wrote letters, incessant letters.

Chapter 70 ❋ A Chapter Meeting of the Discalced; Teresa's New Constitutions for the Order

I

Only the letters that Teresa wrote to Gracián were saved from this effort, but they mention the many others—to Doria, Heredia, Mariano, Roca, Juan de la Cruz, and to the presiding dignitary, Juan de las Cuevas. They were the sole means by which she could take action, and action was needed.

To Teresa, Gracián and Doria represented the middle ground between laxity and fanatic asceticism. If they worked together, Doria's hard good sense would distinguish between what to save and what to put down, and Gracián's *blandura* (softness) would enable them to act without exacerbating the poisonous divisions that existed in the Order. One or the other, she prayed, would win the election, and thereafter both should work in a partnership—a partnership for which her letters must make them both see the need, yet without making either feel belittled.

That in itself was hard enough, but she also had to counter an unscrupulous campaign manager and his dangerously eligible candidate. Mariano was determined that neither of them should be elected. Twenty friars would make up the Chapter, and he intended to direct all their votes to Heredia. His selling points were formidable. Heredia was the Order's elder statesman, its first friar. He was wellborn and had valuable connections; the Duke and Duchess of Alba, once more in high favor with the Crown, were among his closest friends. Above all, he was General Caffardo's choice, which would ease all future relations between the Calced and Discalced.

Teresa knew how well Heredia would suit Caffardo; she also knew him for an envious, pussyfooting worldling, fundamentally blind to her conception of the religious life. The whole corpus of her letters can scarcely produce one good word for "Macario." One of her letters to Gracián begins with its second page, after some obliterations: ". . .the effect Macario has on me, for I don't believe he can hide his temptations. . . . I had a lot to say to Mariano about his temptation to get Macario elected—for he has even written to me about it! I don't understand that man, and I don't want to reach an understanding [about him] with anyone but you. So what I have written you is for you alone.

"Don't stop supporting [Doria] and keep on making it plain that you do not want the position for yourself, and I really can't see how there will be any who can cast their votes in good conscience except between you two."

Those letters are realistic. They advise Gracián to flatter Macario's toady, Fray Gabriel: "You should make friendly inquiries about him as if you were doing it on your own initiative. Even if he is at odds with you, I think it is because they both are jealous because you seem to like others more."

It had to be Gracián or Doria, with the one acting as the other's coadjutor. The nuns need understanding that only Gracián could give, but how easily that understanding can be represented, twisted by his enemies! Teresa knew that the scandalous whisperings would never die: yet she saw that they would be diminished if the friars made a gesture of confidence in him, elected him, and sent him off—but in Doria's company, to guard his good name. But could she make him understand her in all this? Did he feel her caution as a lack of trust in him, of love for him?

"Now, let's talk about what you said about not being elected or confirmed, and what I wrote to the Father Commissary [Juan de las Cuevas]. Realize, father, that so far as my wish to see you free [of authority] goes, it comes from the great love for you that I have in the Lord, not what I want for the good of the Order. A weakness of the flesh comes out of that love, one that makes me suffer so much when others don't realize what they owe you and how much you have suffered that I can't bear to hear a single word said against you. But in the end I have come to see that the general good counts for more, even though it has seemed to me that as you would always be going about with Father Nicoleo [Doria], it would come to the same thing, the one way or the other. But now I see that it would be better for you to bear your burden, and I am saying so to the Father Commissary. If not, then Father Nicoleo, with you going with him, because of the experience you have with friars and nuns.

"I have given the Commissary solid reasons for this and told him that Fray Fernández wanted it that way—though at one time he did want Macario to have the power, for reasons that existed then. But, oh, the damage he could do now! I also named Fray Juan de Jesús [Roca], so it wouldn't look as if I were limiting myself to just two possibilities, though I told him the truth—that he hasn't the art of governing. . .but would be an adequate companion for one of you two because he is so open to reason and influence.

"And I do believe that if [Roca] went with you he wouldn't depart from what you told him in any way, so it would be all right. Besides, I'm sure he won't get any votes.

"May the Lord guide it by the way that will be most to His glory and service—which I can hope that He will seeing that He has already done what counted still more. It's a pity that. . . ."

(Final page missing.)

Gracián took advice badly. He had been happier in the role of Angela's Paul, and I doubt that he ever credited Teresa's letters to the Commissary with having had much effect.

II

Juan de la Cruz did not interrupt his prayers to come to the Chapter. Heredia, having heard rumors that the Commissary was influencing friars to vote against him, stayed away in a sulk. The leading *Descalzos* present were Gracián, Mariano, Doria, Roca—and Elías de San Martín, who had spread the *beatas'* scandals in Seville and made Gracián's imprisonment in Alcalá so unpleasant.

The first business was the election of four Definitors: a governmental body which would be largely honorary. Doria was one; the other three were those conspicuous by their absence: Juan de la Cruz, Heredia, and Heredia's crony, Fray Gabriel. After that came the serious voting in which twenty friars would cast their votes to represent the will of more than three hundred friars and two hundred nuns. Fray Gabriel and Doria got one vote apiece, Heredia seven, and Gracián eleven. The record of the Chapter reads: "Gracián, having received one vote more than half and two more than the others taken together, is left canonically elected Provincial." It was more than he could have hoped for after having tasted Mariano's electioneering and sat through his fiery opening address to the Chapter. Clearly, las Cuevas had chaired the proceedings well.

Teresa had correctly foreseen no votes for Roca; Doria's poor showing indicates that she had let herself be blinded by wishes, for las Cuevas would obviously have preferred a well-born Spaniard with Court connections to a

Genoese businessman; and the friars felt no warmth for the only one of their leaders who had gone scot-free during the time of persecution.

But Teresa, knowing that Gracián had won, assumed that he would thereafter work hand-in-hand with Doria, if only in unspoken acknowledgement that he, not Heredia, had become Provincial thanks largely to her appeals to las Cuevas that Fernández's final wishes be respected.

III

Teresa's happiness at the outcome of that election cannot be exaggerated. The degree to which she saw it as the fulfillment of her life's work can be exaggerated, and almost uniformly has been. A supposed quotation from a letter sent, some say, to María Bautista, and others say to San José, is invariably quoted as her *nunc dimmitis:* "Now, daughter, I can say what the blessed Simeon said, for I have seen accomplished all I desired for the Order of the Virgin, and so I beg and implore you not to beg and implore God that I may live on, but that I may go to my rest, for I can be of service no more."

Teresa's realism allowed of no such ecstasies. She asked for a copy of the brief and had it translated. It did not give all they asked for, she wrote to Gracián. For one thing, it was important that they be allowed to give the university degrees of Maestro and Presentado to such *letrados* as they had, so that future questions of theology could be settled by themselves and not submitted to the General in Rome. Until that should be done, it was of the utmost importance that they establish a friendly relationship with both the General and with the Calced. Gracián must write to the General at once in a tone of the utmost humility, acknowledging himself to be his loyal subject. And, equally important, he must write in the same vein to Father Angel. "Write thanking him for all that he has done and saying that he must consider you his son—*and see that you do it!*"

For once, she did not moderate her tone; perhaps she hoped that Gracián had finally learned his lesson. Alas, Gracián never learned such lessons, and he was riding high. For Teresa's sake we may be glad that she died before she saw the outcome of his ineducability: Gracián expelled from the Order, Doria named Provincial in his place, the final separation from the Calced made far less amicably than it might have been, and Gracián's enemy, Elías de San Martín, become her now fully independent Order's first General.

Mercifully, she foresaw none of that. But in the years since she first wrote her Constitutions she had learned that they were inadequate in many respects. She saw that certain rules must be laid down for her nuns before the Chapter dissolved, and trusted Gracián to present them and see to it that they were accepted. First, no vicar of a convent must ever act as its nuns' confessor: "I have seen grave improprieties start with this, and it will be enough to mention only one: if the Vicar gets fond of a nun, the Prioress can't keep him from having as much to do with her as he likes, since he is the Prioress's superior; and a thousand misfortunes can start from that."

Nor should any Prioress ever be considered the subject of some local Prior:

"They aren't all like my Father Gracián, and we must look to the future." Priors can and do give orders that are in conflict with the Constitutions, creating confusion and discontent.

As for the friars, their sole contact with the nuns must be limited to hearing confessions: brief confessions of actual sins, and nothing else. If they gather from this that the state of the convent is not what it should be, they should then discuss it with the Provincial — not with the Prioress. This limitation will keep some nuns free from the temptation to feel holier-than-thou; and, since friars, like other men, can become the *devotos* of nuns with whom they talk too much, this same limitation will prevent the "occasions which *esos negros devotos* would seize to destroy the brides of Christ." (Without Teresa's letters, as we at long last have them, these warnings about vicars and friars would be read as anxious, puritanical foresight: but not now.)

She goes on to a matter that she had understood from the very beginning. Above all, the Constitutions must be respected as to the freedom they give nuns to choose their confessors, whether from their own Order, from another, or from the secular priesthood. She once discussed this with Father Fray Pedro Fernández, who agreed that it was right. Gracián must stress it that this should not be feared, for "nuns who have this freedom seldom use it, but those who are denied it rarely think about anything else."

None of this means that Gracián cannot visit the convents and advise them. She has told the Commissary how much good his visits do, and indeed Gracián owes such visits to the nuns after all the tears his troubles have cost them. But he should not discuss this particular matter with the Chapter, only with his companion, Doria. (A wise caution. It might well have caused murmurings that she granted visiting rights to Discalced convents exclusively to the *Descalzo* most often accused of misbehavior with the nuns.)

She has collected petitions from the convents as to changes they desire in their rules. Some, Gracián will see, are ridiculous. Others should be taken seriously. Fernández, for example, had insisted that they should not have eggs with their bread at collation, though such a rule could only cause senseless scruples in nuns whose health demanded a good supper. That rule should be struck out, like the one specifying the material to be used in their stockings. Scruples over trivia distract the soul from the essentials of the religious life.

Yet some rules, in themselves trivial, should be kept for the sake of appearances: for example, the rule that the face be kept veiled in the confessional and with all visitors except for the immediate family. And for the sake of appearances, others should be struck out, such as the original rule about founding in poverty. Since more and more houses now have incomes, anyone reading the rule in the Constitutions would say, "You see how soon they went back to the Mitigation?"

The really important thing is to have few rules, and those few firmly enforced. To ensure this, the Constitutions should be printed, for a handwritten copy tempts prioresses to put things in and leave others out.

The Chapter will admit that she has lived with nuns and understands them; so, she hopes, they will let her Constitutions stand as they have evolved from experience: they express a Rule simple enough to command unquestioning obedience, which is essential to a convent's peace, but also one which still allows a nun the freedom and human respect she needs to grow to her full spiritual stature.

To her last day, Teresa would be urging that her Constitutions be set in print. Print is respected by men as well as by headstrong prioresses. Wisely, she did not mention that angle; but she knew that it mattered.

No, Teresa's happiness over the election did not inspire a *nunc dimittis,* a calm conviction that her work on earth was done.

But at least she did not doubt that she would soon be on her way to Burgos, accompanied by a grateful Gracián and his inseparable companion, Nicoleo Doria. No realist is ever wholly free of illusions.

Chapter 71 ❀ *Plan to Found in Soria*

I

Doña Ana Enríquez, Marchioness of Alcañices, had a Jesuit confessor in Valladolid. She had known Baltasar Alvarez and shared Teresa's grief at his death, and she sent Teresa a statue for her Palencia chapel.

It was one more delight, Teresa wrote her, a beautiful thing to have in a place where Doña Ana's cousin, the Bishop, had made everything go so well. "But in spite of it all, I am lonely as far as spiritual matters go, for in all my acquaintance here there isn't a single father of the Company. Though I really feel lonely anywhere, for when our saint was alive, I could write to him about everything."

Doña Ana read letters aloud, and her words were repeated. As Teresa knew, they could even reach Burgos—and disarm any who had learned from the Valladolid Jesuits to think of her as a fortune snatcher. A longing for any Jesuit at all in Palencia was excessive, perhaps, but worth trying. That odd, haunting dread of Burgos kept recurring, Voice or no Voice.

Yet it seemed as if everybody knew that Burgos would be next. A letter from Dr. Velázquez, now Bishop of Osma, came with an invitation for her to found a convent in Soria, which was in his see and lay on the way to Burgos. Doña Beatriz de Beamonte wanted to found a convent for her niece, Doña Leonora.

Teresa asked a few questions, and sent an evasive answer. She is sorry that there would not be time to allow for it, because it would be summer before she could leave Palencia and after Burgos another foundation was waiting. Besides, she hates to involve those she truly loves in such troubles as her foundations always bring.

She wrote Gracián the whole story, her true reasons for hesitating included, and put it out of her mind for a time. Other convents were having their

363

troubles. In Valladolid one hysterical nun had to be confined and another prevented from fasting or being alone. María Bautista blamed it on a girl whom Teresa had transferred from Salamanca — one surnamed Gutiérrez and supposed by some to be Martín's natural child. María Bautista demanded that she be sent to Medina, where, Teresa said, there were too many melancholiacs already. "I think," she wrote Gracián, "I will take her to Burgos — as a penitent, not as a founding nun. As for Inés de Jesús, I think I will leave her there as a prioress, for she likes Burgos much better than Madrid — though she does everything grudgingly."

Inés had worked out even worse in Palencia than she had in Medina. As soon as Teresa brought in a few more nuns, they demanded an election. So by April the Prioress was Isabel de Jesús, from Salamanca — for whom Inés and her small clique made things so unpleasant that both eventually had to be removed, Isabel by her own request going back to Salamanca.

There were also family troubles to be seen to. Father Angel, still believing in Lorenzo's wealth, had called on Don Francisco and his Doña Orofrisia. Teresa urged Gracián to do it, too, when he left Alcalá: "And may God take care of you! The way he's being ruled now will be his perdition, for I tell you, those two women are his bad marriage. I wish with all my heart I were clear of the whole lot. The mother-in-law had struck up such a friendship with me that I'm worn out. What's worse, she's headed for losing everything, for someone has made her believe that he has an income of two thousand a year. I told her the truth, so that she can see how much she's spending." (Amusingly, this page from a letter the rest of which is lost ends, "Tell me how Macario has been acting and for the love of charity, tear up this letter!")

Antonio Gaitán passed on another family problem from Alba. Beatriz de Ovalle's current lover had a wife with a foul, loose tongue. A small town scandal like that did the Foundress's convent no good and disturbed Gaitán's little girl who was boarding there. Teresa wrote back, trying to deny the facts, while admitting that Juana had no control over the girl. The jealous wife is lying, "and even if it were true, her own sense of honor should keep her from saying such infamous things." Poor Juana at least does not deserve the ill-treatment she's getting in Alba: "She has sworn to me again and again that it is all false, and I believe her because she is not a liar. . . . People only look down on her because she is poor."

Family loyalty demanded that denial — though it remains obvious that if poor Juana had thought that Teresa believed her, she would have felt no need to swear once, let alone again and again. But it was an ugly situation, and one that might make the Duchess remove her patronage, leaving the convent to the mercies of Señora de Laiz. She was like that. Similarly, if Doña Orofrisia's too-well-connected mother did not get the money earmarked for Lorenzo's chapel, she would do all she could to alienate the Mendozas and their circle. It all left one desperately tired of being beholden to the nobility.

And a convent in Soria would be more of the same. Doña Beatriz de Beamonte was actually descended from the royal house of Navarre, as La Cardona had pretended to be. Consequently her niece, Doña Leonora, had not found it difficult to purchase an annulment of an unsatisfactory marriage. So she now wanted to enter a convent: not any convent, but one set up in her Aunt Beatriz's palace. Teresa found it an ugly notion, and was taken aback when Gracián embraced it and insisted upon it. They would stop there, he said, on the way to Burgos. Teresa at last gave her reluctant consent.

He would soon be coming, and she had not yet found her nuns a house. She negotiated for others than those so promptly offered by Canon Tamayo, but the negotiations fell through. As the Chapter drew towards its close, she sent Canon Reinoso a note. She would take a house he had finally found for her: Tamayo's were impossible, though as she had believed them as good as sold for the last two and a half months, he might start a lawsuit. Perhaps they could tell him that they needed only one of his houses, and he could get a better price for selling both at once. Or they could tell him that they were only renting the house Reinoso had found until they could afford Tamayo's. Or, would it be best to come straight out with it and take the consequences? "As one of our sisters gracefully put it, we'll all have to be friends again in Holy Week, so we may as well get it over with now."

But Tamayo showed signs of being too hasty. Teresa gave in and settled for his property when she heard that Gracián was actually on his way to Palencia. Tamayo, angered by the delay, had raised the price, and insisted upon getting the full payment, cash down; but he did not trust those who had offered to stand surety for it, he said. Canon Reinoso stopped the Bishop's steward in the street as he was riding past, and began to explain things to him. By Teresa's account, the steward laughed. "You're asking me for a sum like that?" Before Reinoso could answer, the steward had reached inside his cloak, pulled out paper, pen and inkhorn, and signed for the full amount, without even dismounting from his mule. "Which is something to think about in times like these," Teresa says.

Not really. The steward knew what would have pleased his employer. He was coming soon, and the nuns had to be housed. It was too bad that Tamayo had to profit, but constabulary could be appointed to watch that brothel-church at night; it had been a disgrace too long.

II

Teresa knew that she had been weak in consenting to found in Soria: a convent set up in a palace to please a great lady and sanctify the spoiled niece whose marriage had been dissolved—thanks to the happy combination of money and family. . . . But Gracián had wanted it, and promised that he and Doria would go with her. It would be the first of that pair's blessed journeys together, and made with her—to soften whatever differences lay between them, to make each feel himself indispensable to the good of the Order; it was what she had worked for. Roca would come, too, as far as Palencia, for the great day of the formal foundation of the first convent in their newly independent Order.

Gracián came first. He came and left before the others arrived. Heredia had

been consoling himself in the company of his old friend, the Duchess of Alba
He heard of the adulterous niece whose behavior had set the town to dragging
up other tales, tales better forgotten. He knew that such tales are relished in
small places; the riot in Montalbán was a case in point. Heredia had little love
for Gracián, or for Teresa; but his future now lay with the newly independent
Discalced. He had no wish to see them smeared again, and above all in a way
that might cool the patronage of the Duchess, with her ever-ready way out—the
nominal patronage of the steward's wife. When he learned that Gracián's first
act as Provincial would be to join Teresa and set out as her travelling companion, he spelled out the danger.

In Salamanca—where all too many scandals were remembered—the Discalced were about to enjoy their first triumph: their own college in the great
university. Nothing must endanger that, must it? A courtesy call in Palencia,
made in company with Doria and Roca, would of course be unexceptionable.
But the visit must be of the shortest, pointedly so. As for the proposed trip to
Soria, such an invitation to scandalmongers was madness!

Gracián took Heredia's advice. *Peregrinaciones* omits any mention of his
having refused to stay out the week and see the splendid installation ceremony that Bishop Mendoza had arranged. What he does tell about that visit is
still revelatory.

Teresa had called herself "the old hag" for several years, but only because
she no longer looked some twenty years younger that she was. After her
near-fatal illness in Valladolid she took a sudden plunge from her delusive look
of a woman still sexually attractive in late middle-age to that of one far older
than her actual sixty-five years. Gracián found it a shock. The change, he said,
was scarcely believable: "Always before she looked more like a *moza*"—a girl.
One should remember, too, that even an old face can brighten with happiness.
It was not only Gracián for whom that hasty visit was a shock.

Gracián must also have been stunned when she told him of her plans for
the Soria foundation: that noble house, that golden opportunity, though in
Peregrinaciones he told of it as evidence of her reverence for holy humility. Still,
I doubt that in Palencia or later he fully grasped what she was saying about
that foundation in the only way that she could.

For Prioress she chose a lay-sister from Medina, Catalina de Cristo; Teresa
had already made her porteress there, an unusual honor for a peasant girl who
could not read and write. Gracián remembers protesting: "As Prioress? And in
Soria!" Teresa said, "Silence, father! Catalina de Cristo knows how to love God
very much, she has a great, holy soul, and her spirits are always high. Nothing
else is needed to show one how to govern well. She will make a good prioress."

Another choice evoked a further protest. From Salamanca she chose Bañez's
La Parda, the blackamoor slave-girl who had been "crazy with joy" when she
found herself in a convent. Of her, Teresa said, "It will do them good to have a
saint in that foundation."

One should add to Gracián's account that she gave Catalina a literate and
competent subprioress—another Beatriz de Jesús, and the only satisfactory
nun of her five who bore that "name in religion." She had come from Salamanca

and would have been unhappy in Palencia now that her friend Isabel de Jesús had asked to go back. From Segovia she took two; one was a half-sister of the problem girl she had originally meant to take to Burgos as a penitent. The last, another Catalina, was the problem nun from Avila whose ecstasies had so unsettled Teresica. This had one purpose only: to quiet Teresica, who was already under pressure from Francisco and his mother-in-law to leave the convent and take her dowry with her.

These seven, with Inés, San Bartolomé, and Teresa herself made ten: a larger company than Teresa had ever taken to found a new convent, and you'll grant, an odd one.

Before they had begun to gather, Gracián made off for Alba, to join Heredia. Just after his departure Teresa sent him a letter that a better man would not have wanted to keep. Gracián did keep it, as valuable evidence of La Santa's pure love for him — so unjustly treated after her death.

"May the Holy Spirit be with you, my father. Now don't you see what a little time my happiness lasted? I had been longing for that journey, and I know that I should have been sorry when it was over, as I always was when I travelled in the company I expected to have. Expected until only now.

"Well, God be praised, I think the trip has begun to tire me already. I tell you, father, the flesh is weak after all; and so you left me more saddened that I could wish I had been. Very much more. At the very least you could have waited until we were in our new house here. A week, more or less, couldn't have made much difference. You left a great loneliness here, and please God the one who was tempted to take you away acted better than I expected. . . .

"I have only one consolation — that they would have had me as something to bring up against this Santo Santorum (*sic*) — for I tell you I had a great deal of temptation about that, and to keep it from happening I would let everything else rain down on me — as it is raining heavily now, to go by the way I feel.

"Well, it may all turn out for the best, and if that happens, I shall have nothing to complain of, even if I have to suffer still more."

Such self-pity, such laying herself open not only to Gracián but to her amanuensis, San Bartolomé, is unlike Teresa; it comes from sudden heartbreak after joyful anticipation, and it strikes rock bottom with a message from Laurentia — who had been silent so long.

"Nobody else seems to fill this emptiness, so that as things go now with poor Laurentia, everything tires her. She asks very earnestly to be remembered to you. She says that her soul finds no rest or peace when it is not with God or with somebody who understands her, like you. She says that everything else is such a cross to her that no words could exaggerate it. . . . and San Bartolomé is still very sad. Give us your blessing."

But she is still Teresa. Abruptly she pushed Laurentia aside. The nuns in Alba "are strangely afraid of their prioress" and don't tell her all she should know. Gracián himself must look into the matter of those students who are said to be so overhelpful to them.

And within three days she was ashamed of that letter and followed it with one all brisk cheerfulness. The Bishop has come and is putting the finishing touches to the planned activities. Father Nicoleo has just preached a first-rate sermon. She likes talking to Roca. He is fond of Gracián, and Gracián must make him feel that the fondness is mutual: "It's very important to have a good friend nowadays."

Sister Isabel will take this letter when she leaves, en route for Segovia. "Do, for the love of charity, show her the greatest kindness." She should not be blamed or let blame herself for leaving Palencia. A small convent can afford factions even less than friars can — Gracián, Roca, "and even Macario."

Roca and Doria marched in the procession with the cathedral staff of eighty. All carried lighted candles, and the convent annals record a miracle which Teresa failed to observe. A wind blew out all the candles except for those carried by Teresa and her nuns.

Then Teresa set out to found her fifteenth convent.

Chapter 72 ❀ The Soria Founding

I

At some time after Dr. Velázquez left Toledo to become Bishop of Osma, Teresa wrote him a letter of which a fragmentary copy exists, headed in his own hand: "Part of a relation that the Mother sent me in consultation about her spirit and manner of proceeding."

In Toledo, you recall, she made him what was in effect a general confession which, as she said, did not cost one twentieth of the pain it had cost her to cover the same ground with Gracián. He knew about the *arrobamientos* that had frightened Avila after she lost de Prádanos; how they came when she feared, in Salamanca, that being "so bound" to Martín had cost her the blessed "freedom" to "love in Christ," free from all creature love; and how they had not come again until Angela told her Paul that her bondage to him was worth more in God's eyes than the freedom it had cost.

The letter he saved in part is worth considering here, if only because she could not have written it to him after Soria. It begins, "Oh, if I could only make Your Lordship understand the peace and quiet that my soul has found!"

It is not joy, but an inner certitude, as if the knowledge that one is heir to a great fortune made one content with present poverty. She coddles her health, fasts little, does little penance, and despite that her only desire is to serve God. She sometimes has "intellectual visions" concerning the Trinity and Christ's humanity, but "imaginary visions" are part of the past. And while she still sometimes seems to hear the Voice, there are no ecstasies and no desire for suffering. Sometimes it seems to her that she only lives to eat and sleep with her soul in a stupor — and despite that she knows that her love of God and her wish that all should love Him is still growing. Stranger still, she no longer feels her old torment at the thought of souls being lost and her fear that she, too, is in sin. She has even lost that fear of unwitting heresy which used to make her seek out *letrados*, "Fray Domingo, Master Medina, and Fathers of the Company."

Then, the passage we cited before: "Nor have I ceased being given to understand that the souls of some now dead who have inspired me are in heaven; others are not. The loneliness makes me think that one cannot attribute that sense to him 'who sucked the breasts of my mother. . .' The flight into Egypt. . ." (Those who have left Purgatory and are with God are with us, too. The loneliness ceases. Just so, when she had first begun to feel that loneliness for Lorenzo, she lost the assurance that he, too, was in Heaven and wrote to his son that he would only be in Purgatory for a short time—or possibly, just possibly, none.)

Finally—"except when I am ill"—she lives in an awareness of God that has freed her alike from the fear of death and the desire to escape from life. The chance that her prayers can lead a single soul to love God more and praise Him more, "even if only briefly," means more to her than that she herself should be in glory.

It is a remarkable confession of faith. Few in Teresa's day ever conceived of loving God without fear and without desire of reward. Note, too, the honesty which mentions a lessened awareness of God's presence when she is ill, made self-centered by pain. This statement is worth remembering when the outer facts of Teresa's story blur it. She has a vision of life as it should be lived and of God as He is. It gave her stature that is not cheapened by the fact that she was also human and set in the world of things as they are.

II

As with Malagón, *Fundaciones* tells us next to nothing about Soria. She was asked there by the Bishop of Osma, a former confessor with whom she had discussed her spiritual life "with great openness." Her patroness, "a noble widow with no children," was generous, penitent, and "very much God's servant." She wanted more nuns than usual, so Teresa came in a group of ten. A stagecoach was sent from Soria to fetch them.

"Because I had said that I would bring two Discalced fathers, I brought Father Nicoleo de Jesús María, a man of great perfection and discretion, and a native of Genoa." (Two long paragraphs in Doria's praise distract the reader from the absence of one of the promised pair.) The journey was easy, for they had good accommodations on the road. They reached Burgo de Osma in three days "and spent the night in a church which was not at all bad." Then they set out after Mass and reached Soria at five in the afternoon, where the Bishop stood in a window and blessed them as they passed. (Osma, the cathedral town proper, boasted only three hundred souls, and the Bishop's residence was in Soria.) Doña Beatriz de Beamonte was waiting at the palace door. Everything was ready, even a room to serve as a chapel "until the covered way into the church should be finished." The first Mass was celebrated by a father of the Company, as the Bishop went to Burgo de Osma almost daily. The foundation was celebrated with a Mass on the Feast of the Transfiguration (thirty-six days later).

The Bishop of Osma had gone blind in one eye, which was sad. He was a holy character who suffered from false witness and overcame it by his humble way of life.

This is all *Fundaciones* tells about Soria.

From San Bartolomé we know that they caused considerable excitement on the way, as their stagecoach full of nuns, accompanied by a priest and an armed *alguacil* sent from Soria, was taken for a haul of heretics being carried off to the Inquisition.

The first Mass was said by a Jesuit because Doria waited only an hour or so to see the papers notarized before he left. Since he knew of the proposed "partnership," he had been irked by Gracián's shrugging him off so soon — and to be the scapegoat, if more talk sprang up about travelling with nuns.

Teresa's mention of false witness against the Bishop still goes unexplained. His avoidance of Teresa may or may not have anything to do with it, but to her surprise and disappointment she saw next to nothing of him while she was there. Her letters mention with regret at having no chance to talk with him. We do know that before she left Soria he went to Madrid, learned that he was transferred to another see, lost that one, too, and spent his final days in a hermitage. As for the humble way of life that she mentions, he is said to have gone everywhere afoot with his weary, disgruntled staff trudging after him. Something went wrong with him after he left Toledo, but what it was I don't know.

On Doña Beatriz de Beamonte there is more evidence. Shortly after her marriage she left her husband and returned to her parents in Navarre, only coming back to Castile at her husband's death when she was forty-six. Her will provides for an illegitimate daughter, but there were no other children. One can understand her impulse to make a convent for the niece who had also married unhappily. However, as Teresa soon learned, this kindness was bitterly opposed by a nephew who had expected to become her heir, by the niece's ex-husband, and — though somewhat less hotly at first — by the local Jesuits.

The nephew was particularly incensed because his aunt not only gave the convent the use of her palace, one wing excepted, and a generous yearly income, but an immediate gift of three thousand ducats. Some shocking reports of what he had to say to Teresa on the subject are substantiated by a letter in which he tells a friend that, having been "forced" by his aunt to go and pay his respects to the Mother, he offered them "on the end of a pitchfork."

It also turned out that Doña Leonora could not take the habit at once. While there was no doubt that the annulment would be granted, the papers from Rome had not yet arrived. Meantime Doña Beatriz presented the convent with two other well-dowered nieces. The younger of them eventually offered one bit of evidence for Teresa's canonizatin which rings true.

Teresa asked her, "Now tell me, which is the holier, the Prioress or I?" The girl, scarcely out of childhood and wholly tactless, did not hesitate: "Why,

Catalina, of course!" Teresa hugged her, laughing. "Perfectly right! She has the holiness, and I have the reputation for it!" (This same story was later borrowed for the process which made San Bartolomé the Venerable San Bartolomé; it was charming enough to use twice, though San Bartolomé would never have made such an estimate.)

Doña Beatriz moved at once to the few rooms she kept for herself; but a palace and those ill-assorted nuns did not make a recognizable Discalced convent. Teresa was eager to get away — and to Madrid, for she had learned, with a relief she could not deny, that Burgos must be indefinitely postponed. Bishop Mendoza, expecting only smooth sailing, sent a canon of Palencia there to discuss the foundation with the Archbishop — who said that the city opposed the foundation and that he, for his part, had no wish to go through with the sort of trouble that his friend Mendoza put up with when Teresa founded in Avila. Having been a canon of the Avila cathedral at the time, he remembered all that business only too well! On hearing the news, Teresa wrote Canon Reinoso that she has told the Archbishop that she certainly does not want to involve him in any trouble — and will tell the world that she could not have got to Burgos until its cold winter set in, which would endanger her health.

Then she wrote to Quiroga, who had recently become a Cardinal. The Discalced, she reminded him, were now a separate province. To grant them their Madrid licence would no longer mean taking sides in a factional dispute — his previous reason for refusing. And, she added, his niece, Doña Elena, who had previously considered joining the Order, was now still more eager — for she could enter it in Madrid, and be near him.

If Teresa had thought that the Cardinal-Inspector's objections to the Medina convent were largely on its merchant-class patronage, she was sadly mistaken. Teresa was soon reduced to writing to Quiroga's confessor imploring him to clarify things with his Most Illustrious penitent. It was not at her wish that Doña Elena was intending to turn Discalced. Indeed, she had urged her to stay with her children, who needed her! And saintly though the lady was, she, Teresa, had learned by experience that widows with daughters spelled trouble for a convent. She would be deeply grieved if His Most Illustrious Lordship denied the Madrid licence because of a false charge that she or hers had wanted Doña Elena to join them. She had even now consulted the Dominican Prior in Soria, who assured her that Doña Elena's vow to turn Discalced is invalid and should be ignored! (The Prior was also Doña Elena's uncle and Quiroga's first cousin. Teresa could hope that her seeking advice from one of the family would carry weight.)

Teresa truly did not want Doña Elena. She wrote to Gracián instructing him to forbid it if Doña Elena persisted. Long ago, she had asked Baltasar Alvarez to get the notion out of the lady's head "because of her children and her relatives and what we know of the lady herself. And tear up this letter! And don't let anyone think we are refusing her for fear of the Cardinal! They should only think it's because it wouldn't be good for her children — which is true enough. Besides, we've already had enough of these widows!" (Teresa was currently having enough of them and would have more; though she would have consid-

371

ered Doña Elena a small price to pay for that crown of her work, a convent in Madrid.)

She also told Gracián that to avoid making further trouble between Bishop Mendoza and the Archbishop of Burgos, she had written Bishop Mendoza that he must give that foundation no further thought, as Gracián had forbidden her to take the trip because of her poor health. "You did say something like that to me once." And obviously, this is no time to attempt that foundation: "Indeed it looks as if Fray Baltasar will make it first!"

Baltasar Nieto; or, otherwise put, when hell freezes over.

For the time being, Teresa most wanted to get back to Avila. Doria wrote her a disturbing letter about its troubles, financial and otherwise. Her only fear, she wrote Gracián, was that its nuns would make her Prioress, as she hadn't the strength for that, but she could at least straighten things out a little. They had a building problem that she could use as an excuse to Doña Beatriz. . . .

Soria had been a mistake that even a lay-sister-Prioress and a blackamoor saint could not rectify. Doña Beatriz was highhanded. For example, she made a next-door church the convent's property in true de Beamonte fashion: she simply told the parishoners that henceforth they must worship elsewhere. Similarly, when Teresa urged her need to visit Avila, Doña Beatriz said that she must stay and wait for Doña Leonora's annulment to come so that she could give the lady the habit with her own hands—as one of her rank surely deserved of an Order's foundress. She would see to it that nobody in Soria helped Teresa to get away before that, so ungratefully! Teresa had to write again to Canon Reinoso, asking him to arrange her escape.

While Teresa waited she had the second of her two brief meetings with Ribera, who became her first and best contemporary biographer. The first, in Valladolid, had been prompted by his curiosity over the fortune-snatcher of whom he heard so many ugly stories from the fellow Jesuits with whom he was briefly staying. The ailing, aging woman, still so strong in spirit, was nothing he had expected: for Ribera it was love—"a love in Christ"—at first sight. Now, he had spent four days in Soria and was just about to leave when he learned that she was there. The Jesuits with whom he was housed had assumed that he would not want to see her. This, he had written, he would regret to his dying day, for he could talk with her only that one more time before he had to be on his way.

Their meeting, like the first, lived on in his mind. It hardly needed the miraculous preservation—which he alone described so accurately, not "like wax" as others remembered it, but "brown and shrivelled like a walnut"—to move him to research Teresa's life as best he could and produce a book which had something of the living woman in it.

Canon Reinoso sent a good little prebendary, also named Ribera as it happens, with a cart in which to take Teresa and San Bartolomé away. Teresa herself says nothing of that departure. They slipped away by night while the palace slept, reaching Burgo de Osma in time to receive communion at the first Mass.

The celebrant, by an odd coincidence, was the man who would become

Teresa's second biographer, Yepes. He used more inventive source material than Ribera did, chiefly culled from nuns and from Yanguas (who claimed to be the chosen confessor of her last eight years). Nonetheless, I believe his account of that meeting with the Mother.

As he says, when she knelt and lifted her veil, "her face was the color of earth," but when she received the Host, that dusty gray "seemed to turn transparent." In that one moment, she was beautiful.

Though *Fundaciones* skips the departure from Soria, it describes the trip: over fifty leagues of mountain terrain where there was often no cart-road, only a trail. The carter knew the way to Segovia, where she had a week's rest, but thereafter they were lost. The guides they found stayed with them while the road was good, and then vanished. Sometimes they had to get out and walk while the cart skirted a cliff so narrowly that it seemed to hang in mid-air. Somehow, they got back alive.

But, the chapter ends, the foundation itself was made "with no trouble at all." She can only pray with God's help it "will come to be one in which He is served."

That was the most Teresa could make herself say for Soria.

Chapter 73 ❀ *Failure of St. Joseph's and Other Convents to Maintain Teresa's Ideals*

I

During those last weeks in Soria, and all through the journey back to her first convent, Teresa thought things through again and again. Nothing had gone as she had planned it. Gracián left her in Palencia and went to Alba and Salamanca; Doria got away from Soria within hours and went to Valladolid. Gracián sent him orders to go to Rome and pay the respects of the Discalced to the new General. They seemed determined to keep as far away from one another as possible. Letters from Soria did nothing to bring them together.

Still, Teresa's last letters from Soria brought her a promise that Doria would see her in Avila; he would wait on his way to Madrid where he'd get his final orders about leaving for Italy. That was a concession — granted only when she pleaded her need for advice with the convent's affairs: the poverty, for example, which was so oddly caused by Francisco de Salcedo's will. He had left them all he had, and only she and Lorenzo had known that he died on the edge of bankruptcy. What he left, as Teresa figured it, would keep thirteen nuns from starvation for three months; but the myth of de Salcedo's wealth persisted, and it had dried up all alms. Why give to a convent so rich?

An eccentric Flemish widow, Ana Wasteels — always, in Teresa's letters, "La Flamenca" — had professed as Ana de San Pedro; but she was keeping tight hold on most of her money unless her daughter should be professed, too. The girl did not much like the notion, though Doria — en route to Valladolid — had written to say that the money was needed and she'd settle down. "Forbid it!" Teresa wrote to Gracián from Soria, "at least for the time being. . . . I am more afraid of a discontented nun than I'd be of a crowd of devils."

And Francisco, bullied by his mother-in-law (another Doña Beatriz) had almost persuaded Teresica to leave the convent. Then, by Doña Beatriz's plan, the girl could be married off cheaply and Francisco could corner almost two-thirds of Lorenzo's estate and avoid the ludicrous waste of building Lorenzo's chapel.

That same final letter from Soria begged Gracián to deal with still another bad problem. "Please God you've been able to do something about the Beatriz [de Ovalle] business that I've suffered over so long. I have written terrible letters to her and her mother that should have done something to better it all. . . . It's a damnable thing, and I am sure that if they don't take her away from her occasion of sin, it will go from bad to worse — if anything worse is possible, seeing how bad it is now. I can stand the fact that her reputation is already lost, though it grieves me, but I don't want their souls to be lost — and as I see it, that family are so unlike parents and children that there's no cure for it."

In the week she rested in Segovia, Teresa wrote once more to Juana, imploring her to bring Beatriz to Avila; they could stay with Pedro at La Serna, which was still not sold. From an inn in Villacastín, when the dangerous, exhausting trip was nearly over, she wrote to María de San José. She still hasn't got the two hundred ducats that San José says she turned over to Horatio Doria, not to her as she had specifically directed. San José must make sure that she gets it. Lorenzo's chapel weighs heavy on her conscience. She looks forward to seeing Father Nicoleo in Avila.

But Doria had not waited for her. When little Ribera, their escort, went back to Palencia, he took a note to Canon Reinoso: She is in Avila, and only wishes she could get away again. There are "too many people here, too little time, and with it all a great loneliness." The "good little prebendary" will describe their trip. It is strange that everyone who tries to help her only gets into troubles, just as Reinoso himself had done in Palencia. These journeys are always exhausting — all but one. It was easy getting by coach to Soria, and she had "the views of the rivers for company."

Rivers, you note. Not Gracián, nor even Doria.

II

San José de Avila was in decay. Mariá de Cristo was a feeble prioress; there was no discipline. The silent times went unobserved, the rule that all things be held in common was forgotten. Julián de Avila, always overindulgent and overcredulous, had now become another García Alvarez, spending hours in conversation with a nun called Mariana. Doubtless all good and holy, Teresa wrote Gracián, but dangerous to Mariana's overexcited mind and a source of jealousy to the others — a situation that could scarcely be handled without causing resentments that would be still worse. "God keep me from confessors established for years on end!"

In mid-September, Casilda de Padilla's mother removed her, and all hope of her fortune, from María Bautista's convent; simultaneously, she withdrew Casilda's sister from the Convent of St. Catherine of Siena, so at least the defection would not be seen as criticism of the Discalced. Teresa wrote to Gracián that even if the poor little thing tried to come back, it would be a mistake to receive her, ever. It was partly the fault of the subprioress; she had the same Jesuit confessor as Casilda's mother, she disliked María Bautista, and she had got them both worked up over María Bautista's refusal to relinquish the money that Casilda's mother had wanted to give the Jesuits.

Still, Teresa warned Gracián, this must not lead them into any show of resentment against the Jesuits. Some of them were "still helpful," and in time they "could shake them off, little by little." It is sad that she could no longer remember the truth of which she had reminded Baltasar Alvarez: that their Orders "fought under the same banner." Still more sad that she so closely paraphrased Suárez's order that the Jesuits rid themselves of her Discalced little by little, "suavely and efficiently."

News came from Medina that if Doña Elena were not allowed to turn Discalced, she would turn Franciscan. That was worth passing on: the Franciscans were at the bottom of the socio-ecclesiastical heap. Quiroga would see the Discalced as the lesser evil, and Doña Elena would make it clear to him that she preferred Madrid to a market-town. The ploy was distasteful, but it seemed to Teresa that the more she came to detest these snobberies, the more she was forced to use them.

She wrote to Quiroga's confessor. She was sorry to hear such news, she said. Far better if the lady stayed with her children. For herself, she did hope that His Illustrious Lordship would send the Madrid license soon, as she wanted to leave Avila before the cold weather set in.

Yes, like it or not, people had to be used. Like Don Sancho Dávila — whose letter from Alba told of his longing to write a life of his saintly mother, the Marchioness of Velada: but was he worthy? It troubled him that when he said Mass he often couldn't keep his mind on the words he pronounced. And, did Teresa know a good cure for toothache? He had one that nothing seemed to help. . . .

Don Sancho could be used. Báñez passed through Avila while Teresa was thinking it over. Each felt that the other somehow belonged to the past, but face to face they were still old friends. She showed him the letter, for his advice was always sound. Beatriz's parents could not handle her, but couldn't Don Sancho somehow influence her lover? Báñez thought it worth trying; the *hidalguía*, after all, speak a common language.

Indeed, Teresa wrote to Don Sancho, he must write his life of the saintly Marchioness. His scruples about a wandering mind were really nothing. Only that very day she had told their mutual friend Fray Domingo Báñez about having the same trouble herself, and he assured her that it was unimportant. But as for toothache, she had found only one sure cure; have the tooth pulled.

How are the Duchess, and Don Fadrique, and the Countess of Oropesa? She would love to write to them all, but her "head isn't fit for it" because of something "for his ears alone." Conceivably, he can help her; she has failed. He must know about Beatriz de Ovalle: "They tell me it is public knowledge." True or false, Don Gonzalo's wife believes that her husband is Beatriz's lover, "and even if it weren't true, it strikes me that one should run from the tongue of an angry woman as one would from a wild beast." But Beatriz's parents refuse to take her away. Though that wouldn't restore the girl's reputation, it would at least stop the adultery — and the affair is endangering many souls. The woman, they say, has left her husband, and it's all being talked about in Salamanca and even in Avila.

But Don Gonzalo owns a large estate far from Alba. Can't Don Sancho — himself a priest and Don Gonzalo's friend — persuade him of the harm he is doing and get him to spend six months or a year in his other residence? By that time she, Teresa, could surely get Beatriz out of Alba. "I beg you, do anything you can that will leave me free of this trouble."

Don Gonzalo knew what he wanted; there was little chance that Don Sancho would succeed. But Don Sancho would not be overconscientious about an appeal "for his ears alone" since she had made it clear that the scandal was "public knowledge." So at least the Duchess would hear from a source she could trust that Teresa was doing all she could to prevent her niece from bringing shame on her nuns — in the Duchess's convent.

III

Out of sheer loneliness Teresa wrote incessantly to Gracián about the unending troubles in Avila: the poverty, the increasing pressures put upon Teresica to leave the Order, the unruliness of La Flamenca's daughter, that impossible novice, and Mariana's persistent holy cozying with Julián de Avila; "and how peevish Julián is getting!"

It seemed that there were troubles everywhere. In Villanueva de la Jara the prioress and subprioress were constantly at one another's throats; and, in Beas, Ana de Jesús was getting dangerously discontented. Perhaps, if the new foundation in Granada were made, one could send the subprioress of Villanueva there with Ana de Jesús as her prioress? That might calm them down, please God . . . .

Then, a new difficulty. It turned out that much of La Flamenca's money was deeded to the Jesuits. She wanted to annul the deed and give the money to the convent. Any word that the Discalced were again trying to rob the Jesuits would make more trouble; but so would forbidding the annulment. Told less than the truth, Teresa's hungry nuns would be infuriated by her refusing them that money; told the whole truth, they would babble and the Jesuits would accuse her of slander. Talk about being between a rock and a hard place!

And of course, to take the gift meant professing the daughter. She seems more honest and quiet than she was at first: "But I have wondered whether the devil isn't giving her the intelligence to deceive us, after all, and she and her mother won't end up tormenting us even though she is behaving well enough now."

La Flamenca has asked Dr. Castro about it. He says that, as he is a friend to both the convent and the Jesuits, she should ask someone else. Gracián knows Dr. Castro; what is he really like? Can he be trusted? Teresa finds herself attracted by his intelligence, his charm, his way with words. "I don't know whether that doesn't just come from his being so much like you."

He has called there several times, preached them a sermon, and though he doesn't like to hear confessions, it seems he would like to hear hers — probably out of curiosity. He says he believes in no visions, even those of St. Brigid. In the old days, when she feared she was suffering from delusions, that would have made her want to confess to him very much. Still, though she is now at peace, she will confess to him — if Gracián thinks she should.

Why does she ask Gracián's permission? It has always been taken for granted that she would confess to others in Gracián's absence. And why does she have to ask if this gifted, intelligent young man can be trusted? He has shown great discretion, refused to make further trouble by deciding what only Teresa herself should decide. . . . She herself had given the answer: "I don't know whether that doesn't just come from his being so much like you."

Teresa had learned to distrust her own lifelong need for the emotional nourishment that only a man could give her. Still, she wanted it, she was hungry. Surely she was not aware at any conscious level of saying, "Come back — or tell me that I may depend on another man." But, to my ears, she said just that.

Doña Elena's threat to turn Franciscan did, in fact, make Quiroga accept the lesser of two evils. Told of his capitulation, Teresa wrote him a short, dignified note. The Father Provincial would come to Medina, of course, to give the habit to their dear Sister Elena. May this be to God's glory and may He preserve His Lordship for many years.

She was careful not to spoil the effect with any reference to Madrid.

Gracián made a brief stopover in Ávila on his way to Medina. He poured scorn on Castro's timid refusal to advise them. Of course they must profess La Flamenca's daughter and let the good woman annul her deed to the Jesuits at once. More important still, Teresa must assume her rightful place as Prioress. Surely she saw that it was essential to the convent's wellbeing?

Teresa begged him to change his mind. Couldn't he see that she was old, ill, constantly tired, unfit to govern?

Gracián laughed at her. What trouble would it be, with her good cousin San Jerónimo to act as her subprioress? The convent was poor only because Teresa refused to give it standing. She was leaving her friends with a choice of believing that either she had rejected its nuns as unworthy or that they had rejected her.

Teresa implored him to let her husband what strength she still had until she could found her convent in Madrid. Gracián ordered her to kneel on her rigid joints and kiss the floor in subjection to his authority. He made a good story of it in *Peregrinaciones*. "With the greatest grace in the world she got us all to laughing at her because we would not let her rest. When she tried to give her reasons as to why we should make some other nun prioress, I ordered her to set her mouth against the floor, and while she was thus prostrated we all began to sing *Te Deum laudamus*, with great calm and happiness. When she got up, her face was composed and smiling and we began to discuss the foundations of Burgos and Granada."

I do not doubt that Teresa got to her feet smiling. Example is necessary for teaching the obedience which alone can insure a convent's peace.

And they did talk about Burgos. Only that week, at Gracián's urging, Bishop Mendoza's representatives on the fourth of November. Sometime within the which had been based, he assured them, only on the Archbishop's exaggerated memories of a little trouble in Avila a quarter century or so ago. The council's permission for Teresa to found her convent was signed and put in the hands of Mendoza's representatives of the fourth of November. Sometime within the next month or so, Gracián told her, she should be off. Madrid could wait. He might, just possibly, find time to go with her.

As for the priory in Granada, Juan de la Cruz should take it over. He was unhappy at having been moved from his hiding-place in Beas and made Rector of the College of Baeza, but his notion of returning to Castile as a simple friar was nonsense, a waste of his talents. Once installed in Granada he could fetch Ana de Jesús there to found a convent, since Teresa seemed to think that was what she wanted. . . .

In effect, Fray Juan, too, could kneel and kiss the floor.

With this settled, Gracián went on to Medina, and then back to Salamanca with no further delay. But all was not settled in Teresa's mind. She still believed that Madrid should and would come first.

Chapter 74 ❀ *More Problems for Teresa*

I

Teresa's first act as Prioress was to demand that María de San José pay up the money needed to start building Lorenzo's chapel. She opened her letter with the various congratulations and sympathies that San José's last had demanded; she enclosed some pills for San José's most recent ailment and said, "If you do love me then I repay it—and I like to hear you say so." She expressed joy at hearing that García de Toledo was back from the Indies, and urged San José to show him great kindness while he was in Seville. Then she got down to it.

"They" have made her prioress "out of sheer hunger." San José owes Lorenzo's estate four hundred and thirty ducats, and she must pay them.

Months ago Doria wrote to ask her for the installment San José was due to send, saying that it was already owed to his brother Horatio. "I told him no, by no means, and that is why I told you not to send the money to Madrid, because I was afraid of just what happened to it, and it struck me as all wrong as I like straightforward dealings."

She had learned that Horatio Doria's getting the money had been prearranged with San José, and when she wrote him pleading this convent's need, he sent her a hundred with a vague promise of another later and added that he had just sent a thousand to San José. "Out of that you'll be able to pay some part of what you owe me!" San José can explain herself to Doria: "I've had more than enough dealings with Father Nicoleo, and I won't say any more to him about it. The chapel still waits to be built, and if it isn't while I am here, or at least begun, I don't know when it will be, since I hope, God willing, to go from here to make the foundation in Madrid." San José can be sure that she, Teresa, would prefer to drop the whole distasteful business and would if Francisco's marriage hadn't left Lorenzo's estate in such a mess: "It's a pity. That boy was only fit for God."

She laid the letter aside. It had said too much that could anger Doria. "A fortnight later," as it says, she had news that made her pick it up and go on. As before, she talked about the last things first. She got a letter from Rodrigo Alvarez which asks about "things that aren't suitable to put in a letter" though she'd gladly discuss them with him face to face. (The "things of God," that is.) Instead, San José must give him her last chapter of *Las Moradas*, which Gracián left there and San José, she gathers, hasn't troubled to read. She can tell him that her soul has now found just such peace as that last chapter describes. What a comfort it would be to *talk* about it with him! And what a comfort it will be if God brings García de Toledo here! They say he has gone to Madrid, which is why she encloses no letter to him! "He would be amazed to know how much I owe him."

Of the message to Rodrigo Alvarez, one can only say that Teresa made a distinction between peace of soul and peace of mind. As for García, she hoped in vain. Safe in the Indies he had been glad to correspond with her and use his influence as the Viceroy's nephew when her brothers needed it. Back in Spain, he was intelligently mindful of why he had been shipped away from Avila. He neither saw Teresa nor wrote to her again.

Teresa laid this letter aside, half written. She picked it up, finished it, and sent it off, when she learned the intended use of that thousand ducats. With Doria's encouragement San José was about to buy a house in the most expensive part of town. And, she says her say: God forgive the man who has encouraged San José to move into the elegant barrio of San Bernardo! Teresa had loved the house she has now, and so do the nuns who still live there — but even so she would not object to a move by which San José would not plunge them still deeper into debt. "But I will say no more about it, and I have written to Father Nicoleo and asked him not to, either."

She spells nothing out, nor does she need to. One begins to see the pattern in Doria's leaving her so quickly in Soria, and not meeting her in Avila as she had expected. Yes, and why the company she chose to remember on the way to Soria had been that of the rivers.

Doria was no fool. He knew how Teresa had campaigned for him and Gracián, on the understanding that whichever won, the other would act as his coadjutor. And what had her effort effected? One sole vote for himself, and the cold shoulder from Gracián. Moral: neither she nor her Gracián could offer him a future worth having. The only sane course was to build an alliance with Heredia. Heredia had lost by two votes, but he had useful friends, and, better yet, he was old: his warmest supporter would be seen as his heir apparent — once his position was strengthened enough.

Still, Doria saw, Teresa had been right at one point: he should not go to Rome. He must stay in Spain and keep a weather eye out for every chance to sail into better waters — and steer clear of both Gracián and Teresa as best he could, without causing conspicuous, premature trouble.

Nonetheless, he was clumsy at the start. A hundred, already owed, to Teresa; a thousand to San José, to whom he owed nothing. Teresa understood — more than she wanted to understand. She was being ill-treated only as a symbol; Doria's anger was against Gracián — and it was justified. Tipsy with triumph, Gracián had changed.

Perhaps, after all, Madrid should wait. If Gracián, as he had half-promised, would go to Burgos with her, wasn't it possible that with God's help on that long journey she could make him remember all he had ever meant to her, all she had hoped he could give to her Discalced?

But Burgos would cost dear for that chance, that outside chance: the long, hard, cold journey in November weather, the certain resentment of the Jesuits, and, probably, of the Archbishop. And how would Doria react? Had Gracián only urged Burgos on her when she got up from kissing the floor because he hoped for something to go wrong with Madrid? Because Madrid, once founded, would redound to Doria's credit, since he had begun it all by capturing Doña Isabel Osorio?

Burgos . . . and Granada . . . Poor little Fray Juan, homesick for Castile and the peace of a quiet monastery! She had laughed at his belief that one cannot find God until he is dead to the world; but at times it seemed only too true. She would write to him. She could laugh about it a little, say that despite those Andalusians she would gladly exchange his unhappy lot for hers, safe in the south away from aching cold that would come too soon. And then, from her heart, she would ask for his prayers: prayers that her mind and soul be filled, like his, with the knowledge and love of God.

Fray Juan gave her more than his prayers. He took her letter to the Vicar-Provincial of Andalusia, Diego de la Trinidad. Mother Teresa, he urged, was old and ill. If she were to found a new convent, it should be the one now proposed for Granada, not Burgos with its winters of sleety rain and snow. Fray Diego agreed — and just one day after Teresa wrote to Canon Salinas in Palencia about her final decision to go to Burgos, Diego de la Trinidad put his formal order in Fray Juan's hand. "I order Father Fray Juan, Rector of Baeza and under my rule, that he come to Granada and procure conveyances and money with which our Mother may go to found there, bringing her with all the respect and tenderness due to her person and her years, for it seems that as it is the first foundation to be made in that kingdom, it seems that her presence is necessary." This was well phrased: since Burgos was capital of "a new kingdom," it enabled Gracián to point out, if he so wished, that Teresa's presence was equally necessary there.

John of the Cross accepted it in glad good faith. He wrote to Teresa announcing his happy achievement and plunged at once into making the necessary arrangements. It was like him to waste no time on waiting for her letter of thanks. He had gone to Granada, "procured conveyances and money," and set out over the difficult cart-roads to Avila by the time his letter reached her—by a courier on muleback from Baeza. Teresa had no way of communicating with him. He would be weeks on the road and she did not know his route.

Mendoza's representatives were still in Burgos, doing what they could to smooth the way for her, and her mind was made up. They were both brothers of Canon Salinas, in Palencia, and she had sent him a letter just two days before Diego de la Trinidad gave Fray Juan his order. She asked the canon to write to his brothers urging them to plead her case with the Archbishop as strongly as they could. Catalina de Tolosa's eagerness, persisting in the face of so much opposition, had "a mystery about it," as if God had given her that determination for His own purposes. The canon must not let his brothers be discouraged by any opposition they still find but "tell them that if God truly wants the foundation, the devil cannot win." Indeed, it was that very opposition which had wholly convinced Teresa that to weaken before it would be to play into the devil's hands.

The devil, by the way, had chosen the right man to be Archbishop of Burgos. We learn from Pedro de la Purificación that he was Teresa's "relative on her mother's side of the family," and it was a fact that he was anxious to keep hidden. He had come up the hard way—from the *pecheros*, which was at least a certificate of "pure blood"—but who would believe that, if the family connection were known?

As young Canon de Roja in Avila, the Archbishop had heard the junta fulminate against the *converso* woman who had become a protégée of the Jew-loving Mendozas. Since then, he knew, she had had one narrow escape after another from the Inquisition. As titular Bishop of the Canaries, de Roja had felt it safe enough to oblige her powerful friends with a vague show of friendship towards her and her Order. Burgos was another matter. The Jesuits hated the notion of her coming there, and if they discovered the relationship, they would surely spread ugly stories about Jews who rose high in the Church, Jews who stuck together.

The cousinage was not close, though it doubtless existed. Fray Pedro de la Purificación knew the Archbishop's background: Teresa herself would have been the first to understand the Archbishop's anxiety that it remain unknown, and to sympathize with it, even while she saw it as one more bit of the devil's good luck. But it did not weaken her determination to go to Burgos—and to

381

make that long journey with Gracián, God willing, and God helping her to say all that should be said to him on the way.

II

This brings us to the part of Teresa's story which recent times have been most anxious to forget. It can be pieced together from three of her letters. They are preserved in Córdoba as holy relics, and though Silverio de Santa Teresa, the first great modern Teresian scholar, respected them in the 1920's, they are excluded from Efrén and Steggink's superb *Obras Completas* made forty years later: excluded completely, and not even included among those now classified as forgeries. What's more, Efrén and Steggink's *Tiempos y Vida de Sta. Teresa*, a masterpiece of scholarly research, refers to Pedro de Castro only three times in its index of over two thousand names.

Teresa had been back in Avila for seven weeks and two days when she wrote to ask Gracián if this Dr. Castro—so like him in many ways—could be trusted; fifty-one days, all like those in which—first deserted by Gracián and then by Doria—she had written to Canon Reinoso that in Avila she only found "too many people, too little time, and with it all a great loneliness." In that loneliness, we need not wonder that she so responded to Dr. Castro's "intelligence, his charm, his way with words" as to be frightened by that response—responded so intensely that she, who so stressed the importance of a nun's being free to choose her own confessors, this time asked Gracián for his advice and consent.

And within a fortnight of her writing that letter, Teresa was hearing Pedro de Castro's confession. Long ago, Juan de Prádanos, whom she idealized, had suddenly turned the tables and made the confession which drove her to offer herself to be tormented by Satan in his place—on the sole condition that she, too, should not be driven to sin. It had surely been something that Martín Gutiérrez confessed to her that left her unable to believe that he had left Purgatory for Paradise, for she would have believed no slander spoken against him by another. Something about Teresa made men confide in her and ask her help—as Lorenzo had done, and, as she told him, others had done before him.

Teresa had often wanted to put her great confession, her celebration of God's mercy, into the hands of *letrados* for the help that their criticism, their evaluation might give her. Now, as she told both Gracián and the Bishop of Osma, she herself needed no such help any more. But, for the first time, she wanted to put that book into the hands of a priest for the sake of the help it might give him—and the book was impounded by the Inquisition. Then she remembered the copy that de Medina had made for the Duchess of Alba. Don Sancho Dávila, she was sure, could persuade her to lend it to be read by her present confessor, his friend Don Pedro Castro y Nero.

The book came promptly, with a letter from the Duchess. The Duke was ill, and she herself had a cold, but she was going south to visit the Marchioness of Escalona. Gracián would be going with them.

That was bad news. It meant that if Gracián did not weaken and refuse to go to Burgos with her at all, they still could not leave for a month or two in deep midwinter; and it seemed still likelier that he was snatching at an excuse to avoid her.

Yet Teresa's note of thanks is all discretion. Much as she has suffered from knowing what has been going on in Alba, she has wished that she might be there, if only to kiss their Excellencies' hands. She is grieved to hear of their illness. Yet anxious as Gracián must be to go with Her Excellency to Escalona, she must beg that he not be taken just now for he is about to have her convents' Constitutions printed, and all the houses are in great need of them.

Gracián was not just about to have them printed, and it would be long after her death before he got around to it. But Teresa got the book for Dr. Castro; and four days after the Vicar-Provincial signed his order that Juan de la Cruz bring Teresa to Granada with all tender care, she wrote the first of those letters that are preserved in Córdoba: the letters that were never discussed and are now even excluded from the canon as interesting forgeries.

I have felt that same temptation to exclude them. What Teresa felt for Castro was innocent and brief; but I do not like to remember its tragic consequence.

Chapter 75 ❀ Dr. Castro, a Congenial Confessor; Last Meeting with John of the Cross

I

Some patterns persist lifelong. Teresa had been her father's dearest child, her brother Rodrigo's fellow dreamer. She loved men more than women. Her protectiveness towards Juana was motherly; her love for Lorenzo was womanly. In much the same way she expresses awe, respect, a sense of holy duty towards the Queen of Heaven, but her prayers and her love are all for His Majesty Jesus Christ, the Rival who freed her to love men not sinfully but with "a pure love in Christ." The fact remains that one cannot think of any time in her life except for its lonely last weeks when Teresa was not emotionally dependent upon some man: some man whom she felt to be responsive to her spirit and capable of teaching her fine untrained mind.

Furthermore she grew up an unquestioning child of the double standard. After her girlhood she would have worried little about the priest of Becedas — whose saving love for her "might have had more purity in it." True, fornication was "an offense against God"; but its gravity, in her eyes, depended upon the degree of self-betrayal that it cost a priest. One who sought "perfection" and, having determined to offer God a life of unstained holy chastity, still fell from that ideal incessantly and hopelessly was sinning as gravely as any similarly fallen nun.

Pedro Castro y Nero was an outstandingly gifted young man. In time he would hold three bishoprics of ever increasing importance, and he was just about to be installed in an archbishopric when he died in late middle-age. Teresa did not overrate his charm, his intelligence, his style in writing and in speech. And few of us have not felt that awareness of kinship at first meeting which proves that our closest friends are born, not made. Castro and Teresa had, in fact, much in common. Yet the very fact that Gracián had deserted her in Palencia, afraid to stay out the week and see her nuns led into their convent, made her cling all the closer to her faith in what he had once been to her and could be again, Angela's Paul. In Avila she had found "too many people, too little time, and with it all a great loneliness." It is not surprising that when she met Castro, she felt his reality as a threat to a hard-held dream or that, for the first time, she asked to have her choice of a confessor approved — and approved by Gracián.

Castro, Teresa soon realized, was still trapped in "the way of fear": the despair which had made her for twenty years an endlessly self-condemning, sinful nun. His life, his great potential, was being wasted only because he could not find "the way of love," the knowledge of God's unending mercy and the strength that knowledge brings.

She gave him the book. When he had read it, he wrote her a letter that swept her off her feet. Her answer poured out in a flood. Even before she began to thank him for it, she says, she had to say a *Te Deum* in thanks to God. "Now I kiss your hands endlessly and long to thank you with more than words. How great God's mercy is! My evil sins have worked to your healing — and well they might have, for you see I am not in hell where I have long deserved to be. That is why I called my book *Concerning God's Mercies*." Praise God, it has given him hope! Somehow, she had "expected no less" though "his every word of excess" disturbs her. As she does not want to set down more in black and white, will he come to see her tomorrow? If he will, she "can show him a soul which has gone wrong time and time again — and which [she] now puts wholly in his care." Now, she is trying to say, they can help each other. Since he knows of God's mercy to her, he can believe that no soul need despair; and because he so needed that knowledge he can understand her better than those who have never sinned and repented.

Thus far we have nothing more disturbing to saint-watchers than they find in the confessions in the *Life*: only a saint's typical self-condemnation, as if her most trivial "imperfections" were mortal sin. But now comes the passage that cannot be so accepted, for Teresa has not only described the vision at Beas in a *cuenta*, Christ joining her hand with Gracián's in the spiritual marriage which should make her his obedient wife. Angela also wrote to Paul of the bond that was holier than the freedom she had feared to lose to Martín Gutiérrez, since Christ "the marriage-maker" had tied a knot that "even death can only make more firm."

"I trust in His Majesty to give me grace to obey you all the rest of my life. I do not think that absence can change that obedience, nor do I want it to, for I have seen strange things result from a desire for freedom." (Strange, tragic things, as once in Salamanca.) "But it is impossible that this should be anything but a great blessing to me — unless you should forsake me. And you will not."

(Gracián would not stay in Palencia for a few days more: Gracián was off to Escalona. Doria, begged to return the money stolen from her convent, gave back a grudging half, and sent ten times as much to María de San José. Teresa had to trust someone.)

But, she goes on, Castro must bear it in mind that her book did not exaggerate her sins, and God's mercies only show her to be a sinner still, since she repays them so poorly. Yet he, too, must show her the same Godlike mercy, since to one who knows herself, mercy and kindness is the greatest punishment. She will give him some other papers that will show him that in cold justice she "merits only abhorrence." Yet: "I think you'll like them. May God give Himself to you, as I beg Him to, amen."

Nor has he written overmuch, as he seems to fear: The wish to serve God gave him the right words. Nor need he have apologized for calling her Sister: "I haven't been as happy as I am tonight for a long time. I kiss your hands many times for the title you gave me. I think it is a very honorable one."

She had rarely been so incautious in a letter; this was among other things an admission that she had defied the Inquisition and shown him a clandestine copy of her forbidden book. But she had dictated, and she did not sign her name. If the letter went astray, she could disclaim it. She had no reason to leave the other two letters to Castro unsigned and did not.

La Flamenca's daughter would be professed week-after-next. Castro knew that it was a profession to which Teresa had consented only under pressure from Gracián. He also knew that Ana Wasteel's dowry had been enlarged at the expense of the Jesuits. Unsurprisingly, he refused to preach the sermon on the occasion and have it seen as indicating his approval.

His refusal threw the girl into one of her states of hysteric depression. Her mother was enraged, and told Teresa that her son-in-law, Don Alonso, would see to it; his gifts to the Cathedral were nothing that its canons would dare to lose.

Teresa wrote to Castro. Surely he realizes how he has upset *la pobrecita*? She herself, of course, respects his wishes as she would even if she were not bound to him by obedience, for she is incapable by nature of asking a favor that might cause anyone difficulties. She is only writing to prevent Don Alonso's making him think even briefly that she would protest his decision. So, unless the Father-Provincial comes, there had better be no sermon at all, even though the nuns had rather have the partridges spoiled than do without one.

(She had hope, of course, that the Father-Provincial would soon be back from escorting the Duchess to Escalona; it was only a way of indicating that nobody less than the head of the Order could comfort the nuns for their disappointment in losing Castro's sermon.)

The letter worked, but the day had a tragic ending. Teresa could never bear to write about it to anyone.

II

It occasioned a letter far more worth suppressing than the first once its background is known. Castro preached his sermon, and very late that night Teresa wrote him her thanks for the happiness and help that he had given. She was, she said, no longer satisfied with knowing that he was now on his way to heaven; it was her great wish that he should become a powerful influence in God's Church. "And if you do not grant it to me, it would have been better for me not to have known you, for it would grieve me so. . . . I have pleaded with Him that a fine mind like yours should not be wasted."

He should send a messenger to tell her whether the long day left him overtired, but he must not bother to write about it, as she has tired him too much already. "I am tired, too, after spending the evening with a father of the Order. At least he has spared me the necessity of finding a messenger to take a letter to the Marchioness, as he is going back by way of Escalona. The letter to Alba went off in safe hands before."

The evening was tiresome, but at least the Discalced father who tired her can carry a letter which may let her know how soon she can hope to see Gracián. That is all Teresa would ever say of her last meeting with John of the Cross.

He reached Avila on the twenty-eighth of November. Clearly he did not come to the convent until after the sermon and the feast of partridges. He left the next morning, early enough to make use of the short hours of daylight. Crossing the Guadarrama Mountains was not easy even in summer, and Avila had just had its first fall of snow. He took away three nuns. Two of them had been chosen by Gracián for the purpose when, Teresa having kissed the floor, they "talked about Burgos and Granada."

It was a hard pull from Granada to Avila when wagon-wheels must be got across two mountain ranges. Juan de la Cruz, who did not spare himself, had made it in thirteen days. Even a hired muleteer would have demanded a day's rest, at the least, before he headed back. That he left the next morning demands an explanation. He loved Teresa after his own angelic fashion, and he was her "little saint," the one who alone of her friars had never disillusioned her. Why did they give themselves only one tiring evening together?

Fray Juan had reached Avila on an unfortunately busy day, but he would have waited quietly for a good time to bring his news, and he would have accepted it quietly when Teresa told him that her order to go to Burgos was now final. We can also be sure that he would have resented no praise that Teresa might have showered on a priest who risked offending the Jesuits to preach the sermon for La Flamenca's daughter — now Ana de los Angeles. John of the Cross was incapable of jealousy.

We are frequently told that he left the next morning because Teresa was under orders from Gracián to leave at once for Burgos. That, by her own admission, is not true. Her final orders for Burgos come from her Vicar-General, Angel de Salazar, who gave them at Bishop Mendoza's request; it would be a month before Gracián came north from Escalona and they started out.

I believe that I know more about that tragic evening.

Let us begin with a passage from the last chapter of *Fundaciones*.

"One day within the Octave of St. Martin [the first week, that is, of Fray Juan's thirteen-day journey] I began to wonder what I should do if the license there were granted, for I thought that with my bodily infirmities — which the cold always makes worse — I could not bear to go to Burgos, where it is so cold, and that it would be mad to start out on such a long journey when I had scarcely recovered from that hard journey back from Soria. Nor was the Father-Provincial willing to let me go; he thought that once everything was straightened out, it would be better to send the Prioress of Palencia."

(Cousin Inés, the former prioress, she means; and perhaps Gracián did write her something of the sort when he left for Escalona. One is nonetheless reminded of that letter from Soria in which she mentions telling the same story to Bishop Mendoza — with the excuse, "You did say something like that to me once." But let her go on, and remember that she did not doubt her Voice.)

"I was thinking this and very determined not to go when the Lord said these words to me: 'Ignore the cold. I am the true heat. The devil is using all his strength to impede this foundation. Put yourself on My side and it will be made. And so do not give up going in person, for that will do great good.' "

John of the Cross never spoke of that evening in Avila, but his companion, Pedro de la Purificación, remembered it for Teresa's canonization — before *Fundaciones* was published. Nor had he read it in manuscript: Gracián took it with him to Brussels and hesitated long over whether it would, after all, do him more good than harm. Fray Pedro spoke from memory when he said that La Santa told Fray Juan that she could not go with him to Granada because she had heard God's voice commanding her to found in Burgos.

We cannot doubt what John of the Cross would have said. Fray Pedro chose not to quote him, but Fray Juan's convictions are spelled out in the eleventh chapter of his guide for the Discalced, *The Ascent of Mt. Carmel*. There we find his analysis of the bodily delight so often mistaken for the prayer of union: an overflow from the love of God which is felt in the flesh — and with it his warning that if it is mistaken for a "mercy," it can lead the soul astray. This much he had taught Teresa after she brought him to the Incarnation.

But, he goes on, in the same dangerous, delusive way certain persons see visions: "They also apprehend extraordinary words, sometimes from the person represented in the vision, sometimes without seeing the one who speaks. . . ." The more these things seem to come through the bodily senses, the more certain it is that they come from the devil, but all are dangerous even though (as Teresa herself puts it) they are only heard "with the cares of the mind." "It must be grasped that even if these apprehensions come from God, one must never trust them nor accept them. Instead, one should flee from them utterly and have no desire to know whether they are good or bad. . . . One who values these apprehensions is in serious error. . . . Such manifestations should invariably be judged as coming more certainly from the devil than from God . . . for the devil can deceive a soul more easily this way than by working on his inner spirit."

Juan de la Cruz was forthright. He said what he meant and all that he meant. He would have considered it a grave sin not to warn Teresa that the voice which ordered her to Burgos, not Granada, was almost certainly the devil's voice.

As angels love, he loved Teresa, and all that Pedro de la Purificación remembers her as saying could only have left him feeling deeply saddened and futile. He had, in truth, taught Teresa much, but her faith in that "speaking," remembered so, word for word, seemed to deny it. What his love for her and his God forced him to say, what she had to hear from him, her "little Séneca," her saint, was their shared tragedy. Both would gladly have believed the other, neither could, and the issue was central to their very lives.

We can understand why Fray Juan left at dawn the next day. We can understand why Teresa could not so much as name the father of the Order who left her so tired, and why she had to calm herself by writing letters. She wrote to Dr. Castro. She wrote to María de San José, asking her to give Fray Juan two nuns for Granada: "I trust you not to give him your worst." She wrote on, until, as the last of those letters said, it was two in the morning.

We can also understand why all who treasure Teresa and Juan de la Cruz, whether for what they were or for what they were not, want to forget that final meeting and parting. Its tragic inevitability does not erase our wish that it had been different. At least we may be sure that on Fray Juan's part there was no bitterness: only grief for a great soul whom the devil stood to gain so much by deceiving—a grief that surely welled up again as he wrote that stern eleventh chapter of *The Ascent of Mt. Carmel*.

I, at least, am sure that on Teresa's part there remained a doubt that she would never be able to put down. Had she been right? Should she have gone with him? It was a doubt that she could never have shared with another, and above all not with Gracián.

Nor could she have talked about it with Castro, in so many words; but the letter she wrote him that night is, at one level, the quiet closing of a door, the painless relinquishment of an outgrown need. If she has only taught him to save his own soul, that letter says, it would be better if they had never met. She can only pray that a fine mind like his should be wholly given to God (as was—she knew she wrote—that of her little Séneca).

And with that, so far as we know, her correspondence with Dr. Castro ends.

Chapter 76 ❁ *A Ghastly Trip to Burgos*

On the evening after Fray Juan left Avila, Teresa wrote to her brother-in-law. That very day, she says, she has heard from Bishop Mendoza that certain misunderstandings in Burgos are cleared up. "I expect to go there before I go to Madrid." Perhaps Beatriz would consider taking the habit in Avila and then going with her, first to Burgos and then to Madrid. If it were suggested to her only as an experiment which she'd be quite free to abandon at any time, she'd have no reason to resent the suggestion. And if Juana brought her to Avila as if to say goodbye before Teresa set out on such a long journey and they made it appear that the invitation was a spur of the moment impulse, it would give people nothing new to gossip about.

It is a smooth letter; it even manages to imply that Beatriz is a slandered innocent. It contrasts sharply with the one Teresa put off until after it was written. Both kindness and policy prompted her to be gently insincere with de Ovalle, but to write to Gracián after that evening with Juan de la Cruz and his daybreak departure was harder by far. Mercifully, he had only known that Fray Juan was coming to pick up nuns for Granada; there was no need to tell him more.

"The nuns were taken off today, which made me very unhappy and left me with a great sense of being alone. They didn't feel that way, especially María de Cristo [the deposed prioress] who has been dead set on getting away from here. She has been telling everyone about it. And the other wasn't suitable, as you'll find out. All in all, I'd been having great scruples about that, but Dr. Castro helped me to shake them off. Fray Juan would have very much liked to send you some money and figured hard over whether some could be spared from what was given him for the trip, but it couldn't be done. I expect he'll send you some later."

Antonio Ruiz "had somehow got it into his head" that she, too, would be leaving with them, and had come on from Malagón to be her armed escort. He left eight crowns for the college in Salamanca, "though the way things are now it wouldn't take much to tempt me to steal them."

The nuns in Palencia look forward to seeing Gracián again, and Dr. Castro wishes he'd spend Christmas with him. (Four weeks away.) "I wish it, too, but I seldom get what I want." Teresica is being heavily pressured to leave the Order and is unhappy because she must go to Burgos with them.

Then—abruptly and with no mention of Fray Juan—"Ana de los Angeles took the veil yesterday. It all left me terribly tired, I didn't get to bed until two in the morning." And, at once, a count of the nuns to go to Granada: "three from Beas, three from here, two from Seville, and two lay-sisters from Villanueva. Ana de Jesús will take it badly; she likes to give all the orders herself. If you approve, be firm about its being done . . . and if not, stay with God and do what you like for since I went to bed at two and got up at dawn, I have a head like bad luck. I'm doing fairly well otherwise.

"The difficulty that just struck me about Teresica is, what if the other one, Beatriz, has to be taken along? Because it would be unbearable in every way if they went together. She's the trouble; Teresica might be some help. . . . But, well, Beatriz will protect herself from giving me that trouble; and to my way of thinking it wouldn't be suitable if you came with Tomasina."

Tomasina was a nun from Salamanca who did go to Burgos with them, and Beatriz, as the thought of Teresica had suddenly made Teresa hope, refused. The sentence doesn't hang together, but neither does the whole letter. It is interesting only for all it does not say.

But if a dozen years ago Stegginck and Efrén had not published the "orders" for Teresa's journey to Granada which Juan de la Cruz procured from Diego de la Trinidad, Teresa's letter would still leave me wondering — as she meant it to — how Antonio Ruiz ever got the idea that she would forget Burgos and go to Granada with Fray Juan.

As well as anything, this illustrates why Teresa's life has so long needed to be rewritten in the context of her letters, and her letters examined in the context of the available documentary material, in place of hagiography's dependence on so many heavily embroidered "memories." Greatness like hers is not diminished by being made humanly comprehensible. I have tried to take the needed first step, despite my vast limitations.

II

Apparently Heredia suggested that Gracián be the Duchess's escort to Escalona, just as he had seen to it that Gracián should not refresh old scandals by taking Teresa to Soria. And Gracián, once in Escalona, was long in making up his mind to return. Letters from Teresa which express delight at his seeming decision to leave the Duchess are followed by one that says, "For the love of God, I have nobody else to go with! Don't think of leaving me out in the cold."

One letter, referring to Heredia and the Duchess, says, "I simply can't understand some kinds of holiness! I am thinking of the one who never writes to you and of the one who thinks that everything in the world has to be done her way. Oh, Jesus, how little perfection there is in this world!"

It was finally settled that Gracián would come at the start of the new year. An undated letter from Teresa ends with a postscript from Teresica overflowing with delight at the prospect of his coming, to which Teresa added a postscript of her own. "Teresica's message made me laugh. I am sure there is no better cure for anything than love. May God give it to us, along with His Majesty."

May God give us back that love in Christ that we once shared . . . .

Before Gracián came, Teresa wrote to young Lorenzo. He had married the daughter of an *oidor* and as a result was receiving seven thousand ducats a year in tribute from the Indians. This called for more than congratulations. She hopes he will remember poor Aunt Juana. Beatriz would like to enter some unenclosed convent like the Incarnation, but that needs a dowry. And while

Francisco's wife is a nice girl, she is poor; can't he send a wedding present? But above all, he must begin to think seriously about his little daughter.

"I can see how much I love you, because while the offense against God should sadden me, I see you so clearly in that little girl that I can't help from being happy, I love her so much." Now that Lorenzo has the means he must see to it that the child is brought up decently. She can't stay where she is. The money he sends can be invested until she is twelve and then it will be her dowry, for marriage or the convent. Tiny as she is, she hates to leave this convent whenever she comes to visit; she has the same sweet, bright nature as Teresica. "You bear a good father's name, my son. Try to live up to it."

She mentions one more worry which she does not see as Lorenzo's responsibility. Agustín de Ahumada is coming back to Spain. "Please God he'll bring enough to live on, for nobody here will be able to help him!" (She needn't have worried. Agustín managed to help himself in his usual fashion right up to the end, when that silver-framed slice of the miraculously preserved flesh of La Santa's "favorite brother . . . so white that it might have been wax" — insured his veneration and tender care by the Sisters of Charity.)

Teresica did not want to go to Burgos, but Teresa knew that she could not be left behind. We have one letter, probably the last of all the many Teresa wrote to Francisco's mother-in-law, Doña Beatriz de Castilla y Mendoza. It tries for tact. Pedro's claim to La Serna is nonsense, no cause for worry. But Francisco is "acting wrongly" and she, as Lorenzo's executor and as Prioress of San José, must see that his chapel is built. Francisco's pressures on Teresica and any attempt to contest Lorenzo's will could only involve herself and Doña Beatriz in a costly and futile lawsuit, which neither want. The letter was read, correctly, as a threat. Doña Beatriz, warned that Teresa would go to law rather than release Teresica or abandon the plan to build Lorenzo's chapel, went to Valladolid, where she tried to poison as many minds as she could against Teresa with her own tale of woe.

She was not the only Doña Beatriz on Teresa's mind. In Soria, the annulment of Doña Leonora's marriage had finally come from Rome. Teresa's last letter from Avila urges her nuns to treat the new novice, their patroness's niece, with the greatest kindness and respect after she took the habit — and not to expect too much of her. (She wrote with good reason; as she had guessed, Doña Leonora was not cut out for the life of a nun.)

Gracián came, as promised, in the first week of January. His companion was Pedro de la Purificación, who had decided to leave Andalusia for his native Burgos and feel out the chances for a priory there. They brought two nuns from Alba, as well as Mother Inés — to try out her third priorate — and, against Teresa's advice, Tomasina from Salamanca, who in fact turned out much better than Teresa had been led to hope.

From Avila Teresa only took San Bartolomé and another lay-sister. And in one respect, at least, the Voice was true to its word. It snowed only as far as Medina, and that was snow mixed with rain. Thereafter the weather was unusually warm for January. But the almost unending sheets of rain that poured down were phenomenal. They enter the civic records of all the cities which had to cope with the flooded rivers which lay beside or across their way.

III

San Bartolomé tells of how they got to Medina drenched and exhausted. Teresa called the pain from her cancerous throat the start of "a bad cold." (Within a month the physicians would call it a bleeding ulcer.) She had reached Medina with a high fever and had to spend the next three days in bed. However, she managed to dictate a letter to Cardinal Quiroga's confessor about Doña Elena's happiness. She has "settled down wonderfully, as if she had never known any other kind of life." And, Teresa hoped, the Madrid licence would come soon as she was now on her way to Burgos, and would shortly be coming back to make that long-awaited foundation. In later times the nuns in Medina forgot Teresa's illness there; but they did recall several miraculous healings which she performed there—unobserved, apparently, by San Bartolomé and Gracián, who both wrote at length about that journey. (Almost without exception it was the convents which gave Teresa most trouble while she lived that proved the richest source of useful memories for her canonization.)

She was also bedridden for five days in Valladolid. As San Bartolomé recalls, the doctor in Medina had warned her against starting out again. But we owe most of our memories of that stay in Valladolid to Gracián. As he tells us, Catalina de Tolosa wanted her eldest daughter, Catalina de la Asunción, to come back to Burgos. María Bautista was angry, for the girl kept the convent records and accounts. Gracián asked Bishop Mendoza to intervene, but, as he remembered, "the Bishop was very annoyed and said, 'The Mother is terrible. She expects us all to serve her and she doesn't want to please a single friend.'" (On the way, Teresa wrote Catalina de Tolosa, "Don't think I didn't have to do much to bring Asunción along with me, considering the resistance they put up.")

Gracián was also irked by María Bautista's stinginess. As her convent was by far the richest, he asked for a hundred ducats to cover the journey and help with the new foundation. María Bautista unwillingly gave him fifty. Her chapel was a treasure house of gifts from the Valladolid nobility, and Teresa had nothing for the Burgos chapel but a tiny statue of the child Jesus, so he ordered the nuns to see what they could steal from the watchful sacristan.

"And as they were little skilled in theft and strange to the convent, one snatched one part of a three-piece set of vestments leaving the rest behind, and another got so rattled that she gave herself away with her stolen goods in hand; and thus we took off with things that did the one convent harm without doing the other any good.

"When we got to Palencia we disclosed it to the Mother. Her laughter and wit when she told the convent about the terrors those nuns had gone through provided us all with tremendous amusement. And it was still more amusing when María Bautista and her nuns discovered the little thefts and sent us *coplas* and bits of fine prose demanding them back. And I never wanted to give anything back; but because it was so funny—or, to put it better, embarrassing— the Mother insisted that if a prioress wouldn't give us anything in spite of our need, then we should just endure our poverty and be still."

He added that María Bautista, despite being a cousin who had always been shown affection, was very short with the Mother except when it came to giving advice or criticism. Teresa would listen with a look of grave attention and then turn to him with a smile, and say, "Jesus, what this one knows! Why, it makes me a perfect fool in comparison with her. I'm confounded at how ignorant I am and how unsuited for any good works." And often, Teresa "would let her talk and talk and then shut her off with queenly grace: 'God help me, do you hear how much she's said? And she hasn't said anything.'"

Gracián could make anything sound like fun, even five days abed with a high fever, unable to swallow anything but fluids and gruel—and throughout, being lectured and bullied. Teresa's sharp-edged response, which he found so unexceptionable and "affectionate," is only too easy to understand when it is coupled with the report of her faithful nurse, San Bartolomé, who was shocked by María Bautista's unpleasant behavior.

The bad weather grew incredibly worse. They reached Palencia soaked to the skin; but they had been expected, and the whole town turned out to greet them. In Palencia, Teresa did not have to die to become La Santa. The town was the Cathedral's, Reinoso and Salinas were genuinely devoted to her, and the rest of its oversized staff of clerics saw her as one of their Bishop's greatest enthusiasms, at least.

Their coach was surrounded by crowds begging Teresa's blessing. The nuns received her, singing the *Te Deum*.

Her health got no better, and all the attention was fatiguing, though a happier fatigue. Teresa was eager to be on the way again; but the roads, they were assured, were impassable. On January sixteenth she wrote to Catalina de Tolosa that she hoped to start on the nineteenth. She had taken another lay-sister, so she'd have eight to house, but Catalina must not worry about enough beds. They'd manage somehow until they had collected their own property.

It was the twenty-fourth before Gracián, in desperation, decided to start out and get it over with. On the first day they followed the river Pisuerga. The road was visible through the heavy fog because it was whitish, but it was made of an amazingly deep, sticky mud. Often the carts could hardly be pulled out of the hub-deep mess into which they sank. At one point Teresa urged her nuns to get out and walk with her, lightening the load. Gracián warned her that he should go first, and she saw his mule sink so deep that even its strong legs could barely back out. He remembered how she laughed at herself. "Sinner that I am, that's the mud that looked so nice to me! There's the roads of the world for you!"

Once they got through that stretch of mud they came to a puddle which looked, San Bartolomé says, more like a lake. Halfway through it, Gracián's mule abruptly knelt to drink, Gracián fell off, and the nuns all shrieked, believing that he had drowned.

Their guides, supposedly well chosen, had turned out to be incapable boys.

393

Late that night they reached a filthy inn where San Bartolomé could not even manage to make up some sort of dry bed for the Mother, and everyone assured them that they would have to stay several days as the roads were flooded. But the inn was too foul; they decided to push on, unfed, the next morning.

At one point Teresa's cart skidded, the driver pitched forward under the mules, and Gracián was sure that Teresa must have been badly hurt. She offered him wine to calm his nerves, but he suddenly remembered that it was the feast of St. Paul, refused it and insisted that they must push ahead to some place where he could say Mass and let her receive communion. They found a village and church a league further on.

The whole trip was more or less like that until the day they reached the Almazón, in flood just outside of Burgos. There was a pontoon bridge, but it was invisible, totally under the rushing water. Gracián found a local guide who was sure he could get them across by sighting familiar landmarks. His confidence was not contagious. One could be sure of only one thing about the invisible bridge: it was not lying level. A single false step of a mule, a single cartwheel over the edge of a pontoon, would mean certain death.

For once in her life, Teresa admitted to sharing the physical fear of all the rest. But to turn back was also unthinkable; for days they had found no inn not already overflowing with men who knew better than to fight that storm. The whole company confessed, the nuns and muleteers to the friars, and the friars to one another. Somehow or other they reached the other side, all safe, and near a church where Pedro de la Purificación said the second Mass of the day.

Then they entered Burgos. The Cid's old city had become another Venice; the streets were made of water. But Gracián had decided that before the nuns entered enclosure, they should see the Holy Cross of Burgos. This singular artifact, brought to Spain from Bohemia in the Middle Ages and firmly believed to have been made by an eyewitness at the Crucifixion, was in the chapel of an Augustinian monastery on the far side of town.

Neither Gracián nor San Bartolomé say more of it than that they went the extra miles to see it, though it is a disturbing sight. It is now in Burgos proper, and never without a few kneeling before it, apparently transfixed. It is life-sized, startlingly realistic, the crucified body of a tall, thin man, carved from brown wood but having a strange look of sun-browned dead human flesh. It wears a false beard, and its very long black hair hangs loose from the head which has fallen sidewise in death. Ancient, ecstatic accounts say of the hair and beard that they seem to grow on the head, and that the painfully realistic sag of the body and buckling of the knees is achieved by the use of flexible joints. It is naked, except that where one would expect a loincloth, it wears a very short red skirt embroidered in gold, a singular garment which some Spaniard doubtless felt more suitable for His Majesty than whatever He originally wore.

Teresa says only that they saw it and sent an Augustinian lay-brother to tell Catalina de Tolosa that they would come to her after dark, and that Catalina had a great fire ready for them so that they could dry their clothes.

On the next day a number of de Tolosa friends came to tell Teresa how welcome she was to Burgos. She could only lie abed behind a curtain and answer them in a hoarse whisper. Gracián went to stay with his friend Pedro Manso, a canon of the Cathedral, and was off the next day to get the Archbishop's licence and permission to say Mass for the nuns in Catalina's house when he returned.

Chapter 77 ✸ A Founding in Burgos Despite Hostility

I

De Roja had been named Archbishop of Burgos while Teresa, in Valladolid, was fighting her way back to life after the bout with *el catarro universal*. At her request, Mendoza called on him at a nearby Jeronimite monastery where he was staying, to ask him to grant her a convent in his new see. De Roja agreed, trusting to luck that he could block Teresa's arrival without offending too many grandees.

When the Salinas brothers made nonsense of his pretext of potential trouble with the city council — and easily, since they were natives of Burgos and knew the right people — de Roja wrote Teresa an evasive letter which she misread as capitulatory, an invitation. And when Gracián, remembering the troubles in Seville, wrote to ask her if she had a written licence, she replied that none was necessary because Mendoza and de Roja "had exchanged belts or whatever it is that bishops do."

Gracián expected no trouble. The Jesuits, as Señor de Tolosa's confessors during his lifetime, had always said Mass in that house; one room, fitted out as a chapel, had never been used for anything else. Moreover, Gracián had been on pleasant terms with de Roja when he was still titular Bishop of the Canaries. He was staggered to find himself faced by a furious stranger.

Yes, said de Roja, he had written to Teresa that he would gladly meet her if she came to pay Señora de Tolosa a visit. He had certainly not said that she might come with a crowd of nuns and make the lady's house into a convent! And no, they might not have a single Mass said in that house! There were churches in the neighborhood. If Gracián really wanted to serve those women, the best thing he could do was to take them back directly to the convents from which they came. That was final. (As Teresa wrote, "And such nice roads and weather, too!")

Canon Salinas had given Teresa letters to all his influential friends. They pleaded with the Archbishop on her behalf, as did Gracián's friend, Dr. Manso. This produced a mocking offer of compromise: Teresa might found in Burgos *if* her convent had an assured income of forty thousand ducats a year and a house of their own which met with the Archbishop's approval. He could not approve of Catalina de Tolosa's house "because it was damp."

Catalina's large house was one of the finest in the *barrio* preferred by all the wealthiest merchants in Burgos. Her income did not approach forty thousand ducats a year, but she had planned to be generous; inspired by what she had learned of Soria, she intended to follow suit, give her whole house and ask only that she and her two children, a boy and a girl too young to take the habit, might live in a wing that had a separate entrance. The Archbishop's mockery transformed her gently competitive generosity into furious pride. She announced that every penny she owned should go to Teresa's Order; for her and her children, God would somehow provide.

Catalina, indeed, was not only generous and proud; she was also religious and warm-hearted. She had been shocked when the de Padillas withdrew their daughters from their respective convents; and, as Teresa put it, though she was only forty-six, she immediately made herself a loving mother to the nuns now in her care. She could not do enough for them. Indeed, Teresa says, she proved that the noblest spirits are not found among the nobility—adding hastily, "I don't mean to imply that she was not very much the child of someone, or that pure blood was lacking in her family." It was the nearest she could come to the truth without telling a literal lie, though for the better part of her stay in Burgos it weighed on her mind that she was putting Catalina de Tolosa in danger. Better be "of pure blood" if one chose to befriend "the nun, Teresa de Jesús."

Similarly, *Fundaciones* mentions the Jesuits only twice in connection with Burgos: once to say that six years before, a Jesuit had first suggested that she found there, and once, towards the end of the chapter, to call them "an Order to which [she] owes much." The story, as it evolved, was not one that Teresa would have put into a book intended to outlive her, for as she said in one of her letters which tell the whole sorry story, "Others will follow these [Jesuits] who will see things very differently." She knew that religious Orders, like her own, can suffer periods of decadence; but she believed that eventually their original inspiration would win out. Greed was alien to the ideals of Loyola, and the greed she had found in Burgos should not be held against his Company in perpetuity.

But it was a bad business. To begin with, the Jesuits denied Catalina confession and absolution on the grounds that she intended to cheat her own children of their rights. She had only spoken in anger: neither would she have made good on that threat to give her all to the Discalced, nor would Teresa have countenanced it. (For that matter, neither the Archbishop nor the Jesuits had been moved by anxiety for her children's welfare.) In this impasse, Teresa hated to see Catalina suffer. She was also keeping Gracián in Burgos much against his will, and he let her know it, in a way that cut like a knife. Something had to be done, for his sake, for Catalina's and for her own.

Gracián's eagerness to get away was nothing he could discuss with his host, Dr. Manso. Manso would have found it shocking. From their first meeting, when Teresa was only a hoarse whispering from behind a curtain, he had felt a quality of life in her like nothing he had ever met before. As he wrote afterwards, "it went through [his] own body with a stirring of [his] very entrails. The hairs on [his] arms seemed to stand on end." It was as if in her presence one became aware of the presence of God. I believe him. He and the physician Aguilar, who had studied medicine in Salamanca while he was there studying theology, immediately became and remained Teresa's staunch friends and tireless defenders in that place. Still more strikingly, neither ever offered the expected proofs of her sainthood which so many later recalled in describing her last months: "the odor of sanctity," for instance, that celestial perfume which is given off by the bodies of saints, both dying and dead.

But Gracián wanted to go to Valladolid, and both the Archbishop and the Jesuits were determined that Teresa get out of Catalina's house. When Catalina's brother went to Seville, he took a letter from Teresa to María de San José. They were dependent, it said, on Señor de Tolosa's sister; San José could send back her answer by him, and with it the money for Lorenzo's chapel. "And for the love of charity try to send me all you can—and that should be all of it, for I have your written promise to pay me by this year. Don't send it in the way you sent the other, which really made me angry. If you send it as I am telling you, by Pedro de Tolosa, I will be sure to get it."

Gracián is here, and being "very useful." Teresica is here because "they" are trying to get her to leave the Order, and she could not be left alone. They had a bad, wet journey and her throat is so sore that she can only swallow softened food, and no medicine helps it. But she is getting better; they mustn't worry. It will go away if they all pray for her. She hopes for a letter full of their news; she hasn't seen San José's handwriting for a long time.

Pedro de Tolosa came back with promises but no money. Teresa addressed her next letter to San José and another nun, thus ensuring that its contents would be known to the convent. It said that even a small part of the promised money would be welcome if it were sent at once, for it has turned out that they must buy a house. Three letters of the fifty-six to San José now published still remained to be written, but none give thanks for any part of that money which Lorenzo had lent in Seville, seven years before, or sent thereafter to pay off—as he fondly believed—the *alcabala*.

Teresa also sent Pedro de la Purificación to Soria with a begging letter to Doña Beatriz. She sent it unsealed in a letter to her confessor, telling him to read it to the prioress and subprioress, but secretly; the lady must not know. Then, since they cannot found in Burgos without an income, he must assure Doña Beatriz that she will gain much from the Lord by doing what the letter asks.

It was a desperate hope, and no surprise to learn that Doña Beatriz felt she had done quite enough already.

II

There was no house that Teresa herself could buy, and she was determined that Catalina de Tolosa have no more trouble from the Jesuits. It was also hard for her nuns since the Archbishop refused to allow masses to be said in the room that had been used so long as Señor de Tolosa's chapel. The nuns owned only four hooded mantles and four pairs of high clogs, so they went out to Mass in two shifts. Their veiled faces caused at best curiosity and on occasion a kind of pointless fury. Once a drunken prostitute knocked Teresa down in the mud. It was essential that they move anywhere, and after three months and three days, they did.

A hospital for male paupers had a few spare rooms in its attic. Teresa hired two of these rooms and a tiny kitchen. An adjoining third room had been taken by an eccentric widow who intended to move in some six months later; when she learned who her next-door tenants would be, she was not content to have the door bolted against them; she had carpenters come and board it up.

Gracián took them there and left for Valladolid where he hoped to found a new priory. Somehow Manso's unfeigned devotion to Teresa had shamed him into that unwontedly long captivity.

At least, masses were said in the hospital; the nuns no longer had to go out into the streets, which had left several of them with agonizing scruples over breaking their vow of enclosure. Better still, Hernando de Mazanas, the director of the hospital, took pity on them and gave them two more tiny rooms which opened into each other; by setting up a temporary grille in the doorway between them, one of these could be used for a parlor where they could receive guests from the world in proper conventual style.

On the other hand, they were there only on the understanding that they would leave at a day's notice if the Archbishop so ordered; and God only knew when something would vex him into giving that order. Moreover, the endless groans, screams, and whimpering of the dying paupers came through the attic floorboards both day and night. So did the stench of their unwashed bodies and their suppurating wounds.

The stench, San Bartolomé remembered, was particularly hard on Teresa, who had a passion for cleanliness which many would subsequently try to deny as worldly — displeasing to God and unthinkable in a saint. San Bartolomé was not shocked; she alternately washed one or the other of Teresa's two tunics, so that she might enjoy clean underwear next to her skin. But, she says, Teresa never complained of the noise the sufferers made, or of their stench.

On the contrary, she went down into the hospital every day to stand by one bedside or another, speaking so low that San Bartolomé, behind her, could rarely hear many of her words. But she saw their effect. Sometimes a patient smiled, even laughed. Sometimes a contorted face relaxed into a look of rest. She particularly remembered a young man whose shrieks had been hideous as a barber-surgeon opened an abcess on his body.

Teresa bent down to him: "Son, why are you screaming so?"

"They're trying to rip the life out of me!"

It was the love, the pity she gave, San Bartolomé said, that always made them quiet. She did not hear what Teresa said to that young man, but his screaming changed to a soft whimper, and then to silence followed by sleep — the sleep of an exhausted body.

She remembered, too, a day when Señora de Tolosa brought a sack of oranges. They had been Teresa's delight while she lived in her house, as she could chew the sections and swallow their juice with little pain. Teresa was overjoyed and could hardly wait for their giver to leave so that she could take them down to the hospital and distribute them among the worst-off patients whom she called *mis pobrecitos:* my poor little ones.

It is an account embroidered by miraculous healings; for San Bartolomé, the truth was enough. Yet San Bartolomé did report one miraculous healing — on herself. She had a toothache and begged the Mother to ease it as she seemed to ease the pain of those suffering men. The Mother laughed, slapped the cheek she had seen San Bartolomé clutching, and said, "Oh, go cure yourself!"

But the tooth stopped aching, San Bartolomé says, almost at once.

III

Clearly it was imperative that they should find a house. None that Dr. Manso or Licentiate Aguilar, the physician, could locate were even remotely suitable. The director of the hospital heard of one, but on further inquiry it seemed to be both badly situated and much overpriced. At last, in desperation, Manso went to look at it and found that its owners had left town and entrusted its disposal to a priest who was willing to sell it to Teresa at a price which many protested as sheer robbery of its owner; it should have fetched at least twice as much.

The Jesuits had made it clear to Catalina that she could not buy it for Teresa without endangering her immortal soul. But Palencia was being well provided for by Bishop Mendoza, and the convent permitted Catalina's two daughters there to make over their dowries to their mother's foundation in Burgos. That was a start, a down-payment. Teresa believed that she could depend on the other convents, especially the one in Toledo, to pay off the full price, little by little.

In this she was right, for after her death and exhumation everyone became increasingly generous. At the time the purchase demanded a stout share of the first two theological virtues, faith and hope. In fact, her need was so great that she made one more attempt to collect from María de San José for Lorenzo's chapel.

San José had bought her new house, and had also gone to the extra expense of giving it a bell-tower. She had nothing to spare.

A small part of Teresa's response to the news still exists, for a strange reason. After Gracián was expelled from the Order, San José went to Evora, in Portugal, where she worked hard at moulding her now-current image as La Santa's favorite daughter. She had part of that letter copied and properly notarized; the notary certified that it was written by Mother Teresa de Jesús in the March of 1582 — when she began the first attempts to buy the bargain house that Dr. Manso had learned about.

Read in the right tone of voice, it serves San José's purpose. We can thank Gracián for our ability to hear its anger, its sharp-edged laughter, for he gave us Teresa on her sick-bed in Valladolid, mocking María Bautista: "Jesus, what this one knows! . . . I am confounded at how ignorant I am, how unsuited for any good works." And considering the circumstances under which Teresa wrote, plus the depression so often allied with terminal cancer, we can allow for its lapse, rare for her, into self-pity.

San José indicated the passage that she wanted. As Teresa did not paragraph, the notary began a line too soon, but that hardly mattered out of its context — Teresa's response to San José's refusal to repay some part of Lorenzo's money.

"It made me laugh that you justified this with your bell-tower, and if you are as much of a bell-ringer as you say, you have a point. You tell your tale so well that it seems to me that after I die, they should choose you as the Foundress, and even while I'm alive I would be most willing, since you know so much more than I do and are so much better. To tell the truth about this, I do have some slight advantage of you in the way of religious experience; but people have already begun to think little of me, for you'd be shocked at how old I am and little I'm fit for etc."

I suppose that the *etc.* is the notary's, set down automatically at being checked in mid-sentence.

By mid-April the house was bought. The Archbishop saw it, expressed satisfaction, permitted them to move in, made several amiable calls — and continued to refuse them a licence. Once more they had to break enclosure and go to Mass through the streets.

Teresa was reduced to appealing to Mariano, since he was in Madrid. As the Archbishop refused to let them hear Mass in their own chapel, perhaps the new Nuncio could be persuaded to overrule him? He might, if Mariano will get Heredia to urge the Duchess of Alba to make the request in person.

It was futile, of course. She should have known that Mariano would not lift a finger on her behalf. Amusingly enough, at this time she herself received an appeal from Doria, whom Gracián was still appointing to posts far from the reins of government. His knowledge of Teresa's so different plans for his future at Gracián's side led him to hope that she would intervene for him still: a hope in the same class with her own hope of help from Mariano.

Yet even if Doria had waited for her in Avila, or given her some part of the thousand ducats that went towards San José's new house and bell-tower, Teresa's reply would have been the same, though its tone would have been warmer; she knew how little she could influence Gracián about anything, and least of all, about Doria. The Father-Provincial, she said, would not have sent him to any place where he was not needed. It would be quite unsuitable for her to question his judgment. This had clearly been Doria's second appeal, for she also says, "Don't be a hypocrite and neglect to write to our father about the whole thing. Only a short time ago I wrote you another letter by way of Doña Juana" (Gracián's mother who, it seems, had not bothered to forward it).

Teresa saw Alvaro Mendoza as her court of last resort. He had been vexed when she took the useful Asunción away from María Bautista, but that was lost in his anger against his former canon, now Archbishop of Burgos. Unsealed, and under cover of a letter he sent to Teresa, he wrote him one so scathing on the subject of prelates who give their word only to break it that Teresa saw it would do more harm than good. Manso, who knew the Archbishop equally well, agreed with her. She wrote to Mendoza again, begging him to make his approach as conciliatory and flattering as possible.

Mendoza was amused and he complied. His letter must have been a masterpiece, for the Archbishop immediately granted the licence, and on April nineteenth Pedro Manso said the convent's first Mass and reserved the Host upon its altar. Next, the Archbishop offered to give the habit to Catalina's little Elenita, who had just turned twelve. She was an affectionate child, and devoted to Teresa as children invariably were: Teresa called her *mi gordilla,* "my little fatty." (Our standards of beauty change; one is startled when someone as recent as Jane Austen speaks of a girl's having lost her looks and become quite thin.)

The Archbishop's sermon on this occasion was as confusing as all the rest of his conduct. Throughout it he wept copiously, begging forgiveness of Teresa, Catalina de Tolosa, and everyone else he had inconvenienced. It was embarrassing and nobody knew what to make of it, for the tears that poured down his cheeks were beyond any actor's powers of fakery. Clearly, he had undergone some sort of revelation—if only that Teresa's ducal supporters and Catalina's wealthy-burger sympathizers were more useful friends than the Jesuits, friends whom he, by his own folly had nearly cast away.

Suddenly Teresa found Burgos at her feet. Generous leading citizens called daily, giving alms. And money attracts money; Teresa's glowing accounts of such good fortune brought contributions from her other convents towards the purchase of the house. Even San José and her favorite nun, Isabel of the Trinity, wrote to say that they would renounce their dowries to Seville in favor of Burgos. Teresa, thanking them as "foundresses," said that she hoped she would get their money soon. She never did, but at least San José had expected to get around to it sometime.

This quickened Teresa's hopes for Madrid. She wrote her cousin-Prioress Ana in Toledo instructions: she must let Quiroga know "how well this foundation has gone, even though the Archbishop held it up." She should also write to Doña Luisa de la Cerda (one of his friends) and remember to sympathize with all her latest troubles. As for her troubles up here, she now dares hope that God will release her from them soon. (While she does not mention it, the hospital had not been the ideal place in which to handle either cousin Inés or Teresica.)

Don Fadrique, Duke of Huéscar, wrote to say that his wife was pregnant and to ask for her prayers. She promised them gladly, saying that she would have written to him before this if illness and the problems of making a foundation had not made her a bad correspondent.

In a letter to Roque de Huerta's friend Cassademonte she mentions the exhausting difficulties the foundation had cost. Nonetheless, she has done and is doing all she can to hurry the Madrid foundation along.

The Burgos foundation was made; Madrid seemed closer. We would think, as we're always led to think by Teresa's biographers, that except for her failing health it was now all roses, and wonder what detained her—if a letter she wrote in the third week of May did not set things straight. . . .

Chapter 78 ❀ Trouble with Jesuits; Beginning of Teresa's Fatal Illness; Burgos Flooded

I

The Burgos Jesuits had been prepared for Teresa by their brothers in Valladolid and Avila: Teresa, the woman of impure blood and dubious reputation whose writings were impounded by the Inquisition; the woman who stole and taught her prioresses to steal large fortunes to which their Company had prior claims. They were not soothed when the Archbishop let himself be swayed by a notorious Jew-lover like Mendoza, and not only gave Teresa a licence to found a convent for Catalina de Tolosa, but made a public spectacle of himself, weeping as he gave her child the habit of the Discalced Carmelites.

They shared their emotions with their far-flung brothers. Avila, Soria and Valladolid all reacted: Valladolid most furiously, as both de Padilla and de Tolosa money would have been theirs if Catalina had not gone back to Burgos. As Teresa learns, the Valladolid Jesuits would be capable of disturbing many of María Bautista's most valued patronesses, such as Doña Ana Enrique, Marchioness of Alcañices, to whom she had written sincerely about "their saint," Baltasar Alvarez, and more politically about the loneliness of being in Palencia "without a single Father of the Company" there.

Canon Reinoso had well supplied that lack. We have her letter to him from Avila, and her mention, in another, of one she wrote him from the hospital in Burgos. Now, she wrote him enclosing an unsealed letter to the Jesuit Rector in Valladolid. She wanted him to read it before he sent it along with his regular post to the Bishop. He could see from it, she says, "what is going on with the Jesuits, for now their enmity is really beginning to line up." (Not separate communities, that is, but one for all and all for one.) "Now they are telling Catalina de Tolosa that they want to have no more to do with the Discalced for fear that they may become infected with their way of prayer. . . . The devil must care a great deal about estranging us, considering the rush he's in to do it!"

The Jesuits had also told her that their General was coming from Italy to put things straight. Since Reinoso's uncle, Don Francisco, is General Mercurian's great friend, will he please see to it that Mercurian learns the truth? (This had been only a threat; General Mercurian was not coming to Spain.)

"The devil sets it up, making them blame me in matters for which they actually owe me gratitude. He even inspires them to bear false witness against certain men. Everything that I have said, or wanted, or tried to do—it's a wonder they don't even tell about what I think—is, according to them, intended to check their own black self-interests—and since I don't believe that they tell lies, it is clear that the devil is at work in this tangle of tricks."

What Teresa had to say to the Rector in Valladolid, we can guess. They "blamed [her] in matters for which they actually owed [her] gratitude." She had tried in vain to get María Bautista to renounce the de Padilla money; she had been unhappily overruled when she tried to prevent La Flamenca's cancellation of her deed of gift to the Avilan Jesuits. She discouraged Catalina's intention to turn over the whole de Tolosa fortune to the Discalced and finally — to make assurance doubly sure — called in a notary and drew up a formal renunciation of all or any part of Catalina's property.

For the rest, she wanted to blame the devil: a handful of rare souls in the Company had inspired her with Loyola's teachings, and she truly believed that, according to God's will, Loyola's spiritual sons and her Discalced should have made an alliance that the devil feared. Yet she knew that the devil was greatly helped by "black self-interests" — simple human greed.

Even while blaming the devil she cannot omit that factor in her letter to Reinoso; nor omit something else, something painfully familiar throughout her past twenty-seven years. "He even inspires them to bear false witness against certain men." Manso and Aguilar among them, I suppose. And the fact that Teresa was so old and ill at sixty-seven as to make sexual scandals ludicrous left Gracián no less afraid of them. He came back to Burgos to taste her sudden triumph, but he cut his visit unexpectedly short.

Manso, with whom he stayed, was about to preach the sermon when the convent took in a novice: its first, if we except the child Elenita. Manso would have expected only a protective anger like his own when he told Gracián of how the greed for Catalina's money was being reinforced with "false witness" against all men known to be Teresa's friends, Gracián's own obviously innocent self included. Teresa begged Gracián to stay and see that novice take the habit, as she had begged him in Palencia to stay and see her nuns enter their convent. But Gracián hurried away, pleading the urgent series of visitations with which Teresa explained his departure to his friends, only saying, "It makes me very unhappy, for I don't know when we will see him again."

San Bartolomé has more to say about Gracian's cruel neglect of La Santa and the pain it caused her: so much more, indeed, that she is no longer believed on that point — for after Teresa's canonization, Gracián had to be rewritten, as Angela's flawless Paul.

But the Jesuits, as I see it, have nothing to apologize for, no need to pretend that their present evaluation of Teresa was ever other than what it is today. Sixteenth-century Spain was sixteenth-century Spain; Teresa was half-Jewish, the author of a forbidden book and a self-proclaimed much-fallen Magdalen. The marvel is that in an Order still on the defensive she found a few great souls willing to trust her. She, too, was of her day and on the defensive. Burgos had added cruelly to her already heavy burden of weariness. It may have eased her to turn her final disillusionment with Gracián outwards in anger against Jesuit injustice and "black self-interest."

Having notarized the papers in proof that she had renounced Catalina's money, she planned to leave Burgos at once. She had done what she could. Those five months in Burgos had not been of a kind to strengthen Teresica's wish to stay in the Order, and her sixteenth birthday was in the offing. Teresa was anxious to get back to Avila and have her professed at once. It was necessary if poor Lorenzo were to get his chapel.

That she did not leave Burgos for a matter of months to come was due to what the legal profession calls an act of God. It's high drama, as reported by San Bartolomé, Dr. Manso, and numerous historians of the city, is not mentioned in *Fundaciones*. She had finished the Burgos chapter shortly before she wrote Reinoso about her continuing troubles with the Jesuits; and the flood that swept away so much of Burgos occurred only five days later.

II

Burgos, like London and Paris, is bisected by a river, but a river unlike the Thames or the Seine. In summer, it is no more than a creek running through a deep gulley. In winter, the creek becomes a river, and nowadays the sides of the gulley are built up with heavy stone walls. These walls, like the bridge which replaced the pontoons that Teresa had crossed to reach the city, were built after the flood that began on the night of May 21, 1582. Up to that year, the river had been an occasional winter nuisance, nothing more.

The acts of the city council describe the damage done by that unseasonable flood to "the squares and streets, homes and public buildings and the water supply," and to the bridge in the center of town, "a most sumptuous structure whose foundation stones were swept away." All sections suffered, but the worst hit was the La Vega *barrio* in which "monasteries, convents and churches as well as private residences were utterly destroyed." This was because a section of the original city wall still stood and acted as a dam, making La Vega a temporary lake.

As the waters began to rise, the residents of that *barrio* fled to high ground to wait it out. Those who passed the new convent beat on its doors and shouted warnings to the nuns to save themselves. The Archbishop gave orders that Teresa and her nuns be given formal protection as they were led to safety. Teresa simply refused to leave the house that she had won against such difficulties. It was not wise, it was not admirable, and it was nothing that she cared to discuss later.

San Bartolomé says: "The waters continued to rise until they came into the house, and with every wave of the river the building shook and threatened to fall in on us, for it was old, and La Santa's room was in such bad condition that one could see the light of the sky through the roof and the walls were all cracked, and it grew terribly cold, as it sometimes does in that city. The river rose up to the level of the first storey.

"Since we were in that danger, we took the Holy Sacrament up into the attic, and we all recited litanies, for we expected to be drowned at any minute. And we were in that danger from six in the morning until midnight of the next day, without food or rest. Our Santa was the most wretched soul in the world, for she had just finished the foundation of the convent and the Lord seemed to have deserted her and she did not know whether she should have stayed or left the way all the other monks and nuns had done at that time.

"We were all so upset that we couldn't agree to pay any attention to our Santa. After a long time she said to me, 'Daughter, see if there isn't a bit of bread left.' That broke my heart. And a novice who had been strong enough to go

404

down and get a loaf from under the rising water and hide it under her girdle gave it to us then, because none of us had anything else. And if some swimmers hadn't got in, we all would have died.

"They looked more like angels of God to me! They dove underwater and shattered the doors to get in — and that, little by little, let the water drain out of the rooms. So much litter and mud and stones was left behind that they had to take off more than eight cartloads after the waters finally went down, and the room that had been La Santa's cell eventually fell in."

Oddly enough, the city's reaction to all this was the exact opposite of Teresa's and of the nuns whom she had so nearly condemned to death. As San Bartolomé said: "Many people including the Archbishop cried out that she had tied the hands of God so that the whole city should not perish."

But reconstructing the house was quite as much of a task as the getting of it had been, though, for the first time, Teresa was unable to oversee and encourage her workers, laughing with them, urging them on, and passing the wineskin when they showed fatigue. She was gravely ill and confined to her bed throughout.

Dr. Manso spent much time with her, as her confessor. He talked with her about "the things of God" and San Bartolomé heard him "mutter behind his teeth, and still so that [she] should hear him, 'Oh, blessed woman! Blessed woman!' "

Teresica remembered hearing her say, "Oh, you bad man! What do you think one would have to do to merit our God's sending his soul to hell for good and all?"

She did not hear the rest of her hoarse whispering concerning God's forgiveness; but Manso wrote later that he learned more Christian truth from her than he had learned from many *letrados,* and that unlettered as she was, she seemed to know and understand the Gospels better than those who were allowed to read and study them.

Nonetheless, ill as she was, and inspired as Dr. Manso found her, she was able within a week to dictate a furious, long, long letter to Ana de Jesús in Granada. "I laugh at the hubbub you are making with your complaints against the Father-Provincial." Far from snooping into her affairs as Ana believes, Gracián knows only what she herself had written to San José — as Ana and her nuns had not seen fit to tell her, Teresa, anything. So she's buying a house for twelve thousand ducats? If she's as rich as all that she should hardly be bothered by Gracián's suggestion that she might help other convents!

But Mother Ana's successful efforts to set an example of disobedience to the whole Order are a cause for grief. Her camping out in the houses of gentry with her nuns was pretty bad; it was still worse for her to have shipped the two poor things from Villanueva back again when she found that the crowd she had decided to take with her made two more an inconvenience. Why not send back some of those she had taken from Beas without permission?

"I laughed at your fears that the Archbishop [of Granada] might try to suppress your convent. He not only doesn't want to, he couldn't, not if he tried for the rest of his life." Not that it wouldn't be a good thing if he could and did; a convent founded in disobedience is no gain to the Order. As for the number of nuns Gracián had told her she might take from Beas, Ana had paid him no more attention than as if he held no office at all.

The diatribe runs on: Beatriz de Jesús (yes, an odd source to quote) writes that Mother Ana plans to send the Seville nuns back to their house, despite the illness and deaths from the plague that are still going on there. Can't Ana realize that there are worse sufferings than being a bit overcrowded—by one's own fault? It's the nuns from Beas who should be sent back, all so blindly besotted on their prioress that they can't see anything as brides of Christ should!

"I don't want that house to develop the way the one in Beas did. I'll never get over the letter they wrote me from Beas when you left. A Calced nun wouldn't have written one to equal it! . . . I suppose you took the ones who were your greatest enthusiasts with you. Oh, holy spirit of obedience!"

Can't Ana realize that she is starting work in a new kingdom and teach her nuns to act like brides of Him Crucified, not like spoiled children? And what difference did it make that Gracián addressed her as President, not Prioress? María de Cristo wrote her about this, shocked—as if titles make people worth more in the eyes of God! How can nuns learn humility if their Prioress sets them a bad example? She, Teresa, has sent word to Beas that she will pay for having their nuns sent back, and she only wishes Avila weren't so far from Granada so that she could retrieve the ones sent from there too!

She has written enough news from Burgos to Fray Juan and to other prioresses; they'll pass it on. María de Cristo, Antonia del Santo Espíritu and Fray Juan should all read this letter.

(Pointedly, she sends none of them her regards.)

No doubt Fray Juan had left Teresa on the defensive after that "tiring" evening in Avila, and Burgos had done little to disprove his opinion on the source of her Voice. But it is sad that she now seems to rebuke him along with Ana de Jesús and the nuns chosen by Gracián for Granada despite her protests—the deposed prioress María de Cristo and the "unsuitable" Antonia del Santo Espíritu.

It is also strange that this weary, angry letter survived the beatification of the Blessed Ana de Jesús, Teresa's sole known letter to her, except for the fragments which were copied and notarized to further the canonization of Juan de la Cruz: the one expressing shock that Ana can complain of "that divine, heavenly man," and the other urging her to treat him with more honesty. It is in accord with the letter in which Teresa, having listed the nuns for Granada, says, "Ana de Jesús will take it badly. She likes to give all the orders herself." But it squares ill with that long-respected forgery cited for the Blessed Ana's beatification, which begins: "My daughter and my crown!"

Indeed, this letter's survival is all the more puzzling since the Blessed Ana made such a good thing of her memories of La Santa and John of the Cross once they were dead. But Teresa's having dictated that letter to San Bartolomé in her painful, protracted, angry whisperings is no puzzle. She was played out, and sick at heart over the difference between the dream that gave birth to her Order, and her Order's developing reality.

After the flood it would be two months before she was well enough to get out of bed and leave Burgos.

Chapter 79 ❀ *Visit to Palencia; Last Letter to Gracián*

I

In early June, Teresa wrote again to Quiroga's confessor urging that her convent in Madrid be licenced even before the King got back from Portugal (Quiroga's latest excuse). Her work in Burgos is finished, glory be to God. Surely He will give the Cardinal light?

Three weeks later, she wrote to Gracián. He has answered none of her letters; it would be a great relief to hear from him. "For the love of God, don't go to Seville!" The plague, he must know, is only one of her anxieties about his being there again. Next comes a passage so cross-hatched with censorings that one can only see that it concerns money, the devil, Pedro de Tolosa and his Jesuit confessors. Another, beginning, "Oh, since Teresica . . . ," is totally obliterated. The next, left slightly more legible, worries over the convent in Salamanca which is still not properly housed. May God guide him, for her sake. Her "throat is no worse than usual, which is a great thing." And she must beg him at once to send her convent here a Discalced confessor.

A July letter to María de San José sympathizes over deaths from the plague, and scolds her bitterly for sending nuns to Granada "mounted on mules for all the world to see."

One seeks Dr. Manso's remembered Teresa in these letters in vain. But she still lives. A letter to Doña Leonora, the ex-wife in Soria, brings her back. Doña Leonora on taking the habit experienced a brief wave of religious enthusiasm which quickly drained away. She felt it as a lost happiness and wrote to ask Teresa the way back. Teresa offered her no hope of further delights in prayer. She appealed to Doña Leonora's first determination to serve God, and she told her about old María Díaz:

"She gave away all she owned for God and kept only a blanket that she covered herself with at night, and then she gave that away, too. At once she was overwhelmed with the greatest aridities and spiritual troubles imaginable, and she said, 'Are you like that, God? After You left me with nothing, are You leaving me, too?'

"His Majesty is just like that, daughter. He repays great services with trials, and there can be no better payment, for it is only in our trials that we discover a true love of God . . . . Do not let what you feel distress you. Value yourself for helping God bear the Cross and don't strain for those delights, like common soldiers who expect their daily wages. Serve him for nothing, as grandees serve their King.

"May He who is King of Heaven be with you."

That was her final faith, her final strength. With all her human faults she had learned to live by it. She did not deserve to have that faith demeaned, as it soon would be, by the celebration of her raptures — once needed, but their purpose long since served. Only one who knows how God repays the greatest services can bear to hear that cry from the Cross: "My God, my God, why hast Thou forsaken me?"

A second note to Doña Leonora reminded her again of what she had said. But she could not, as the lady wished, go to Soria and talk it out with her. She must husband her strength; for when the King got back to Spain, she would be founding a convent in Madrid.

That is all from Brugos, except for a note to María de San José, again sending sympathy to nuns who had lost members of their family in the plague, and adding that as none of their own number died, they might be sure that it was because God thought none of them ready for their reward as yet. It was too bad that Gracián had promised Palencia she would be there for a month, as she was anxious to see Teresica professed in Avila: "You — and all of you there — must pray for her, for though she's a dear little thing, she's just a young girl, after all." Doria has written her from Genoa. All here are well and send their best.

It is an unusual letter to San José, for it never mentions money — even though the convent in Burgos, not yet fully paid for, now had to be virtually rebuilt. But Teresa had relinquished that problem to Tomasina Bautista. Tomasina had been elected prioress as soon as the foundation was made. Cousin Inés had endeared herself to the nuns in Burgos even less than she did to those in Palencia.

II

In decent weather the trip from Burgos to Palencia could be made in two days; it seemed incredible when one remembered the way up, through the sheets of rain, the floods, the hub-deep mud. Dr. Manso and the physician, Aguilar, took the first day's journey with Teresa and left her in a convent of the Poor Clares — whose abbess managed to slip a gift of two ducats into her belongings secretly.

Manso hated to part with Teresa and did so with an odd word of comfort. "I told her," he recalled, "that she was going to her death." Teresa smiled it away. First, Teresica must be professed, and then she would found her convent in Madrid. Still, she spent the promised month, less three days, in Palencia.

Teresica, testifying for her aunt's beatification, was honest about her reaction to the last stages of Teresa's illness. An unhappy girl, not quite sixteen, she had been frightened and repelled by what she saw. "Sometimes I saw her so afflicted with pain, with such tremblings of the head and shrinking as if she felt blows on her body that I not only could not bear it, but it seemed to me that

408

the fury that was tormenting her surely came from demons who were doing her violence." She was less honest about the trouble that she herself had been giving. She had wanted to leave the Order, she said, "to join another," but was so gravely dissuaded that "in confusion" she consented to be professed in Avila. When she gave this statement, fourteen years after Teresa's death, she did not want to remember that she had been determined to leave the religious life for good and all.

Teresa let little of this show in her letters. In one to Mother Tomasina she let it slip that Teresica was being less "amiable" than she had been in Burgos, but she dropped the subject immediately for suggestions as to how Mother Tomasina might save on the laundry bill and directions about repairing the worst remaining gap in the convent wall. Her throat, she went on, felt better; she had not felt so well for a long time — even though the moon was at the full. (The moon still affected her body as well as the mind.) And, best of all, General Caffardo had come to Genoa and made Doria treasurer of all the Discalced. Mother Tomasina must have "some sort of procession and give thanks to God" that their finances were in such good hands.

To Teresa, the news meant that Gracián and Doria would have to work in partnership after all; however unwillingly, each would supply what the other lacked. Las Cuevas, the Dominican who had chaired the Chapter that elected Gracián, reacted otherwise. When he testified for Teresa's beatification, Gracián had been expelled from the Order and Doria was its provincial, but I do not think that this colored his memory of a visit he paid Teresa during that month's stay in Palencia.

They talked, he said, about her impounded book, and she assured him that her visions were things of the past. Then she expressed her hope that Gracián and Doria would eventually work hand-in-hand. Gracián, he had reminded her, was elected on just that condition, but from the start he ignored it, setting himself above the law. He was too proud to reflect that even Moses had his Aaron, and that they, in turn, consulted with the elders in their company.

She saw Gracián otherwise, las Cuevas went on, and he asked her to visit Valladolid quickly and talk with the friars of their new priory. Then she could see what discontent the man's imperious ways were creating and warn him, as the mother of a headstrong son. Gracián, he hoped, would respond to that deep, motherly love — which alone had caused their names to be slanderously coupled by her enemies; she alone had any chance of persuading him that his proud self-isolation was destroying all harmony in their Order.

That much, at least, Teresa wanted to believe. She hoped against hope that even if Gracián could not be dissuaded from going to Andalusia, she could set him straight before he started out. But the hope was faint; and the news from her convents was uniformly disturbing.

The nuns in Toledo were moving to another house. She warned them that Diego Ortiz must not bear the full expense, and they must not let him see that his ill-nature disturbs them: "He's always like that." And on no account must they accept Brianda's sister; she's fit to be a *beata*, but not a nun.

Catalina de Tolosa's troubles with the Jesuits continued. Teresa wrote to her that they had failed to make trouble for her daughters in Palencia when they sent their dowries to Burgos; both "those angels" were well and happy. Other news from Burgos was still more distressing. Tomasina did not wear well under the pressures of illness and want that followed the flood. She became unreasonably demanding, harsh with the nuns and habitually overworking the lay-sisters. Worse still, she had begun to beg.

This was both an infringement of the Constitutions and bad policy; nothing succeeds like success or the appearance of success. Tomasina needed both rebukes and reassurances. "Move slowly, " Teresa urged her; little by little Catalina would manage to make over her daughter's share of the estate to them; but, if Tomasina seemed to want more than that, or talked poor-mouth, she would lose more than she tried to gain.

But no convent was in worse state than Alba de Tormes. The Duchess, as long feared, had finally washed her hands of it, and Teresa wrote her only known letter to Teresa de Laiz: No, Señora Laiz could not get Tomasina back. In Burgos, when she had first made that request, "the poor creature trembled from head to foot." If the Señora only wanted her for fear that Mother Juana would be reëlected, she needn't worry. Mother Juana wrote Teresa that nothing in the world could ever persuade her to act as Prioress there again. Indeed, no prioress would stay there long; the nuns are infantile, they have schoolgirl crushes and are impossible to govern. No convent could be further from the Discalced ideal.

"May God forgive you! I beg you to consider it as your house [not Her Excellency's] and realize that it is impossible to serve God where there is no peace and quiet, and so you are very wrong to play favorites with them in anything . . . and if God gives me strength I will manage to go there myself and work out this tangle. . . . I have learned that the friars of another Order [the local Franciscans] have spread a highly indiscreet account of it, and it is making talk even among the laity a long way from Alba." She ends with a hope that Gracián, at least, will get there soon. "A house like that can hurt the whole Order. People will think that the Discalced are all alike."

She also wrote to thank Don Sancho Dávila for his efforts there, with a wish that she could see him "to discuss things not fit to put in a letter. . . . Oh, Lord, what I went through with my niece's parents to make them leave her in Avila before I went to Burgos!" (Beatriz had stayed with a second cousin, Señor Cimbrón. It was too little too late, but all Teresa had been able to manage.)

Bad news of a very different kind came from Salamanca. Illness, poverty, and bad housing had driven the Prioress to defying the Constitutions with fanatic excesses of bodily penance and fasting. Perhaps the poor woman only wanted to bribe God, but she was creating an atmosphere of religious hysteria as far from the Discalced ideal in its own way as were the infantilisms and scandals in Alba.

Her letter to cousin-Prioress Ana made no impression. Her letter to Gracián brought only an order that she visit Salamanca and Alba herself before she went back to Avila. He could not spare the time; he had cut short his stay in Valladolid and gone to Almodóvar, planning to leave shortly for Seville. He had

410

cancelled the plan to go to Medina and preach when Quiroga's niece took her final vows; Quiroga was still withholding the licence for Madrid, and since there was clearly no pleasing him, one might as well forget it.

Nonetheless, Teresa knew that Valladolid had to come before Avila, for more reasons than one. Her body and will to live had come very close to the end of the line, but even at her strongest she would hardly have been equal to the situation that she found there.

III

María Bautista was not waiting for Teresa with open arms. Doña Beatriz de Castilla y Mendoza had found her a good audience when she took her case to Valladolid for Mendoza support: Teresa, intending to let her young nephew starve along with his bride, the Bishop's poor young kinswoman! And why? In order to use the better part of her dead brother's estate to build a chapel to the greater glory of—her family! María Bautista, after so many years among the Mendozas, could surely see the situation as it was? Somehow, she must bring her mad old aunt to her senses . . . !

María Mendoza heard the same tale. She, too, was old, and wisdom had never been her outstanding virtue. She was also none too well, and the sight of illness in others depressed her. When she heard that Teresa was so ill, she decided to keep out of the picture.

Alvaro Mendoza would have been wiser and kinder, but the day that Teresa reached Valladolid was the day on which he had to leave to attend a council of bishops which had been called in Toledo. He offered to take a letter to her convent there. Teresa wrote "in great haste because the Bishop wants to start off. . . ." They must show him the utmost gracious attention and send someone frequently to wait upon his wishes, for they owe him everything. They must also humor Diego Ortiz: "Don't pay any attention to his worrying you. . . . Just give way to him in everything. I don't see how I could get down there now. You'd be shocked at my condition and the troubles I'm having here. Pray for me to His Majesty. This is August twenty-sixth, and by the end of this month I'll be in Avila, if it is to His service. It hurt me deeply that the Father-Provincial left at a time like this." But she has sent Heredia the patents for their third house in Toledo, and if he is willing to take over Gracián's duty their move can be managed well. (Gracián, in preparation for his move to Andalusia, had named Heredia Vicar-Provincial of Castile.)

The next day she sent a note to Tomasina. She is pretty well and won't be here long. It's good that the Jesuit Rector came to see them; Tomasina must show him great courtesy and ask him to preach to them. Too bad about that new novice, but it's only a temptation that she'll get over, and meanwhile the girl must write to nobody but herself or San Bartolomé. And nothing Catalina de Tolosa says should trouble them; she is so distracted with her own worries that she'll say one thing one day and quite another the next. Warmest greetings to Dr. Manso and the physician; she needs Dr. Manso's prayers and when she has time she'll write and tell him about that. And, once again, Tomasina must

411

learn to accept others' limitations and not expect them to be perfect, and remember to put her kindness into words. "I have warned you about such things. I don't want you to cast them into oblivion."

On September first, the day she had hoped to be halfway to Avila, she wrote her last letter to Gracián. So he'll write often? That does not lighten her sorrow. His reasons for leaving Valladolid were all inadequate. He could have written his orders, correcting the friars' studies, forbidding them to confess *beatas*, and trusted their monasteries to take care of themselves for another two months while he put the convents here in order.

"I don't know why, but I felt your leaving so badly that I lost all desire to write to you and I couldn't until today — and it is the day of the full moon and I have a headache to match it." But it's only the moon, and she'll feel better tomorrow; the sore throat is better, though it is not yet gone. "I have gone through a lot here with Don Francisco's mother-in-law. She is strange — and absolutely determined to invalidate the will. And although there's no justice on her side, she's in high favor and quite a few have agreed with her and have advised me that I'll have to agree or Don Francisco will lose everything and we [Discalced] will have to pay for it. This would leave the convent in Avila ruined; please God it doesn't happen. Teresica is being badly pressured, but she has behaved well. Oh, how she grieved at your not coming! In a way, that pleased me because it went to teach her that we must trust nobody but God — and it even did me no harm!"

It was less than the whole story. She could hint at Doña Beatriz's fury, which San Bartolomé has described; but she could not tell how María Bautista had joined the attack, or how wretchedly confused it all left Teresica. (And the girl deserves pity; Doña Beatriz was not an attractive person, but neither was the sick old woman, pain-wracked in a way that suggested demonic possession.) But that letter, so long put off, had still harder things to say.

She "could not get out of it," she said. Little as she wanted to, she would have to speak out. In Palencia she had tried to discount much that las Cuevas said, but events had proved him right. They had agreed that the Vicar-Provincial appointed for Castile when Gracián went to Andalusia should be Doria, who was now getting on so well with their new General, but instead Gracián had appointed Heredia, and even for him he had invented new limitations; he could not, for instance, preside over the elections of priors, though that was the proper function of a Provincial or his Vicar. The enclosed letter from Heredia has something to say about that.

"It surprised me that he has gone back to the position of being my friend . . . though even if he weren't, it would be insufferable in every way to have somebody else oversee the elections. I don't understand how you kept yourself from realizing that." And the very idea of having Doria found a house in Rome when Doria is needed here, and Gracián needs Doria! Gracián cannot see to everything by himself. . . .

"Father de las Cuevas said that to me several times. He very much wants you to act wisely. . . . In fact, he made it my obligation, and he even told me that you were defying the decision [of the Chapter] which was that if you found yourself without one companion, you should immediately take another as it was impossible for you to be adequate alone, and Moses had I don't know how many to help him. I told him that there was nobody, that you couldn't even find anybody you thought fit to be a prior. He said that was his main point.

"After I came here they [the Discalced friars in the new priory] told me that they noticed how much you dislike going around with anyone important. Oh, I see that it's because you feel you can't do otherwise, but now that a Chapter is going to be held, I don't want to have anything like that attributed to you. Think about it, for the love of God. . . ."

He must also watch his words in Andalusia. He says that his friars are being slandered? May God not do her the bad turn of letting her see him one of them! "As you say, the devil never sleeps." She would suffer less if he were going to Granada—where he should have sent Heredia. "Don't think of turning yourself into an Andalusian now, for you haven't the right temperament for being among them . . . and as for that preaching, I beg you again that even if you preach seldom, you still watch your words carefully."

As for the new priory, the friars are fairly well thought of, but there is constant illness; the house, like her first convent here, is malarial, and it was "inhuman" of Gracián to leave them without even appointing a prior. María Bautista can't understand why he didn't name Roca, and she agrees.

A friar from Salamanca tells her that the Prioress is about to ruin them by buying a house at three times its market value: "She is *tan mujer,* so head strong, that she carries on as if she had a definite licence from you, neither more nor less, and she tells the Rector that everything she does is by my orders. . . . It is one of the devil's tangles because she wouldn't deliberately lie, but her determination to get that devilish house is driving her mad. The friar says that he keeps telling the Prioress that every time he helps her with her machinations he goes to confession because he is encouraging her sinful disobedience—but he always breaks down under her hysterical pleadings."

She herself has asked Heredia to do what he can to stop it. She will get there by the end of October, and she has warned the guarantor of the proposed loan that he will never get his money back. It's lucky that the nuns lent so much to Gracián, or that, too, would have gone into their secret down-payment. (A broad hint that the Prioress bought Gracián's approval before he left Salamanca, immediately clarified with one last plea.) "For the love of God, think what you're doing! Don't believe the nuns, for if they want something they'll give you a thousand reasons for it, and it's far better for them to take a little house, like poor people, and enter it with humility—which could, in time, improve their spirit—than to be left with heavy debts. . . .

"It did a lot of good in Alba when I wrote them how angry I was and that I would certainly come there. That will come out right. With God's help I'll be in Avila by the end of this month. Try to believe that it isn't suitable to drag this girl from one place to another. Oh, father, how hard-driven I have felt, these days!"

A long, long, bitter, disillusioned letter. What can she say that will better its tone and still warn him again about the troubles he is inviting in Seville? I see

413

her lie back, eyes closed, looking for words while San Bartolomé dips her quill again and waits. . . .

Then she ends it briefly: It has been a relief to hear that he is well. He should read this letter to María de San José and the sisters; she begs them to treat him with tender care, but to do nothing indiscreet. Regards to Fray Juan de la Cruz. San Bartolomé sends her best wishes.

"God take care of you and guard you from dangers as I pray Him to, amen." It is hard to love those whom we cannot respect or trust.

Chapter 80 ❊ *A Bad Reception in Valladolid; Teresa Kidnapped by Heredia; a Mess in Alba de Tormes*

I

Teresica, pressured by Francisco and his mother-in-law, and confused, poor child, by her seven months in Burgos, was in delicate balance. If she were not taken to Avila and professed soon, Teresa saw, she would settle for whatever cut-rate marriage Doña Beatriz could arrange for her. In time she herself would admit how hard to handle she became, and how she was haunted by the memory of Teresa's grave, gentle rebukes during those last days in Valladolid.

Teresa wrote to the convent's confessor in Alba: his letter, she said, was a relief. She still hoped to get there at a time when they could discuss things at their leisure, but there was no hurry, "for though the devil has disturbed them, the sisters are basically good souls and God won't let them out of his hand."

On the night before she left Valladolid she wrote to Catalina de Cristo in Soria. She wishes that she could go to Doña Leonora's profession: "It would be more enjoyable than what I now have on my hands, for here . . . [Censored]. I will be just a short time in Avila, for I can't avoid going to Salamanca, so you can write me there, or in Madrid" (where she hoped to be soon thereafter).

Then comes a line concerning a certain ill-feeling never elsewhere mentioned in still extant Teresiana: Inés de Jesús was embittered when Teresa made her former lay-sister, the illiterate Catalina, not her, the Prioress of that nobly patronized convent in Soria. "I am writing to Mother Inés de Jesús in the hope that you two may become reconciled. In the matter of the Jesuits, I am glad that you are doing what you can with them because it is necessary, and the good and the bad that we show them in . . . [censored].

For the rest, Catalina should tell Doña Beatriz de Beamonte anything she thinks she'd like to hear. But they must be certain that their hesitation about professing the other novice, Isabel, is wholly due to her personality; if her lowly origins have anything to do with their decision, "she must be professed at once."

The letter is dated Valladolid, September 15. It has a postscript written at

414

night on the following day. "Now we are in Medina and so busy that I can't say anything more than that we had a good trip. Use a little dissembling about Isabel's profession, so that she won't even imagine that it is because she is not of good family, since that is not your main reason for not doing it." Apparently humble Catalina, given her place as an example of the Divine disregard for social position, had absorbed the Beamonte atmosphere and become another disappointment. But what has so broken Teresa since the previous night? She gave her orders, and she no longer expects them to be obeyed.

San Bartolomé had little imagination, no ambition, and nothing to lose when she told how Teresa started out on her last journey. San José, Ana de Jesús, and María Bautista all stood to lose much by not supporting one another's claims to have been La Santa's triple tiara, all equally worthy to have been called "my daughter and my crown." But San José outdoes herself in her description of Teresa's leave-taking in Valladolid: the tears, the embraces, the tender farewells from every soul in that convent, and Teresa's parting words to them! "I am amazed at what God has wrought here in the perfection of your religion. Take care that you never fall from it. Do not be content with ordinary goodness, but perform heroic deeds of still greater perfection . . . I am deeply comforted to see the poverty and love for one another that is in this house. Strive that it may always be so." Valladolid . . . holy poverty, so perfectly embodied . . . Either San José knew where María Bautista's character most needed a helpful touch-up, or she had an ironic sense of humor, or both.

San Bartolomé told the facts. Don Francisco's wife and mother-in-law had influenced all the nobility in the matter of Teresica's dowry—which Teresa intended to waste on that chapel for Lorenzo! There was, of course, no question as to whose side María Bautista was on. San Bartolomé says: "The Prioress of that convent was very winning with those gentry, and in spite of her being one whom La Santa loved much, on this occasion she paid her no respect whatsoever, and said that she wished us godspeed from her house. And when I was going out of it, she shoved me at the door and said, 'Get out of here, both of you, and don't come back again!' "

According to San Bartolomé, they left Valladolid in a covered cart, without escort. (You will see presently why the improved version sends them off in a coach sent by the Duchess of Alba, accompanied by Heredia and another friar.) They reached Medina after nightfall.

"The night we got there," San Bartolomé says, "she had to give the Prioress a piece of advice which did not go down at all well." Mother Alberta was so angry and expressed herself so freely that "La Santa winced with pain," and retired to the cell provided for her. Mother Alberta doubtless had a good deal to say about the misuse of Teresica's dowry, as she had learned of it from María Bautista, and still more to say about Teresa's mismanagement of her golden opportunity in Soria. But all that we know of that night is that Teresa neither ate nor slept—and that she added her sorry postscript to the letter which told Catalina del Cristo that she must leave for Avila and then Salamanca before she got to Madrid.

The evidence for her beatification process in Toledo does not mention her letter to Catalina, or any disagreement (heaven forbid) with Mother Alberta, but it tells instead of an evening writing letters to Dr. Castro, Ana de Jesús, Gracián, and Gracián's mother. No such letters were ever produced in evidence of their having been written, but these supposed last words from La Santa all had their use. Long letters to Gracián, her saint, and Doña Juana, his blessed mother, were to be expected as the last that Teresa would ever be well enough to dictate; rumors about her displeasure with Ana de Jesús had to be laid to rest with the suggestion that her last letters included words of love and inspiration to "her daughter and her crown"; and (in case some part of the actual story leaked) there should have been a note to Dr. Castro, to explain why Teresica's profession in Avila would have to be delayed.

For when Teresa left the next morning, she was not setting out for Avila, as she still believed.

II

How this happened gets conflicting explanations.

According to Gracián, Heredia took Teresa to Alba (with her full consent) "to give light to the Duchess" and preside over the election of a new prioress, after which she would go back to Avila to serve as its prioress once again. By Teresica's account, Teresa was "called to Alba to console [sic] the Duchess at the birth of her nephew," though Teresa told her that "no act of obedience ever cost her so much."

Others, chiefly nobles, say that she came when Don Fadrique asked her to be present and pray for the safe delivery of an heir who would eventually succeed him as Duke of Alba.

A nun from Valladolid says that Teresa went to Alba at the Duchess's invitation, another that she went at orders from Father Angel, and a third that she went gladly, despite the opposition of Doña María Mendoza.

All came near to the truth.

It was plain to Heredia that Gracián was giving Teresa short shrift, and he needed her support in his dealings with Gracián. Hence the child that Don Fadrique expected was Heredia's golden opportunity, for Fadrique could easily be persuaded that Teresa's prayers would work best at close range, in the castle; a healthy child would be credited to Teresa; the Duchess, a silly woman, would react by putting Teresa de Laiz back where she belonged—a name on a best-forgotten scrap of paper—and Teresa would be grateful, see her folly in having insisted that Avila and Salamanca should come first, and not only forgive his little practical joke of having kidnapped her but thank him for it.

I daresay he had to confide in Mother Alberta—at least to the extent of saying that he would come in the morning to take her and Teresica and San Bartolomé away.

Teresa assumed that after the hasty profession in Avila he intended to urge her to come back with him to Alba; she only learned the shocking truth when she was captive in the *carroza* he brought for her. They would make the day-and-a-half journey direct to Alba; apparently Don Fadrique wanted no delay, though the child was not due for another two or three weeks.

When she realized that she had been kidnapped, she was too ill to make any effectual protest. She was running a high fever, coughing blood, and in extreme pain; the jolting *carroza* and the day-long journey left her weak and confused.

Once it was clear that Teresa had reached a point of no return, Heredia rode ahead to Alba. He did not notice that Mother Alberta had provided the women with nothing to eat or drink on the way, and as San Bartolomé says, Teresa had eaten no supper the night before, and was given no breakfast. After dark, with leagues yet to go, they found a *posada* which could give them a room but no food.

As San Bartolomé tells it: "When we got to a tiny village near Peñaranda, the Mother was so weak and in such pain that she nearly fainted—such pain that it made one suffer to see her. . . . I didn't know how to find something to eat, and she said to me, 'Daughter, see if you can find something to give me for I am faint.' And there wasn't anything but dried figs, and she had a fever!

"I had two reales to spend so that I could buy a couple of eggs no matter how much they cost, and I couldn't find anything for my money but those figs and so I had to come back. I couldn't look at La Santa without crying, for her face was almost like one that was dead.

"I could not hide my grief at that moment, for it seemed as if my heart would break and I couldn't do anything but cry at seeing myself so helpless when I saw her dying with nothing I could do to help her. And she said to me, with the patience of an angel, 'Don't cry, daughter, for this is what God wants now.' And she went on comforting me and telling me not to grieve, because they were very good figs and many poor people would consider them a treat and that she was very well satisfied with the fig she ate."

That night Don Fadrique's wife went into labor, slightly before her time, and bore a healthy boy. Her priest later wrote a life of Isabel de San Domingo, the Prioress of Segovia; in it he says, "A grateful murmuring went around the castle, 'Praise God, now we don't need that saint!' "

It's a good story and one that would have appealed to Mother Isabel. She always blamed Heredia for Teresa's death, saying that he had made her a martyr to obedience, which was unjust. Heredia brought about the unhappiness of Teresa's last days, true enough; but it had been plain to Dr. Manso and the physician Aguilar before she left Burgos that she could not last out many more months.

San Bartolomé would never join the chorus which blamed Teresa's death on Heredia. She only said, "That trip and the troubles she was bearing and the shattering she took from it all brought on the crisis of the illness from which she had been suffering." That is fair; in Avila Teresa would probably have lived long enough to see Teresica take the veil.

María de San Francisco, a nun of Alba and at that time no friend to La Santa, diagnosed her fatal illness for her canonization in a way that offended none, including Heredia's friends. The death, she said, "resulted from her love of God."

417

In the morning, Teresa, Teresica, and San Bartolomé started out again. After a league and a half they got to another village where San Bartolomé called a halt and managed to find "a dish of overboiled cabbage with a lot of onions." At least it was watery enough for Teresa to swallow.

Heredia, having long since reached the castle, stayed there. He saw no advantage to bringing Teresa to the Duchess now; her condition was a disappointment. Not having seen her for many months, he had not realized that she was dying when he arranged his kidnapping. He only perceived that, once they had been for some time on the road.

Teresa reached Alba that afternoon. San Bartolomé says, "She was so shattered she couldn't talk to her nuns and told me that she felt as if she hadn't a single sound bone left in her body."

According to Gracián she said, "Oh, God help me, daughters, how long is it since I went to bed so early! Thank God I fell ill in your midst."

After those days and nights of bodily and mental pain she probably did say, "Thank God, I can get to bed." But she was in no condition to say more. She was hemorrhaging from the mouth, and once she was put to bed they called a physician.

San Bartolomé says, "He immediately gave her up for lost. That was a very hard thing for me to bear, and worse for its being in Alba."

The next morning, though Teresa could not move without help, she insisted on being got out of bed to hear Mass and take communion. And for eight days more she managed to be in and out of bed while she tried to talk some order into the convent and prevent the election of a nun favored by Teresa de Laiz — a local girl whose "name in religion" made her yet another Inés de Jesús. Teresa believed that because of her letters and the help of the convent's confessor, Dr. Sánchez, Mother Juana had been sufficiently straightened out to deserve reëlection and could be persuaded to accept it.

The election was held on September twenty-seventh. Teresa de Laiz had been more persuasive, and Inés won, hands down.

Teresa had just heard the news when she was told that she had a visitor, the Rector of the new Discalced College in Salamanca. She had herself helped into the parlor to see him. The Rector, Agustín de los Reyes, brought bad news and wished to clear himself of blame. Mother Ana de la Encarnación had finally bought the shockingly overpriced house which would plunge the nuns into debt. She had managed it with the help of the friar who had seen Teresa in Valladolid, that weak soul who had alternately let himself be bullied by Mother Ana into carrying on the negotiations, and then hurried to confess his sin in having helped her to defy authority.

Father Fray Agustín, witnessing for Teresa's beatification, left us a vivid memory of that meeting, his only meeting with her. Teresa, he says, protested that purchase with him for almost three hours. Why had he not managed to stop Mother Ana? Why could nothing be done about it now? "I said, 'Mother, I agree with you, that's all so. But it is done. Once something is done, what cure for it is there, after all?' "

He remembered that her body seemed to crumple as she slumped down in total exhaustion. Then suddenly her back straightened, and her voice had all the vigor, the *brío* of a strong woman not past early middle-age. "Is it done, son? Well then, I tell you that it is not done and it will not be done and they will not set foot in that house, because it is not the Lord's will."

He left her shaking his head and feeling an uneasy confusion. And within a few days something happened which he found increasingly hard to dismiss as coincidence.

"It was something to marvel over, because the next Thursday, a week later, the contract was cancelled and the whole business so completely dropped that it was as if it had not been negotiated over the past five years. And the thing that still stuns me is that nobody said a word about it, or went into that house, or as much as tried to set foot in it."

Teresa would live for six more days after that meeting, but it was the end of her public life.

Chapter 81 ❀ *Teresa's Death and Burial; Exhumation at Gracián's Orders; Author's Last Words on St. Teresa*

I

In time the convent wove many edifying tales about those six days, with Teresa lying surrounded by her adoring nuns and often visited by the Duchess, who on one occasion came with a flask of angel-water, a perfume, which she realized at once to be superfluous as she breathed the celestial odor of sanctity that rose from the deathbed.

In plain fact, the Duchess was wholly absorbed in arranging the christening party for the Duke's first legitimate grandson. Fray Antonio de Jesús was equally absorbed in the Duchess's plans and joys. And the new Prioress, adding spite to the obvious incompetence that Teresa had seen in her, let it be known that the dying old woman should be ostracized.

Juana del Espíritu Santo, the despised prioress, dared call on her only twice. Teresica was there, and remembered that Teresa said to her "Don't be sorry, sister. When I am a little better we will go to Avila together, where we will all be buried some day. We'll go to my own convent, San José."

Teresa, Teresica adds, was constantly unhappy over not being there. "She said that as soon as she was a little better she would hire a litter that would carry her to Avila 'and bring her down there, for she was very ill."

On the Sunday, St. Michael's Day, she managed to get to communion. "But, " says San Bartolomé, "it gave her such a hemorrhage that she had to be got back into bed at once."

St. Michael's Day is the last day of September. According to Gracián, on

419

October first Teresa asked to have an altar set up in her cell so that she might hear Mass from bed, and he lets his readers assume that this was done. If it had been, either Teresica or San Bartolomé would have mentioned it.

San Bartolomé stayed with Teresa constantly, long after Teresica could bear it no more. She remembered the hour when Teresa gave up that last hope of being carried back to die in Avila. "I myself was more dead than alive two days before she died when she said to me, 'Daughter, the hour of my death has surely come.'"

At two in the morning, San Bartolomé sent for Heredia to confess her. Despite the newly elected Mother Inés, one or two nuns came in, and one of them, a young girl named Constancia, would offer a memory that has the ring of truth. Heredia, she said, knelt by her bed and said, "Mother, pray the Lord not to take you from us now and do not leave us so soon." Teresa said, "Be still, father. And you, *you* have said that? By now I am not needed in this world."

On the following day, the Duchess did actually come to see her. Juana del Espíritu Santo mentioned that call in a report dated only five years later: "She was sick of the illness of which she died, and the Duchess of Alba, now Dowager Duchess, visited her bed." Mother Inés, the new Prioress, bears this out, though at the time she was still keeping away and telling her nuns to do likewise: "Since the Mother Teresa was so sick the Duchess paid her visit, in her cell where she was in bed, so I do not know what they talked about."

A barber-surgeon was also called that day, for the singular purpose of cupping and bleeding a patient whose chief symptom was hemorrhage. His name was Jerónimo Hernández, and called as a witness at the canonization process, he said only that he had performed this service at her physician's order, that "he had found her very exhausted from the illness of which she died," and that his own age, at the time, had been twenty-eight.

Gracián says that after the bleeding, Teresa began to recite the *Miserere*. She might well have done so, if strength had remained for it.

Much would be written of Teresa's ecstatic passing, her smiles and inspiring words to the nuns all gathered and kneeling by her bed. I find Teresica more credible. "For the last few days she suffered greatly, for God had let her feel the pain of her illness very much, and all the other slights that she had to bear; and a little before she died He ordained that she should not break free from fear of the shades of death, for the memory of her sins afflicted her so much as if they had been very great. And she could not do anything but beg God to forgive them, and not to consider the evil way she had served Him, but His own Mercy, by which and by His precious blood she was hoping to be saved.

"Many times she repeated the beginning of David's verse, '*Cor contritum et humilem, Deus, non despicies.*'" A humble and contrite heart, O Lord, thou wilt not despise . . . Only the first words, over and over . . . "*Cor contritum . . . cor contritum et humilem.*"

Teresica also recalls that Teresa implored the few nuns who came to her cell to study her Constitutions and keep them, and overlook her own failings.

At five in afternoon of that day, Teresa asked to be given the *Viaticum*, the last communion given to the dying.

Juana del Espíritu Santo told San Bartolomé that it should be put off until morning. The great ducal christening party was going on at the castle, and Heredia would be unwilling to leave it. Teresa insisted, and Heredia came. The few nuns who had not voted for Mother Inés came and knelt by the bed. Teresa could not lift her head, but Juana and San Bartolomé held her upright.

In Medina, twenty-eight years later, long paragraphs of Teresa's inspiring last words were offered in evidence for her canonization. I find it enough to know that Teresa, in unqestioning faith, received the body and blood of His Majesty, in humble love and in hope for His mercy on a life that had tried to teach His will, though with small success — and as she saw it, small success through her own fault. *Cor contritum . . . contritum . . . .*

Constancia, the young nun who remembered her saying to Heredia, "Be still, father. And you, you have said that?" also says that when Juana and San Bartolomé had laid her down, Teresa lay with her hands clasped, whispering, "After all, Lord, I am a daughter of the Church."

At nine that night, Heredia came back to give Extreme Unction. Teresa, Constancia says, "spoke the responses with deep feeling and went back to thanking God for the grace that had made her a child of the Church."

Heredia may have felt some guilt, for he asked her if she were willing to be buried there, not in Avila. Juana del Espíritu Santo probably believed her own memory when many years later she witnessed that Teresa said, "Jesus, do you have to ask that, father? Can't they spare me here a bit of earth?" But Juana imagined that rebuke to a convent which she herself had not forgiven.

San Bartolomé, too, remembered Heredia's question, and she says, "Without answering one word she showed by the look on her face how it sorrowed her that anyone could even ask her that."

Heredia should have known.

In the hands of Teresa's first biographers, Juana's memory grew into a touching dialogue, with San Bartolomé insisting that the Prioress of Avila should be buried in her own first convent, and Teresa gravely reminding her that the Son of Man had no place to lay His head. They would have done better to let honest San Bartolomé's story stand, drawing their Gospel reference from Christ before Herod: "But He answered him never a word."

Teresa died between three and four in the morning, gasping and struggling for breath, while San Bartolomé held her in her arms.

II

A lay-sister helped San Bartolomé wash the body and dress it in its habit. An undertaker's services were dispensed with: as several would witness, "She was buried guts and all." That same day, October fourth, the convent held its wake. Heredia and a fellow friar, Fray Tomás, led the prayers. Antonio Gaitán's little girl, Mariana, much enjoyed being let stay up all night. When she took the veil, some years later, she wrote, "We all spent the night with her body with great pleasure."

In time the whole Alba community but one testified to the odor of sanctity which that night filled the convent with celestial fragrance. Only the lay-sister who had helped San Bartolomé wash and clothe the body admitted that she had missed it; her nose had been stuffed up with a bad head-cold.

If only for the delight of that fragrance one would have thought that the convent would have been unwilling to waive the usual three days between a death and a burial, but the wake began when the body was barely cold and the funeral was set for ten the next morning. The Duchess of Toledo, a guest at the christening party, sent "a rich cloth of white brocade" to use as a pall. In later years she witnessed that this fulfilled a prophetic vision granted her in childhood, in which she laid just such a covering on the body of a saint.

No coffin was used in the church. The body was placed on a litter, before the church was opened: so placed that it might be removed without a moment's delay, once the office of the dead had been sung. There would be no funeral Mass, though Teresa had once protested in a letter to Gracián that nuns were given such short shrift and buried without a Mass, in a way unworthy of a bride of Christ.

At ten the doors were opened and the church was packed, for besides the nuns and the local Franciscan friars (so recently spreading deplorable tales about them), the Duchess came with her household and the entire christening party. A stunning list of those present does not mention the poor de Ovalles; it is unlikely that Teresa's sister knew of that unseemly haste and even tried to get in. But the convent record boasts of so many grandees present, Dukes, Duchesses, Marquises and Marchionesses, Counts and Countesses, that one doubts a much later memory of one Mariana de Jesús that the small church also held "many leading gentry of the town." More to the point, no Mendozas or Mendoza connections are named as among those present.

Laid on her litter, Teresa's face was covered, but her feet were left bare. Don Sancho Dávila kissed them, and other clerics followed suit. Many later reported their dazzling whiteness and flowery scent.

That final tribute offered, the body was whisked out by way of the porter's lodge, the Duchess of Toledo's fine brocade was removed, and a blanket substituted. A coffin, hastily knocked together of thin pine wood, received the body.

Mother Inés, conspicuous by her absence throughout Teresa's last days, was now the center of activities. A quarter-century later she claimed her part in having made the miraculous preservation just that, miraculous. "I had warned," she says, "that she should be buried without taking out her guts or embalming her or using any artificial means to prevent corruption, but to put her, in her habit, into a box."

A stone-mason, Pedro Barajas, described having gathered efficient laborers and overseen their work; it should be "such that anybody who wanted to make off with the body could not do it." They had been at work for the better part of the day on which Teresa died, breaking out mortar, removing stones, and "making a very deep hole in the wall of the church" down in the crypt. Thereafter, Pedro and his fellow workers were ordered to pack so much stone and mortar around "the box" that it could never be removed. (This broke the fragile lid, and as Ribera conscientiously notes, it flawed the miracle with a broken nose.)

Mother Inés, who oversaw the reconstructing of the wall says, "It was done as thoroughly as if they were building an edifice meant to last forever." Barajas supports this, and Teresica was told that when the work was undone, the men who had done it in a day and a half were four days at breaking it down again.

The Duchess was lucky that Mother Inés had been elected. She might have had trouble with a Prioress who insisted that all things be done decently and in order. The Duchess wanted Teresa to be buried in Alba — to put Bishop Mendoza in his place. Avila had been his convent, the first of an Order now in high favor with the King, and she knew Mendoza would want the body there. The Duchess was small-minded, and years of toadying to her had taught Heredia how to please her. The first suggestion may have been his, but I doubt that, for we do have San Bartolomé's word for it that he asked Teresa's permission to bury her in Alba.

Almost at once Heredia had reason to regret his acquiescence, or his inspiration, whichever it was. Juana de Ahumada protested that her sister's hasty burial had been "indecent." Father Pedro González, a local priest, put himself on record with these words: "It almost makes me cry to think that the body of the holy Mother Teresa de Jesús should have been treated like that." The indignation grew, reaching such a pitch that Heredia made a public statement that the body had not been actually buried in Alba, only "deposited" with intent to remove it as soon as a chapel already proposed for the convent in Avila was ready to receive it. However, the porteress in Alba, one of the very few who had voted for Mother Juana, went on record with Father González, stating that they saw Heredia view the reconstructed wall and heard him say, "The Mother is going to stay there for eternity, and I will be the one who speaks for her times."

The repercussions were showy and had little to do with Teresa herself. At Court, the grandees were split in furious dissention, pro-Toledo faction against pro-Mendoza. This in turn encouraged dissent among Teresa's friars. Long-present distrust and covert enmities flared into open war: war between Gracián's supporters and the new Heredia-Doria alliance. As San Bartolomé puts it, "They all became entangled with the world."

At the Chapter held in Almodóvar during the following May, Gracián discovered how much he needed friends. A few weeks of thought convinced him of his holy duty to snatch the body from the de Toledos and see that Teresa was buried in Avila as the Mendozas had so rightly desired.

He got to Alba secretly in July. By that time, he had the support of all the Order's nuns except for an insignificant few scattered here and there, since the very prioresses who had given Teresa the most trouble while she lived were the most convinced of her sanctity once she was dead — and of the fervor with which they had always served her. Almost all of them could recall the supernatural experiences by which they had known the very moment of Teresa's entry into eternal glory. For example, Ana de Jesús had been at death's door and made what she took to be her last confession to John of the Cross when the room filled with light and La Santa stood before her saying, "Do not grieve. I have not died but entered into life." Nor was it, Ana goes on, a dream; for when the vision faded she found herself miraculously fever-free and restored to perfect health.

Gracián, in Alba, found that Mother Juana's faction far outnumbered that of Mother Inés. Many described a haunting, sweet fragrance that filled the crypt and rose to their cells, penetrating brick and mortar, though nine months earlier it had been blocked by the stuffiness in a lay-sister's nose. The others, including Mother Inés, were afraid of ghosts; they constantly heard strange tappings from behind the rebuilt section of wall.

Even without these manifestations, none would have dared to protest the secret disinterrment ordered by their Provincial. To cheat the Duchess could only mean trouble in this world; but to disobey the man who stood over them in the place of Christ meant unending trouble in the world to come — the price of mortal sin.

All were awed when no stench of corruption came from the shrivelled, brown body, still intact except for the broken nose.

The body was not long intact. As the wonder grew, bits of it began to be distributed, an arm, a finger, a rib. . . . Simultaneously, the ink began to flow. A saint was born; an endlessly enraptured, levitating saint at whose birth Teresa would have laughed and wept if she had not been in the place that knows only the Beatific Vision.

III

It is said that when the Duchess discovered the theft she ran through the streets, shrieking, "They have stolen my saint!"

That is hearsay. It is fact that at the Chapter which finally read Gracián out of the Order, leaving him to pursue his literary career first in Italy and then in Flanders, only one voice was not raised against him.

Juan de la Cruz never had any interest in politics.

But Juan de la Cruz grieved that Teresa was remembered only for the dubious "mercies" which he had believed her to have outgrown until that night in Avila when he felt, quite wrongly, that his teaching had been largely wasted. But, by God's grace, not utterly wasted: though the devil had known what he stood to win by winning that great soul, while Teresa lived and could speak for herself, his winnings had been small. Now she was dead, and he stood to win all that she had accomplished. Juan de la Cruz wrote his *Ascent of Mt. Carmel* — and most specifically its eleventh chapter — as his attempt to protect Teresa's Order from the devil's most cunning deceits, the only deceits that can win those who truly love Christ. He wrote it in the hope that her Order might grow in her own unwavering desire to serve her God.

True, he had not understood her. The angels must always be baffled by humankind. But he understood her ideals. That in itself was remarkable. Until the last century or so, men have rarely made a serious effort to understand women, their fellow humans.

424

Still, we should remember that if Teresa had not been falsified by her contemporaries, she would have been forgotten; and even in her time the falsifications did some good. Ribera, who wrote her soundest contemporary biography, was a Jesuit; and the miracles he reported along with the facts did much to leave her Order and his as she had longed to see them, brothers-in-arms, fighting under the same banner.

Furthermore, these same falsifications were what enabled Luis de León, a descendant of converted Jews once jailed by the Inquisition, to edit and publish the *Life*, with an appendix chosen from Teresa's *cuentas*. The book's immediate appeal did much to make things easier for him, and for Luis de Santander, and numerous other *conversos* who could claim that they had known and helped her.

Christians always admit that Herod was part of the Plan. Those who call the Church its worldly fulfillment should not be ashamed to admit that Teresa, by now, would be forgotten if the Duchess of Alba had not wanted to spite the ducal Mendozas — or if Gracián's jealous fear of Doria and Heredia had not led him to order the exhumation which changed Teresa from a potential liability to an ace of trumps in Philip's long game of one-upsmanship with the Papacy.

Because of the ugly haste with which she was sealed away into cold-storage and the ugly cowardice which led to exhumation, Teresa's letters, though still seen as unfit for publication, were preserved as holy relics. I should like to believe that God wanted her to be remembered, and used the world as it then was in the hope that what was so saved of her reality would be better understood in an age that could respect her life, and, yes, her sanctity, for what it is.

The End.

Index

10, 77, 35; death, 223, 273

Cepeda, Juan de (grandfather). *See* Sánchez, Juan

Cepeda, Juan de (half-brother), 5, 9, 10

Cepeda, Leonor de, 69

Cepeda, Lorenzo de (brother), xxv, xxxii, 19-20, 77, 136, 234; chapel for, Teresa's concern about, 347, 348, 351-352, 354, 374, 378, 379, 391; death and will, 346-347, 348, 349, 351-352; estate bought by, 251; financial situation, 242, 258, 273; goes to Indies, 35; religious life of and Teresa's advice to, 273-274, 277, 278-279, 282; returns from Indies, xxviii, 222-223; Seville convent aided by, 214, 223, 242, 251, 288; sexual drive of, 35, 56, 279-280; use of title by, 242-243

Cepeda, Lorenzo de (nephew), xxxii, 223, 310, 339; illegitimate child of, 345, 355, 391; marriage, 390

Cepeda, Lorenzo de (uncle), 4, 15, 29, 54; enters Church, 5

Cepeda, María de (half-sister), xxv, 14, 17, 77; birth, 5; death, 86; marriage to Martín de Guzmán, 15, 16

Cepeda, María de (cousin), 96

Cepeda, Pedro de (uncle), xxv, 33; religious life of, 17, 25

Cepeda, Rodrigo de (brother): birth, 7; as child with Teresa, xxv, 11-12, 18-19; in Indies, xxv, 19; will of, 19, 23

Cerda, Luisa de la, xxvi, xxxii, 83, 84 165, 301; *Life* manuscript and, 119, 120, 122, 134; and Malagón foundation, xxvii, 116, 117, 120, 121; relations with Teresa, 79-80, 117, 125, 129; and relocation of Malagón convent, 246, 247-248, 251. *See also* Malagón convent

Cetina, Diego de (confessor), 44, 45, 55; removed as Teresa's confessor, 46

Charles V (of Germany), 8, 50, 92

Chávez, Beatriz, 237, 245, 283, 284, 311, 352; accusations by, 259, 322-323; and García Alvarez, 265; background and relations with Gracián, 214-215, 263, 264; at Seville convent, 218, 249; Teresa's advice about, 328; as Vicar-Prioress, in Seville, 323, 324. *See also*, Alvarez, García

Chávez, Diego, xxxii, 317

Cisneros, Cardinal, 1

College of St. Gil, 48, 50

Concerning God's Mercies, 41; additions to, 101, 102; and *Camino*, relationship between, 107; initial writing of, 83

Confessions of St. Augustine: effect of, on Teresa, 40

Confessors: nuns' relationship with, 105; Teresa on, 26, 166, 168.

Contreras, Ana de (Ana de Jesús), 332

Convent of the Angels, 69, 79

Convent of the Image, *See* Jesús, María de

Convent of the Incarnation, *See* Incarnation convent

Convents: financial difficulties of Teresa's, 245, 256 (*see also* entries for individual convents); founded in poverty, 84; reforms and, 23-24, 98, 108-109,; Teresa's decision to start, xxvi (*see also* St. Joseph's Discalced Convent); unenclosed, dangers of, 21, 22, 25, 32; Teresa's advice for Visitors to, 256-258

Conversos, 69; heresy associated with, 41, 51; Inquisition's interest in, 53, 152; persecution of, 78, 79. *See also* Anti-Semitism; Jews, Spanish

Corro, María del, xxxii, 262; accusations against Teresa, 228, 231, 234

Cota, Pedro de: Discalced opposed by, 231, 244

Council of Palencia, 229

Council of Trent, 23-24, 36, 37, 109, 131

Counter-Reformation, 50

Court of Blood, 176

Covarrubias, Bishop, 187, 298, 300

Cristo, Catalina de: selected prioress at Soria, 366; Teresa advises about, Soria, 414-415

Cristo, María de, xxxiv, 374, 389, 406

Cruz, Isabel de la, 163, 164, 165

Cruz, Juan de la, xxvii, xxviii, xxxiii-xxxiv, 139, 150, 186, 237, 277, 328, 406, 424; background and character, 116; Beas foundation opposed by, 192-193; captured by Calced, xxviii, 298-299; and Discalced Chapter meetings, 253, 313; Duruelo monastery prepared by, 123-124; escapes from Calced, 311; Granada priory to be headed by, 378; in hiding, 318; at Incarnation, 168, 169-170, 229, 259, 288; miracles and, 177-178; Pastrana monastary examined by, 139; secures permission for Granada convent, 380-381; and Teresa, 170-171, 173, 341, 342; Teresa's last meeting with, 386-388; visions and locutions distrusted by, 172, 205, 387, 424

Cuentas de conciencia, Teresa's, 75, 151; as defense for Seville trial, 238-239; on endowment of Toledo convent, 135; for Pedro de Ibáñez; on return to Incarnation, 160-161; on vow of obedience to

Martínez de Hiniesta, Hernando, 186-187
Mascarénas, Leonora de, 40, 131; and María de Jesús, 118-119
Matías, Pedro, and Bernarda Gutiérrez, 222; and Seville convent, 242, 286
Mazanas, Hernando de, 398
Medina, Bartolomé de, 140, 147, 151, 162, 181, 192, 239, 310; attitude towards Teresa, 156-157, 175, 176; Beas foundation opposed by, 188
Medina, Luis de, 113, 115
Medinaceli, Duke of, 176
Medina (del Campo) convent, 127, 162, 310-311, 356; election of prioress, controversy over, 148; financial situation, 114, 116, 118, 157; founding of, xxvii, 112-115; girls' school at, opposed by Teresa, 178, 268; house donated for, 116; initial nuns for, 114. *See also* Quiroga, Elena de
Medina Sidonia, Duke of, 184
Meditaciones sobre los Cantares, xxvi, xxviii, 152; Báñez refuses to accept, 224-225; copies of, 344, 345; Teresa ordered to burn, 344-345
Mejías, María, 122, 191, 195
Mendoza, Alvaro, xxxiv, 82, 140, 192, 305, 329, 411; Burgos convent aided by, 400-401; *converso* priests supported by, 78, 79; and Mendoza-de Toledo feud, 181; and Palencia convent, 339, 356, 358; reaction to Medina foundation, 113; and St. Joseph's founding, xxvi, 78, 79, 80, 86, 87-88, 91, 92, 93, 98, 99; Teresa writes about Gracián and Seville, 207-208; transfer of, 293, 294
Mendoza, Ana de, xxxiv, *See also* Eboli, Princess of
Mendoza, Bernardino, 114, 119
Mendoza, Cardinal, 132
Mendoza, Diego de, 88, 132; and Inquisition, 195; Teresa rejects his ex-mistress as novice, 349-350
Mendoza, Luis Hurtado de (Count of Tendilla), 311; defends Discalced and confronts Sega, 320
Mendoza, María (Sarmiento) de, xxxiv, 80, 118, 119, 329, 339, 411; friendship with Teresa, 79, 167; and Jesuit-sponsored novices at Valladolid, 166, 167; and St. Joseph's hermitages, 99; Teresa seeks help of, for Báñez, 162; Valladolid convent aided by, 124, 126
Mendoza (y Castilla), Orofrisia de, xxxv; marriage to Francisco de Cepeda, 355
Mendoza, Pedro, 78-79, 140

Mercedarians, 187, 190
Mercurian, General, 180
Military Order of Alcántara, 79
Military Order of Santiago; and license for Beas convent, 185, 188, 190
Miseria, Juan de la, xxxiv, 139, 184, 202, 207; background, 131; and Catalina de Cardona, 159; defection from Discalced, 312; and Catalina Gordóñez, 198; portrait of Teresa by, 244; profession of, xxvii, 132
Mogador, Alonso, de, 216
Monasteries: Teresa permitted to found, 111. *See also* Discalced Carmelites; Duruelo monastery; Pastrana monastery; Pastrana movement
Monks of the Good Woman, 335
Monterrey, Count and Countess of, xxvii, 150, 151
Montoya, Canon, 341; as emissary to Rome for Discalced, 315, 318, 326
Mora, Juan de, 109
Morades, Las, 239, 299-300, 379; genesis of, xxviii, 286-288; Diego de Yanguas reviews, xxix, 344
Moya, Rodrigo de, complains about Caravaca convent, 291; offers convent, 199; Teresa writes about Caravaca, 241. *See also* Caravaca convent
Mysticism, 50, 51
Nanciano, Gregorio, xxxiii, 200, 246, 247
Narduch, Juan, *See* Miseria, Juan de la
Nieto, Baltasar (Baltasar de Jesús), xxxi, 222, 285, 320; and Catalina de Cardona, 159; and Discalced expansion into Andalusia, 184; Gracián accused by, 294, 295; as prior at Pastrana monastery, 134, 139, 174; retires to Portugal, 295; and scandals in Andalusia, 109-110, 139
Nieto, Gaspar, 109-110
Nieto, Inés, 220-221, 229
Nieto, Melchor, 109-110
Nuns, confessors and, Teresa on, 105, 362; direction of, Teresa on, 117-118, 142; life and foibles of, Teresa on, 104, 105-106; relations with friars, Teresa on, 247-248; rights of, 86
Obras Completas, 117, 137
Ocampo, María, 69. *See also* Bautista, María
Ocampo, Teresa de, 7
Of Christian Works (Borgia), 46, 55
Olea, Francisco de, 189; and Bernarda Gutiérrez, 224, 225; novices offered by, 256, 260, 265
Ordóñez, Ana. *See* Angeles, Ana de los
Ordóñez, María, 95, 96

434

391

Quesada, Teresa de, 114, 157, 160, 162; made prioress at Medina, 148
Quiroga, Elena, 115, 392; and Medina convent, 116, 178, 267-268; possibility of becoming a nun, 347, 351, 371, 375
Quiroga, Gaspar de (Grand Inquisitor), xxxv, 306, 310, 357; Gracián consults, 298; Madrid license sought from, 371, 407; reaction to *Life*, 282, 343; Sega rebuffed by, 320; Teresa meets, 343. *See also* Inquisition, Spanish

Ramírez, Alonso, 126, 127, 129
Ramírez, Margarita, 228, 265, 311, 329; accusations by and appearance before Inquisition, 224, 237, 322-324; sent to Calced convent in Pastrama. 283
Ramírez, Martín, 125, 150
Raptures, Teresa's, 49, 50, 63. See also *Arrobamientos*, Teresa's
Reformation, 50
Reforms, religious, 23-24, 65, 98, 108-109. *See also* King's Reform; Philip II, and reform of monastic orders
Reinoso, Canon, 372, 402; and Palencia convent, 356, 357, 365
Reinoso, Cardinal, 87
Reyes, Agustín de los, xx, 418-419
Ribadeneira, Father, 67
Ribera (Teresa's first biographer), 12, 81, 87, 343, 425; on Rodrigo de Ahumada's death, 19; on María Dávila, 97; on Heredia, 116; on Salamanca foundation, 145; Teresa meets, 372; on Teresa's vow of perfection, 68
Ripalda, Jerónimo (confessor), xxxv, 238, 271; directs Teresa to write *Fundaciones*, xxviii, 138, 141; and Bernarda Gutiérrez, 225; novices sponsored by, 167; opinion of Teresa, 179; Palencia foundation supported by, 356
Roberto, Mencía, 164
Roca, Juan (Juan de Jesús), xxxiv, 158, 260, 306, 335, 357; and Discalced Chapter meetings, 253-254, 255, 313; jailed in Madrid, 318; Teresa advises on appeal to Rome, 326
Rojas y Sandoval, Cristóbal (Archbishop of Seville), 216-217, 221, 350
Rossi, Giovanni Battista. *See* Rubeo, Juan Bautista
Royal Council, Spanish, 94, 283, 317, 320; accusations against Gracián considered

by, 294, 295; Discalced autonomy supported by, 310; Gracián prohibited from resigning Visitorship by, 298; powers of, 92; St. Joseph's closing appealed to, 91, 93; and Tostado, 270, 281, 285
Rubeo, Juan Bautista, xxvii, xxxv, 127, 134, 139, 229, 243; character, 109, 110; death, 314; Discalced expansion authorized by, 111; Gracián and Discalced expansion opposed by, 199, 213, 219; Incarnation visited by, 24, 32-33, 38; and Medina convent, 310; Spanish religious orders examined by, 109-111; Teresa excommunicated by and ordered under house arrest, 231; Teresa's disobedience of, and efforts to explain herself, 205, 208, 212, 218-219, 220, 236; Teresa's worsening situation with, 293, 310
Rueda, Dr., 306, 325
Ruiz, Antonio, 389; lends money to María de San José, 251; warns Teresa about Malagón convent, 246
Ruiz, Simon, 114, 148
Sáchez, Gabriel, 2
Sacramento, María del, xxvii, 143
St. Joseph's Discalced Convent, 69-72, 75, 77, 79, 90, 91; briefs for, 72, 85, 86, 92, 96; chronology of founding, xxvi; endowment for, rejected by Teresa, 93; financial situation, 77, 84, 88, 89, 97, 98, 373-374; founding in poverty, reactions to, 84-85, 86; hermitages for prayer at, 98, 99; Inquisitor Soto visits, 100, 101; life in, 103-104; nuns for initially, 88-89, 95-96, 97; opening of, 85, 89; opposition to and attempts to close, 90-92, 93, 98-99, 103; problems at, 374-375, 376-377; rules and Constitutions for, 96; Teresa forced to leave and then returns, 90, 93, 94, 95-96; Teresa returns to from Toledo, 293, 294
Salamanca convent, 178, 410, 413; condition of, 151; financial situation, 179; founding of, xxvii, 140-146 passim 175; new house for, controversy over, 418-419; problems at and Teresa's visit to, 330; Teresa's desire to found, 136-137, 138-139
Salazar, Angel de, xxxv, 80, 85, 110, 156, 159, 192, 231, 236, 258, 286, 294, 296, 339, 354; appointed Vicar, xxviii, 326; and election of prioress at Incarnation, 86, 87; Gracián opposed by, 219, 229-230, 335; and Medina convent, 148; and nobility, 94; and St. Joseph's, 70, 72, 75, 77, 80, 86, 87, 91, 93, 95; Teresa excommunicated by, 148; Teresa permitted to resume travels by, 329;